Enterprise Architecture for Connected E-Government:

Practices and Innovations

Pallab Saha
National University of Singapore, Singapore

Information Science
REFERENCE

Managing Director:	Lindsay Johnston
Senior Editorial Director:	Heather A. Probst
Book Production Manager:	Sean Woznicki
Development Manager:	Joel Gamon
Development Editor:	Hannah Abelbeck
Acquisitions Editor:	Erika Gallagher
Cover Design:	Nick Newcomer

Published in the United States of America by
Information Science Reference (an imprint of IGI Global)
701 E. Chocolate Avenue
Hershey PA 17033
Tel: 717-533-8845
Fax: 717-533-8661
E-mail: cust@igi-global.com
Web site: http://www.igi-global.com

Library of Congress Cataloging-in-Publication Data

Enterprise architecture for connected e-government: practices and innovations / Pallab Saha, editor.
    p. cm.
  Includes bibliographical references and index.
  Summary: "This book addresses the gap in current literature in terms of linking and understanding the relationship between e-government and government enterprise architecture"--Provided by publisher.
   ISBN 978-1-4666-1824-4 (hardcover) -- ISBN 978-1-4666-1825-1 (ebook) -- ISBN 978-1-4666-1826-8 (print & perpetual access) 1. Internet in public administration. 2. Public administration--Technological innovations. 3. Management information systems. 4. System design. I. Saha, Pallab, 1970-
   JF1525.A8E67 2012
   352.3'80285--dc23
                          2012000167

British Cataloguing in Publication Data
A Cataloguing in Publication record for this book is available from the British Library.

All work contributed to this book is new, previously-unpublished material. The views expressed in this book are those of the authors, but not necessarily of the publisher.

This book is dedicated to my father, the late Shri Jagatbandhu Saha.

Table of Contents

Foreword xvii

Preface xix

Acknowledgment xxviii

Section 1
The Connected Government Paradigm

Chapter 1
Connected Government as the New Normal: A Strategic Thinking Approach to
Whole-of-Government Enterprise Architecture Adoption 1
  Pallab Saha, National University of Singapore, Singapore

Section 2
Government as a Complex Adaptive System

Chapter 2
A Problem Oriented Enterprise Architecture Approach Applied to Wicked Problems 57
  Bernard Robertson-Dunn, Australian Government Information Management Office, Australia

Chapter 3
The Power of EA Taxonomies in Enhancing Portfolio Visibility and
Optimising Decision Making 78
  Don Ashdown, Queensland Government, Australia
  Vanessa Douglas-Savage, Queensland Government, Australia
  Kirsten Harte, Queensland Government, Australia
  Ee-Kuan Low, Queensland Government, Australia

Section 3
Frameworks for Connected Government

Chapter 4

Integrating Agency Enterprise Architecture into Government-Wide Enterprise Architecture:
The Case of Korean Government Initiatives 105

Young-Joo Lee, National Information Society Agency, South Korea
Shinae Shin, National Information Society Agency, South Korea

Chapter 5

Government Enterprise Architecture: Towards the Inter-Connected Government in the
Kingdom of Saudi Arabia 121

Ali S. AlSoma, Ministry of Communications and Information Technology, Saudi Arabia
Hasan M. Hourani, Ministry of Communications and Information Technology, Saudi Arabia
Dato' Mohd Salleh Masduki, Ministry of Communications and Information Technology, Saudi Arabia

Chapter 6

National Enterprise Architecture Framework: Case Study of EA Development
Experience in the Kingdom of Bahrain 152

Ali AlSoufi, University of Bahrain, Bahrain
Zakaria Ahmed, eGovernment Authority, Bahrain

Chapter 7

Towards Whole-of-Government EA with TOGAF and SOA 177

Awel S Dico, BMO Financial Group, Canada & The Open Group, UK & Addis Ababa
University, Ethiopia

Chapter 8

Enterprise Architecture in Countries with Volatile Governance:
Negotiating Challenges and Crafting Successes 205

Saleem Zoughbi, UN-ESCWA, Lebanon
Sukaina Al-Nasrawi, UN-ESCWA, Lebanon

Section 4
Transforming to Connected Government

Chapter 9

A Case Study in the Emergence of Coherence through Cultural Change 219

Charles Solverson, City of Tacoma, USA
Susan Coffman, City of Tacoma, USA
David Johnson, City of Tacoma, USA
Linda I. Paralez, Demarche Consulting Group, Inc., USA

Chapter 10

Whole-of-Enterprise Approach to Government Architecture Applied for Implementing
a Directive of EU 247

Ivo Velitchkov, European Commission, Belgium

Chapter 11

The Role of Services in Governmental Enterprise Architectures:
The Case of the German Federal Government 262

Dominik Birkmeier, University of Augsburg, Germany
Sabine Buckl, Technische Universität München, Germany
Andreas Gehlert, Federal Ministry of the Interior, Germany
Florian Matthes, Technische Universität München, Germany
Christian Neubert, Technische Universität München, Germany
Sven Overhage, University of Augsburg, Germany
Sascha Roth, Technische Universität München, Germany
Christian M. Schweda, Technische Universität München, Germany
Klaus Turowski, University of Augsburg, Germany

Chapter 12

An Investigative Assessment of the Role of Enterprise Architecture in Realizing
E-Government Transformation 288

Leonidas Anthopoulos, Technological Education Institute (TEI) of Larissa, Greece

Chapter 13

Architecting for Connected Healthcare: A Case of Telehomecare and Hypertension 306

Torben Tambo, Aarhus University, Denmark
Nikolai Hoffmann-Petersen, Regional Hospital Holstebro, Denmark
Karsten Bejder, Aarhus University, Denmark

Chapter 14

An Approach to Multi-Agency and Intra-Agency Unification with Enterprise
Architecture Driven e-Government in South Africa 326

Robert Benjamin, Nanograte Knowledge Technologies, South Africa

Chapter 15

An Architecture Driven Methodology for Transforming from Fragmented to
Connected Government: A Case of a Local Government in Italy 350

Walter Castelnovo, University of Insubria, Italy

Chapter 16

Moving towards the Connected Transformational Government: Perspectives from
Malaysia and Beyond.. 374

Dzaharudin Mansor, Microsoft Corporation, Malaysia
Mohd. Rosmadi Mokhtar, National Universiti (UKM), Malaysia
Azlina Azman, Malaysian Administrative Modernisation and Management Planning Unit (MAMPU),
Malaysia

Chapter 17

Enterprise Architecture for Personalization of e-Government Services:
Reflections from Turkey 389

    Alpay Erdem, Middle East Technical University (METU), Turkey

    İhsan Tolga Medeni, Middle East Technical University (METU), Turkey & Turksat, Turkey &
        Çankaya University, Turkey

    Tunç D. Medeni, Turksat, Turkey & Middle East Technical University (METU), Turkey & Yildirim
        Beyazit University (YBU), Turkey

Chapter 18

IT and Enterprise Architecture in US Public Sector Reform: Issues and Recommendations............. 412

    Terry F. Buss, Carnegie Mellon University, USA

    Anna Shillabeer, Griffin Information Solutions, Australia

Section 5
Public Value Management in Connected Government

Chapter 19

Assessing the Value of Investments in Government Interoperability 442

    Anthony M. Cresswell, SUNY Albany, USA

    Djoko Sigit Sayogo, SUNY Albany, USA

    Lorenzo Madrid, Microsoft Corporation, USA

Chapter 20

A Public Economics Approach to Enabling Enterprise Architecture with the Government
Cloud in Belgium 467

    Marc Rabaey, University of Hasselt, Belgium

Chapter 21

Addressing the U.S. Federal Government Financial Crisis: A Case for a U.S. Department
of Defense Enterprise Architecture-Based Approach 494

    William S. Boddie, National Defense University iCollege, USA

Compilation of References 515

About the Contributors 546

Index 558

Detailed Table of Contents

Foreword..xvii

Preface...xix

Acknowledgment..xxviii

Section 1
The Connected Government Paradigm

Chapter 1

Connected Government as the New Normal: A Strategic Thinking Approach to
Whole-of-Government Enterprise Architecture Adoption...1
Pallab Saha, National University of Singapore, Singapore

The United Nations has acknowledged that transition towards the future of government requires a holistic and coherent framework, which cannot be delivered with piecemeal fragmented thinking and approach. Governments in the future will be more connected than ever before, by being FAST (Flat, Agile, Streamlined, and Tech-Savvy). With its ability to manage complexity, Government Enterprise Architecture (GEA) has emerged as the essential means to drive public sector transformation and realize connected government with demonstrable benefits. Elevating effectiveness and quality of government services is not merely a matter of leading edge technologies, but also demands visionary leadership, strategic wisdom, foresight, clear directions, and sound execution mechanisms. With collaboration, connectedness, and co-innovation as the cornerstones of the governments of the future, this chapter explores and elaborates the role of enterprise architecture in making this happen. As the anchor chapter, it also sets the context for the subsequent chapters of this book.

Section 2
Government as a Complex Adaptive System

Chapter 2

A Problem Oriented Enterprise Architecture Approach Applied to Wicked Problems 57
Bernard Robertson-Dunn, Australian Government Information Management Office, Australia

Enterprises more often than not operate in an environment of plentiful problems, most of which are difficult to comprehend and almost impossible to act upon with any sense of certainty given their complex adaptive nature. These are called wicked problems. This chapter takes a problem-oriented approach to enterprise architecture with special focus on government enterprises. It is based on the assertion that the more frequently encountered, requirements based approaches to enterprise architecture have limited effectiveness when dealing with large scale and socially oriented systems development. The chapter presents an alternative approach by taking a problem-oriented perspective.

Chapter 3

The Power of EA Taxonomies in Enhancing Portfolio Visibility and
Optimising Decision Making 78

Don Ashdown, Queensland Government, Australia
Vanessa Douglas-Savage, Queensland Government, Australia
Kirsten Harte, Queensland Government, Australia
Ee-Kuan Low, Queensland Government, Australia

Taxonomies provide mechanisms to organize and use information in a coherent manner. This chapter describes how the Queensland Government and several of its large agencies embraced enterprise architecture taxonomy to bring forth better and smarter decisions pertaining to investments and managing such investments as a portfolio with the intent to minimizing losses by spreading risks. The chapter further demonstrates use of this approach for making evidence based policy development and compliance.

Section 3
Frameworks for Connected Government

Chapter 4

Integrating Agency Enterprise Architecture into Government-Wide Enterprise Architecture:
The Case of Korean Government Initiatives 105

Young-Joo Lee, National Information Society Agency, South Korea
Shinae Shin, National Information Society Agency, South Korea

South Korea ranks amongst the most advanced in e-government. Over the years, the country has openly embraced ICT within the government and utilized it to propel its digital government agenda aimed at national prosperity. As part of its e-government, enterprise architecture is an important and mandatory element. Towards this end, the government of South Korea has developed and deployed the Korean Government-Wide Architecture (KGEA) that lends structure and basis for influencing the national ICT agenda, enhances investment management practices across the government, and enables government-wide transformation. This chapter describes South Korea's voyage of the conception, development, and deployment of KGEA and shares the key learning points.

Chapter 5

Government Enterprise Architecture: Towards the Inter-Connected Government in the
Kingdom of Saudi Arabia 121

Ali S. AlSoma, Ministry of Communications and Information Technology, Saudi Arabia
Hasan M. Hourani, Ministry of Communications and Information Technology, Saudi Arabia
Dato' Mohd Salleh Masduki, Ministry of Communications and Information Technology, Saudi Arabia

Discerning citizens demand better and more efficient services from their Governments. This requires governments to be receptive to the requirements and expectations of their citizenry. Saudi Arabia is one of the countries in the GCC region that has used ICT to deliver better services. Their propensity to ensure that the ICT supports the business of government has led them to use EA. The Kingdom of Saudi

Arabia has taken the lead in developing the Yesser Enterprise Level Architecture Framework (Y-ELAF) for adoption across the Kingdom. This chapter describes the Y-ELAF and demonstrates its adaptation in a government agency. The experiences and lessons learned from the agency are now being used as benchmark and illustration for adoption in other agencies within the Kingdom.

Chapter 6
National Enterprise Architecture Framework: Case Study of EA Development
Experience in the Kingdom of Bahrain 152
    Ali AlSoufi, University of Bahrain, Bahrain
    Zakaria Ahmed, eGovernment Authority, Bahrain

Bahrain has one of the most advanced and well respected e-governments across the GCC region. This is according to the UN's e-government readiness survey conducted every two years. Bahrain's primary motivation to build an effective government EA is its strong belief that effective EA in the government directly influences the e-government capability and maturity. In order to realize its vision, Bahrain embarked on developing its National Enterprise Architecture Framework (NEAF). This chapter is a first-hand description of NEAF's development journey, its primary objectives, and its expected impact and contribution to Bahrain's Economic Vision 2030.

Chapter 7
Towards Whole-of-Government EA with TOGAF and SOA 177
    Awel S Dico, BMO Financial Group, Canada & The Open Group, UK & Addis Ababa
        University, Ethiopia

It is acknowledged across the world that to bring real transformation in governments, countries must take a Whole-of-Government (WOG) perspective. However, it is also understood that such initiatives and changes are fraught with political landmines. In this context, governments are embracing EA as the means to deliver the WOG perspective. That said, it is also true that current EA frameworks and methodologies are designed for single agency contexts. The WOG perspective brings forth different kinds of requirements, challenges, and complexities; and the current EA frameworks and methodologies fall short in meeting these. This chapter takes a look at The Open Group Architecture Framework (TOGAF), and analyses it from a WOG perspective. It then discusses the modifications and extensions that are required to make TOGAF applicable in the WOG context.

Chapter 8
Enterprise Architecture in Countries with Volatile Governance:
Negotiating Challenges and Crafting Successes 205
    Saleem Zoughbi, UN-ESCWA, Lebanon
    Sukaina Al-Nasrawi, UN-ESCWA, Lebanon

EAs in countries with stable governance have the advantage of continuity, predictability, and reliability. This has been instrumental in creating a perception that EA has higher applicability in countries with stable governments. However, the reality is that there are countries that exhibit characteristics of volatility, political instability, low quality of regulations, absence of rule of law, and widespread chronic corruption. Such countries are assessed and ranked by the World Bank Institute. Such countries come with their own peculiarities and complexities in terms of governance. This chapter explains how a disciplined approach brought in by EA can be adapted for adoption in countries with volatile governance. The chapter is a practical description of how the challenging environment can be negotiated and successes crafted.

Section 4
Transforming to Connected Government

Chapter 9

A Case Study in the Emergence of Coherence through Cultural Change 219

Charles Solverson, City of Tacoma, USA

Susan Coffman, City of Tacoma, USA

David Johnson, City of Tacoma, USA

Linda I. Paralez, Demarche Consulting Group, Inc., USA

The Building and Land Use Services (BLUS) in the City of Tacoma in the United States of the America used EA to spearhead reengineering of business processes, automation of service delivery enabled by enterprise-wide interoperable information technology. Technology considerations aside, this chapter highlights the criticality of collective decision making, codes, culture, and vision on the success of government transformation. These are mechanisms that are often sidelined, despite the fact that these can actually be the showstoppers. This chapter further elaborates how this journey enabled an enhanced partnership between the city government and the community, thus making architecture driven government transformation an ongoing and continuous improvement practice.

Chapter 10

Whole-of-Enterprise Approach to Government Architecture Applied for Implementing
a Directive of EU 247

Ivo Velitchkov, European Commission, Belgium

More often than not enterprises fail to take a holistic perspective to EA. This leads to questionable and short term benefits that organizations derive from their architectures. This chapter describes the journey taken in Bulgaria where the Whole-of-Government (WOG) perspective was embraced to identify legal, political, organizational, and technological factors relating to compliance with a new regulation established by the European Union (EU), and how the passage helped in the improvement of e-government services. Supporting the realization of a single market within EU, the chapter demonstrates the role of WOG EA in identifying areas where administrative procedures could be simplified for authorization of service providers, consistent with the expectations of the new regulation.

Chapter 11

The Role of Services in Governmental Enterprise Architectures:
The Case of the German Federal Government 262

Dominik Birkmeier, University of Augsburg, Germany

Sabine Buckl, Technische Universität München, Germany

Andreas Gehlert, Federal Ministry of the Interior, Germany

Florian Matthes, Technische Universität München, Germany

Christian Neubert, Technische Universität München, Germany

Sven Overhage, University of Augsburg, Germany

Sascha Roth, Technische Universität München, Germany

Christian M. Schweda, Technische Universität München, Germany

Klaus Turowski, University of Augsburg, Germany

Europe's Digital Agenda addresses issues pertaining to political goals and actions needed to develop Europe's IT with the aim of designing government services around the needs and expectations of its citizens. The European Interoperability Strategy and the European Interoperability Architecture provide the foundation for bringing business process and service orientation into the fold. It realizes the importance of communication between administrations, businesses and citizens, and directly supports efficiency and effectiveness of public services both in design and delivery. ICT plays a crucial role in providing such efficient services. This chapter presents an approach adopted in the German Federal Government of systematically deriving services from business processes, so that these services are amenable to IT enablement and automation. The described method follows principles and guidelines from design science to deal with applicability. This is a critical success factor as different stakeholders bring different requirements and expectations to the table, thereby making it extremely difficult to codify services that fulfill requirements across the entire federal government.

Chapter 12
An Investigative Assessment of the Role of Enterprise Architecture in Realizing
E-Government Transformation 288
Leonidas Anthopoulos, Technological Education Institute (TEI) of Larissa, Greece

Across the world, countries have adopted EA to enable government transformation. As part of their programs countries have expended resources in developing their own frameworks, methods, guidelines, and tools. These are supported by legislations, regulations, procedures, and policies. While the detailed goals differ from country to country, the broad aim of realizing public sector reforms and government transformation through EA remains a common thread among all these programs. This chapter presents the findings from an assessment of such EA programs from different regions and countries around the world. It provides a comparison and contrasts various programs, their respective nuances, and distinguishing success factors. Further, the chapter evaluates the contribution of such EA programs to the overall vision of achieving connected government.

Chapter 13
Architecting for Connected Healthcare: A Case of Telehomecare and Hypertension 306
Torben Tambo, Aarhus University, Denmark
Nikolai Hoffmann-Petersen, Regional Hospital Holstebro, Denmark
Karsten Bejder, Aarhus University, Denmark

Healthcare is one of the sectors, which requires deep interactions between the government and its citizenry. Furthermore, these interactions are being influenced by emerging trends in demography, medical sciences, and technology, leading to greater connectedness. Transformation in the healthcare sector demands new ways of delivering services, often in non-hospital settings, e.g. telemedicine, telehealth, e-health, and home care. Rising healthcare costs bring in more complexity to the already complex scenario. In summary, the situation is characterized by several unknown factors and how these factors play out in different countries. This chapter presents two case studies from Denmark discussing the benefits of telemedicine focusing on collaboration and communication, the two key elements for realizing connectedness. It shows the use of EA in bringing about changes in mental models as to how different stakeholders in the system should strive to connect, collaborate, and co-create in the context of the healthcare sector.

Chapter 14
An Approach to Multi-Agency and Intra-Agency Unification with Enterprise
Architecture Driven e-Government in South Africa 326
Robert Benjamin, Nanograte Knowledge Technologies, South Africa

EA in countries with initial levels of e-government capability and maturity bring in a different set of challenges. The need to address the change in mindsets pertaining to bringing in structure, discipline, standards, shared vision, and political will to deliver effective e-government cannot be understated.

South Africa, as a fledgling democracy, after coming out of its checkered past, presents an excellent learning platform for all developing economies. This chapter demonstrates how South Africa used EA, adapted EA to be precise, to suit its special requirements due to its unique characteristics. The chapter discusses the criticality of improving quality of life and retention of societal values when architecting government services.

Chapter 15
An Architecture Driven Methodology for Transforming from Fragmented to
Connected Government: A Case of a Local Government in Italy 350
    Walter Castelnovo, University of Insubria, Italy

Many European countries are characterized by a fragmented form of local government. While this provides some obvious advantages, it creates enormous pressures on national or central governments to realize integration and operate coherently. Integrated aggregations of municipal governments are a plausible approach to achieve connectedness. Such aggregations provide the potential to reap in economies of scale benefits. Such benefits are even more welcome when Europe in general faces massive financial and economic challenges over next decade and beyond. As a case study, this chapter describes the journey, of a local government in Italy (Region Lombardia), of how aggregated integration was achieved using a standard transformation process that was enabled by back-office reorganization, inter-agency collaboration, interoperability, governance, and innovative service design.

Chapter 16
Moving towards the Connected Transformational Government: Perspectives from
Malaysia and Beyond.. 374
    Dzaharudin Mansor, Microsoft Corporation, Malaysia
    Mohd. Rosmadi Mokhtar, National Universiti (UKM), Malaysia
    *Azlina Azman, Malaysian Administrative Modernisation and Management Planning Unit (MAMPU),
        Malaysia*

In an era where governments are increasingly interacting with citizens and vice versa, moving from traditional bureaucratic forms of governance to one that is more collaborative and participatory is not a non-trivial shift. It offers and demands transformation in the models and approaches with which public services are designed and delivered. Taking the case of Malaysia, this chapter provides insights into the role of interoperability in delivering such joined-up government services. It demonstrates how ICT can be used to lower boundaries to move towards connected government. The chapter presents the role of EA in envisioning and realizing the benefits of transformational connected government in a scenario wherein the citizenry are becoming more tech-savvy, knowledgeable, and vocal about their rights.

Chapter 17
Enterprise Architecture for Personalization of e-Government Services:'
Reflections from Turkey 389
    Alpay Erdem, Middle East Technical University (METU), Turkey
    *İhsan Tolga Medeni, Middle East Technical University (METU), Turkey & Turksat, Turkey &
        Çankaya University, Turkey*
    *Tunç D. Medeni, Turksat, Turkey & Middle East Technical University (METU), Turkey & Yildirim
        Beyazit University (YBU), Turkey*

Often EA has been viewed as a means to deliver broad-based and non-granular government services. Currently, there is a gap in research literature describing the use of EA in designing and delivering fully integrated, knowledge-based, and personalized services. Taking the example of Turkish E-Government Gateway, this chapter describes Turkey's journey in embracing EA to enhance its e-government services. Using the Capgemini Framework, the decision to deliver personalized services brings in several challenges and opportunities. In making this shift, a deliberate decision to adopt the one-stop-shop philosophy characterized by a high degree of centralized coordination and also a high degree of integration. With the advent of open platforms, cloud computing for government, the chapter positions personalization of services as a plausible pathway to engagement, collaboration, and transformation.

Chapter 18

IT and Enterprise Architecture in US Public Sector Reform: Issues and Recommendations............ 412
    Terry F. Buss, Carnegie Mellon University, USA
    Anna Shillabeer, Griffin Information Solutions, Australia

Over the past two decades the United States has undertaken significant public sectors reforms, especially under the last two and the current President. While the political rhetoric has been abundant, the reform initiatives themselves have largely failed to meet the expectations of the policy makers, public servants, citizenry, and other stakeholders. Within this larger context of public sector reforms, IT reforms have also been ineffective and unsustainable. Using the Federal Government as a case study, this chapter investigates the true motivations of public sector reforms, the reasons for the relatively ineffective IT reforms and how they relate to the broader public sector reforms and the systemic factors that have prevented EA from realizing its full potential to deliver on the reforms. The chapter then discusses plausible ways to make public sector reforms through IT and EA more effective with the eventual goal of delivering better government.

Section 5
Public Value Management in Connected Government

Chapter 19

Assessing the Value of Investments in Government Interoperability 442
    Anthony M. Cresswell, SUNY Albany, USA
    Djoko Sigit Sayogo, SUNY Albany, USA
    Lorenzo Madrid, Microsoft Corporation, USA

Investments in interoperability of ICT systems are potentially a big contributor to governments in making them more efficient and responsive. The diversity in stakeholder expectations and needs lends complexity to the equation, thereby necessitating the need for effective architecture. Assessing and monetizing the value derived from such architecture driven interoperability in government is a complex problem for policy makers, managers, and analysts. This chapter presents two approaches to assess the value of interoperability that go beyond the traditional return on investment analyses. The approaches are based on socio-economic returns derived by extending government network interoperability and public value framework, and supported by illustrations of application via two case studies.

Chapter 20

A Public Economics Approach to Enabling Enterprise Architecture with the Government
Cloud in Belgium 467

Marc Rabaey, University of Hasselt, Belgium

Embracing Cloud Computing demands a very high level of architectural maturity, especially when government service delivery enabled by supporting business functions and processes are impacted by the Cloud. This chapter, therefore, proposes an additional stage in EA planning, when governments aim to bring Cloud Computing into the fold. This additional stage focuses on the investment aspects of Cloud Computing and is designed to align them to government-wide strategies and operational activities. Inherent flexibility is provided within the approach by using and extending from a real options paradigm. The chapter presents the case study of the Belgian government and is intended to enrich EA with its investment and economics oriented perspective.

Chapter 21

Addressing the U.S. Federal Government Financial Crisis: A Case for a U.S. Department
of Defense Enterprise Architecture-Based Approach 494

William S. Boddie, National Defense University iCollege, USA

The United States' current national debt stands at $ 14 trillion and the national deficit at $ 1.3 trillion. These statistics present a grim reality about its current economic crisis and an extended period of sluggish economic growth over the next decade or so. In response, as the government tries to improve government-wide performance, reduce operating costs, national debt, and national deficit, this chapter asserts that current ways to doing so will likely deepen the crisis even further, leading to a downward spiral. This is because the underlying systemic issues need to be tackled first. Taking the case of United States Department of Defense (DoD), this chapter elaborates how EA has been used to achieve the often conflicting goals of performance improvements, reduction in operating costs, and improvements in debts and deficits.

Compilation of References 515

About the Contributors 546

Index 558

Foreword

Governments around the world increasingly rely on online services to accomplish core mission functions with citizens, industry, and other governments. Effective, cost-efficient designs for these Electronic Government (E-Government) functions require a robust, scalable approach to Enterprise Architecture (EA) that integrates strategic drivers with business requirements and technology solutions. EA began as a technology design discipline in the late 1980's, as a need arose to integrate systems and share data across organizational boundaries. Since those early beginnings, EA has evolved into a management and technology best practice that has a global following and is singularly able to provide authoritative views of current and future states for various types of enterprises; including organizations, consortia, supply chains, lines of business, programs, and systems.

This book provides valuable insights from authors who are active in government, business, or academe, and have a common interest in how EA can support and promote the creation of a new generation of E-Government services that will more effectively function within and between agencies at the international, national, regional, and local levels. Because resources are often tight, there is a tremendous need for E-Government services that more effectively cover horizontal mission and support functions, and that vertically link various levels of government in a way that eliminates waste and duplication.

My own experiences as a U.S. Federal Government executive, management consultant, and university instructor have reinforced the view that EA is the only management and technology discipline capable of serving as a meta-context and source of standards for developing enterprise-wide E-Government services. The problem is that agency leaders are often not aware of the ability of EA to enable the transformation of mission and support functions, despite their desire to do just that. Perhaps it is because EA is still viewed by many as an IT discipline, or that EA projects in the past have sometimes delivered expensive shelfware instead of scalable designs using agile / rapid application development methods. The EA community's record for adding value needs improvement, and the material in this book provides many recommendations and case studies for doing that. Thank you to the authors of this material and especially to my long-time friend and colleague, Pallab Saha, for providing this book during a time that it is needed by governments that are looking for ways to create and improve E-Government services.

Scott Bernard
Syracuse University, USA

Scott Bernard *is currently the Federal Chief Architect with the Office of Management and serves as Co-Chair for the Federal Enterprise Architecture's Security and Privacy Profile for the U.S. Federal Chief Information Officers Council, Architecture and Infrastructure Committee. He has previously served on the faculty of Carnegie Mellon University's Institute for Software Research, School of Computer Science, where he developed a professional certificate program in enterprise architecture, and he served for over a decade on the faculty of Syracuse University's School of Information Studies. Dr. Bernard has thirty years of experience in information technology management, including work in the academic, federal government, military, and private sectors. He has held positions as a Chief Information Officer, IT Management Consultant, Line-of-Business Manager, Network Operations Manager, Telecommunications Manager, IT Systems Security Manager, and Project Manager for several major IT systems installations. He has served as a senior IT executive for a federal agency, started an enterprise architecture practice for an IT management firm, developed his own consulting practice, and lectured on the topic of enterprise architecture worldwide. Dr. Bernard was the founding editor of the* Journal of Enterprise Architecture, *and served as Chief Editor from 2005-2010. In 2004, he wrote the first textbook on enterprise architecture that is now in use at universities and in training programs around the world. He also created the EA3 Cube TM framework and methodology that is featured in this book, as well as the design for an on-line architecture repository that is called Living Enterprise™. Dr. Bernard earned his Ph.D. at Virginia Tech in Public Administration and Policy, a Master's degree in Business and Personnel Management from Central Michigan University, a Master's degree in Information Management from Syracuse University, and a Bachelor's degree in Psychology from the University of Southern California. He is a graduate of the United States Naval War College, and earned a Chief Information Officer Certificate and an Advanced Program Management Certificate from the National Defense University. Dr. Bernard is also a former career naval aviator who served on aircraft carriers and with shore squadrons, led IT programs, and was the Director of Network Operations for the Joint Chiefs of Staff at the Pentagon.*

Preface

The United Nations has played a pivotal role in elevating the need for connected government through its biennial e-government readiness surveys. Specifically, the surveys in 2008 and 2010 elaborate the criticality of governments to connect seamlessly across functions, agencies, and jurisdictions to deliver effective and efficient services to citizens and businesses. Governments of the future will have to be *connected*. This is also emphasized in the World Economic Forum's *The Future of Government* report published in 2011. In this context, the role of enterprise architecture as a disciplined and structured approach for planning and realizing connected government cannot be overstated. Connected governments have deeper *engagement*, encourage *participation* and *collaboration*, and exhibit greater *openness* and *transparency*. Resultingly, connected governments deliver services that are more *personalized* and *choice-based* anchored around the *whole-of-government* paradigm. The focus shifts from efficient delivery of e-services to value of services delivered that are enabled by *blurring boundaries, user driven governance*, and *open government*. This transition is being further accelerated by the advent and proliferation of social media. In short, democratization is a significant and visible outcome of connected government. In terms of scale, intensity, and impact, this transition is nothing short of transformational.

This book covers a subject matter that has gained prominence in the recent years. The need arises from the fact that there is a dearth of literature demonstrating field tested concepts substantiated with real examples of countries embracing enterprise architecture and its role in realizing the vision of connected government. The lack of literature and guidance oftentimes acts as an impediment. Over the years, I have had the privilege of working directly in several national enterprise architecture and electronic government programs in various capacities. These experiences triggered my earlier book *Advances in Government Enterprise Architecture* in 2007. As part of my ongoing work, I received a Microsoft grant for my research titled *Enterprise Architecture as Platform for Connected Government* in 2010, which eventually triggered this book. In the course of my research, it was all too evident that despite the existence of adequate literature in electronic government and enterprise architecture as separate disciplines, governments still struggle to embrace enterprise architecture as a means to realize the vision of connected government. The current situation is further exacerbated by the unavailability of credible reference material. Put together, this book, a first of its kind in the world, aims to address this gap and provide governments across the world a comprehensive compilation of high quality chapters that form a definitive reference for national and local governmental initiatives. With the intention of balancing theory and practice, this book aims to:

1. Demonstrate the importance of government enterprise architecture in elevating the effectiveness of e-government programs;

2.   Disseminate current advancements and thought leadership in the area of enterprise architecture in the context of connected government;
3.   Provide national e-government initiatives with evidence-based, credible, field tested, and practical guidance in crafting their respective architectures; and
4.   Showcase case studies and experience reports of innovative use of enterprise architecture in enhancing national e-government initiatives.

The book is structured into five (5) sections consisting of twenty-one (21) chapters in all. The chapters were carefully selected after being subjected to a rigorous review process spearheaded by the Editorial Advisory Board (EAB). In addition to rigor, relevance, and applicability, I have also attempted to make the book representative of the different regions in the world. Most chapters are in-depth case studies symbolizing different types of governments, cultures, and practices. This selection is deliberate as it allows readers insights into a multitude of country-specific challenges, peculiarities, and nuances. It is obvious such initiatives would be ongoing activities; thus, the chapters represent snapshots in time, representing the current state of practice. The following paragraphs provide an overview and summary of book sections and chapters.

SECTION 1: THE CONNECTED GOVERNMENT PARADIGM

The first section, consisting of one chapter, establishes the context for the entire book. Chapter 1, "Connected Government as the New Normal: A Strategic (Systems) Thinking Approach to Whole of Government Enterprise Architecture Adoption," presents the dimensions of connected government and positions it as a multi-dimensional construct with crucial constructional elements that the governments aspire for. The chapter then discusses the policy and strategy levers available to positively influence the dimensions of connected government. The role of enterprise architecture in impacting the levers is then proposed and elaborated. Despite good intentions, it is well known that governments face increasing challenges in realizing connected government by making enterprise architecture effective. If not tackled early on, these challenges have the potential to derail initiatives. The chapter uses strategic (systems) thinking to uncover the systemic challenges faced by governments to embrace connected government with a whole-of-government paradigm. The facilitators and inhibitors are presented and analyzed. Given the complexities involved, the chapter proposes plausible intervention strategies that countries can cogitate in order to accelerate their respective initiatives. This chapter is the genesis for the rest of the book.

SECTION 2: GOVERNMENT AS A COMPLEX ADAPTIVE SYSTEM

Consisting of two chapters, this section takes forward the ideas presented in Section 1. It takes a systemic view of governments, wherein it is imperative to understand and tackle inherent complexities within governments. This section aims to make evident the benefits of taking a problem-oriented approach to enterprise architecture and how taxonomies, a first class citizen of government transformation initiatives, are used to enhance the effectiveness of management decisions.

Chapter 2, "A Problem-Oriented Enterprise Architecture Approach Applied to Wicked Problems," argues that a problem oriented approach to enterprise architecture can deliver better outcomes than one based upon needs and requirements, especially when dealing with wicked problems. The chapter draws a distinction between what an enterprise architect does (i.e. solve business problems) and what the architect produces (i.e. descriptions of the end states). It also suggests that the approach to modelling and understanding business problems can have significant impacts on the quality, effectiveness and efficiency of potential solutions, and the decisions made in identifying optimal solutions and implementation projects. Finally, the chapter discusses the use of the proposed approach to wicked problems in the context of e-Government.

Chapter 3, "The Power of Enterprise Architecture Taxonomies in Enhancing Portfolio Visibility and Optimising Decision Making," describes the efficacy of using enterprise architecture taxonomies in making sense of organizations and its components to support portfolio visibility and optimise decision making. It describes the use of taxonomies in a manner that has been successfully applied across a range of medium to large organizations particularly at a whole-of-government level within the Queensland Government, the Gold Coast City Council, and at an agency level within the Queensland Department of Justice and Attorney-General. These taxonomies enable increased visibility of the organization's investment portfolio in supporting more structured decision-making and provide a basis for evidence-based policy development. At the whole-of-government level, this supports optimisation of information and IT investments across the entire connected government portfolio.

SECTION 3: FRAMEWORKS FOR CONNECTED GOVERNMENT

Actualization of connected government using enterprise architecture requires methods, practices, guidelines, tools, and mechanisms. These play a crucial role in bringing in structure and standards in the way architecture outputs are developed and used. These also bring about a certain degree of maturity in the way the outputs are communicated and outcomes derived. Section 3, consisting of five chapters presents enterprise architecture frameworks developed by various countries. All the chapters in this section are descriptions of initiatives undertaken in various countries. I do not subscribe to the notion that a framework developed for one country will be applicable to another without any adaptation. That said, I do believe there is still a lot to learn from the experiences of other countries.

Chapter 4, "Integrating Agency Enterprise Architecture into Government-Wide Enterprise Architecture: The Case of Korean Government Initiatives," describes the successful case of government enterprise architecture implemented by the Korean Government. First, a brief history and current status of the Korean government enterprise architecture program are introduced. Next, the characteristics of Korean government enterprise architecture are reviewed using an analytical framework. Finally, the strength and potential weakness of the case is discussed in terms of its relevance in realizing connected governments and furthering future advancement. The fact that South Korea ranks first in the world for e-government maturity makes this chapter immensely valuable, enriching the potential learning.

The growth of ICT-mediated services in the private and public sectors demands that organizations become more focused in delivering efficient services to well-informed and demanding consumers. Governments being very large enterprises are increasingly under pressure to optimize and align their ICT strategies and resources to support the business of government. The Kingdom of Saudi Arabia responds to this challenge by adopting the use of enterprise architecture to transform traditional government services into eGovernment services or eServices. Y-ELAF (Yesser Enterprise Level Architecture Framework) is an enterprise architecture framework that is an adaptation of the industry-recognized framework TOGAF Version 9 (The Open Group Architecture Framework Version 9), modified to fit the government environment of Saudi Arabia. Chapter 5, "Government Enterprise Architecture: Towards the Inter-Connected Government in the Kingdom of Saudi Arabia," elaborates the iterative phases of Y-ELAF used to develop the enterprise architecture of a government agency. Further, the chapter describes the outcomes and lessons learned.

Building on the belief that there exists a positive correlation between the desired level of e□government capability and maturity and the required level of architectural maturity, the eGovernment Authority (eGA) of the Kingdom of Bahrain embarked on a three year eGovernment program aimed at improving service delivery to citizens through seamless integration and connected governance. In order to achieve this objective, eGA realized the need for a Kingdom-wide strategy and holistic guiding plans, and hence decided to design and develop a National Enterprise Architecture Framework (NEAF). NEAF is an aggregation of models and meta-models, governance, compliance mechanisms, technology standards, and guidelines put together to guide effective development and implementation of an enterprise architecture by different government entities across the Kingdom. Chapter 6, "National Enterprise Architecture Framework: Experiences in the Kingdom of Bahrain," describes a NEAF development project success story, its objectives and its importance to Bahrain's economic vision 2030. It describes the NEAF development lifecycle and highlights at each stage the findings and challenges faced during the development of the framework.

Governments around the world have acknowledged the complexity associated with public sector transformation and have initiated enterprise architecture programs to help manage those complexities and enable the desired strategic transformation. However, most of those EA programs are of limited scope in both EA and SOA practices, and are not comprehensive enough to deal with and manage the associated complexities. As a result, EA programs suffer from the inability to leverage EA and SOA benefits across agencies or jurisdictional boundaries. Currently, the majority of government agencies use EA and SOA within the confines of agency boundaries to deliver solutions by focusing on technical factors that define detailed blueprints of systems, data, and technology. Research has pointed out that whole-of-government enterprise architecture is currently at the conceptual level and still has a long way to go to reach the maturity level required for true value realization. Chapter 7, "Towards Whole-of-Government Enterprise Architecture with TOGAF and Service Oriented Architecture," gives a brief analysis of the current state of enterprise architecture in governments to highlight the current challenges. It discusses various scopes of whole-of-government enterprise architecture and recommends the plausible approaches to enable sustainable connected government based on The Open Group Architecture Framework (TOGAF) and SOA.

Architecting in countries with stable governance has the advantage of continuity, predictability, and reliability. This has been instrumental in creating a perception that enterprise architecture has higher applicability in countries with stable governments. However, in reality there are countries exhibiting characteristics of volatility, political instability, low quality of regulations, absence of rule of law, and widespread chronic corruption. Such countries are assessed and ranked by the World Bank Institute. Such countries come with their own peculiarities and complexities in terms of governance. These countries, too, require architecture and planning. This chapter explains how a disciplined approach brought in by enterprise architecture can be adapted for adoption in countries with volatile governance. Chapter 8, "Enterprise Architecture in Countries with Volatile Governance: Negotiating Challenges and Crafting Successes," is a practical description of how the challenging environment can be negotiated and successes crafted.

SECTION 4: TRANSFORMING TO CONNECTED GOVERNMENT

Connected government requires fundamental changes in the way governments operate and interact. This necessitates challenging and transforming several long-held and strongly ingrained mental models. For nations to realize this transformation, the role of methods, practices, guidelines, tools, and mechanisms cannot be overstated. This section, consisting of ten chapters, is primarily a collection of cases. This compilation of chapters represents experiences from both national and local governments, developed and developing economies, and large and small countries. I have selected this mix deliberately so as to provide a wide perspective to the readers. However, I expect countries to use their own discretion and judgment when adopting the methods, practices, and tools described in the chapters.

The emergence of e-governance within Tacoma, WA, a progressive, midsized, U.S. city located in the Pacific Northwest, has been a process of insights and solutions. The interrelationships of e-government, enterprise architecture, and sustainable practices as a means to e-governance are examined through the case study of one Tacoma city division, Building and Land Use Services (BLUS). BLUS managers have redesigned business processes to automate service delivery by the optimization of enterprise-wide interoperable information technology. Chapter 9, "Emergence of Coherence through Cultural Change: A Case of the City of Tacoma," discusses the consideration of the influences that collective decision-making, codes, culture, and vision have on governmental transformation. The identified gap between enterprise architecture and e-government systems is consistent with the emerging convergence of knowledge for developing enterprise architecture maturity, developing best practices for shared information management, and expanding human potential. Internal and external stakeholders have experienced the successful emergence of BLUS into rationalized data and applications, in which the optimization of existing interoperable technology has enabled an enhanced partnership between the city government and the community.

Sustainable benefits of enterprise architecture efforts can only be realised if all structures and behaviour are taken into account together with their drivers and controls. Chapter 10, "Whole-of-Enterprise Approach to Government Architecture Applied for Implementing a Directive of the European Union," tells the story of an e-Government project in Bulgaria where a whole-of-enterprise approach is applied to identify together legal, organizational, and technological measures related to achieving compliance with a new regulation and improvement of a set of e-Government services. One of the main objectives of the project was to discover the potential for simplification of administrative procedures for authorisation of service providers in line with a new regulation in the European Union supporting realisation of a single market of services. The obtained analytical results and the defined target state are not limited to improvement of online services but include pertinent legislation harmonisation and other non-IT related changes. The applied agile EA approach helped with completing the project within six (6) months, realising results exceeding its scope.

In the public sector, Information Technology (IT) as means to support governmental processes is as important as in the industry. Delivering high quality eGovernment services requires an efficient and effective IT support. This IT support can only be provided if the requirements specified in the processes are correctly and completely transformed into IT solutions. Services are seen as major means to support this transformation. Chapter 11, "The Role of Services in Governmental Enterprise Architectures: The Case of the German Federal Government," proposes a method which systematically translates business processes into services. The method contains: (1) a data model describing the structure of the work products of the method, (2) a technique for emergent data modeling, which allows its users to customize the data model according to the government's needs, (3) a role model describing the required competencies for each step, and (4) a process model describing the required steps to derive services from business processes. To succeed in a governmental context with diverse, federative organizational structures, the method needs a high degree of flexibility. In particular, the proposed method has been designed to be compatible with different process modeling techniques.

Chapter 12, "An Investigative Assessment of the Role of Enterprise Architecture in Realizing E-Government Transformation," investigates important e-strategies concerning the existence and contribution of enterprise architecture to strategic implementation and transformation. Different architecture frameworks are compared, and architectures are aligned to strategic and to transformation objectives, in support of Connected Government. Moreover, the necessity of the alignment of enterprise architecture to the strategy is underlined, and a maturity roadmap to Connected Government is considered. Major e-strategies around the world are being implemented for more than a decade and they have resulted in digital public service delivery and in internal efficiency for further transformation. Most of these strategies have or are being updated and their current versions focus on cross-departmental service delivery leading to Connected Government. Enterprise architecture offers the ability to determine and close departmental gaps, and in this context, it can support the migration to Connected Government.

The healthcare system in many countries is operated by the governments, and interaction with the healthcare system is one of the most frequent interactions between citizens and governments. Demographic, medical, and technological changes are likely to bring new aspects of connectedness into the everyday life of people and place healthcare and homecare professionals in new roles. A transformation is underway where hospital best practices are constantly reducing in-hospital stays to alternative, less-costly care—notably at home. Telemedicine, telehealth, eHealth, home monitoring, and self-care are essential aspects of this transformation. Many issues are influencing this transformation and new barriers are showing up where others are being removed. A broadly oriented enterprise architecture effort is adopted for the underpinning of the change process. The architectural approach encompasses views of the citizen, the healthcare system, the information infrastructure, and the citizen-oriented technology. Chapter 13, "Architecting for Connected Healthcare: A Case of Telehomecare and Hypertension in Denmark," is a case of telemonitoring and self-care using mobile hypertension measurement on a large-scale population cohort. Evaluation of the acceptance and success of the solutions is done within a combined understanding of elements like technology, economy, organization, and culture.

Chapter 14, "Government Enterprise Architecture in Countries with Initial Levels of E-Government Capability and Maturity: Experiences from South Africa," introduces an emerging enterprise architecture approach to e-government. Within the South African context, it is fair to expect e-governance to achieve a minimum level of standardized, data-management practices. For the purposes of this chapter, this level of governance is viewed as the desired strategic objective for e-government. For the past four years, an approach for engaging with government was prototyped and tested. Its intent is to deliver governance-oriented, ICT solutions. Its main objective is to provide data integrity to multi-agency requirements and help design solutions aimed at satisfying those requirements. The diplomatic path towards standardizing data-management practices within government is not always direct. Due consideration is given to organization, business process, technology, and people aspects. It would seem that the outcomes, which resulted from employing the ontology, addressed an underlying need of governmental agencies across the board, namely the need for unification. This chapter explains how multi-agency and intra-agency unification was facilitated through the described initiative.

Connected government implies that citizens and enterprises can interact with governments as with a single entity rather than with a number of different public authorities. In countries characterized by a highly fragmented system of local governments, connected government at the local level can be achieved only through a process of progressive integration on a wider area of systems of local government already integrated at the local level. Chapter 15, "An Architecture Driven Methodology for Transforming from Fragmented to Connected Government: A Case of a Local Government in Italy," argues that this process should be based on a maturity model and a reference model that defines the technological and organizational conditions that allow the establishment of more integrated aggregations of municipalities. With reference to a study funded by the Region Lombardia (Italy), the chapter introduces the concept of Integrated System of Local Government (ISLG) and describes the process that leads to the establishment of ISLGs as an intermediate step toward connected government at the local level. Moreover, the chapter discusses the conditions that can induce different aggregations of municipalities to comply with a set of standard requirements in the implementation of their integration processes.

Chapter 16, "Moving towards the Connected Transformational Government: Perspectives from Malaysia and Beyond," provides insights into interoperability from the point of view of delivering government services. It shows that today, technology and industry have progressed to such an extent that the technical barriers to interoperability can be overcome in many ways. The real challenge is to address business interoperability that involves the interplay of technical, architectural, strategic, organizational, policy dimensions, and even legal dimensions. This in turn has influenced the evolution of government interoperability frameworks, wherein some governments have incorporated enterprise architecture based approaches. Today, new socio-economic challenges require policy makers to rethink their approaches in ways that will enable them to constantly improve and evolve citizen-centric services powered by ICT enabled Connected Transformational Government.

As there has not yet been enough work on enterprise architectures for fully integrated knowledge-based, highly-sophisticated (citizen-oriented) personalized services, this chapter aims to articulate upon a perspective to design architectures for the development and provision of such services. In doing so, the authors benefit from their knowledge and experience gained via the Turkish e-Government Gateway (eGG) and general e-government services development and provisioning. Chapter 17, "Enterprise Architecture for Personalization of E-Government Services: Reflections from Turkey," is a discussion on development of eGG services in Turkey, and provides a visionary suggestion for knowledge-based personalized, citizen-centric e-government. Among the suggested perspectives, an E-Citizen Decision Support System, and Entity-Utility and Information Flow Model could be useful for eGG development in Turkey and elsewhere.

Chapter 18, "IT Reform and Enterprise Architecture in the United States' Public Sector Reforms: Issues and Recommendations," looks at whole-of-government public sector reforms from an IT focused enterprise architecture perspective. The chapter summarizes reforms carried out under three US presidents—Clinton, Bush, and Obama—and discusses how they have too frequently failed to meet expectations of policy makers, public servants, the public, and other stakeholders. We find that IT reforms in support of larger public sector reforms have been ineffective and unsustainable, although many IT reforms have been successful in a narrower context. Enterprise architecture has suffered as a once promising methodology that did not become the "silver bullet" in managing the IT and information infrastructure to support reforms, knowledge management, and decision-making. It is also seen as an important tool for reducing information management silos that successive governments have unsuccessfully tried to reduce. This chapter raises the spectre of endemic barriers to reforms that must be overcome if enterprise architecture and IT reforms are to realize their potential, and offers recommendations for overcoming these hurdles in the context of whole-of-government public sector reforms.

SECTION 5: PUBLIC VALUE MANAGEMENT IN CONNECTED GOVERNMENT

Countries make large investments in numerous initiatives in their quest to be more connected. Furthermore, a large proportion of these investments are for ICT. This is necessitated because these countries realize the contribution of ICT to national economies leading to digital prosperity. Developing countries, in general, face the spectre of digital divide, which at times undermines the benefits derived from connected government. Additionally, many times the benefits that are derived tend to be subjective and socio-cultural in nature. These are difficult to quantify and monetize. Proliferation of connected government-centric architecture programs can lead to competition for resources and influence. Thus, it is imperative, that all such initiatives and programs are accompanied with rigorous value assessment, and such assessments become integral elements of any methods, practices, guidelines, and mechanisms. The rigor alleviates any concerns about inadequate value and benefits that the citizens demand and expect. This section, consisting of three chapters, shows how.

Government investments in enhancing the interoperability of ICT systems have the potential to improve services and help governments respond to the diverse and often incompatible needs and interests of individual citizens, organizations, and society at large. The diversity of stakeholder needs and the complexity inherent in interoperable systems for connected government require an architecture that is up to the task. The value propositions that underlie the architecture's performance assessment or reference model are fundamental. The propositions must be broad enough to span the full scope of the government program goals. Chapter 19, "Assessing the Value of Investments in Government Interoperability," puts forward two perspectives for assessing the value of interoperable ICT investments incorporating outcomes beyond financial metrics. The first is the network value approach to assessment of investments in interoperable ICT systems for government. The second is the public value framework developed by the Center for Technology in Government, which expands on the network value approach to include a broader range of public value outcomes. These approaches are illustrated via two case studies: (1) the I-Choose project designed to produce interoperable government and private sector data about a specific agricultural market and (2) the government of Colombia's interoperability efforts with expanded metrics based on the expansion of interoperability networks.

Cloud computing is a very demanding technology regarding the level of maturity (stages) of enterprise architecture, and more so when the business processes of the governments are directly affected by the implementation of cloud computing. Therefore, an extra stage in enterprise architecture and an extra service model are conceived to better map the opportunities and risks while investing in cloud computing. Chapter 20, "A Public Economics Approach to Enabling Enterprise Architecture with the Government Cloud in Belgium," proposes a holistic generic investment framework aimed to align cloud computing and other investments with the strategy and operations of the government. Real options and option games (along with classical investment techniques) are used to give the public management the flexibility to adjust the course of actions of the (investments) projects. In this framework the move of legacy systems to the Cloud and the overall risks related to the implementation of cloud computing are discussed. The main question addressed is whether governments can implement ambitious cloud computing projects without enterprise architecture, and if not, then, which stage should be used.

The United States' Federal Government is in an extreme financial crisis. The national debt is $14 Trillion and the national deficit is $1.3 Trillion. The Federal Government seeks to improve government-wide performance, reduce operating costs, reduce national debt, and reduce national deficit. If the Government continues its current enterprise management approach, the national debt and national deficit could become greater and the Government could default on its debt. Chapter 21, "Addressing the United States' Federal Government Financial Crisis: A Case for Department of Defense Enterprise Architecture Based Approach," proposes that the DOD institutionalize an enterprise architecture based approach to improve department-wide performance, reduce operating costs, reduce national debt, and reduce national deficit.

I expect this book to be greatly useful and have direct application benefits to a wide spectrum of audiences. The intended audience and potential uses include:

1. Government Leaders, Chief Architects, Analysts, and Designers seeking better, quicker, and easier approaches to respond to needs of their internal and external customers;
2. Policy Analysts, Line-of-Business Managers concerned with maximizing business value of IT and business competitiveness;
3. CIOs/CTOs of business software companies interested in incorporating government enterprise architecture to differentiate their products and services offerings and increasing the value proposition to their customers;
4. Consultants and practitioners desirous of new solutions and technologies to improve the productivity of their government clients;
5. Business management, public policy, and IS management educators interested in imparting knowledge about this vital discipline;
6. Academic and consulting researchers looking to uncover and characterize new research problems and programs; and
7. Electronic government professionals involved with organizational technology strategic planning, technology procurement, management of technology projects, consulting and advising on technology issues, and management of total cost of ownership.

In being the first book that explicitly investigates the role of enterprise architecture as a means to connected government, this is seminal. The subject matter covered in this book has been my passion for a decade. I take immense pride in sharing my work and the outstanding works of the other contributing authors to a wider audience. In the coming years I envision a greater maturity in government enterprise architecture initiatives, and I anticipate that the book will make a direct contribution to that vision.

This book is about the future and how steps are being taken to realize that future. The book, through a confluence of ideas and practices, demonstrates foresight and is a guide to inventing tomorrow's good practices today. In this context, my assumption is that countries would rather lead than follow. If that happens to be your goal too, then welcome aboard.

Pallab Saha
National University of Singapore, Singapore
2012

Acknowledgment

This book reflects the ideas and contributions of many individuals. I have always been deeply interested in the discipline of enterprise architecture. Given that the government sector presents some very complex challenges, it has been my area of research for several years now. As part of this journey, I have been privileged to contribute to Singapore's Government Enterprise Architecture; collaborate with some outstanding experts at the United Nations and the World Bank; advise several national governments through their journeys and be part of the government enterprise architecture community globally. All of the above have reinforced my passion and interest, and provided the trigger for me to conceive this book. This book is an excellent example of team effort.

First and foremost, I would like to thank IGI Global for giving me the opportunity to continue my wonderful collaboration with them. This is my third book with IGI Global, and it has been a great partnership so far. Secondly, I would like to thank all contributing chapter authors. Their contribution has been invaluable. They are all well experienced and respected experts representing both academia and practice.

Last, but not the least, the contribution of the Editorial Advisory Board (EAB) cannot be overstated. These are globally recognized experts who took time off their busy schedules to review the chapters and provide constructive feedback to improve the overall quality of chapters. Thus, the EAB played a crucial role in enhancing the quality of the book. Interacting with them over the years has enriched my understanding in many ways.

This book would not have become a reality without the blessings of my mother, Shrimati Anima Saha, and my father, the late Shri Jagatbandhu Saha. I thank Neeta, my wife, for her love, support, and patience, while this was being written. A special word of love goes to our most adorable daughter Anushka. Neeta and I were blessed with Anushka when I started working on my first book, and now with this fourth book, she is on the verge of entering primary school.

Pallab Saha
National University of Singapore, Singapore

Section 1
The Connected Government Paradigm

Chapter 1

Connected Government as the New Normal:
A Strategic Thinking Approach to Whole–of–Government Enterprise Architecture Adoption

Pallab Saha
National University of Singapore, Singapore

ABSTRACT

Around the world, governments are constantly facing new demands, greater expectations, and an increasingly more vociferous and assertive citizenry calling for better governance. In such a scenario, governments can ill-afford to ignore such demands and expectations. The current challenges faced by governments, for example in Europe, the United States, and the Middle East, represent a complex mix of political, legal, social, and economic issues. These are increasingly not limited to national boundaries, and the underlying inter-linkages cannot be overstated. This confluence of demands, expectations, challenges, and trends require governments to be connected in the broadest and deepest sense. The traditional governments operating in relative isolation and projecting an image of infallibility are rapidly being replaced by governments that are more networked, responsive, collaborative, and participative. Co-creation of services leading to co-production of government is the new paradigm. This transition requires fundamental change in current mental models, supported by a structured and disciplined approach to conceive and design the connected government. Taking a whole-of-government perspective is a

DOI: 10.4018/978-1-4666-1824-4.ch001

critical success factor. It is imperative to think strategically to elevate the role of enterprise architecture. This chapter identifies the key dimensions of connected government, presents their distinctive attributes, explores the powerful, but, in some cases, controversial, concepts of connected government, and by embracing a systemic approach, investigates the criticality of enterprise architecture in powering connected government. The foundational ideas in this chapter lay out a broad framework for understanding and benefiting from enterprise architecture, actualized via the edifice of connected government.

1. INTRODUCTION

Enterprise Architecture (EA) is defined as the ongoing process of building the ability to tackle complexity, with the pivotal goal of creating and sustaining coherent enterprises. EA is often used to plan and implement efficient and effective transformation efforts. However, the strongest driver for EA is to improve service delivery and overall performance within the organization's business segments. The principal challenge faced by chief architects today is to institute an EA program that is able to coordinate sustainable changes throughout the enterprise, while simultaneously mentoring the specific transformation planning that is needed to support the mission (Saha, 2007).

In a nutshell, EA is a robust planning function which helps organizations understand the process by which business strategies turn into operational reality. Hence, establishing a standard methodology for conducting architecture planning and implementation is vital. Metaphorically, an EA is to an organization's strategy and operations as a set of blueprints is to a city and its buildings. Traditionally, by following an architecture-based approach, organizations strive to address issues pertaining to: (1) business alignment; (2) information accuracy and integrity; (3) infrastructure management; (4) security; (5) technology compatibility; (6) business value of IT; (7) enterprise governance; (8) business collaboration; and (9) procurement among several others. Though EA is often assumed to follow an organization's strategy and to enable alignment of IT with business objectives, increasingly, evidence of the reverse is also surfacing. In other words, organizational strategies are being influenced by IT capabilities (Saha, 2007, 2008).

Conventionally, EA consists of a collection of interconnected architectural domains (also called viewpoints or perspectives). These are:

- *Policy and strategy architecture*, which establishes principles, rules and guidelines aimed at providing direction to the entire enterprise.
- *Business architecture*, which defines enterprise business outcomes, functions, capabilities and end-to-end business processes, and their relationships with external entities required to execute business strategies;
- *Data / information architecture*, which deals with the structure and utility of information within the organization, and its alignment with its strategic, tactical and operational needs;
- *Application architecture*, which specifies the structure of individual systems based on defined technology; and
- *Technical architecture*, which defines the technology environment and infrastructure in which all IT systems operate.

The above five domains largely represent the current state of practice in the discipline of EA. In their book, *Coherency Management: Architecting the Enterprise for Alignment, Agility, and Assurance*, authors Doucet, Gotze, Saha, and Bernard present and discuss the **extended** and **embedded** modes of EA in addition to the **traditional** mode. They assert that as organizations start embracing the more advanced **extended** and **embedded** modes, the need for synergy and consistency amplifies, thus facilitating the attainment of **organizational coherence**, the ultimate goal of EA (Doucet, et al., 2009). Successful EA not only captures the above five (5) domains, but also the relationships between them. Having linkages between the five (5) domains provide line-of-sight (or traceability) to the relevant stakeholders of the EA. Figure 1 depicts the key domains of EA, with special focus on government EA.

EA effectively supports the business, enables information sharing across departments / divisions / organizations, enhances management's ability to deliver effective and timely services and improves operational efficiencies. Committing to an ongoing EA practice within an enterprise enables a business-aligned and technology-adaptive enterprise that is effective efficient and agile (Burns, et al., 2009).

Most governments worldwide are in the midst of substantial public sector transformation activities. A majority of these initiatives is triggered by the need to have better and seamless government services delivered online. The focus on automating government services often is largely limited to specific ministries and agencies. However, such initiatives lack the cross-ministry / agency viewpoint and coordination. This creates challenges in embracing a Whole-Of-Government (W-O-G) approach with its associated benefits, which are much more than the benefits derived by merely taking agency-centric viewpoints. These shortcomings are clearly evident in the findings of the UN Global E-Government Survey 2010. According to the UN, the value of e-government will be increasingly defined by its contribution to national development. Lack of coherent strategy is often cited as the primary reason for underdevelopment of e-government. Moving forward, more and more countries are adopting national e-government strategies and multi-year action plans, and EA is the strategy that governments are increasingly looking toward (UNDESA, 2008; UNDESA, 2010). According to Haiyan Qian,

Figure 1. Components of government enterprise architecture

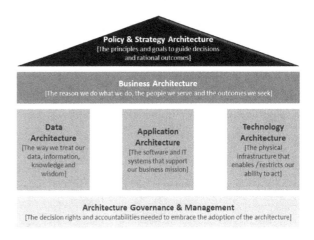

Director of the Division for Public Administration and Development Management, United Nations Department of Economic and Social Affairs (UNDESA), "EA is an effective strategic planning tool for governments by [facilitating] creation of linkages and improving interoperability among government agencies, benefiting both internal operational processes as well as improved public service delivery to citizens." Adoption of IT for government services and programs plays an important role in designing and furthering the e-government initiatives. Robert Atkinson and Andrew Mackay, in their report titled "Digital Prosperity-Understanding the Economic Benefits of Information Technology Revolution," clearly demonstrate the role and influence of IT adoption to national productivity and overall economic prosperity (Atkinson & Mackay, 2007). This is not surprising given the ability of IT to enable nearly every aspect of a modern knowledge based economy that countries increasingly aspire to be. The ubiquity of the IT makes it even more compelling to embrace and derive benefits out of. Figure 2 depicts the systemic view of this phenomenon.

Figure 2. Information and communication technology (ICT) enabled economic growth and digital prosperity

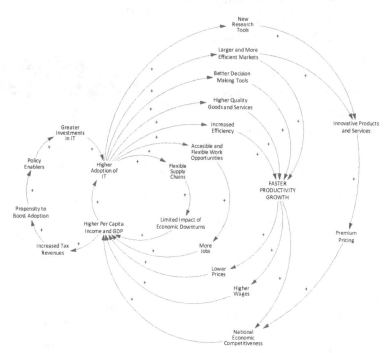

2. BACKGROUND: UNDERSTANDING CONNECTED GOVERNMENT

Connected government *enables governments to connect seamlessly across functions, agencies and jurisdictions to deliver effective and efficient services to citizens and businesses.* The United Nations (UN), in its Global E-Government Survey of 2008, used to connect governance as its primary criteria to evaluate and rank national e-government programs. According to the survey, the concept of connected government is derived from the W-O-G approach which utilizes technology as a strategic tool and enabler for public service innovation and productivity growth, the key outcomes being public service **innovation** and digital **prosperity** (UNDESA, 2008).

In continuation of this theme, the UN Global E-Government Survey of 2010 takes the concept of connected government even further, adding "citizen centricity" as the watchword. This ap-

proach to government service delivery requires countries to shift from a model of providing government services via traditional modes to integrate electronic modes wherein the value to the citizens and businesses gets enhanced. According to the UN, such IT-enabled services (e-services) can actually improve the rate and quality of public service delivery in times of economic crises (UNDESA, 2010).

Thus connected government, of which e-services are a crucial component, leads to several benefits, both internally to the provider agencies and governments, and externally to the consumer citizens and businesses. Figure 3 lists the benefits (UNDESA, 2008).

Government transformation is a long term endeavor that is seldom impacted by any short term technology trends. In their transition toward connected government, all governments typically traverse through the four primary stages of e-government capability and maturity, each stage representing a progressively higher level in the

Figure 3. Benefits from IT-enabled connected government

Benefits from Connected Government	
Internal (To Provider Agencies and Governments)	**External** (To Consumer Citizens and Businesses)
1. Avoidance of duplication	1. Faster service delivery
2. Reduction in transaction costs	2. Greater efficacy
3. Simplified bureaucratic procedures	3. Increased flexibility of service use
4. Greater efficiencies	4. Innovation in service delivery
5. Richer communication & coordination	5. Greater participation and inclusion
6. Enhanced transparency	6. Greater citizen empowerment
7. Greater information sharing	7. Greater openness and transparency
8. Secure information management	

government transformation continuum. The four widely used stages of e-government capability and maturity are; **Web presence**, **interaction**, **transaction**, and **transformation**. Furthermore, connected government is the desired state that countries strive to reach as part of their **transformation** journey of e-government maturity (UN-DESA, 2008). However, there is no straightforward way to describe what exactly connected government means and its implications for countries.

Based on the current state of the practice and available literature, connected government is expected to entail certain characteristics and capabilities. These characteristics and capabilities, described below, are clearly stated to be the key contributors to e-government development according to the UN E-Government Survey 2010, and in turn contribute to national development (UNDESA, 2010). These characteristics and capabilities, structured as dimensions, allow connected government to be viewed as a multi-dimensional construct. The dimensions of connected government are:

- **Citizen centricity**: This refers to viewing governments from the outside-in, i.e. understanding the requirements and expectations of the citizens becomes the pre-eminent guiding principle for all government policies, programs and services. In short, this represents the service-dominant logic which requires governments to operate as

one enterprise and organize themselves around citizen demands and requirements (AGIMO, 2010; Cisco IBSG, 2009). Aside for the citizens per se, other government constituents, such as businesses and civil organizations, are captured in the **social inclusion** dimension described later;

- **Common infrastructure and interoperability**: This refers to the use of standards and best practices across governments so as to encourage and enable the sharing of information in a seamless manner. Interoperability is the ability of organizations to share information and knowledge within and across organizational boundaries (APDIP, 2007). The underlying foundation for effective interoperability comes from standardized common infrastructure;

- **Collaborative services and business operations**: Connected government requires ministries and agencies to collaborate. It is not difficult to uncover success stories about integration and interoperability at the technology level. However, to collaborate at the level of business services and functions requires political will. This is because collaboration at this level leads to shallower stovepipes, elimination of redundant or overlapping services and discovery of common and shared services, which in turn lead to loss of authority and control for some (Saha, 2008);

- **Public sector governance**: This refers to the decision rights and the accountability framework required for implementing all the other strategies for connected government. Good governance is a non-negotiable factor in the success of connected government, more so in countries that have multiple levels of governments (i.e. federal / central; state / provincial; and town / city) where various levels could be administered by different political parties (Cisco IBSG, 2004);

- **Networked organizational model**: As Theresa Pardo and Brian Burke discuss in their work on government interoperability, this refers to the need to accommodate new organizational models wherein the enterprise (in the context of the W-O-G) is a network of relatively autonomous ministries and agencies working in a coherent manner to deliver value to both citizens and businesses. This makes the whole-of-government a networked virtual organization (NVO) that operates seamlessly toward a common mission (Pardo & Burke, 2008);

- **Social inclusion**: This refers to the ability of governments to move beyond horizontal and vertical integration of government service delivery to engaging the citizens and businesses at relevant points in the policy and decision making processes. E-democracy and social inclusion ensure that delivery of government services is not a one-way exchange. Innovative ways of using technology to facilitate constituent participation and building a consultative approach are imperative for the success of connected government (Microsoft, 2010); and

- **Transparency and open government**: This refers to the political doctrine which holds that the business of government and state administration should be opened at all levels to effective public scrutiny and oversight. In its broader construction it opposes reason of state and national security considerations, which have tended to legitimize extensive state secrecy (Halstead, et al., 2009).

The levers that contribute to performance along the dimensions are presented in this chapter. In addition, connected government is expanded to include four evolutionary stages, described in a subsequent section of this chapter. Together, they allow much greater clarity and granularity in the description, role, structure and implications of connected government that so many countries seek to achieve.

According to the UN, moving to connected government requires a holistic and coherent framework, which cannot be achieved by piecemeal approaches and mechanisms. Such a framework recognizes the integrated presence of e-government both as an internal driver of transformation within the public sector and an external driver of better governance. Typically governments are the largest organizations. They are further characterized by complex federated structures where individual government organizations work in their respective silos. This often leads to fragmented business processes and duplicated systems and technologies, creating obstacles in cross-agency interoperability. Government-wide architecture allows end-to-end business processes, standard technologies, rationalized the data structure and modularized e-services that can be assembled as required to deliver e-services (UNDESA, 2008).

EA is a critical success factor for all types, scale and intensities of e-government programs. The key goal of EA in government organizations is to make them citizen-centered, results-oriented and market-based. Governments usually pass through different evolutionary stages in their EA journeys. There is no dearth of literature that identify leadership as the most important success factor for e-government. Taking **leadership** and **orientation** as the two dimensions, the

Figure 4. Design and evolutionary stages of EA

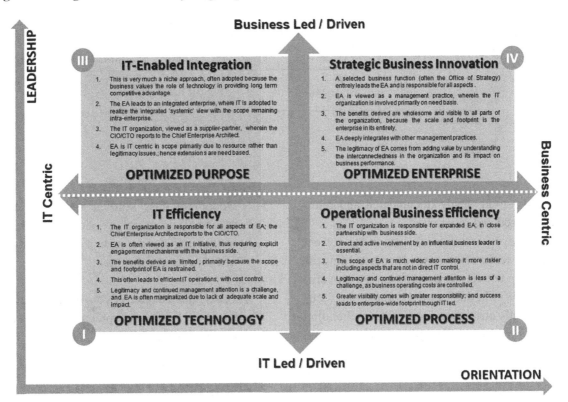

four designs and evolutionary stages of the EA are; **optimized technology, optimized process, optimized purpose** and **optimized enterprise**. Even though optimization of technology is not a prerequisite, it is a valid entry point into the EA journey for many countries. The primary reasons being: (1) EA programs are largely driven by the CIO / IT departments, hence they have maximum control over the technology infrastructure; and (2) this is an area where tangible benefits can be demonstrated fairly quickly. These two reasons make technology optimization an attractive entry point, even though countries (and governments) must move beyond this to other stages of EA evolution to derive full benefits. However, the caveat is that transitioning to higher levels of evolution requires greater involvement of a broad range of stakeholders and government constituents. The characteristics of the four EA design and evolutionary stages are shown in Figure 4.

Interestingly, there exists a positive correlation between the **desired level of e-government capability and maturity** and the **required level of architectural maturity**. Figure 5 shows this relationship, from which the ability to build and manage advanced government EA is a necessary prerequisite for countries aiming to elevate to higher levels of e-government maturity and capability (Saha, 2008).

Connected government as a goal is gaining acceptance and popularity. This is demonstrated by various e-government surveys that are conducted regularly by different organizations including the UN. The expanding role of EA as a central component of e-government programs is substantiated by the fact that several countries have taken a legislative approach to embracing and adopting EA. Furthermore, there have been several EA surveys conducted in the past few years. Hence, individually (e-government and EA) are

Figure 5. Mapping e-government maturity to government EA evolution

E-Government Maturity Stages	Government EA Maturity Stages			
	Optimized Technology	Optimized Process	Optimized Purpose	Optimized Enterprise
1. Web Presence	√			
2. Interaction	√	√		
3. Transaction		√√	√	
4. Transformation (Connected Government)			√√	√√√

well understood, richly documented and regularly assessed and researched.

This chapter addresses the gap in the current literature in terms of linking and understanding the relationship between e-government and government EA. Within this broader context, the focus is specifically on uncovering and comprehending the relationship between government EA and connected government. The primary reason for focusing on connected government is that it is the area where government EA has the highest potential for influence and as a result the highest levels of benefits derived, as is evident from Figure 5.

The aim is to address the questions: (1) **can enterprise architecture act as a platform for connected government?**; and (2) **what will it take for enterprise architecture to do so?**, substantiating any claims with empirical evidence. The research objectives are to:

1. Identify and develop dimensions of connected government and position it as a multi-dimensional construct.
2. Specify levers that positively influence the various dimensions of connected government.
3. Understand the role of enterprise architecture (either as a facilitator or inhibitor) in achieving connected government.
4. Identify enterprise architecture capabilities and structure them as a meta-framework to act as a positive factor in connected government.

5. Document case studies and experience reports of successful use of enterprise architecture in transitioning to some or all stages of connected government.

Broadly, this chapter covers objectives 1, 2, 3, and 4. The remaining chapters of the book collectively cover objective 5.

3. ASSESSMENT FRAMEWORK AND FINDINGS

In order to evaluate current government EA frameworks an assessment framework has been established and utilized for the rest of the study. In alignment with the research objectives delineated earlier, the **Enterprise Architecture Assessment Framework for Connected Government (EAAF-CG)** is based on the dimensions of connected government presented here. Figure 6 shows the assessment framework along with the **dimensions** and **levers**. Connected government is systemic in nature. This makes the relationships between **dimensions** and **levers** causal and mutually reinforcing among and between themselves by design.

Section 2 identifies and describes the dimensions of connected government and Section 3 presents the levers that contribute to the dimensions of connected government. The EA assessment framework is derived from these two, wherein the impact of government EA on the

Figure 6. EA assessment framework for connected government

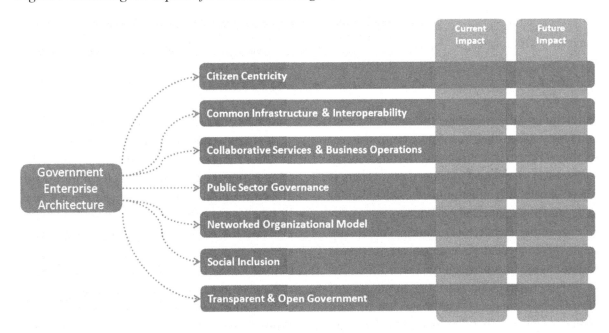

Enterprise Architecture Assessment Framework for Connected Government	
Dimensions of Connected Government	**Levers to Connected Government Dimensions**
1. Citizen Centricity	A. Citizen requirements & expectations B. Government appears and operates as one C. Multiple channels of engagement D. Adaptability of government services
2. Common Infrastructure & Interoperability	A. Technology standards B. Government-wide applications & systems C. Data exchange standards D. ICT & infrastructure management
3. Collaborative Services & Business Operations	A. Collaborative business functions B. Shared services C. Shared information D. Service innovation & back office reorganization
4. Public Sector Governance	A. Business function ownership B. Business outcome accountability C. Governance structures, policies and practices D. Institutionalization of governance
5. Networked Organizational Model	A. Multi-stakeholder cooperation B. Ministry / agency and government level autonomy C. Cluster based approach & common mission D. Value network
6. Social Inclusion	A. Citizen engagement at various levels B. Citizen outreach C. Responsive government
7. Transparent & Open Government	A. Public scrutiny & oversight B. Data discovery, availability & accessibility C. Performance management & accountability D. Legal Framework(s)

Figure 7. Modeling the impact of EA on connected government

levers and the dimensions of connected government are analyzed. Figure 7 represents the purpose and approach taken in this research study. For deeper analysis, six levels of impact are defined.

The levels of impact (influence) are specified in Figure 8.

It is important to note that the **dimensions** and **levers** of connected government and **impact levels** of government EA together form the foun-

Figure 8. Levels of impact of EA on connected government

Levels of Impact of EA on Connected Government	
Impact Level	**Descriptions**
Level 0 → None	This indicates that EA has no influence on connected government. There may be elements of this connected government dimension existing in the e-government programs, but they are isolated and independent of EA.
Level 1 → Marginal	This indicates, if at all, EA has minimal influence on connected government. It is characterized by ad-hoc, spotty and inconsistent influence. The elements of EA that have the potential to influence are being put in place.
Level 2 → Localized	This is indicative of the partial influence on connected government. The elements of EA with clarity of purpose are specified, and the influence is ad-hoc and localized to a few lines-of-business, ministries and agencies.
Level 3 → Defined	This is indicative of the continuous and consistent influence on connected government. The elements of the EA are clearly defined, their roles in e-government programs specified and outcomes established. However the EA itself may be positioned a recommended good practice, but not mandatory.
Level 4 → Institutionalized	This is indicative of the continuous and consistent influence on connected government. The elements of the EA are clearly defined, their roles in e-government programs specified, outcomes established and continuously tracked. Government EA efforts are internalized and embraced widely across the whole-of-government. However there could be a tendency that linkages between the various dimensions of connected government are ambiguous.
Level 5 → Optimized	This exhibits all the characteristics applicable to Level 4. In addition, the linkages between the different dimensions of connected government are made explicit and the EA activities and programs are optimized around these interconnected / correlated dimensions to derive the highest levels of benefits.

dation for countries reaching the connected government stage in their respective e-government journeys. However, connected government is too coarse as an assessment index or metric. There is a need to establish a fine-grained mechanism for understanding connected government as a desirable capability. Hence, four granular evolutionary stages of connected government are presented and discussed in subsequently.

This section presents a qualitative evaluation of the role of government EA programs in achieving connected government. The evaluation, based on publicly available information (i.e. information available via government websites and other literature) focuses on countries in the Asia-Pacific region. To put this in perspective, the key point that influenced the research design and objectives is the availability of several surveys on EA conducted for both the government and private sectors. However, the underlying commonality in all of these surveys is the primary objective of assessing the maturity of EA itself as a stand-alone strategic technology management practice. In other words, these surveys typically tend to evaluate EA as an end. Currently there are no surveys that investigate the role and influence (impact) of government EA to various aspects of e-government, i.e. evaluating EA as a lever to connected government, and (2) the assessment of government EA programs is based on publicly available information. In the situation wherein government websites for countries in the Asia-Pacific region may not share all the information, the survey findings are adequately tempered. The intention of the survey in this phase is not to pin-

Figure 9. Current impact of EA on connected government in selected countries

Current Impact of Enterprise Architecture on Connected Government

DIMENSIONS	UAE	AUSTRALIA	JORDAN	NEW ZEALAND	SAUDI ARABIA	SOUTH KOREA
Citizen Centricity	Marginal	Localized	Defined	Defined	None	Institutionalized
Common Infrastructure & Interoperability	Localized	Defined	Defined	Institutionalized	Localized	Institutionalized
Collaborative Services & Business Operations	Marginal	Defined	Defined	Institutionalized	Marginal	Institutionalized
Public Sector Governance	Marginal	Localized	Defined	Localized	None	Institutionalized
Networked Organizational Model	None	Localized	Defined	Institutionalized	Localized	Defined
Social Inclusion	None	Marginal	Marginal	Defined	Marginal	Localized
Transparent & Open Government	None	Marginal	Marginal	Localized	None	Localized

point inadequacies, but to derive a general sense of direction in an aggregated manner.

Figure 9 shows the current impact of EA on connected government in selected countries. The survey of the six countries clearly reveals that connected government is a desirable long-term goal for national e-government programs. This is further evidenced by the UN Global E-Government Survey of 2010 wherein the four stages of online service development include **emerging**, **enhanced**, **transactional,** and **connected** (UNDESA, 2008). The e-participation is considered separately. The above considers connected government (i.e. the connectedness) from the point of view of government being a service provider and its goal of doing this in the most efficient way. The service consumer point of view is partly captured via the e-participation dimension. It is obvious that there is a need to unify both the service provider and service consumer points of view and extend the definition of connected government.

The countries surveyed were deliberately selected for their wide range of characteristics that include e-government capabilities, government EA practices, national plans, and formally directed efforts (Liimatainen, et al., 2007). From the country assessments, the following levels of connectedness are identified and proposed. The levels represent the **evolutionary stages** of connected government.

- **Intra-governmental**: Connectedness among and between government ministries and agencies that usually leads to the W-O-G perspective and being viewed as a single virtual and networked enterprise. This also includes interactions and coherency at multiple layers of government (national, state, province, district, city). Notwithstanding the richness of interactions, the extent of connectedness is limited within the boundaries of government.

- **Inter-governmental**: This is connectedness between sovereign nations driven by common and shared goals and objectives on issues that have multi country or global repercussions (examples include law enforcement, customs, counter-terrorism, health, intellectual property, free trade agreements, etc.).

- **Extra-governmental**: This refers to the connectedness between government and associated business organizations and partners outside of the government. This type of connectedness allows the creation of services that may be planned and delivered in collaboration with non-governmental entities, seamlessly integrated, and usually leading to service ecosystems. Coproduction of government is the outcome.

- **Ubiquitous**: This refers to connectedness that facilitates multi-dimensional multi-channel all pervasive communication between all stakeholders (but focusing more on citizens) by way of participation, engagement, openness, government transparency, and accountability. This is the stage wherein government itself acts as a platform and coherency is imperative as connectedness is fully diffused, comprehensive and encompasses the emotional aspects as well.

Figure 10 shows the four evolutionary stages of connected government derived by expanding the connected stage in the approach used by the UN. Figure 11 depicts their key characteristics, and the relationship between government connectedness and performance.

It is crucial to view the four evolutionary stages of connected government is the context of intensity of participation that is needed to make it happen. Greater engagement leads to better outcomes at lower cost, more innovative solutions and services, acceptability of greater diversity, better use of resources and higher compliance to

decisions. Participation 2.0 requires a paradigm shift in the way interactions between governments and other entities take place.

The varying degrees and approaches that countries use EA as a means to achieve connected government is noticeable from the assessments carried out. The following are the key findings and issues for discussion that can be extracted.

Government EA programs have traditionally been used to establish common underlying infrastructure and interoperability. The technology, application, data, and security architectures directly contribute to this. This is not difficult to explain as EA has generally been viewed as a structured and disciplined approach for IT management and planning, in most cases, led by the IT department (CIO office) in the government. Common infrastructure and interoperability also require the least amount of involvement from the service consumers and users, thereby making it (politically) easier to progress. The emergence of cloud computing is making the move to common infrastructure even more justifiable. Collaborative services and business operations incorporate interoperability at the business layer. Even though government EA efforts have tried to address this dimension in their bid to achieve connectedness, real progress is often hampered by weak governance. In scenarios wherein traditionally government ministries and agencies operate with a good degree of autonomy (and hence in their own stovepipes), getting them to collaborate is not necessarily easy. Government entities can often consider this as an intrusion into their autonomy (Fishenden, et al., 2006). At the intergovernmental level this could be equated to intrusion into national sovereignty. Furthermore, identifying collaborative services and business functions is only part of the issue. The biggest factor for all types of connectedness is to get common agreement on ownership and management of such collaborative services. With government EA efforts pushing the W-O-G viewpoint, it is not entirely uncommon to this being realized. Successful national EA programs have created the no-

Figure 10. Evolutionary stages of connected government

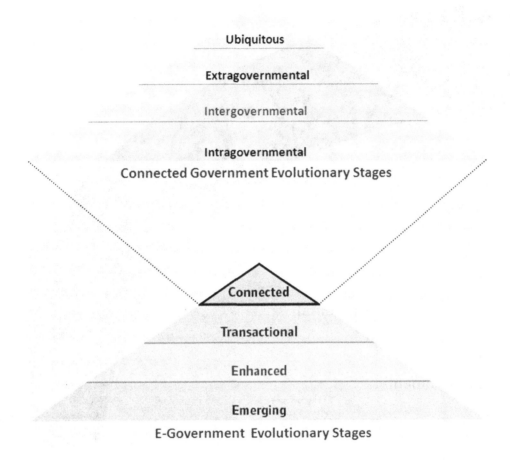

tion of governments operating as large integrated enterprises, allowing citizens to interact with the government though multi-channel engagement mechanisms. Advanced implementations, as in South Korea, even allow the possibility of citizens being provided individually customized intelligent services (Leechul, 2010). This is realized through building service modularity capability during service analysis and design (Janssen & Hjort-Madsen, 2007). The prospect of having customized services encourages citizens to interact more with the government, thus contributing to ubiquitous connectedness.

Advanced and successful e-governments have effective authority and accountability structures at the core. The underlying technology can only do so much. Without good governance, e-government programs can have severely limited benefits. Overall, public sector governance is a critical success factor as it eliminates ambiguity in terms of stakeholders, their roles and responsibilities, enforcement mechanisms and practices, expected outcomes, and mission effectiveness. Most government EA frameworks are limited to the governance of the architecture during and after the development. There are not many instances of utilizing EA as a means to enhance the broader public sector governance. The role of public sector governance gains importance as countries try to extend the degree and intensity of their connectedness from intragovernmental to ubiquitous. Viewed in conjunction with collaborative services

Figure 11. Evolution of connected government mapped to government performance

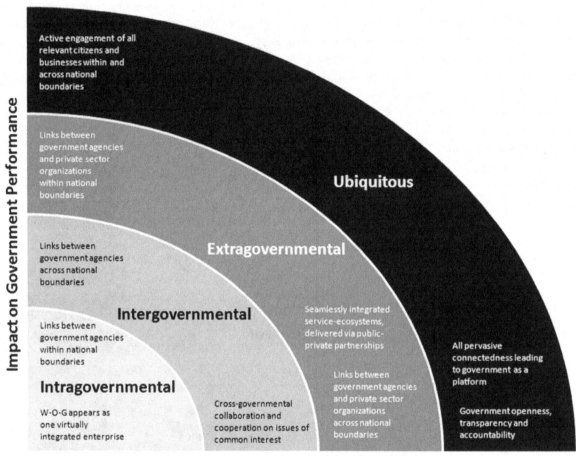

and business operations, the centrality of effective governance cannot be overstated.

For governments to provide citizen centric seamless services that are adequately modularized for necessary flexibility, there is a need to understand complete value networks, their constituents and stakeholders and levels of required coordination and cooperation. This becomes non-trivial if the value network includes a mix of providers from the government and the private sectors as these two groups typically have a divergent set of goals, objectives and operating models. Government EA has not been fully utilized to address this dimension of connected government. Key areas where EA could be used include: (1) articulation of the

shared business purpose; (2) delineation of targets and goals; (3) continuous tracking of performance; (4) collaboration factors and needs; and (5) legal and governance issues. **Service Canada** (http://www.servicecanada.gc.ca/eng/home.shtml) is a good example of citizen centric services being provided by a multitude of service providers both from the public and private sectors. As it should be, the service consumers (citizens) are completely transparent to the complex networks of providers that work together to provide consumable services (Microsoft, 2009).

Social inclusion and open government are relatively new dimensions in the context of connected government. These bring the "softer" aspects into the picture. Trust, openness, and accountability play a critical role. Traditional EA programs have viewed and designed government services largely from a service provider perspective, wherein the emphasis is on getting the various government entities to be "connected" to one another. EA frameworks that addressed the issue of citizens being "connected" to the government via active engagement and participation are weak or altogether missing. Government EA frameworks must factor in the influence of social media and the paradigm shift that it brings in to participation, as discussed earlier. The four most likely operating models for e-governments of the future can be derived by addressing two most basic questions: (1) what is the level of trust in government from the citizens; and (2) will public administration focus on increased participation or will the main goal be to deliver government services in the most efficient manner. Plotting these two questions as two distinct dimensions, four quadrants, each representing an operating model, are derived (Nordfors, et al., 2009). These are:

- **Government goes private**: The strong demand for government services, which government entities alone are unable to fulfill, powers the need to trust service providers in the private sector.
- **The limits of efficiency**: Government itself is subject to several rounds of reengineering and other improvement initiatives, leading to greater efficiencies, including reduction of overlaps, gaps, and economies of scale benefits. That said, the regime of low trust reigns supreme; hence, as demand for services increase, governments become the bottleneck.
- **Chaotic government**: Though this represents citizens demonstrating high participation in government matters, they have a low trust in the government. This leads to stakeholders aiming to influence decisions and support individuals. However, this

takes place without any focus or structure, leading to unbridled interactions.

- **Co-production of government**: Characterized by high trust and high participation, government services are delivered in a coherent manner with ample collaboration between government and private sector service providers. Co-production represents the most desirable form of connected government.

Moving up the connected government maturity levels and selecting the relevant government operating model necessitates governments are viewed in a holistic manner. Government EA provides that capability, and this is discussed in the next section.

4. STRATEGIC (SYSTEMS) THINKING IN THE GOVERNMENT

Government EA has gained the center stage as an essential discipline to enable and even drive government transformation. To be considered the "**architecture of the enterprise**," it is thus an imperative to understand the enterprise that is to be architected, an understanding that permeates the entire enterprise (Saha, 2008; Doucet, et al., 2009). Yet, all current government EA activities focus entirely on the operational aspects, completely ignoring the more important strategic aspects. In order for government leaders and policy makers to comprehend the role and intended outcomes from government EA programs, it is imperative that they view such programs from a strategic viewpoint in the way these are planned, designed, embraced, managed, and governed. It would be an understatement to say that enterprises are complex (Sterman, 2000).

Going a step further, governments are even more complex and at times paradoxical. This stems from the fact that governments are by far the largest enterprises and with size comes

Figure 12. Characteristics of complex adaptive systems (governments)

Common Characteristics of Complex Adaptive Systems (Governments)	
1. Constantly changing	6. Self-organizing
2. Tightly coupled	7. Adaptive
3. Governed by feedback	8. Counterintuitive
4. Non-linear	9. Policy resistant
5. History dependent	10. Trade-off dependent

complexity. Complexities in governments are of both types—**combinatorial complexity** and **dynamic complexity**. Complexity arising due to the sheer number of components and elements that are interconnected refers to combinatorial complexity. Dynamic complexity, on the other hand, arises due to the velocity of change and the quantum of interactions between the components and elements (Sterman, 2000; Reed, 2006). In addition, unpredictable delays between decisions and their effects (and counter-effects) completes the picture of what constitute, according to Gartner, "**wicked problems**" (Gall, et al., 2010). Chapter 2 describes a problem oriented enterprise architecture approach in addressing wicked problems.

In short, governments are excellent examples of **complex adaptive systems**. A system is *defined as a set of interrelated things encompassed by a well defined and permeable boundary, interacting with one another and an external environment, forming a complex but unitary whole and working toward a common overall goal*. Complex systems are characterized by: (1) large number of interacting components; (2) non-linear interactions leading to disproportionately major consequences; (3) dynamic behaviors where in solutions cannot be imposed, rather they arise from circumstances (emergent); (4) existence of history that influence the present and the future; (5) substantial unknown unknowns; and (6) inability to predict the future. Governments around the world are facing several challenges (wicked problems) and are under pressure to address these challenges in more open, accountable, and transparent ways

from active and vocal citizens and businesses alike. From a leader's point of view, it is hence imperative to probe, sense and respond; create environments that allow for patterns to emerge; encourage interactions and diversity to deal with such complexities. The emergence of pattern-based leadership provides the necessary impetus and direction (Reed, 2006).

In order for governments to transform, it is critical that they are understood and, as complex dynamic systems governments, exhibit the characteristics shown in Figure 12 (Sterman, 2000).

Enterprises (in this case government) characterized by Figure 12, require much more than conventional thinking in order to understand the system and the challenges that the system faces. The success of government transformation programs thus becomes dependent on comprehending the entire system (Senge, 1990). Ambiguity in understanding the system is one of the primary reasons for public sector transformation showing less than satisfactory results and success rates. It is amply evident that countries are adopting W-O-G EA as the meta-discipline to trigger, design and realize government transformation, and taking a systemic perspective is the most logical way to move forward.

However, in the past decade or so the focus of W-O-G EA programs has been on developing frameworks, methodologies, languages, guidelines, best practices, reference architectures and other capacity building activities. This is evident in the surveys done and summarized in Figure 9 of this chapter. Despite all these seemingly im-

Figure 13. Comparing conventional (open-loop) and systems (closed-loop) thinking

Comparing Conventional and Systems Thinking	
Conventional (Open-Loop) Thinking	**Systems (Closed-Loop) Thinking**
Static thinking Focusing on particular events.	**Dynamic thinking** Framing a problem in terms a pattern of behavior over time.
Systems-as-effect Viewing behavior generated by a system as driven by external forces.	**System-as-cause** Placing responsibility for a behavior on internal factors and actors.
Fragmented Believing that really knowing something means focusing on the details.	**Holistic** Believing that to know something requires understanding the context of relationships.
Factors thinking Listing factors that influence or correlate with some results.	**Operational thinking** Concentrating on causality and understanding how a behavior is generated.
Straight-line thinking Viewing causality as running in one direction, ignoring the interdependence and interaction between and among the causes.	**Loop thinking** Viewing causality as an ongoing process, with effect feeding back to influence the causes and the causes affecting one another.

pressive efforts, the adoption of W-O-G EA has been less than impressive. This is evidenced by Gartner's *Hype Cycle for Government Transformation 2011*, wherein W-O-G EA would require another ten (10) years before reaching full maturity and delivering benefits justifying its immense potential (Bittinger, 2011).

On the upside, however, Gartner's *Hype Cycle for Enterprise Architecture 2011* does state that W-O-G EA is past the bottom of the trough of disillusionment. There is no dearth of literature and other enabling resources for countries to build their enterprise architectures. Yet, after the initial enthusiasm, things are difficult to sustain with questions often being raised regarding the efficacy of government EA efforts (Burton & Allega, 2011). This is not surprising at all. EA efforts in the past decade or so have concentrated on building what could be termed as solutions to the EA problems. As it is evident from this research, nearly all EA efforts currently focus on building frameworks, methodologies, guidelines, principles, best practices and tool support. Without fully understanding the underlying system, the success achieved

through the above has been limited. This leads to two logically explainable reactions: (1) frantic efforts to improve the frameworks, methodologies, guidelines, principles, best-practices, and tool support; and (2) discontinuing the W-O-G EA altogether by terming it as "too difficult" and "too complex."

The need of the moment is not better solutions, but better thinking about the problems. Gary Hamel in his book *The Future of Management* states that solving a systemic problem requires understanding its systemic roots. This is the first of the ten (10) rules for management innovation. It is in this context that conventional open-loop thinking to solving business problems needs to be replaced with systems (closed-loop) holistic thinking (Hamel, 2007). A systemic perspective is used to understand how the numerous components of the governments act, react and interact with one another with the intent of improving the adoption of W-O-G EA for connected government. This provides a comprehensive, holistic and a more coherent way of anticipating synergies and mitigating negative emergent behaviors, which would facilitate the development of policies and other relevant intervention mechanisms. Using a systemic perspective encourages strategic thinking (Zokaei, et al., 2011). Figure 13 shows a comparison of systems thinking with conventional thinking.

This chapter uses causal loop diagrams to capture non-linear cause and effect relationships in order to realize the systems thinking. The primary purpose of building causal loop diagrams is to gain insight into the underlying structure of a messy, complex situation. A system model (output from the causal loop diagramming) depicts how the variables interrelate, and where there are opportunities to intervene in the modeled system to influence its behavior. A causal loop diagram is an intellectual device that forces deep thinking, and one of the most effective mechanisms to visualize, understand and communicate complexity (Butland, et al., 2007). The conventions of causal-loop diagrams are not described here, as excellent literature is already available in this area. Unfortunately, the same cannot be said about the reasons for less than optimal adoption of W-O-G EA by many countries. Gartner's *Hype Cycle for Enterprise Architecture 2011* clearly states that W-O-G EA is currently immature and is still about ten (10) years from attaining full maturity and adoption. It does not provide the reasons for the current state and what needs to be done to address this "wicked problem" that connected government is. The steps used to develop system models in the next section are as follows (Butland, et al., 2007):

A. **Systemic understanding**: Creating a shared understanding and mutual appreciation of the priority / issue in consideration;

B. **Systems synthesis and modeling**: Synthesizing inputs into conceptual models of the situations involved in the real world;

C. **Systemic analysis and extension**: Analyzing system models and extending them through intensive negotiations;

D. **System transformation**: Establishing relationships between the desired and the current views for a change program; and

E. **Systemic interventions**: Identifying actions and responses aimed at addressing the priority / issue in consideration.

With the primary aim of advancing the adoption of W-O-G EA for connected government, there is a clear need to: (1) uncover the critical influencing factors; (2) indentify the relationships between and among the factors; (3) recognize the underlying dynamics; (4) propose plausible intervention strategies to address the situation (Sterman, 2000). It can be mentioned with a high degree of confidence that the systems thinking approach presents the highest potential to view W-O-G EA adoption from a holistic perspective, which also happens to be a major gap in the current literature.

5. SYSTEM MODELING FOR W-O-G ENTERPRISE ARCHITECTURE ADOPTION

The general approach to system modeling is one of building from a core towards a periphery. The process is initiated by developing a core "nodal loop." This nodal loop is the central engine that captures the essential dynamic of the issue / priority / concern that is being investigated. The criteria for the nodal variable is usually based on: (1) scientific relevance; (2) decision making relevance; and (3) heuristic power (Butland, et al., 2007).

Governments around the world are under increasing pressure to demonstrate their performance to all key stakeholders. They are at times being expected to do things that have very little precedence. Business models and technologies are changing rapidly and stakeholders expect governments to embrace these changes ever more quickly (Hjort-Madsen, 2009). This puts unprecedented pressure on the governments not only to focus on efficiency, but also remain effective and agile. The current economic and geo-political situation exacerbates the need to perform and deliver even further as citizens are demanding (not merely expecting) high performing governments. With this background and the discussion in Sections in 1 through to 4 earlier in this chapter, **government transformation**, stands out as the common theme underlying all government programs and initiatives. Hence, this is adopted as the nodal variable to build the system model, which is described in the subsequent sections.

5.1. The Transformation Imperative as the Genesis

According to the UN, many governments are experiencing the transformative power in revitalizing public administration, overhauling public management, fostering inclusive leadership and moving civil service toward higher efficiency, transparency and accountability. Countries recognize the increasingly central role e-government will play in reaching these goals (Bittinger, 2011; Cisco IBSG, 2009). There are example abounds of the positive influence of high performing governments on the overall national development of countries and in turn the size of their economies itself. It is fairly straightforward to state that countries with growing economies (rising GDP) tend to be more complex simply because expectations from these governments are higher and as a result such governments tend to provide greater number of (and more complex) services (Muehlfeit, 2006). As government services permeate more into the economy (i.e. more and more constituents use these services) they without fail become complex and dynamic as governments are forced to cater to a wide range of needs, wants, expectations, and aspirations. This increases the pressure on the governments to organize their services as there arises the need to: (1) change the way services are delivered and consumed; (2) change the way internal back office operations are executed; and

(3) change the way resources and processes are sourced and combined (Moon, 2010). The role of enabling policies in making this happen cannot be overstated. It is in this context that governments are looking at e-government to bridge the policies and outcomes, leading to even more government services that are offered electronically. These factors are all interrelated in a single reinforcing loop that forms the trigger for government-wide transformation. This is depicted in Figure 14 in the variables 1 through to 9 combining to form the reinforcing loop **(R1: complexity triggered transformation)**.

5.2. Powering ICT Capability and Industry Development

Information and Communication Technology (ICT) is increasingly a central part of the national competitiveness strategy and plays a key enabler of socio-economic progress and development, productivity enhancement, modernization, economic growth and even poverty reduction (World Bank, 2008; World Economic Forum, 2009). The reinforcing loop R1 described in Section 5.1 creates the initial trigger for governments to embrace ICT enabled transformation. A positive influence of this is that the pressure to transition to e-government also creates pressure to improve the overall e-government maturity. A capable and mature e-government allows countries to showcase their achievements and those are further fuelled by the several e-government surveys and rankings that are currently in use. An interesting downstream impact of high e-government capability is that it directly impacts the overall national ICT capability. A country's e-government focus and capability provides the raw material to improve its overall national ICT capability by way of resources, talented and trained people, investments, research and development expertise, supporting policies and governance among other enabling inputs (Mickoliet, et al., 2009).

Figure 14. Complexity triggered government transformation

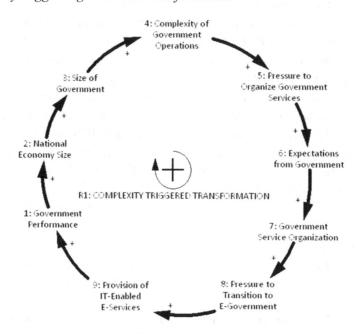

Greater national ICT capabilities provide the necessary fodder to the emergence of national ICT industry (World Bank, 2008; World Economic Forum, 2009). There are several countries who have utilized their foray into e-government as an entry point to build their national ICT industries, notable among them being South Korea, Singapore, Taiwan, Turkey, Malaysia, Egypt, South Africa, and Brazil. Several other countries like Bahrain, Oman, Vietnam, United Arab Emirates, Philippines, and Macau are also in the process of attempting the same. The above list of countries is only indicative of the diffusion of this approach. A common underlying element in all these countries is that the national e-government and ICT strategy typically is derived from the national ICT plans where the primary focus is increasing the ICT penetration. An example is Singapore, wherein the national e-government plan (eGOV 2015, the current one) is derived from the national ICT plan called the iN2015. An interesting observable phenomenon is as the national ICT industry matures; it also facilitates the joint delivery of selected e-government

services in the Public-Private Partnership (PPP) mode based on business needs.

The impact of national ICT industries to the overall economy and GDP is immense, albeit sometimes it takes time to fully realize the potential. According to the World Economic Forum "a fluid and ever-changing ICT touches nearly every industry sector with innovative, personalized and efficient solutions." The World Bank's *Global Economic Prospects 2008 – Technology Diffusion in the Developing World* further substantiates the link between the technology diffusion and its impact of the national economies (World Bank, 2008). In short, technology is both a critical determinant and an outcome of rising national incomes. These factors and their impacts are captured as two reinforcing loops **(R2: capability multiplier)** and **(R3: IT industry in motion)**. The variables covered include 9, 10, 11, 18, and 19, which in turn feeds into variable 2, further reinforcing the loop R1. These are depicted in Figure 15.

Figure 15. Impact on ICT capability and industry development

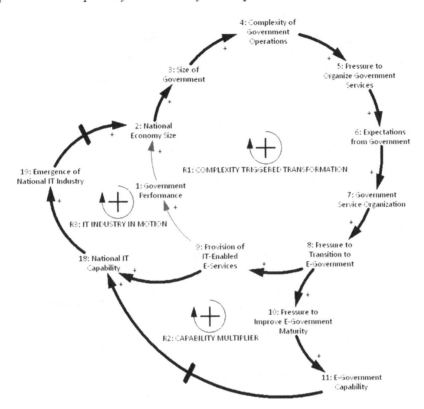

5.3. Enabling ICT Adoption and Savvyness

The highly interconnected and interdependent reinforcing loops R1, R2, and R3, if utilized correctly, provide tremendous momentum for countries to embrace e-government and make use of them for government modernization and transformation, enhancement of national ICT capability and even development of the national ICT industry, each feeding into the other and growing stronger. A few countries have understood these dynamics and used it to their advantage. The positive churn that loops R1, R2, and R3 create is further instrumental in creating and sustaining another reinforcing loop that allows countries to be power-consumers of ICT. As the national ICT industry matures (discussed in Section 5.2), an ecosystem is created. This facilitates the adoption

of ICT both across the government and the private sector organizations. Knowledge on ICT and its capabilities makes organizations ICT savvy, i.e. they develop the ability to utilize ICT to address business issues and ICT becomes an integral part of the overall government and corporate strategy. Such organizations are able to balance supply-side leadership along with demand-side leadership by adopting advanced practices and techniques such as portfolio management, ICT strategic planning, risk management, business continuity planning and ICT service management among several others (World Economic Forum, 2011). These in turn augment their ability to embrace new technologies quickly as it allows them to be on the "leading edge," even though, as experience has shown, this may not always be the best strategy. The *World Economic Forum's Global Information Technology Report of 2010/2011* provides

Figure 16. Impact on ICT diffusion and leverage

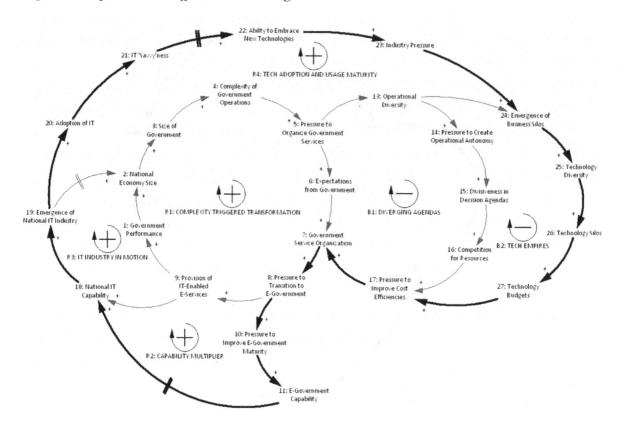

an excellent example of this phenomenon of ICT diffusion and leverage. In short, ICT readiness facilitates ICT adoption and usage. Countries that demonstrate a high degree of ICT diffusion and leverage usually tend to have the position of Government Chief Information Officer (GCIO) and similar roles across the government. This is indicative of the seriousness that is lent to ICT (Zenghelis, 2010). Interestingly, a majority of these organizations also tends to pressurize their vendors to deliver and deploy the latest technologies, some of which may not even be field proven. The chase to embrace and showcase new technologies, gives rise to large projects that are implemented in isolation. Examples include next generation broadband, cloud computing, and green ICT among others, which in turn feeds to encourage the development of technology silos. This will be discussed further in subsequent sections. The

reinforcing loop **(R4: Technology adoption and usage maturity)** consisting of new variables 19, 20, 21, 22, and 23 is shown in Figure 16.

The discussions above have identified four reinforcing loops: R1, R2, R3, and R4, wherein the key points are as below:

A.   According to John Zachman, the two primary reasons for organizations to embrace EA as a disciplined approach to planning and implementation are management of complexity and change. Loop R1 is in line with this. Countries use e-government as a way to trigger and sustain government transformation. As shown in the UN E-government maturity levels, transformation (i.e. achievement of connected government) is the highest level and is much more than mere automation of government services.

B. Government modernization and transformation positively influences e-government capability, leading to more mature national ICT capability, which in turn plays a critical role in the emergence of the national ICT industry, captured through loops R2 and R3.

C. Aside from the supply-side viewpoint captured in loops R1, R2, and R3, these factors also provide a positive momentum to the demand-side, i.e. ICT diffusion and leverage, captured in loop R4.

It is not difficult to understand that countries would typically go through several cycles of loops R1 to R4 connected as a group of virtuous spirals, in the process advancing their e-government maturity. It has already been established in Section 2 (Figure 5) that transitioning to higher levels of e-governments maturity requires disciplined planning and implementation—capabilities provided by Government EA. To make this happen, it is important that countries as part of their national strategies provide resources and dedicate efforts to create the necessary ecosystem and the supporting infrastructure. The influence of ICT adoption and savvyness can be summarized as follows (Tamara & Damuth, 2009; Zenghelis, 2010):

A. ICT aids in providing positive thrust to the technology frontier.

B. ICT enables equitable capabilities by diffusion of ideas and financing.

C. ICT enables opportunities for growth and innovation.

D. ICT aids in the reduction of systemic risks.

E. ICT modifies the way spatial-location decisions are made and executed.

5.4. Diverging Agendas

As a long term endeavor, government transformation influences several other factors. Despite the fact that the four highly interconnected virtuous spirals provide positive momentum to W-O-G

EA adoption, the fundamental principles of business make it clear that there would be limits to growth. Any system with unchecked growth will ultimately destroy itself if it is not balanced with relevant factors. In this context, the limits to growth refer to factors that typically slow down or obstruct the W-O-G EA adoption. It is important to understand that there are potentially multiple limits and countries have to: (1) identify them; (2) prioritize them; and (3) address them according to their specific requirements. However, the state of affairs in the case of W-O-G EA adoption for connected government is not one of moving at breakneck speed, but of overcoming the inertia to get it to move. Hence the need to slow down using balancing loops is not immediate. This phenomenon is elaborated in the subsequent sections.

Focus of countries on government transformation leads to pressure on the government to organize and structure its business and services in a manner that is intuitive and has a citizen centric outside-in perspective. Countries with advanced government EA programs typically capture the outside-in view of the government through their Business Reference Models (BRM). The BRM provides a business-centric view of the government operations and usually organizes government operations through components like business areas, lines-of-business and business functions at the W-O-G level. Such standard approaches tend to discourage and overlooks the need for operational diversity that is needed at the agency level. Resulting from the need to have operational diversity, governments (and their agencies) are under pressure to retain and even enhance operational autonomy. As agencies start functioning in an autonomous manner, their strategies, goals, objectives, procedures and business focus diverge. This creates competition for resources and usually the larger and more influential agencies are able to garner a greater amount of resources. Aside from certain country specific issues, the general trend described above is globally prevalent. Such a scenario creates avoidable duplications and overlaps leading to wastage of precious resources. According to Scott Bernard of Syracuse University, who has been deeply involved with the United States' Federal Enterprise Architecture program, "agencies are often funded individually and cross-agency initiatives therefore require a designated "lead" that receives much or all of the money for implementation, which is less than optimal. Also, a lack of complete standards for workflow, data, systems, and infrastructure inhibit multi-agency initiatives." For lower and middle income countries this situation is further exacerbated by the constraints of finance and available capabilities. As a result, the primary focus of government transformation has undoubtedly become achieving cost efficiencies. **"Doing more with less"** is the mantra that is all too common in government parlance. The 2008 financial and economic crisis and the unfolding austerity measures by governments around the world makes the goal of cost efficiencies even more pronounced. Efficiencies and performance gained as a result of cost cutting may provide some benefit to individual agencies and organizations; however, aggregated at the national level, it brings deflationary pressures. Without fail this hurts the country and a downward impact on the economy is inevitable. This is a classic example of "racing to the bottom." The above phenomenon is captured via variables 13, 14, 15, 16, and 17, getting initiated with variable 5 and completing the circle linked to variable 7, and joining the rest of the loop R1. This is shown in Figure 17 and represents (perhaps) the most important balancing loop **(B1: Diverging agendas)** in terms of its role and impact on successful adoption of W-O-G EA. From the countries and their government EA programs surveyed it can be stated without any doubt that the trend of agencies operating with a high degree of autonomy leading to diverging agendas is common and instrumental in putting breaks on government-wide transformation activities.

5.5. Feudalism in Governance

It would not be an overstatement to say that governance is the most important factor contributing to the success or failure of W-O-G EA adoption. Clearly defined governance and allocation of decision rights increase the probability of successful and effective adoption of W-O-G EA manifolds. A direct and unquestionable impact of operational diversity amongst agencies within the government is the emergence of business silos that operate in their own stovepipes. Amplified by the diverging agendas (discussed in Section 5.4), the business silos are instrumental in creating and abetting the feudal form of operation.

In the context of the agency IT organizations, the CIOs almost operate their "little" empires with negligible serious interactions both with the business side and IT organizations of other agencies (characterized by low inter-agency and intra-agency communication, cooperation and collaboration). In other words, these artificially created silos lead to technology diversity (each agency invests in technology that is suitable only for itself), which leads to technology stovepipes and bulging technology budgets at the W-O-G level. This, in turn, intensifies the pressure to demonstrate cost efficiencies with regard to any expenditure made on ICT. Hence the single minded focus on measuring and reporting the business value of IT for all CIOs and their IT organizations becomes paramount. This has a direct impact on the credibility of the CIO leadership. Interestingly, this whole series of factors gets boosted by the earlier discussed reinforcing loop R4, thus augmenting the overall impact at the W-O-G level by slowing or even pulling down the government-wide transformation efforts. These variables are collectively captured as a balancing loop **(B2: Technology empires)**. The technology diversity phenomenon elaborated above, in all cases is not a bad characteristic. The problem gets amplified when the diversity leads to investments in isolated, unrelated and irrelevant areas. Man-

Figure 17. Limit to government transformation with diverging agendas

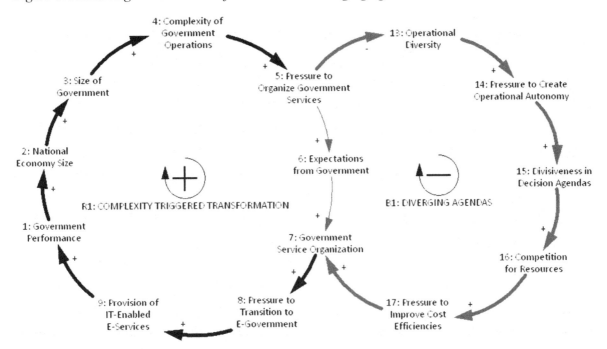

aged diversity allows for risks to be distributed across technologies and their supplying vendors, without compromising the autonomy agencies so greatly value.

The feudal mindset is even more ingrained on the business side of the operations. Government agencies (and their constituent departments) like to and demand to operate in their respective stovepipes in the name of operational autonomy. From a business operations perspective, most agencies rank very low in: (1) the extent to which their business functions depend on business functions of other agencies (by way of sharing, collaboration and commonalities); and (2) the extent to which their business functions are replicated across different constituents. In other words, the primary operating model is overwhelmingly diversified. Some of this can definitely be attributed to history (and legacy). Historically, ministries and departments within governments have been encouraged to operate as relatively independent organizations due to the need to distribute political authority. The concept of W-O-G as a single

coherent enterprise is new, transformational and unsettling. Mostly operating in a monopolistic environment, it necessitates a huge mindset change, hence the cynicism and impatience. The diversified operating model naturally leads to the same functions and activities being replicated across different parts of the agencies and the government organizations, in turn pushing up their operating budgets in support of the wasteful replications and redundancies. Resulting from fragmentation and overlaps are situations wherein there could be multiple departments doing the same thing (oversupply) as well as certain business activities which no department or agency is responsible for (starvation), both having a negative impact on the operational efficiencies and costs, further pushing the pressure to improve cost efficiencies and in turn on the government-wide transformation efforts. These variables are collectively captured as a balancing loop **(B3: Business empires)**. Loops B2 and B3 are depicted in Figure 18.

Figure 18. Feudalism as the predominant governance archetype

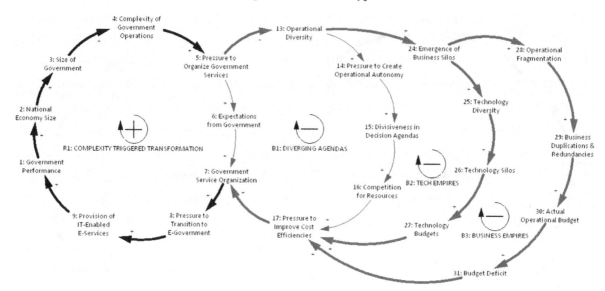

5.6. Building the Ecosystem and Critical Mass

Even as the emergence of business silos within the government amplifies the feudal form of governance and the diversified operating model, the reverse influence also comes forth at the same time. There is a definite move to federate operations of the government so as to derive the benefits of both centralization and decentralization without slowing the government transformation activities. Though it could be argued that at different stages of architecture maturity, centralized and decentralized approaches have their utility, nonetheless more stable and sustainable governance approach in the longer term happens to be federated. This has a long tradition in several forms of government and attempts to balance the accountabilities and the allocation of decision rights between multiple governing bodies. This makes the federated approach by far the most difficult to embrace for effective decision making, entailing suitable adaptations by countries taking into consideration respective cultural, political, social, technological and economic factors (Burns, et al., 2009).

Getting the federated form of governance right brings with it several benefits and positive impacts, one of the primary ones being getting the different constituents of the government to collaborate and share. Collaboration and sharing in this context could potentially include (but are not limited to) (Hjort-Madsen, 2009):

A. Adoption of and conformance to common technology standards and best practices.
B. Establishment of data exchange standards, and adherence to such standards.
C. Rationalization of data to address issues of redundancies, security, and integrity.
D. Sharing of common data and other business information.
E. Common and shared applications and application components, leading to use and reuse.
F. Collaboration and sharing between agencies dictated by common overarching business functions.

The extent of collaboration and sharing depends on the maturity and comfort levels of agencies to do so. Each of the above directly

Figure 19. Government EA ecosystem and the lead adopters

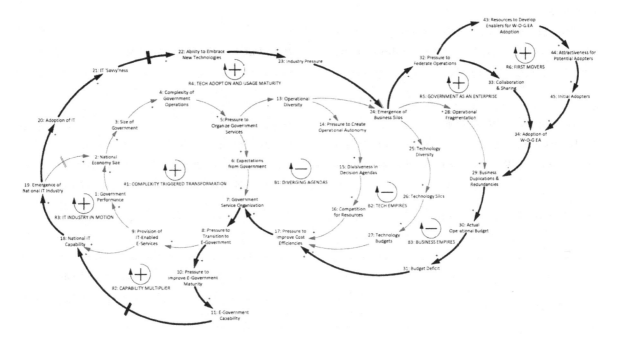

influences the adoption of W-O-G EA by addressing key issues pertaining to strategy, business, information, data, application and technology infrastructure, leading to reduction of business duplications and redundancies and standardization of the underlying technology infrastructure. These factors are captured through variables 32, 33, and 34, and combined to form the reinforcing loop **(R5: Government as an enterprise)** which is shown in Figure 19.

An interesting and useful phenomenon that gets triggered as a result of the pressure to federate government operations is the push to expend the resources required to develop enablers for W-O-G EA adoption. The enablers for W-O-G EA adoption are an aggregated factor that typically consists of: (1) reference architectures; (2) frameworks; (3) methodologies; (4) guidance documents; (5) case studies; (6) tool support; (7) awareness and advocacy sessions; (8) legislations and policies; and (9) capacity building. Developing and making these components available increases the attractiveness of embracing EA to

potential adopters. This is important, because many times, due to the broad and deep nature of work that EA requires, it becomes confusing, in turn leading to trepidation in "taking the plunge." The enablers listed above help alleviate the fear and encourage governments to take the initial concrete steps. This then creates a pool of initial adopters, "the first movers." These factors are captured through variables 43, 44, and 45, and combined to form the reinforcing loop **(R6: First movers)**.

Figure 18 shows the two reinforcing loops R5 and R6. Interestingly, these two loops get further reinforced and augmented by loops R2, R3, and R4. This phenomenon is explainable by the fact that parts of the government (or agencies) having higher capabilities in delivering e-services and the ability to embrace new technologies also have an observable preference to adopt government EA. Such organizations and agencies are willing to experiment and take the lead in creating the ecosystem by being the first movers. This, in turn, positively influences the government-wide transformation journey by extracting the benefits of diffusion effect.

Thus far we have seen six reinforcing loops (R1 through to R6) that collectively play a critical role in the adoption of W-O-G EA centered on the government-wide transformation area. These loops provide the initial momentum, but in order to sustain this momentum and make W-O-G EA a self sustaining program, it is important to build up the critical mass of adopting agencies so as to cross over the tipping point. Loops R5 and R6 provide a good build up to get to the tipping point. Through the lead adopters, governments are able to create a pool of agencies that adopt EA. As adoption grows, the fear of the unknown subsides as more experience is gained. As experience is gained, agencies learn to avoid the traps and work their way to success, in turn leading to improved business outcomes resulting from EA. In other words, as more agencies initiate their EA programs, the more they traverse the learning curve, moving progressively ever more quickly. This makes it even more attractive to potential adopters thus increasing the adoption rate even further creating an effective virtuous spiral. This phenomenon is captured through variables 35, 46, 54, 51, 44, 45, and 34 and consolidated as a reinforcing loop **(R8: Success breeds success)**. The only caveat here is that agencies usually take some time to succeed in their efforts. This is a very powerful mechanism that governments can use as a lever to push the adoption of W-O-G EA.

A minor reinforcing loop that gets created as a result of loop **R8 is the "bandwagon effect."** These are agencies that, with not necessarily sufficient knowledge just join the lead agencies in adopting EA because they perceive it to be a good thing to do. In itself the bandwagon effect could be a double-edged sword, which means it can provide fodder by contributing to the critical mass, but if not managed well could lead to dissatisfaction and negative word-of-mouth. However, with good enablers (as discussed earlier in loop R5) the bandwagon effect is usually has positive

impacts. Reinforcing loops R7 and R8 are shown in Figure 20.

5.7. Expanding Horizons

In most cases EA remains within the discipline of ICT strategy and management. This is further strengthened by the fact that currently almost all EA efforts are initiated and managed by the IT organization / CIO office. This constrained way of looking at EA is reinforced by several factors, the key ones being: (1) current literature "conveniently" using **Enterprise Architecture** and **Enterprise IT Architecture** interchangeably; (2) emergence of the discipline itself from the IT side of the organization; (3) EA initiatives historically assigned to and managed by the IT organization with limited linkages to other areas; and (4) lack of awareness on the business side in appreciating the true scope and potential of EA. Gartner terms this as the "traditional" approach of EA.

In the government context, EA programs are typically managed by the Ministry of ICT (or equivalent), though there are a few cases wherein the organization responsible for government administration or public service development managing EA programs are emerging. This is important, as it points to the partial transformation of the ingrained mindset and also recognition of the role and impact of government EA spanning much more than mere ICT and related issues (Burns, et al., 2009).

Advanced and effective government EA programs demonstrate a very interesting phenomenon, i.e. they permeate through the organization spanning all key business functions and departments. These EA programs are not confined to the IT organization (or the CIO office). Largely initiated and generally managed by the IT organization, EA initially faces an uphill task to get active involvement and sponsorship from the rest of the organization. Initial efforts to get the senior leadership involved invites resistance, cynicism and even outright rejection. It naturally takes the

Figure 20. Critical mass adopters and the implementation learning curve

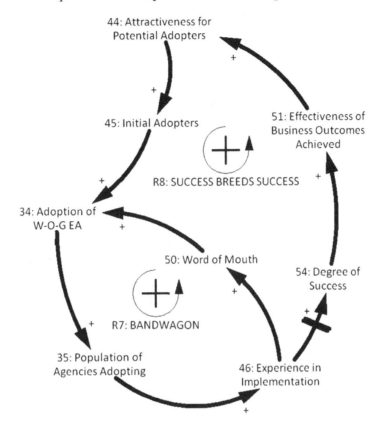

organization some successes to begin with and traversal of the steep learning curve, leading to greater chances to succeed and more importantly to demonstrate such successes to the rest of the organization. These have already been discussed in the context of reinforcing loops R7 and R8. An important outcome of loops R7 and R8 is that as EA initiatives succeed, they tend to be more effective in terms of business outcomes, leading to expansion of the program scope and expectations. The expansion of the scope happens by linking government EA to other management practices and disciplines like portfolio management, strategic planning, corporate governance and innovation among others. This kind of integration of EA to other management disciplines contributes to the overall penetration of the EA into the whole of the organization. At this juncture EA becomes the **"architecture of the enterprise."** The caveat

here is that organizations usually take time and experience to get to this level of architecture maturity. These phenomena are captured through variables 52 and 53 and is collectively depicted as reinforcing loops **(R9: Facilitated diffusion)** and **(R10: Architecting the enterprise)** shown in Figure 21.

5.8. Understanding the Business Value Hurdle

Despite the fact that reinforcing loops R6, R7, and R8 are instrumental in creating the critical mass of adopters and providing the opportunity for much needed experience, there is an interesting downside attached to these. The negative impact of adopters and their success stories starts from the variable 34 (i.e. W-O-G EA adoption), which leads to increase in the number of agencies and

Figure 21. Enterprise architecture as the architecture of the enterprise

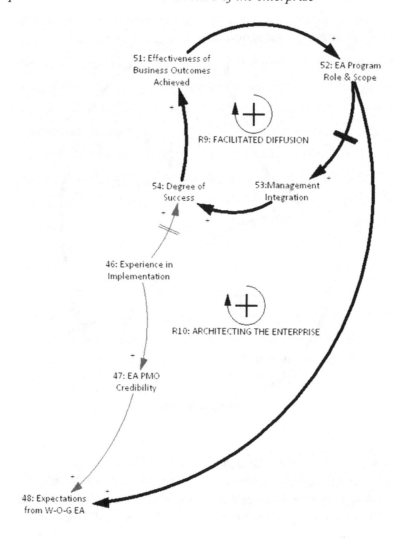

other organization structures in the government that start and derive benefits out of EA. As the adoption of government EA becomes more prevalent and widely diffused, the financial resources required to keep the program afloat keep escalating. This escalation in the financial burden creates a reduction in the actual program value. This captures an interesting behavior, i.e. the doubters about the W-O-G EA, already cynical about the whole initiative get ignited when made aware about the amount of resources that is ploughed into the program (Burns, 2009; Microsoft, 2010). Constantly looking for cracks, these groups start questioning the benefits that are derived from W-O-G EA. In addition, the information about the financial resources expended makes them more vocal and vociferous. This in turn leads to the program owners and other key stakeholders scrambling to demonstrate the program Return On Investment (ROI), sometimes using dubious ways. This itself is not a desirable behavior as it shows the core EA group to be insecure and unsure, which could at times lead to slowing or total stoppage of the government transformation journey, thus jeopardizing even the national development agenda. It is interesting to note that such

Figure 22. The ROI conundrum and its impact on program continuity

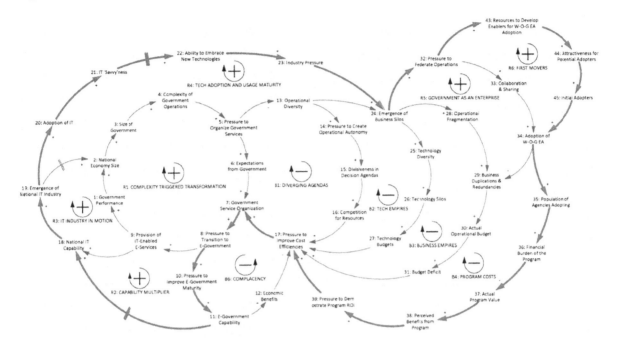

behaviors also impact the organization's ability and willingness to adopt new technologies as the risk-averse behavior becomes highly pronounced and visible. It usually is a show-stopper for the innovation culture. This is captured through the variables 34, 35, 36, 37, 38, 39, and 17 combined together into the balancing loop (**B4: Program costs**) and is depicted in Figure 22.

In an interconnected loop, as there is more adoption of government EA leading to valuable experience gained by the core group of the implementation team, it elevates the credibility of the Government EA Program Management Office (PMO) and in turn directly influences in raising the expectations from the program itself. This state is now a victim of its own success. The expectations lead to stiffer and stretched targets and gets further amplified by the factors coming in from loop R10. Together, the heightened expectations raise the desired program value, thus negatively impacting the actual benefits derived by the organization and pushing the pressure to demonstrate the program ROI even higher. This

is captured through the variables 34, 35, 46, 47, 48, 49, and 38 combined together into the balancing loop (**B5: Burden of stretch targets**) and depicted in Figure 23.

5.9. The Political Dynamics

One of the crucial and largely under-addressed factor that systematically resists the adoption of W-O-G EA is the prevailing political dynamics in the government. Done to its full potential, government-wide transformation that is driven by EA can bring in major changes to the way government is planned, designed, operated and managed. It can lead to redistribution of authority, rebalancing of finances, changes in organizational structures, redefinition in job roles, perceived intrusion into individual autonomy among many other related but very fundamental impacts. For most governments (and civil servants) that (usually) have a limit to their tenure in a given position, bringing in such fundamental changes all at one go is neither a priority nor a desire. As a result,

Figure 23. EA office and the burden of stretch targets

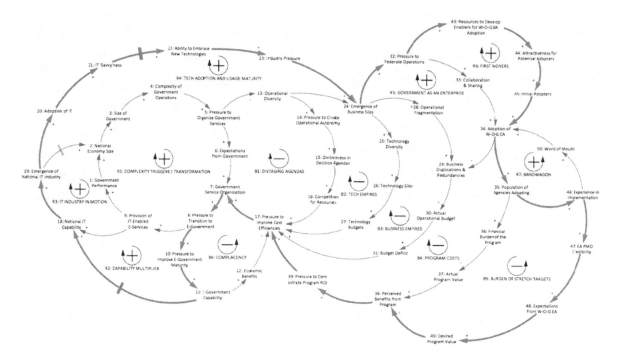

in most cases, the urge to "cling to power" takes precedence over everything else and government transformation is the first casualty. With such a background, pushing W-O-G EA invites irrelevant scrutiny and questioning. Often such scrutiny has been, in reality, a delaying tactic. These kinds of political tactics can often manifest into operational obstacles. For instance, some common reasons provided by parts of the government (ministries and agencies) include: (1) insistence on maintaining own version of all business processes citing operational uniqueness (we're different); and (2) refusing to share information and collaborate citing confidentiality and state secrecy. If analyzed in depth, these operational obstacles are in some form an expression of the feudal form of governance (discussed earlier). Many countries are attempting to address the issue of refusal to share government information through open government initiatives. It is early days now, before the actual rules of engagement are codified and implemented widely across in the national governments. Political ob-

stacles impact overall architecture governance effectiveness, which in turn affects the business outcomes. The most difficult part of this whole phenomenon is that it is almost impossible to fully comprehend the actual power-equation, because, like the proverbial iceberg, the part that is visible constitutes less than ten percent (10%) of the total. As a result the attractiveness for potential adopters to support and embrace government-wide transformation and W-O-G EA wanes, which deepens the silo mindset among the ministries and agencies. This further slows down the overall momentum toward the transformation along with all the associated affects already discussed earlier. The phenomenon of the underlying political dynamics is captured with variables 40, 41, 42, and 51, and collectively put into the balancing loop **(B7: Political landmines) (see Figure 24)**.

An interesting behavior that is widely observable and can be considered a manifestation of agency autonomy and the feudal form of governance is the "not invented here" syndrome. In

Figure 24. Extending the feudalism

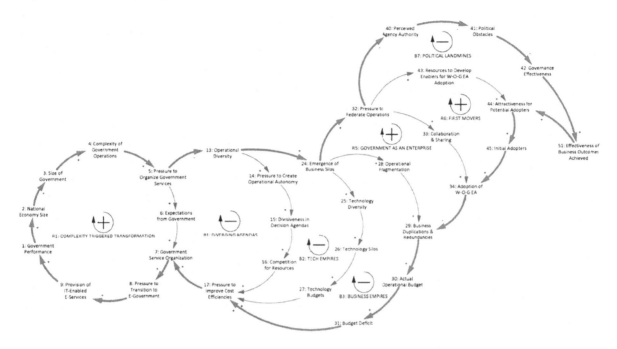

operational terms, this means that ministries and agencies while not directly refusing to accept government-wide frameworks, policies, standards, methodologies, and other guiding materials, actually attempt to delay the progress by initiating activities and assigning resources to develop the same (or similar) materials specifically for the agency. The reason often cited is that "they're different" and centrally developed material would not suit their specific requirements. In a general scenario of aggressively pushing to achieve cost efficiencies, such replicated efforts amounts to wasteful use of scarce resources. Such behavior further demonstrates the ingrained divisiveness and the complete lack of "W-O-G as a single enterprise" mindset. The phenomenon is captured into the balancing loop (B8: Not invented here) and strengthens the loop B7 discussed earlier.

In some governments, the initial momentum and enthusiasm brings in a good disciplined effort to adopt e-government. This is demonstrated via commendable performance and also manifests itself as a high ranking in the various e-government surveys. As a result the countries reap in economic benefits affected from good governance and also become role models for other countries that aspire to emulate similar successes. Notwithstanding the initial success, sustaining the same level of momentum and senior government leadership involvement to ensure continued success is a different ball game altogether. In most cases, the classic "S" curve of performance, when extended, is likely to be a "rise-stagnancy-fall" curve of performance. The stagnancy and fall part of the performance happens due to two reasons: (1) the country in question actually falls back in performance; and (2) other countries emulate, catch-up and even exceed the role model countries. Both cases, at times are instrumental in deepening the complacency and inertia to keep up the momentum (see Figure 25).

This is an important phenomenon, because most countries publicly do not state complacency and inertia as a reason for slowing down or even reversing government reforms and transformation.

Figure 25. Self-sufficiency as a perceived virtue

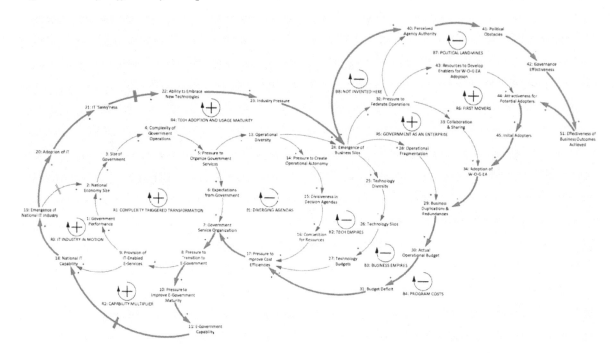

This would amount to sacrilege for the government in power and provide fodder for opposition parties to pull down the government. Hence, this phenomenon of complacency and inertia indirectly manifests itself through the several other balancing loops discussed earlier. Figure 26 shows the balancing loop **(B6: Complacency)** along with its variables 10, 11, 12, and 17.

5.10. Connecting the Dots: The Confluence

Earlier studies partially identified key challenges that countries face embracing government EA as a decision making and management framework. Nonetheless, the key word is "partially." Current literature on government EA is incomplete in two regards: (1) the coverage of challenges i.e. all the challenges have not been identified; and (2) the challenges and (hence their) solutions have been looked at and analyzed in a piecemeal approach. In other words, architecture driven connected government has not been addressed as a complex

messy problem, and then in taking the W-O-G approach, governments have not been studied as complex adaptive systems (Meadows, 1999; Stroh, 2000).

Sections 5.1 through to 5.9 presented and discussed ten (10) reinforcing loops and eight (8) balancing loops connecting over fifty (50) variables in a single linked and coherent way. The loops and their constituent variables have deliberately been kept generic to ensure wide applicability subject to local adaptations. Figure 27 depicts the full system model. The purpose is to:

A. Understand the dynamics of W-O-G EA adoption aimed at achieving connected government via government-wide transformation.

B. Identify enablers and inhibitors impacting W-O-G EA driven government transformation.

C. Develop intervention strategies that are likely to provide the highest degree of leverage to encourage and push the W-O-G EA adoption,

Figure 26. Complacency and inertia as system constraints

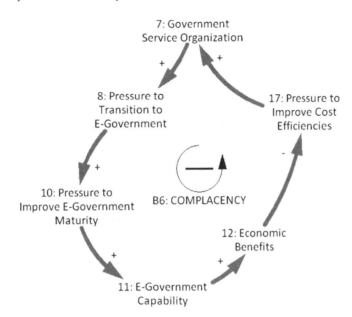

so as to create a framework for W-O-G EA that takes into consideration the enablers and inhibitors.

Sections 5.1 through to 5.9 address A as above, while Sections 6 and 7 will address B and C. It is interesting to note that all the "difficult-to-solve" challenges that countries face in W-O-G EA adoption have very little to do with technology, EA frameworks, best practices, methodologies, tools and the like. Yet that is where most countries spend their efforts and resources. Hence, the divergence between **where the resources are being spent** and **where they need to be spent** is growing. There is a mismatch in both understanding and expectations. The chasm between **perceived show-stoppers** and the **actual show-stoppers** is enormous and widening. In other words, governments are spending resources to develop "solutions" without fully understanding and articulating the underlying "problems." The dimensions of connected government have been listed in Section 2. It is very clear that current forms of management, bureaucracy and organization design are insufficient to address issues

related to the connected government dimensions, as the challenges to be surmounted in future will not be solvable by solutions of the past. The need would be for management innovation. Gary Hamel defines management innovation *as anything that fundamentally alters the way in which the work of management is carried out, or significantly modifies customary organizational forms, and, by doing so advances organizational goals*. Current forms of management, established during the Industrial Engineering era in the seventeenth (17th) and the eighteenth (18th) centuries are not suitable for today's modern knowledge based economies. Yet, very little advancement has actually taken place in the management itself. This is the very essence of W-O-G EA for connected government. Current EA efforts focus on lower level innovation, for example, process or operational innovation, product or service innovation and, at best, strategy innovation (Dettmer, 2007). The "solutions" seldom look at the management innovation that is absolutely essential for government-wide transformation to gain traction and sustain.

Furthermore, this variance gets exacerbated by the fact that most government EA programs are

Figure 27. W-O-G EA adoption for connected government: full system model

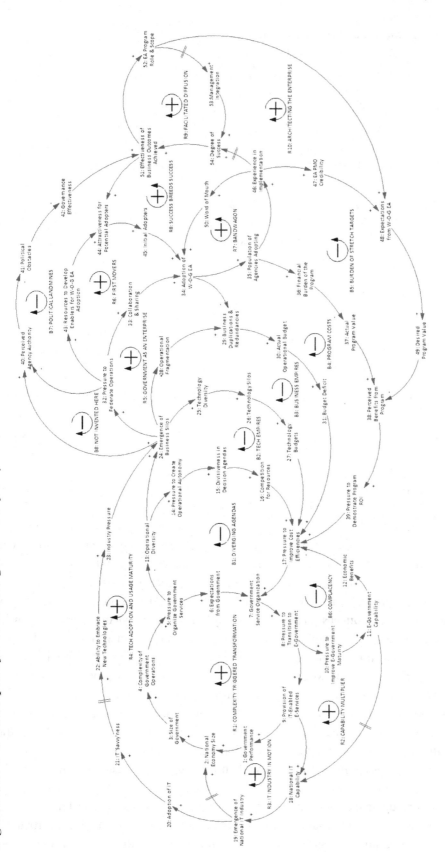

initiated and managed by the Ministry of ICT (or equivalent). This group perceived to be the "technicians," who are not even privy to high-priority strategic issues and challenges are expected to make W-O-G EA programs successful by practically operating in the dark. While assigning W-O-G EA to the ICT group, there is usually a leadership failure in recognizing that it requires clear authority and power to influence for the EA to be effective. This entails from the fact that most EA activities require ICT groups to operate in areas that are beyond their jurisdiction, and without adequate authority most activities cannot be completed to derive the intended outcomes. With respect to W-O-G EA, senior government leaders operate in a realm of bewildering uncertainty and staggering complexity and a result find limited success or even fail (and hence discontinue the whole effort).

Interestingly, analyzing all the ten (10) reinforcing and the eight (8) balancing loops reveal the existence of behaviors captured in all the ten (10) system archetypes described by Peter Senge. This is important as it facilitates the design of intervention strategies and is discussed later.

6. INTERVENTION STRATEGIES

6.1. Emergent Systemic Profile

Peter Senge in *The Fifth Discipline* argues that to solve difficult problems one needs to understand the "interrelationships rather than things, for seeing patterns of change rather than static snapshots." Taking a holistic synthesized view, the ten (10) reinforcing and the eight (8) balancing loops together capture the systemic structure of W-O-G EA adoption for connected government. Each causal loop represents a set of interrelationships between multiple factors / variables. Collectively, they represent the overall systemic structure that connects more than (fifty) 50 critical factors / variables. The principle of parsimony is thus achieved (Sterman, 2000).

To design effective intervention strategies, it is critical to "diagnose" the issues correctly. In this regard, this research proposes defining and comprehending the **emergent systemic profile**. Ideally, the aim is to develop a profile for a country intending to adopt W-O-G EA for connected government and then use the profile to design the intervention strategies based on suitability and effectiveness contexutalized to specific requirements. This profile based approach allows for configurability of the interventions and actions. Figure 28 shows the basic approach to construct the emergent systemic profile.

The causal loops and their interconnected constituent factors / variables provide senior government leadership with the inputs to initiate the process prognostication in the context of W-O-G EA adoption for connected government. However the prognosis needs to be validated by a detailed examination and analysis to ascertain the underlying systemic issues. This leads to a detailed diagnosis by constructing the emergent systemic profile (Meadows, 1999). The intent is for a country to have a single unique profile. This facilitates a coherent response. However, it is likely that countries with multiple levels of government may have one national level profile and multiple sub-profiles to address localized issues. In constructing the profile and performing the diagnosis, countries must factor in the targeted evolutionary stage of connected government. The diagnosis performed with the profile information is followed by the relevantly designed intervention strategies. For better effectiveness, the **prognosis → diagnosis → intervention** cycle is repeated as a continuous learning and improvement process.

The emergent systemic profile points to the existence of enablers and inhibitors on two different dimensions (vectors) which are largely orthogonal in nature. In other words, absence of or weak inhibitors do not necessarily mean the presence of strong enablers. From an execution viewpoint, there are ramifications that governments need to understand and factor in when designing interven-

Figure 28. Approach to construct emergent systemic profile

Approach to Construct Emergent Systemic Profile for W-O-G EA Adoption		Intensity of Impact [H, HM, M, L]	Likelihood of Occurrence [H, HM, M, L]	Composite Rating [H, HM, M, L]
Enablers	R1: Complexity Triggered Transformation			
	R2: Capability Multiplier			
	R3: IT Industry in Motion			
	R4: Technology Adoption & Usage Maturity			
	R5: Government as an Enterprise			
	R6: First Movers			
	R7: Bandwagon			
	R8: Success Breeds Success			
	R9: Facilitated Diffusion			
	R10: Architecting the Enterprise			
Inhibitors	B1: Diverging Agendas			
	B2: Technology Empires			
	B3: Business Empires			
	B4: Program Costs			
	B5: Burden of Stretch Targets			
	B6: Complacency			
	B7: Political Landmines			
	B8: Not Invented Here			
Legend: H → High; HM → High-Medium; M → Medium; L → Low				

tion strategies. The two dimensions (i.e. enablers and inhibitors) are used to build four unique quadrants called the **systemic states**, depicted in Figure 29, that provide a concrete basis (rationale) for designing appropriate interventions.

The systemic states derived from the emergent systemic profile provide the means to develop **strategic navigation pathways** for countries. The most plausible pathways that are observed in reality are listed below, depicting the defining milestones in a country's W-O-G EA journey:

A. Initial ⟷ [Diminished / Discontinued]
B. Initial ⟷ Arduous ⟷ [Diminished / Discontinued]
C. Initial ⟷ Profligate ⟷ [Diminished / Discontinued]
D. Initial ⟷ Arduous ⟷ Profligate ⟷ [Diminished / Discontinued]
E. Initial ⟷ Optimal ⟷ [Expanded / Sustained]
F. Initial ⟷ Arduous ⟷ Optimal ⟷ [Expanded / Sustained]
G. Initial ⟷ Profligate ⟷ Optimal ⟷ [Expanded / Sustained]
H. Initial ⟷ Arduous ⟷ Profligate ⟷ Optimal ⟷ [Expanded / Sustained]

Pinpointing the exact systemic state requires profound evaluation; if not, the intervention strategies are likely to be tenuous. Effective intervention

Figure 29. Systemic states for intervention design

		Enablers	
		Low	**High**
Inhibitors	**Low**	**Initial** [This is characterized by absence of both the reinforcing and balancing loops, thus in all likelihood pointing to an relatively immature program, requiring further substantial resources and efforts. This also includes re-initiation.]	**Optimal** [The program is characterized by existence of a majority of reinforcing loops which are collectively dominant, and existence of weak balancing loops. Care must taken to maintain status quo.]
	High	**Arduous** [The program existence of a majority of balancing loops which are collectively dominant, and existence of weak reinforcing loops.]	**Profligate** [This is characterized by existence of both strong reinforcing and balancing loops. By itself, this is unsustainable as it is terribly wasteful, and requires sincere efforts to move to the 'optimal' state.]

strategies are an imperative because these dictate the strategic navigation pathway that is traversed. The links depicted in the pathways are deliberately bi-directional as W-O-G EA programs can traverse in either direction. This is especially more likely in the government context as major changes (like change of political leadership) have the potential to disrupt, revive, weaken, or strengthen existing programs. The chapters in this book provide ample examples of pathways E, F, G, and H.

6.2. Designing Intervention Strategies

The emergent systemic profile and the strategic navigation pathways form the basis for designing intervention strategies. The specific interventions would depend on the context of country specific nuances. Nonetheless, designing the right interventions are as important as the locations these interventions would be applied to. In a complex system, there are places where a small shift in one thing can produce large changes in (almost) every-thing. The places are termed "leverage points—the points of power." Donella Meadows in her article *Leverage Points–Places to Intervene in a System* identifies and elaborates generic leverage points where interventions are most likely to be impactful and results bearing (Meadows, 1999). The next few paragraphs elaborate on the leverage points suitably adapted to the context of W-O-G EA for the connected government. The leverage points then lead to the plausible interventions which are discussed in the subsequent sections (Meadows, 1999; Stroh, 2000; Dettmer, 2007). As a caveat, leverage points and associated interventions are not an exact science, so discretion is expected and recommended.

A. **The mindset out of which the system arises**: According to John Zachman, any organization that aspires (and expects) to manage complexity and change needs architecture. This is absolutely true. Organizations (governments included) view EA as an IT management and strategy discipline. Following

Figure 30. Comparing current and recommended paradigms for W-O-G EA

W-O-G EA for Connected Government Paradigms	
As they are	**As they should be**
Governments are primarily hierarchical in structure, characterized by creative apartheid, over administration, and risk aversion.	Governments embrace a lattice-based structure that potentially connects every stakeholder in the organization to everyone else, enabled by direct communication channels. There are multiple nodes that are lateral in a dense network of interpersonal connections where information flows unfettered.
Organizations that have not embraced a formal architecture framework or methodology do not have any architecture.	All organizations have an architecture. The only point of contention is whether the architecture is informal and implicit or formal and explicit.
W-O-G EA is a project and there is a point when it is considered complete.	W-O-G EA for connected government is a journey that has no end. Following from the earlier point, as long as the organization exists, it needs to be continually architected.
The techniques, tools and approaches used in the process of architecting are new, and have nothing to do with any existing management practices	Most techniques, tools and approaches used are well accepted. The newness comes from the way they are applied and interconnections between them created so that the line-of-sight can be established and maintained.
Organizational coherency is not important	Management of complexity and change are great reasons to do formal architecture. Nonetheless, as a result of the architecture the organization becomes more coherent.
The architects do all the architecting.	The architects establish the rules, procedures and shared understanding. The actual activity of architecting is done, to a large extent, by the people themselves. The actual role of the architects is to ensure consistency and completeness holistically.
Enterprise architecture is an IT management and IT strategic planning discipline and remains stuck in the IT trap.	The barriers between business and IT in the context of EA are artificial and constrain its role and derived benefits. Organizations with mature EA view it as a management and strategic planning discipline, which in some literature gets mentioned as second generation EA.

from this obviously flawed view, emerge paradigms that are deeply ingrained and are the most effective candidates of leverage. Listed below are a few such paradigms as to **what they currently are** contrasted with **what they should be changed to** in the context of W-O-G EA for the connected government. It is evident from Figure 30 that the current paradigms are not only flawed but also severely restrictive. Transitioning to the new paradigms is a gradual process and impacts the very fundamentals of the system but has the power to transform the way W-O-G EA is viewed and along with its influence all the loops discussed earlier.

They constitute the most potent of the leverage points.

B. **The goals of the system**: EA is the very essence of good organization design. To move toward connected government and evolve through its various stages, countries need to design their government(s). In most countries the formation of the structure and behavior of the governments has been organic and gradual. They seldom have been subjected to any disciplined and structured processes of planning, design and adoption. There may have been some initiatives and programs in parts of the governments, but in such cases the scope and coverage are piecemeal and the W-O-G continues to remain inefficient in the larger context. Section 2 of this chapter identifies seven dimensions of connected government: (1) citizen centricity; (2) common infrastructure and interoperability; (3) collaborative services and business operations; (4) public sector governance; (5) networked organizational model; (6) social inclusion; and (7) transparent and open government. These are excellent goals for any government and stand the test of time. In Section 2 these dimensions are well elaborated and the role of W-O-G EA in impacting these dimensions have also been explained, including how countries need to progress along these dimensions to evolve through the various stages of connected government.

C. **The rules of the system**: This is an area many countries proactively look at seriously as a way to enable W-O-G adoption. These are important as they establish the scope of the system by way of its boundaries and its degrees of freedom. The rules get operationalized through legislations, policies and procedures. The Clinger-Cohen Act of 1997 is an example of a rule operationalized as a legislation that mandates the need to have formal EA in all federal agencies in the United States as part of the Presidential Management Agenda. This legislation is very specific to EA in the federal agencies. However, this is supported by a host of other legislations concerning e-government in the United States. Similar legislative approach to establish the rules of the system exist in Bahrain, South Korea and Singapore. Rules may differ in scope, coverage, specificity and operationalization, but the underlying intent remains consistent, i.e. to define the boundaries and expectations of the system. Rules are strong leverage points. Nonetheless, when setting rules to enable W-O-G EA for connected government, it is critical to identify and understand: (1) expected impact of the rule(s); (2) conflicting and supporting rules, if any; and (3) support system required to enforce the rule(s).

D. **The structure of the system**: Governments are bureaucratic organizations. Their primary purpose is to administer. Transformation and innovation is not business as usual for governments. There have been efforts around the world targeting public sector reforms. Beyond the political rhetoric, in most cases successes have been limited, the primary reason being the structure of the system itself as one of the most deeply ingrained constraining factors. This is because the structure of the system in some sense (both directly and indirectly) reflects authority or the power structure, thereby making it relatively resilient to change. However, if there are ways and means for the system to modify governance structures, add new negative or positive loops, dynamically reallocate resources and make new rules, it gives the ability for the system to self-organize, stay responsive and adapt more effectively. Gary Hamel in his book *The Future of Management* describes the demise of management in the way it is practiced presently due to its inadequacies in addressing current and future organizational issues. Hamel proposes ten (10) rules for management innovators, all of which are applicable to government organizations (Hamel, 2007). The rigid organization structure that governments relish having in the name of stability more likely than not comes in the way of government-wide transformation efforts, i.e. the structure becomes a drag on the system.

E. **The structure of information flows**: In many situations citizens and businesses believe that information sent to governments tends to go into a "black-hole"; it goes in, and seldom anything useful ever comes out. The virtual non-existence of feedback loops and information sharing makes it necessary to provide the same information more than once. Governments are (usually) the largest collectors and sources of information. However, the appropriate flow of this information is generally impaired and way less than optimal. The feedback loops that enable the information flows bring in accountability in performance. For example, UN E-Government surveys and the published ranking make many countries start taking e-government seriously. A low rank that is publicly visible makes it embarrassing for national governments.

As part of open government programs, countries like India, Australia and New Zealand have or are instituting legislations pertaining to freedom of information. From a W-O-G EA perspective this is both necessary and radical as governments tend to hold back on information citing security and confidentiality concerns (State Services Commission, 2006; Office of the Chief Information Officer, 2007; NIA, 2008; NIA, 2009). It does not require deep analysis to realize that to successfully traverse the evolutionary stages of connected government, three things pertaining to information are absolutely essential: (1) clarity and understanding in the information collected; (2) clarity in how the collected information is aggregated for decision making; (3) clarity in establishing the channels through which the information flows and who receives the information. The technicalities of frequency, format, protocol and the like are more implementation issues. Thomas Davenport and Jeanne Harris in their book, *Competing on Analytics: The New Science of Winning,* aptly describe the importance of information, information flows and the raw material they provide organizations for building and using analytics as a competitive weapon (Davenport & Harris, 2007).

F. **The strength and intensity of the balancing (negative loops)**: Loops B1 to B8 in Figure

27 are the key negative loops identified and elaborated in the previous sections. Negative loops per se are not bad for the system. These loops, also called balancing loops, correct the system and keep the system in a stable state. Goldratt's Theory of Constraints (TOC), another systems thinking approach, rightly urges organizations to uncover the constraints and address them before anything else. Even though negative loops correct the system and keep it in a stable state, if dominant, they slow down the performance of the system. Almost all governments usually try to ignore the existence and impact of negative loops, hence not acting on them. Instead their focus is on the positive loops and the tendency to make them stronger. Fundamentally there is nothing wrong in making the positive loops stronger and dominant via proper interventions. However, strengthening the system by making the positive loops dominant, without weakening the negative loops is akin to accelerating a vehicle without releasing the brakes. It produces friction, leading to intense heat in the engine and ultimately break-down. It is critical that role of negative loops is fully understood in the context of the current system behavior prior to proposing ways and means to use them as leverage points. In a system that is accelerating without control (as a result of highly dominant positive loops), collapse and destruction are very likely. In such scenarios, negative loops are used to full positive effect to slow down the system and bring it down to a more manageable and sustainable level of performance. However, this is not the case with regards to W-O-G EA for the connected government.

As has already been explained in the previous sections and also evidenced by Gartner's *Hype Cycle for Enterprise Architecture 2011,* W-O-G

EA currently faces tremendous headwinds and inertia before it can even start to move, though its adoption is on the upside. The negative loops B1 and B8 directly contribute to the inertia becoming the system's constraints thus preventing the system to move (Fishenden, et al., 2006; Bittinger, 2011; Burton & Allega, 2011). The primary source of the inherent inertia that exists in governments and their organizations comes from the short-sighted belief that these entities operate in a monopoly, unless forced to, there is no urgency to bring in change. Hence it is imperative for governments to fully understand the impact of negative loops and design appropriate interventions.

G.   **The strength and intensity of the reinforcing (positive loops)**: Loops R1 to R10 in Figure 27 collectively represents factors that have the ability to push forward and have a multiplier effect on W-O-G EA adoption for the connected government. Used correctly, they have the ability to provide the rationale for moving toward connected government using W-O-G EA. In the situation wherein efforts are required for governments to embrace W-O-G EA, the positive loops provide the necessary impetus. From a government perspective these loops need to be strengthened to a level where they can overcome the inertia presented by the negative loops in the system. As discussed earlier, if the strengthening of the positive loops happens in unison with the weakening of the negative loops, the system moves and provides the desired performance. However, it is critical to realize that completely eliminating negative loops altogether is neither possible nor desirable, as they provide the levers to slow down the system when the system moves at a greater than sustainable pace.

H.   **The lengths of delays**: Delays are a critical dynamic characteristic of any system. Figure 27 identifies some of the key delays that exist in the whole system. Delays are

strong leverage points, even though they could be double-edged swords. On the positive side, delays act as buffers in the system that can absorb the shocks and gyrations in the system, whilst on the negative side they seemingly slow down the impact of another change in the system. Delays are common causes of oscillations. In the context to W-O-G EA adoption, the area where delay has a negative impact on the overall system is time needed to reach the critical mass of EA adoptions across the government. As explained earlier, as critical mass is achieved, the system "tips-over" to the new state, thus facilitating system success. However, when the response to specific change is not visible with a reasonable period of time, there is a tendency to believe that the system is not responding, hence the reaction to "push the throttle," until there is an overcorrection followed by oscillations. Despite the fact that delays are strong leverage points, it is important to realize that delays are often not easily changeable. Things take as long as they take.

Applying the above interventions would depend on the emergent systemic profile. Leverage point H through to leverage point A are sequenced in increasing order of effectiveness. Interestingly, the sequence also captures the order of ease of adoption, i.e. as expected, changing the mindset is definitely the most difficult (and not surprisingly) the most effective leverage point for which appropriate interventions can be designed and implemented. Hence an observable trend is that there is a direct correlation between the evolutionary stage of connected government to the leverage points (and intervention strategies) that countries are required to employ. In other words, as countries target higher stages of connected government they employ the more difficult (and more effective) intervention strategies at points which give them more effective leverage aptly selected to fulfil the

Figure 31. Mapping systemic interventions to stages of connected government

Evolutionary Stages Of Connected Government	Length of Delays	Strength and Intensity of the Reinforcing Loops	Strength and Intensity of the Balancing Loops	Structure of Information Flows	Structure of the System	Rules of the System	Goals of the System	Mindset of which the System Arises
Intragovernmental	vvv	vvv	vv	v	v	v		
Intergovernmental	vvv	vvv	vvv	vv	v	v	v	
Extragovernmental	vvv	vvv	vvv	vvv	vv	v	v	v
Ubiquitous	vvv	vvv	vvv	vvv	vvv	vv	vv	vv

Legend: vvv → Imperative | vv → Important | v → Substantive

higher requirements and expectations. To attain the **ubiquitous** level of connected government, countries would usually require multiple "cycles" of W-O-G EA programs such that it allows the governments to traverse through and learn from progressively more complete and advanced generations of EA, even as they move through the various systemic states introduced earlier. Figure 31 maps the intervention strategies and leverage points needed versus the evolutionary stages of connected government as a general guideline for countries to adapt and adopt.

A common underlying thread in many countries is the current focus on government data. Availability of government, usually as **Open Data** initiatives, provides the enabling impetus for governments to be more connected, win trust and even spur innovation by encouraging co-creation of new services to meet the growing demands and expectations of the populace (Huijboom & Van Den Broek, 2011; Lee & Kwak, 2011).

The role of Open Data in enabling this journey through the various evolutionary stages of connected government cannot be over-emphasized.

Moving from **Intragovernmental** to **Ubiquitous** demands innovative services, that can be conceived and delivered only if government data is openly available. The innovation maturity with government data can be summarized as four quadrants, as shown in Figure 32. For governments to be **Ubiquitous**, they must be in the **Innovation Leaders** quadrant.

6.3. Manifesto for Government Leaders

Government EA efforts around the world have penetrated deep into e-government programs. There is a realization that moving toward higher levels of e-government capability and maturity (especially achieving connected government through government transformation) makes an effective government EA an imperative. Government EA programs surveyed in this study clearly evidence that even as governments across the world are attempting to become more collaborative and pervasive, they are also trying to balance these with being less intrusive. Connected government

Figure 32. Innovation maturity with open government data

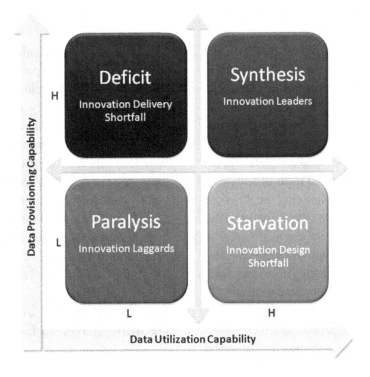

is no longer limited to being what governments are trying to be, but what citizens and businesses are demanding of governments. Yet, in adopting the W-O-G EA paradigm in the context of connected government, countries overly focus on improving the **operational enablers** at the cost of **strategic wisdom and direction**. **Ignorance**, **complexity** and **capability gaps** are cited most frequently as the primary reasons.

Operational enablers main components that countries typically develop as part of their EA program. These include: (1) frameworks; (2) methodologies; (3) reference architectures and models; (4) tool capabilities; (5) competency building activities; (6) guidelines and standards; (7) best practices and the like. Abundance of operational enablers is clearly evident in the government EA programs reviewed and presented in Section 3. The skewness in favor of operational enablers is hard to miss. Though operational enablers are important, they, by no means have the ability to

supplant the strategic perspective. Their role is primarily in supplementing strategic wisdom and direction. In the absence of strategic perspective, countries unknowingly drift between different systemic states, in an arbitrary manner without comprehending the underlying reasons. In such scenarios, which are all too frequent, the program virtually navigates blind leading to cynicism, lack of persistence, erosion of confidence and loss of attention by the government leaders. It almost takes a crisis to make a deep change. And when it is time to address the crisis, the focus is on symptoms, not causes (Snowden & Boone, 2007).

For many governments, connected government is a concept and a long term vision. It is the new normal. To make it simple and intuitive, this concept could be manifested and realized as a Government 2.0 program. Government 2.0 is gaining traction as a means to achieve part of the capability dimensions of connected government. Government 2.0 involves the use of Web 2.0 family of technologies to power government reforms, openness, collaboration, and engagement. To actualize the vision of connected government, government leaders have to demonstrate the willingness to challenge conventions and question some long-standing assumptions, which contribute to the existence of some fallacies. These fallacies include: (1) government EA not designed to address national priorities; (2) accepting fragmentation on the basis of government layers and jurisdictions; (3) no questioning the traditional form of authority, taking it as sacrosanct and ignoring the power of influence; (4) government as the absolute owner of all public data; (5) government as the creator, operator and regulator of all government services; (6) government entities operating in monopolistic situations and not required to compete; and (7) underestimating the impact of digital divide.

From the above leverage points and their impact on the evolutionary journey towards connected government it is absolutely clear that this cannot be accomplished by merely the involvement of the IT department (or the CIO Office). As a management practice, whose scope and coverage includes the entire government, EA needs to be freed up from the constraints that comes with being with the IT department. The six primary reasons why EA must not be assigned to the IT department are:

A. Enterprise Architecture (EA) ≠ Enterprise IT Architecture (EITA);
B. True EA leads to redistribution of authority and reallocation of accountability, both beyond IT department jurisdictions;
C. The value proposition delivered and benefits from EA are solely business realizable;
D. The primary goal of EA is to build a coherent enterprise, not better IT systems;
E. Factoring complexities in the organizations, holistic synthesis takes precedence over fractional analysis;
F. Resistance to EA by the business, is a consequence of failure, not the cause for it;

and EA failure is not an IT failure, but an organizational failure.

These six reasons should not come as a surprise, as empirical evidence points to the beginning of this major shift. According to Gartner: (1) nearly 70% will have delivery of business value and business transformation as their primary focus; (2) about 5% of the organization had their EA functions reporting to roles outside of the IT department; and (3) 40% stated that business leaders were an integral part of the EA programs (Burton & Allega, 2011). While the above data includes both public and private sectors, aside from the actual numbers, the trend is all too evident. The aspirations of the W-O-G EA are clearly reflected.

6.4. Escaping the Shackles: Designing W-O-G EA Adoption

This section presents a brief summary of the steps for designing or rethinking W-O-G EA adoption to power the vision of connected government (Snowden & Boone, 2007).

A. **Articulate** the goals and objectives of connected government, along with the intended level of connected government maturity. The inability to concisely describe the above is symptomatic of a lack of clarity.
B. **Catalog** the reinforcing and balancing loops that are applicable. Tailor the systems model as required.
C. **Construct** the emergent systemic profile. It is important to fully understand the underlying nuances and inherent characteristics (both implicit and explicit) that give rise to the emergent systemic profile.
D. **Validate** the emergent systemic profile. Iterate and refine as needed factoring in the presence of ambiguity, confounding variables, dynamic complexities and implicit linkages.

E. **Ascertain** the systemic state and determine the strategic navigation pathway. This evaluation needs to be supported by an adequate supporting explanation and rationale.

F. **Identify** the leverage points that are pertinent and exploitable. Be sure to take into consideration cultural, economic, political and technological factors that may impact the effectiveness of the leverage points.

G. **Craft** the specific intervention strategies to support the leverage points. In the first pass, articulate the intended impact on the system (i.e. W-O-G EA adoption). Iterate until the desired impact is achieved and implement interventions in full scale.

H. **Scrutinize** the performance of the whole system against the initial set of goals and objectives and make mid-course corrections as new information is gathered and as required. The consequences of the interventions are as important as the interventions themselves.

The above steps ought to be repeated for countries to continuously practice the strategic (systems) thinking and advance W-O-G EA adoption for connected government. Chapters 9 through to 18 demonstrate the application of these steps through case studies and experience reports of transformation to connected government.

7. TOWARDS GOVERNMENT ENTERPRISE ARCHITECTURE FRAMEWORK

Sections 5 and 6 have clearly demonstrated the centrality of architecture in the new form of government—*the connected government*. The connected government paradigm is new and alien to many countries. The current understanding of this paradigm is limited to connectedness within the government and its agencies (or in other words the *intra-governmental* state). Based on a survey of available literature there have been some instances

of *inter-governmental* and *extra-governmental* states, but these are limited to specific issues and scenarios and seldom broad-based. As a result, current government EA frameworks are overly conceptualized and designed for the intra-governmental state of connected government. In a sense, this reflects the current state of thinking and practice which limits the benefits that governments accrue from EA. Section 6.1 identifies and elaborates the factors (enablers and inhibitors) that influence the W-O-G EA adoption. Needless to mention, the current government EA frameworks perform poorly in addressing the larger systemic issues that so often hold back or even stall major government EA initiatives and programs.

As clearly articulated by the UN, W-O-G EA initiatives need to be preceded with major public sector reforms to allow for the move toward connected government. This obviously requires a strong political will, which (usually) are not forthcoming. To complicate and confuse matters further, countries are enthusiastically jumping on to the *Open and Connected Government* fad, often referred to as Government 2.0. Notwithstanding the observed and emergent characteristics and dimensions of connected government, countries are attempting to circumvent the need for major reforms in the public sector, by embracing the Web 2.0 technologies. This is with the expectation that embracing Web 2.0 technologies in the context of the government will automatically and effortlessly catapult countries to higher and more mature levels of connected government. Based on current adoption and use of Web 2.0 technologies (e.g. social media), it is not difficult to categorize the countries in terms of their intent and maturity (Dutta & Mia, 2011). Figure 33 depicts the connected government maturity matrix. The matrix is based on two dimensions: (1) Technology Adoption; and (2) Government Culture and Management.

As is seen in the figure, a combination of the dimensions above creates four distinct quadrants, which are elaborated in the paragraphs below:

Figure 33. Connected government categorization matrix

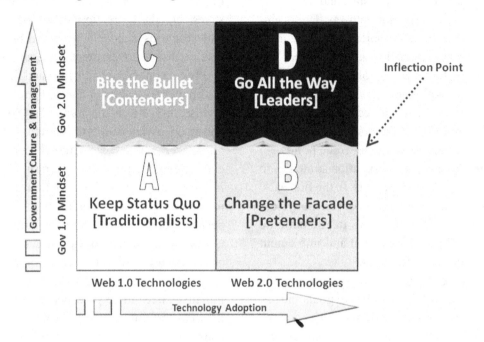

- **Traditionalists**: These are countries that prefer to maintain their current forms of governance, for numerous reasons. These are focused on adopting the more conventional ICT (e.g. websites and portals) primarily used to automate government services. This group is classified as the **traditionalists**; Quadrant A. Not to undermine this group in any way, a few nations in this quadrant can have very efficient and seamlessly delivered government services via the electronic medium. The main point to be highlighted is that governments in this group are rigidly hierarchical, practice top-down (centralized) form of governance along with other key characteristics.

- **Pretenders**: These are countries that prefer to maintain their current forms of governance, for numerous reasons. The difference between this group and the traditionalists is that countries in their attempt to cover-up traditional forms of governance, and (usually) to showcase modern thinking to the world at large, enthusiasti-

cally embrace Web 2.0 technologies. These (social media) technologies could include Facebook, Twitter, Flickr, Twitter, Orkut, Wikipedia, as well as innovations like next generation broadband, crowd sourcing and cloud computing among several other up and coming ways and means. Countries in this group continue to be rigidly hierarchical, practice top-down (centralized) form of governance, but embrace Web 2.0 technologies in a superficial manner (i.e. they only change the façade). Countries in this group view social media as an exciting new medium (that often supplants the more traditional media like Television and Print) and nothing more. Inherently, the governance does not change. Hence these countries are categorized as the **pretenders**: Quadrant B.

- **Contenders**: In this category are countries, which have embraced broad government-wide reforms. Thus, they are the ones to portray the next generation of governance and the much needed mindset change coupled with political reforms have taken place. In terms of technology adoption, primarily due to economic reasons, they continue to utilize the conventional ICT, usually in an efficient manner. The main point to highlight is that countries in this category have made the required reforms and innovations in the governance, but yet to fully technology enable it with the more contemporary Web 2.0 technologies. This group classified as the **contenders**; Quadrant C. This category represents countries that have 'bitten-the-bullet' with regards to political reforms and mindset transformation. According to the UN this paradigm shift leads to much greater bottom-up empowerment, coupled with non-physical communication, borderless interaction and blurring of classical boundaries between constituents and governments.

- **Leaders**: Countries in this category demonstrate all the characteristics of next generation forms of governance (as contenders). In addition, these countries are able to extract the full benefits of such forms of governance via the broad-based adoption and use of Web 2.0 technologies. The countries in this quadrant are classified as **leaders**; Quadrant D.

Among the four quadrants shown and described above, the key is the existence of a deep chasm between quadrants 'A,' 'B,' and 'C,' 'D.' This deep chasm results from the fact that countries categorized as C and D have embraced the more difficult political reforms and mindset change. These are the critical success factors to move towards connected government. In other words, it represents the inflection point of government transformation. Needless to mention, very few countries have fully envisioned what crossing this chasm actually entails, let alone traverse it successfully. The ensuing change is disruptive and because it will mean redistribution of authority

(and power) it is reasonable to expect that not everyone will embrace it willingly.

Thus, it is imperative that any government EA framework fully factors in the existence of this inflection point and is designed accordingly. The intent is to ensure that these emergent characteristics are taken as inputs to the design of the government EA framework. It is beyond the scope of this chapter to provide a detailed description of a government EA framework that would be suitable in the context of connected government. Chapters 4 through to 8 provide examples of such frameworks. Nonetheless, as a starting point, Figure 34 provides a graphical representation of the key elements and dimensions that W-O-G EA framework should capture. The intention is for it to be used as a reference structure and benchmark for assessing any EA framework for completeness. The dimensions depicted in Figure 33 are imperative to cover the whole of government; the elements shown within each dimension are representative.

Current EA frameworks—**public sector** (e.g. Federal EA Framework, European Interoperability Framework, Nederlandse Overheids Referentie Architectuur); **defense** (e.g. US Department of Defense Architecture Framework, UK Ministry of Defense Architecture Framework); **industry-specific** (e.g. Enhanced Telecom Operations Map); **vendor-specific** (e.g. Oracle EA Framework, SAP EA Framework); **consortium** (e.g. The Open Group Architecture Framework); and **consultancy** (e.g. Capgemini, Logica)—are not designed for W-O-G EA, hence require substantial adaptation. They address some but not all the dimensions as in Figure 34. Chapter 7 describes how The Open Group Architecture Framework can be adapted for use in the context of W-O-G EA.

Irrespective of how the frameworks are designed and adapted, it is imperative to demonstrate the public value of the investments made in such programs. Chapters 19 through to 21 delineate how this is done, through substantive examples.

Figure 34. W-O-G enterprise architecture framework structure

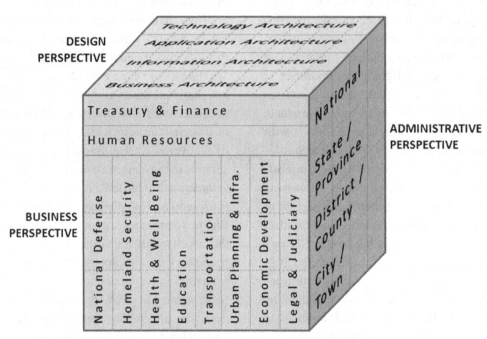

Whole-of-Government Enterprise Architecture Framework Structure

8. CONCLUSION AND WAY FORWARD

A few years back Michael Porter asserted "strategic planning in most organizations has not contributed to strategic thinking." In the case of W-O-G EA adoption for connected government this statement cannot be disputed. Strategic (systems) thinking makes it possible to translate complex information that is interconnected into simple, yet compelling explanations of not only what is happening, but more importantly "why." There is no dearth of literature that identifies pitfalls to EA and proposed solutions to avoid such pitfalls. There is also abundant guidance literature available as to how governments (and other organizations) must adopt EA. On the other hand, none of the currently available literatures explain the underlying complexities of EA adoption per se. Gary Hamel's contention that **operational efficiency does not equate to strategic efficiency** makes absolute sense in a scenario where governments are gradually transforming from a hierarchy to a lattice (both by necessity and design).

EA is a very large undertaking for any organization. W-O-G EA is even larger, more complex and more dynamic, making it an imperative to comprehend the underlying complexities in a holistic and coherent manner. Current thinking positions EA as an IT strategy and management discipline. This research intends to dispel this thinking and positions EA as the "architecture of the enterprise." For this to be true, it is crucial that EA is positioned outside of the IT department (and CIO jurisdiction). It is well-known that adopting EA at the W-O-G level requires and demands much more than good frameworks, methodologies, tools and technical capabilities. There have been some efforts to identify such influencing factors. However, all these efforts have looked at such influencing factors in a piecemeal manner and hence their proposed solutions are seldom convincing or effective.

The systems thinking approach addresses the "why" of W-O-G EA adoption in the context of connected government and uncovers non-obvious interdependencies between the factors such as:

A. Different organizational units within the government (e.g. central structure, ministries, and agencies).
B. Corresponding actions taken by these organizational units.
C. Quantitative tangible variables (such as national economy size) and qualitative ones (such as operational diversity).
D. Short and long term consequences of government decisions.

W-O-G EA for connected government is a long term endeavor. The technical process of architecting is difficult enough, but understanding the underlying complexities and the interconnected dynamics that contribute to particularly intractable and difficult-to-solve problems makes it intimidating for many countries. Systems thinking, used in this chapter, looks at these problems and analyzes them with the core intent of: (1) motivating people to change; (2) generating collaboration between groups that blame each other for the current situation; (3) concentrate limited resources to the points of greatest leverage; and (4) ensure continuous ongoing learning after key decisions with regard to interventions have been made.

To ensure that the potential of connected government is realized and the benefits derived, policy and decision makers play an essential role. W-O-G EA provides the enabling mechanism to understand the holistic viewpoint that is so very crucial. Through the use of tools like the emergent systemic profiles, systemic states and strategic navigation pathways proposed and described in detail in this chapter, countries have the means to assess, design, and advance their W-O-G EA

agenda. As Haiyan Qian of UNDESA succinctly puts it "W-O-G EA is more a reform process of the government sector rather than the streamlining of the government ICT structure." To make this happen, government EA frameworks must be designed and applied keeping in view the systemic nature of government business and strategic thinking that is required to attain connected government, which countries aspire for. The purpose of this chapter is not to predict and design the future of W-O-G EA, but to assist countries in inventing it, thus giving every nation the ability to take full advantage of the extraordinary opportunities that lie ahead.

REFERENCES

AGIMO. (2010). *Engage: Getting on with government 2.0. report of the government 2.0 taskforce*. Canberra, Australia: Government of Australia.

APDIP. (2007a). *E-government interoperability: A review of government interoperability frameworks in selected countries*. Bangkok, Thailand: United Nations Development Program Regional Center.

APDIP. (2007b). *E-government interoperability guide*. Bangkok, Thailand: United Nations Development Program Regional Center.

Atkinson, R. D., & McKay, A. S. (2007). *Digital prosperity – Understanding the economic benefits of information technology revolution*. Washington, DC: The Information Technology & Innovation Foundation.

Bittinger, S. (2011). *Hype cycle for government transformation 2011*. Gartner Industry Research ID Number: G00214747. Retrieved from http://www.gartner.com.

Burns, P., Neutens, M., Newman, D., & Power, T. (2009). Building value through enterprise architecture: A global study. *Booz & Company Perspective*. Retrieved from http://www.booz.com/media/file/Building_Value_through_Enterprise_Architecture.pdf.

Burton, B., & Allega, P. (2011). *Hype cycle for enterprise architecture 2011*. Gartner Industry Research ID Number: G00214756. Retrieved from http://www.gartner.com.

Butland, B., Jebb, S., Kopelman, P., McPherson, K., Thomas, S., Mardell, J., & Parry, V. (2007). *Tackling obesities – Future choices*. London, UK: Government Office for Science.

Cisco, I. B. S. G. (2004). *Connected government: Essays from innovators*. London, UK: Premium Publishing.

Cisco, I. B. S. G. (2009). *Realizing the potential of the connected republic: Web 2.0 opportunities in the public sector*. Cisco Systems Incorporated White Paper. Palo Alto, CA: Cisco Systems Incorporated.

Davenport, T. H., & Harris, J. G. (2007). *Competing on analytics – The new science of winning*. Boston, MA: Harvard Business School Press.

Dettmer, H. W. (2007). *The logical thinking process: A systems approach to complex problem solving*. New York, NY: ASQ Quality Press.

Doucet, G., Gotze, J., Saha, P., & Bernard, S. A. (2009). *Coherency management: Architecting the enterprise for alignment, agility and assurance*. Bloomington, IN: AuthorHouse.

Dutta, S., & Mia, I. (2011). *Global information technology report 2010-2011: ICT for sustainability*. Geneva, Switzerland: World Economic Forum.

Fishenden, J., Johnson, M., Nelson, K., Polin, G., Rijpma, G., & Stolz, P. (2006). *The new world of government work: Transforming the business of government with the power of information technology*. Microsoft Public Services and e-Government Strategy Discussion Paper. Palo Alto, CA: Microsoft.

Gall, N., Newman, D., Allega, P., Lapkin, A., & Handler, R. A. (2010). *Introducing hybrid thinking for transformation, innovation and strategy*. Gartner Research ID Number: G00172065. Retrieved from http://www.gartner.com.

Halstead, D., Somerville, N., Straker, B., & Ward, C. (2009). *The way to gov 2.0: An enterprise approach to web 2.0 in government*. Microsoft US Public Sector White Paper. Palo Alto, CA: Microsoft.

Hamel, G. (2007). *The future of management*. Boston, MA: Harvard Business School Press.

Hjort-Madsen, K. (2009). *Architecting government – Understanding enterprise architecture adoption in the public sector*. Doctoral Dissertation. Copenhagen, Denmark: IT University of Copenhagen.

Huijboom, N., & Van Den Broek, T. (2011). Open data – An international comparison of strategies. *European Journal of ePractice, 12*, 4 – 16.

Janssen, M., & Hjort-Madsen, K. (2007). Analyzing enterprise architecture in national governments: The cases of Denmark and Netherlands. In *Proceedings of the 40th Annual Hawaii International Conference on Systems Sciences (HICSS 2007)*. HICSS.

Lee, G., & Kwak, Y. H. (2011). *An open government implementation model – Moving to increased public engagement*. Washington, DC: IBM Center for The Business of Government.

Leechul, B. (2010). Building an enterprise architecture for statistics Korea. In *Proceedings of the Management of Statistical Information Systems (MSIS 2010)*. Daejeon, Republic of Korea.

Liimatainen, K., Hoffman, M., & Heikkilä, J. (2007). *Overview of enterprise architecture work in 15 countries*. Helsinki, Finland: Ministry of Finance, Government of Finland.

Meadows, D. (1999). *Leverage points: Places to intervene in a system*. Hartland, VT: The Sustainability Institute.

Mickoliet, A., Kounatze, C. R., Serra-Vallejo, C., Vickery, G., & Wunsch-Vincent, S. (2009). *The role of the crisis on ICT and their role in the recovery. Organization for Economic Development and Cooperation (OECD) Report*. Washington, DC: OECD.

Microsoft Corporation. (2009). *Government service center – A Microsoft vision for high performance citizen service*. Microsoft Corporation White Paper. Palo Alto, CA: Microsoft.

Microsoft Corporation. (2010). *Connected government framework – Strategies to transform government in the 2.0 world*. Microsoft Corporation White Paper. Palo Alto, CA: Microsoft.

Moon, Y. (2010). *Different – Escaping the competitive herd*. New York, NY: Crown Business.

Muehlfeit, J. (2006). *The connected government framework for local and regional government*. Microsoft Corporation White Paper. Palo Alto, CA: Microsoft.

NIA. (2008). *2008 informatization white paper*. Korea: Ministry of Public Administration and Security, Government of Republic of Korea.

NIA. (2009). *2009 yearbook of information society statistics*. Korea: Ministry of Public Administration and Security, Government of Republic of Korea.

Nordfors, L., Ericson, B., Lindell, H., & Lapidus, J. (2009). *eGovernment of tomorrow – Future scenarios for 2020*. Vinnova Report VR 2009:28. Gullers Group. Retrieved from http://www.gullers.se.

Office of the Chief Information Officer. (2007). *South Australian government ICT strategy*. Adelaide, Australia: Government of South Australia.

Pardo, T. A., & Burke, G. B. (2008). *Improving government interoperability: A capability framework for government managers*. Albany, NY: SUNY Albany.

Reed, G. E. (2006). Leadership and systems thinking. *Defense AT & L*. Retrieved from http://www.au.af.mil/au/awc/awcgate/dau/ree_mj06.pdf.

Ross, J. W., Weill, P., & Robertson, D. C. (2006). *Enterprise architecture as strategy: Creating a foundation for business execution*. Boston, MA: Harvard Business School Press.

Saha, P. (2007). *Handbook of enterprise systems architecture in practice*. Hershey, PA: IGI Global. doi:10.4018/978-1-59904-189-6

Saha, P. (2008). *Advances in government enterprise architecture*. Hershey, PA: IGI Global. doi:10.4018/978-1-60566-068-4

Senge, P. (1990). *The fifth discipline*. New York, NY: Doubleday Currency.

Snowden, D. J., & Boone, M. (2007). A leader's framework for decision making. *Harvard Business Review*. Retrieved from http://www.mpiweb.org/CMS/uploadedFiles/Article%20for%20Marketing%20-%20Mary%20Boone.pdf.

State Services Commission. (2006). *Enabling transformation: A strategy for e-government 2006*. Wellington, New Zealand: Ministry of State Services, Government of New Zealand.

Sterman, J. D. (2000). *Business dynamics – Systems thinking and modeling for a complex world.* Boston, MA: Irwin McGraw-Hill.

Stroh, P. D. (2000). Leveraging change: The power of systems thinking in action. *Reflections: The SoL Journal, 2*(2). doi:10.1162/15241730051092019

Tamara, R., & Damuth, R. (2009). *Estimating the effects of broadband penetration on GDP and productivity in south east Asia.* Nathan Associates Business Report. Retrieved from http://www.nathaninc.com.

UNDESA. (2008). *United nations e-government survey 2008: From e-government to connected governance.* New York, NY: United Nations.

UNDESA. (2010). *United nations e-government survey 2010: Leveraging e-government at a time of financial and economic crises.* New York, NY: United Nations.

World Bank. (2008). *Global economic prospects – Technology diffusion in the developing world.* Washington, DC: The World Bank.

World Economic Forum. (2009). *ICT for economic growth – A dynamic ecosystem driving the global recovery.* Geneva, Switzerland: World Economic Forum.

World Economic Forum. (2011). *The future of government – Lessons learned from around the world.* Geneva, Switzerland: World Economic Forum.

World Economic Forum. (2011). *The global information technology report 2010/2011 – Transformations 2.0.* Geneva, Switzerland: World Economic Forum.

Zenghelis, D. (2010). *The economics of network powered growth.* CISCO IBSG White Paper. Palo Alto, CA: CISCO Internet Business Solutions Group (IBSG).

Zokaei, K., Seddon, J., & O'Donovan, B. (2011). *Systems thinking – From heresy to practice.* London, UK: Palgrave Macmillan.

ADDITIONAL READING

ADSIC. (2009). *Abu Dhabi IT architecture & standards version 2.0.* Abu Dhabi, UAE: Abu Dhabi Systems and Information Committee (ADSIC).

AGIMO. (2007). *Cross-agency services architecture principles.* Sydney, Australia: Department of Finance and Administration, Government of Australia.

AGIMO. (2010). *Engage: Getting on with government 2.0: Report of the government 2.0 taskforce.* Sydney, Australia: Department of Finance and Deregulation, Government of Australia.

AGIMO. (2011). *Australian government architecture reference models version 3.0.* Sydney, Australia: Department of Finance and Deregulation, Government of Australia.

Al Khouri, A. M., & Bal, J. (2006). E-government in GCC countries. *International Journal of Social Sciences, 1*(2), 83–98.

E-Government Authority. (2007). *Bahrain e-government strategy 2007 - 2010.* Manama, Bahrain: E-Government Authority.

E-Government Authority. (2009). *Bahrain e-government program: Looking beyond the obvious.* Manama, Bahrain: E-Government Authority.

Enterprise Architecture Working Group. (2006). *Egyptian Government enterprise architecture framework version 4.0.* Cairo, Egypt: Ministry of State for Administrative Development.

Gartner Incorporated. (2007). *An Assessment of Ksa Yesser program.* New York, NY: Gartner Incorporated.

MOICT. (2006). *Jordan e-government program: E-government strategy 2006 – 2010*. Amman, Jordan: Ministry of Information and Communication Technology.

MOICT. (2007). *Jordan e-government architecture*. Amman, Jordan: Ministry of Information and Communication Technology.

State Services Commission. (2006). *Enabling transformation: A strategy for e-government 2006*. Wellington, New Zealand: Ministry of State Services.

State Services Commission. (2008). *New Zealand e-government interoperability framework version 3.3*. Wellington, New Zealand: Ministry of State Services.

State Services Commission. (2009). *New Zealand federated enterprise architecture framework version 0.9*. Wellington, New Zealand: Ministry of State Services.

YESSER. (2006). *The national e-government strategy and action plan*. Riyadh, Saudi Arabia: Ministry of Information and Communication Technology.

Section 2
Government as a Complex Adaptive System

Chapter 2
A Problem Oriented Enterprise Architecture Approach Applied to Wicked Problems

Bernard Robertson-Dunn
Australian Government Information Management Office, Australia

ABSTRACT

This chapter proposes that a problem oriented approach to Enterprise Architecture can deliver a better outcome than one based upon needs and requirements, especially when dealing with Wicked Problems. A distinction is drawn between what an Enterprise Architect does, solve business problems, and what the architect produces, descriptions of end states. It also suggests that the approach to modeling and understanding a problem can have significant impacts on the quality, effectiveness, and efficiency of potential solutions and the decisions made in identifying optimal solutions and implementation projects. Finally, the chapter discusses the use of the proposed problem oriented Enterprise Architecture approach to Wicked Problems in the context of e-Government.

INTRODUCTION

Successful problem solving requires finding the right solution to the right problem. We fail more often because we solve the wrong problem than because we get the wrong solution to the right problem (Ackoff, 1974).

DOI: 10.4018/978-1-4666-1824-4.ch002

This chapter makes a number of assertions about why wrong problems are solved, how this error can be prevented, and how problem solving can be made more effective by utilising an approach that will result in more optimal solutions.

The assertions in this chapter are that:

1. The current needs/requirements based approach to Enterprise Architecture is not

suitable when applied to large scale and socially oriented systems development;

2. Business goals are achieved by identifying and solving business problems;
3. Implementing a solution to a business problem will create or result in new problems;
4. The way that a problem is understood and analysed can significantly impact the effectiveness of the solution; and
5. Taking a problem oriented approach to Enterprise Architecture will bring a better result than the current approach.

The objective of this chapter is to propose that a problem oriented approach to understanding how an enterprise should best achieve its goals is a more effective mechanism than the current approach based on needs and requirements.

The structure of this chapter is as follows:

1. An overview of current needs and requirements based approach to Enterprise Architecture and reasons why it is not optimal when applied to Wicked Problems
2. An outline of a problem oriented approach to Enterprise Architecture and why it is preferable to the current approach.
3. A discussion on techniques and methods of problem solving.
4. The application of a problem oriented approach to Enterprise Architecture to e-Government.

BACKGROUND

The Role and Purpose of Enterprise Architecture

Enterprise Architecture is a means to an end.

For Enterprise Architecture to be of use to the enterprise, the end needs to be of benefit. The means is the mechanism by which it delivers that benefit.

It is suggested that the purpose of Enterprise Architecture is to deliver benefit to the business by identifying and solving business problems. Solving business problems often, but not always, results in solutions that utilise information systems.

For too long, enterprise and information systems architectures, and the projects that implement these architectures have been driven by needs and requirements. Unfortunately, needs and requirements are not a good way to describe problems or the solutions to those problems.

If Enterprise Architecture does not bring, or enable, business benefit by solving problems, and is not recognised by the business for doing so, then it is doubtful that Enterprise Architecture will be perceived as being of any use to the enterprise.

It is useful to distinguish between what Enterprise Architects do (the process) and what they produce (architecture).

The Enterprise Architecture Process

The architecture process is the set of activities that develops end states and other architecture artefacts.

Requirements engineering approaches to Enterprise Architecture such as that of The Open Group Architecture Framework (TOGAF) Application Development Method (ADM) start with business needs and then develop requirements for a system that will satisfy those needs. (TOGAF, 2009).

Figure 1 illustrates the relationship between needs and requirements that the TOGAF ADM defines.

The difficulty with this approach is that needs and requirements are both solution oriented. Needs are satisfied, requirements are met. Neither describes goals or problems.

TOGAF has been used here only as an example of a needs and requirements based approach. Most, if not all, architecture frameworks make the assumption that the business has identified, analysed, and solved the problem to be addressed. In many cases, especially in large information

Figure 1. A needs and requirements approach to enterprise architecture

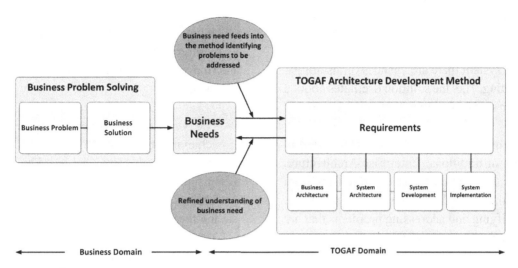

A Needs/Requirements Approach To Enterprise Architecture

system based projects, the business problem has not been fully identified, let alone solved. Most business cases incorporate a sketchy view of the proposed solution but also contain a detailed project plan and a firm cost.

The reality is that the needs and requirements that form the basis of a business case do not describe the problem sufficiently well so as to define an optimal solution. At best, they describe some characteristics of a solution, at worst they are incorrect, incomplete and lead to a solution that does not actually solve the business problem.

What the business is not equipped to do is describe how the system should be architected, designed, and constructed. This is the role of the Enterprise Architect who, among other things, is expected to define an "as-is" or target architecture of a system that will exhibit the behaviour required to solve the business problem.

In order to make decisions regarding the best "as-is" architecture, the architect needs criteria against which to assess the various options. Needs and requirements, because they describe the solution, do not provide the necessary criteria. This means that the architect is mostly disconnected from the real problem, a situation reinforced by most formal project management approaches, which position needs and requirements as being the only necessary inputs and drivers for a project.

It is preferable that the Enterprise Architect should assess candidate solutions against the business problem, not against needs and requirements.

Agile System Development

Agile has been promoted as a better approach to system development than the large scale, waterfall style of which most Enterprise Architecture activities form a part.

However, Agile is really only another needs and requirements based approach to creating a solution. It recognises that business people have trouble defining what they actually want, i.e. the requirements do not sufficiently represent the problem.

In order to address this shortcoming, Agile promotes the approach of rapidly creating solutions and testing them with the business to see if they solve the business problem.

The answers to the testing process enable the developers to modify the solution and test again. Hopefully, the process will converge to an acceptable solution. Unfortunately, like any feedback system there are chances of instability, and "hunting," i.e. the solution oscillates about a particular solution, without actually getting any closer.

Agile has some advantages over the waterfall approach of traditional Enterprise Architecture, but it is still solution focused and suffers from most of the same difficulties, including that of not identifying and addressing problems that are likely to arise from a particular solution.

A PROBLEM ORIENTED APPROACH TO ENTERPRISE ARCHITECTURE

This section discusses a problem oriented approach to Enterprise Architecture. It covers:

1. The definition of the approach;
2. The advantages of a problem oriented approach over a needs and requirements approach;
3. A description of the process required to undertake the approach; and
4. The architectural artefacts that the process can produce.

Definition of a Problem Oriented Approach to Enterprise Architecture

A problem oriented approach to Enterprise Architecture is a modelling approach that directly and explicitly identifies business goals and the problems facing the enterprise in achieving these goals. It is an approach that focuses on problems, solutions, and business value.

It provides a business oriented justification for solutions and the allocation of resources in developing and maintaining them.

A problem oriented approach to Enterprise Architecture utilises the same modelling and architecture development techniques as a needs and requirements based approach, however it starts from different assumptions. These assumptions include:

1. The purpose of a business can be related to achieving its goals;
2. Business goals can be achieved by solving business problems;
3. The business can allocate a value to achieving the goals;
4. The value of a solution exists in the problem it solves and the business goals achieved;
5. Implementing solutions incurs costs as well as creating new, consequential problems. These include dependencies on vendors, the cost of operating and maintaining the solution and the effort required to bring about changes that the new solution may require.

An overview of the problem oriented approach to Enterprise Architecture is shown in Figure 2.

The structure of the approach is intended to ensure that business problems are the main drivers for the Enterprise Architecture and are properly identified, described, analysed, and solved.

Details and justification of these issues are included later in this chapter; however, the most important aspect of problem solving lies in understanding the right problem and in the right way.

Identifying and understanding the right problem requires that the problem be described and modelled in such a way that it leads to an optimal solution. To achieve this, it is critical that correct assumptions are made about the problem and about what needs to be understood.

This is especially important when addressing Wicked Problems. These present the greatest challenge because of the difficulty in defining the problem and the way in which solution options can change the problem. Wicked Problems are discussed in more detail later in this chapter.

Figure 2. A problem oriented approach to enterprise architecture

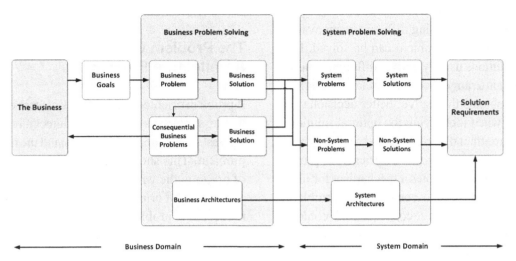

A Problem Oriented Approach To Enterprise Architecture

The measurement or assessment of value in order to make decisions in a problem oriented approach is important. Values can be, but do not have to be, financial. Decisions can be made based upon features, flexibility, risk, time to implement etc. However, it is important to relate these to business problems, rather than to solution characteristics.

It may also be possible to derive a value statement by analysing the place of the problem in a hierarchy of problem/solution chains. Those problems closest to achieving business goals may be deemed to have higher intrinsic values than those in a support or enabling position. However, those enabling problems/solutions with many dependencies may be deemed to have high relative value and hence importance.

By basing the model on value, the business is able to understand why the various systems and subsystems exist, the role they play, and why they are important to the enterprise.

The problem oriented approach also recognises that solving a business problem will probably create new problems when the solution is implemented. These consequential problems do not necessarily create business value. They may be

of value to the business because they are solved but do not in themselves create business value.

It is not suggested that a problem oriented approach should replace other architecture views. However, because solving problems creates value, the problem oriented approach can provide a firm foundation which connects and underpins the different perspectives of the other views.

The Benefits of a Problem Oriented Approach to Enterprise Architecture

If Enterprise Architects are to be of benefit to the business, they should explicitly demonstrate that their activities solve business problems. If Enterprise Architects cannot achieve this, then the business will not value their contribution.

By taking a problem oriented approach from the start, the risk of taking the wrong approach to understanding the problem is minimised. The approach properly identifies both the problem and the optimal solution, it engages the business in a manner that the business best understands, it provides a solid foundation for implementation projects and minimises the risk of implementing solutions that deliver little or no business value.

A problem oriented approach provides an opportunity to question the value of solving the problem, or of proposing different or innovative ways in which the problem can be solved. Different solutions usually deliver different benefits and result in a range of costs. By relating solutions to the problems they solve, better decisions can be made when identifying the optimal solution.

An important differentiator between the traditional approach and a problem oriented approach is that the latter promotes a mechanism for identifying and addressing consequential problems and their solutions. These consequential problems are frequently not addressed in implementation projects and can give rise to unintended consequences both to the business and within the ICT environment. These include system fragmentation, a proliferation of product sets and technology, islands of information, and an inordinate amount of maintenance just to keep systems running.

A problem oriented approach, when extended appropriately into the implementation domain, provides a framework for monitoring solution development to ensure that the original problem is solved. There are many large scale ICT projects that eventually deliver a solution to a problem that has either disappeared or changed so that the solution is no longer of use.

The reason this happens is usually because the project team is focused on delivering the solution. Any distraction that results in significant changes to the project plan, especially one that recommends stopping the project, is not looked upon favourably.

It is suggested that the project team include an Enterprise Architect as a peer of the project manager. This person would have responsibility for ensuring that the business problem was still current and valid and that any changes in the problem domain were matched by appropriate modifications to the solution.

The Enterprise Architect would also be responsible for approving all the seemingly small decisions made during system construction in order that the project delivers an optimal and valuable solution.

The Problem Oriented Architecture Process

A problem oriented approach to Enterprise Architecture should start with the Architect identifying the best way to model and understand the business problem. This should be done to avoid the trap of bringing the wrong approach to the problem.

A problem oriented approach simultaneously models the problem's potential solutions and implementation options using a problem solving methodology. Requirements still play a part in the method but are outputs of the problem solving process.

An Enterprise Architect is a bridge between the business that has the problems and those who acquire, develop, and/or implement solutions. Ideally, the Enterprise Architect should maintain an active role in the solution implementation in order to ensure that the right problem is being solved and that any new problems are recognised and appropriately accommodated.

It should be recognised that an Enterprise Architect does not necessarily use technology to solve business problems. In fact, one of the most efficient ways of solving a business problem not is to have the problem in the first place. This can often be achieved by making changes to an enterprise so that the problem disappears. Assuming that the solution is an Information System usually precludes this option.

Problem Oriented Enterprise Architecture Artefacts

The artefacts developed by problem oriented Enterprise Architects include:

1.   A description of the problem;
2.   Analysis of the problem;

3. Confirmation from the business that solving the problem will create value;
4. Potential solutions;
5. Analysis of the solutions, including implementation issues and identification of problems that will be created as the result of implementing the solution;
6. Justifications for selecting the optimal solution, including how and why decisions were made; and
7. A preferred solution description and implementation approach, including how the consequential problems will be, or could be resolved. It should be noted that consequential problems do not always get resolved when the solution to the business problem is implemented. However, it is essential that solving consequential problems be part of the identifying the optimal solution.

In the context of a problem oriented approach, requirements are an outcome of the problem solving activity and feed into the implementation project as the project charter.

There should be very little requirements gathering in an implementation project other than how to conduct the project from a project management perspective.

A Problem Oriented Approach Applied to the Enterprise

Modelling the enterprise based upon business problems assumes that achieving a business goal can be described in terms of the problems that must be solved in order to achieve that goal.

An integral part of a problem oriented approach of the enterprise is the relationships between business problems, their solution and the consequential problems created by implementing the solutions. This is a view of the business that often cuts across traditional business boundaries because it is the problem being solved that has the focus, not the particular business structure at any point in time.

Business problems usually cut across organisational structures and, if the consequential problems are properly identified and addressed, then issues such as change management, industrial relations, etc. will be appropriately dealt with.

A problem oriented model of the enterprise could initially be based upon a business process model. A business process view defines the processes that a business performs in order to interact with the external world and to internally create and deliver appropriate products and/or services.

Starting with the business processes, the first problems an enterprise must solve are how to deliver these processes. Most business processes are delivered by using human and automated systems. The next set of questions, therefore are concerned with how to create human and automated systems that support business processes. This is an example of the solution to one problem creating new problems. By using a problem oriented modelling approach, a set of interlocking solutions, connected by, and solving, problems can be developed.

A Problem Oriented Approach Applied to Specific Goals or Problems

Modelling the whole enterprise from a problem perspective will often be difficult and unnecessary, however a problem oriented modelling approach that focuses on individual symptoms, issues, business cases and potential projects can bring significant benefits. This is because of the understanding that can be derived from a perspective that cuts across traditional viewpoints and which is based upon business value. It also provides a decision making framework that relates more easily to business values and, by derivation, business priority.

It is suggested that every project proposed by the business should demonstrate that it solves a business problem and that solving the problem creates value for the business. In order to achieve

Figure 3. A problem oriented approach to strategy

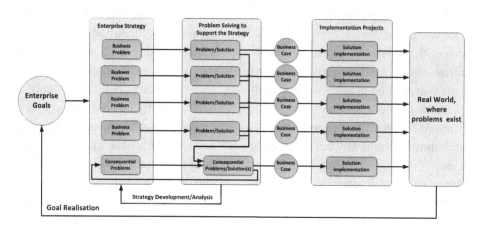

A Problem Oriented Approach To Strategy

this it is necessary to model an individual problem and potential solutions.

Business Strategy in a Problem Oriented Approach

In a problem oriented approach, a strategy can be defined as a group of problems that require solving in order to achieve a business goal. In developing a strategy, it needs to be recognised that problems and solutions are likely to have complex interactions and dependencies.

Like architecture, strategy relies heavily on modelling and it is highly likely that the problems will be wicked in nature. Therefore, it is very important that the optimal approach to both strategy and problems be identified early in the strategy development process.

Figure 3 illustrates the relationships between strategy, problems, and solutions when taking a problem oriented approach to understanding the enterprise.

INDIVIDUAL ASPECTS OF A PROBLEM ORIENTED APPROACH

This section describes in more detail the individual aspects of a problem oriented approach to Enterprise Architecture. These are:

1. Modelling, which is the basis of understanding all facets of problem solving;
2. Problems, which are usually phrased as questions;
3. Solutions, which are potential answers to questions from the problem domain;
4. Decision making; and
5. Problem solving.

Modelling

A model is a description or representation of something. That something may be real, in the sense it has a physical manifestation, or it may be a concept, a problem, a plan, or even other models.

Creating models is fundamental to documenting and understanding the world. It is also part of the process of planning and of creating projects, objects, and systems.

Modelling enables predictions to be made about the behaviour of the real world either as time passes and/or as changes occur. These changes can include modifications to what is there already, or to the development and implementation of new objects, structures and systems.

A model is always incomplete, in that it can never be a full replication of the real thing, otherwise it would be the real thing. All modelling involves simplification. However, sometimes simplification can destroy the model's ability to replicate the behaviour of the object or system being studied. Simplification needs to be undertaken with great care, recognising that it may reduce the usefulness and effectiveness of the model.

Models designed to support problem solving need to be flexible, dynamic, goal oriented and be aimed at decision making. Solution models are more directed at end states and implementation projects.

There are two critical decisions that are made when a model is developed. The first is the scope of the model, i.e. what is included in the model and what is deemed to be irrelevant or unimportant to the model. The second is the approach to be used in the model, and includes decisions regarding the use of hard or soft modelling techniques. A brief overview of these techniques follow:

Types of Models

Models can be categorised in many ways, including:

Hard or Soft Models Hard models tend to be mathematically and/or diagram based. In this context, diagrams should use well-defined concepts and relationships. Science and engineering use hard models.

There are inherent limits to hard models. The world is non-linear and chaotic by nature. Models of systems where errors grow exponentially, such as in chaotic systems, cannot reliably predict the future.

Sometimes mathematics is used to model concepts and relationships that cannot be defined well enough to justify such a hard approach. Economics is a prime example of this.

Soft models tend to be picture and/or textual based. Pictures are images of objects that are not well defined and which have more general or fuzzy relationships.

They often deal with concepts that are hard to define and where there are relationships that are unclear or which are not able to be enumerated.

Enterprise Architecture most often uses diagrams and text to define the state of a system, usually the current state, and the future state.

Conceptual and high level diagrams tend to be softer than physical and implementation oriented diagrams, which describe very well defined objects and their relationships.

Static or Dynamic Models Static models use textual and diagrammatic methods.

Dynamic models usually involve software and computers, although there are other techniques, for example, miniature engineering, physical model making, and mock-ups, where only part of the real system is constructed.

Modelling and Systems Thinking

Systems Thinking takes a whole-of-system approach to understanding the real world. It is based upon Systems Engineering (also known as Cybernetics) which is an interdisciplinary approach that uses a combination of scientific and mathematical understanding of the real world and a systemic approach to problem solving.

The systemic approach is based upon analysing and modelling the problem holistically, developing and evaluating solution options, selecting the best and then implementing that solution. Systems Engineering works very well in the hard world of the physical sciences and engineering.

Systems Thinking tries to adopt Systems Engineering principles in the area of soft problems. These are areas where concepts, entities, and relationships are very much less certain than those in the physical sciences and engineering.

Systems Engineering principles of holistic modelling and a systemic approach can provide useful results when applied to soft problems, as long as the potential for errors and unwarranted conclusions is recognised and managed.

Approaches to Systems Thinking that may provide benefit to a problem oriented approach of the enterprise include:

System Dynamics (SD) is a technique which uses hard, usually mathematical, models to understand problems and to develop and analyse solutions.

SD is useful in analysing causal and feedback loops, often involving non-linear relationships in complex dynamic systems. A major component of SD is simulation, using dynamic, computer based mathematical models.

Viable Systems Model (VSM) assumes that a viable system is an adaptable system organised in such a way as to meet the demands of surviving in the changing environment.

VSM is a hierarchic model of the organisational structure of a viable or autonomous system. The hierarchic nature of the model means that it recognises that reality is often recursive. A system is composed of sub-systems, which in turn are composed of more sub-systems.

Soft Systems Methodology (SSM) is an approach aimed at dealing with the multiple perspectives that are encountered in understanding systems, particularly in situations that require change.

It involves documenting, analysing and assessing the viewpoints of the various stakeholders involved in a system, building operational definitions of the existing and/or any proposed system, and modelling the activities necessary to carry out the defined objective.

SSM is a soft methodology rather than being based on soft models. It places great emphasis on getting the best approach to understanding and addressing the problem.

The Importance of Identifying the Correct Approach for a Model

This is one of the most critical issues when modelling. When creating a model, certain assumptions have to be made about the intended model. The first issue centres on the purpose of the model: what part of reality should the model represent and be used to understand?

Making the wrong decision regarding the modelling approach can have disastrous impacts on subsequent activities. It limits information gathering, analysis, and decision-making. It also misrepresents the problem to the extent that the wrong problem gets solved.

Proponents of specific methodologies can easily fall into this trap. Just because an approach has been successful in the past with certain types of problems does not mean that it is the best approach for the next problem. Unless there is an initial step of validating the proposed modelling approach there will be a significant risk of solving the wrong problem.

Here are two examples that illustrate the importance of approach and assumptions when understanding and solving a problem.

An Incomplete Model: The Millennium Bridge

A high profile example of where this resulted in issues with the solution was the Millennium Bridge in London. The engineers modelled the bridge using all the traditional mathematical and computer based techniques they had in the past. Unfortunately, the walking behaviour of the pedestrians who used the bridge was not fully understood and the bridge, when it was first opened, started to sway in a manner that was totally unpredicted by the designers (French, 2003).

Assumptions had been made in understanding the problem and modelling the solution. The engineers had neglected to incorporate into their models the sideways forces, which pedestrians generate when walking, so the solution did not solve the problem appropriately.

It is critical that the modelling approach and techniques be suitable for the problem being addressed. The only way that this can be achieved is by constantly questioning the base assumptions that have been made when identifying the modelling approaches.

The most dangerous assumptions are those that have been made unconsciously and which are therefore the hardest to evaluate and test.

Getting the Model Right: A Number Puzzle

Another example where the modelling approach can have a significant impact on the ability to solve a problem is illustrated as follows:

What comes next?

1, 11, 21, 1211, 111221, 312211

If you try and model this problem assuming it is a numeric sequence then you will not solve the problem.

If you tried to link the numbers to some other sequence, such as the alphabet or days of the year, then you will also fail.

The secret is in the algorithm used to create the groups of character. It uses a mixture of cardinal numbers and numeric characters. In other words, depending on where it is used, "1" can be a quantity or it can be a character that just happens to have the shape of the number 1.

This is the algorithm: to form the next group: count the numbers (as characters) in the current group. As you do, write down the quantity of the characters followed by the character being counted. Write the quantity and the characters as numbers.

In illustrating the algorithm, the quantities will be written as words, the characters as numbers.

The first group is 1.

The second group describes the first group, which is one 1. This is written as 11.

The third group describes the second group, which is two 1s, written as 21

The fourth group describes the third group, which is one 2 and one 1, written as 1211

The fifth group describes the fourth group, which is one 1, one 2, two 1s, written as 111221

The sixth group describes the fifth group, which is three 1s, two 2s, one 1, written as 312211.

And the solution, i.e. the next number in the sequence is one 3, one 1, two 2s, two 1s, written as 13112221.

These examples illustrate the importance of making valid assumptions about a problem and in applying the correct model when identifying a solution.

Problems

Some problems are so complex that you have to be highly intelligent and well informed just to be undecided about them- Laurence J. Peter (Peter & Hull, 1969).

Problems from an Enterprise Architecture Perspective

An Enterprise Architect will have a very different perspective of problems from that of the business or from those who implement solutions. To an Enterprise Architect, a problem is a question that needs answering. A business problem is a question that, when answered, will achieve a business goal.

The Enterprise Architect needs to select the appropriate approaches and modelling techniques that best enable problems to be solved. As stated earlier, this can be one of the most important and critical decisions when problem solving

It should be noted that it is likely that multiple models will be required in order to understand a problem. For example, in the case of enterprise information systems there are the perspectives of business processes, applications, information, and

IT infrastructure. Different types of model may be used in each of these perspectives.

Identifying the best approach to problem solving is important because of the need to recognise that solutions cause consequential problems. This is as much a solution issue as a problem issue. Some solutions may create more consequential problems than others.

From the Enterprise Architect's perspective, problems can be divided into three broad types, Tame, Complex, and Wicked:

Tame problems (sometimes called simple problems) are able to be solved by pattern recognition. It is possible to identify a particular solution because the problem type has been solved before and any tailoring or modification of the solution to fit a particular instance of the problem does not materially impact either the solution or the problem. It is also possible to easily identify that the problem has been solved.

For a problem to be considered as tame, it is also necessary that implementing the solution will not create new problems that are complex and/or wicked. If the solution to a tame problem creates other, also tame problems, then the whole group of problems and solutions can be considered to be tame.

The value of solving a tame problem is easy to calculate and is agreed by all stakeholders

Complex problems are not solvable by recognising the problem and applying a known solution. A large amount of fact-finding, analysis and investigation of potential solutions may be required to identify the optimum (or sometimes, only) solution.

Once a solution has been identified, it is easy to confirm that it is a solution to the problem.

For a problem to be considered as complex it is also necessary that implementing the solution will not create new problems that are wicked. If the solution to a complex problem creates other, tame and/or complex problems, then the whole group of problems and solutions can be considered to be complex.

Wicked Problems are the hardest type to understand and solve. The term was originally coined by Horst Rittel (Rittel & Webber, 1973) in the context of a general theory of planning and was applied to problems that had a high degree of social complexity.

As information and communication systems move out of the purely technical and data processing worlds into on-line environments, instant communication and entertainment, and most importantly, involve the general public, the more the problems become wicked.

In addition, as information systems become larger and more complex, systemic non-linearities due to issues such as scale, speed of change and response times start to dominate. This leads to problems with many of the same characteristics as those found in the social context.

Characteristics of Wicked Problems that are relevant to a problem oriented approach to Enterprise Architecture are:

1. A Wicked Problem is difficult to model and understand. Entities and concepts can be difficult to define and their relationships may be unclear or change radically as events occur or over time. Selecting the best way to approach the problem becomes a problem itself;

2. A Wicked Problem comprises a number of interlocking issues. Addressing one can change one or more of the others;

3. A Wicked Problem has never been encountered before, not in its present form. Even if it is similar to other problems, small differences can have major and significant impacts. This is because of the non-linear and chaotic nature of the real world;

4. It is difficult to confirm that a proposed solution will fully or adequately solve a Wicked Problem;

5. There are many stakeholders, each with different views of the problem;

6. It is difficult to assess potential solutions because of the number of stakeholders and their different value systems;
7. There are no opportunities to create test solutions and assess them against the problem or each other;
8. A Wicked Problem can often change when a solution is considered or implemented;
9. There are many consequences to implementing a solution. Managing these consequences can lead to new Wicked Problems; and
10. Sometimes the solution appears to be simple, but the wickedness lies in the difficulty of implementation.

The value of solving a Wicked Problem is never easy to calculate. This is because of the difficulty of defining the problem and the different perspectives and self interests of the stakeholders.

Solutions

The world is far more focused on solutions rather than problems, on symptoms rather than causes and activity rather than progress. External pressures on a business are also solution focused. Vendors and service providers all offer solutions; that is what they sell.

It is probable that vendors will only promote the positives of their products and services. Often they do not know themselves what the downsides are, and in many cases the downsides are related to specific implementations.

Therefore, it is up to the business, as the buyer, to understand its own business problems. No one else is likely to.

It is also the case that the business usually focuses on the cost of a solution rather than the value of the problem being solved. Symptoms and solutions are far more obvious and tangible than causes and problems.

The business sees and suffers from symptoms and proposes solutions it is familiar with. It hopes, expects, or assumes that they are solutions to the symptoms it is experiencing.

Technical specialists, and often to some degree, Enterprise Architects, know, and are familiar with, their solutions. They know the solutions have been used to solve business problems in the past but, unfortunately, they may not understand enough about the new problem to determine if their solution is appropriate.

What are Solutions?

Solutions are answers to the questions posed by problems. They are often actions that, when taken, change the environment to such an extent that the problem either disappears or its impact and effect are greatly reduced.

There are two aspects to a solution: the plan, and the implementation.

The plan is what is proposed and comprises a model and description of the end state and a description of how the solution is to be implemented. Implementation is the project that results in a physical manifestation of the solution.

Some problems are such that various solutions can be tried and their effectiveness assessed. Other problems do not permit this. One characteristic of a Wicked Problem is that it is not possible to try multiple solutions and then select the one with the best performance.

It should always be possible to assess a proposed or planned solution against the problem, using various models, but as previously discussed, models are not reality.

Investigating problems that a solution might create after implementation requires predictions and involves uncertainty. The problem may change in unforeseen ways; the environment within which the problem and/or enterprise works may change; and values, as perceived by the business, may change.

However, some assessment of the flexibility of a solution can always be made and appropriate decisions taken when comparing alternative solutions.

Fundamental to a problem oriented approach is the assertion that solutions in themselves only incur costs they do not create value. It is the fact that the problem has been solved that creates value.

It should be recognised that only hard models of solutions can be costed. Soft models, including conceptual and logical models are not suitable for costing, only physical models.

Identifying Potential Solutions

There are two main ways to identify potential solutions, re-use existing and known solutions and develop new solutions.

Re-using existing and known solutions. A problem can be identified as one of a known type. Therefore, solving the problem can potentially re-use existing and proven solutions.

Developing new solutions. The alternative way is to develop a new solution from scratch. This will require more time and effort in understanding and analysing the problem. It is likely there will be re-use of known and proven techniques and or components. However, there are likely to be new features and/or sub-components.

When new technologies or methods are involved in the solution, as is often the case with modern information systems, it is wise to assume that a new solution needs to be developed.

Analysing and Evaluating Solutions

A solution represents only part of the problem solving activity. Analysing and evaluating a potential solution can involve such questions as:

1. How is it possible to assess if a solution will solve the problem? The answer to this question will be needed when comparing different solutions;

2. Will solving the problem change the problem? It can happen that when a business solution is implemented, other parts of the business, not previously identified as being part of the problem, decide that they want the solution as well. This increased usage can have a significant impact on the performance of the solution. In addition, other parts of the business may wish to make changes to the solution so that it better suits their needs. What was a small scale problem with an appropriate small scale solution can rapidly become much larger and require a significantly different solution;

3. What problems will the solution create after implementation? Most solutions need to be operated, maintained, and enhanced as the business changes. This will involve costs, trained staff with particular skills, and potential disruptions as the system is upgraded. There may also be dependencies on the vendor for ongoing support and enhancements;

4. How will it be implemented? and

5. What are the implementation issues?

Implementing Solutions

It is suggested that combining problem solving and solution implementation into a single project is unwise. Many failed projects have been analysed and the most common reasons for the failure are associated with requirements. They are unclear, have been changed, etc. It is suggested that the fundamental reason is two-fold. The first has been covered elsewhere in this chapter and is that requirements do not define the problem or solution. The second is that an implementation project should not have to define the solution.

If the project has to both define the solution and implement it there is a paradox. The paradox lies in the relationship between the plan and the solution. Part of the project plan is to define the solution, but the solution is what the project needs to achieve.

A project that implements a solution should be given the description of the solution in the project charter. The problem that the solution is trying to address should have been solved and developing the project plan should have been part of the problem solving process.

The project should also be monitored by someone who understands the problem being solved in order to make sure that decisions made during the solution implementation do not inadvertently change the solution in a way that negatively impacts the problem being solved. In addition, it is necessary to ensure that new problems that are created do not reduce the net value of the problem being solved.

That is why before a project to implement a solution is initiated, it is important to have analysed these consequential problems, because the solution may change when they are encountered.

Implementation projects should only ask "how do I implement this solution?" not "what solution should I implement?"

Decision Making

A decision consists of making a choice between at least two options.

Good decisions are made when known and measurable criteria are used on which to base a choice between the options. This can be difficult to achieve, especially when there are multiple criteria of different kinds.

A problem oriented approach endeavours to relate solutions to problems and problems to business value. This facilitates decision making because comparisons can be made in terms of a common criterion, business value, and by comparing business problems and their priorities to the business.

This contrasts with the needs and requirements based approach where comparisons can usually only be made in terms of solution cost.

Modelling for Decision Making

All modelling for problem solving must in some way support decision making. Understanding and analysing a problem, documenting and analysing potential solutions should all support the processes of identifying the optimal solution. This needs decisions.

It can be very useful to create a specific model of the decision making process. The decisions and options can be identified and their relationships modelled in exactly the same way as any for any architecture.

Decision tree analysis can also provide insights into the problem.

Decision making when solving tame and complex problems is relatively straight forward and sequential. Decision making when solving a Wicked Problem is much more difficult and is never sequential, or even iterative, it is highly interconnected. It is often the case that making a single decision is not possible because of the ripple through, or feedback effect. In this case, a number of decisions must be made as a group.

Decision-making is a deceptive activity. It is easy to make a decision, it is harder to make a good decision and even harder to justify a good decision that satisfies people who have not been part of the decision making process and who are impacted by the subsequent problems. Relating decisions to business value assists in addressing this issue.

Problem Solving

Problem solving requires an understanding of the problem, the generation of potential solutions and a decision-making process that identifies the solution that best solves the problem according to some criteria defined by the business.

Problem solving requires the drawing together of the three activities discussed above: understanding the problem, identifying potential solutions and making decisions.

It is important to note that this does not describe a sequential process; it describes activities that are undertaken when solving a problem.

Sometimes these activities follow a structured process, sometimes it seems that the process is somewhat random and will never end. This usually depends on the type of problem being solved.

It should also be recognised that implementing a solution is likely to create new problems. When solving a problem it is important to assess what these consequential problems are and re-apply the process to these new problems.

That is why, before a project to implement a solution is initiated, it is important to have analysed these consequential problems, because the solution may change when they are encountered and addressed.

Problem solving requires a range of skills and techniques. Documenting and analysing a problem and defining the required outcomes has need of a different set of skills from those involved in developing and selecting solutions. Depending on the nature of the problem/solution type, it may also be necessary to be creative, innovative, cunning, and sometimes even misleading, especially when it comes to addressing Wicked Problems.

It should also be noted that the set of skills involved in implementing projects once a solution has been identified and defined are different from those needed for problem solving. Not understanding this difference has led to many a failed project.

When problem solving in an enterprise context it needs to be recognised that enterprises are inherently feedback systems; outputs are monitored against inputs and control decisions made by operational systems and by management. In fact most enterprises are unstable feedback systems. Very often, they are either growing or shrinking. Wicked Problems are often wicked because they are systems with very strong and complex feedback. The output of the problem solving activity feeds back and changes the problem, a classic feedback loop.

A PROBLEM ORIENTED APPROACH APPLIED TO CONNECTED e-GOVERNMENT

For this chapter, e-Government is defined as:

the use of information and communication technologies in government to provide public services to improve managerial effectiveness and to promote democratic values and mechanisms; as well as a regulatory framework that facilitates information intensive initiatives and fosters the knowledge society (Gil-Garcia & Luna-Reyes, 2003).

Examination of this definition leads to the observation that there is no single enterprise, goal or problem involved in achieving e-Government. This means that Enterprise Architecture will need to be applied to individual goals and problems.

The Goal of e-Government

The goal implicit in the definition above is "the use of Information and Communication Technologies (ICT)." This goal is solution oriented, i.e. ICT is the assumed solution mechanism.

It should be recognised by those working in the field that this assumption could potentially lead to solutions that use ICT just because it is available, not because they solve problems in the best way or facilitate the achievement of e-Government.

It is suggested that by taking a problem oriented approach to e-Government, any proposed solutions can be more easily justified by demonstrating that they are part of resolving problems associated with e-Government.

A more appropriate and explicit goal of e-Government that minimises potentially restricting assumptions could be:

To improve the effectiveness and efficiency of government by utilising modern technologies and practices

The advantage of this goal is that it defines an outcome: "the effectiveness and efficiency of government" followed by a mechanism "by utilising modern technologies and practices."

The goal provides a focus from which problems can more easily be derived. It also suggests a measurement and decision making framework, that of effectiveness and efficiency.

This is an example of identifying early assumptions and validating them, before moving on to problem solving activities.

The assumption in the Gil-Garcia and Luna-Reyes definition is that the driving force is the use of ICT. In a problem oriented approach, the assumption is that the driving force is to improve government by making it more effective and efficient.

e-Government as a Wicked Problem

Reasons for concluding that e-Government is a Wicked Problem:

1. The problem is difficult to model and understand: there are multiple sub-goals, each with different problem characteristics;
2. The problem comprises a number of interlocking issues: addressing a specific sub-goal is likely to impact one or more other sub-goals;
3. The problem has never been encountered before: the enabling characteristics of today's and tomorrow's ICT have never been previously available. What complicates the problem even more is that these enabling characteristics are likely to change in the relatively short term;
4. There are no obvious solutions to any of the problems;
5. There are many stakeholders, each with different views of the problem: there are at least three groups of stakeholders, Governments, Citizens and Vendors of products and services.

These groups form a complicated set of entities. Citizens have relationships with vendors; they purchase products and they may also be shareholders. Citizens in democracies have a power over governments, citizens also make use of public services, Governments control the regulatory frameworks and also purchase products and services;

6. It is difficult to assess potential solutions because of the number of stakeholders and their different value systems;
7. There are no opportunities to create test solutions and assess them against the problem or each other;
8. ICT, on its own, is not sufficient to solve any of the problems. There will be many other issues to be identified and addressed;
9. There will be many consequences when implementing solutions to the problems. These are likely to also be Wicked Problems; and
10. Implementing any solution to the problems of e-Government is likely to be a Wicked Problem of its own. Appropriate change management strategies will be essential.

An Example of a Problem Oriented Approach to Identity Cards

In a democracy, the government, in its various forms, has relationships with its citizens.

When a person is born, the birth is recorded and a birth certificate is created based upon that record. The birth certificate can then be used to create other forms of identification, which may be used during interactions with various government agencies. These practices vary from democracy to democracy, but this description is suitable for the purposes of this example.

Before today's electronic communication became ubiquitous, all interactions with government was by physical means, either via letters and forms or by attending a government facility.

In some cases, it was possible for a citizen to access public services without having to establish their identity.

With citizens making more use of on-line interaction with government agencies, the old physical means of identification are no longer sufficient. On-line access, facilitated by ICT, has changed the problem of how a citizen proves their identity.

The old problem was "How can a citizen prove what their name is, when necessary?" The solution was for the citizen to provide their birth certificate or some other form of documentation such as a drivers license or passport.

Now the problem has become "How can the government be assured that the citizen with whom they are interacting on-line is the person they claim to be?"

What was a citizen's problem has now become a government's problem.

One solution to the new problem is to give every citizen an identification number. This immediately creates a large number of new problems, including:

1. When and how do you allocate the number?
2. How do you relate the number to the citizen?
3. How do you maintain that relationship over the life of the citizen?
4. How do you create groups of citizens (e.g. married couples, families, dependents etc) and identify the groups?
5. How do you deal with citizens who have dual nationality?
6. How do you protect the information about citizens that the government collects and manages?
7. How do you deal with citizens who lose their means of identification?
8. What other information do you collect on citizens to facilitate government's interactions with its citizens?
9. Who has access to this information?
10. How do you control access?
11. How long do you retain the information?
12. How do you convince citizens that allocating them an identification number will be of benefit to them, and not just the government?

This list is not comprehensive, however it illustrates that solutions can change problems and that they can also create consequential problems, many of which are more difficult and more wicked than the original problem being solved.

It may be that, in an on-line world, an identification number is the only sensible solution. However, when contemplating solutions, unless the consequential problems are addressed as well, then the selected solution may fail.

In the UK and Australia, national identity schemes have been proposed and attempts have been made to implement them. In neither country have they been successful, primarily because the governments did not adequately address the problem of convincing their citizens that it was in the best interests of the country, not just the government.

FUTURE DIRECTIONS

Achieving e-Government in a connected world will require solutions to many problems, many of them Wicked Problems. These solutions will need to solve many problems that have never been encountered before.

The history of major, large-scale systems development is littered with embarrassing failures.

Development of systems in the future will need to address the issues inherent in current approaches. A problem oriented approach utilises many of the current techniques and methods in use today, it changes only the initial approach and focus.

The greatest difficulty will not be in adopting a problem oriented approach. It is more likely to be in changing the culture and ingrained habits of today's Enterprise Architects and the business communities that engage them.

CONCLUSION

Current framework approaches to Enterprise Architecture take needs and requirements as their primary input. The first step of these architecture projects is to gather or identify business requirements in order to develop architectural and system solutions.

These requirements do not describe problems, they describe characteristics of solutions. Current approaches assume that the business has analysed and solved its business problems such that solutions can be developed based upon these requirements.

In reality, in most cases the business has not properly analysed, understood, and solved its business problems.

In addition, because a problem has not been properly identified, the fact that the implementation project will deliver an inappropriate solution will not become apparent until the solution fails to meet expectations.

The needs and requirements approach upon which most architecture frameworks are based, disconnect the solution from the problem. This means it is difficult to identify if the proposed solution will solve the business problem it is supposed to be addressing.

In fact, it is not uncommon to see projects that are solving the wrong problem—in the sense that the stated reason for the project does not match the outcome of the project.

Needs and requirements are also deficient in identifying problems that will arise when a particular solution is implemented. Implementation projects concentrate on the solution at hand. Problems that need to be solved tend to be associated with system construction and delivery, not support, maintenance or other whole-of-life issues.

It is proposed that a better approach is to base Enterprise Architecture activities on the primary input of business goals and problems. The business can then identify business value in achieving these goals and to solving the problems that arise when achieving them.

A problem oriented approach has the following advantages:

1. The primary driver is achieving business goals;
2. It explicitly addresses business problems;
3. The business can understand the purpose of the architecture and the solution because they relate to an environment the business understands;
4. The solution explicitly solves a well defined, documented and analysed business problem;
5. Problems that the solution will create once implemented are identified early in the problem solving process and can be accommodated when assessing solution options; and
6. Implementation projects commence with a well-defined solution.

It is suggested that problem solving, supported by a problem oriented approach to Enterprise Architecture is much more likely to result in optimal solutions to today's complex and Wicked Problems.

ICT is being widely used in today's society. The use of this technology in the context of e-Government presents a large number of Wicked Problems.

Wicked Problems will always arise when problems involve people. It is safe to assume that forecasting what people want, how they will behave when given a new technology, and how their opinions and choices will change over time is impossible.

The consequence of this is that the implementation of ICT to support e-Government will not be easy.

By taking a problem oriented approach, rather than one based on needs and requirements, it is more likely that the development of capabilities, systems and supporting infrastructure and services will deliver better outcomes which create greater value for the communities of the world.

REFERENCES

Ackoff, R. L. (1974). *Redesigning the future: A systems approach to societal problems.* New York, NY: John Wiley & Sons.

French, S. (2003). *Soft modelling and problem formulation.* Retrieved from http://www.sal.hut.fi/TED/slides/Soft_modelling.pdf.

Gil-Garcia, J. R., & Luna-Reyes, L. F. (2003). Towards a definition of electronic government: A comparative review. In Mendez-Vilas, A., Mesa Gonzalez, J. A., Mesa Gonzalez, J., Guerrero Bote, V., & Zapico Alonso, F. (Eds.), *Techno-Legal Aspects of the Information Society and the New Economy: An Overview.* Badajoz, Spain: Formatex.

Peter, L. J., & Hull, R. (1969). *The Peter principle: Why things always go wrong.* New York, NY: William Morrow and Company, Inc.

Rittel, H., & Webber, M. (1973). Dilemmas in a general theory of planning. *Policy Sciences, 4,* 155–169. doi:10.1007/BF01405730

TOGAF. (2009). *Introduction.* Retrieved May 2011, from http://www.togaf.info/togaf9/chap01.html.

ADDITIONAL READING

Australian Public Service Commission. (2009). *Smarter policy: Choosing policy instruments and working with others to influence behaviour.* Retrieved from http://www.apsc.gov.au/publications09/smarterpolicy.htm.

Australian Public Service Commission. (2009). *Policy implementation through devolved government.* Retrieved from http://www.apsc.gov.au/publications09/devolvedgovernment.htm.

Chapman, J. (2004). *System failure: Why governments must learn to think differently* (2nd Ed.). London, UK: Demos. Retrieved from http://www.demos.co.uk/files/systemfailure2.pdf.

Checkland, P. (1981). *Systems thinking systems practice.* Chichester, UK: John Wiley & Sons.

Conklin, J. (2005). *Dialogue mapping: Building shared understanding of wicked problems.* Retrieved from http://cognexus.org/wpf/wickedproblems.pdf.

Farmer, N. D. (2002). *A mathematical model of the causes of the lateral oscillations of the millennium bridge.* Retrieved from http://www.enm.bris.ac.uk/teaching/projects/2002_03/nf9811/FinalProject.pdf.

Flowers, S. (1996). *Software failure: Management failure.* Chichester, UK: John Wiley & Sons.

Hall, P. (1980). *Great planning disasters.* Berkley, CA: University of California Press.

Whelton, M., & Ballard, G. (2002). *Project definition and wicked problems.* Paper presented at the International Group for Lean Construction, 10th Annual Conference. Gramado, Brazil.

KEY TERMS AND DEFINITIONS

Business Goal: An objective or outcome that the business wishes to achieve. External business goals might be to achieve an increase in profit and/or asset values, or to abide by laws and regulations. An internal goal is necessary to support the business itself. Examples are ICT and Enterprise Architecture.

Business Problem: A question, which when answered will achieve a business goal.

Business Value: That which is created when an external business goal is achieved.

Need: Something the business wants or deems necessary. A need can be satisfied.

Requirement: A characteristic that must be met by a person, object, or system.

Solution: An action which, when taken, or a system which, when implemented will solve a problem. An answer to a problem.

Value to the Business: That which is created when an internal goal is achieved.

Chapter 3
The Power of EA Taxonomies in Enhancing Portfolio Visibility and Optimising Decision Making

Don Ashdown
Queensland Government, Australia

Vanessa Douglas-Savage
Queensland Government, Australia

Kirsten Harte
Queensland Government, Australia

Ee-Kuan Low
Queensland Government, Australia

ABSTRACT

This chapter describes the power of using Enterprise Architecture (EA) taxonomies in making sense of an organisation and its components to support portfolio visibility and optimise decision-making. It describes the use of taxonomies in a manner that has been successfully applied across a range of medium to large organisations particularly at a whole-of-government level within the Queensland Government, the Gold Coast City Council, and at an agency level within the Queensland Department of Justice and Attorney-General. These taxonomies enable increased visibility of an organisation's investment portfolio to support more structured decision-making and provide a basis for evidence-based policy development. At the whole-of-government level, this supports optimisation of information and IT investments across the entire connected government portfolio.

DOI: 10.4018/978-1-4666-1824-4.ch003

INTRODUCTION

This chapter outlines the theory behind taxonomies, their role in providing context and scope for EAs, and how they can be leveraged to support:

- business management, particularly in service design and strategic planning
- portfolio management, particularly in investment management and investment planning
- policy development and compliance.

This chapter has a primary focus on taxonomies for enhancing portfolio visibility and optimising decision making across an organisation.

Although this chapter includes examples of how EA taxonomies have been applied in Queensland Government, the data is fictitious.

Before the power of taxonomies can be demonstrated, it is pertinent to distinguish taxonomies from other related tools.

BACKGROUND

Humans use a range of tools to make sense of the world around them, in order to classify and tag concepts so definitions and relationships are drawn to provide context to particular subject domains.

Within the EA and information architecture context, sense-making tools include folksonomies, keywords, ontologies, taxonomies, thesauri, and vocabularies.

Sense-making tools can emerge from social relationships, or can be formally constructed. The focus of this chapter is on formally constructed taxonomies, as distinct from other formally created tools, but we will briefly touch on a selection of sense-making tools. The main types of sense-making tools are briefly described below.

Folksonomies. An emergent sense-making tool that are typically non-hierarchical. These user-created category structures are not edited for consistency or full coverage of a subject area (Mathes, 2004; Vander Wal, 2007).

Keywords. Short descriptions for artefacts which may or may not be edited or formally controlled, and hence straddle the boundary of emergent and designed tools. In that regard, it is not dissimilar to folksonomies.

Ontologies. Formal description of the concepts and relationships within a defined subject area, and includes constraints on logical application of the concepts and relationships. Ontologies are used to reason about concepts within a domain as well as describing the domain itself (Ontology, 2011).

Thesauri. Groups of words with similar meanings (synonyms), and often also include related terms and antonyms. Thesauri differ from vocabularies in that they strive to include all terms used within a subject area, not just those that are preferred, as well as relationships between terms (Thesauri, 2011).

Vocabularies. Vocabularies are a formal collection of terms within a subject area, often arranged alphabetically and with definitions. Controlled vocabularies are characterised by carefully selected terms that represent the preferred terminology within a subject areas.

FRAMEWORKS

The growth and evolution of EA has led to various endeavours to formalise and capture the most useful aspects of the EA practice into EA frameworks. These frameworks represent a body of knowledge and structural arrangements for repeatable application of EA techniques.

EA frameworks range from the well known and broadly applied Zachman Framework and The Open Group Architecture Framework (TOGAF) to lesser-known local frameworks such as the Queensland Government Enterprise Architecture

(QGEA). Although each of these frameworks has a common objective, to provide structure and repeatability to the application of EA practices to planning and managing ICT, the approaches taken by the frameworks can vary considerably. Possible approaches include process-based, structural, pattern-based, governance, or contextual.

- TOGAF is primarily process-based but it also includes some structural and pattern elements.
- The Microsoft Connected Government Framework (CGF) is a structured layered framework spanning business, services, ICT solutions, and infrastructure with patterns for common elements of government service delivery.
- The Cisco Connected Government Framework is a collection of tools and processes for raising the maturity level of government e-service delivery.
- The Zachman Framework is entirely structural. It provides a matrix of related viewpoints from which to understand the business to varying levels of depth.
- The Standards and Architectures for eGovernment Applications (SAGA) has several viewpoints with the main emphasis on interoperability and architecture and infrastructure patterns and standards. SAGA uses a taxonomy for classifying business services but does not apply the concept through deeper layers of the framework.
- The QGEA is both a governance and taxonomy-based architecture.
- The Australian-Government Architecture (AGA) and the U.S. Federal Government Enterprise Architecture (FEA) from which it is derived are both taxonomy-based architecture frameworks.

Understanding the approaches taken by these EA frameworks enable them to be mixed and matched to provide a more comprehensive mechanism for undertaking EA activities.

This chapter however is specifically about taxonomies and their use in EA. Some frameworks are heavily reliant on taxonomies whilst others only use them lightly. This chapter reviews taxonomies in depth, which provides the reader with a foundation for either using them in isolation or in conjunction with a complete EA framework. One final point to note with EA frameworks. Even those that are heavily based on a specific taxonomy should be assessed by the reader with the view that taxonomies are to some degree interchangeable. If an EA framework suits your purposes in all manner except for its taxonomies then consider using the framework but substituting an alternative taxonomy. There are pros and cons to this, and it should not be done lightly, but this chapter will provide the reader with a good basis for making such a judgment.

TAXONOMIES

A taxonomy is a hierarchically-structured classification scheme. The hierarchical nature of a taxonomy distinguishes it from other sense-making tools. Taxonomies are usually purpose-built and used to represent knowledge within a particular subject area. Some of the earliest and most broadly recognised taxonomies are those of "animal, mineral, or vegetable" (Linnaean Classification, 2011) and biological classification (Biological Classification, 2011). A taxonomy typically includes both preferred terms and alternatives (synonyms), to ensure consistency of meaning and coverage within the defined subject area.

Taxonomies have also been labelled classifications, reference models, and frameworks, particularly within the EA discipline.

Characteristics of taxonomies:

- purpose-built to cover all possibilities within a specific subject area

Figure 1. Domain levels within a taxonomy (Queensland Government, 2011 – used with permission)

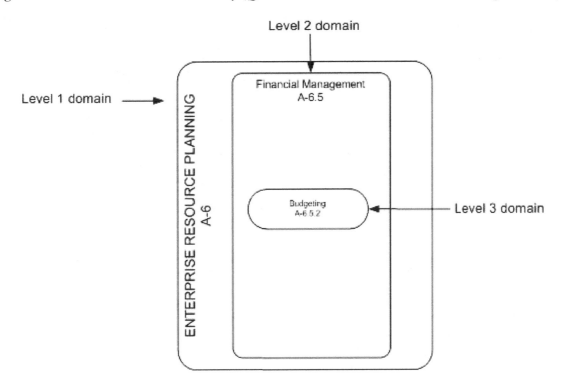

- uses a hierarchy that shows relationships between different domains. This hierarchy is also the basis for showing broader and narrower terms (parent-child relationships) as well as terms at the same level
- includes aspects of vocabularies and thesauri, in that elements are typically defined and represent preferred and alternatives terms for the subject area.
- typically stops short of including ontological elements such as logical application constraints
- A well-designed taxonomy is easy to use and understand and allows for any relevant element to be classified into one or more mutually exclusive categories (often called domains).
- A taxonomy should also be complete in its hierarchical classification scheme i.e. every possible element that exists must have a place in the taxonomy

A poorly designed taxonomy by contrast would have overlapping domains, incomplete coverage and be non-intuitive to use. An extreme, contrived example of such is Borges' classification, otherwise known as the *Celestial Emporium of Benevolent Knowledge* (Borges Classification of Animals, 2006).

Hierarchy. By using a hierarchy, taxonomies become a powerful tool for analysis. They provide a *bird's eye* view of the range of topics within a subject area at varying levels of detail. For example, a book's table of contents can be used to understand the *breadth* of its sections by looking only at the highest level of the hierarchy (typically chapter headings). A table of contents can also be used to understand the *depth* of a subject area, for example by looking at a chain of nested subheadings within a chapter. Figure 1 shows the concepts of breadth and depth within a hierarchy.

Table 1. Taxonomies associated with a number of EA frameworks

EA framework	Taxonomies are known as	Examples
Australian Government Architecture (Australian Government Information Management Office, 2009).	reference models	Performance Reference Model Business Reference Model Service Component Reference Model Data Reference Model Technical Reference Model
Federal Enterprise Architecture (Office of Management and Budget, 2007).	reference models	Performance Reference Model Business Reference Model Service Component Reference Model Data Reference Model Technical Reference Model
QGEA (Queensland Government, 2011).	classification frameworks	Business Service Classification Framework Business Process Classification Framework Information Classification Framework Application Classification Framework Technology Classification Framework
Singapore Government Enterprise Architecture (Singapore Government, 2010).	reference models	Business Reference Model Data Reference Model Solution Reference Model Technical Reference Model
TOGAF (The Open Group, 2011).	reference models	Technical Reference Model

A Spread of Taxonomies

There are already a number of EA taxonomies in existence. A selection of the more common taxonomies are summarised in Table 1.

Taxonomies within the Queensland Government EA

The QGEA is segmented into four horizontal layers: business, information, application and technology; and one vertical slice: information security (see Figure 2).

Within each segment one or more taxonomies (also called QGEA classification frameworks) exist.

- Business layer: Business Service Classification Framework (BSCF) and Business Process Classification Framework (BPCF)
- Information layer: Information Classification Framework (ICF)

- Application layer: Application Classification Framework (ACF)
- Technology layer: Technology Classification Framework (TCF)
- Information security slice: Information Security Classification Framework (ISCF).

A summary of each QGEA classification framework is provided in Table 2.

Each QGEA classification framework is a hierarchical taxonomy and consists of a set of *domains* which are defined with possible alternative terms.

Levels of Classification

The hierarchical structure of the QGEA taxonomies allows for multiple levels of domains, as shown in Figure 1. The QGEA taxonomies generally identify three levels of domains, although in some cases only two levels may be defined. While three levels is sufficient for analyses that compare multiple business units across the Queensland

Figure 2. QGEA (Queensland Government, 2011 – used with permission)

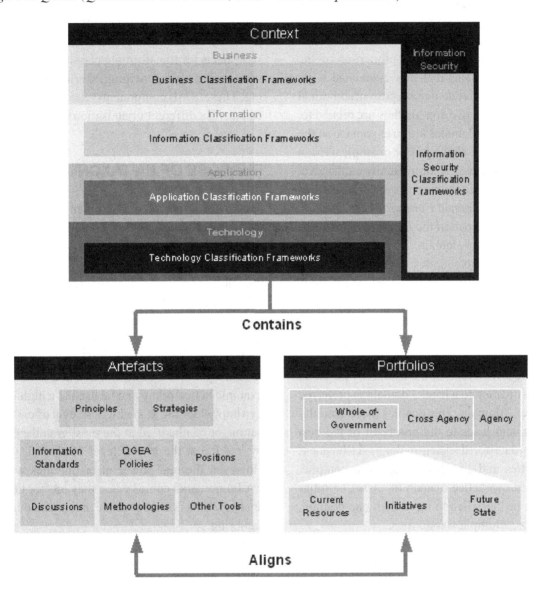

Table 2. QGEA taxonomies

Taxonomy	Description
BSCF	Used to classify the types of government services, and mechanisms used to deliver these services.
BPCF	Used to classify the business processes enacted across government.
ICF	Used to classify information assets to information subject types.
ACF	Used to classify automated business solutions termed *applications*. Applications are distinguished from technologies by the presence of embedded business rules and logic.
TCF	Used to classify technology assets that form part of an organisation's infrastructure and are usually provided as commodity technologies to the organisation.
ISCF	Used to classify the different bodies of work relating to information security.

Government, in many cases level four or lower domains have also been defined and used locally by various government departments.

Each domain inherits the properties of the higher-level domains that it is associated with. That is, all level three domains represent additional detail of the level two domain they are related to, and all level two domains are an expansion of the level one domain above it. For example, within the application classification framework the level three domain of *Budgeting* is a specialised area of the level two domain *Financial Management*, which in turn is a part of the *Enterprise Resource Planning* level one domain.

The QGEA taxonomies are primarily used to classify capabilities or assets. For example, a business service (capability) is classified to the BSCF; information assets are classified to the ICF.

Importantly, when the taxonomies are used, organisations are encouraged to classify their assets at the lowest level of the taxonomy possible, i.e. classification to a level 3 domain is preferred to a level 2 domain. This enables more granular analysis, and leads to the provision of the best possible data for decision-making. As business capabilities and IT-related assets are complex structures, in practice, a capability, asset, or initiative can be classified to more than one domain, and across multiple taxonomies.

Representations of Taxonomies

A taxonomy can be represented in various ways. These range from a simple text list (with indentation to show hierarchy), a list with domain identifier numbers, a spreadsheet, a database, an Extensible Markup Language (XML) document, and visual representations such as 'city plans.' The selection of representation is dependent on the proposed use of the taxonomy, e.g. ad-hoc discussions regarding scope of an initiative or merging repositories of classified items. The authors use multiple representations of which the primary ones are pictorial, spreadsheet (being the most flexible)

and XML. The XML version is controlled by an XML Schema Definition (XSD) schema and supported by Extensible Stylesheet Language (XSL) stylesheets for transforming classified content to various formats for merging, sharing and analysing. These XML components ease the sharing of data across different organisational units.

PURPOSE OF EA TAXONOMIES

The most obvious use of a taxonomy within an EA is to establish and define a common vocabulary within a given subject area. When used, this leads to better communication among stakeholders as common terms reduce misunderstandings, and allows for the identification of commonalities, which may not otherwise be apparent from the names given to an asset by organisational units.

Using a taxonomy within EAs also allows for multiple levels of abstraction and detail. For example, a taxonomy can be used at a high level by simply looking at the highest level of classification, or can be used at the most granular level by looking at the lowest level of classification. However, the real power of taxonomies within EA frameworks comes when they are applied to analysis. This is the true value of that taxonomies can bring.

Figure 3 demonstrates the areas that an EA taxonomy can provide context for and combined with analysis, enhance visibility of an organisation's portfolio and optimise decision making. The following sections detail how the QGEA classification frameworks are used to:

- support business management
- create an EA baseline (as is)
- support portfolio management to inform the development and realisation organisation's desired future state (initiatives and to be)
- support informed policy development and compliance analysis.

Figure 3. Integrating EA taxonomies to increase portfolio visibility and optimise decision-making

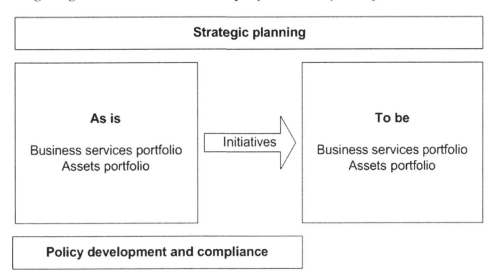

EA TAXONOMIES IN BUSINESS MANAGEMENT

Business service taxonomies provide powerful support for business planning and managing an organisation's services as a portfolio. They enable an organisation to:

- Manage services as a portfolio through understanding an organisation's current service offerings (services portfolio) and assessing these against its business intentions. This assists with decisions for service modification/improvement, new service design, and service decommissioning.
- Support strategic planning by providing a more structured way of assessing the comprehensiveness of an organisation's strategic plan.

This section discusses how the BSCF is used to achieve these purposes.

Managing Services as a Portfolio

The BSCF defines a business service as "sets of activities that deliver value to or enable outcomes

for Queenslanders through the delivery of business outputs" (Queensland Government, 2010a). The BSCF (Figure 4) defines a business service as having two aspects that it can be classified to:

- Service line – the business segment that the service operates within. This may be a direct service to the community (constituent service) or a supporting service to different parts of the government (administration services)
- Service mechanism – the intended outputs that are delivered by a service. These may be engagements or products (Queensland Government, 2010a).

Business service design. The following example demonstrates the use of a business service taxonomy for new service design. An education organisation has identified that the need for a counselling service for its students as many students have been dropping out of courses due to stress and personal difficulties and dilemmas. As the service will be consumed by students who are in fact constituents, the organisation has determined that the most appropriate industry segment to classify the service to will be within the *Constituent*

Figure 4. BSCF (extract) (Queensland Government, 2010b – used with permission)

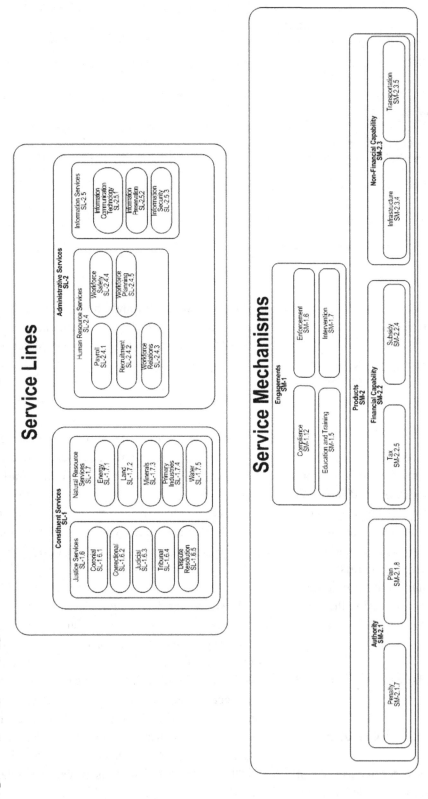

Table 3. Example of business service classification

Business service name	Service line	Service mechanisms
Student Counselling service	Constituent services: Community services Constituent services: Education services	Engagements: Care and rehabilitation Engagements: Marketing and advocacy Product: Subsidy

Services domain within the QGBSCF. Utilising the definitions within the QGBSCF, the organisation determines that the most appropriate service lines for this service would be *Community Services* given its focus on counselling and *Education Services* given that the service is to be delivered to students. To provide this Community Service and Education Service, one clear mechanism for service delivery is through *Care and rehabilitation*. However, there may be other possibilities and by classifying the proposed service to the QGBSCF it is easier to identify what these may be. For example, is it likely that the education organisation would offer such a service and not promote it? On reflection, the organisation may then choose to classify the service also to *Marketing and Advocacy*. Perhaps it is common for students dropping out of courses to be experiencing financial difficulties? The organisation may identify that an emergency loan scheme or food vouchers should be offered as part of the service and also classify the service to *Subsidy* (see Table 3 and note that the use of a colon to indicate moving down the hierarchy of the BSCF).

This example demonstrates how the business services taxonomy can be a powerful tool to support the thinking process when designing services. It encourages the service designer to consider alternative aspects of service mechanisms by looking at all *types* of service mechanisms. This also enables the service designer to understand the true scope of the service so that its delivery can be scheduled and resourced appropriately.

Business services portfolio view. If this organisation has a complete service catalogue,

it could classify all of its services to the BSCF, providing a portfolio view of all its service offerings. In Figure 5 and Figure 6 below, the education organisation has indicated in shading what service lines and mechanisms it currently has service offerings.

This portfolio view enables the organisation to understand:

- what service lines it currently operates within
- what service mechanisms (engagements and products) it currently delivers to these service lines

This view allows the organisation to abstract the detail of a large number of service offerings to a logical view of the *types of services* that are being offered to its customers. A business services portfolio view challenges an organisation to evaluate its service offerings. Typical questions that a portfolio view addresses are summarised in Table 4.

The following heat map shows how further data can be overlaid over the BSCF domains to provide a visual representation to the organisation of the number of services it provides within each service line and mechanism. In this case, we can see that the organisation's main focus is on delivering services with an Education and Training engagement and there are several services with Care and Rehabilitation engagements. The main industry segment that it has service offerings within is Education Services.

As demonstrated in Figure 7 by counting the number of times a business service is classified to

Figure 5. BSCF - service lines (Queensland Government, 2010b – used with permission)

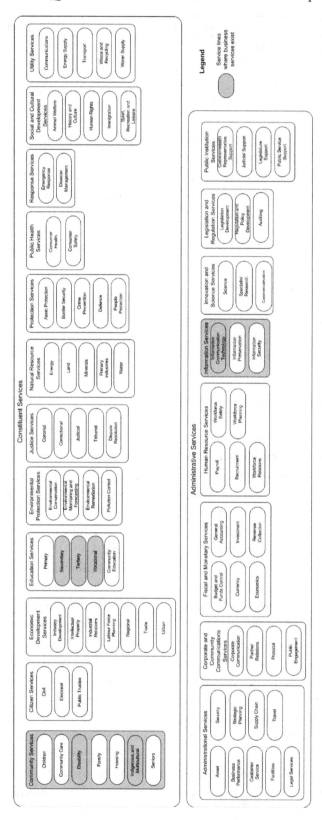

Figure 6. BSCF - service mechanisms (Queensland Government, 2010b – used with permission)

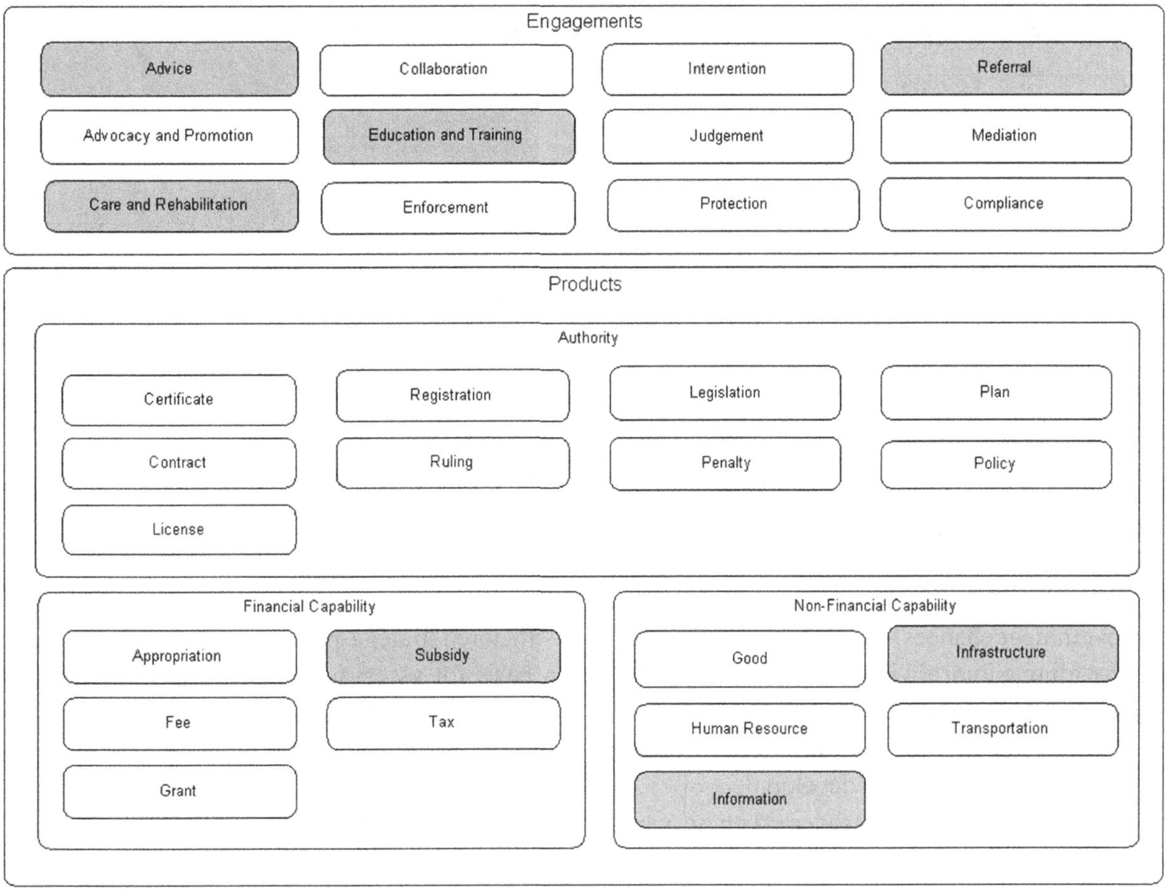

Table 4. Business services taxonomy to analyse portfolio coverage, alignment, and gaps

Coverage	• Is this what we expect our spread of service types to look like?
Alignment	• Are these service types aligned to what we understand as our organisation's purpose and vision? • Which ones of these domains are our *core services* (i.e. high value services delivered to our customers)? • Are any of these service types regarded as *non-core* (e.g. internal administrative services that are business imperatives)? Are there opportunities to outsource some service offerings so we can focus on our *core services*?
Gaps	• What service lines do we not currently operate within? • What service mechanisms do we not currently deliver? • Are there service lines or service mechanisms that present opportunities to capture a larger part of our customer base or to better improve our service delivery?

a service line or service mechanism, the organisation can ask the following questions:

- Have we over-invested in some areas?
- Is there overlap and duplication in some of our service offerings?

For example in the scenario above, we know that the organisation is planning a new Student Counselling Service. It would be prudent for the service designer to examine what existing services are already delivering Care and Rehabilitation

Figure 7. Business service taxonomy – counts (Queensland Government, 2010b – used with permission)

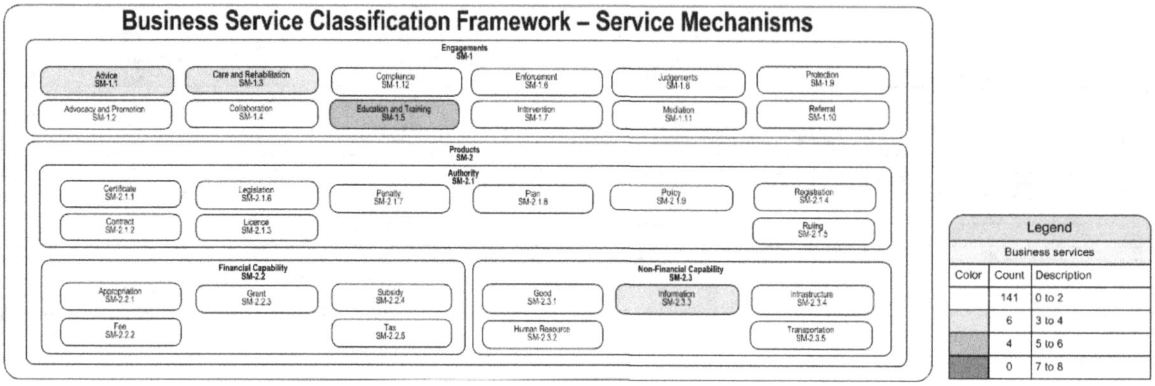

engagements to identify any potential overlap or duplication.

In addition, transition activities as a result of business mergers and acquisitions (machinery-of-government changes) can be better supported by providing a logical view of business services across two or more organisations.

Further analysis of cost data for business services would then enable development of cost management strategies in tandem with service optimisation strategies.

In the example below the education organisation may determine that as it wants to focus on retaining students, it may be appropriate to increase its expenditure in areas such as Care and Rehabilitation, Advice and Referral. The organisation may determine that it is not as concerned with providing Infrastructure services to its students and there may be an opportunity to reduce the proportion of expenditure there. Assessing the level of spend per domain enables the organisation to ask the following questions:

- Is the level of expenditure in these domains aligned to what we understand as our organisation's purpose and vision?
- Are there opportunities to reduce expenditure in some domains?

EA Taxonomies to Support Strategic Planning

EA taxonomies can also be used to support a more structured strategic planning process by providing a basis for assessing the comprehensiveness of strategic plans, including the portfolio coverage of performance indicators. Figure 8 provides a view of using the BSCF within the Queensland Government for this purpose.

By classifying each performance indicator to service lines in the BSCF, the following view is generated. From this view, it is identified that there are a number of gaps i.e. service lines with no performance indicators. A few of these service lines e.g. *Civil* and *Electoral* are federal government services and hence, are valid gaps. Other gaps are apparent in the *Justice Services* and *Protection Services*. This requires further investigation.

Is the government interested in measuring the performance within these service lines? If so, performance indicators need to be included, or perhaps, this government has other peripheral business plans specifically targeted at integrated justice and people protection, and that performance indicators have already been identified within those plans.

A business services taxonomy can prove to be an effective high-level tool for assessing the

Figure 8. Business services taxonomy to analyse completeness of strategic plans (excerpt) (Queensland Government, 2010b – used with permission)

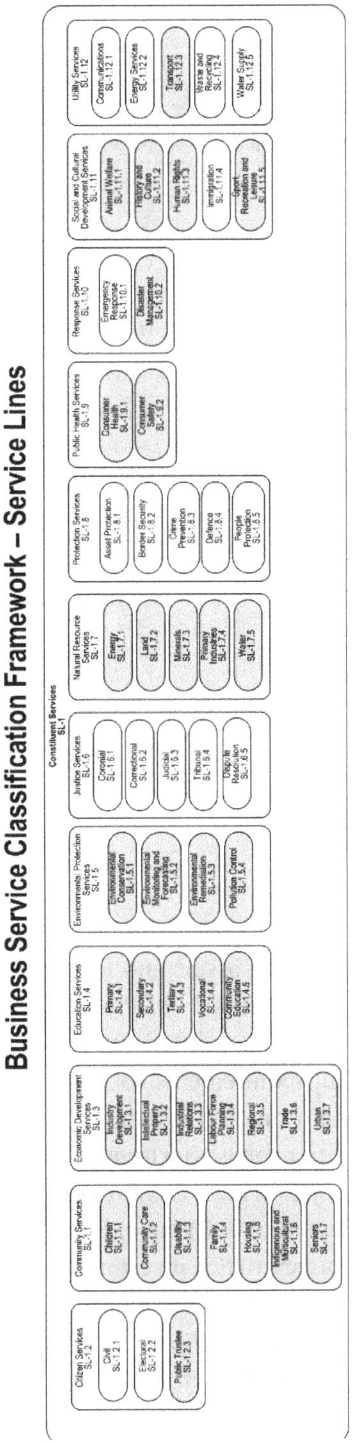

completeness of an organisation's performance management activities, particularly in relation to its strategic intentions.

USING TAXONOMIES TO CREATE A BASELINE

One of the first steps in building a good EA practice is to develop a good understanding of business and its components (Schekkerman, 2008; The Open Group, 2011). This can be achieved by describing the organisation as it exists now and as it is intended to look and operate in the future. This section discusses the development and evolution of an ICT baseline within the Queensland Government with the use of taxonomies to provide coherent portfolio analysis for optimising decision-making.

In 2004, the Queensland Government (QG) published its Smart Directions Statement for Information and Communications Technology (hereafter known as the Qld SDS)—this was a strategy document designed to support the government in achieving better efficiencies and cohesion across its ICT investment portfolio—including current assets and ICT-enabled initiatives. One of the performance indicators in the Qld SDS was to deliver an ICT baseline to support improved ICT decision-making. This is often touted as the first concerted attempt within the Queensland Government to create a portfolio view of its ICT investments across QG's portfolio of its 24 departments at the time.

In essence, the ICT baseline was the first step in increasing the maturity of using portfolio analysis techniques at a whole-of-Queensland Government.

To deliver the ICT baseline, two major questions were addressed.

- First, what approach would be used to create a cohesive and consistent ICT baseline across the diverse QG portfolio, i.e. what will the ICT baseline data look like?

Table 5. Applications register

	Sample attributes
Definitional attributes	name purpose
Cost attributes	capital cost estimated replacement cost operational cost
Planning attributes	Anticipated end of life
Relationship attributes	mappings to business objectives that the application supports
Assessment attributes[1]	business impact score condition score future business value score

Figure 9. Applications taxonomy – classification (Queensland Government, 2011 – used with permission)

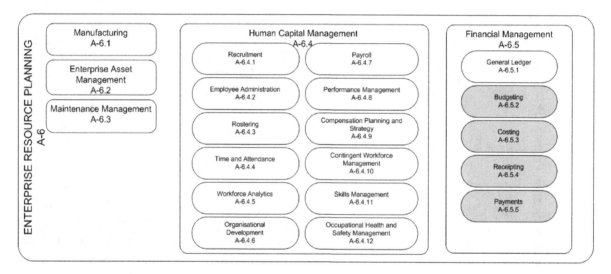

• Second, how can a coherent ICT portfolio view be derived that would support evidence-based decision-making.

The answers lay in the QGEA taxonomies that had already been published, albeit used sparingly at the time, across the QG.

The Approach

Each department was tasked to populate on an annual basis two main registers: applications register and technologies register. Essentially, departments were asked to provide data relating to application assets and technology assets. In subsequent iterations of the ICT baseline, an information assets register was added to the list of reporting requirements to instil a culture of managing information as assets.

This section focuses on the application register and how the use of the QG Application Classification Framework (ACF) moved the QG closer to generating a view of ICT investments as a *portfolio*.

Table 5 provides a summary of the types of attributes collected for each application within the applications register.

In addition to these attributes, each asset in the application register was also classified to one

Figure 10. Applications taxonomy – classification and percentage of use (Queensland Government, 2011 – used with permission)

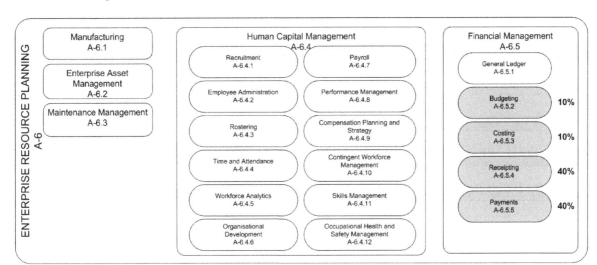

or more domains from the ACF, i.e. classified to a standard taxonomy. See Figure 9 for an example of classifying SAP Financials to the QG ACF.

It is worth noting that this technique of classification to a standard taxonomy applies across the EA stack. To gain a better understanding of the *type of asset*, assets are classified to its respective taxonomy e.g. information assets to the ICF, application assets to the ACF and technology assets to the TCF.

Aside from achieving language consistency in classifications, this approach provides further benefits:

- provides a completeness check in data collection by allowing organisations to answer the question "Does my organisation have any assets in this domain?" thus allowing for more comprehensive and complete ICT baseline data set.
- provides a foundation for managing assets as a portfolio and not individual line items in a particular layer. This provides a basis for using portfolio analysis techniques to support improved ICT decision-making. The next section provides further evidence of this.

USING TAXONOMIES TO SUPPORT PORTFOLIO MANAGEMENT

Portfolio management enables a central oversight of all current and potential investments – the portfolio view. Through the use of portfolio analysis techniques, the organisation's portfolio can be adjusted to determine whether to continue or divest investments. These adjustments are made based on evidence relating to multiple facets including cost, risk, strategic alignment, demand, capability (skills and knowledge) and capacity (time and effort).

Comprehensive portfolio management will involve two perspectives:

- *assets* portfolio management – *current investments* (business-as-usual) including information assets, applications and technologies
- *initiatives* portfolio management – *current and future change initiatives* including projects and programs

Figure 11. Application taxonomy – spend

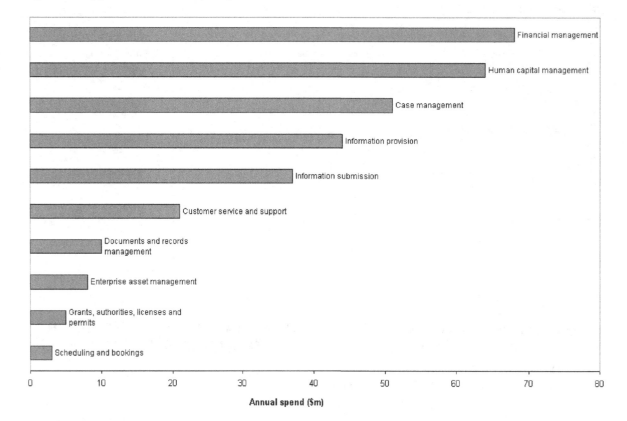

Asset Portfolio Management

Assets that are gathered as part of an EA baseline process can be classified to standard taxonomies providing a sound foundation to support asset portfolio management. The following sections provide examples of analyses that support decisions relating to adjusting an organisation's asset portfolio.

Portfolio balance Portfolio balance refers to the extent to which a portfolio aligns with its business intentions. For example, an application that is based on SAP Financials is used for financial management. Typical classifications for the SAP Financials system would be as shown in Figure 9 .

These classifications become more powerful when other supporting data from the registers are overlayed on to the standard taxonomy. Figure 10 provides the same classification overlayed with percentage of use. The figure indicates that

SAP Financials is primarily used for *Receipting* (40%) and *Payments* (40%), and to a lesser extent, *Budgeting* (10%), and *Costing* (10%).

Classifications to the standard taxonomy with percentage of use, coupled with annual operational cost provide the following cost-centric portfolio view.

Figure 11 shows how a portfolio view provides insight to the applications portfolio. Rather than just seeing a list of assets by their annual spends, a portfolio view provides answers to the following:

- What are the types of applications that the organisation spends on?
- Is this spending balanced against the organisation's business intentions?

As an example of analysis, suppose that Figure 11 represented the application portfolio view for a government organisation. Initial analysis of

Figure 12. Application taxonomy - count

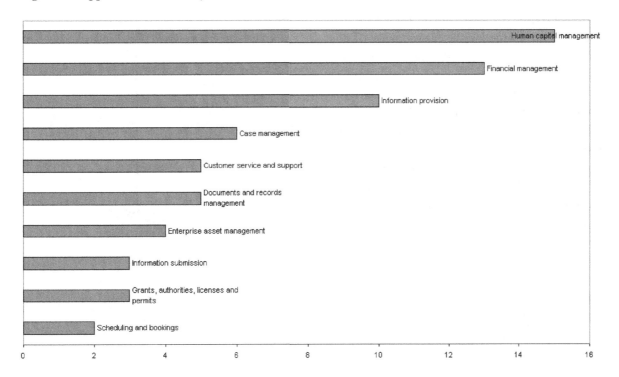

the chart indicates that this organisation has high spend to support internal business, i.e. *financial management* and *human capital management* and proportionally less for *customer-centric* business including *customer service and support* and *grants, authorities, licenses and permits.*

A view such as this provides a more informed comparison of application costs—a reduced focus on line items in an application register and an increased focus on "How much is my organisation spending in supporting the various *application capabilities?*" Based on the view above, it can be seen that this organisation is spending a high percentage of its IT costs in supporting internally-focused capabilities, i.e. *human resource management* and *financial management*, and proportionally less on service delivery.

Based on an organisation's business context, in this case, a government organisation, this may be regarded as an *unbalanced portfolio*. It can be argued that government organisations exist for the purpose of providing services to the community,

and not to manage its finances and pay its staff, although these are necessary activities. Without even going into the specifics of the data, the chart has revealed an area for further investigation: Is this organisation spending too much to support its internal services at the expenses of customer service delivery? A government organisation may see a need to explore opportunities to reduce costs in human resources and financial management, as these application capabilities do not directly support its focus of community service delivery.

Portfolio duplication A domain with multiple assets classified to it may represent duplication in a portfolio. This allows an organisation to discover duplicates for potential rationalisation, standardisation, and/or decommissioning. Figure 12 represents the application domains against the number of applications classified to each domain.

This portfolio view can be used as a catalyst for an organisation to clean up its current *application backyard*. For each domain with duplicates, further data on each potential duplicate such as assessments of current business impact, condition, fit-for-purpose and cost can be used to make decisions on subsuming the functionality of duplicate assets with a stronger performing asset, leading to the decommissioning of weaker assets to reduce the level of portfolio duplication. This brings with it the benefits of streamlined support for a smaller number of assets, consolidated information sources and ultimately reduced costs and complexity within the application portfolio.

Cost benchmarks Taking this cost-centric portfolio view one step further, an organisation can provide cost benchmarks for each domain. For example, within the Queensland Government, each department can compare their cost against the state benchmarks using box plots. A sample box plot is shown below to identify the minimum, 25th percentile, median, 75th percentile and maximum values for operational costs in a domain (see Figure 13).

These cost benchmarks are only possible with the use of standard classification taxonomies and assist individual departments to measure them-

Figure 13. Box plot for cost analysis

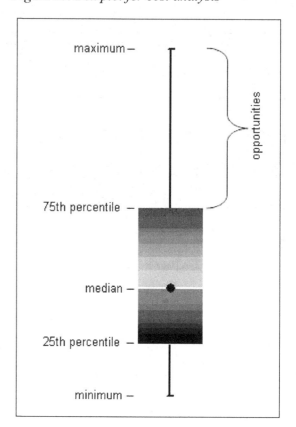

Figure 14. Box plots for cost benchmarking

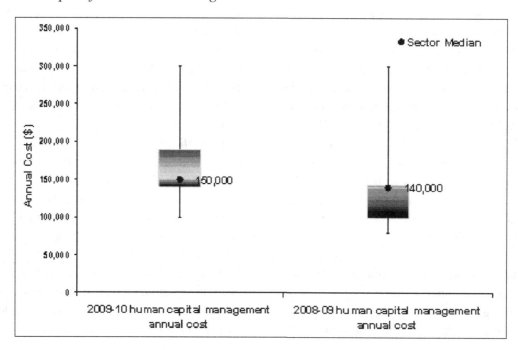

Figure 15. Annual spend over time

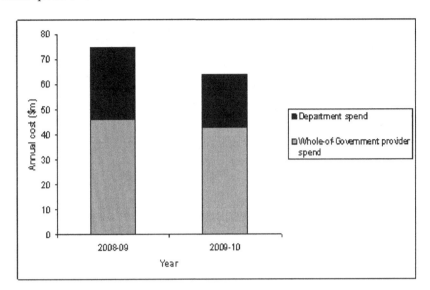

selves against the rest of the government (see Figure 14).

By searching for data on the annual unit cost for all ICT assets classified to human capital management in the application classification taxonomy for the last two financial years, we are able to establish a benchmark (i.e. the median) expenditure for these assets for the sector.

The example above shows that there has been a growth in the maximum per unit cost across the enterprise. Departments within the enterprise that are spending in the 75th plus percentile could investigate opportunities to reduce their expenditure by talking to departments with lower costs. Likewise, at a whole-of-enterprise level, there may be an opportunity to develop initiatives focused on reducing the enterprise's overall spend (see Figure 15).

How effective has a Whole-of-Enterprise Shared Service Arrangement Been? Are There Further Opportunities?

This enterprise has a whole-of-enterprise human capital management shared service arrangement. Human capital is acknowledged as an ongoing

area of high spend. Again, because all departments of the enterprise classify their ICT assets to the same taxonomy we are able to investigate how effective the whole-of-enterprise arrangement has truly been in reducing overall costs and proliferation. In this case, we are investigating the sum of expenditure on applications classified to the human capital management area/domain within the applications taxonomy. As we can see from the graph there has been a reduction in department spend in other human capital related applications from 2008/09 to 2009/10. The cost to provision the whole-of-enterprise solution from 2008-09 to 2009-2010 has remained relatively stable. However, overall spend for the area/domain of human capital management has decreased. This trend should be monitored to ensure that the benefits of an overall cost reduction are realized and whether there are further opportunities to standardize within the area/domain of human capital management.

It is timely to note that these analyses are relevant and applicable across the EA stack, to support portfolio management for business services, business processes, skills, information assets, applications, and technologies.

Figure 16. Defining an initiative using a solution model based on standard taxonomies

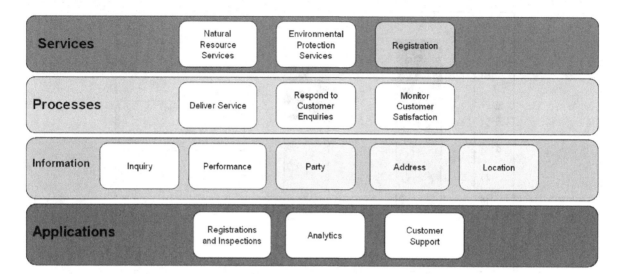

Initiatives Portfolio Management

In addition to gathering capabilities and assets that are owned, used and delivered by the organisation, there is also a need to gather existing and potential initiatives. These initiatives can be projects, programs and other major change activities. In a typical planning and initiative implementation life cycle, three sources of information are used to derive a comprehensive initiatives portfolio:

- existing initiatives that are part of the or-ganisation's existing change portfolio
- potential initiatives derived from analys-ing quantitative data as per assets portfolio management, mostly relating to cleaning up the existing assets portfolio to achieve a more balanced portfolio – in terms of cost, risk and strategic alignment; and to capi-talise on opportunities to reduce portfolio duplication
- potential initiatives derived from analys-ing qualitative data from business planning and business visioning activities including environmental analysis, business focus, and improved business models.

Initiatives portfolio management aspires to provide a central oversight of all existing and potential initiatives in order to:

- identify overlaps between initiatives that could lead to consolidation and rationalisa-tion of multiple initiatives
- support collaboration opportunities and open up communication between owners of similar initiatives
- identify potential to practise the principle of share-before-buy-before-build by corre-lating data from both the initiatives portfo-lio and the assets portfolio.

In a large and complex organisation such as the public sector, it is imperative to use a structured and evidence-based approach to achieving these outcomes as the quantity of initiatives are high, and the variation on how initiative definitions are produced makes it difficult to compare *like with like* initiatives.

In the Queensland Government, the approach recommended for use across the departments is to link components of each initiative to domains that are part of common taxonomies – these are

Table 6. QGEA products to support compliance

QGEA governance product	Scope	Purpose
Principles	Mandatory	Espouse fundamental values and beliefs
Strategies	Mandatory	Describe long-term direction
Policies and positions	Mandatory with compliance reporting	Describe behavioural changes to support strategies, including the definitions of targets for compliance reporting
Supporting tools	Better practice and implementation advice	Other documents such as guidelines, checklists, and fact sheets.

the same taxonomies used to classify capabilities and assets. This process produces a *solution domain model*. Figure 16 is an example of a solution domain model for a *Lands Registration* initiative. Note that each component is labelled using the same domain names as the standard taxonomies.

By tracing down the EA stack of business services, business processes, information, applications and technologies using the standard taxonomies, the scope and context of an initiative can be defined in a more structured manner.

When all initiatives within a department (and at a whole-of-government) are represented as solution domain models, a portfolio manager can more easily analyse:

- *Portfolio overlaps* across any domain to support focused communication between initiatives that have overlap in domains
- *Portfolio leverage* for all initiatives to identify existing capabilities or assets that future initiatives can share before considering building or acquiring new dissimilar capability.

Another benefit of using this approach is improved cost estimation for initiatives. On the basis of quality data collected as part of a baseline on the implementation costs and ongoing costs for assets within a domain, statistical techniques can be used to benchmark costs. These benchmarks support a more rigorous approach to cost estimation for new initiatives, and provides a more realistic projection for ongoing costs post implementation.

Closing the Loop between Assets and Initiatives

If *investment management* is defined as the management of current portfolio (assets) and *investment planning* is scoped as the management of the change portfolio (initiatives), the Queensland Government encourages the use of standard taxonomies to:

- improve the use and management of assets across the state to minimise duplication and optimise spend against key business intentions
- obtain powerful insight into how efficiently an organisation's investments are performing (i.e. benchmarking)
- improve the rigour of scoping and defining the initiatives
- streamline the identification of overlaps and *like* initiatives
- support the philosophy of share-before-buy-before build by increasing the visibility of the current portfolio (assets) to support the change portfolio (initiatives)
- inform innovation and leverage learning and best practice across the sector

USING TAXONOMIES TO SUPPORT POLICY DEVELOPMENT AND POLICY COMPLIANCE

The QGEA framework describes a hierarchy of governance products to communicate the government's business intentions. Table 6 summarises each product and its purpose.

We have seen how capabilities, assets, and initiatives are classified to the standard QGEA taxonomies. In addition to this, each QGEA governance product that is produced is classified to one or more domains within the standard QGEA taxonomies. This can be useful in two scenarios where a department:

- modifies (i.e. development and enhancement projects) its **capabilities**
- is in the early stages of defining an **initiative**.

In both of these scenarios, the department can easily navigate the repository of QGEA governance products to determine whether any constraints apply or guidance is available. The department can then focus its decision-making on those aspects of the project or initiative that are not constrained.

For example, a department has an initiative that requires a new Document and Records Management capability. The department can cross-reference if and what QGEA governance products have also been classified to this domain. The department finds that there is a QGEA policy and position that requires it to select 1 of 3 products from a panel of providers. The department does not need to expend effort researching the market and can instead focus on other aspects of the initiative. The department also finds that there is a guideline that provides implementation advice on how to ensure its Document and Records Management capability meets its legislative recordkeeping obligations.

Departments within the Queensland Government departments are required to report their level of alignment with mandatory QGEA governance products annually. Because each QGEA governance product is classified to the standard QGEA taxonomies, the whole-of-Government EA team is able to examine the level of alignment with the QGEA by domain, layer and slice. This is further able to be correlated with benchmarked asset profiles to align policy focus with significant investment domains.

FUTURE DIRECTIONS

The future of EA taxonomies is influenced by its *network effect* (Network effect, 2011). Fundamentally, the network effect states that the value of a product or service increases as more people use it. Telecommunications and the internet are replete with examples of this e.g. fax machines, email, FaceBook, Wikipedia etc.

In terms of EA taxonomies, experience confirms that the more people contributing to a pool of classified capabilities (assets) or initiatives, the greater the value for those that need to search or analyse the classified assets.

Promoting the Use of Taxonomies

The network effect for EA taxonomies is slightly more complex due to the fact that participation (by individuals) is generally asymmetrical, i.e. those individuals that contribute to populating a classified repository are not necessarily the same individuals that derive value from the repository. Consider an analogy of a book library with two types of participants; authors and readers. Authors write and contribute books to a library whilst readers choose and read said books. Putting financial aspects aside for the purpose of this analogy, what would then motivate authors to write books? Possible answers are altruism, a love or writing, a responsibility (orders or direction). The answer that applies most effectively is potential role reversal. Most authors also like to read books so contribute on the basis that they will also gain a benefit by being able to read others' books.

We have found that those who are best placed to classify ICT assets to EA taxonomies are often the same people that later come looking for answers from our repositories of classifications and this tends to reinforce the value of contribution.

The shortcoming of any system reliant on the network effect is the need to prime the system before it reaches sufficient size to be self-sustaining i.e. the point at which returned value to any new participant is higher than their cost of participating. In the case of the Queensland Government, such initial priming was achieved through mandated participation coupled with a dedicated support team. Consistent classification is the key to putting the repositories of classifications to good use. This consistency can only be achieved through proactive and just-in-time education and training. Over time, emphasis has changed from mandated participation to demonstrating value through active marketing and advocacy through demonstrating analysis capabilities from gathered data.

The network effect is further promoted by de-emphasising these taxonomies as ICT classifications, and instead promoting these taxonomies in practical business disciplines i.e. investment planning, portfolio management, business analysis and evidence-based policy development. This has led to a change in emphasis from classification of just ICT assets (applications and technologies) to classification of business capabilities and assets (business services, business processes, skills and information assets).

Quality of Classifications

An important aspect of the use of EA taxonomies is the quality of the classifications. A good taxonomy will be easy to use and leave no ambiguity with regard to which domain(s) items should be classified. Even so, in enterprise-scale use the participants using the taxonomy are diverse people with different skills, contexts, and level of familiarity with the classifications. This can lead to mis-classification of items, which then reduce the overall value for either ad-hoc or structured portfolio analysis. Techniques to reduce error rates include independent checking of a sample of items,

rich descriptions of domains with examples, and tools, which can automatically suggest default classifications based on other attributes.

Adopting a Spread of Taxonomies

A general rule is that the more taxonomies that are adopted by an organisation the less active participation each taxonomy gets, thus reducing the value of all taxonomies. It is recommended to commence with only one or two taxonomies and putting effort into embedding these into operational practices and gaining the benefits from this rather than attempting to institute a comprehensive suite of taxonomies that will likely become shelf-ware.

A variety of options exist for organisations wishing to invest in the use of EA taxonomies. There is a spread of existing taxonomies already available to choose from. The decision then becomes one of customising an existing taxonomy, developing a new taxonomy, or producing a synthesis from existing taxonomies. There are pros and cons to each approach.

Developing a taxonomy This approach is time-consuming, but results in a fit-for-purpose taxonomy without any need for compromises. However, the resultant taxonomy may need validation to ensure it is complete and comprehensive, and can introduce a high learning barrier if its underlying building blocks are different to those already in use. To enable successful adoption of a fit-for-purpose taxonomy, a range of change management and ongoing support processes such as training will need to be introduced.

Choosing or modifying a taxonomy Choosing from existing taxonomies is not always straightforward. Evaluating different taxonomies can be time consuming, although generally less so than developing one from scratch. Using or modifying an existing taxonomy generally requires compromises, and the chosen tool may not meet all organisational requirements. However, existing tools have the advantage of being proven and tested, and also have the additional benefit of cross-pollination of lessons learned and a philosophy of continuous improvement as a result of cross-organisational use of the same taxonomies.

Convergence of Taxonomies

The *utopic view* sees a world where all organisations use standard taxonomies for classifying their capabilities and initiatives, where standard taxonomies can be defined for particular industries, and of these taxonomies being published through international standards. With an increasing number of state jurisdictions in Australia already sharing knowledge and lessons learnt from their EA practices—including taxonomies, this convergence may indeed be one small step closer.

CONCLUSION

This chapter began with defining sense-making tools to assist humans in understanding the world around them. One of these sense-making tools, taxonomies, was discussed within the context of EA practice, and specifically within the Queensland Government. A number of techniques were presented on how taxonomies can provide strength of support in business management, EA baseline, portfolio management, and policy development and compliance. Finally, this chapter discussed approaches for promoting managed use of taxonomies and the possible convergence of taxonomies.

The authors believe in the value of EA taxonomies and continue to pursue their use in supporting connected E-Government initiatives.

REFERENCES

C2. (2006). *Borges classification of animals.* Retrieved May 12, 2011, from http://c2.com/cgi/wiki?BorgesClassificationOfAnimals.

Australian Government Information Management Office. (2009). *Australian government architecture reference models.* Retrieved March 3, 2011, from http://www.finance.gov.au/e-government/strategy-and-governance/aga-rm/AGA-RM.html.

Biological Classification. (2011). *Wikipedia.* Retrieved May 1, 2011, from http://en.wikipedia.org/wiki/Biological_classification.

Federal Republic of Germany. (2008). *Standards and architectures for egovernment applications (SAGA).* Retrieved 18 August, 2011 from http://www.cio.bund.de/saga.

Linnaean Classification. (2011). *Wikipedia.* Retrieved August 18, 2011, from http://en.wikipedia.org/wiki/Linnaean_taxonomy.

Mathes, A. (2004). *Folksonomies – Cooperative classification and communication through shared metadata.* Retrieved August 16, 2011, from http://www.adammathes.com/academic/computer-mediated-communication/folksonomies.html.

Network Effect. (2011). *Wikipedia.* Retrieved April 9, 2011, from http://en.wikipedia.org/wiki/Network_effect.

Office of Management and Budget. (2007). *Federal enterprise architecture.* Retrieved March 30, 2011, from http://www.whitehouse.gov/omb/e-gov/fea/.

Ontology. (2011). *Wikipedia.* Retrieved May 1 2011, from http://en.wikipedia.org/wiki/Ontology.

Open Group. (2011). *The open group architecture framework (TOGAF).* Retrieved May 5, 2011, from http://www.opengroup.org/togaf/.

Queensland Government. (2010a). *Queensland government business service classification framework definitions.* Retrieved April 28, 2011, from http://www.qgcio.qld.gov.au/SiteCollectionDocuments/Architecture%20and%20Standards/QGEA%202.0/Business%20Services%20Classification%20Framework%20Definitions.pdf.

Queensland Government. (2010b). *Using the business services classification framework*. Retrieved April 28, 2011, from http://www.qgcio.qld.gov.au/SiteCollectionDocuments/Architecture%20and%20Standards/QGEA%202.0/Business%20Services%20Classification%20Framework%20Definitions.pdf.

Queensland Government. (2011). *Queensland government enterprise architecture*. Retrieved March 30, 2011, from http://www.qgcio.qld.gov.au/qgcio/architectureandstandards/qgea2.0/Pages/index.aspx.

Singapore Government. (2010). *Singapore government enterprise architecture*. Retrieved 2 May, 2011, from http://www.ida.gov.sg/Programmes/20060419144239.aspx?getPagetype=34.

Thesauri. (2011). *The free dictionary*. Retrieved May 10, 2011, from http://www.thefreedictionary.com/thesaurus.

Vander Wal, T. (2007). *Folksonmy coinage and definition*. Retrieved 2 May 2011, from http://www.vanderwal.net/folksonomy.html.

ADDITIONAL READING

Finkelstein, C. (2006). *Enterprise architecture for integration: Rapid delivery methods and technologies*. Boston, MA: Artech House.

Microsoft. (2011). *Connected government*. Retrieved August 16, 2011, from http://www.microsoft.com/government/ww/articles/pages/connected-framework.aspx.

Ross, J., Weill, P., & Robertson, D. C. (2006). *Enterprise architecture as strategy*. Boston, MA: Harvard Business School Press.

Saha, P. (2009). *Advances in government EA*. Hershey, PA: IGI Global.

Spencer, P. (2007). *Connected government: Creating a springboard for transformation and innovation*. Retrieved August 16, 2011, from http://www.cisco.com/web/about/ac79/docs/wp/ctd/Connected_Govt_PoV_1030_finalCB.pdf.

Wilson, J. A., Mazzuchi, T., & Sarkani, S. (2011). Evaluating the effectiveness of reference models in federating enterprise architectures. *Journal of Enterprise Architecture*, 7(2), 40–49.

KEY TERMS AND DEFINITIONS

Classification: The practice of categorising entities to defined domains according to their qualities and characteristics.

Taxonomy: A sense-making tool that is structured as a hierarchical classification scheme.

Portfolio: A collection of programs, projects, activities, investments or assets selected, managed and monitored to align with the business direction.

Policy: An instrument used to support or constrain organisational behaviour.

Asset: An entity that is of value to an organisation.

Initiative: Projects, programs or change activities that form an organisation's change portfolio.

Domain: A discrete, atomic element within a taxonomy.

ENDNOTE

[1] QG departments were provided with standard evaluation categories that they rank against to provide a final score for each asset reported.

Section 3
Frameworks for Connected Government

Chapter 4

Integrating Agency Enterprise Architecture into Government–Wide Enterprise Architecture:
The Case of Korean Government Initiatives

Young-Joo Lee
National Information Society Agency, South Korea

Shinae Shin
National Information Society Agency, South Korea

ABSTRACT

Since the Korean government mandated public entities to adopt Enterprise Architecture (EA) in 2005, 75.8% of central agencies, municipal governments, and other public organizations have adopted EA. Following a two-year project, which defined all government-level architecture components and collected relevant data from each agency's EA, the Korean Government-Wide EA (KGEA) was rolled out. As of the end of 2010, KGEA manages IT projects, information systems, work processes, data, hardware, and other related information of 809 agencies in a single repository. All information is shared with all the agencies through the KGEA portal (www.geap.or.kr). This chapter illustrates a case of how EA works for aligning an agency's IT resources with the national IT agenda and enhances IT investment management at a government-wide level. By applying the analytical framework suggested by Janssen and Hjort-Madsen (2007), the development and accomplishments of KGEA are then discussed in terms of connected government—specifically national IT investment and resource management, public service improvements, and interoperability across agencies. This case may offer practical guidance to government CIOs of other countries when implementing Government-Wide EA (GEA).

DOI: 10.4018/978-1-4666-1824-4.ch004

INTRODUCTION

Beginning with the development of the Technical Architecture Framework for Information Management (TAFIM) by the US Department of Defense in 1992, 67% of countries in the world are in the process of developing EA or similar programs in order to improve interoperability among public administration information systems, mitigate project duplication, and maximize the return on investment (Liimataine, et al., 2007).

Government-Wide EA (GEA, also known as National Enterprise Architecture, NEA) is aimed at ensuring interoperability, avoiding the duplication of efforts and enabling government-wide reuse. Under this conception, the term 'enterprise' refers to the scope of the architecture dealing with multiple agencies in a given country. However, the public sector EA is carried out in common but also differs slightly in form according to the geographical, cultural, and regulatory characteristics of each country, and its degree of utilization also varies because of various regulatory factors (Hjort-Madsen, 2007).

At the same time, there are challenges in the GEA programs related to integration and interoperability within and between public agencies. Some researchers find these challenges very hard to overcome (Hjort-Madsen & Burkard, 2006). Other researchers observe that EA in the public sector has yet to be transformed from an IT-centric to a business-centric, and a governance system at the entire national viewpoint is often times seen as unattainable (Hjort-Madsen & Gotze, 2004; Isomäki & Liimataine, 2008). These schools of thought are often associated with the loss of confidence within; many countries are not confident especially in terms of realizable benefits and performance of EA, which are among the most important drivers in the continued advancement of EA projects (Liimataine, et al., 2007).

Korea is one of the world's best in national IT competitiveness, as indicated by being ranked no. 1 in the evaluation of e-government readiness conducted by the UN in 2010. At the same time, it has been actively driving the deployment of EA to ensure efficient management of IT investments. As a result, Korea has been able to create an enabling environment highly conducive to actual deployment and utilization of EA at the working level, unlike many other countries still remaining at the early stage of defining conceptual definition and methodology of EA. In particular, the recent Korean GEA (hereafter KGEA) program has unified EA of individual agencies enabling a holistic view at a whole-governmental level.

The objective of this chapter is to introduce the successful case of GEA implemented by the Korean Government. The chapter will be structured as follows. First, a brief history and the current status of KGEA program is introduced. Next, the characteristics of KGEA will be reviewed using the analytical framework suggested by Janssen and Hjort-Madsen (2007). Finally, the strength and potential weakness of the case will be discussed in terms of its relevance in realizing connected governments and furthering future advancement.

BACKGROUND: FRAMEWORK FOR ANALYZING THE KGEA CASE

Previous case studies on EA were mostly conducted at the organizational level with an interpretative approach and ad-hoc analysis (i.e. Armour, et al., 2003; Hjort-Madsen, 2006; Pulkkinen, 2006). However, an analytical framework which is well-suited for the analysis on the government level is needed because of the dynamic regulatory characteristics of the public sector. The seminal study on the government-level EA case was conducted by Janssen and Hjort-Madsen (2007). They developed an analytic framework based on the institutional theory (Scott, 1995) in order to provide insights into institutional aspects such as policies, actors, frameworks, principles standards, and implementations. The framework was used to compare GEA cases in Denmark and the

Figure 1. The analytic framework (adapted from Janssen & Hjort-Madsen, 2007)

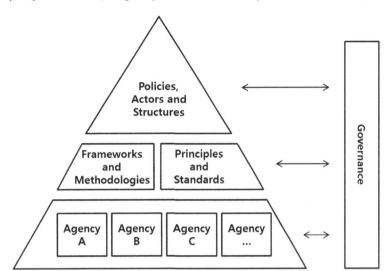

Netherlands, and later was also used by the Finnish government to assess the EA maturity level of different countries (Liimataine, et al., 2007).

The framework aims to take a broad view of GEAs within the public sector. It assumes that designing public organizations involves designing them to reflect the political perspectives and public managers' decisions at a strategic level in operational activities and decisions. Because GEAs are often initiated at the executive level and diffused using different governance mechanisms, the architecture models, principles, and standards make up the specific feature of a GEA. This results in the following aspects which need to be analyzed to understand a GEA case (see Figure 1).

Policies, Actors, and Structures

This aspect encompasses the environmental and political drivers of EA. Political vision affects the configurations of GEA programs and how far reaching the outcome can be, which is proportionate to the level of ambition. Likewise, the number and types of agencies involved in an EA might be considerably different, and the structure of the public administration determines the way

GEA programs can be designed, disseminated, and adopted.

Governance

Architectures evolve over time and consequently governance structures and mechanisms are important for guiding and encouraging the desired behavior. Enterprises generally design three kinds of governance mechanism: decision-making structures, alignment processes, and formal communications (Weil & Ross, 2005).

Architecture Frameworks and Methodologies

Designing takes a resource-based view of public administration, and uses frameworks and planning process methodologies. The GEA model(s) chosen determine which aspects can be captured at which level of abstraction.

Architecture Principles and Standards

Architects use standards, principles, and guidelines for guiding the implementation of EA. Principles

Table 1. EA adoption in Korea at the agency level

Type	No. of agencies	No. of EA adoption		2010	2009	2008	2007	2006	~2005
Central Administrative Agencies	40	36	90%	-	4	5	10	12	5
Local Municipalities	16	16	100%	-	13	2	-	-	1
Other Public Agencies	76	48	63.2%	1	10	15	11	5	6
Total	132	100	75.8%		27	22	21	17	12

restrict architectures and set the direction for the future, while standards can be enforced at various levels, including standard business processes, standard technical building blocks, standardization of interfaces and interaction patterns.

Implementation

The scope operates across multiple implementations among many agencies and disciplines. Specifically, this aspect provides indications for how (parts of) the GEA are adopted, used, and updated. It also contains change support to enable the adoption and diffusion of the GEA.

CASE: KOREAN GEA INITIATIVES

Brief History

The Korean Government enacted a law to mandate the adoption of EA in 2005 to efficiently manage the complex and vast information resources in the public sector and induce methodical approach for information technology planning. In the following year, the 1st Phase EA Master Plan (2007~2009) was established, which contained directions and objectives for public sector in adopting EA.

The first work in accordance with the 1st EA Master Plan was to develop EA standard, guidelines and assessment tools, which mostly benchmarked the US Federal EA(FEA) practices. In addition, the training program for the agency personnel in charge of EA management was de-

veloped and initiated. Based on the master plan, agencies including central departments and local governments have been actively adopting EA since 2007 (see Table 1).

As a result of consistent efforts of the public sector for EA application, currently 100 public agencies have adopted EA and the rest are preparing for adoption by 2015. In 2009 alone, 27 agencies adopted EA as the 1st EA Master Plan ended. As intended by the government's EA initiatives, agencies began to build capacity in managing information resources using EA and several best practices were identified. However, from a government-wide perspective, duplicated systems were still being developed and operated by different agencies, and investment in information technology were planned in the interest of each agency not aligned with government-wide policy goal. As an example, The Board of Audit and Inspection of Korea reported in September 2009 that agencies wasted KRW 50 billion on 11 duplicated investments after a large-scale audit of agencies' investments in information technology projects.

As such, the KGEA program was initiated to eliminate cross-agency duplication of Information systems and related resources as well as to improve services for citizens and increase efficiency of national IT projects. In this context, the program designed the initial architecture model so as to view all agencies' IT resources. The model provides the whole view of as-is architecture, to-be architecture and corresponding transition plan of the whole government business by abstracting currently operating public service, supporting information systems, transactional data, including software and hardware of each agency.

In 2008, the KGEA program was crystallized into the Government EA management system, which was then renamed to Government EA Portal (GEAP) in 2010. Every agency EA was integrated into the GEAP by providing agency's current EA information in compliance with the KGEA meta-model, whose details will be introduced later in this chapter.

As of the end of 2010, the Government EA portal stores the latest information of 809 agencies' IT resources[1]. These data are shared over the website by the stakeholders concerned with national IT policy. The portal also provides information for IT portfolio and investment management information in a dashboard format. Stakeholders can browse current status of IT projects aligned with national IT agenda, and oversee which agenda are being supported by which agency's IT investments. Consequently, GEAP is now being widely used by administrations for management of IT investment such as identification of duplicate IT projects among agencies, discovery of new public IT initiatives for seamless public service to taxpayers, and maintaining interoperability of applications. Below is the detailed description of current KGEA implementation.

Policies, Actors, and Structures

The EA legislation and the 1st EA Master Plan were led by the Ministry of Information and Communications (MIC). The first GEA program started as one of the 30 e-government initiatives in 2005. MIC funded pilot EA programs for the Ministry of Government Administration and Home Affairs (later changed to Ministry of Public Administration and Security, MOPAS) and the Ministry of Maritime Affairs and Fisheries. After verifying the feasibility from the two pilot projects, mandatory adoption of EA was stipulated in the Act of the

Efficient Adoption and Operation of Information Systems (NIA, 2010).

The Act prescribes Chief Information Officer (CIO) of an agency to be responsible for EA implementation and he (or she) should take appropriate measures to efficiently manage the organization's information resources by utilizing EA. The agency CIO is also obliged to report a directory of an agency's current information systems and related assets. After the presidential election and subsequent reorganization of central departments in 2007, the role of overseeing the GEA was transferred to MOPAS. Afterwards, EA related legislation was merged into e-Government Act at the end of 2010. Specifically, Section 47 of e-Government Act made MOPAS eligible for implementing and managing government-wide EA in which agencies' EA information are integrated and analyzed for policy improvement. Not to mention that this provision motivated MOPAS to develop KGEA model not merely promoting agency-level EA.

While the major policy focus of MIC was to boost IT industry in Korea, one of the important mission of MOPAS is to enhance government's organizational capacity and build an accountable and efficient fiscal management system for local governments. The leadership transfer to the administration-focused department gradually formed unique institutional environment and governance structure for GEA adoption and use. As of 2010, the structure for planning, managing, and promoting GEA program is shown in Figure 2.

The EA policy resides in the structure of national IT investment decision-making. The President's Council on Information Strategies (CIS), which oversees the national IT policies, has the highest decision-making authority. The council reviews and endorses the national EA master plan. MOPAS is responsible for execution of the national EA program, development, and distribution of EA guidelines, and evaluating the performance of agency's EA. On a yearly basis, MOPAS reports to the council regarding the cur-

Figure 2. The governance structure of KGEA program

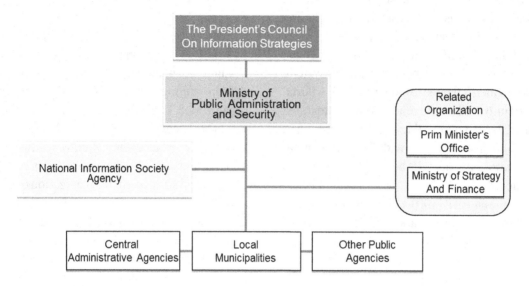

rent state of national EA progress. The National Information Society Agency (NIA) is an organization designated as an EA facilitator and provides specialized expertise in developing and implementing the national EA program as well as consulting service to agencies.

All of the central administrative agencies and local municipalities are subject to the provision of mandatory adoption of EA. Public agencies whose previous three-year's average IT budget exceeds KRW 2 billion or one year's budget exceeds KRW 5 billion are subject to mandatory adoption. However, there is no penalty clause for not adopting EA. Agencies can still choose when to adopt EA or just not adopt.

Governance

As can be seen in the Korean IT policy structure, responsibility for e-government program and national EA program is concentrated in a single organization structure. Although MOPAS has taken the exclusive role of leading EA policy, it spares no effort in consulting a wide spectrum of views from all government organizations. Some Measures to ensure proper communication with

other agencies include forming a committee of CIOs from central administrative agencies, and holding workshop for the personnel in charge of EA at the agencies. Specifically MOPAS holds yearly national EA workshop to introduce the direction of EA policy, collect opinions from agencies, and provide a forum for sharing EA best practices. The education program provided by NIA is another channel of communication for EA policy with regard to standards and guidelines.

Although there is no specific incentive or penalty for agencies' EA adoption, the KGEA policy created institutional environments where agencies are under coercive and normative pressure to utilize EA. For instance, when MOPAS reviews national IT investment plan to identify cross-agency duplication, agencies are required to register related EA information into the GEAP as guided by the reference model. Another example is that the EA maturity level of the central administrative agencies is reported and reflected in one of the measure of IT management performance, which is a part of yearly evaluation conducted by the Prime Minister's Office (PMO) Lastly, in annual IT budget request to Ministry of Strategy and Finance, it is mandated that agencies request

Figure 3. The conceptual framework of KGEA

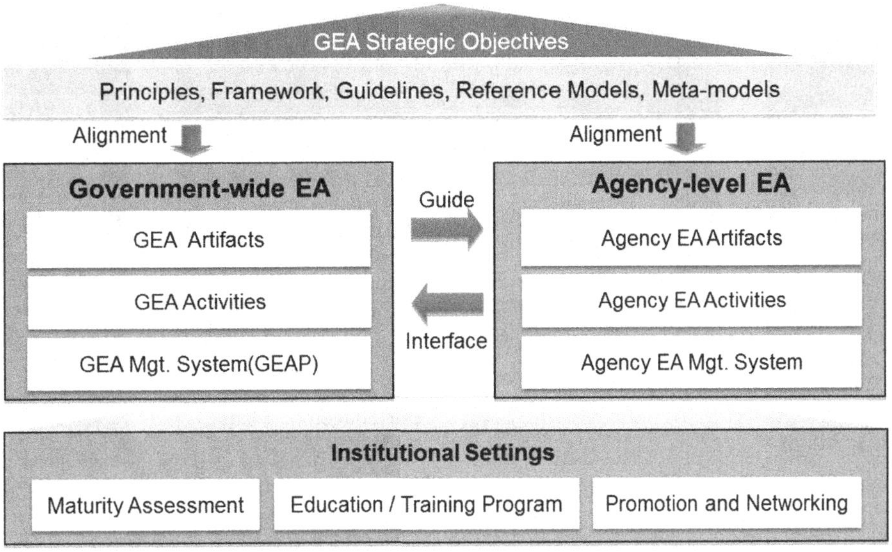

the maintenance cost of information system that is registered to GEAP in one of the component of as-is architecture.

Frameworks and Methodology

Figure 3 depicts the conceptual framework of KGEA. It defines every component that needs to be considered related to the development, operation, and management of government-wide EA. Under the GEA strategic objectives, common principles, guidelines, and reference models are defined by MOPAS and updated by NIA. Under the common standards, the hierarchical structure presents the government-wide EA and agency-level EA, which are closely connected with each other by institutional settings such as regulative maturity assessment, education and training programs, and other mutual communications. Specifically GEA Meta-model acts as a guidance of abstraction level with which aspects can be captured at agency-level architecture information.

The GEA methodology is defined as a set of processes, activities, and recommendations for public agencies to successfully introduce agency-level EA. The methodology also provides infor-

mation on how to comply with regulations and standards required by government. The methodology was developed from the need to maintain a certain level of self-reliance on the part of agency users and limit excessive reliance on EA vendor's methodologies. Therefore, in order to maximize ease of use, it focuses more on the processes rather than the artifacts or deliverables

All phases in the EA lifecycle are covered in the methodology with which every agency can implement EA through a systematic approach by providing step-by-step guidance, forms, examples, detailed techniques. Under the GEA methodology, the Guideline on the Adoption and Operation of the Information Technology Architecture describes the activities and consideration needed for each life cycle of EA implementation by each agency (Figure 4). In the *Preparation Phase,* activities related to setting a strategic direction of EA and organizing a team for preparing EA introduction are defined. In the *Development Phase,* various activities are defined related to actual implementation of agency-level EA including definition of the agency-level framework, redefinition of agency reference models by inheriting from GEA reference models, establishment of as-is and to-

Figure 4. The KGEA methodology for agency-level EA

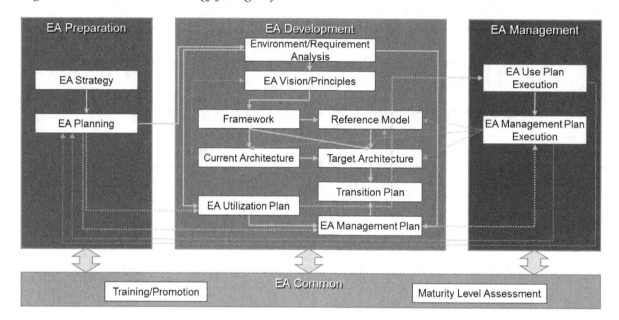

be architecture, transition plan, and management system development. In the *Management Phase*, activities related to communication with internal stakeholders in order to plan EA management are described.

Architectural Principles and Standards

The guiding principles of KGEA implementation has been characterized as *alignment*, *integration*, and *transformation*. Alignment refers to the defining and managing of the government IT strategy and IT investment allocation to each agency to be aligned through the KGEA. Integration refers to the connection and integration of the businesses, services and data of agencies so as to improve the efficiency of government process and the service provided to the taxpayers. Transformation refers to the continuous enhancement of the business process and IT based on KGEA.

In order to uphold these principles, MOPAS provided the relevant standards such as the GEA reference model, meta-model and maturity model,

on which each agency develops and manages its EA.

GEA reference model includes Performance Reference Model (PRM), Business Reference Model (BRM), Service Component Reference Model (SRM), Data Reference Model (DRM), and Technical Reference Model (TRM). PRM defines a framework to assists in visualizing cause-and-effects of IT investments and generating performance indicator on each IT projects for better decision making on strategic IT planning and day-to-day IT management. By providing a clear line-of-sight from IT project performance to business performance, PRM helps predict and manage the outcomes of IT investment. BRM is a model that classifies and defines business functions and related information. BRM provides standards to serve as a guideline for government and agencies in identifying redundancies or affinities in their business functions. SRM is a model that lists business/agency-independent service components, providing a unified and comprehensive component classification for the government's services to citizens. In the KGEA case, SRM combined with BRM plays a key role in promoting service

Figure 5. The meta-model for agency-level EA (initial version)

mandatory
optional

	Business	Application	Data	Technology	Security
Overview	CV1 Vision & Mission CV2 ITA principle CV3 Terminology				
Reference model	RV1 Business reference model, RV2 Service Component reference model, RV3 Data reference model, RV4 Technology reference model/standard profile. RV5 Performance reference model				
CEO/ CIO	BV1 Organization structure diagram/ description BV2 business structure diagram/ description	AV1 Application system structure diagram/ Description	DV1 Data structure diagram/description	TV1 Technology structure diagram/ Description	SV1 Security policy SV2 Security structure diagram/description
owner	BV3 Business relationship diagram/description BV4 Business function deployment /description	AV2 application system relationship diagram/ description AV3 application function deployment/description	DV2 Concept data relationship diagram/ description DV3 Data exchange description	TV2 Technology relationship diagram/description	SV3 Security relationship description
designer	BV5 Business process design/description	AV4 application function design/ description	DV4 Logical data model Data exchange design description	TV3 Technology design/description TV4 System performance design description	SV4 Management Security design description SV5 Physical security design description SV6 Technical security design description
builder	BV6 Business manual	AV5 Application program list	DV6 physical data model	TV5 Product list	SV7 security manual

integration and reuse by identifying redundant or correlated services among agencies. Specifically, Shared Service Component in the SRM facilitates a service component marketplace where all types of agencies develop, store, and distribute reusable application components. DRM is a model that classifies data and defines standard data structures to support development of Data Architecture (DA), and it promotes data standardization and reuse, as well as effective data management. TRM is a model that classifies and defines technologies and technical standards/specifications which provides a comprehensive list of unit technologies, technical standards, and commercial products. It also provides an IT resource classification to support agency's systematic IT resource management.

Finally, the GEA meta-model is a set of standard EA deliverables required by agencies to create and report for the sake of the government-wide EA success. It is a backbone model used to construct an agency's EA, by defining required architectural information and their relationships. Agencies can develop its own EA by defining architecture model or meta-model aligned with the agency's EA objectives, however, agencies' model must include the information required by the GEA Meta-model.

The initial meta-model (ver. 1.0) is defined by a 5x4 matrix of EA artifacts classified by the views and perspectives. For the views, the five domains of business, application, data, technology, and security are defined. For the perspectives, the four levels of CEO/CIO, manager, designer, and builder are defined (see Figure 5).

Although the initial meta-model helped agencies to adopt EA without much confusion, it had a weakness of directing every types of agencies to homogeneous EA artifacts without taking the heterogeneous requirements of regional agencies sufficiently into consideration.

Figure 6. The KGEA meta-model (ver. 2.0)

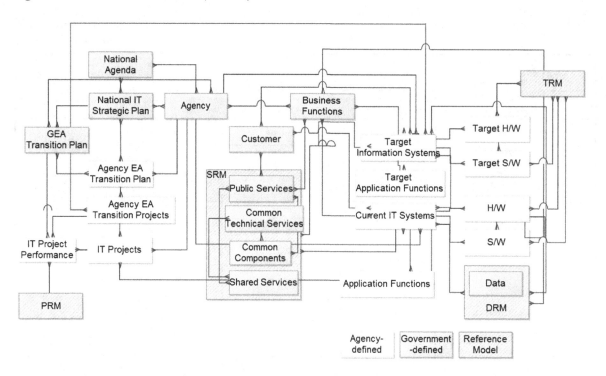

Therefore, along with KGEA program the meta-model ver. 2.0 has been developed to allow autonomy to agencies and require compliance to a set of common requirement of GEA. As seen in Figure 6, current meta-model is composed by attributes of agency's EA information, not specifying EA artifacts as in the initial model. Now each agency has flexibility to develop its own EA framework and model as long as it meets GEA meta-model requirements. In addition, the model provides a whole view of GEA in a single diagram overarching reference models, as-is and to-be architecture, government-wide EA components and agency-level EA components, thus making it easy for every EA stakeholders to be able to forge a common understanding.

Another distinctive deliverable of KGEA is government-wide to-be architecture patterns based on the *Public Services* derived from Service Reference Model (SRM). Public Service of SRM is a standard service catalog that classifies all governmental activities from the end user's point of

view in order to fulfill customer-centric service integration regardless of functional separation throughout agencies. To facilitate continuous improvement of the service to citizens, each Public Service has been defined to follow evolution patterns based on its level of data integrity and functional standardizability (Figure 7). Besides, other architectural components such as current IT projects, as-is information systems are attributed to related Public Service components. The relation along with architectural patterns becomes the reference for how duplicated IT services or IT projects should be integrated from the end user's viewpoint and which data can be merged. For instance in the target information system component of the meta-model, the government knowledge management system is targeted to the *unification* pattern in which every agency use a single system to share business knowledge, while national disaster alarm system is targeted to the *collaboration* pattern so that related orga-

Figure 7. The public service architectural patterns of KGEA

		Coordination	Integration	Unification
Data Integrity	**Integration**	- Although it is composed of multiple independent information systems, the data needed to deliver the administrative services are integrated.	- Although the common data of the agencies are utilized, the administrative service domain performs partially unified or connected business functions.	- The administrative service domain performs the unified business functions based on the common data of the agencies.
		Connection	**Cooperation**	**Collaboration**
	Connection	- Although it is composed of multiple independent information systems, the data needed to deliver the administrative services are integrated.	- Based on data sharing through the collaboration of agencies, the administrative service domain performs those business functions requiring the cooperation of the agencies at each business step.	- Based on data sharing through the collaboration of agencies, the administrative service domain performs the same business functions.
		Diversification	**Negotiation**	**Standardization**
	Distribution	- Multiple independent information systems and data needed to deliver the administrative service are operated independently.	- Although the independent data of the agencies are utilized, the administrative service domain can have similar business functions.	- Although there is no direct interchange of data concerning business execution among the agencies, the administrative service domain performs the same business function.
		Individual	Group	Whole

Business Function Standardization

nizations quickly arrange countermeasures against natural disasters.

Implementation and Use

Functionally, enterprise architecture explains how all agencies' Information Technology (IT) elements work together as a whole. When enterprise architecture needs to encompass the various perspectives and abstractions of different stakeholders within the enterprise, a System Of Systems (SOS) approach is required (Morganwalp & Sage, 2003). The resultant KGEA management system successfully addresses the complexity of nationwide IT projects, resources, and assets by incorporating hierarchical levels of the architecture. The KGEA has a two-level structure of agency-level EAs and government-wide EA that abstracts agency EA elements. Such a structure requires the government-wide EA to not only present common guidelines and a set of reference model but also to mandate the agencies to generate and manage the EA information to substantiate the model.

As shown in Figures 8 and 9, the contents of meta-model are stored in the KGEA repository by the input from agencies, and the government EA management system (GEAP, Government Enterprise Architecture Portal) provides processed information in a dashboard format in which combinations of meta-model elements are visualized. The comprehensive information from GEAP is used for identification of duplicated IT investments, current status information systems,

Figure 8. The operational structure of KGEA

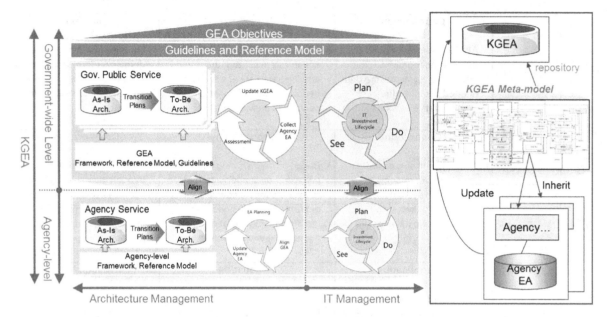

data and so forth. Each agency can directly input agency EA information through the portal website or install an Application Program Interface (API) that automatically updates whenever agency EA information is changed. Through such a process, the GEAP currently stores the installed base of 809 agencies' 13,700 information systems, 68,406 hardware devices, 62,157 software programs, and 12,619 IT projects throughout the public sector, all of which relation are linked to upper level IT agenda (www.geap.go.kr; Figure 6) Information is disseminated from the portal to not only top-level stakeholders for reviewing current state of national IT investments but also to agency-level practitioners for exploring opportunities of sharing IT services and related resources. For example, based on the information from GEAP, MOPAS evaluates every year IT investment plan submitted by the central administrative agencies to eliminate duplicated IT projects among agencies and suggest inter-agency collaboration to enhance service quality. In 2010, MOPAS proactively identified twenty areas of Public Services and ten types of data that should be integrated or merged, and

also funded agencies to execute integration initiatives. Even when an agency voluntarily identifies new e-government program, which can integrate siloed services, it should be reviewed whether it corresponds with the targeted service integration model guided by the to-be architecture of GEA.

FUTURE DIRECTION

Proceeding from what has been described above; the KGEA case can be summarized as having the following characteristics

- Strong leadership from the centralized IT governance and EA governance
- Mandatory adoption of agency EA, but autonomy in actual implementation
- No explicit incentives but institutional environments for utilization
- IT investment control based on the government-wide architectural information
- Central mechanism for service and data integration among agencies

Figure 9. The KGEA web portal (illustrative)

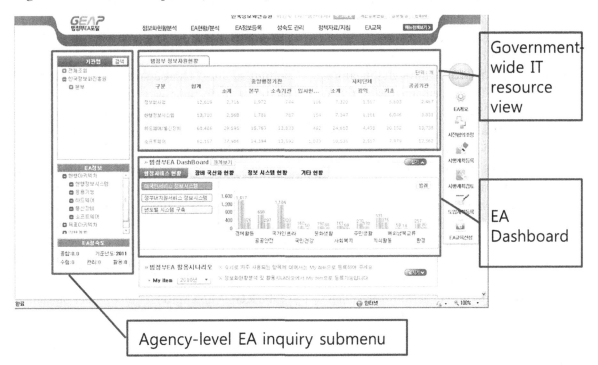

More focus on the redundancy management rather than interoperability

The recent trend of public sector EA is to ensure connected government (Saha, 2008). The KGEA case illustrates some of the features of a connected government; viewing the government in a holistic manner and as a single entity instead of a collection of piecemeal agencies or departments, with focus on delivering core government services in an efficient manner through an outcome oriented approach; the establishment of government-wide policies and standards, allowing autonomy to individual agencies and departments, and focusing on core government functions and business processes (Saha, 2009). We further believe that merely sharing the standard and guidelines does not lead to the foundation of connected government. That is, our case implies the implementation of GEA meta-model and its repository as well as continuous collaboration between agencies as crucial factors in realizing connected government.

On the other hand, the advantages of highly centralized architecture and governance raised controversial issue among researchers. While centralized development suggest more standardization and consequently a high level of interoperability, decentralized development suggest a faster development and acceptation of e-government at the local level (Aagesen, et al., 2011). In the KGEA case, there is potential weakness of relatively long lead time for a service to be actually deployed to citizens due to the process of review from top-level management. Another argument is that while centralized EA governance indeed facilitates the diffusion of data standards, as in the KGEA case resulting increase in nationwide interoperability; it might hinder efficient integration of public services. It is mainly because coordination might be more complex when using EA to integrate business applications across government organizations (Boh & Yellin, 2007). Although the KGEA model was useful in identifying the potential areas of public services, it is likely to require stronger forms of horizontal coordination to realize successful implementation of the desired service (DeSantics & Jackson, 1994).

From a practitioner's perspective, KGEA utilization needs to penetrate through the entire process of national IT management. Ideally, GEA must be utilized in all the lifecycle of IT investment management. Vertically integrated IT governance structure in Korea contributed to the efficient diffusion of EA, but at the same time, it constrains broad utilization throughout the administration. As in the CPIC (Capital Planning and Investment Control) system of the US Federal Government, the Office of Management and Budget (OMB) and the General Accounting Office (GAO) are integrated into IT governance in order to ensure consistency and leadership in performance management. On the contrary, in the KGEA case the budgeting department and the auditing department are not completely integrated into the governance structure. Therefore, the KGEA face challenges in adjusting EA governance structure and expanding the role of KGEA to the performance management throughout the IT investment life cycle, which needs to overcome boundary issues among departments

CONCLUSION

This chapter introduced the recent progress on GEA after a few years of effort by the Korean governments. A balance of such factors as top-down leadership, facilitating governance system, and workable architecture model, standard and supporting information systems led to the present accomplishment of KGEA implementation and utilization. Overall, the KGEA seems to be passing through a transition phase as it evolves from technical interoperability to the interoperability of the government services. However, several challenges remain to be overcome before reaching the next level.

Finally, along with some criticisms towards EA by practitioners that EA is failing to deliver the promised benefits (Lagerstrom, et al., 2011), Gartner predicts that GEA has just passed the bottom of the "Thorough of Disillusionment" phase in their famous Hype Cycle (Gartner, 2010). Under the circumstances, EA practitioners should be able to break away from the notion that EA is just 'something IT guys do.' As many previous studies have pointed out, the change management program should be implemented via a stakeholder's approach, and we have to continuously persuade stakeholders of the value of EA while minimizing the resistance (Isomäki & Liimatainen, 2008; Biggert, et al., 2009). Our future work should be the persistent advancement of the KGEA and introduction of other outstanding practices that present tangible outcomes and business values of EA.

REFERENCES

Aagesen, G., Veenstra, A. F., Janssen, M., & Krogstie, J. (2011). The entanglement of enterprise architecture and IT-governance: The cases of Norway and the Netherlands. In *Proceedings of the 44th Hawaii International Conference on System Sciences*. Hawaii, HI: System Sciences.

Armour, F. (2003). A UML-driven enterprise architecture case study. In *Proceedings of the 36th Hawaii International Conference on System Sciences*. Hawaii, HI: System Sciences.

Biggert, T., & Suryavanshi, K. (2008). Using enterprise architecture to transform service delivery: The U.S. federal government's human resources line of business. In Saha, P. (Ed.), *Advances in Government Enterprise Architecture*. Hershey, PA: IGI Global. doi:10.4018/978-1-60566-068-4.ch014

Boh, W., & Yellin, D. (2007). Using enterprise architecture standards in managing information technology. *Journal of Management Information Systems, 23*, 163–207. doi:10.2753/MIS0742-1222230307

DeSanctis, G., & Jackson, B. M. (1994). Coordination of information technology management: Team-based structures and computer-based communication systems. *Journal of Management Information Systems, 10*(4), 85–110.

Hjort-Madsen, K. (2006). Enterprise architecture implementation and management: A case study on interoperability. In *Proceedings of the 39th Annual Hawaii International Conference on System Sciences (HICSS 39)*. Kauai, HI: System Sciences.

Hjort-Madsen, K. (2007). Institutional patterns of enterprise architecture adoption in government. *Transforming Government: People. Process and Policy, 1*(4), 333–349.

Hjort-Madsen, K., & Burkard, J. (2006). When enterprise architecture meets government: An institutional case study analysis. *Journal of Enterprise Architecture, 2*(1), 11–25.

Hjort-Madsen, K., & Gotze, J. (2004). Enterprise architecture in government – Towards a multi-level framework for managing IT in government. In *Proceedings of European Conference on e-Government*, (pp. 365-374). Dublin, Ireland: ECEG.

Isomäki, H., & Liimatainen, K. (2008). Challenges of government enterprise architecture work – Stakeholders' views. In M. A. Wimmer, H. J. Scholl, & E. Ferro (Eds.), *International Conference on Electronic Government*, (vol 5184), (pp. 364–374). Berlin, Germany: Springer.

Janssen, M., & Hjort-Madsen, K. (2007). Analyzing enterprise architecture in national governments: The cases of Denmark and The Netherlands. In *Proceedings of the 40th Annual Hawaii International Conference on System Sciences*, (p. 218a). Hawaii, HI: System Sciences.

Lagerström, R., Sommestad, T., Buschle, M., & Ekstedt, M. (2011). Enterprise architecture management's impact on information technology success. In *Proceedings of the 44th Hawaii International Conference on System Sciences.* Hawaii, HI: System Sciences.

Liimataine, K., Hoffman, M., & Jukka, H. (2007). *Overview of enterprise architecture work in 15 countries.* Helsinki, Finland: Finnish Enterprise Architecture Research Project.

Morganwalp, J., & Andrew, P. (2003). A system of systems focused enterprise architecture framework and an associated architecture development process. In *Information, Knowledge, Systems Management* (*Vol. 3*, pp. 87–105). Thousand Oaks, CA: Sage.

NIA (Ed.). (2010). *Information white paper 2010.* Seoul, South Korea: NIA.

Pulkkinen, M. (2006). Systemic management of architectural decisions in enterprise architecture planning: Four dimensions and three abstraction levels. In *Proceedings of the 39th Hawaii International Conference on System Sciences 2006.* Hawaii, HI: System Sciences.

Ross, J. W. (2003). Creating a strategic IT architecture competency: Learning in stages. *MIS Quarterly Executive, 2*(1), 31–43.

Saha, P. (Ed.). (2008). *Advances in government enterprise architecture.* Hershey, PA: IGI Global. doi:10.4018/978-1-60566-068-4

Saha, P. (2009). Architecting the connected government: Practices and innovations in Singapore. In *Proceedings of the 3rd International Conference on Theory and Practice of Electronic Governance (ICEGOV2009)*. Bogota, Colombia: ICEGOV.

Scott, W. R. (1995). *Institutions and organizations.* Thousand Oaks, CA: Sage.

Weill, P., & Ross, J. W. (2005). A matrixed approach to designing IT governance. *Sloan Management Review, 46*(2), 26–34.

ENDNOTE

[1] Agencies that have not adopted EA should submit the information to GEAP mandatorily by the e-government act.

Chapter 5

Government Enterprise Architecture:
Towards the Inter-Connected Government in the Kingdom of Saudi Arabia

Ali S. AlSoma
Ministry of Communications and Information Technology, Saudi Arabia

Hasan M. Hourani
Ministry of Communications and Information Technology, Saudi Arabia

Dato' Mohd Salleh Masduki
Ministry of Communications and Information Technology, Saudi Arabia

ABSTRACT

The growth of ICT-mediated services in the private and public sectors demands that organizations become more focused in delivering efficient services to well-informed and demanding consumers. Governments, being very large enterprises, are increasingly under pressure to optimize and align their Information and Communications Technology (ICT) strategies and resources to support the business of government. The Kingdom of Saudi Arabia responds to this challenge by adopting the use of Enterprise Architecture (EA) to transform traditional government services into eGovernment services or eServices. Yesser Enterprise Level Architecture Framework (Y-ELAF) is an Enterprise Architecture Framework that is an adaptation of the industry-recognized framework, The Open Group Architecture Framework (TOGAF) Version 9, modified to fit the government environment of Saudi Arabia. This chapter describes the seven iterative phases of Y-ELAF to develop the Enterprise Architecture of a government agency, the outcomes, and lessons learned.

DOI: 10.4018/978-1-4666-1824-4.ch005

INTRODUCTION

Since the 1950s, when computers became commercially viable, governments have utilized their data processing capabilities to resolve issues on repetitive activities such as local administrative and accounting system. Governments, as early adopters of computer systems, become increasingly dependent on these systems to automate certain processes and functions, and as this dependence increases, the situation becomes more complex in terms of systems that are isolated, dispersed, incompatible, as well as hard and expensive to sustain and maintain. As technology continued to mature, different approaches were introduced as a way to deal with the increasing complexities. Such approaches included Client-Server Architecture, Distributed Processing, Distributed Databases, etc. These approaches also introduced their own inherent complexities and issues. Technology advances, particularly the Internet and mobile technologies, coupled with the increasing demand of more competitive and efficient services and products, result in a more demanding and a well-informed clientele—the Customer is King. More focus was needed on becoming more and more service-oriented and technological developments continued to change and mold to fulfill the ever-increasing demands. Great emphasis was placed on Service Oriented Architecture (SOA) as a way to become more service-oriented and more resilient to change. For large enterprises and conglomerates, the challenges were multifold. The enterprise could no longer operate as a set of isolated functions. The enterprise had to function like an ecosystem where business, technology, infrastructure, people, and the environment all work in harmony. This was the birth of Enterprise Architecture (EA). Some Governments, being large enterprises, saw the potential for a long term, more organized and well planned approach for fast tracking e-transformation initiatives through Enterprise Architecture across the public sector.

The need to optimize the use of ICT (Information and Communication Technology) resources to support the business of government has become increasingly critical. Governments, large corporations, and ICT industry associations need to use Enterprise Architecture to align ICT, government business processes, and other components required to deliver government services efficiently and effectively. In order to unify and standardize approaches to Enterprise Architecture development, several frameworks have evolved over the past few years.

The Saudi eGovernment Program (Yesser) opted to develop its own EA framework called Y-ELAF (Yesser Enterprise Level Architecture Framework) based on TOGAF Version 9 (The Open Group Architecture Framework Version 9). Y-ELAF provides Yesser with a set of tools to develop Enterprise Architectures for agencies in a rigorous and repeatable fashion. The development of Enterprise Architectures for agencies using Y-ELAF helps agencies to document their eGovernment Transformation Strategic Plans in a systematic way. Y-ELAF is a comprehensive Enterprise Architecture Framework containing all the tools required for developing an Enterprise Architecture including reference architecture models, development guidelines, checklists, templates and the use of a common vocabulary to name a few. The use of Y-ELF has greatly enhanced the success of implementing eGovernment projects in the Kingdom of Saudi Arabia. This chapter introduces Y-ELAF as the framework adopted in the government of Saudi Arabia to address the need to align ICT resources with the business of providing efficient and effective online services (eServices) to the nation.

WHAT IS eGOVERNMENT?

The definition of the term eGovernment ranges from "… refers to the use by government agencies of information technologies (such as Wide Area

Networks, the Internet, and mobile computing) that have the ability to transform relations with citizens, businesses, and other arms of government." (World Bank, 2011) to "... the use of technology to enhance the access to and delivery of government services to benefit citizens, business partners, and employees." (Deloitte & Touché, 2003). The common theme behind these definitions is that eGovernment involves the automation of existing paper-based government procedures. It will prompt new styles of leadership, new ways of debating and deciding on strategies through public eParticipation, new ways of transacting the business of government, new ways of listening to citizens and communities (again through eParticipation), and new ways of organizing and delivering information and public services. Ultimately, eGovernment aims to enhance access to and delivery of government (i.e. public) services to benefit citizens, businesses and the government itself. More importantly, it aims to help strengthen government's drive towards effective governance and increased transparency to better manage a nation's social and economic resources for all aspects of development.

eGOVERNMENT IMPLEMENTATION IN SAUDI ARABIA

The genesis of eGovernment in the Kingdom of Saudi Arabia (KSA) came with the Royal Decree 7/B/33181 to develop and implement the Kingdom's eGovernment Strategy and Action Plan with the goal of achieving benefits for the whole country by:

- providing better government services to individuals, businesses and government users, thus raising satisfaction with government services and increasing quality of life;
- improving the efficiency and effectiveness of the public sector, thus decreasing cost,

increasing productivity, creating a more business-friendly environment, and leading to economic growth and higher Gross Domestic Product; and

- spreading information, knowledge, and use of eServices, thus contributing to the establishment of an information society in Saudi Arabia and supporting society's advancement.

The development and implementation of the eGovernment Strategy and Action Plan is led by Yesser, an organ of the Ministry of Communications and Information Technology; with the collaboration of the Ministry of Finance and the Communications and Information Technology Commission, Kingdom of Saudi Arabia. Yesser's primary role is that of an enabler and facilitator of the individual eGovernment projects implemented by the various government agencies (eGovernment Program, 2005).

The Saudi eGovernment program has successfully implemented its phase-one projects and is currently entering phase two covering the period of year 2011-2015.

ISSUES AND CHALLENGES

As mentioned in the introduction, governments were early adopters of computing to resolve local business process challenges such as accounting, administration, statistical analysis, and reporting. Naturally this perpetuates the organizational culture of protecting turf—ownership of information, ownership of procedures and processes, protecting the boundaries of organizational mandate, and so on—leading to the development of silos or islands of automation.

Government agencies, like other organizations are composed of departments and units performing specific functions very much like pieces of a jigsaw puzzle that can only form the intended beautiful picture shown on the box cover when correctly assembled to make a whole. Jigsaw puzzle pieces has structure and will only fit one way to form the picture shown in the box. Similarly, application systems will only contribute effectively towards an optimized discharge of an organization's responsibilities and functions if they conform to a structure that aligns them to the business processes of the organization. In order to meet the challenges of aligning organizational components, governments, large corporations, and ICT industry associations developed various systematic frameworks to help align application systems with business needs. These are known today as Enterprise Architecture frameworks.

WHAT IS ENTERPRISE ARCHITECTURE?

Enterprise Architecture is the process of translating business vision and strategy into effective enterprise change by creating, communicating, and improving the key principles and models that describe the enterprise's future state and enable its evolution towards realizing that future state.

A well-defined Enterprise Architecture can help a government agency to align its ICT resources to its Strategic Plan of enabling citizen services through these ICT resources. It helps in cutting costs and complexity, and enabling business flexibility and process optimization. Enterprise Architecture can improve ICT agility by adopting standardization, consistency, and scalability, while at the same time providing increased security and compliance. The Enterprise Architecture framework is a promising tool for implementing integrated eGovernment initiatives and has been thoroughly tested and deployed in various countries. EA addresses most systems architectural issues giving rise to the following benefits:

a. Improves business flexibility, and at the same time, improves business processes and system optimization.
b. Helps reduce process, system, and infrastructure costs and complexity.
c. Helps ensure enterprise security and compliance.
d. Drives standardization, consistency, and scalability.

Thus, the primary objective of EA development is to align ICT with the business of the agency, thereby optimizing the service delivery capability of the agency (eGovernment Program, 2009e).

WHAT IS NOT ENTERPRISE ARCHITECTURE?

Like most terms, Enterprise Architecture may mean different things to different people. For some it is a set of rules. For others, it is a logical and technical design, and for some others, it is a methodology for achieving an effective design. Nevertheless, all EA development projects have a common goal—*to create order out of chaos*. However, achieving this goal is easier said than done, especially since Enterprise Architecture must provide structure and efficiency, and at the same time remain flexible to accommodate changing business strategies, functions, rules, and components. Sometimes, the intent of Enterprise Architecture is misunderstood:

a. **EA is not business strategy**: Business leaders and senior executives define a business strategy, and it articulates the strategic business goals and directions of the organization as a whole. The business plan turns strategies into specific tactical plans designed to achieve the strategic goals. The EA team must leverage the strategic guidance from the business strategy and specific tactical guidance from the business plans to guide their EA efforts overall.

b. **EA is not ICT strategic planning**: EA and ICT strategic planning are complementary efforts that must be coordinated and integrated, but they are not the same. While a CIO most often leads ICT strategic planning, EA teams should serve as an advisor into ICT strategic planning, along with the CTO, senior ICT staff, and business leaders and users.

c. **EA is not ICT governance**: ICT governance is composed of processes with the inputs, outputs, roles and responsibilities that are inherent in a process definition. ICT governance is the process that ensures the effective and efficient use of ICT in enabling an organization to achieve its goals.

d. **EA is not program management**: Program management is the coordinated planning, management and execution of multiple related projects that are directed toward the same strategic, business or organizational objectives. EA is a planning discipline, while program management is an execution discipline. EA is responsible for defining the future state of the enterprise, analyzing the gaps between the current state and the future state, and developing the standards and guidelines that support the realization of the future state.

e. **EA is not portfolio management**: Portfolio management is the processes, governance, and tools used to plan, create, access, balance, and communicate the execution of the ICT portfolio. Portfolio management techniques can be applied to the application portfolio, the infrastructure portfolio, the project portfolio, the ICT investment portfolio, or any of these in combination.

f. **EA is not business process management**: Business process management is a systematic approach to improving the way an enterprise does business by analyzing the strategic goals of the enterprise, then aligning the stakeholder interest with shared process performance objectives. As part of the common requirements vision process, EA provides the analysis of the strategy and identifies the most critical strategic imperatives.

g. **EA is not performance management**: Performance management is the combination of management methodologies, metrics, and ICT that enable users to define, monitor, and optimize results and outcomes to achieve personal or departmental objectives while enabling alignment with strategic objectives across multiple organizational levels. EA teams must participate in performance management efforts relating to critical business processes. This will allow them to track key business metrics that demonstrate the business value that EA is delivering.

h. **EA is not implementation:** Enterprise architects do not dictate implementation details for the entire organization or for specific practice areas. EA provides the foundational principles, guidelines, standards, and constraints that enable implementation teams to make better decisions.

i. **EA is not a technology or application inventory**: Many organizations fall into a trap of believing that EA is a map of all their technologies and applications and/or that EA is solely about technology. EA development is a much broader process that is directly reflecting the business vision and strategy, and represents people, processes, organization, information, and technology that are critical to the business strategy.

j. **EA is not change management**: Change management is a structured approach to change that encompasses individuals, teams, and organizations, with the objective of facilitating the human side of change. EA provides the strategic context for the change through the common requirements vision or some similar vehicle, and it provides the view of the future state from a process, organization, information, and technology perspective.

EA must support, facilitate, enable, and collaborate with all of these efforts to reach the mutually defined future state.

THE TRANSFORMATION APPROACH

Development of the Enterprise Architecture is a complex process as ICT systems development moves from vision to implementation to operation. The process is far from linear—it is a mistake to view the process as one that moves from point A to point B. The use of Enterprise Architecture frameworks to model ICT implementation projects is a continuous process that aims to ensure continuous enhancement of the value of ICT.

Enterprise Architecture is about business transformation enablement and its program to facilitate change. It provides a disciplined method that will allow the transformation agenda to move forward; providing design and alignment tools to enable rapid change in business processes and the infrastructure that supports them. As such, the Business Transformation Enablement Program is not about producing a solution for the transformation of all of the Government's business processes and information systems. Rather, it is developing a standardized means by which such solutions can be planned, designed, and cost-effectively implemented by departments and agencies. It supports more rigor and due diligence at the project level, and increases the likelihood that economies of scale, adaptability, and enhanced productivity will result from business transformation across the full spectrum of government operations. This makes the business of planning, designing, managing, communicating, and implementing business transformation itself a more efficient process.

ENTERPRISE ARCHITECTURE FRAMEWORK IN SAUDI eGOVERNMENT

In order to meet the challenges of nurturing the implementation of eGovernment in Saudi Arabia, Yesser developed a customized EA Framework called Y-ELAF based on the industry recognized Open Group Architecture Framework Version 9 (TOGAF Version 9, 2011). Enterprise Architecture developments in government agencies are carried out by Yesser's internal consulting arm, the Yesser Consulting Group (YCG). The following sections introduce Y-ELAF, the EA framework used in the Kingdom of Saudi Arabia to develop the eGovernment Transformation Strategic Plans in government agencies (eGovernment Program, 2009d).

INTRODUCTION TO Y-ELAF (YESSER ENTERPRISE LEVEL ARCHITECTURE FRAMEWORK)

Figure 1 represents a high-level outline of the Y-ELAF Enterprise Architecture development process (Yesser Consulting Group, 2009).

Based on an agency's request for assistance to develop its eGovernment Transformation Strategic Plan, Yesser provides EA consultants from the YCG to perform an EA development consultancy engagement. The consulting team then uses the agency's Enterprise Strategy (Vision, Mission, Goals, and Objectives) plus stakeholder interviews to determine the baseline EA of the agency. The outcome of this phase of the EA development engagement is a comprehensive baseline EA and Architecture Vision to be used in the development of the agency's target EA. The iterative process of developing the target EA across all architecture segments—Business, Applications, Data, and Technology—provides a robust target EA from which a gap analysis between what is desired and what is currently available can be performed with

Figure 1. Y-ELAF iterative EA development process (source: Y-ELAF EA Development Toolkit, 2010)

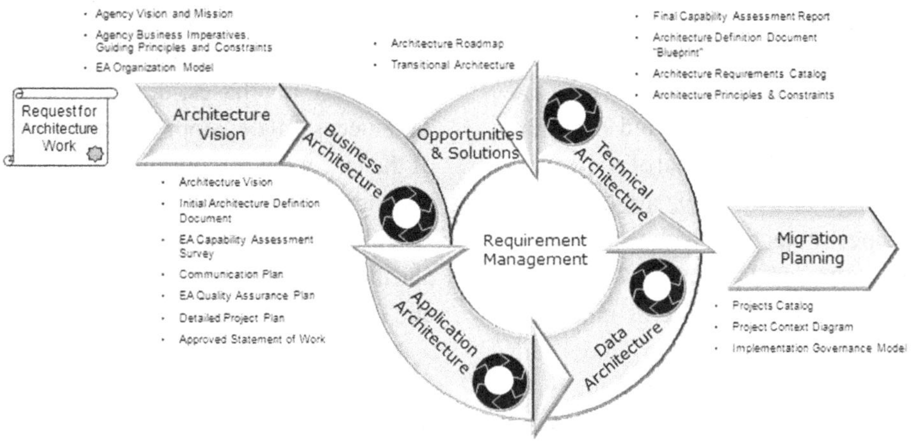

confidence. Based on the gap analysis a detailed architecture roadmap providing transitional Enterprise Architectures, implementation roadmap, and governance will then be developed providing the agency with a clear and achievable eGovernment Transformation Strategic Plan.

WHAT IS Y-ELAF?

The Yesser Enterprise Level Architecture Framework provides a collection of development processes, best practices, standards, tools, deliverables list, and templates to assist in the creation of the Enterprise Architecture for an agency.

Y-ELAF comprises the following:

a.   Common vocabulary, models, and taxonomy.
b.   Processes, principles, strategies, and tools.
c.   Reference architectures and models.
d.   Guidance, best practices, guidelines, checklist.
e.   Architecture Development Methodology.
f.   Enterprise Architecture deliverables and its templates.
g.   Enterprise Architecture deliverable Samples.
h.   Enterprise Architecture Consulting RFP.

i.   Enterprise Architecture Development Toolkit.

Utilizing an Enterprise Architecture framework streamlines the process for creating and maintaining Enterprise Architectures and enables an agency to leverage the value of architecture best practices. It also helps to maintain consistency throughout the various Enterprise Architectures developed for the Saudi government.

WHY IS Y-ELAF REQUIRED?

Development of an Enterprise Architecture is a complex task as it involves various domain expertise and skills, a lot of collaboration and a need to address various types of enterprise issues. An Enterprise Architecture team may lose project objectives during EA development due to various project issues such as lack of current architecture information, non-availability of business or application architect resources, difficulty of understanding current business issues, and so on. Enterprise Architects may be too focused in the study and understanding of current situations that they stray from the reasons for undertaking the EA development project in the first place. Moreover, it is difficult to build consistent and repeatable Enterprise Architecture framework from multiple resources for multiple organizations.

A number of generalized EA frameworks exist in the industry such as TOGAF and Zachman Enterprise Framework, with the goal of addressing the basic challenge of assessing, aligning, and organizing business objectives with technical requirements and strategies. There are also a number of EA frameworks focused on specific industries such as eTOM (enhanced Telecom Operations Map) for the telecom industry. Each framework possesses different strengths and weaknesses; making it difficult to utilize any one existing framework that is ideal for all situations and meets government organizational requirements. To overcome these challenges, Yesser developed the Yesser Enterprise Level Architecture Framework (Y-ELAF) based on the industry recognized EA framework, TOGAF Version 9. This framework streamlines architecture development activities and makes the development process consistent, repeatable and independent of execution resources.

HOW IS Y-ELAF USED?

Developing Enterprise Architecture from scratch is a demanding task, thus EA frameworks are created to simplify the process and guide an architect through all areas of architecture development. Yesser uses Y-ELAF for Enterprise Architecture development in areas such as scope definition, project planning, process, review, guidelines, document templates, and list of deliverables. For example:

a.   Enterprise Architecture deliverables format (with help of templates).
b.   Enterprise Architecture Tasks Project Plan (with help of development methodologies).
c.   Guidelines for development of deliverables.
d.   Checklist for artifacts review.

Enterprise Architecture describes the interrelationships between business processes, information, applications, and underlying infrastructure for an agency, and provides best practices for technology purchases, design, and deployment. The successful development and implementation of the target EA is a highly collaborative process and depends on the strength of the Enterprise Architecture framework, governance structure and the commitment of the participants to its goals and guiding principles.

Y-ELAF COMPONENTS

Y-ELAF comprises the following core components:

a.   **Project Charter** to document the project purpose and scope, project objectives and success criteria, list of deliverables, stakeholder information, and communications plan comprising the communications matrix, responsibility table, escalation process, and the approvals matrix.
b.   **Detailed Project Plan** to document project tasks, dependencies, duration, resource allocation, and so on.
c.   **Architecture Vision Document** to show agency business drivers, business goals, principles, and the high-level conceptual target EA.
d.   **Architecture Requirements Document** containing the EA requirements information, and EA functional and non-functional requirements.
e.   **Architecture Definition Document** providing the EA model (business, application, data, and technology architectures) for the baseline and target Enterprise Architectures.
f.   **Architecture Roadmap and Project Initiatives Catalog** to show the EA migration roadmap, the catalog of projects to be

initiated, and projects high-level schedule and costs.

BENEFITS OF USING Y-ELAF

The Yesser Enterprise Level Application Framework (Y-ELAF) provides significant value to an agency, including:

a. Continuous alignment of ICT with business needs.
b. Improved Return On Investment (ROI) through better execution of the business strategy using ICT, and more efficient utilization of ICT resources.
c. Leveraging technology to create new business strategies.
d. Using a single architecture framework to combine services, ICT and architectures.

For an enterprise architect, the Y-ELAF provides a number of key benefits.

a. The Y-ELAF's practical approach allows the architects to focus on the architecture and not be bogged down with excessive processes and artifacts, or creating their own processes.
b. The agile nature of the Y-ELAF enables continuous improvements and adaptation to changing business conditions and new technologies.
c. The Y-ELAF uses industry EA concepts and terminology and leverages the best of other frameworks.
d. Access to a set of best practices, tool sets, templates, reference architectures, and tailored architecture processes around specific problems (such as developing a consulting RFP) will significantly reduce the time required to develop enterprise-level architectures.

DIFFERENCES BETWEEN TOGAF AND Y-ELAF

Y-ELAF was developed using TOGAF V9 as the base. This adaptation was needed to fit the TOGAF framework into the Saudi government operating environment. Table 1 shows the differences between TOGAF and Y-ELAF. The main differences are in the manner that each of the EA development phases are executed.

ENTERPRISE ARCHITECTURE DEVELOPMENT USING Y-ELAF

Transforming a government agency's traditional services into online transactional services is a multidisciplinary endeavor, involving strategic planning, government process reform, business planning, project management, and systems development. Enterprise Architecture is used to define and scope the eGovernment initiatives and projects needed to enable effective implementation of an agency's business plans and to ensure that all new information systems contribute effective results in the increasingly integrated government business and technology environment. The architecture of an enterprise is the set of models that represent and describe it. Enterprise models serve as a basis for analysis, and aiding managers to determine the changes needed to achieve agency goals and objectives. They act as blueprints to guide and coordinate the efforts of those engaged in building new enterprises or changing existing ones.

Globally, Enterprise Architecture has been promoted as a key tool for the transformation and modernization of government as part of eGovernment implementation programs. Enterprise Architecture offers a model that connects ICT strategy to business objectives, and creates a formal communication structure to support the attainment of a common vision. The success of this highly collaborative process will depend on the strength of its governance structure and

Table 1. Differences between TOGAF and Y-ELAF

Comparison Items		TOGAF	Y-ELAF
1	Framework Phases	1. One Time Preliminary Phase 2. Requirement Management 3. Phase A: Architecture Vision 4. Phase B: Business Architecture 5. Phase C: Information Systems Architectures 6. Phase D: Technology Architecture 7. Phase E: Opportunities & Solutions 8. Phase F: Migration Planning 9. Phase G: Implementation Governance 10. Phase H: Architecture Change Management	1. Optional Pre-assessment/Assessment Phase 2. Phase A: Architecture Vision 3. Phase B: Business Architecture 4. Phase C: Information Systems Architectures 5. Phase D: Technology Architecture 6. Phase E: Opportunities & Solutions 7. Phase F: Strategic Roadmap and Migration Planning 8. Phase G: Implementation Governance
2	Preliminary Phase	1. Prepares an organization to undertake successful Enterprise Architecture projects. 2. Defines the organization context and governing structure to carry Enterprise Architecture projects	1. Optional Pre-assessment / Assessment Phase 2. Defines the scope of work and resources required for the development of the Enterprise Architecture. 3. Identifies and measure the organization's maturity level, strengths and weaknesses.
3	Vision Phase	1. Does not use specific project management methodology or approach to manage Enterprise Architecture engagements. 2. Delivers an approved statement of architecture work. 3. Establishes communications plan	1. Adopts a tailored PMI based project management process to manage Enterprise Architecture engagements. 2. Delivers a project charter for the architecture work. 3. Establishes a detailed project plan that defines several sub-plans including project schedule, communication plan and others as per PMI standards.
4	Requirement Management Phase	A separate process to manage architecture requirements throughout the phase of the ADM cycle	Requirements are managed implicitly within each phase of the Y-ELAF framework
5	Change Management Phase	Separate process to ensure that changes to architecture are managed in a controlled manner	Integrated implicitly within the Implementation Governance phase
6	RFPs templates	NA	Adopts tailored RFP templates that are used to minimize implementation risks.

the commitment of the participants to its goals and guiding principles. In developing Enterprise Architecture for an agency, Yesser (through its consulting arm, the Yesser Consulting Group—YCG) uses a streamlined process to perform EA development:

a. **Phases**: YCG's approach enables many phases of the EA development project to be run concurrently to reduce the time associated with creating architectures of various scopes. The process is highly iterative because architectures are developed and refined using feedback from stakeholders.

b. **Tasks** in each phase use prescriptive guidance for performing them in a practical and most efficient manner by leveraging YCG's EA Repository of reusable architecture artifacts.

c. **Deliverable Artifacts Created in Each Phase**: Individual models and diagrams provide a simplified documentation approach

Figure 2. Enterprise architecture development activities (source: Y-ELAF EA Development Toolkit, 2010)

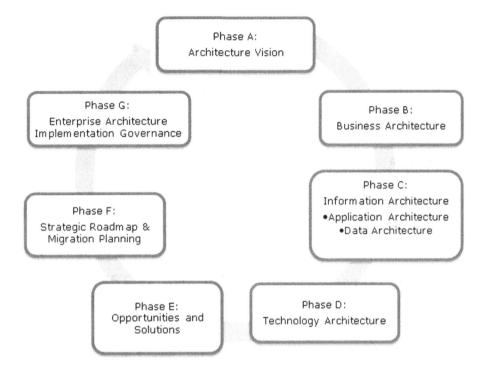

with sufficient detail without requiring excessive overheads associated with creating documentation.

From the base process, YCG creates tailored EA processes to target a specific segment, i.e. a domain architecture development based requirement. These tailored EA processes use the basic structure and phases of the base EA process; and they are further streamlined by emphasizing the critical path for a given architecture engagement, and using prescriptive guidance, case studies, sample artifacts, and applicable reference models for executing these critical tasks and for creating key artifacts.

YCG develops an agency's Enterprise Architecture in phases and iteratively to fine tune the agreed target EA using feedback from stakeholders. Often the EA development engagement starts with a pre-assessment and capability maturity assessment to understand at a high-level the structure and maturity of the agency. Figure

2 shows diagrammatically the various phases of the EA engagement. As implied by the circular movement of these phases, the development of an agency's EA is an iterative process (Yesser Consulting Group, 2009).

PRE-ASSESSMENT PHASE

The objective of this phase is to determine the maturity level, strengths and weaknesses, and other factors to be used for determining the scope and resources needed to perform the EA development engagement. Figure 3 shows the inputs, activities and outputs of this phase (Yesser Consulting Group, 2009).

The following Y-ELAF guidelines are used for the Pre-Assessment Phase:

a. Pre-Assessment exercise should be completed within a short duration.

Figure 3. Pre-assessment activities (source: Y-ELAF EA Development Toolkit, 2010)

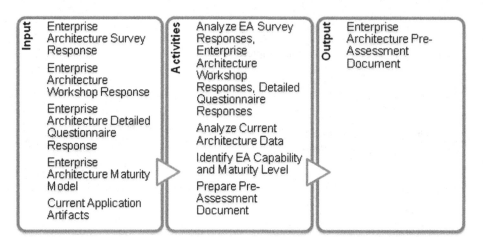

b.   Development of any baseline architecture artifacts is out of scope for Pre-Assessment phase.

c.   The Enterprise Architecture scope should be clearly identified (or validated) as part of the Pre-Assessment.

d.   Critical business processes and related information systems and technology should be Pre-Assessed.

e.   The business units for the Pre-Assessment phase must be identified accordingly and the participation of all critical stakeholders is mandatory.

f.   Recommendations should be provided at a high-level and should be categorized based on criticality.

g.   Identification of projects (or project details) for implementation of recommendations is out of scope for the Pre-Assessment phase.

h.   Existing maturity models may be adopted and customized according to the needs of the organization to avoid delays in getting the organization's agreement of the maturity model.

PHASE A: ENTERPRISE ARCHITECTURE VISION DEVELOPMENT

The objective of this phase is to develop a high-level view of the target Enterprise Architecture that the agency aspires towards. The outcome of this phase reports on information such as the agency's business drivers, goals, and the conceptual target EA. Figure 4 shows the input, activities and output of this phase (Yesser Consulting Group, 2009).

The Enterprise Architecture Vision development guidelines are as follows:

a.   The purpose of the Enterprise Architecture Vision is to agree at the outset what the desired outcome should be for the Enterprise Architecture, so that architects can then focus on the critical areas to validate feasibility.

b.   The Enterprise Architecture Vision provides a high-level and informal view of the Target Enterprise Architecture that the agency aspires to. Depending on the scope and requirements of the architecture, the Enterprise Architecture Vision may provide target architecture details, but it serves as a directional guideline to assist in the architectural planning and decision-making

Figure 4. Enterprise architecture vision development (source: Y-ELAF EA Development Toolkit, 2010)

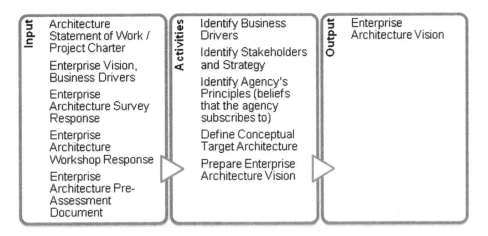

of the Target Architecture. It also needs to describe how the new capability will meet the business goals and strategic objectives, and address the stakeholder concerns when implemented.

c. The Enterprise Architecture Vision typically covers at a high level, the breadth of scope identified for the project.

d. Principles represent the highest level of guidance for ICT planning and decision-making. Principles are simple statements of an organization's beliefs about how it wants to deploy ICT infrastructure and services over the long term, and are derived from business goals and vision.

e. Principles should be few in number, future-oriented, and endorsed and championed by the agency's senior management. They provide the organization a foundation for making architecture and planning decisions, framing policies, procedures, and standards, and supporting the resolution of contradictory situations.

PHASE B: BUSINESS ARCHITECTURE DEVELOPMENT

The objective of this phase is to develop the Business Architecture model that will be used for understanding the baseline Business Architecture and the development of the target Business Architecture.

The agency's Business Architecture aligns its operating model, strategies and objectives with ICT. It also creates a business case for ICT transformations and provides a business-centric view of the enterprise from a functional perspective.

This part of the Y-ELAF provides the following key areas of information about the agency:

a. **Business Strategy**: Key agency business requirements, objectives, strategies, key performance indicators, business risks, and the agency's operating model.

b. **Business Function**: The key agency services, processes, and capabilities that will be affected by the Enterprise Architecture effort.

c. **Business Organization**: The high-level organizational structures, business roles (internal audiences, external customers, and

Figure 5. Baseline business architecture development (source: Y-ELAF EA Development Toolkit, 2010)

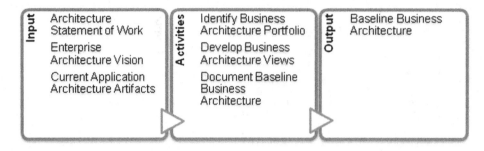

Figure 6. Target business architecture development (source: Y-ELAF EA Development Toolkit, 2010)

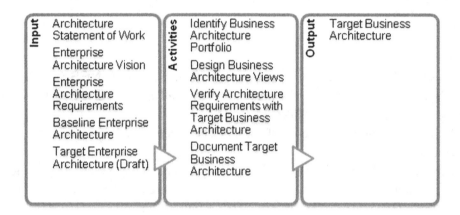

partners), the decision-making process, and the agency's budget information.

Baseline Business Architecture Development

The Baseline Business Architecture describes the current organizational structure of the agency, roles and responsibilities chart, business requirements, PMO details and so on. The Baseline Business Architecture inputs, activities, outputs are shown in Figure 5 (Yesser Consulting Group, 2009).

The Baseline Business Architecture development guidelines are:

a. Document baseline process models.
b. Identify baseline Business Architecture stakeholders.

c. Document current Key Performance Indictors.
d. Document current project management methodologies.

Target Business Architecture Development

The Target Business Architecture defines the target organization structure, roles and responsibilities chart, business requirements, roles and responsibilities, PMO details, etc. Figure 6 shows the inputs, activities and outputs of the Target Business Architecture (Yesser Consulting Group, 2009).

The Target Business Architecture development guidelines are as follows:

a. Design the target business service processes with industry standard notations.

b. Prioritize target service process maps.

c. Create Architecture Definition Document.

d. Establish key performance indicators.

e. Create Business Scenarios.

f. Identify the human and ICT actors to solve the identified business problems.

g. Structure information captured in such a way that it can be reused later.

h. Stay focused on what needs to be accomplished and the means of achieving it.

i. Use the help of domain experts to uncover critical business rules.

j. Check if the Business Architecture conforms to the security standards adopted.

k. Document all security related aspects to the business.

PHASE C: INFORMATION ARCHITECTURE DEVELOPMENT

The objective of the Information Architecture development phase is to define the Application and Data Architecture components.

Application Architecture

Application Architecture describes the major logical grouping of capabilities that manage the data objects necessary to process the data and support the business processes of the agency. Application Architecture identifies the criteria and techniques associated with the design of applications (eGovernment Program, 2009b). These techniques help the environment to be easily modified to respond quickly to changing business needs, as well as to the rapidly evolving information technologies available to support those needs. The Application Architecture provides an application- and services-centric view of the agency and it ties business functions and services to application processes; and services to application components in alignment with the application strategy. The Application Architecture's scope, strategy, standards are a consequence of the Business Architecture.

The Application Architecture is composed of the following:

a. **Application Strategy**: The key application architecture principles, application governance and portfolio management, and a set of Reference Application Architectures relevant to the agency.

b. **Application Services**: An inventory of the key application services exposed to internal and external audiences that support the business services.

c. **Application Processes**: A series of application-specific processes that support the business processes in the Business Architecture.

d. **Logical Components**: An inventory of the relevant product-independent enterprise application systems that is relevant to the stated business objectives.

Baseline Application Architecture Development

The Baseline Application Architecture models the current applications portfolio, system/organization matrix, system/function matrix, and the application communication diagram. Figure 7 outlines the Baseline Application Architecture inputs, activities, and outputs (Yesser Consulting Group, 2009).

The Baseline Application Architecture development guidelines are as follows:

a. Define current application building blocks in detail.

b. Assess and baseline current security-specific architecture elements.

c. Do not create system design documentation for the applications; but describe them as logical groups of capabilities that manage the data objects.

Figure 7. Baseline application architecture development (source: Y-ELAF EA Development Toolkit, 2010)

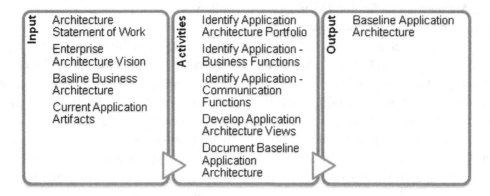

Figure 8. Target application architecture development (source: Y-ELAF EA Development Toolkit, 2010)

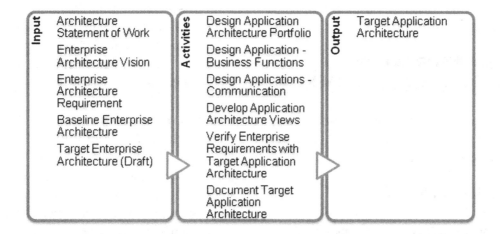

Target Application Architecture Development

The Target Application Architecture provides a model of the future application portfolio, system/organization matrix, system/function matrix, and the application communication diagram. Figure 8 outlines the Target Application Architecture inputs, activities and outputs (Yesser Consulting Group, 2009).

The Target Application Architecture development guidelines are:

a.   Architect/Design applications should be highly granular but loosely coupled.

b.   Plan for extensibility and scalability as part of the Application Architecture.

c.   Design applications to re-use components.

d.   Design integration for bridging the gap between heterogeneous operational application systems while still maximizing the investment in existing hardware and client platforms.

e.   Integration Architecture addresses the correlating components of data interchange, business processing issues, and end-user presentation.

f.   Integration Architecture meets the needs of linking heterogeneous operational application systems while protecting existing investments.

g. Provide maximum flexibility to integrate heterogeneous systems when enhancing existing end-user functionality with a middle service tier.

h. Minimize the impact on existing application systems.

i. Design for the N-tier service oriented architecture.

j. Generalize application interfaces.

k. Implement business rules as discrete components.

l. Design network-neutral applications.

m. Minimize data movement between applications.

n. Keep the integration strategy as simple as possible.

o. Choose XML as a preferred mode for all application integration for new systems, wherever possible.

p. Align to 'Open Standards.'

q. Implementation of Web Services should comply with Service Oriented Architecture (SOA).

r. Build detailed Application Building Blocks for the target architecture.

s. Build the Target Application Architecture based on documented security requirements.

Data Architecture

Data Architecture describes the logical and physical data assets and data management resources of the agency. It is one of the fundamental components of the Enterprise Technology Architecture. At the agency level, the consultant needs to look at how data is managed, accessed, and stored in databases across multiple applications in the agency. The data infrastructure is also an area that needs to be architected. The Data Architecture describes all of the moving pieces and parts for managing information across the enterprise, and the sharing of that information with the right people at the right time to realize the business objectives stated in the business architecture. The key components for describing the data architecture include:

a. **Information Strategy** is the Information Architecture principles, information governance and compliance requirements, canonical data models, and industry data model, support strategy. A set of reference information exchange as well as dissemination patterns and reference models also supports strategy.

b. **Information Assets** is a catalog of critical business data types and models (such as user profiles, service data, links with information providers) and the relationships between these business data types and all the services and processes that interact with that data.

The Data Architecture provides an information- and data-centric view of an agency, focusing on key information assets that are used to support critical business functions.

Data Architecture establishes an infrastructure for providing access to high quality, consistent data wherever and whenever it is needed. This infrastructure is a prerequisite for fulfilling the requirement for data to be easily accessible and understood by authorized end users and applications within the agency and other agencies across government (eGovernment Program, 2009a).

Baseline Data Architecture Development

The Baseline Data Architecture defines among others the current database portfolio, information model, data dissemination, and data lifecycle diagram. Figure 9 shows the inputs, activities, and outputs diagram for the Baseline Data Architecture development (Yesser Consulting Group, 2009).

The Baseline Data Architecture development guidelines are as follows:

Figure 9. Baseline data architecture development (source: Y-ELAF EA Development Toolkit, 2010)

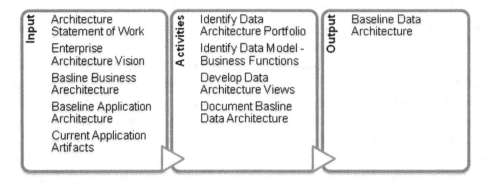

Figure 10. Target data architecture development (source: Y-ELAF EA Development Toolkit, 2010)

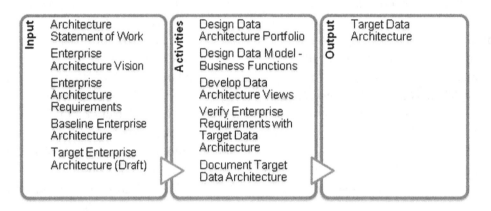

a. Design the data infrastructure to easily accommodate changes in the data model and database technology. The data infrastructure is a crucial component of establishing an overall adaptive architecture.

b. Design the enterprise Data Architecture such that it enhances and facilitates the sharing of data across the agency.

c. Design the enterprise Data Architecture so that is business driven, as opposed to technology driven, and aligned with the Application Architecture.

d. Separate the data sources for Online Transaction Processing (OLTP) data and Online Analytical Processing (OLAP) information.

e. Document the current standards governing how data is stored and used.

f. Document the current security requirements for the data architecture.

g. Capture how data integration is done in the current architecture.

Target Data Architecture Development

The Target Data Architecture defines among others the future database portfolio, information model, data dissemination, and data lifecycle diagram. Figure 10 shows the inputs, activities, and outputs diagram for the Target Data Architecture development (Yesser Consulting Group, 2009).

The Target Data Architecture development guidelines are:

a. The Target Data Architecture should be designed to be reusable.

b. The target entities should address how the business functions, processes, and services utilize the data entities.

c. Target Data Architecture should conform to all the data security standards.

d. Identify the requirements for data integration and the Target Data Architecture should address these requirements.

e. Data governance should be set in place for the Target Data Architecture.

f. If an enterprise-wide data model is possible then it should be created.

g. The Target Data Architecture should be consistent.

h. The Target Data Architecture should be designed in a way such that data is shared and accessible.

i. Data should be highly available, correct, secure, and consistent.

j. Data should be easily accessible to authorized stakeholders.

k. Point-to-point data integrations should be avoided.

l. Data ownership and data governance should be clearly defined.

m. Data redundancy should be minimized.

n. Generally, the Data Architecture consists of the following sub components:

1. Centralized Metadata.
2. Data Modeling.
3. Database Management System.
4. Data Access Middleware.
5. Data Access Implementation.
6. Data Security.

PHASE D: TECHNOLOGY ARCHITECTURE DEVELOPMENT

The objective of the Technology Architecture development is to map application components defined in the Application Architecture phase into a set of technology components, which represent the software and hardware components. Technology Architecture is the logical software and hardware capabilities that are required to support the deployment of business, data, and application services. This includes ICT infrastructure, middleware, networks, communications, business processing, and standards (eGovernment Program, 2009c). As Technology Architecture defines the physical realization of an architectural solution, it has strong links to implementation and migration planning. Technology Architecture shows baseline (i.e. current) and target views of the technology portfolio, detailing the roadmap towards the Target Enterprise Architecture, and helps to identify key elements in the roadmap (eGovernment Program, 2009d).

The key components are:

a. **Technology Strategy**: The Technology Architecture principles, technology asset governance and portfolio management strategy, and technology standards, patterns, and reference architectures used for developing specific technology solutions.

b. **Technology Services**: An inventory of the specific technology services and their relationships, and the business services, application services, information assets and logical or physical technology components that realize those services.

c. **Logical Components**: The product-agnostic components that exist at the technology infrastructure tier to support each technology service.

d. **Physical Components**: The set of technology products that exist behind each of the logical technology components to implement the technology service.

The Technology Architecture provides a technical reference model, that is used to align technology purchases, infrastructure, and solution implementations with the enterprise ICT strate-

Figure 11. Baseline technology architecture development (source: Y-ELAF EA Development Toolkit, 2010)

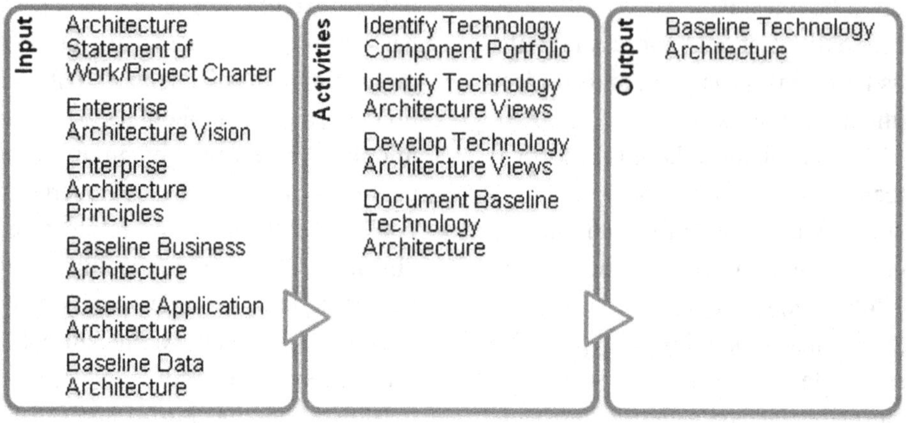

Input	Activities	Output
Architecture Statement of Work/Project Charter	Identify Technology Component Portfolio	Baseline Technology Architecture
Enterprise Architecture Vision	Identify Technology Architecture Views	
Enterprise Architecture Principles	Develop Technology Architecture Views	
Baseline Business Architecture	Document Baseline Technology Architecture	
Baseline Application Architecture		
Baseline Data Architecture		

gies, architecture principles, standards, reference architectures, and governance model.

Baseline Technology Architecture Development

The Baseline Technology Architecture provides a model of the current technology architecture portfolio, application and user location, network computing/hardware, environment landscape, platform decomposition, communication engineering, datacenter components, monitoring and operations, and security details. The Baseline Technology Architecture inputs, activities, outputs are shown in Figure 11 (Yesser Consulting Group, 2009).

The Baseline Technology Architecture development guidelines are as follows:

a. The Baseline Technology Architecture needs to represent the current technology environment details only.

b. The Baseline Technology Architecture needs to be developed based on industry standard notations such as UML (Unified Modeling Language), a standardized modeling language used in object-oriented software engineering.

c. Technology Architecture should not be mixed with other architectures such as Business, Application, or Data Architectures.

d. Technology Architecture is the implementation details of the organization's business processes and necessary details should be documented.

e. A Technology Architecture document is very close to implementation details and the depth of details to be documented should be done accordingly.

f. Document the security standards followed by the current Technology Architecture.

Target Technology Architecture Development

The Target Technology Architecture provides a model of the target technology architecture portfolio, application and user location, network computing/hardware, environment landscape, platform decomposition, communication engineering, datacenter components, monitoring and operations, and security details. The Target Technology Architecture inputs, activities, outputs are shown in Figure 12 (Yesser Consulting Group, 2009).

Figure 12. Target technology architecture development (source: Y-ELAF EA Development Toolkit, 2010)

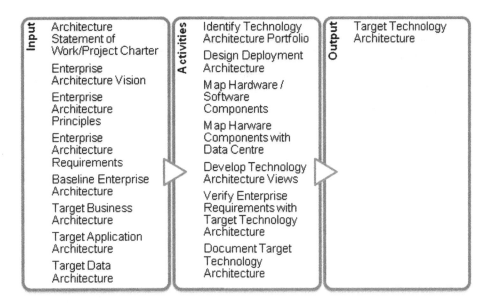

The Target Technology Architecture development guidelines are as follows (eGovernment Program, 2009e):

a. Network.
    1. Networks must be positioned for future growth in traffic and expansion of services.
b. Security.
    1. Authentication and Authorization of users prior to accessing services.
    2. Use PKI (Public Key Infrastructure) technology for authenticating the users' access to sensitive transactions.
    3. Use appropriate security service levels for each part of the technical infrastructure according to agency-wide standards.
c. Availability.
    1. Implement a fault tolerant solution (as per requirement).
d. Performance.
    1. Architecture must support performance requirements.
e. Scalability.

    1. Architecture must be scalable for future growth needs.
f. Technology Neutral.
    1. Architecture must conform to open standards and should avoid vendor specific technology.

PHASE E: OPPORTUNITIES AND SOLUTIONS

This phase of the EA development performs the gap and impact analysis based on the Target and Baseline Enterprise Architectures. The work done at this phase also derives a series of Transition Architectures that delivers continuous business value and is directly concerned with how the Target Enterprise Architecture will be implemented. The Enterprise Architecture gaps and impact analysis inputs, activities, outputs are shown in Figure 13 (Yesser Consulting Group, 2009).

The Gaps and Impact Analysis development guidelines are as follows:

a. Gaps and impact analysis are consolidated and their inter-dependencies closely assessed

Figure 13. EA gaps and impact analysis development (source: Y-ELAF EA Development Toolkit, 2010)

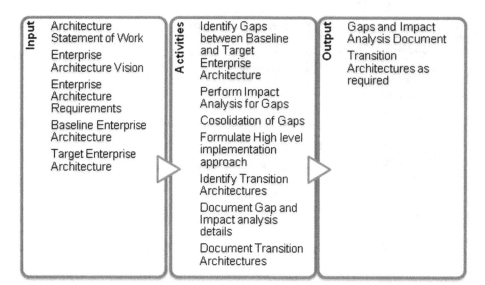

to derive an initial critical path. The overall intent is to simplify the transformation process by reducing the number of building blocks to be created as well as reducing the administrative overhead associated with portfolio and project management.

b. A high-level Implementation and Migration Strategy (that will be part of the Implementation and Migration Plan) is created to illustrate the overall implementation approach based on the outline critical path resulting from the dependencies analysis.

c. Transition Architectures consisting of a set of coordinated and well-defined building blocks grouped into work packages that define the scope of delivery vehicles (i.e., portfolios, projects, and initiatives) are developed. The Transition Architectures incrementally implements building blocks focusing on the delivery of a continuous flow of business value in support of agency business objectives.

PHASE F: STRATEGIC ROADMAP AND MIGRATION PLAN DEVELOPMENT

This phase develops the Strategic Roadmap that recommends the progressive implementation of a Migration Plan to evolve toward the future state architecture that:

a. maximizes the value from each phase of the roadmap;

b. minimizes the risk and cost for the proposed EA initiatives and solution implementation;

c. considers technology dependencies across phases; and

d. provides the flexibility to adapt to new business priorities and to changing technology over time.

The drafting of the Migration Plan starts with the creation of a prioritized list of architectural changes that drive the development of an implementation plan to achieve the future state. The risks and costs for each project in the implementation plan are then defined and a high-level transition plan developed. Migration from a current state to a

Figure 14. Enterprise architecture roadmap development (source: Y-ELAF EA Development Toolkit, 2010)

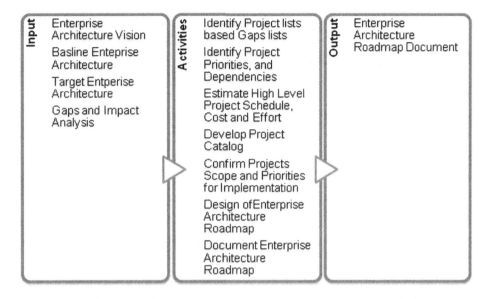

future state based on a "big bang" approach is not recommended. An incremental approach whereby implementation of the Target EA deliverable recommendations are broken into several phases based on business priorities and dependencies would likely bring about early successes. Once these transition phases have been defined, the transition architectures that act as checkpoints in the progressions towards the future state are developed. This incremental approach manages risks better and also provides the feedback to allow the fine-tuning of subsequent phases.

The Strategic Roadmap should produce the following key artifacts:

a.   A prioritized list of architecture recommendations based on the list from the Target Enterprise Architecture development phase.
b.   A set of transition architectures that progress the current state to the desired future state using those architecture recommendations.
c.   A project implementation plan implementing each transition.

d.   A cost analysis of each project implementation and a benefit analysis from each transition architecture.

The outputs and recommendations from the Strategic Roadmap would give a clear picture to all stakeholders regarding timeframe and investment requirements for achieving at the desired Target Enterprise Architecture.

It must be emphasized that the development of the Strategic Roadmap and Migration Plan must be performed with the close collaboration of the agency stakeholders. The Enterprise Architecture Roadmap inputs, activities, outputs are shown in Figure 14 (Yesser Consulting Group, 2009).

The Enterprise Architecture Roadmap development guidelines are as follows:

a.   Develop viable implementation and migration plan in cooperation with the agency EA program managers.
b.   The migration plan should be based on a prioritized list of projects.
c.   Assign a business value to each project.

Figure 15. EA implementation governance development (source: Y-ELAF EA Development Toolkit, 2010)

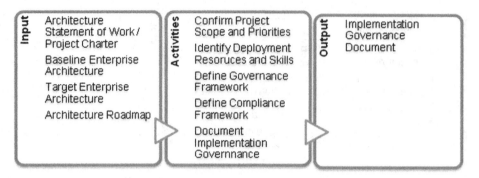

d. Prioritize the migration projects by conducting a cost/benefit assessment and risk validation.

e. Align implementation and migration plan with business/capability planning.

PHASE G: ENTERPRISE ARCHITECTURE IMPLEMENTATION GOVERNANCE

Enterprise Architecture governance provides the structure and processes for implementing an agency's business strategy and objectives through Enterprise Architecture. An EA governance body is used to guide each project and ensure its alignment with the EA during ICT transformations and solution implementations. Implementation governance includes:

a. **People**: Teams, individuals, roles and responsibilities of the governance board.

b. **Processes and Policies**: Architecture life-cycle management, change management, reviews cycles.

c. **Technology**: Infrastructure for implementing the processes and policies of Enterprise Architecture governance

d. **Finance**: ICT cost allocation, project-funding models, business case tools to

continuously monitor a positive return on investment.

The EA Implementation Governance inputs, activities, outputs are shown in Figure 15 (Yesser Consulting Group, 2009).

The EA Implementation Governance development guidelines are as follows:

a. Establish an implementation program that will enable the delivery of the Transition Architectures agreed during the Migration Planning phase.

b. Adopt a phased deployment schedule that reflects the business priorities embodied in the Architecture Roadmap.

c. Follow the organization's standard for corporate, ICT, and architecture governance.

d. Use the organization's established portfolio/program management approach, where it exists.

e. Define governance/compliance framework to ensure the effective long life of the deployed solution.

SUCCESS STORIES

Y-ELAF has been used successfully on numerous engagements to develop the Saudi eGovernment Transformation Strategic Plan among agencies in Saudi Arabia. This has resulted in the following successes for the Kingdom's eGovernment implementation, which started in 2006.

- 694 online services (eServices)
- 179 other services (informational)
- 23 Mobile and SMS services

The following is the latest example of where Y-ELAF was used to develop the plans for transforming traditional paper-based government services into online services.

The Saudi Commission for Health Specialties

The EA engagement for the Saudi Commission for Health Specialties (SCHFS) started in January 2011 and was successfully completed in June 2011. SCHFS was established under Royal Decree No. M/2 dated 6/2/1413H. It is headquartered in Riyadh and linked across the Kingdom to fourteen branches in the provinces. A Board of Trustees that includes all the stakeholders in the healthcare ecosystem, i.e. Health Regulators, Medical Institutions, Colleges, and Hospitals, supervises SCFHS' operations. SCFHS is responsible for the professional development and regulation of healthcare practitioners in the Kingdom of Saudi Arabia. Some of the functions performed by the agency include the registration and classification of healthcare professionals, continuous education, and training of healthcare professionals, and accreditation of hospitals, clinics, and medical training institutions.

The following is a list of SCFHS' Strategic Priorities.

1. Manage healthcare classification and registration activities and resources in an efficient and cost effective manner.
2. Optimise the use of technology to improve efficiency and customer satisfaction.
3. Manage documentation activities and resources in an efficient and cost effective manner.
4. Align the legal framework with the needs and best interests of the medical community.
5. Improve the quality standards of medical and healthcare training centres across the KSA.
6. Improve the governance and effectiveness of Boards and Committees within SCFHS.
7. Manage training activities, internal resources, policies, and procedures in an efficient and cost effective manner.
8. Maximise opportunities to enhance healthcare examination service levels by leveraging on ICT.
9. Enhance available healthcare examination question banks to improve relevance and quality of the examination process.
10. Improve customer experience and the image of the SCFHS.
11. Ensure quality and comprehensiveness of services being provided and ensure minimum standards are maintained across the whole Kingdom.

Challenges

SCFHS realizes that it has to modernize its operating model to serve its stakeholders better. It faces many challenges including the fact that much of SCFHS' services are delivered as traditional paper-based processes leading to inconsistencies and delays. Many processes cannot be completed in the branches making it necessary for healthcare professionals to visit the SCFHS headquarters in Riyadh to complete their service requests. Measurement of performance is also difficult to arrive at, as there is no published Key Performance Indicators (KPI) available. Computer network connectivity from headquarters to the 14 SCFHS branches is also limited as connectivity is via 512K bps leased DSL lines or through the Internet. The bandwidth of his connectivity is too slow to allow for good integration of ICT-mediated services (Yesser Consulting Group, 2009).

Solution

SCFHS requested the Yesser Consulting Group (YCG) to assist in developing an eGovernment Transformation Strategic Plan that will bring the agency into a modern customer-centric organization by leveraging ICT to deliver better services. YCG formed a three-man team to perform an EA development project over a period of four months. The team comprises a Team Leader who also acts as the project manager, an Enterprise Architect and a Business Analyst. The team used the following broad guiding principles in the performance of their assignment.

1. **Consistency:** The team adopts a common and consistent approach that treats users equitably and provides them with certainty and reliability. A common approach, typified by reuse of components, helps to reduce risk and cost, increase interoperability, and certainty.
2. **Focus on delivering customer value:** Customer needs determine how the agency functions as well as ensuring healthcare professionals deliver quality practices. Functions include direct services and regulating how healthcare professionals serve their customers.
3. **Information management is everybody's business:** All departments and units in the agency participate in information management decisions needed to accomplish business objectives.
4. **ICT is aligned and supports business requirement:** Information Systems and Technology exist to support the needs of the business at SCFHS and not the other way round. Changes to applications and technology are made only in response to business needs. Leverage on the Government Service

Bus (GSB) to expose Business Services to other agencies.

Outcomes

The ultimate outcome of the SCFHS EA engagement is an eGovernment Transformation Plan for SCFHS containing among others, a roadmap for transforming the agency's services from a largely paper-based manual delivery model into an electronic online service delivery model (eGovernment Program, 2005). The strategic eGovernment Transformation Plan describes the interrelationships between business processes, information, applications and underlying infrastructure for the organization, and provides best practices for technology purchase, design and deployment.

The plan addresses the following:

1. **Optimization of the business processes**: The adoption of Service Oriented Architecture (SOA) and Business Process Management (BPM) approach for the design of the eServices platform ensures the delegation of authority within and across the SCFHS departments, and branches. This is possible by the new empowerment of the SCFHS business units, where they can configure several aspects of the business processes (authorization, approvals, notifications, Business Rules and Reports) by themselves (by leveraging the intuitive screens developed using BPM standards) with minimum ICT intervention.
2. **Automation of Services:** Emphasis has been laid throughout the proposed solution on replacing manual activities with automated ones wherever possible to reduce the turnaround time and increase the productivity of the SCFHS employees.
3. **Adopt Service Oriented Architecture:** Service-oriented Architecture helps organizations to transform their business processes into high performance entities by simplifying

Figure 16. SCFHS service delivery model (source: YCG, SCFHS Target Architecture Document, 2011)

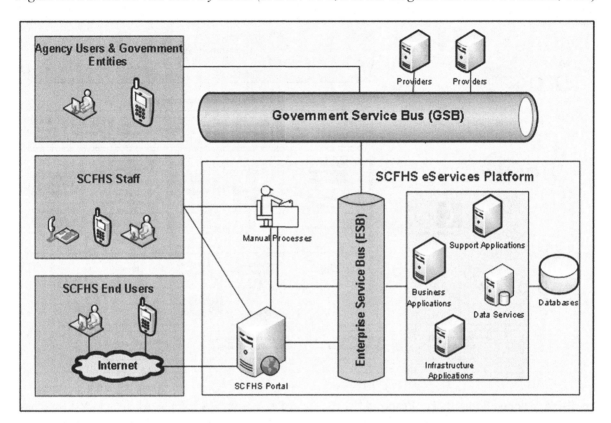

the underlying information systems. Old architectural approaches that once expanded business opportunities now limit growth. Service-oriented architecture gives existing systems the flexibility and agility to respond to rapidly changing business environments.

4. **Facilitate and accelerate exchange of information:** The end objective of the eGovernment initiative is to enable SCFHS to consume the information that is provided by other government agencies via the GSB, and to publish information on the GSB to be used by other agencies so that G2G, G2B, G2C interactions can be facilitated. The proposed solution would address this objective by linking the automated systems of the SCFHS with those of other government bodies through the GSB to facilitate

the exchange of data among government agencies involved.

5. **Expand service delivery channels.** In the past SCFHS primarily uses face-to-face counter services to deliver its services. The target architecture implements all forms of delivery channels—Internet, mobile device services, IVR, service call centres, as well as traditional counter services.

Figure 16 shows graphically the service delivery model of the agency after analyzing the various inputs obtained during the EA development engagement. The diagram shows that the agency's systems will be fully integrated within the agency and with other government entities in the Kingdom. Figure 17 depicts the Service Interaction Model developed for the SCFHS. The agency, with the help of the YCG EA project team,

Figure 17. SCFHS service interaction model (source: YCG, SCFHS Target Architecture Document, 2011)

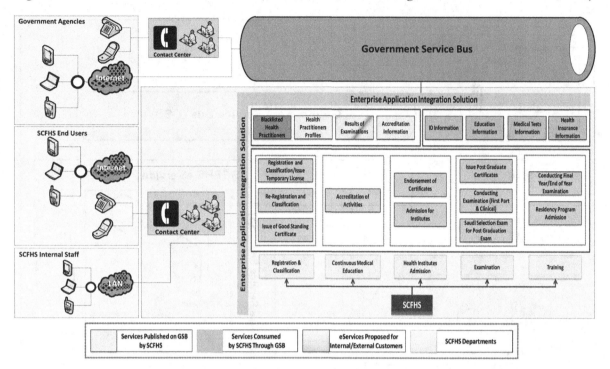

has also developed Requests For Proposal (RFP) documents that will soon be published for ICT companies to respond with bid proposals. Three RFPs are currently under consideration:

1. Business Solutions RFP to design, develop, deploy and maintain ICT-mediated solutions for identified business needs.
2. eServices Portal RFP to design, develop, deploy and maintain an eServices Portal through which SCFHS services will be exposed.
3. Project Management Office (PMO) RFP to invite bidders to establish and operate a project management office.

LESSONS LEARNED AND MOVING FORWARD

Planning and implementing a government-wide e-Transformation is obviously a major undertaking, with its own set of unique challenges. The use

of a rigorous EA framework such as Y-ELAF has made it possible for Yesser to develop Enterprise Architectures in Saudi Government Agencies that ensures these e-Transformations are carried out with success. The use of Y-ELAF has also made it possible for agencies to quickly learn and understand the benefits of using a structured methodology to plan for an optimized implementation of eGovernment services or eServices. Yesser's goal in using Y-ELAF is to institutionalize the discipline of using Enterprise Architecture to plan, implement and govern the delivery of eGovernment services to the nation as a whole. By doing so scarce business and ICT expert resources would be utilized optimally, and "the whole of government" concept of delivering services achieved—the idea that government services will be available anytime and from anywhere, thus breaking down the barriers of time, space and form. Enterprise Architecture, as a relatively new discipline that is gaining mainstream popularity in the public sector, comes with a number of substantial challenges that must be addressed. One of the main challenges is proving the value of Enterprise Architecture. Being a long-term undertaking, it is not easy to show return on investment in the short term. Therefore, education and awareness to all stakeholders is important.

A second challenge is the ability to establish, implement, and sustain an EA Governance Framework across the agency. This is particularly difficult in large government environments. It is therefore important that a governance structure is established and provided with the necessary resources, tools, and authority to ensure compliance across the agency.

A third challenge is the ability of the agency to hire and retain the necessary qualified human resources or alternatively partner with third party service providers who have a proven track record of successfully delivering Enterprise Architecture projects.

Despite these challenges, Yesser has been able to promote the use of Enterprise Architecture as a framework for aligning ICT strategies with the business needs of government agencies. Ultimately, the goal is to institutionalize the use of EA as the primary tool for governing the delivery of eGovernment services to the whole of the Kingdom of Saudi Arabia.

REFERENCES

Deloitte, & Touché. (2003). *At the dawn of egovernment: The citizen as customer.* Retrieved from http://epractice.eu/files/At%20the%20Dawn%20of%20e-Government%20-%20The%20Citizen%20as%20Customer.pdf.

Institute for Enterprise Architecture Development. (2011). *Website.* Retrieved from http://www.enterprise-architecture.info/.

Version, T. O. G. A. F. 9. (2011). *TOGAF 9 online documentation.* Retrieved from http://pubs.opengroup.org/architecture/togaf9-doc/arch/.

World Bank. (2011). *Website.* Retrieved from http://web.worldbank.org/WBSITE/EXTERNAL/TOPICS/EXTINFORMATIONANDCOMMUNICATIONANDTECHNOLOGIES/EXTEGOVERNMENT/0,contentMDK:20507153~menuPK:702592~pagePK:148956~piPK:216618~theSitePK:702586,00.html.

YCG. (2009). *Enterprise architecture development toolkit.* Riyadh, Saudi Arabia: Yesser Consulting Group.

Yesser. (2005). *The national egovernment strategy and action plan.* Riyadh, Saudi Arabia: Kingdom of Saudi Arabia.

Yesser. (2009a). *Interoperability framework.* Retrieved from http://www.yesser.gov.sa/en/BuildingBlocks/Pages/interoperability_framework.aspx.

Yesser. (2009b). *Government secure network (GSN).* Retrieved from http://www.yesser.gov.sa/en/BuildingBlocks/Pages/e-Gov._network.aspx.

Yesser. (2009c). *Government service bus (GSB).* Retrieved from http://www.yesser.gov.sa/en/BuildingBlocks/Pages/government_service_bus.aspx.

Yesser. (2009d). *eGovernment transactions' methodologies & handbooks.* Retrieved from http://www.yesser.gov.sa/en/Methodologies/mechanisms/Pages/e_government_transactions.aspx.

Yesser. (2009e). *Best practices for government agencies' IT managers.* Retrieved from http://www.yesser.gov.sa/en/Methodologies/Pages/best_practices_government.aspx.

KEY TERMS AND DEFINITIONS

ADM: Architecture Development Method. A methodology used in TOGAF for EA development.

Application Architecture: Application Architecture describes the major logical grouping of capabilities that manage the data objects necessary to process the data and support the business of the agency. It is a blueprint for the individual application systems to be deployed, their interactions, and their relationships to the core business processes of the agency.

Architecture: Architecture is the fundamental organization of a system, embodying its components, their relationships to each other and the environment, and the principles governing its design and evolution.

Architecture Framework: An architecture framework is a foundational structure, or set of structures, which can be used for developing a broad range of different architectures. It describes a method for designing a target state of the agency in terms of a set of building blocks, and for showing how the building blocks fit together. It contains a set of tools and provides a common vocabulary. It also includes a list of recommended standards and compliant products that can be used to implement the building blocks.

Architecture Landscape: The architecture landscape is the architectural representation of assets deployed within the agency at a particular point in time. The views are segmented into strategic, segment, and capability levels of abstraction to meet diverse stakeholder needs.

Artifacts: An EA artifact is an architectural work product that describes architecture from a specific viewpoint. Examples include a network diagram, a server specification, a use-case specification, a list of architectural requirements, and a business interaction matrix. Artifacts are generally classified as catalogs (lists of things), matrices (showing relationships between things), and diagrams (pictures of things).

Baseline Architecture: The baseline architecture is the existing defined system architecture before entering a cycle of architecture review and redesign. It is also called the As-Is Architecture or Current Architecture.

BPM: Business Process Management

Business Architecture: The Business Architecture describes the business strategy, governance, organization, and key business processes information, as well as the interaction between these concepts.

CIO: Chief Information Officer

CTO: Chief Technology Officer

Data Architecture: The Data Architecture describes the structure of an agency's logical and physical data assets and data management resources. It is a structure of the agency's logical and physical data assets and data management resources.

EA: Enterprise Architecture is a logical framework that establishes the links between strategy and the organizational structures, business processes, and information and technology needed to fulfill that strategy and deliver the agency's business vision. The purpose of enterprise architecture is to optimize across the enterprise the often fragmented legacy of processes (both manual and automated) into an integrated environment that is responsive to change and supportive of the delivery of the business strategy.

Enterprise: An Enterprise is a collection of organizations that has a common set of goals.

eParticipation: eParticipation comprises processes that allow citizens to interact online with government through information access thus providing citizens the ability to participate in public debate, public decision-making on policies, and to provide feedback to government.

Framework: A framework is a structure for content or process that can be used as a tool to structure thinking, ensuring consistency and completeness.

Governance: Governance is the discipline of monitoring, managing, and steering a business (or IS/ICT landscape) to deliver the required business outcome.

GSB: Government Service Bus

ICT: Information and Communications Technology

KPI: Key Performance Indicators

PKI: Public Key Infrastructure

Reference Architecture: Reference architecture is an abstraction of multiple architectures that have been designed and successfully deployed to address the similar types of business problems. Reference architectures incorporate the knowledge, patterns, and best practices gained from many project implementations. Reference architecture provides detailed architectural information in a common format such that solutions can be repeatedly designed and deployed in a consistent, high-quality, and supportable fashion.

Requirement Traceability: Requirements traceability refers to the ability to define, capture and follow the traces left by requirements on other elements of the software development environment and the trace left by those elements on requirements. Requirements Traceability is concerned with documenting the relationships between requirements and other development artifacts. Its purpose is to facilitate: (a) the understanding of product under development and its artifact; and (b) the ability to manage change.

RFP: Request For Proposal

Roadmap: A roadmap is an abstracted plan for business or technology change, typically operating across multiple disciplines over multiple years. Normally used in the phrases Technology Roadmap, Architecture Roadmap, etc.

SCFHS: Saudi Commission for Health Specialties

SOA: Service Oriented Architecture

Target Architecture: The target architecture is a description of a future state of the architecture being developed for an agency. There may be several future states developed as a roadmap to show the evolution of the architecture to a target state. This is also called as To-Be Architecture

Technology Architecture: The Technology Architecture describes the logical software and hardware capabilities that are required to support the deployment of business, data, and application services. This includes ICT infrastructure, middleware, networks, communications, processing, standards, etc.

TOGAF: TOGAF (The Open Group Architecture Framework) is an ICT industry recognized architecture framework. TOGAF provides the methods and tools for assisting in the development, production, use, and maintenance of enterprise architectures. It is based on an iterative process model supported by best practices and a re-usable set of existing architecture assets.

YCG: Yesser Consulting Group, a Yesser internal consulting department that assists agencies to develop their eGovernment Transformation Plans

Y-ELAF: Yesser Enterprise Level Architecture Framework

Yesser: The Saudi eGovernment Program

Chapter 6
National Enterprise Architecture Framework:
Case Study of EA Development Experience in the Kingdom of Bahrain

Ali AlSoufi
University of Bahrain, Bahrain

Zakaria Ahmed
eGovernment Authority, Bahrain

ABSTRACT

Building on the belief that a positive correlation between the desired level of e-government capability and maturity and the required level of architectural maturity exists, the eGovernment Authority (eGA) of the kingdom of Bahrain embarked on a three-year eGovernment program aimed at improving service delivery to citizens through seamless integration and connected governance. In order to achieve this objective, eGA realized the need for a Kingdom-wide strategy and holistic guiding plans, and hence decided to design and develop a National Enterprise Architecture Framework (NEAF). NEAF is an aggregation of models and meta-models, governance, compliance mechanisms, technology standards, and guidelines put together to guide effective development and implementation of an Enterprise Architecture by different government entities across the Kingdom. This chapter will describe a NEAF development project success story, its objectives, and its importance to Bahrain's economic vision 2030. It describes the NEAF development lifecycle and highlights the findings and challenges faced at each stage of the project.

DOI: 10.4018/978-1-4666-1824-4.ch006

INTRODUCTION

Governments around the world are leveraging advances in Information and Communication Technologies (ICT) to enhance their service delivery mechanism so as to improve citizen's satisfaction towards government as well as gain competitive advantage over other nations in attracting investments.

Building on the belief that there exists a positive correlation between the desired level of eGovernment capability and maturity and the required level of architectural maturity, the eGA embarked on a three-year eGovernment program aimed at improving service delivery to citizens through seamless integration and connected governance. In order to achieve this objective, eGA realized the need for a Kingdom-wide strategy and holistic guiding plans, and hence decided to design, develop, and implement NEAF for the Kingdom of Bahrain.

Aspirations for economy, government, and society in accordance with the guiding principles of sustainability, competitiveness, and fairness have been described in the "economic vision 2030" of the Kingdom of Bahrain. NEAF was designed and developed in alignment with this vision.

NEAF would help in managing complexity, managing IT portfolio, delivering a road map for changes, supporting system development, supporting business and IT budget prioritization, etc. Different issues in any organization like legacy transformation, business changes, infrastructure renewal, and application systems renewal and business/IT alignment can be resolved by designing an Enterprise Architecture (EA).

The chapter will start with objectives and scope of the project, and after a brief theoretical background on EA concepts, the approach taken to developing NEAF is described. Each stage of the approach is then discussed and the findings and challenges are highlighted. During the architecture assessment stage (As-Is), an EA maturity view is established and concluded. This builds a foundation to developing the target architecture along with the design of governance and compliance process. Additionally, the definition of a set of standards and guidelines, to help government entities focus on certain technologies and reduce their cost and interoperability in the long run, will be highlighted. Finally, the gap identified between the as-is and to-be architectures that triggered a set of initiatives at national level and specific to government entities will be described. The chapter is closed by a summary of NEAF development outcomes.

WHAT IS NEAF?

NEAF is an aggregation of models and meta-models, governance and compliance mechanisms, technology standards, and guidelines put together to guide effective development and implementation of EA by different government entities across the country.

The Open Group Architecture Framework (TOGAF), an industry standard architecture framework, was adopted to develop NEAF. NEAF was designed to be an extensible and scalable framework, one that would be able to adapt to the changing environments and needs of the Kingdom.

PROJECT OBJECTIVE AND SCOPE

EA is practiced in many industries; private and public sectors. It is very important before embarking an EA project that the objectives to be achieved are defined clearly. As a trend, EA could serve different objectives: to lower the cost of IT, fix its effectiveness, fix its strategic value, use IT to generate new strategic value or in many cases to transform the business with IT. For instance, EA could help with coping legacy complexity and cost, reintegrating the supply chain, integrating public services, enhancing channel capabilities, or even delivering better customer service.

The main objective of NEAF is to assist the kingdom of Bahrain to design, develop, deploy, and use enterprise architecture for better strategies, processes, plans, structures, technologies, and systems across the government entities for successful implementation of e-Government. Specifically, in case of Bahrain, the focus was to:

- Simplify and speed up services deployment to citizens
- Diversify services delivery channels
- Ease and improve integration between various ministries and government authorities.
- Achieve cost benefits of consolidation and standardization. Hence, reinvest the savings into modernizing the service delivery and provide more innovative services to citizens

Used as a guiding tool, NEAF was believed to provide a structured and comprehensive process for evaluating the impact and consequence of changes in business direction, business processes, avoiding silo base IT decision making and achieving the required alignment in the acquisition and implementation of technology tools.

The first iteration of NEAF (development phase) covered 167 services across 26 government entities (ministries and authorities). The aim was to move the government entities from business silos state towards standardized technology and rationalized data and applications. The output of the first iteration of the initiative was:

1. Target architecture for government service delivery
2. Technology standards and guidelines
3. Initiation of EA maturity program
4. Governance and compliance framework to guide all the above

Apart from the above initiatives, the project also identified a set of projects to be implemented to achieve the target architecture. These projects range from simple enhancements to a system through major introduction of new application systems. Several awareness building sessions and training workshops for all involved government entities were also conducted under this initiative, as final deliverable of the project.

ENTERPRISE ARCHITECTURE: A THEORETICAL BACKGROUND

Enterprise architecture defines the business, the information necessary to operate that business, the technologies necessary to support the business operations, and the transitional processes necessary for implementing new technologies in response to the changing needs of the business.

As illustrated in Figure 1, EA is simply defining the four layers of Business, Information, and Application and Infrastructure architectures. These layers are usually called domains and can be described as follows:

1. **Business domain:** represents the functions and processes that support the business, the organizations that perform the business processes and the locations where the business is performed, and the factors that could cause the business to change.
2. **Information domain:** identifies the major types of information needed to support the business functions. It identifies and defines the information model, data sets, metadata repositories, and their relationships to the business functions and to application systems.
3. **Application domain:** identifies and describes applications and modules, as well as their relationships to business processes and other application systems and modules. The application architecture identifies the major applications needed to support the crosscutting business processes of the enterprise.

Figure 1. Enterprise architecture layers and definitions

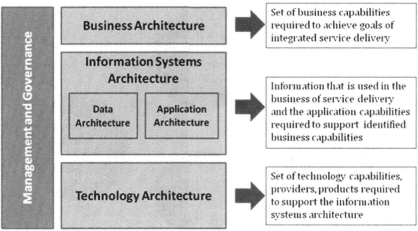

4.   **Infrastructure domain:** identifies the major technologies, or *platforms,* necessary to support the enterprise's applications and data systems, and associates those platforms with the various applications in the architecture.

In every EA project, the above current domains status (As-Is) architecture are first defined to measure their EA maturity of the organization. Then and based on a comprehensive study of the organization, the target architecture (To-Be) would be developed. The journey of moving the organization's current to target architecture with a set of action plan is called the Transitional plan.

Finally, and in order to complete the circle, such a transitional plan would not be possible without management and a governance process. These processes provide policy guidance, advice and assistance in the definition, design and implementation of the enterprise architecture discipline and practice throughout the company, an understanding of the process for making co-operative and collaborative IT investment decisions and designate who within Flabella is responsible for making these decisions.

THE DEVELOPMENT PROCESS AND METHODOLOGY OF NEAF

Alignment of Bahrain's economic vision 2030 with the vision, mission, goals, and objectives of each ministry or government agency would drive their Business Architecture. Business-IT alignment for better Return Of Investment (ROI) and efficient service delivery to the citizens would drive the IT architecture covering Application, Data, and Technology. Common infrastructure for the service delivery on multiple channels and national data set for Symantec interoperability are primary contributors for the standardization and seamless integration across the ministries and agencies. These are the key drivers for the adoption of enterprise architecture across the Kingdom of Bahrain.

eGA has taken initiative to design the EA framework at the national level (NEAF) which consists of reference architecture, standards & best practices, guidelines and policies along with governance and compliance to be adhered by each ministry/agency.

NEAF was developed in cooperation with WIPRO, an international consulting house, home grown EA methodology called ASSIMPLER. It stands for and focuses on Availability, Scalabil-

Figure 2. NEAF development methodology

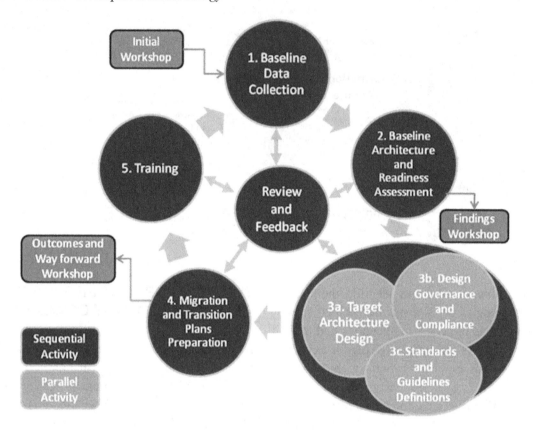

ity, Security, Interoperability, Maintainability, Performance, Low Cost of Ownership, Extendibility, and Reliability. ASSIMPLER is based on two well known EA frameworks: The Open Group Architecture Framework (TOGAF) from the Open Group, which is a process and methodology oriented framework (Aurenmalik, 2010), and Zachman enterprise architecture framework, one of the most popular enterprise architecture frameworks developed by Mr. John A. Zachman and which is more perspective and taxonomy oriented (Zachman, 2003).

As shown in Figure 2, the design of NEAF follows a stage approach covering the baseline architecture (As-Is), target architecture (To-Be), gap analysis, and finally, the implementation roadmap, as well as migration plan. The baseline architecture for all the ministries/agencies provides business and IT landscape in current

scenarios and the interactions/integration between different entities. Target architecture in the context of NEAF is Reference architecture with project/opportunities to be implemented by relevant ministries/agencies. Gap analysis is required to ensure the reusability of existing assets (business and IT) as well as the additional components required to achieve the EA vision at the national level, aligning with Bahrain economic vision 2030. Implementation roadmap and migration plan is the list of initiatives/projects to be taken by each ministry/agency to ensure target architecture at the national level is achieved.

EA maturity model has been designed for the kingdom of Bahrain to assess the capability of each ministry/agency to be able to implement the initiatives/projects recommended as the outcome of NEAF. Overall assessment of the EA in different ministries/agencies has been summarized at the national level with the maturity level matrices ministry wise and domain wise. This will be elaborated further in the coming sections.

The success factors of the NEAF project was education, communication, and awareness. Therefore, throughout the project, several workshops, awareness meetings, focused discussion groups for both data gathering, gap analysis and finally EA/NEAF training were conducted to all key members of the government entities involved in the project. Some of the key workshops are shown in Figure 2. In the last phase of the first iteration of development of NEAF, more specific and targeted training was conducted for those personnel from government entities who would play critical roles within the specific government body. Eighty-five trainees from twenty-six different government entities attended the training.

Overall, the development process follows sequential activities, except for stage 3, where three key deliverables are developed in parallel, as by this stage, all the necessary data would be available. These are the target architecture design, the governance and compliance design, and the definition of NEAF standards and guidelines.

In summary, built on the pillars of business, data, application and technology, design and development of NEAF involved following steps:

1. Creation of awareness about the EA initiative amongst the government entities.
2. Collection of data for the government entities' vision, goals, business processes, IT organization, skill sets, capabilities, systems, infrastructure deployment, IT planning and budgeting.
3. Validation of data collected with the stakeholders from the government entities. Missing data wherever identified was also collected.
4. Based on the data collected, assessment of the baseline architecture of the individual government entities and also the kingdom as a whole was carried out. This assessment shed light on the EA readiness of the government entities (measured on EA maturity model developed specifically for the project), technology landscape across the government entities, IT planning, governance and policy related issues such as data sharing, source code management, documentation of systems and IT ownership.
5. Development of target architecture to address the requirements of integrated service delivery for government entities.
6. Comparison of the target architectures vis-à-vis the baseline architectures to identify the gaps between the two states.
7. Preparation of the migration plan, spanning over three years, identifying the projects and initiatives to be undertaken by the government entities to migrate from baseline to target architecture. The projects were prioritized based on the readiness of the government entities, business alignment and functional and data dependency.
8. Discussion regarding the migration plan with the individual government organization to align the projects to their plans and requirements.

The NEAF initiative was designed to be dynamic in nature. The target architectures and the migration plan have to be periodically evaluated and refined to align them to the constantly changing environment, priorities and requirements of the Kingdom. This will ensure that the NEAF initiative will drive the government entities in the direction of achieving the economic vision 2030.

In the coming sections, NEAF development process will be described in detail including outcomes, challenges, and recommendations for the next phase of NEAF implementation.

ARCHITECTURE BASELINE ASSESSMENT (AS-IS STAGE)

The findings of the baseline architecture assessment provided crucial insights into the architectural landscape of the government entities. The assessment identified factors that were either conducive or impeding the movement towards target architecture. A few favorable factors identified include:

1. Employing Balanced Scorecard systems to ensure alignment between visions, objectives, and business services.
2. Defining and implementing different layers of access controls in information systems, and
3. Taking initiatives in improving the reliability and availability of services.

However, it was identified that such factors were restricted only to few government entities. The hindering factors, which were more prevalent amongst the government entities, include:

1. Lack of a policy framework for defining and governing ICT investments in the kingdom. This resulted in poor utilization of government funds and investment in redundant IT systems, data sharing, and system interoperability.
2. Absence of defined standards and guidelines.
3. Duplication of work due to lack of definition and availability of reusable components.
4. Lack of an application integration framework.

These factors led to delayed and poor quality of services delivered to citizens.

EA MATURITY LEVEL (ARCHITECTURE READINESS ASSESSMENTS)

The comprehensive data collected from the targeted government entities, also enabled the project team to assess their EA maturity, both at entity level and overall government level. All four domains (business, data, application, and technology) of the architectures of the government entities were assessed across eleven architecture elements on a five-point maturity scale. As briefly described in Figure 3, the eleven architecture elements considered for assessment were governance, planning, framework, blueprint, communication, quality of service, compliance, integration, security, process, and involvement.

The maturity levels in eleven elements across four architecture domains were used to calculate weighted mean enterprise architecture maturity level for the government entities. On the scale of 0 to 5 (0 being the lowest and 5 being the highest maturity level), the architecture maturity levels of government entities varied from a low of 0.21 to a high of 1.22. The average enterprise architecture maturity of all government entities stood at 0.77. Relatively low levels of architecture maturity indicate presence of wide ranging opportunities for improvement in the architectures of government entities. The architecture elements average maturity measured across all the government entities are shown in Figure 4.

EA ASSESSMENT STAGE: FINDINGS AND HIGHLIGHTS

The methodology and maturity framework description are not the focus of this chapter, therefore no more elaboration will be given in this regard. However, what is more important are the key finding and observations identified from the above maturity assessment exercise. These findings helped the project team as an input to

Figure 3. Architecture elements and their description

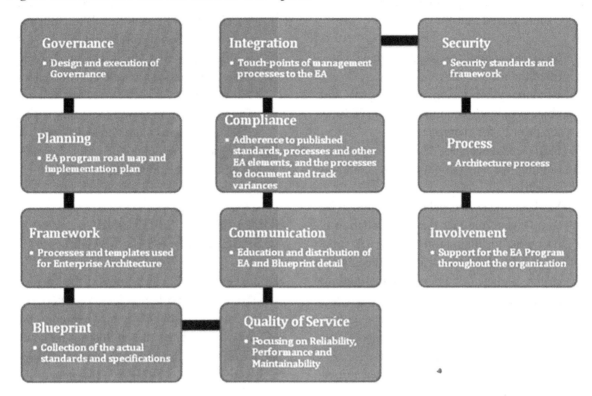

Figure 4. Average maturity of architecture elements measured across all government entities

development of the target architecture, and they can be summarized as follows:

- Most of the ministries/agencies have identified the need for EA.
- Alignment their vision, mission, goals and objectives with economic vision 2030 is top priority for everyone.
- Skill enhancements, resource pooling, funding for new initiatives are common concerns.
- Skill shortage or en-balance is common issue. Despite the fact that ICT adoption is becoming the main target of every government entity, IT/IS departments/directorates suffer shortage of human resources both in quality and quantity.
- Overall need to have centralized governance to assist their EA and to support their businesses is common consensus.
- Data/information sharing between ministries/agencies is major concern for delivering the business services by most of the ministries/agencies.
- Well-established frameworks for seamless integration between ministries/agencies to deliver the services are high priority action point considered by everyone.
- Architectural artifacts are partially created across the ministries/agencies due to missing EA initiative either at the national level or at the ministry/agency level.
- Business-IT alignment is ad-hoc and inconsistent in most of the ministries/agencies and hence IT investment and ROI is not completely justified.
- Security has been addressed in ad-hoc way in most of the places except few who has adopted industry standard and recommendations.
- Senior management involvement is visible as initial stage but not to the expectation to deliver the business services in effective and efficient manner across the ministries.

- Ownership of the services is not very clearly defined and Service Level Agreement or Operational Level Agreement (SLA/OLA) is missing across the kingdom between ministries/agencies as well as with vendors and suppliers.
- Training programs, awareness, knowledge management are major areas of improvement in the kingdom to drive the EA initiatives across the ministries/agencies.

SUMMARY OF BASELINE ASSESSMENT (AS-IS STAGE)

National enterprise architecture for the kingdom of Bahrain will be a key vehicle for successful implementation of the eGov strategy and other key initiatives across the ministries/agencies. Several focus areas in economic vision 2030 can be directly linked with NEAF, and hence, it is very critical for each government entity to align their EA with the national EA.

Service delivery to the businesses, citizen and within the government in seamless integration manner by executing processes owned by different government entity can become reality only if all these entities adopt a common framework for the business and IT architecture and adhere to the national standard for the business and IT service design and implementation.

National level bus infrastructure (*National Service Bus*) for the service mediation and integration, message routing, transport and transformation, and also to offer message broker supporting Web service standards are few of the justification to invest and utilize for the effective service delivery as per agreed SLA and OLA.

Symantec Interoperability between all the government entities can be achieved by defining enterprise-standard like metadata schema and industry-standard vocabularies for service delivery area and support of service delivery areas as scalable way for boundary-less information flow, and by incorporating Symantec technology within the infrastructure across the Kingdom. This can be achieved by mapping the data between different ministries, by providing Symantec integration across the country as well as exchanging data in consistent, flexible way for the providers and consumers of the services. Metadata repository at the national level can be leveraged to define National Data Set (NDS) as well as the key sources for the services to access the required information from different ministries/agencies.

The kingdom of Bahrain as one enterprise or rather "ONE BAHRAIN" consisting of different government entities as separate enterprises will be delivering the services using multiple delivery channels and hence authentication and authorization process will cut across multiple enterprises. This requires robust security architecture for different types of delivery channels and federated identity management to provide assembled identity of the user's information stored across multiple distinct identities management systems. Single Sign On (SSO) at the national level can be another initiative to align with EA needs.

Governance will play key role to ensure that government entities within the kingdom of Bahrain will comply with the standards and policies to provide the quality of the services as per the SLA with the customers and OLA between the enterprises. EA Governance Authority with proper roles and responsibilities will guide and mentor the ministries/agencies to design their own EA in line with national level EA.

THE TARGET ARCHITECTURE (TO-BE STAGE)

In this stage the findings of the baseline architecture along with the kingdom's economic vision 2030, eGovernment strategy and other business requirements and current planned initiatives will be used as an input to developing the target architecture (To-Be). To achieve this the architecture

vision, principles, requirements, constraints was defined; service delivery architecture was developed, which consisted of Business, Data, Application and Technology architectures; conducted an architecture trade-off analysis, to decide what items from the current identified architecture to be reused, and what are obsolete and have to be changed when developing the target architecture. Additionally, two more important deliverables are the outcome of this stage; the definition of architecture Governance and Compliance and the design of Standards and Guidelines. These are described in detail in the following sections.

ARCHITECTURE GOVERNANCE

The aim of enterprise architecture is to improve the alignment between IT and business by enhancing the ability of the organization to better control IT-related changes in a manner that supports the overall business strategy. To do this, the organization is required to map its current and future EA states of the organization in relation to the business and IT perspectives and consequently prepare a transition plan that closes the gap between the two states - in other words, the organization's IT blueprint.

Architecture governance is the set of mechanisms through which architecture is enacted in the enterprise. Governance is essentially about ensuring that business is conducted properly. It is less about control and strict adherence to rules, and more about guidance and effective and equitable usage of resources to ensure sustainability of an organization's strategic NEAF objectives (Hrdinová, 2009).

Architecture governance provides a practice and orientation by which architectures can be effectively managed and controlled at an enterprise level. During the assessment of the baseline architectures of the government entities, it was observed that a major factor that has resulted in lower values of architecture maturity in these

Figure 5. The governance council structure

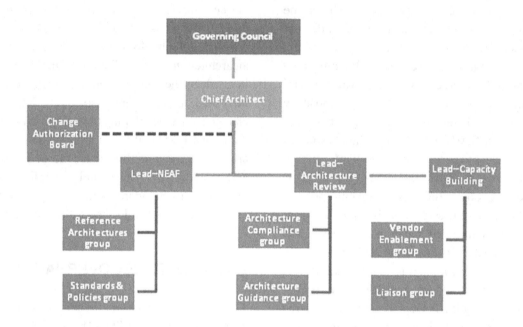

government entities is lack of an architecture governance framework. This led the NEAF team to propose the formation of an architecture governance body and the design and development of architecture governance framework.

The recommended governance structure for NEAF is a federated architecture governance model and it provides advantages in cost, schedule, autonomy, scalability, and robustness. The federated governance structure maintains a good balance between enterprise-wide standards, reference architecture and frameworks, and localized business-area driven innovation (Seifert, 2008). Four steps Governance process model namely (Enable, Ensure, Evolve, and Enhance) was recommended for NEAF, as follows:

- **Enable**: identify strategic projects and secure funding for the identified projects.
- **Ensure**: conduct architecture reviews for NEAF compliance, perform EA maturity assessment, and guide government entities on IT initiatives.

- **Evolve**: keep NEAF up to date and manage standards, policies and guideline.
- **Enhance**: manage capacity building and perform vendor enablement with regards to NEAF.

A central enterprise architecture team, shown in Figure 5, has a primary responsibility for reference architecture, standards, and frameworks that are common across the kingdom of Bahrain.

As shown in Figure 5, the governance structure was proposed to be comprised of the governance council, which is the decision-making arm and the execution arm. Under the guidance of the governance council, the execution arm of governance authority led by a Chief architect would play a key role in successful implementation of the roadmap identified in NEAF. The chief architect would be supported by NEAF reference architecture team, architecture review team and capacity building team. The governance authority would provide guidance and assistance to the government entities and enable them to enhance

Figure 6. NEAF governance context

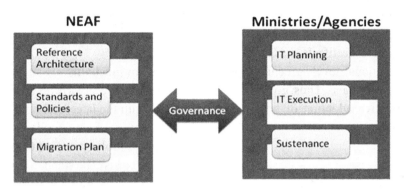

the architectural maturity level. One of the key responsibilities of the governance authority would be to guide and assist the IT architects in the government entities. This would be aimed at enabling these architects to guide the initiatives in the government entities in alignment with the key infrastructure initiatives identified in the roadmap.

NEAF GOVERNANCE CONTEXT

As shown in Figure 6, NEAF is constituted by reference architecture, set of standards and policies, and a migration plan. Reference architecture is a resource containing a consistent set of architectural best practices for use by all the teams in the enterprise and these can be embodied in many forms: prior project artifacts, guidelines, design patterns, frameworks, and so on. The purpose of reference architecture is to provide guidance for the development of architectures for new versions of the system or extended systems. Thus, reference architecture provides an asset base that projects can draw at the beginning of the project lifecycle and add to at the next version of the project. The mission, vision, and strategy of each of the government entity get elaborated in the specific of its architecture which is guided by the reference architecture.

Reference architecture is supported by a set of standards and policies that oversee the adoption of the reference architecture. Standards provide a base that foster consistency in the architecture procedures and policies guide the decision-making procedures and thus help in achieving rational outcomes that provide guidance for future. This will be further elaborated in the coming sections.

Migration plan is another major component of NEAF that outlines the roadmap for the transition of the current state of architecture of various information systems to the future state that is aligned to the mission, vision, and strategy of the various ministries/agencies of the kingdom of Bahrain. This will also be further elaborated in the coming sections.

Various government entities, on the other hand, formulate their respective IT plans, execute those plans, and then sustain the IT systems developed. NEAF and its components would act as the guiding factor for formulation and implementation of the plans of government entities. The architecture specific to the government entities would be guided by reference architecture and supported by the standards, policies, and migration plan that constitute NEAF. Governance aims to act as the bridge between the components of NEAF and the way ministries/agencies plan, execute, and sustain their IT initiatives. Governance processes would be essential to identify, manage, audit, and disseminate all information related to architecture management, contracts, and implementation. These governance processes would also be used to ensure that all architecture artifacts and contracts, principles, and operational-level agreements are monitored on an ongoing basis. Thus, governance would help in effective adoption of NEAF by government entities.

TECHNOLOGY STANDARDS AND GUIDELINES

NEAF tries to achieve interoperability across platforms and services, while ensuring that technology is used cost-effectively to support the business. Technology standards and guidelines form a critical component of NEAF and guide cross-ministry standardization. Thereby improving enterprise efficiency and effectiveness by incorporating consistent integration, improved resource utilization, reduction in overall costs and risks, optimization of project schedule, efficient IT operations, optimize technological diversity, and provide increased opportunities for sharing and collaboration between the government entities.

Products and technologies currently being used across ministries/agencies were compared to the leading products and technologies in various technology areas of interest, together with understanding of maturity level and transformational values of existing and emerging technologies by studying analysts' reports and predictions on products and technologies, to develop and define the technology standards.

Domains: Technology standards and guidelines across fifty-nine technology areas have been defined under NEAF. These standards and guidelines would be adopted by the government entities of Kingdom ensuring that the technology is used in a standardized manner to support the services being provided. The fifty-nine technology areas were categorized under seven technology domains, viz. Application, Collaboration and Productivity, Data, Enterprise IT Management, Network, Platform and Security. These domains and technology areas are further elaborated in Appendix A.

Review mechanism: Standards and guidelines will have to be regularly reviewed to keep them up to date with the latest technology developments. Maintenance of the standards will ensure that current technology is used to support kingdom's business needs. The standards and policies group of the NEAF team of governance authority for NEAF will be responsible for conducting reviews as per the review schedule for the standards and publishing updated versions of standards and guidelines. Impact on existing as well as future planned investments by ministries/agencies should be duly considered while standards and guidelines are reviewed.

While the architecture review team of the governance authority for NEAF will be responsible to ensure compliance to the approved standards and guidelines, any ministry planning to deviate from the approved standards and guidelines shall request for an exception and follow the agreed exception process.

MIGRATION PLAN

The migration plan established as a part of NEAF definition identified more than 60 critical initiatives that would be undertaken for enhancing the setup and service delivery at the Kingdom as well as the government body level. Prioritized on the basis of business alignment, dependency of government entities on each other (for functionality and data), complexity, business value, organizational impact, and readiness of government entities, these initiatives have been distributed for implementation over a period of 3 years

Figure 7 shows the approach taken to develop these initiatives. The identified consolidated gaps and solutions between the As-Is architecture and To-Be architecture were filtered through the

Figure 7. Approach of developing transition plan for government initiatives

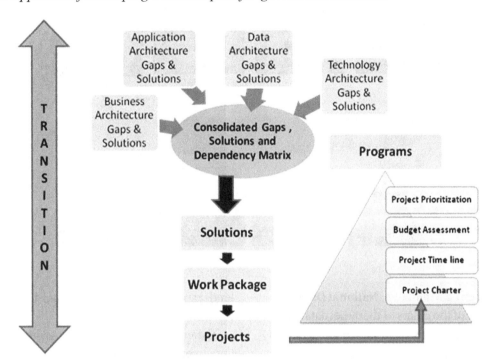

dependency matrix. It resulted into sets of solutions and work packages. These packages were then grouped into projects. Based on the above mentioned priority matrix, these projects were then organized and grouped under a Program, where it would be managed and governed by the eGovernment NEAF Implementation team. Sample work package and projects are shown in Appendix B.

In general, these initiatives are divided into two categories; government entity specific projects and national level projects. The former are initiatives that would be managed by concerned government entity, as they are either introduction of new specialized system or enhancement of an existing one, whereas the latter are initiatives that do not have specific owner and they impact all or several government entities.

CRITICAL NATIONWIDE INITIATIVES

The nation-wide initiatives would be aimed at improving the interoperability of the Information systems, ensuring availability of accurate data and information across government entities and providing improved returns on IT investments.

A critical initiative, **National Gateway Infrastructure** (NGI) provides a crucial integration framework required to connect the services offered by various government entities and provide a seamless integrated environment to the consumers (citizens and residents). It enables optimized distribution of information between different types of applications across multiple locations. NGI has been architected over an Enterprise Service Bus (ESB), which forms the basis of communication between various disparate systems. NGI would provide various services such as adapters, Web services connectivity, data services to facilitate interactions between the systems.

Figure 8. NEAF target system landscape

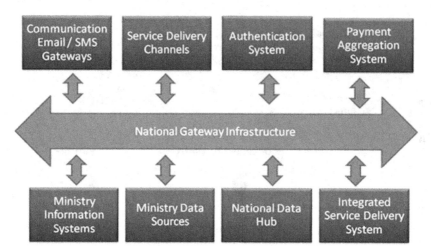

Another critical initiative, **National Data Hub** (NDH) is one of the pillars of the target data architecture. NDH system would realize the concepts and functionalities being sought for improving the exchange of information between the government entities while maintaining the accuracy. The core of NDH system would be formed by the National Data Set (NDS), the master data, and the system to manage this master data. The NDH system would be integrated with the data sources in the government entities. Data integration services would facilitate this integration that would happen through the NGI. The NDH system would clean and blend/merge data from multiple sources and populate the master data set according to the defined schemas. Concepts of metadata would be utilized to manage and govern the data. The NGI and NDH would form the core IT components for realizing the unified service delivery. Providing unified services to the customers is identified as one of the key element of the vision of eGovernment Strategy 2007-2010.

Along with the NGI and NDH important initiatives such as **Authentication system**, **centralized Email** and **Short Message Service (SMS) gateways**, **Payment Aggregation system** and **Central Enterprise Management** systems have also been recommended. Figure 8 shows the target system landscape, where all the national level systems are interconnected by the NGI.

Other than the critical nation-wide initiatives, the government entities need to undertake initiatives that would enhance the existing systems and enable them to enact the role of being a constituent of Service Oriented Architecture (SOA). These initiatives are primarily aimed at enhancing the functionalities in existing information systems and migrating the systems to next generation of technologies.

SHARED SERVICES CONCEPT

Two key initiatives that have been developed as local service but over the time the owners, encouraged by the government, started offering services to other government entities on request basis. These initiatives are Human Resource Management System (HRMS) that is owned by Civil Service Bureau (CSB), and Financial Management Information System (FMIS) owned by Ministry of Finance (MOF). Based on the analysis conducted by NEAF team, it was found that they both lack many functionalities that encouraged some government entities to seek alternatives and invest unnecessary in other expensive solutions. Additionally, the way these services were provided lacked many good operational and services features, such as SLA and customer service. Therefore, the NEAF team decided to adopt these systems and manage them under their national initiatives to support the concept of formal shared services. This initiative, as believed by the NEAF team, would have a big impact on the cost and service quality on the long run, and would meet one of the key strategic objectives of the NEAF project and Bahrain 2030 strategy.

IT RETURN ON INVESTMENT

The initiative also included an attempt to calculate the returns on IT investments that have been made by the government entities. However, the analysis could not be carried out to the required degree due to unavailability of the necessary data on the IT investments. It was found that there was:

- Lack of IT investment measures: Capital expenditure (Capex), Operating expenditure (Opex), and IT assets were not recognized.
- Lack of proper co-ordination between ministry of finance, Bahrain Tender Board (TB) and other government entities through a robust IT investment framework, made controlling of IT investments difficult.

Simply no one, even ministry of finance, have the answer to the IT investment (Capex, Opex, and IT assets). This has highlighted the requirement of establishing a framework for tracking the IT investments, and thereafter using it for calculating IT's ROI. Therefore, it was recommended to conduct:

- A strategic exercise to link budgets to spending involving all types of agencies (MoF, TB, and other government entities)

under the leadership of EA governance authority.
- Such exercise should aim at developing and standardizing the budget formats, with various exhibits and procurement categories.
- IT procurement manual should also be developed.
- Possibility of developing a tool for IT Portfolio Management should be explored.

SUMMARY OF NEAF DEVELOPMENT PHASE

NEAF was a very strategic but challenging project that has been carried out as one of the major initiatives of eGovernment authority of kingdom of Bahrain. The project was one of the few ones that met its objectives, completed on time (1 year) as planned and within the allocated budget. This success would not have happened without the full support received from eGA and government's top management. The other key success factor was the NEAF team composition. Both the consultants and the eGA team were selected carefully considering their strength, experience, and team work capabilities. May be the most challenging point in the project was dealing with big number of government entities, that had no clue on EA or its benefits. In fact, the very low EA maturity identified proved this claim. However, with well-planned communication strategy and full top management support this gap was bridged and the project team was able to meet the tough deadlines.

To summarize the development phase, a snapshot of NEAF project achievements, are listed below:

1. NEAF developed on four pillars of EA: viz. Business, Data, Application, and Technology.
2. Recommendation to establish and architecture governance body approved by Bahrain

Supreme Committee for Information and Communication Technology (SCICT).

3. Established the baseline architectures and carried out assessment to define the EA maturity levels for government entities.

4. Defined target architectures for Business, Data, Application, and Technology for use by government entities.

5. Defined a roadmap spanning a period of 3 years recommending the critical nation-wide as well as government entities specific initiatives required by the Kingdom.

6. Nation-wide initiatives include NGI, NDS, central Authentication system, Payment Aggregation system, and others. Ministry specific initiatives include implementation of EA, SOA enablement of IT systems and initiatives to achieve target architectures.

7. Defined 59 technology standards categorized under 7 technology domains.

8. Conducted regular workshops to increase awareness about EA and associated concepts.

9. Training conducted to develop capacities in terms of skills and competencies to effectively utilize the benefits and outcomes from NEAF attended by 85 people from 26 government entities. This is shown as the last stage of NEAF development methodology (Figure 2).

10. Enterprise architecture tool was evaluated and selected. This system would assist in architecture change and compliance management, conducting what-if scenario analysis, identifying critical project to be undertaken and generating holistic view of architecture in public sector of the Kingdom.

CONCLUSION

In this chapter, the development lifecycle of the national Enterprise Architecture framework of kingdom of Bahrain was discussed. Starting with objectives and scope of the project, and after a brief theoretical background on EA concept, the approach taken to developing NEAF was described. Each stage of the approach was then discussed and findings and challenges were highlighted. During the architecture assessment stage (As-Is), and with the large number of the data collected from 26 government entities, an EA maturity view was established and concluded. This built a foundation to developing the target architecture along with the design of governance and compliance process, and definition of a set of standard and guidelines to help government entities focus on certain technologies and reduce their cost and interoperability in the long run. The gap identified between the As-Is and To-Be architecture triggered a set of initiatives at national level and specific to government entities. These initiatives were sorted through certain criterion in migration and transition plan stage. The awareness and training was the key to the success of the project, hence it was a core activity at each stage of the development process. The outcome of phase I (Development phase) became the objectives of phase II of NEAF (Implementation phase). Since at the time of writing this chapter, NEAF implementation was still going on, it was not possible to shed further light on the progress on phase II.

WAY FORWARD

Whereas the development (phase I) of NEAF initiative aimed to establish the foundation for utilizing the enterprise architecture concepts in realization of the eGovernment strategy and vision 2030 of the kingdom, the implementation (phase II) would strive to build capabilities in the government organizations to enable them to best utilize the foundation created.

Adopting an objective based program approach; the team in Phase II would pursue a number of goals in the architecture development and architecture governance areas. Closely aligned and complementary in nature, the activities to be performed under these goals would create an appreciation and deeper understanding of Enterprise Architecture in government organizations.

Implementation of Enterprise Architecture Maturity Improvement Program (EAIP) to raise EA maturity of organizations, development of an IT investment framework to support informed decision making about IT spending, imparting of enterprise architecture training to increase self-sustenance of the organization in developing their own architectures, and providing support to the development of architectures of critical national level IT initiatives are of the significant to achieve in planned phase II.

Realization of the vision 2030 will require government organizations to assess and plan their landscapes in close alignment with the strategic direction of the Kingdom. This would be boosted when the ministries embrace introspection and capacity planning exercises supported by NEAF. A governance council with an oversight over planning and development of the architectures of the government organizations of the Kingdom is also essential to ensure the architectures that are planned and developed are able to best utilize the IT as a strategic enabler for achieving the vision 2030.

Various events have happened during the last 18 months particularly at eGA of which development of eGovernment Strategy 2 being a most notable one. In addition, there were changes in the government organizations such as mergers and development of the concept of IT shared services. These changes and the learning developed and challenges faced during the development of EA Phase I, have given sufficient inputs for us to structure the road ahead in the National Enterprise Architecture journey in the Kingdom.

Finally, the four steps Governance process model namely (Enable, Ensure, Evolve and Enhance) that was recommended will ensure that NEAF stays up to date and continuously enhanced. One of the methods used would be to compare NEAF setup with other country's experiences, with similar size and environment, in EA development and implementation.

REFERENCES

Aurenmalik. (2010). Core concepts of TOGAF. *Architect's Journal*. Retrieved from http://archjournal.wordpress.com/tag/core-concepts-of-togaf.

Hrdinová, J., Helbig, N., & Raup-Kounovsky, A. (2009). Enterprise IT governance in state government: State profiles. *Center for Technology in Government*. Retrieved from http://www.ctg.albany.edu.

Seifert, J. W. (2008). *Federal enterprise architecture and e-government: Issues for information technology management. CRS report for Congress.* Washington, DC: USA Government.

Zachman, J. A. (2003). *The Zachman framework: A primer for enterprise engineering and manufacturing.* Retrieved from http://www.zachman-international.com.

ADDITIONAL READING

Bellman, B., & Rausch, F. (2004). Enterprise architecture for egovernment. In *Proceedings of EGOV 2004 Conference*, (pp. 48–56). Zaragoza, Spain: EGOV.

Chief Information Officers Council. (1999). *Federal enterprise architecture framework, version 1.1.* Retrieved September 1999, from https://secure.cio.noaa.gov/hpcc/ docita/files/federal_enterprise_arch_framework.pdf.

Chief Information Officers Council. (2001). *A practical guide to federal enterprise architecture version 1.0.* Retrieved February 2001, from http://www.gao.gov/ bestpractices/bpeaguide.pdf.

Chief Information Officers Council. (2007). *Architecture principles for the U.S. government.* Retrieved August 2007, from http://www.cio. gov/documents/Architecture_Principles _US_ Govt_8-2007.pdf.

eGU. (2005). *eGovernment interoperability framework, version 6.1.* Washington, DC: US Government.

Guijarro, L. (2004). Analysis of the interoperability frameworks in eGovernment initiatives. In *Proceedings of EGOV 2004 Conference,* (pp. 36–39). Zaragoza, Spain: EGOV.

Mcauly, A. (2004). Enterprise Architecture design and integrated architecture framework. *Microsoft Architect Journal.* Retrieved from http://msdn. microsoft.com/library/en-us/dnmaj/html/aj1entarch.asp.

Ministry of Science. Technology and Innovation. (2003). *White paper on enterprise architecture.* Retrieved from http://www.oio.dk/arkitektur.

Office of Management and Budget. (2003a). *Implementing the president's management agenda for e-government, e-government strategy, simplified delivery of services to citizens.* Retrieved April 2003, from http://www.whitehouse.gov/ omb/ egov/2003egov_strat.pdf.

Office of Management and Budget. (2003b). Federal enterprise architecture program management office. *The Business Reference Model Version 2.0.* Retrieved from http://www.whitehouse.gov.

Office of Management and Budget. (2003c). Federal enterprise architecture program management office. *The Performance Reference Model Version 1.0.* Retrieved September 2003, from http://www. whitehouse.gov/omb/egov/documents/feaprm1. PDF.

Office of Management and Budget. (2003d). Federal enterprise architecture program management office. *The Service Component Reference Model (SRM) Version 1.0.* Retrieved June 2003 from http://www.whitehouse.gov.

Office of Management and Budget. (2003e). Federal enterprise architecture program management office. *The Technical Reference Model (TRM) Version 1.1.* Retrieved August 2003 from http:// www.whitehouse.gov.

Office of Management and Budget. (2005a). *Enabling citizen-centered electronic government 2005-2006: FEA PMO action plan.* Retrieved March 2005, from http://www.whitehouse.gov/ omb/egov/documents/2005_FEA_PMO_Action_Plan_FINAL.pdf.

Office of Management and Budget. (2005b). *FY07 budget formulation: FEA consolidated reference model document.* Retrieved May 2005, from http:// www.whitehouse.gov/omb/egov/documents/ CRM.PDF.

Office of Management and Budget. (2005c). Federal enterprise architecture program management office. *The Data Reference Model Version 2.0.* Retrieved November 2005, from http:// www.whitehouse.gov/omb/egov/documents/ DRM_2_0_Final.pdf.

Office of Management and Budget. (2005d). Federal enterprise architecture program management office. *EA Assessment Framework Version 2.0.* Retrieved December 2005, from http://www.cio. gov/documents/EA_Assessment_2.zip.

Office of Management and Budget. (2006). Federal enterprise architecture program management office. *FEA Practice Guidance.* Retrieved December 2006, from http://www.cio.gov/documents/ FEA_Practice_Guidance.pdf.

Schekkerman, J. (2004). *How to survive in the jungle of enterprise architecture frameworks.* Victoria, Canada: Trafford.

KEY TERMS AND DEFINITIONS

Architectural Framework: An architecture framework is a tool, which can be used for developing a broad range of different architectures. It should describe a method for designing an information system in terms of a set of building blocks, and for showing how the building blocks fit together. It should contain a set of tools and provide a common vocabulary. It should also include a list of recommended standards and compliant products that can be used to implement the building blocks.

Architecture Maturity Models: Organizations that can manage change effectively are generally more successful than those that cannot. Many organizations know that they need to improve their IT-related development processes in order to successfully manage change, but don't know how. Such organizations typically either spend very little on process improvement, because they are unsure how best to proceed; or spend a lot, on a number of parallel and unfocussed efforts, to little or no avail. Capability Maturity Models (CMMs) address this problem by providing an effective and proven method for an organization to gradually gain control over and improve its IT-related development processes. The US Department of Commerce (DoC) has developed an IT Architecture Capability Maturity Model (ACMM) to aid in conducting internal assessments. The ACMM provides a framework that represents the key components of a productive IT architecture process. The goal is to enhance the overall odds for success of IT architecture by identifying weak areas and providing a defined evolutionary path to improving the overall architecture process. Further

info can be obtained from http://pubs.opengroup.org/architecture/togaf8-doc/arch/.

Bahrain Vision 2030: is a comprehensive economic vision for kingdom of Bahrain providing a clear direction for the continued development of our economy and at its heart is a shared goal of building a better life for every Bahraini. Vision 2030 has been developed over the course of four years in consultation with over 1000 Bahrainis from the public sector, private sector, academia and civil society. The Vision will be underpinned by a national economic strategy detailing strategic initiatives across a range of sectors which together will deliver the long term aspirations outlined the within the Vision.

EA: Enterprise Architecture defines the business, the information necessary to operate that business, the technologies necessary to support the business operations, and the transitional processes necessary for implementing new technologies in response to the changing needs of the business.

eGA: eGovernment Authority is a government entity that was established in 2006 aiming to drive electronic government in kingdom of Bahrain (www.ega.gov.bh). eGA embarked on a three year eGovernment program aimed at improving service delivery to citizens through seamless integration and connected governance. So far more than 200 electronic services have been developed, which are delivered through several channels such as website (Bahrain.BH), mobile, kiosks, etc. Additionally, major initiatives have already been implemented such as national call center, national data center and citizen service centers. In 2010, Bahrain was ranked on UN eGovernment readiness index as 13th worldwide, 3rd Asian, and 1st Arab world level.

NEAF: National Enterprise Architecture Framework (NEAF) is an aggregation of models and meta-models, governance and compliance mechanisms, technology standards and guidelines put together to guide effective development and implementation of EA by different government entities across the country.

TOGAF: The Open Group Architecture Framework (TOGAF) is a framework—a detailed method and a set of supporting tools—for developing an enterprise architecture. TOGAF was developed by members of The Open Group, working within the Architecture Forum (www.opengroup.org/architecture). The original development of TOGAF Version 1 in 1995 was based on the Technical Architecture Framework for Information Management (TAFIM), developed by the US Department of Defense (DoD). The DoD gave The Open Group explicit permission and encouragement to create TOGAF by building on the TAFIM, which itself was the result of many years of development effort and many millions of dollars of US Government investment.

APPENDIX A

Standards and Guidelines: Technology Areas and Domains

1. Application
    a. Application Development Frameworks for Handheld Devices
    b. Application Development Frameworks
    c. Geographic Information Systems
    d. Modeling, Design and Development
    e. Programming Languages for Application Development
    f. Software Configuration Management
    g. Technologies for Application Development
    h. Web Services
2. Collaboration and Productivity
    a. Business Intelligence
    b. Contact Center Infrastructure
    c. Electronic Mail Systems
    d. Enterprise Content Management
    e. IP Telephony
    f. Office Suites
    g. Project and Portfolio Management
3. Data
    a. Character Set and Encoding
    b. Data Exchange Formats
    c. Data Exchange Transport Technologies
    d. Data Warehouse Database Management Systems
    e. Database Connectivity and Access Technologies
    f. Database Management Systems
    g. Storage
4. Enterprise IT Management
    a. Backup and Recovery
    b. Helpdesk Software
    c. IT Operations Management Systems
    d. Network Management and Monitoring Systems
5. Network
    a. Local Area Network
    b. Network Hardware Components
    c. Network Protocol Suites
    d. Supporting Network Services
    e. Web Browsers
    f. Wide Area Network Technologies
    g. Wireless Networks
6. Platform

    a.   Application Servers
    b.   Desktop Operating Systems
    c.   Directory Services
    d.   Enterprise Server Operating Systems
    e.   Enterprise Server Virtualization
    f.   Hardware Platforms
    g.   Mobile Operating Systems
    h.   Portal Servers
    i.   Web Servers

7.   Security

    a.   Access Management
    b.   Anti-Spam
    c.   Anti-Virus and Anti-Spyware
    d.   Authentication, Authorization and Accounting
    e.   Enterprise Perimeter Firewalls
    f.   Identity Management
    g.   Intrusion Detection and Prevention Systems
    h.   Secure Transport
    i.   Virtual Private Network

APPENDIX B: NATIONAL LEVEL PROJECTS (SAMPLES)

Figure 9.

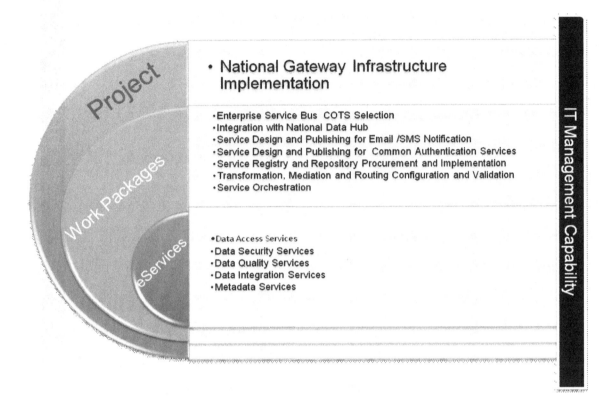

Figure 10.

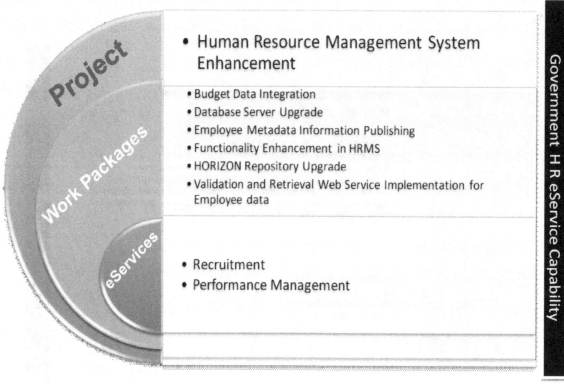

Chapter 7
Towards Whole–of–Government EA with TOGAF and SOA

Awel S Dico

BMO Financial Group, Canada & The Open Group, UK & Addis Ababa University, Ethiopia

ABSTRACT

Governments around the world have acknowledged the complexity associated with public sector transformation and have initiated enterprise architecture programs to help manage those complexities and enable the desired strategic transformation. Along with the EA program, governments have adopted some sort of EA framework and/or Service Oriented Architecture (SOA) individually or in integrated form. However, the majority of those EA programs are of limited scope in both EA and SOA practices, and are not comprehensive enough to deal with and manage the associated complexities. As a result, those EA programs suffer from the inability to leverage EA and SOA benefits across agencies or jurisdictional boundaries. Currently, the majority of government agencies use EA and SOA within the agency boundaries to deliver solutions by focusing on technical factors that define detailed blueprints of systems, data, and technology. What is needed rather is effective Whole-of-Government Enterprise Architecture (EA) that facilitates the alignment of individual agencies' visions with the Whole-of-Government vision to enable sustainable government transformation. Research has pointed out that the Whole-of-Government EA is currently at the conceptual level and still has a long way to go to reach the maturity level required for value realization. This chapter first gives a brief analysis of the current state of enterprise architecture in governments to highlight the current challenges. It then discusses the various scopes of Whole-of-Government EA and recommends the plausible EA approach to enable sustainable connected government based on The Open Group Architecture Framework (TOGAF) and SOA.

DOI: 10.4018/978-1-4666-1824-4.ch007

BRIEF ANALYSIS OF THE CURRENT STATE OF WHOLE-OF-GOVERNMENT EA

This section presents a brief analysis of the current state of Enterprise Architecture and Service Oriented Architecture initiatives in governments by highlighting the successes and challenges associated with the practice.

Maturity of Whole-of-Government EA

Enterprise architecture has gained attention as a tool for planning and managing government transformations to enable sustainable connected government. As a result many countries around the world have initiated Enterprise Architecture programs to help manage government transformations. However, EA programs in most of the countries are of limited scope. According to a report on government enterprise architecture work in 15 countries (Liimatainen, et al., 2007), at the time of the report not all countries had national (Whole-of-Government) enterprise architecture programs. The report also pointed out the lack of holistic view on collaboration between different agencies. Saha (2010a), in his qualitative analysis report on the impact of EA on connected government, clearly states the lack of Whole-of-Government enterprise architecture context in 9 countries surveyed.

This fact is also evident from US General Accounting Office report on EA in United States (Hite, 2004). Back then (in 2004) the report pointed out that the government wide EA management practice was limited. Various agencies were at different levels of maturity, and only a few agencies were successfully using EA while others were struggling. In another report, the US General Accounting Office (Hite, 2003) states the various agencies have identified the lack of high level management support as one of the major obstacles for EA practice in agencies. The observation that government wide EA was limited (and that there

was a lack of agency leadership in support of EA practice) indicates that there was no high level Whole-of-Government EA to guide and support the various agencies. According to recent report (Dodaro, 2011), these issues are still a challenge to government agencies enterprise architecture practice. Dodaro (2011) states that "… the real value in the federal government from developing and using enterprise architectures remains largely unrealized" (p. 14). With such a lack of high-level Whole-of-Government EA context, a wide spectrum of EA maturity differences in agencies can be a major limiting factor for collaboration and interoperability between agencies.

Most recent Gartner research (Bittinger, 2011) points out that even though EA has been recognized as an essential tool for driving sustainable government transformation, much of EA efforts have not gone beyond a mere compliance exercise. The same Gartner report also pointed out that there are few examples of the successful use of EA across agency boundaries. What this implies is that government EA programs are active only in the agency level and that those agency level EA programs are independently operated without or with minimal cross agency collaboration. The results from these reports clearly indicate that the Whole-of-Government EA is lacking or immature.

Effectiveness of Tools Developed by Governments without Whole-of-Government EA Framework

One may ask a question why agencies in United States struggle with their EA practice while they have support from Office of Management and Budget (OMB), which developed and promote Federal Enterprise Architecture Framework (FEAF) for that purpose.

While FEAF is one of the useful frameworks out there, its use did not equally move the various agencies to the expected maturity levels. The reason is that FEAF does not have all that is required to define and manage government wide enterprise architecture. The purpose of FEAF is to provide a common taxonomy for agencies individual enterprise architecture development (Hite, 2004). To be effective and create value, the FEAF needs to be framed in a bigger Whole-of-Government EA framework. The lack of mature Whole-of-Government EA and the primary focus on agencies' EA alone without that bigger context reduces the effectiveness and slows the maturity of agencies' enterprise architecture practice.

Another interesting example to mention here is the Canadian Government Business Transformation Enablement Program (BTEP). BTEP provides a transformation toolkit that helps and facilitates consistent transformation across government agencies and departments towards the Whole-of-Government transformation (Treasury Board of Canada Secretariat, 2004; Institute of Citizen Centred Service, 2011). One of the tools developed under BTEP is the Government of Canada Strategic Reference Model (GSRM). The GSRM provides models, semantics and reusable patterns for describing public sector business architecture. Even though the level of detail and approach varies, at high level GSRM and FEAF have a similar purpose. The main difference is that GSRM gives reusable patterns in addition to reference models and business semantics.

It is interesting to compare the effectiveness of FEAF and GSRM in establishing cross agency interoperability and collaboration. Unlike FEAF use in US government agencies, the use of GSRM by Canadian government agencies has shown some success in establishing cross agencies interoperability and collaboration. This difference is not because GSRM is much better than FEAF. It is rather due to the context in which they are used. The use of GSRM in agencies business architecture is supported by higher-level Whole-of-Government EA context established through Canadian Government Business Transformation Enablement Program (BTEP) (Treasury Board of Canada Secretariat, 2004; Institute of Citizen Centred Service, 2011). As discussed earlier, such

Whole-of-Government EA context is lacking or immature in US government agencies use of FEAF. This observation again stresses the importance of high-level strategic Whole-of-Government EA.

To further illustrate the importance Whole-of-Government EA, another interesting example is that of the Australian government EA approach. The Australian government EA framework, namely, Australian Government Architecture (AGA) reference model, is based on the Federal Enterprise Architecture Framework (FEAF) (Australian Government Information Management Office, 2009). Saha (2010a) did a qualitative analysis of the Australian government EA approach and pointed out the following three observations:

A. There is no clarity as to how the architecture frameworks, standards, principles and policies between the federal level and states are coordinated. Based on available information, the associations and the inter-dependencies are unclear at this stage.

B. The AGA currently consists of only the principles and the four reference models. For AGA to be implementable and its goals realizable, it needs to be augmented with several other key components.

C. AGIMO over the years has developed and published several best practices, frameworks, standards and policy documents in areas of IT management. Linkages to and from IT management practices to AGA are still not available (p. 20).

Again, these observations indicate the lack of Whole-of-Government EA that could have provided larger context to address these observed gaps.

Some countries also use UN/CEFACT Modeling Methodology (UMM) for modeling business collaborations in a technology-neutral and implementation-independent manner (Liegl, et al., 2007). Like FEAF and GSRM discussed above, the use of UMM provides more value when used within the context of the Whole-of-Government EA framework.

Connected Government Frameworks from Solution Providers

It is not only governments that have developed frameworks to help with government transformations. Technology suppliers like CISCO (Spencer, 2007) and Microsoft (Muehlfeit, 2006; Microsoft, 2010) have also developed connected-government frameworks based on their experience with e-Government projects. Those frameworks provide larger context within which their technology offerings are placed to demonstrate value to the governments. It is important to note that those frameworks are largely technology oriented and may not be comprehensive enough to develop the Whole-of-Government EA. However, such frameworks can be used within the Whole-of-Government EA framework if the government is partnering with those solution providers. Similar to the government developed frameworks (such as FEAF or GSRM) (which could be used for strategic business architecture within Whole-of-Government EA framework), the solution provider frameworks, such as Microsoft and CISCO Connected Government Frameworks, can be used for strategic technology architecture within the Whole-of-Government EA framework.

SOA and Whole-of-Government EA Framework

The above analysis and observations highlights the current issues associated with the lack of mature Whole-of-Government EA in governments. In addition to enterprise architecture initiations, governments have also adopted Service Oriented Architecture (SOA). According to Gartner's Hype Cycle for Government Transformation 2011 (Bittinger, 2011), unlike Whole-of-Government EA, the practice of SOA is mature in government organizations. This maturity of SOA is mainly

within technical context addressing concerns related to technology/software systems. With respect to business context, the maturity of SOA in governments is questionable because the majority of organizations place SOA in technology scope. Bittinger (2011) states that "Many government IT organizations have adopted SOA as a technology architecture without embracing the fundamental principles that make this approach truly transformative" (p. 55). Governments' investment in SOA has been limited because of several factors including shortcoming in EA, business processes, and overall SOA governance. Lack of clear understanding of operational requirements and poor communication strategies are also among the factors (Bittinger, 2011). These limiting factors indicate that holistic SOA approach in governments is still immature and its maturity is linked to the maturity of the Whole-of-Government EA. In other words, for SOA to have transformation impact it must be approached at strategic level within the Whole-of-Government EA context. Example of such approach can be found in Canadian government SOA strategy (Treasury Board of Canada Secretariat, 2007) which is developed within the context of the Canadian Government Business Transformation Enablement Program (BTEP) to reinforce the use of GSRM based business services identification, modeling, and design.

Therefore, for SOA to be truly transformational, SOA should not be limited to a technology aspect only. Instead, Whole-of-Government EA should understand the benefits of a SOA approach within the context of government transformation and adopt a SOA style at a strategic level by incorporating the service orientation concept starting with high-level business services modeling. SOA should not be left for a solution project scope only. Instead, it should be incorporated within larger enterprise architecture frameworks and proper SOA governance should be established to facilitate cross-agency interoperability and business and technical capability reuse. This will be discussed in detail later in this chapter.

The Overall Effect of the Lack of Whole-of-Government EA Framework

The above observations may also indicate that the focus on government agency enterprise architectures without Whole-of-Government EA guidance may create silos in governments, which could slow the transformation change and rather enhance disconnected incremental change in governments. Abramson, Breul, & Kamensky (2005) define the transformational change as strategic and disruptive whereas incremental change as more of evolutionary, with modest and quick value realization as a goal. Such disconnected incremental changes in individual agencies may initially create quick value to agencies, but are not able to move the government to the realization of the overall connected government vision.

Moreover, government transformation is much more complex involving very diverse stakeholders with complex (sometimes conflicting) interaction between them (Saha, 2010b). These stakeholders may include individual agencies, citizens, employees, and external partners such as private businesses. The primary goal of Whole-of-Government EA is thus to manage this complexity and enable desired transformational change on a timely manner. To achieve this Whole-of-Government EA requires a comprehensive framework that incorporates people, processes and technology in order to manage the associated complexities and translate government business vision into effective transformational change.

In summary, the current state of Whole-of-Government EA in various governments is not mature enough to enable truly connected government. Gartner's Hype Cycle for Government Transformation 2011 (Bittinger, 2011) clearly shows that Whole-of-Government EA is currently immature and is still 10 years from reaching full maturity and adoption. For the Whole-of-Government EA to mature, governments should adopt an EA framework that links and incorporates other

best practice tools (such as FEAF, GSRM, and UMM), and provides the necessary context for various government agencies. By doing so, the Whole-of-Government EA framework facilitates the linkage of various EA initiatives across agency boundaries. Such a framework should also support incorporation of a SOA concept at various levels of architecture scope and enable iterative architecture development to facilitate incremental value add to the Whole-of-Government objectives. The objective of this chapter is to recommend such a plausible EA approach for governments based on TOGAF and SOA.

WHY TOGAF AND SOA?

The Open Group Architecture Framework (TOGAF) is a generic architecture framework that is architecture style agnostic. The current version 9 of TOGAF has major enhancements compared to the previous versions (Forde, et al., 2009). It can be used with any architecture style, such as Service Oriented Architecture (SOA). TOGAF being so generic framework, it is very overwhelming if one tries to follow TOGAF document line by line. This is because the various artifact types and approaches provided in TOGAF may not be applicable to all situations. Fortunately, TOGAF is customizable to any enterprise scope and enterprise needs. The other benefit of TOGAF is that its Architecture Development Method (ADM) can be used with other frameworks, such as Federal Enterprise Architecture Framework (FEAF), US Department of Defense Architecture Framework (DoDAF), UN/CEFACT Modeling Methodology (UMM), industry governance frameworks, and other reference architectures or models. For example, Blevins et al. (2010) provided analysis of the TOGAF and DoDAF frameworks and concluded that the DoDAF models can be used within TOGAF ADM phases to develop a visual, integrated model of architecture. Thus, using TOGAF as Whole-of-Government enterprise architecture

(EA) framework will allow the government to select and mix best of breed frameworks and methods into a single architecture development process.

SOA adoption in the Whole-of-Government EA is not limited to technology aspect of service orientation. Instead, the principle of a SOA approach should be applied to high-level conceptual and logical business architectures. For this to be practical, various SOA activities need to be guided by larger EA framework. Bennett et al. (2011) lists the risks associated with adoption of SOA without enterprise architecture. Some of the risks of not adopting SOA at the strategic level within the EA context include: limited business agility, exponentially growing governance challenges, limited interoperability, and limited service reuse. For governments, if SOA is not part of the strategic architecture of Whole-of-Government EA, the fragmented SOA implementations within various agencies will not enable the required interoperability and service reuse. It may even add complexity and service governance overhead, resulting escalated cost of interoperability across agencies. The combination of TOGAF (as a guiding architectural process) and SOA (as architectural style) will allow the Whole-of-Government EA to structure and manage the various architectures and associated risks effectively. The objective of this chapter is to provide detail discussion on how TOGAF and SOA can be adapted for the Whole-of-Government EA to enable sustainable connected e-Government.

WHOLE-OF-GOVERNMENT EA

Whole-of-Government EA is about enabling sustainable government transformation. The main driver of government's transformation requirement is the vision of delivering sustainable citizen-centric and citizen-driven services with active empowerment of the government employees. Citizen-centricity is the government capability for delivering services to its citizens consistently through single government access point with the support of multiple consumer channels. A service consumer (i.e. citizens) can come through many channels (for example Web portal, mobile devices, and kiosks) to interact with the government or access the services they are entitled for. These services are normally implemented by various government agencies. Regardless of which agency implemented the services, the citizens access the service from channels that are accessible to them through a single government service access point. Citizen-driven services extend the citizen-centric services by empowering the citizens to actively participate in the government service delivery process. When achieved, this is indeed a major transformation in governments. However, such a transformation would not be possible without strategically linking people, processes, and technology in a coherent manner. Whole-of-Government EA is expected to establish that linkage and facilitates translation of this government vision into effective transformation change. Figure 1 shows the four key questions Whole-of-Government EA must answer in order to enable such a transformation.

Whole-of-Government Strategic Architecture translates a government's transformation strategy into effective change that transforms the government to a desired state. For Whole-of-Government EA to enable the desired change, the government transformation vision must be defined by specifying:

- Why the change is required – this sets a clear transformation strategy to drive remaining activities. This is driven by whole of government vision, goals, and objectives to clearly define and communicate why a transformational change is needed now.
- What needs to be changed – this sets a clear higher-level scope as to what changes are going to be done. This again is driven by the government vision, goals, and objectives to set high-level priorities and de-

Figure 1. Key questions that the whole-of-government EA should ask, understand, and answer

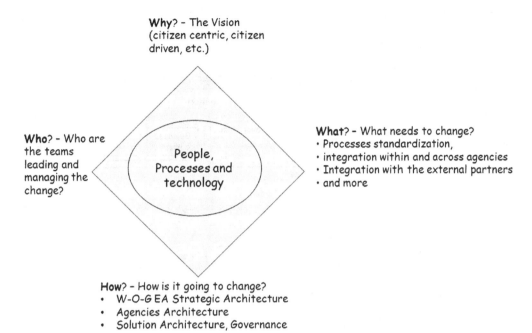

fine the high-level scope of things that will change.

- Who has accountability for the change – this sets the high-level responsibilities at senior leadership level. Depending on what needs to be changed, the roles and responsibilities are specified to lead the change.
- How the change is going to happen – this sets high-level context to give a mandate to the enterprise architecture to define the guidance on how the change will be managed, governed, and executed. This is where most of the activities of the Whole-of-Government EA is going to be as will be discussed later.

Enterprise Architecture Scopes and Associated Architecture Types

Government is a complex enterprise. Saha (2010) discussed the complexities in government as of two types, namely, combinatorial complexity and

dynamic complexity. Combinatorial complexity in government arises from the fact that governments have many constituents and agencies that are interconnected. Dynamic complexity in government arises because of the magnitude of change that occurs within government agencies, continuous interaction between these agencies and changing expectations of various stakeholders. It is due to these complexities and the not so effective approach taken to deal with and manage them that Enterprise Architecture in majority of governments fall short of supporting the required transformational objectives. To manage these complexities within architectural context and properly address diverse stakeholder needs throughout the government, the Whole-of-Government EA landscape needs to be partitioned in to three levels of granularity as depicted in Figure 2.

The first type of architecture is the Whole-of-Government Strategic Architecture. Driven by government's business vision, goals, and objectives, the Whole-of-Government Strategic Archi-

Figure 2. The three levels of whole-of-government end-to-end architecture

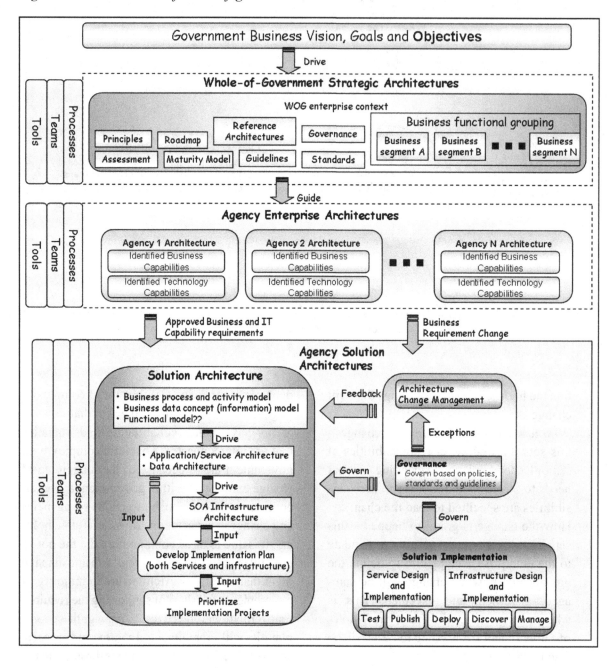

tecture provides bigger enterprise direction and context and guides the transformation by facilitating the required change towards realization of the government vision. As will be discussed in the next section, the Whole-of-Government Strategic Architecture defines business segments based on

functional grouping (independent of how agencies are structured within a government) and develops principles, standards, guidelines, roadmaps, reference models, and governance structure to guide government wide architectural activities.

The second type of architecture is the Agency Enterprise Architecture. Agency Enterprise Architecture provides agency specific high-level context to guide agency's service delivery within the larger Whole-of-Government enterprise context. With the input from Whole-of-Government Strategic Architecture, the Agency Enterprise Architecture addresses one or more business segments identified in the Strategic Architecture. This architecture also needs to specify the environment in which the agency is operating and define the various internal and external stakeholders' interaction with clear requirements and boundaries. Agency architecture complies with the Whole-of-Government conceptual and logical architectures and/or models and specifies detail business and technical capabilities to implement the business functional segment(s) identified at the Whole-of-Government strategic level.

The third type of architecture is Agency Solution Architecture. Agency Solution architecture develops a detailed architecture and design of a solution for the business and technical capabilities defined in the Agency Logical Architecture.

The following sections discuss how TOGAF may be used to deliver these architectures types.

USING TOGAF FOR THE WHOLE-OF-GOVERNMENT STRATEGIC ARCHITECTURE

As a part of its preliminary work, the Whole-of-Government EA should specify and develop the overarching Whole-of-Government context at strategic level to facilitate the various activities implementing change. Based on a clear understanding of the government transformation vision, goals and objectives, which clearly defines why government transformation is required, the Whole-of-Government EA in collaboration with key stakeholders identifies what needs to change to achieve the vision. To do that, first the Whole-of-Government EA needs to have a clear under-

standing of the government transformation vision, goals and objectives. The government transformation vision clearly defines why government transformation is required. Guided by this vision, the Whole-of-Government EA, in collaboration with the key stakeholders, identifies what needs to change to achieve the government transformation vision. After identifying and clearly describing all the things that need to change to enable the transformation vision, the Whole-of-Government EA will create its own vision on "how" to achieve the required change. Some of the concerns that need to be addressed in the Whole-of-Government EA vision include:

- Whole-of-Government EA scope
- Whole-of-Government EA driving principles, standards and guidelines
- Governance and change management capabilities to enable sustainable transformation
- Current architecture maturity assessment and the desired target maturity level
- How the change will be implemented towards that desired target maturity

This section discusses how TOGAF could be used to structure Whole-of-Government EA strategic activities in order to define and describe how the government transformation vision will be enabled and sustained. TOGAF ADM divides the architecture work into phases as shown in Figure 3. The key activities of Whole-of-Government Strategic Architecture in each of these phases are discussed below.

Preliminary Phase (P): Building Whole-of-Government EA Capability

The objective of this phase is to establish some key architectural capabilities to guide, manage, and govern the Whole-of-Government architecture initiatives. For the Whole-of-Government EA to be effective, the following key capabilities should be established:

Figure 3. TOGAF ADM for whole-of-government strategic architecture

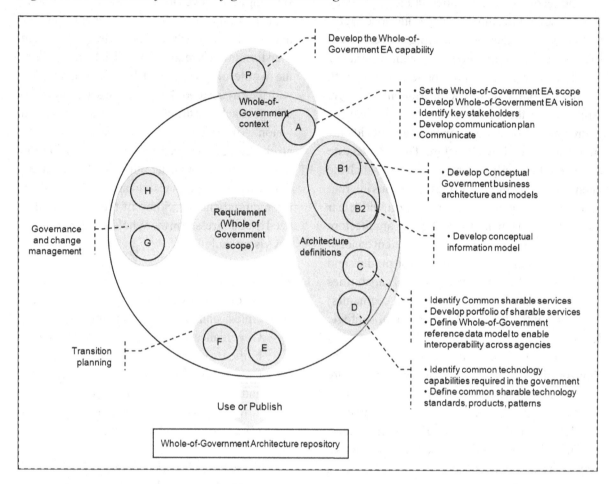

- Organizations, skills, roles and responsibilities to establish and operate the Whole-of-Government EA.
  ○ Build an effective team
    ▪ Identify key high-level government stakeholders responsible for initiating and supporting the Whole-of-Government transformation vision and confirm their commitment. Effective leadership and teamwork is critical for the success of the transformation.
    ▪ Identify all key stakeholders that may be impacted by the Whole-of-Government transfor-

mation vision and communicate the vision. This allows involving stakeholder agencies from the start and building a larger team working toward a common vision.
  ○ Establish Architecture Governance structure and processes
    ▪ Define a high-level Governance strategy that links various governance bodies and processes—Business governance, IT governance, EA governance, and SOA governance.
    ▪ It is important to have governance process in place for SOA.

The governance process and team are best identified and established during this phase.

- Establish EA-SOA centre of excellence and define the SOA goals and strategy for the enterprise in light of the current pain-points and long-term strategies.

- Adapt maturity models and assess the current maturity and determine the desired target maturity level

  - Government needs to have some sort of maturity model against which it can measure its maturity level. These maturity models include an architecture maturity model and SOA maturity model. An architecture maturity model can be used to evaluate overall government architecture capability. A SOA maturity model such as The Open Group Service Integration Maturity Model (OSIMM) may be used for assessing if the government and its agencies are positioned for service orientation and determine the required activities and roadmap.

  - In support of maturity assessment, it is necessary to assess the transformation readiness of individual agencies. This can be done, for example, by adopting the approach of Canadian Government Business Transformation Enablement Program (BTEP) (Forde, et al., 2009). It is necessary to conduct a business transformation readiness assessment to identify business transformation issues. This assessment can be done at this preliminary phase or phase A of TOGAF.

- Adapt or develop Reference Architectures or Models

  - To guide and facilitate architectural activities in subsequent phases and agency architectures, it is important to adopt applicable industry or government reference models and/or develop own government specific reference models. For example, the adaption of Federal Enterprise Architecture models combined with the adaption of industry SOA reference architectures or models can be a powerful guiding tool for the Whole-of-Government and agency architecture initiatives. It is particularly important to adapt the industry SOA Reference architecture to the needs of the Whole-of-Government enterprise architecture. SOA Reference Architecture is a general abstract reference that specifies known elements of SOA and building blocks that could be common for the whole government across agencies. Reference architecture may consist of set of architectural patterns that clearly describe and define the various elements of reference architecture. The other industry framework to adopt at this stage is the SOA Governance Framework (for example, the Open Group SOA Governance Framework).

- Develop Architecture Principles, standards and guidelines (e.g. service orientation, shared service, and interoperability principles)

  - In addition to other high-level architectural principles defined at this stage and also described in TOGAF, high level SOA related principles need to be identified. These principles must support the Whole-of-Government EA objectives which in turn supports sustainable government transformation vision.

  - To facilitate governance activity and allow for effective architecture compliance assessments, standards and guidelines need to be developed based on Whole-of-Government Reference Architecture. Usually, these standards and guidelines are identified based on known patterns that the government enterprise develops in support of the Reference Architecture description. A governance or architecture assessment body would use these standards and guidelines to assess architectural deliverables and check compliance with the architecture principles.

- Develop communication plan
  - The vision and various artifacts mentioned above must be communicated across the government agencies and other stakeholders.
  - Based on the vision, develop statement of direction on architecture approaches, frameworks, and styles (e.g. SOA as architectural style) that must be communicated to the whole enterprise.

It is very important that these capabilities are established in this TOGAF preliminary phase before moving on to the next phase of the strategic architecture.

Phase A: Defining the Scope and Creating the Vision

The deliverables from the previous phase (preliminary phase) are the input to phase A. The main objective of this phase is to develop architecture vision within a given scope. Based on initial contexts that are available as input to this phase (e.g. government vision, principles, guidelines, maturity levels, etc.), the Whole-of-Government EA strategic vision should be developed to show how the change will be implemented towards that desired maturity and set clear scope and constraints for each change initiative. It is very important to

define a clear scope of the Whole-of-Government and all the stakeholders at this stage. The scope could be defined in four dimensions, namely: Whole-of-Government focus; architecture domains (i.e. business, information, and technology); vertical scope (i.e. level of details); and time period (architecture activity schedule). It is important to note here that an overly ambitious scope will not succeed and a scope that is too small will not deliver the expected result.

In this phase of the strategic level of the architecture, it is also important to communicate the high-level service orientation concepts and SOA benefits for the stakeholders (e.g. government agencies). Define how SOA style will contribute and/or enable sustainable government transformation vision. SOA is not just about technology. For the Whole-of-Government EA, service orientation concept extends to business architecture and determines how business capabilities should be architected. Examples of such SOA approach can be found in Government of Canada SOA strategy (Treasury Board of Canada Secretariat, 2007).

The key deliverable from TOGAF phase A is a high-level conceptual architecture vision to facilitate stakeholder communication and validate stakeholder concern. This is important before doing any detailed business segments and capabilities architecture work. Here, all stakeholders will agree on the scope and vision of the Whole-of-Government EA and understand its impact on current agency architecture and operations.

Phase B: Business and Information Architecture

The focus of phase B of Strategic Architecture is to identify the business segments of the Whole-of-Government independent of how the various government agencies are structured to deliver government services. If any business reference model has been adopted in the preliminary phase that could then be reused from architecture repository. As depicted in Figure 4 example, this

Figure 4. Example structure of business reference model

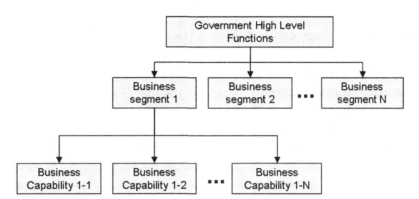

involves identification of high-level government business functions and breaking them down into functionally cohesive business segments with their own set of business capabilities. Modeling government business functions in this way will enable a phased delivery of the transformation vision and facilitate identification of potential redundant overlapping functions across agencies. An example of this type of approach can be found in Canadian Government Service Reference Model (Treasury Board of Canada Secretariat, 2004) as a part of Canadian Government Business Transformation Enablement Program (BTEP). BTEP is initially based on Zachman framework and Canadian Government recently standardized on TOGAF (Bryson & Perry, 2009). Another example is the Australian Government Architecture (AGA) Reference Model (Australian Government Information Management Office, 2009) based on Federal Enterprise Architecture (FEA) models. However, it is not clear from the reference documentation whether the Australian Government Architecture has adopted TOGAF or similar EA framework in conjunction with the FEA models.

Ideally the business segments map directly one-to-one to government agencies. However, there could be a case where business capabilities in a given business segment may be distributed across more than one agency. In any case, the agency structure-independent business model will

facilitate a consistent delivery of required business capabilities and also allows for managing changes associated with the agencies' restructuring. This also enables agencies to align their business architecture with the Whole-of-Government business model and clearly define what is expected of them.

The current version TOGAF 9 (Forde, et al., 2009) lacks Information Architecture in its ADM phases. However, in order to deliver end-to-end government services, the various business segments need to interact and interoperate through information exchange. The interoperability at business level is better handled through information interoperability. This means it is important to develop a high-level conceptual information model and semantic definitions to guide and simplify the information exchange between business segments. For this reason it is important to adapt TOGAF in such a way that information architecture can be done either as a part of this phase or as a separate phase as shown in Figure 3. Again, the adaption and reuse of Federal Enterprise Architecture models or similar can simplify the effort of developing such models. It would be useful also to define possible cross business capability relationships in the form of information and functionality provided.

Some of the key activities of this phase include:

- Identification of government business areas or functions
- Identification of business segments within each area or function
- Identification of high level business capabilities within each business segment
- Developing a roadmap as to when those business capabilities are required within Whole-of-Government transformation context
- Developing high level conceptual information model and semantic definition

SOA related activity at this stage is very high-level identification of the business segments (or capabilities within business segments) for which a SOA approach can be of benefit. Service orientation may not be applicable or required for all business capabilities identified in this phase. Identifying the capabilities for which a SOA approach is of benefit at strategic level would guide the subsequent agencies architectures as to where they must enforce SOA principles.

In addition to developing conceptual business and information reference models, the Whole-of-Government EA may have to define certain government business processes that transcend multiple agency boundaries. Such business processes may integrate with multiple agency specific business process. If such business processes exist, it is beneficial to define those processes at this strategic level to simplify interoperability with agency specific business processes. This can be done, for example, by applying service orientation principles and identifying information requirements with their semantics.

Note that the Whole-of-Government Strategic Architecture develops business and information models at a conceptual level. The conceptual business and information architectures developed here are input to the agency EA that develops agency logical architectures as will be discussed later.

Phase C: Service Architecture

TOGAF ADM uses the term "Information Systems Architecture" for phase C, which includes Application and Data Architectures. When TOGAF is used for Whole-of-Government Strategic Architecture, which defines high-level conceptual architectures, it is wise to use the term "Service Architecture" instead of "Information Systems Architecture." This is because services at this stage are still highly conceptual and no detail service and data modeling is required. The focus of this phase of strategic architecture is the identification and description of common cross agency sharable business services. This will enable reuse of capabilities across agencies and reduce cost by avoiding redundancy and duplication of similar capabilities within Whole-of-Government portfolio of services.

The main activities of this phase are:

- To identify government wide common sharable business services (possibly at business capability level or one level below within business capability).
- Grouping of sharable services into manageable Portfolio of services, which will be developed by various agencies.
- For the identified shared business services, define Whole-of-Government reference information model to enable reuse and interoperability across agencies

To enable such a reuse of common capabilities across multiple agencies it is important to adhere to service orientation principle in modeling those capabilities.

The information/data model and semantic model gets more specific as we go from strategic to agency architecture levels. For common sharable business services (or capabilities), it is generally advisable to define canonical data exchange models at this level. The other option is to identify the conceptual exchange model at this level and delegate the detail canonical data model to the agency implementing those capabilities. This is possible because, regardless of which agency implements them, those shareable services are governable in the scope of the Whole-of-Government information and service governance. Once the common shared business services are identified and described in this phase, the next phase will identify and describe the common sharable technical capabilities required to support those services.

Phase D: Technology Architecture

The main goal of this phase of strategic architecture is not to define detailed technology architecture. It is rather to identify and define the high-level technical capabilities at a conceptual level. Similar to what has been discussed for common sharable business services in phase C, this phase focuses on identification of common sharable technical capabilities, standards and patterns across the Whole-of-Government. Depending on the maturity level of the Whole-of-Government EA, it may also be possible to identify standard technology products at this stage. It is important to note that the technical capabilities identification is driven by business capability requirements.

If industry or government technical reference models have been adopted at the preliminary phase, these would be in the architecture repository for reuse in this phase. Those generic reference models can be reused or customized to define the required Whole-of-Government technical capabilities. Example of technical reference model is a SOA reference architecture, which includes definitions of end-to-end capabilities required for service orientation in general. Moreover, the various options and benefits of cloud services should also be assessed and the applicable cloud services strategy and guidelines should be developed at this phase.

The technical reference model delivered from this phase should be comprehensive enough to be reused and guide the agency technical architectures. The output from this phase will be an input to the agency technology architecture phase as will be discussed later in this chapter.

Phases E and F: Planning and Delivering the Architecture

The main goal of these phases is to formulate how to move from the conceptual architectures done in earlier phases to logical and physical realization of the architecture. All of the stakeholders (including the various government agencies and the Whole-of-Government EA) will be working together to rationalize the various activities that will move the strategic architecture to the next step. Guided by the Whole-of-Government objectives and roadmap, the collaborative team will map the conceptual business segments and associated business capabilities to various agencies. At this phase, the various stakeholders (mainly agencies) get aligned with the government transformation vision and understand what their role and responsibilities are within the bigger Whole-of-Government context. A high-level migration strategy is developed to communicate the overall approach and the dependencies. This way the various initiatives at the agency level will get a clear context as to how those initiatives will contribute to the overall transformation.

At this stage, it is important to align the Whole-Of-Government and agency priorities so that the government service delivery creates value in incremental fashion. If such an alignment is not done, agencies service delivery can be out of sync with the expected Whole-of-Government service delivery schedule. Such an alignment also allows for optimization of the cost of service delivery and government fund allocation. Government transformation is a multi-year initiative and as such, it requires developing a service delivery roadmap to align priorities and allow for incremental value realization over a sequence of short periods of time. It is not practical to plan to implement and deliver the government services all at the same time. That will take a long time, and if short-term wins are not created, the support and momentum will fade away. The practical and recommended approach is to deliver value incrementally under strong governance to manage changes and sustain the incremental values contributing to the overall transformation over time.

This is also where the readiness and architectural maturity of stakeholder agencies could be assessed and their impact and risk on the expected government service delivery can be evaluated. Any interoperability issues need to be examined and clarified to provide clear guidance for the stakeholder agencies architectures. It is also important at this time to confirm the federated governance approach between the Whole-of-Government EA governance and the individual agencies governance in such a way that end-to-end architecture compliance can be achieved and the architecture can continuously contribute to the delivery and sustainability of the Whole-of-Government transformation.

Phases G and H: Governance and Change Management

TOGAF Phases G and H focus on governance and change management. The previous phases (P, A-D) of Whole-of- Government strategic architecture have developed principles, standards, reference models, and conceptual architectures to facilitate the required government transformation. It is therefore important to make sure that these artifacts are properly incorporated into the government agencies' and other participating stakeholders' architectures. Otherwise, the Whole-of-Government enterprise architecture will not deliver the expected value and eventually may fail. It is important to ensure the various agency architectures are complaint with the Whole-of-Government conceptual architectures, reference models, principles, standards and guidelines. This is done through collaboration between the agency

architecture governance teams and the Whole-of-Government EA governance team. The agency architecture governance team is responsible for making sure that the agency architecture is properly implemented to deliver the expected value. By doing so the agency architecture will be in compliance with the Whole-of-Government Strategic Architecture, which means that the business services implemented at the agency level will meet the requirements set at the higher strategic level.

The other key aspect of this phase is architecture change management. Changes are inevitable and can come from any part of the government. From top-down, government strategic objectives may change over time as the citizens' demand or political landscape may change. From bottom-up, changes may result from agencies themselves—for example, agencies may face difficulties in complying with the published architectures because of agency specific business or technical reasons. For this and many other reasons, managing changes to the architecture in a cohesive manner is critical. To deal with such a dynamic change, it is a must to develop a change management process to ensure that the architecture enables the expected government transformation.

USING TOGAF FOR THE WHOLE-OF-GOVERNMENT SEGMENT: AGENCY ENTERPRISE ARCHITECTURE

This section explores how to deliver agency enterprise architecture using TOGAF by discussing the key architectural activities performed at each TOGAF ADM phase. Figure 5 shows the various TOGAF ADM phases as applied to the agency architecture.

Preliminary Phase (P): Building Agency Architecture Capability

The objective of TOGAF preliminary phase for Agency Enterprise Architecture is to develop or

Figure 5. TOGAF ADM for whole-of-government segment (i.e. agency) architecture

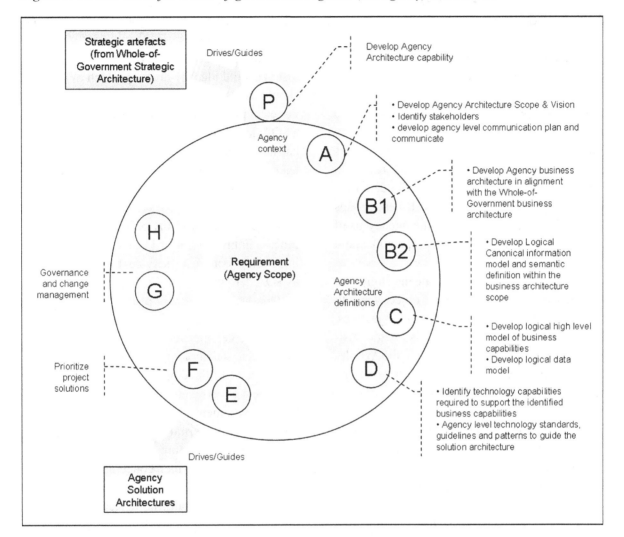

establish agency level architecture capabilities within Whole-of-Government context. Some of these capabilities are:

- Agency EA organization or architecture team
- Overall scope definition for the agency EA and alignment with the Whole-of-Government EA scope
- Agency EA governance body and governance processes
- Linkage path to the Whole-of-Government EA governance and change management processes
- Standard architecture tools specification
- Ensuring that the WOG reference models, standards, principles, guidelines, and patterns are adopted at the agency level

The deliverables at this preliminary phase will set agency EA context and as such, it is important that these capabilities are established before moving to the other architectural phases.

Phase A: Agency Architecture Scope and Vision

The main objectives of this phase are to define scope for the agency architecture, identify the stakeholders, develop the architecture vision, and obtain approval. Practical architecture scope should be defined and all stakeholders within that scope should be identified. The stakeholders concerns must be understood and addressed in the architecture vision. These stakeholders may include the Whole-of-Government EA and groups from the various areas within the agency itself (e.g. agency business, information, operations, and other groups). The architecture team collaborates with these stakeholders to validate the alignment of the agency's business goals and objectives with the Whole-of-Government goals and objectives. If not done already, guided by the strategic business reference model developed at the Whole-of-Government Strategic Architecture level, the agency EA identifies the business capabilities that the agency need to develop in order to fulfill the business goals and objectives of the agency within the context of the Whole-of-Government business strategy. Once the required business capabilities are defined, the agency's technical capability required to support those business capabilities can be identified. The architecture vision is then created to describe how the proposed business and technical capabilities will meet the government and agency business goals and objectives and address the stakeholders concerns.

Architecture vision is not detailed architecture—it is a high level conceptual architecture that is used to set the agency context within a defined scope and used to communicate with stakeholders for approval of the direction specified in the vision. Architecture vision includes conceptual description of business capabilities (in terms of business services), information and technical capabilities at high level without details. This is to the level that is just enough to make sure that the stakeholders concerns are addressed for the

scope of the architecture about to be done and to secure formal approval to proceed with the work in subsequent phases.

From a SOA perspective, the architecture vision should identify areas in which SOA style should be followed and describe the driver for it. For example, the architecture vision may identify a SOA driver coming from high level integration and interoperability requirements including cross-agency service reuse guided by the requirements defined earlier by the Whole-of-Government Strategic Architecture. Other agency objectives such as agency business agility or innovation through process improvement or IT simplification (with integration focus using services) can be identified as SOA derivers.

One key part of this phase, which is often overlooked, is the importance of communication. In order to get approvals and commitment from the various stakeholders (internal or external) it is important to develop a communication plan. Because a government agency operates within a larger government context consisting of diverse internal and external stakeholders, different views of an architecture vision must be created to communicate how their concerns are addressed in the overall architecture vision. It is also necessary to identify or confirm the Key Performance Indicators (KPI) associated with the architecture vision. If Federal Enterprise Architecture (FEA) reference Models are adopted earlier at the Whole-of-Government strategic level, then the FEA performance reference model can be used as guidance. The key output of this phase is the scoped and approved architecture vision along with its communication plan.

Phase B: Agency Business Architecture

The main objective of this phase is to develop an agency's target logical business architecture to support the conceptual business capabilities agreed upon in the previous phase (Phase A:

Architecture Vision). As will be discussed later in the solution architecture section, the logical business architecture defined here will guide the solution architecture projects.

TOGAF discusses the development of baseline and target architectures—the description of the current state and target state of agency business architecture. Given that the conceptual target business reference model is defined at the Whole-of-Government strategic level, it is not recommended to initially spend significant amount of time and money on developing agency current state architectures. This is about government transformation and as such the target state should be done first. Once the description of the target state business architecture is done, then the current state architecture—that is just enough to understand the current capabilities and create a roadmap to the future state—can be put together.

The major activities of this phase of Agency Architecture include:

- Develop business services model for common cross-agency shared business capabilities. These common sharable business capabilities should have been identified earlier at phase B of the Whole-of-Government strategic architecture and delegated to this agency at phases E and G of the Whole-of-Government Strategic Architecture.
- Identify business capabilities of this agency that are not shareable across agencies but specific to this agency and develop the corresponding business service model. This will enable the agency to be agile in providing these services as shared services when required (for example, due to change in government business vision). This is the case for example if after a period of time the government vision is augmented to include the citizen-driven services that require agency specific capabilities.

- Identify business services corresponding to all business capabilities in the scope.
- Develop (or adopt if it exists) logical Canonical information model and semantic definition for each capability area and business services
- Identify the high-level Key Performance Indicators (KPI) associated with each capability or business services

This phase will produce the description of the target state business architecture for the agency. Figure 6 shows an example where agency A is given responsibility for realization of the business capability 1, business capability 2, and business capability 3, which are identified at the Whole-of-Government strategic business architecture level. Agency A would then model the capabilities through identification of business services required to support those capabilities. The business services identification should be at the right level of granularity depending on the level of reuse required and other agency business goals. Business service granularity is related to the scope of service functionality. For example, if a business service is to be reused across government agencies, then the granularity should be determined in such a way that the scope of its functionality does not impede the reuse of the service—i.e. by including the functionality, which is not required by the consumers (other agencies). Where applicable, SOA principle should be applied to business services modeling.

The completed target business architecture should be reviewed by the stakeholders before moving to the next architecture phase. The stakeholders that need to review this target business architecture would have been identified earlier in phase A where the main architecture vision is developed and approved. The review should confirm that the target business architecture described in this phase will enable the agency to achieve that vision.

Figure 6. Example of decomposing the capabilities into business services

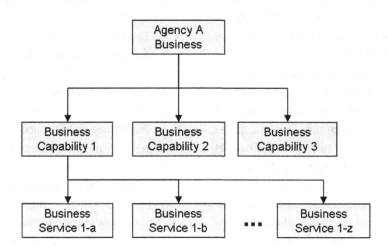

Figure 7. Example showing high-level business service decomposition into business processes and business activities

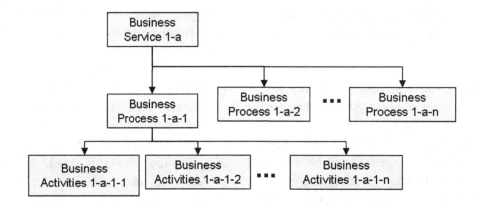

Phase C: Agency Services Architecture

The objective of this phase is to provide a detailed description of the business services identified and defined in phase B. Here the high-level business services are further modelled in terms of agency business processes and business activities. Again, SOA principles should be applied to business processes and business activities modeling. To achieve the desired level of reuse and interoperability it is important to model the services and processes at the right level of granularity determined by ser-

vice cohesion and dependencies. Figure 7 shows an example top-down decomposition of business service (modeled earlier in phase B) into business processes and business activities.

At this stage, the business services and business processes description should include the high level logical descriptions of the service contracts between business services and/or business processes (within the same or different business segments) to enable interoperability and cross-segment service reuse.

The output from this phase is a logical description of business services in terms of business processes descriptions (which are composite business activities). These business processes and activities identified here will be prioritized for implementation at phase E and G. The actual detail analysis and detail modeling of processes and activities is done in the agency solution architecture projects as will be discussed later in this chapter.

Phase D: Agency Technology Architecture

The objective of this phase of Agency Enterprise Architecture is to define the agency's logical technical capabilities. The technical capabilities defined at this stage are driven by the architecture descriptions of the previous phases. The technology architecture must support the business and technical requirements specified in phases A, B, and C. As discussed in the previous section, the Whole-of-Government Strategic Architecture has adopted (or developed) a technical reference model that defines conceptual technical capabilities common or sharable across government agencies. The agency technology architecture is therefore constrained (and should be in compliance) with the strategic conceptual technical reference models or architectures. With this as an input to Phase A of the agency EA, the agency wide technical capabilities should have been described at a conceptual level within the context of the business capabilities defined in the agency's architecture vision (also done in Phase A). As the architecture work progresses from phase A to C, the technical capabilities requirements get more specific. In phase D, with the technical conceptual capabilities and other requirements as input, a detail logical technology architecture should be developed to guide the technology use and decisions within the agency.

From a SOA perspective, the technical capabilities required for a SOA should have been identified conceptually in the technical reference model developed at the strategic level. It is possible that this phase may be able to reference (or

reuse) the SOA technical capabilities defined and deployed as sharable capability elsewhere in the government (for example, as private government cloud services). If cloud services strategy has been developed at Whole-of-Government Strategic Architecture level, this should be taken into account in the agency logical technology architecture as well.

Phases E and F: Planning the Agency Solution Delivery

The main goal of Phase E at Agency EA level is to formulate how to move from the logical agency architectures completed in the earlier phases to implementation solutions of the architecture. Based on agency's business services delivery roadmap, the solution projects are prioritized and get initiated. The solution projects are packaged in such a way that each delivery of solution set adds value and contributes to the agency business objectives.

Some TOGAF users state that solution architecture is not part of EA and as such, TOGAF cannot be used in the solution architecture scope. This assumption is incorrect because TOGAF ADM is a process and it does not dictate on the content of a particular architecture. Solution architecture is still architecture and needs to be managed properly. With this in mind, this phase should structure the solution projects in such a manner that each solution project will go through its own TOGAF ADM phases. Note that each solution project should deliver business value to the government agency and the deliverables (solution set) should be published (managed for reuse) in the agency's solution portfolio. Solution architecture using TOGAF ADM is discussed in the section below. Figure 8 depicts the relationship between Whole-of-Government EA, Agency EA, Agency Solution Architectures, and solution portfolio.

Since some agencies may have already some capabilities in place, Agency Architectures may need to assess current capabilities and develop a

Figure 8. Relationship between whole-of-government EA, agency EA, and agency-level solution archi-tectures

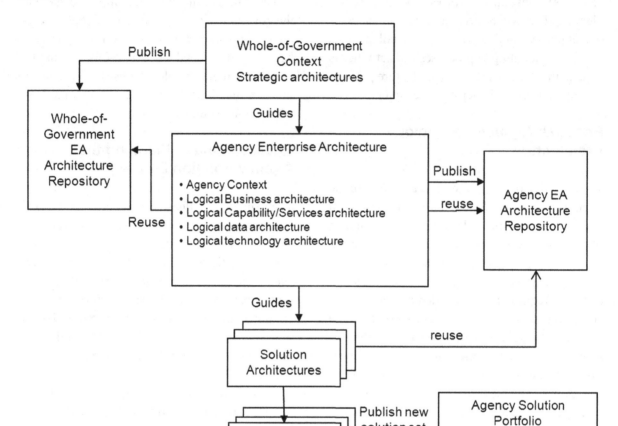

roadmap towards the target capabilities required by the Whole-of-Government strategy. As a result, agency architecture should guide the grouping and initiation of solution projects to deliver the required solution sets.

Phases G and H: Implementation Governance and Change Management

At Agency EA level, the TOGAF Phase G and H focuses on Agency Architecture governance and change management within the context of

the Whole-of-Government EA governance. The agency governance body should work closely and collaboratively with the Whole-of-Government EA governance body. It is thus important to ensure the various Agency Architectures are complaint with the Whole-of-Government conceptual architectures, reference models, principles, standards, and guidelines. This is done through collaboration between the Agency Architecture governance teams and the Whole-of-Government EA governance team. The Agency Architecture governance team is responsible for making sure that the agency architecture is properly implemented to deliver

Figure 9. TOGAF ADM for agency solution architecture

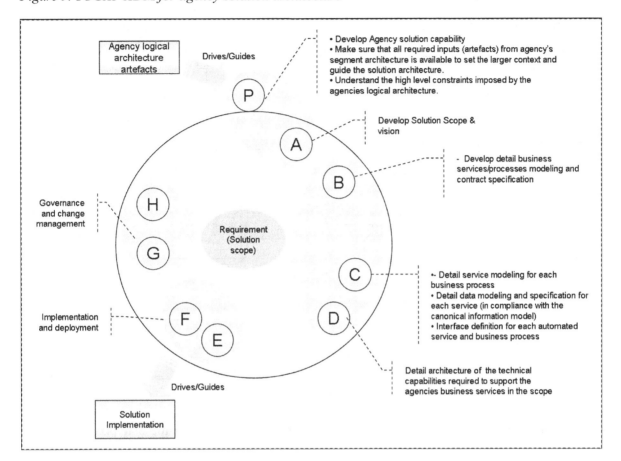

the expected value. By doing so the Agency Architecture will be in compliance with the Whole-of-Government Strategic Architecture—which means that the business services implemented at the agency level will meet the requirements set at the higher strategic level.

From change management perspective the agency, governance body should effectively manage the architectural changes that have impact on the business services delivery.

USING TOGAF FOR AGENCY SOLUTION ARCHITECTURE

This section presents how TOGAF could be used to structure, manage, and deliver Agency Solution Architectures in compliance with the agency's logical architectures developed earlier by the Agency EA. The key activities and deliverables of each TOGAF ADM phase of the Solution Architecture are discussed below. As depicted in Figure 9, guided by the government guidelines (standards) and the agency logical architectures, the Agency Solution Architecture will develop:

- Detailed solution vision that sets clear and practical scope of the solution
- Detailed business process model
- Detailed data models to support the identified business services
- Detailed service/application model to support the business services

Figure 10. Agency solution architecture details

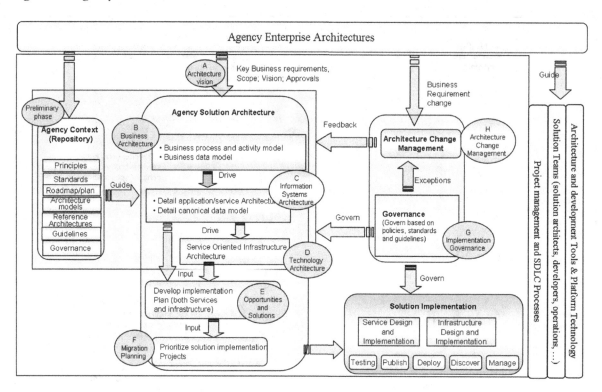

• Detailed technology model to implement the services and applications

Figure 10 shows how the Agency EA and Agency Solution Architectures are linked. The guiding agency context has been developed by the agency EA and published in the Agency Architecture repository. The agency context guides all solution architectures within the agency scope.

The input to solution architecture work is a concrete and specific business requirement. Multiple projects, each with its own concrete business requirements and architecture work, can be initiated simultaneously in a given enterprise—which is the most likely case for the government agencies. All of these projects are then guided by the guidelines, standards, reference models, and logical architectures that are supported by governance process. The architecture governance (including SOA governance) ensures that the various

projects comply with the enterprise guidelines and standards and agency logical architectures.

Solution Implementation is not architecture, but a realization of the architecture. Though implementation is not part of the architecture, it is part of end-to-end service delivery work. Services are composed or orchestrated to implement the required business process. It is only through implementation that the architecture's value is realized by business. The solution implementation stage includes: detailed solution design, development of the solution, service testing, service deployment, service monitoring and management. It is only after services are developed, deployed, and managed that the business impact and value can be measured. Services are deployed, monitored, and managed in an infrastructure that is specified by the agency's technology architecture (discussed earlier in phase D of Agency Architecture).

Preliminary Phase (P): Setting Context for Agency Solution Architecture

The objective of the TOGAF preliminary phase for solution architecture is to create solution project teams (if they do not already exist) that include solution governance. This is to make sure that all required artifacts of agency logical architecture are available to set the context and guide the solution architecture. These artifacts are normally managed in the Agency Architecture repository for reuse by the solution architecture projects (see Figure 8). The service portfolio plan including the business service and business process model and related descriptions developed earlier by Agency EA are input to this phase. At this stage, all of the architectural constraints imposed by the agency logical architecture are clearly communicated to the solution architecture team.

Up until now, the service orientation principle was used conceptually to identify and define business services and processes at the granularity level that is fit for the purpose. At the solution architecture level, more technology oriented SOA principles will be used within the context of a conceptual technical reference model. For this reason, if not done at the agency EA level, it is important to define applicable additional SOA related technical terminologies and communicate at this stage.

Phase A: Setting Solution Scope and Creating Solution Guiding Vision

Each Solution Architecture addresses part of agency business capability, which is defined in terms of business services (composed of business processes). The objective of this phase of Solution Architecture is to set that solution scope and identify the solution stakeholders and their concerns (e.g. security, operations, vendor partners, etc.) to develop high-level overview (vision) of how

the solution pieces are going to be delivered. The solution scope should not be too big or too small. If scope is too big, besides the risk of increasing complexity in implementation, the solution delivery may take so long with unexpected cost and may not deliver the expected business value. If it is too small, the solution's business value and impact may not be visible, making it hard to justify the overall value of the architecture. The solution vision should not be detailed to the level that is going to be done in the TOGAF phases B, C, and D. It should however reflect the SOA approach that will be used in the solution.

The scope and the high-level solution overview should be communicated with all stakeholders. Once all internal and external stakeholders are onboard and approve the solution scope and approach, then the next phase of solution architecture (phase B) commences.

Phase B: Detail Business Services Solution Description

The objective of this phase of Solution Architecture is to model the details of business services (consisting of one or more business processes) with their service contract specification. The inputs to this phase are the logical business services and business processes models together with their corresponding logical information model developed earlier. At this stage, the business services and processes are further modelled in detail to the level that it can be translated into the basic SOA services form which business applications will be created. The detailed information entity model done here is also going to drive the creation of concrete canonical data models and service contracts in phase C using applicable technology standards. For each business service, concrete and measurable business metrics are also defined in detail and validated based on the KPI defined earlier in the agency logical business architecture.

Phase C: Information System Services Detail Description

TOGAF uses the term Information System Services for business services that are translated into technology based services (software services). The objective of phase C of solution architecture is to define SOA based information system services based on the business service model input from phase B. Business processes are described in terms of orchestration or composition of atomic information system services. Detail service specification is done here so that the implementation team can use them to develop a software implementation of the service. The logical information model is used to create a concrete canonical data model and associated schemas (for example XML schemas).

Phase D: Detail Description of Technical Capabilities

The objective of phase D of Solution Architecture is to create a detailed architecture for the technical capabilities required to support the business services that are in the solution scope. The work in this phase is highly constrained by the agency logical technology architecture completed earlier. This is the case because technology standards, product standards, and other technology decisions may have been made in the agency logical target architectures; and the solution technology architecture must comply with those standards or decisions. The solution architect should identify all technical capabilities required for the implementation and deployment of the business services defined in earlier phases. Once the required capabilities are identified, the architect should look into the agency repository for technical capabilities that may have already been implemented and deployed as sharable infrastructure. If the current solution requires new capabilities (i.e. have not been implemented as common service in the government infrastructure),

then the solution project team is going to provide detailed architecture and design to implement and deploy as agency sharable technical capability (if those technical services are common across the government agency). Agency or government wide technology standards and products should be used. If cloud services are specified in the agency logical architecture, the detail cloud service integration design should be done at this level.

Phases E and F: Implementation Projects and Plan

The objectives of phases E and F of solution architecture are to package the work into implementation projects and prioritize (or plan) the implementation. The implementation projects develop software, configure standard products or packaged applications and deploy into agency standard platforms in the infrastructure. Services are composed or orchestrated to implement the required business process. Solution Implementation is not architecture, but a realization of the architecture. Though implementation is not part of the architecture, it is part of end-to-end business service delivery. As depicted in Figure 10, the solution implementation stage includes the following: (1) detailed solution design, (2) development of the solution, (3) testing, (4) deployment, and (5) monitoring and management. The business sees the value only after services are developed, deployed, and managed. Services are deployed, monitored, and managed in an infrastructure that is specified by the Agency technology architecture.

If the service delivery option includes cloud services provided by government or external providers, the detailed cloud service integration plan should be described at this stage. Once tested and deployed, the new services are packaged into solution set and published into agency's service portfolio for future reuse or reference.

Phases G and H: Solution Governance and Change Management

The objectives of Phase G and H of Solution Architecture are to provide governance and change management for the solution architecture and implementation. The main goal is to improve the quality of business service delivery by ensuring that the solution architecture and solution implementation are in compliance with the Agency Logical Architecture. If for some reason the Solution Architecture or solution implementation fails to comply with the Agency Logical Architecture or guidelines, then the risk associated with such non-compliance should be evaluated carefully. If the risk is manageable and exception is granted, then the exception should be managed by the agency's governance team. Too much an exception at the solution architecture and implementation level is a good sign that some parts of Agency Architecture or guidelines need a review (with those exceptions as input to the architecture review process). This can also be a feedback to Whole-of-Government EA, and as a result, the guidelines, standards, and models developed at the Whole-of-Government EA or Agency EA level may be re-visited to improve the end-to-end effectiveness of the architecture.

CONCLUSION

Whole-of-Government Enterprise Architecture (EA) focuses on enabling government strategic transformation to achieve public sector reform and government modernization. To properly manage the associated complexity and enable the expected strategic transformational change, this chapter proposed the partitioning of the Whole-of-Government architecture work into three levels. These architecture levels are: Whole-of-Government Strategic Architecture, Agency Enterprise Architecture, and Agency Solution Architecture. These architectures and their relationships are discussed in some detail. This chapter also provided a detailed discussion on how TOGAF and SOA may be adopted to Whole-of-Government EA to develop those three architecture types. The combination of TOGAF (as a guiding architectural process) and SOA (as architectural style) will allow the Whole-of-Government EA to structure and manage the various architectures and the associated risks effectively.

REFERENCES

Abramson, M. A., Breul, J. D., & Kamensky, J. M. (2005). *Six trends transforming government*. IBM Center for the Business of Government Report. Retrieved from http://www.businessofgovernment. org/report/six-trends-transforming-government.

Australian Government Information Management Office. (2009). *Australian government architecture reference models*. Retrieved from http://www.finance.gov.au/e-government/strategy-and-governance/docs/AGA_RM_v2_0.pdf.

Bennett, S. G., Carrato, T., Dico, A., Gejnevall, M., Harrington, E., & Hornford, D. (2011). Using TOGAF to define and govern service-oriented architectures. *The Open Group*. Retrieved from https://www2.opengroup.org/ogsys/jsp/publications/PublicationDetails.jsp?publicationid=12390.

Bittinger, S. (2011). *Hype cycle for government transformation, 2011*. Retrieved from http://www.gartner.com.

Blevins, T., Dandashi, F., & Tolbert, M. (2010). *The open group architecture framework (TOGAF™ 9) and the US department of defense architecture framework 2.0 (DoDAF 2.0)*. Retrieved from https://www2.opengroup.org/ogsys/jsp/publications/PublicationDetails.jsp?catalogno=w105.

Bryson, R., & Perry, A. (2009). *Government of Canada enterprise architecture- A collaborative practice.* Retrieved from https://www.opengroup. org/conference-live/uploads/40/20078/Mon_-_ am_-_2_-_Perry.pdf.

Dodaro, G. L. (2011). *Opportunities to reduce potential duplication in government programs, save tax dollars, and enhance revenue.* Retrieved from http://www.gao.gov.

Forde, C., Varnus, J., Fehskens, L., Josey, A., Doherty, G., & Fox, C. (2009). *TOGAF version 9: The open group architecture framework (TOGAF).* Reading, UK: The Open Group.

Hite, R. C. (2003). *Leadership remains key to agencies making progress on enterprise architecture efforts.* Retrieved from http://www.gao. gov/cgi-bin/getrpt?GAO-04-40.

Hite, R. C. (2004). *The federal enterprise architecture and agencies' enterprise architectures are still maturing.* Retrieved from http://www.gao. gov/cgi-bin/getrpt?GAO-04-798T.

Institute of Citizen Centred Service. (2011). *Business transformation enablement program (BTEP).* Retrieved from http://www.iccs-isac. org/en/practice/btep/.

Liegl, P., Mosser, R., Hofreiter, B., Zapletal, M., & Huemer, C. (2007). *Modeling e-government processes with UMM.* Retrieved from http://epress. lib.uts.edu.au/research/handle/10453/5899.

Liimatainen, K., Hoffmann, M., & Heikkilä, J. (2007). *Overview of enterprise architecture work in 15 countries. Report of the Finnish Enterprise Architecture Research Project.* Helsinki, Finland: Ministry of Finance.

Micrsoft. (2010). *Connected government framework strategies to transform government in the 2.0 world.* Retrieved from http://www.cstransform. com/resources/index.htm.

Muehlfeit, J. (2006). *The connected government framework for local and regional government.* Retrieved from http://download.microsoft.com/ download/7/f/0/7f08183b-c84f-491b-9b3f-%20 c3d4b0521758/MS_LRG_CGF_Overview_new. pdf.

Saha, P. (2010a). *Enterprise architecture as platform for connected government: Understanding the impact of enterprise architecture on connected government: A qualitative analysis. Phase 1 Report.* NUS Institute of Systems Science.

Saha, P. (2010b). *Advancing the Whole-of-Government Enterprise Architecture Adoption with Strategic (Systems) Thinking. Phase 2 Report.* Singapore, Singapore: NUS Institute of Systems Science.

Spencer, P. (2007). *Connected government: Creating a springboard for transformation and innovation.* Retrieved from http://www.cisco.com/ web/about/ac79/docs/wp/ctd/Connected_Govt_ PoV_1030_finalCB.pdf.

Treasury Board of Canada Secretariat. (2004). *Business transformation enablement program (BTEP): GSRM service reference patterns.* Retrieved from http://www.collectionscanada.gc.ca/ webarchives/20071125180244/www.tbs-sct. gc.ca/btep-pto/index_e.asp.

Treasury Board of Canada Secretariat. (2007). *Government of Canada service oriented architecture strategy.* Retrieved from http://www. tbs-sct.gc.ca/cio-dpi/webapps/architecture/sd-eo/ sd-eotb-eng.asp.

Chapter 8
Enterprise Architecture in Countries with Volatile Governance:
Negotiating Challenges and Crafting Successes

Saleem Zoughbi
UN-ESCWA, Lebanon

Sukaina Al-Nasrawi
UN-ESCWA, Lebanon

ABSTRACT

The growing adoption and use of Information and Communication Technologies (ICTs) in public administration enables global alteration of functions and business processes used by Governments hoping to convert into viable and successful e-governances. The main objectives are not limited to the traditional e-government goals, but also to improve public sector efficiency, transparency, and accountability, and lower cost across all government administrations, thus leading to the reengineering of the public sector. This could happen at different levels. The success rate is related to results achieved in e-democracy, e-transparency, citizen's involvement in public management, and other controversial outcomes, which may not be welcome in some countries. With the advent of EA, one sees a more comprehensive method of solving customization problems. The number of difficulties and obstacles may increase when dealing with issues related to the transformation into e-governance at the micro level; hence, a more efficient way is to introduce an EA framework where one can leverage these difficulties before the actual transformation.

DOI: 10.4018/978-1-4666-1824-4.ch008

THE PROBLEM / CHALLENGE

Despite the advancements in developing EA solutions for governments, much of the work remains a fine piece of achievement in design and good will, but very little has been implemented. In many instances, consulting firms are contracted to do comparable EA design and development in some countries, but these remain only partially realized. There are numerous reasons stopping the implementation of EA solutions (Spewak, 1993). These include:

- The decision makers involved in such EA development are not "decision makers" in the sense that a serious political figure has enough leverage on them so they can hinder, or even in some cases stop, any implementation on EA plans that were already agreed upon;
- The resources upon which the EA development planning is based are not clearly committed by the governments concerned, and even after starting implementation, priorities are changed, as well as financing plans and other reasons.
- Partners in the EA development have to stand their ground. One of the main worries is that higher-level managers and government officials change very frequently, and the project may run into a "reinventing the wheel" situation.

The problem here is to investigate if EA development can be processed in a way where the effect of obstacles could be minimized. There are risks to EA practitioners in such countries where governance is very volatile. With the lack of good governance, even qualified professionals will encounter risks (Spewak, 1992). They could be affected by the opinions of decision makers, results of inadequate decisions, and poor work coordination. These risks are numerous and they include:

- Lack of Alignment;
- IT centric;
- Stand-alone initiatives;
- Lack of cross-functional process owners;
- Enterprise Optimization focus is in the wrong place; and
- Too much focus on the micro level.

MEASURING GOVERNANCE

The World Bank Institute led a project named Worldwide Governance Indicators (WGI). The project's indicators were designed to measure six main dimensions of governance. Reports covered 213 economies over the period of 1996–2009. The six dimensions of governance were:

1. Voice and Accountability;
2. Political Stability and Absence of Violence;
3. Government Effectiveness;
4. Regulatory Quality;
5. Rule of Law; and
6. Control of Corruption.

The issue of governance is not the subject of this chapter; however, there is a need to distinguish between different kinds of governance (Weill & Ross, 2004). The definitions of governance could vary in form; however, they all are focused on a few important issues, such as exercising authority and formulating effective policies and mutual respect, especially for government institutions. For each of these focus areas, some indicators were devised to measure the success in each area. These are called the World Governance indicators. Table 1 is a listing of the definitions of the World Bank Institute indicators.

All of these measures have a defined set of empirical values and a way to measure them, aggregated into a single number as a value of each of these six indicators. These six dimensions of governance should not be thought of as being independent of one another. There is a lot more

Table 1. Measures of governance used by the world bank

Two measures of governance are constructed corresponding to each of these three areas, resulting in a total of six dimensions of governance. These are as follows:
a. The process by which governments are selected, monitored, and replaced:
    1. Voice and Accountability (VA) – capturing perceptions of the extent to which a country's citizens are able to participate in selecting their government, as well as freedom of expression, freedom of association, and a free media.
    2. Political Stability and Absence of Violence/Terrorism (PV) – capturing perceptions of the likelihood that the government will be destabilized or overthrown by unconstitutional or violent means, including politically-motivated violence and terrorism.
b. The capacity of the government to effectively formulate and implement sound policies:
    3. Government Effectiveness (GE) – capturing perceptions of the quality of public services, the quality of the civil service and the degree of its independence from political pressures, the quality of policy formulation and implementation, and the credibility of the government's commitment to such policies.
    4. Regulatory Quality (RQ) – capturing perceptions of the ability of the government to formulate and implement sound policies and regulations that permit and promote private sector development.
c. The respect of citizens and the state for the institutions that govern economic and social interactions among them:
    5. Rule of Law (RL) – capturing perceptions of the extent to which agents have confidence in and abide by the rules of society, and in particular, the quality of contract enforcement, property rights, the police, and the courts, as well as the likelihood of crime and violence.
    6. Control of Corruption (CC) – capturing perceptions of the extent to which public power is exercised for private gain, including both petty and grand forms of corruption, as well as "capture" of the state by elites and private interests.

http://info.worldbank.org/governance/wgi/index.asp

Table 2. Worldwide governance indicators for selected countries

SOMALIA	SOM	-3.31		MONACO	MCO	1.09
PAKISTAN	PAK	-2.76		SWEDEN	SWE	1.10
AFGHANISTAN	AFG	-2.75		QATAR	QAT	1.12
SUDAN	SDN	-2.65		AUSTRIA	AUT	1.13
IRAQ	IRQ	-2.33		NORWAY	NOR	1.19
YEMEN	YEM	-2.31		SWITZERLAND	CHE	1.21
Congo, Dem. Rep.	ZAR	-2.13		FINLAND	FIN	1.36

than just simple calculations. However, these figures are used as an indicator in a good sense of how governance is viewed or "measured" in terms of governance. The values are normalized. The aggregate indicators combine the views of a large number of enterprise, citizen, and expert survey respondents in industrial and developing countries. The individual data sources underlying the aggregate indicators are drawn from a diverse variety of survey institutes, think tanks, non-governmental organizations, and international organizations. Definitions of these six aggregate indicators and the underlying data sources can be found at the World Bank Institute home page (http://info.worldbank.org/governance/wgi/index.asp). For example, for the indicator of po-

litical stability and absence of violence, values ranged from negative to positive. Table 2, shows Somalia as politically very unstable with a lot of violence (-3.31), while Finland enjoyed a high degree (+1.36) of political stability and absence of violence.

If there is no political stability, and we are not referring to the highest governing level, it will be very difficult to implement a sustained EA practice. That encourages us to seek other ways of finding sustained EA practices rather than step back and refrain from doing anything. In fact, there are many qualities in these indicators, and once analyzed, some hints may be drawn regarding which route could be followed to achieve the desired goal. In this chapter, the term Volatility of Governance refers to instability and unpredictability of governing authorities when it comes to institutional change, organization behavior, and politics and rules of governance. Consequently, these countries will be referred to as Countries with Volatile Governance (CVG).

RETHINKING E-GOVERNANCE

The growing adoption and use of Information and Communication Technologies in public administration enables the global alteration of the functions and business processes used by all Governments and leads to E-Government (Federal Enterprise Architecture Framework Version 1, 1999). E-Government provides citizens with speedy and convenient services, improves public sector efficiency, transparency, and accountability, and lowers cost across all Government administrations. Although e-government implementation has been successful in many developed countries, the majority of developing countries, including Arab countries in Western Asia, are still struggling, despite all their efforts to implement e-government. This raises many questions related to the obstacles that are stopping developing countries from emerging into the world of e-Governance. In fact, e-Governance is a wider issue than e-Government focusing on the whole spectrum of the relationships and networks within government, on a larger level, it is the application of ICT as a driving force to ensure success of the delivery of e-services. This includes definitely the relationships between lower level government offices and public servants and the wider society *(civil society organization in addition to the citizen and the private sector)*. The basic requirements for e-governance include the ability to deliver information across platforms and from different government sources (information and databases). Certainly, it must be able to interact efficiently (faster and reliable communications). In all aspects, it has to depend on backend operations, and therefore, maximize them and minimize user

involvement (Process optimization). It is worth mentioning that there are axioms that have been observed worldwide:

- Differences between poor and good governance can be easily identified and quantized;
- During the transformation towards e-governance, introducing ICT to either kind of governance (good or bad) will inherit the problems and difficulties; and
- There is a need to restructure and "reengineer" governance at the micro level in each governmental body or ministry to fit such necessary "reengineering."

No matter how advanced and mature e-government applications are, their final destination is well defined by the ***spread of democracy, transparency, and efficiency of serving the citizen***. Well-established e-government systems cannot avoid the need to assume an additional characteristic, function, and trend, namely the complex task of ***coordinating, networking, and "connecting"*** all providers of e-services, such as different government agencies within the same government, or in between governments (Chen & Vernadat, 2004). Hence, "connected governments" are connected, not in terms of networking only, but also of data and applications.

EA AS AN ENABLER FOR E-GOVERNANCE

Overview

EA started around twenty years ago because of two major reasons:

- **System complexity**—government organizations were spending lots of resources on building IT systems;

- **Poor business alignment**—these organizations were facing difficulties in keeping information systems in alignment with business needs and continuous technological evolution.

EA did not provide magic solutions to these two chronic problems. In fact, implementing systems in government organizations continuously exhibited two characteristics: *more cost, less value*. The cost and complexity of IT systems have exponentially increased, while the chances of deriving real value from those systems has dramatically decreased. This is why, as even large government organizations cannot sustain such systems alone, EA became a very promising solution to them. So it is not only the struggle of overpower, silos, and lack of cooperation with the same government, it is becoming more of "connect or perish" (Van den berg & Steenbergen, 2010).

Looking at the e-government applications from the larger picture, we realize there are four important requirements that determine their success.

- **Citizen development:** It is important that citizens become involved on a participatory approach. Their e-participation can be measured and monitored; thus, a new citizen is becoming a full partner.
- **Governmental reform:** Unless government is ready to implement reform, nothing will move. This reform would be at the process level, organizational level, behavioral, and most of all, strategic level. This will necessitate transparency measures to be put in place.
- **Geopolitical changes:** As a result, many political changes in the organizations and their management will take place; these changes will often involve geopolitical changes as well.
- **ICT development:** The driving force is of course technology. The proper technology, be it infrastructure, platforms, applica-

tions, communications, or data, are the true mechanisms for implementing all logical designs and architectures.

The combination of these four major areas of change will enable what we call true EA for e-governance. That is a simple, yet incomplete introduction of EA.

Application to e-Governance

Why would we use an EA? Once a decision is taken to adopt EA for a government ministry, a specific purpose or reason has motivated that decision. Architectural changes should be implemented with a specific purpose. Most common reasons and purposes are:

- Business process reengineering;
- Systems acquisition;
- System-of-systems migration or integration;
- User training; and
- Interoperability evaluation.

The architecture aims at facilitating such reasons, yet maintaining the ministry's (or organization's) strategic plan. Certainly, it should not violate the legislative aspects of it. The changes that the organization would look for are the starting point in looking for the appropriate architecture and way to implement it. An analytical study before doing anything is very crucial, since it will affect the design of any EA selected. Such study would include questions the architecture is expected to help answer (Graves, 2008). It is not the intent of this chapter to discuss such practices; however, many resources can be located. As the architecture is being studied, one attains and compiles a lot of information. A need for a very concise, yet efficient logical structure for this data should be selected (Heeks & Bailur, 2007). This is called the EA Framework. A well-defined procedure can be found easily to provide guidance in initiating, developing, using, and maintaining enterprise architecture, offering an end-to-end process to initiate, implement, and sustain an EA program. Such a procedure can describe the necessary roles and associated responsibilities for a successful EA program. In all cases, there must be two major principles behind any EA practice:

1. Create a citizen-centered, customer-focused government that maximizes technology investments to better achieve the government vision and its mission outcomes.
2. Encourage the incremental and continuous architecture development with segment architecture approach.

The second principle advocates an approach that is not all-or-none, leading to a W-O-G (Whole Of Government). In fact, we suggest that this incremental step approach would lead to a P-O-G (Part Of Government) (Minoli, 2008). Guaranteeing these two practices, the stability of any EA adoption will be normally sustained. It is worth mentioning that Chief of Information Officers (CIOs) of a government practically look into adoption of EA for improving practices in the design, modernization, use, sharing, and performance of national information resources (Land, et al., 2008). There are certain advantages to this fact:

*   GCIOs are highly educated and they know each other from work or even from university education. Hence, they would be more open to discussion and cooperation and working together. As long as they do not break the regulations that affect the power domination of their superiors and do ask for funding, there will most likely be an initial approval for possible actions along EA development.
*   The young generation of CIOs in these countries are looking for better positions, better experience, and opportunities to advance. They would be more than willing

to get involved in new technical practices, such as adopting EA models on a minor level in their departments.

Leading Government Transformation

The impact of EA on governance is seen clearly within the development of a more efficient structure and processes whereby public sector performance gets better, resources are optimized, and the overall function of the government becomes better (in terms of good governance) (Godinez, et al., 2010). However, it is not as simple and structured as it looks. This impact can be realized and measured, but many factors play a major role in the success of this task. To better understand this issue, let us consider a simple model of a governance level structure. In Figure 1, three concentric circles, labeled 1, 2, and 3 represent the government structure vis-à-vis the governing process. Think of the innermost circle (1) as a particular ministry or government organization. Naturally, there are many circles of this kind running in parallel. Within this circle, one can apply EA in mostly technical terms. Within this context, the involvement of higher governing officials from the government is not likely, and

Figure 1. Government structure vis-à-vis the governing process

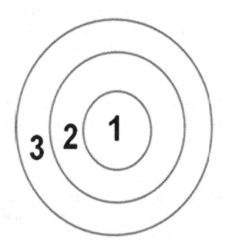

least resistance for change is expected. The impact of applying EA within this limited concept would result in specific technical improvement. Normally, government officials would always welcome better technical performance as long as it does not interfere with existing ways of running the government. In other words, as long as it does not step into level 2, application of EA would be most accepted. Defining level 2 as that of government operations involving mid-level management and decision-making, EA would be have a high potential of application. However, this involves some change of how government may do business. This results in a higher impact than that in level 1. Consequently, taking this to a higher level, such as level 3, EA at this high level government business would have a high impact. Table 3 summarizes this paradigm.

Looking at this paradigm from outside, the active and efficient application of EA would result in requirements for change in the way governments do business. The ability of a government to accept such change and go through this transformation is subject to several factors, such as sufficient resources, adequate decision support on management and planning, intergovernmental coordination, and network and others. However, specific high-level impact of EA at this level would directly touch governance (Federal Enterprise Architecture Framework Version 1, 1999). Critical issues such as transparency, citizen-empowerment, and e-democracy would become the transformation challenge of these governments. Naturally, in countries with volatile governance, a wide controversy would engulf any EA activity at

level 3, at least, and hence, government transformation would be very much in question.

CURRENT GOVERNMENT PROBLEMS AND OBSTACLES TO EA

In many countries, particularly Countries with Volatile Governance (CVG) there are always risks and obstacles to EA:

- Lack of Alignment: In many organizations, several parts and processes, including data are rarely aligned harmonically. This raises the chances for redundancy, duplication of work, inefficient public performance, and certainly of unnecessary spending;
- IT centric: The focus on IT and technology becomes obsessive and raises costs.
- Solo initiatives: This is in fact the most hated attitude of development in any government organization, and logically speaking nowadays, is unthinkable.
- Lack of cross-functional process owners: Efficient process reengineering and design.
- Enterprise Optimization focus is enforced incorrectly: Not much trust and power is given to EA professionals to clear and implement their findings and designs, especially in such countries.
- It can be ruled out that by the time EA work is going on, weak designs and implementers get lost in the details, without proper professional monitoring from the government.

Table 3. Impact of enterprise architecture on governance transformation

Level	Scope of operation	Potential of EA application	Impact on governance transformation
1	Technical	Limited	Least
2	Management & processes	High	Medium
3	Policy	Could vary significantly	High

REVISITING EA MODELS

Many enterprise-architectural methodologies have come and gone in the last 20 years. Today, it is estimated that perhaps 90% of EA work uses one of these four methodologies (Zachman, 1996; The Open Group Architecture Framework, 1999; Federal Enterprise Architecture Framework Version 1, 1999; Rechtin & Maier, 1997):

- The Zachman Framework for Enterprise Architectures: Although self-described as a *framework*, it is actually more accurately defined as *taxonomy;*
- The Open Group Architectural Framework (TOGAF): Although called a *framework*, is actually more accurately defined as a *process;*
- The Federal Enterprise Architecture: Can be viewed as either an *implemented EA* or a *proscriptive methodology* for creating an enterprise architecture;
- The Gartner Methodology: Can be best described as an *enterprise architectural practice;*

How should a governmental organization choose from among these four different approaches to enterprise architecture? Each carries within itself characteristics that facilitate implementation and provide room for professionals to be creative and efficient.

None of these methodologies is complete by itself, and by examining weaknesses and strengths of each, one can find some hybrid and blended approach that may fit the practical need.

It is worth mentioning that one can view the main goal of EA as the improvement of the government organization competitiveness in an increasingly competitive world. It is also important to keep in mind that, as professionals say: *"EA means architecting the enterprise to enable change."*

AN ADOPTED METHOD

Most of the models of EA are driven by stepwise logical development, and that makes them all candidates for modifications in order to fit particular country cases. As an example, we have chosen to pick the Open Group TOGAF ADM (Architecture Development Method). For many reasons, this method can be adaptable to countries with volatile governance. Some of these reasons include generality of design constraints, flexibility of low-level decision-making, etc. The method itself, ADM, is concerned with actual development of the four architectures:

1. Business architecture;
2. Application architecture;
3. Data architecture; and
4. Technology architecture.

The data and application architectures together are called the information system architecture. They are composed of six different steps. These steps are iterative in the sense that we can reapply them repeatedly, hoping to get better results each time. While doing so, constant evaluation and decision-making should be taken as to how wide this method is applied in the organization or enterprise, how details can be defined while doing so, time constraints, and in particular, much of the architectural assets to be leveraged in the organization, including assets created in previous iterations of the ADM cycle within the enterprise and the assets available elsewhere in the industry. It also focuses on respecting a practical assessment of resource and competence availability, and the value that can realistically be expected to accrue to the organization/enterprise from the chosen scope of the architecture work (The Open Group Architecture Framework, 1999) (see Figure 2).

This method depends on steps of work. Originally, these phases were grouped into four steps.

Figure 2. Modified methodology for enterprise architecture

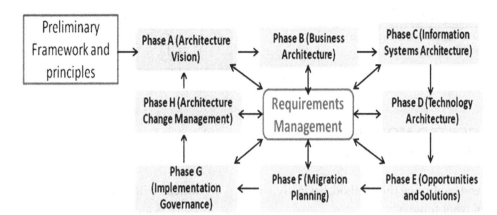

Step 1

Getting the organization committed and involved. This step is composed of the following phases:

- **Preliminary Phase** describes the preparation and initiation activities required;
- **Phase A: Architecture Vision** includes information about defining the scope, identifying the stakeholders, creating the Architecture Vision, and obtaining approvals.

Step 2

Getting the architecture right, which includes:

- **Phase B: Business Architecture** describes the development of a Business Architecture to support an agreed upon Architecture Vision.
- **Phase C: Information Systems Architectures** describes the development of Information Systems Architectures for an architecture project, including the development of Data and Application Architectures.

- **Phase D: Technology Architecture** describes the development of the Technology Architecture for an architecture project.

Step 3

Making the architecture work:

- **Phase E: Opportunities and Solutions** conduct initial implementation planning.
- **Phase F: Migration Planning** addresses Transition Architectures with a supporting Implementation and Migration Plan.
- **Phase G: Implementation Governance** provides an architectural oversight of the implementation.

Step 4

Keeping the process running:

- **Phase H: Architecture Change Management** establishes procedures for managing change to the new architecture.
- **Requirements Management** examines the process of managing architecture requirements throughout the overall process.

Table 4. Illustrations of modifications to the methodology

Step 3	Phase E	Phase F	Phase G
Applying SOA with case study analysis for the particular indicators	⇩	⇩	
Modified Step 3	Phase E'	Phase F'	Phase G'

THE SUGGESTED MODIFICATION ON THE METHOD FOR CVG

We recommend modifying this method, basically as detailed in what follows:

- Modify Step 3 (Phases E, F, and G).

Once the results of Step 2 are completed, that is the architectural designs of the business, information systems, and technology architectures, a study of the viability of implementing such designs should be conducted. This is needed to explore the possible changes that are not necessarily technical, but rather related to government, resources, intentions, intergovernmental cooperation, and others. These were well studied in Steps 1 and 2, but it is important at this stage to reexamine how steady these answers and values are, and how probable changes could take place within a time frame. Perhaps examining these in a matrix-oriented set of issues and parameters and seeing the correlation among them, enables one to reach some empirical assessment probabilities of future failure, which could be taken into consideration for Phases E, F, and G.

- Using Service Oriented Architecture (SOA) for this particular analysis of the completed design in Step 2 may be of help (see Table 4).

There is no standard set of indicators and parameters that can be adopted to examine the risks and develop the modified designs. However, the characteristics are very closely tied not to technical issue, but to others such as:

- Political will in administration, especially if there is a change in leadership while the EA designs are being implemented
- Sudden cuts of resources, mostly financial; thus, it is important to note which ones are at risk and which ones have to be modified

As an example, consider the following case:

Suppose in Step 2 that a certain process was reengineered that spreads over ministry A and ministry B. The design was consulted with both ministries and previously agreed upon, and therefore the architecture was defined as to how to implement this component.

However, knowing that the EA professionals who were working have realized how fragile this agreement was and there may be lack of decision-making to enforce it should there be a problem, they should have examined the risk and explored "what if" scenarios. If ministry A has introduced cuts, and ministry B is willing to fill in, who would own it if originally the owner was A? Knowing that would have implied a change in the structure of one of the departments of either ministry, preventing EA plans from sailing through in Step 3. Some decisions have to be taken, and that should try not to come up with a new architecture. Definitely, the designs in Step 2 have to remain since they are technically the best suited. The need now is for change management issues and scheduling, rather

Table 5. General framework for countries with volatile governance

EA Actions	Task	Recommendations for CVG
Strategize		
	Business strategic planning	Steer it intelligently between government stakeholders who do not differ much
	IT strategic planning	This is the most straightforward.
	Build the business context	Again, partnerships of stakeholders have to work for a relatively short term
Architect		
	Document current state	regular documentation
	Develop future state	Pragmatic and with least ambition possible
	Develop gap analysis and road map	It has to be a short-lived roadmap to allow complete implementation
Lead		
	Promote, encourage, and motivate	Normal work
	Evolve architecture process	Normal work
	Develop human capital	Normal work
Govern		
	Establish decision processes	Minimize decisions to take
	Establish oversight	Work closely with the decision-maker in the Ministry
	Link to related disciplines	Only if and when necessary
	Evaluate performance and adapt	Continuously

than come up with new architectures to meet the changed situation.

In this hypothetical example, no matter how trivial it may look, in countries of vulnerable governance, it could surely block the whole development of EA implementation.

This concept of responding to cases like this, and many more, needs to be customized greatly depending on particular situations, and there would have been no need for them if they can be easily characterized and defined in generic terms. Some research is needed in this regard.

However, we suggest here a general framework for some recommendations for such situations (see Table 5).

BEYOND THE EXAMPLE

Adopting the above method to illustrate the concept of this chapter does not constitute a particular and specific case. It is simply a pragmatic choice for illustration. In general, the basic goal for applying any level of EA is to create and maintain a body of knowledge about the intersection of structure and objective across the whole enterprise (or government) implementing changes in almost any type of structure, which may be physical, organizational, informational, or other. In fact, it is acknowledged that TOGAF's ADM (Architecture Development Method) is not sufficient to satisfy these requirements. It emphasizes a great deal 'anything not-IT that might impact on IT.' This is important in the case of CVGs, as the issue of IT is, in general, the easiest step in decision-making. Therefore, focusing on IT and related issues would be "natural" to government authorities in such countries. Therefore, adopting TOGAF ADM will enable the architects to focus on other issues that relate directly to IT and provide an entry point to non-IT issues in enterprise architecture concerns. This would be an optimal issue for decision-makers. In fact, that may prove to be in many cases perhaps the only efficient way of penetrating walls that the political system with its government leadership can use to block any modification in the government architecture that has its primary focus on governance directly. It is for this reason that the authors have decided to adopt TOGAFR ADM as an example, and for reasons that may be expressed as follows:

- Governments in CVG are least resistant to IT inclusion and technology
- Governments in CVG are most resistant to non-IT issues, particularly focusing on rules and policies at a high level, affecting managers and decision makers in governing positions.
- Countries in this category are not well developed as whole-of-government structures, and hence, being connected is not a strict requirement for applying EA in CVG.

Other methods, such as FEAF, SGEA, DODAF, and AGA would not pose a much different situation to the need for modification to fit the particular situation of decision-making and policies in CVGs. For example, in the case of DODAF, the dependency of the operations view and the systems and services view will not pose as an exclusive method that TOGAF cannot adapt to (such as in itineration for example). In another example, considering SGEA (Singapore Government Enterprise Architecture), one could apply it to provide a holistic view of business functions, common data standards, and shared ICT systems and infrastructure. This will not be preferable in general in CVG environment in a direct straightforward application. Phased and separated steps have to be discovered to enhance the chance of being approved and welcomed by the policy makers.

CONCLUSION

It has been shown that there are characteristics, risks, and parameters that are temporal, which change from time to time and during the study and design of EA solutions. These parameters cannot be taken as a constant set. In fact, this change period could vary from country to country depending on the governance practiced in it. Developed counties would have a longer period of time, increasing the possibility of treating them as constants. In such a case, there is no risk to any EA implementation plans made. However, in countries with volatile governance, this period of time is small, and often smaller than the time needed to transfer within EA development from planning to implementation and change management. This is the crucial problem that was addressed. Further decision-making to adjust to these changes may prove impossible due to several political reasons. Hence, a modification was suggested. The most affected parts of EA would be the processes being part of the architecture. A mixture of service-oriented architecture practices and cross checking with indicators and parameters that may cause such problems may have to be developed. Future research would have to rely on empirical data and case studies in particular countries, which would give more insight as to how to fine tune the modification.

REFERENCES

Chen, D., & Vernadat, F. (2004). *Standards on enterprise integration and engineering – State of the art.* Retrieved from http://www.cimosa.de/Standards/ChVe04.html.

Federal Enterprise Architecture Framework Version 1. (1999). *Website.* Retrieved from http://www.itpolicy.gsa.gov/mke/archplus/fedarch1.pdf.

Godinez, M., Hechler, E., Koenig, K., & Lockwood, S. (2010). *The art of enterprise information architecture: A systems-based approach for unlocking business insight.* Boston, MA: IBM Press.

Graves, T. (2008). *Adapting the TOGAF ADM for government architectures.* Retrieved from http://www.gtra.org/component/content/article/829?format=pdf.

Heeks, R., & Bailur, S. (2007). Analyzing e-government research: Perspectives, philosophies, theories, methods, and practice. *Government Information Quarterly, 24,* 243–265. doi:10.1016/j.giq.2006.06.005

Land, M., Proper, E., Waage, M., & Cloo, J. (2008). *Enterprise architecture: Creating value by informed governance.* Berlin, Germany: Springer.

Minoli, D. (2008). *Enterprise architecture A to Z: Frameworks, business process modeling, SOA, and infrastructure technology.* Boca Raton, FL: Auerbach Publications. doi:10.1201/9781420013702

Rechtin, E., & Maier, M. W. (1997). *The art of systems architecting.* Boca Raton, FL: CRC Press.

Spewak, S. H. (1993). *Enterprise architecture planning: Developing a framework for data, applications, and technology.* New York, NY: Wiley.

The Open Group Architecture Framework. (1999). *Technical reference model, version 5.* Retrieved from http://www.opengroup.org/togaf.

Van den Berg, M., & Van Steenbergen, M. (2010). *Building an enterprise architecture practice: Tools, tips, best practices, ready-to-use insights.* Berlin, Germany: Springer.

Weill, P., & Ross, J. (2004). *IT governance: How top performers manage IT decision rights for superior results.* Boston, MA: Harvard University Press.

Zachman, J. A. (1996). *The framework for enterprise architecture: Background, description and utility.* Retrieved from http://www.eiminstitute.org/library/eimi-archives/volume-1-issue-4-june-2007-edition/the-framework-for-enterprise-architecture-background-description-and-utility.

Section 4
Transforming to Connected Government

Chapter 9
A Case Study in the Emergence of Coherence through Cultural Change

Charles Solverson
City of Tacoma, USA

Susan Coffman
City of Tacoma, USA

David Johnson
City of Tacoma, USA

Linda I. Paralez
Demarche Consulting Group, Inc., USA

ABSTRACT

The emergence of e-governance within Tacoma, WA, a progressive, midsized, U.S. city located in the Pacific Northwest, has been a process of insights and solutions. The interrelationships of e-government, Enterprise Architecture (EA), and sustainable practices as a means to e-governance are examined in the chapter thorough the case study of one Tacoma city division, Building and Land Use Services (BLUS). BLUS managers have redesigned business processes to automate service delivery by the optimization of enterprise-wide interoperable information technology. The discussion includes consideration of the influences that collective decision-making, codes, culture, and vision have on governmental transformation. The identified gap between EA and e-government systems was consistent with the emerging convergence of knowledge for developing EA maturity, developing best practices for shared information management, and expanding human potential. Internal and external stakeholders have experienced the successful emergence of BLUS into rationalized data and applications, in which the optimization of existing interoperable technology has enabled an enhanced partnership between the city government and the community.

DOI: 10.4018/978-1-4666-1824-4.ch009

INTRODUCTION

Enterprise Architecture (EA) is a blueprint for organizational change as defined in models (i.e., words, graphics, and other depictions) to describe in both business and technology terms how the organization is operating currently and how it will operate in the future. EA models also include a plan for the organizational transition to this future state (US GAO, 2006).

The EA approach is a path to knowledge management through the linking of information across disciplines to create a common groundwork for e-government, and ultimately, the opportunity for an informed public to participate fully in the government that serves them (Wilson, 1998). In a context broader than e-government, Wilson (1998) discussed consilience as the key to unification, literally a 'jumping together' of knowledge by the linking of facts and fact-based theory across disciplines to create a common groundwork of explanation (p. 8).

The abundant promise of e-government is the capability for leaders to deliver meaningful governmental services to people worldwide. Based on the potential to improve the human condition, as with all endeavors of such significance, many government leaders eagerly are watching to learn and apply the practices to their circumstances. With the focus on innovation and adaptation that has been achieved in the private sector through the delivery of e-services, expectations for the public sector to experience similar results have increased (Albert, Flournoy, & LeBrasseur, 2009).

The three interrelated and overlapping phases of e-government have been defined as follows:

- **Infrastructure:** Creating an information infrastructure based on reliable and affordable Internet connectivity for citizens, businesses, and stakeholders in a given jurisdiction within the public sector and across society.

- **Integration:** Leveraging the new infrastructure within the public sector to share information (internally and externally), and to bundle, integrate, and deliver services using more efficient and citizen-centric governance models that encompass multiple delivery channels.

- **Transformation:** Pursuing service innovation and e-government across a broader prism of community and democratic development using more networked governance patterns to be applied (a) within government, (b) across various government levels, and (c) among all sectors in a particular jurisdiction (United Nations, 2008, p. 77).

Members of the public have high expectations for e-government; however, our experience in Tacoma has shown that e-government lacks the foundation of a universally accepted, systematic approach to the collection, use, and sharing of information between multiple governmental authorities. Public expectations of e-government have not been met yet in Tacoma.

EA has been used successfully in private enterprise as a structured approach to move from using information silos to using information sharing and process modularity (Gruman, 2006). Enterprise architecture has the agility and flexibility in which organizational leaders can foster the necessary innovation to fulfill the promise of e-government (NUS Institute of Systems Science, 2010).

Researchers at the MIT Center for Information Systems Research (Ross, Weill, & Robertson, 2006) have identified four evolutionary stages of EA relevant to what we are observing in the City of Tacoma: (a) business silos, (b) standardized technology, (c) optimized core architecture, and (d) business modularity. The stages have been defined as:

- **Business silos:** Locally optimal business solutions.

- **Standardized technology:** Enterprise-wide technology solutions.
- **Optimized core:** Standardized enterprise processes/data.
- **Business modularity architecture:** Standard interfaces and business componentization (MIT Sloan Management, 2006, p. 11).

Our experience in Tacoma has shown that cultural and organizational change has been the hurdle to EA maturity, more than the availability of technology. The organizational capacity for evolving architecture is based on organizational behaviors of teamwork, trust, and turf (Schein, 1996).

The dependencies between e-government, EA, and cultural change, together with the altruism and collective decision-making characteristics of public enterprises require leaders to consider all these concepts in developing a conceptual framework for transformation to e-governance. The case study shows that the successful emergence of the City of Tacoma's Building and Land Use Services (BLUS) division into business modularity was the result of a structured approach to organizational coherence and change. The structured approach to change was supportive of an enhanced partnership between the city government and the community it serves (Reddick, 2011).

BACKGROUND

The City of Tacoma encompasses 49 square miles in the Pacific Northwest and has a population of 200,000. The metropolitan area has a population of more than 3.8 million people. The City employs 3,500 workers and operates within an annual budget of $2.2 billion. Tacoma was one of the first U.S. cities to have a municipally owned electric utility install a fiber network throughout its entire service area. The city leaders began their efforts to provide e-government shortly after deregula-

tion of the telecommunications market under the Telecommunications Act of 1996 (City of Tacoma Office of the Mayor, 2011). On April 8, 1997, the Tacoma City Council voted to build the "Click! Network" to provide high-speed Internet and cable television to Tacoma and the surrounding communities (Click! Network, 2007). At the time, this made Tacoma the largest city to build and run its own broadband network.

The investment in broadband infrastructure was accompanied by an economic development initiative in which the City of Tacoma was marketing itself as "America's #1 wired city" (Washington City Managers Association, 2002) and touting its business-friendly climate. The infrastructure development was followed in 2000 by an effort to standardize technology through implementation of Enterprise Resource Planning (ERP) software across all city government departments. The overhead and support costs of maintaining business silos, with IT efforts focused on specific departmental needs and on the complexity of maintaining multiple platforms, led the city leaders to adopt standard platform and database technology for all departments (Eger & Becker, 2000).

The City had a burdensome service delivery process with more than 100 obsolete or obsolescent legacy systems, some of which dated back 25 years, and were written in COBOL. These legacy systems included the (a) customer information system, (b) human resources application, (c) financials, (d) utility billing, (e) budgeting, (f) permitting, (g) tax and licensing, and (h) various work-management systems. In addition, the city officials were entering data into six different, nonintegrated databases thorough 650 individual and largely manual business processes (City of Tacoma, 2006). A fear these systems would fail, and what that failure might mean to the city's revenues, had persisted among city officials. As the leaders identified issues, they determined the key challenges and objectives of the technology standardization for city departments were to:

- Replace nonintegrated legacy systems;
- Eliminate duplicate data entry and redundant information;
- Integrate several disparate databases;
- Improve efficiency of business and customer service processes;
- Consolidate business information to afford more strategic decision making;
- Clean up and centralize citizen, financial, and operational data;
- Improve business process efficiency, from automating to improving workflow; and
- Provide 24-hour, 7-day-a-week, multi-channel customer self-service capabilities (City of Tacoma, 2006, p. 1).

In September 2002, Tacoma city officials selected a global software corporation based in Germany to transform from the city from business silos to standardized technology. The standardization project called for the transformation to be completed within 18 months. Multiple types of business software were installed under the project including (City of Tacoma 2006):

- Finance/Accounting: General ledger, payables, cash management, fixed assets, receivables, and budgeting.
- Human Resources: Payroll, training, benefits, recruiting, and diversity management.
- Manufacturing: Engineering, work orders, scheduling, workflow management, quality control, cost management, manufacturing process, manufacturing projects, manufacturing flow, and activity-based costing.
- Project Management: Costing, billing, time and expense, performance units, and activity management.
- Customer Relationship Management: Sales and marketing, service, customer contact, and call center support.
- Data Services: Various self-service interfaces for customers, suppliers, and employees.

- Access Control: Management of user privileges for various processes (CIS World, 2002).

On October 6, 2003, the city went live. A press release at the time read "City of Tacoma Successfully Launches Most Diverse ERP Solution Worldwide; Improved Customer Service, More Efficient Operation Expected" (PR Newswire, 2003). The new system was promised as support for the City of Tacoma's general government departments, as well as Tacoma Public Utilities through (a) management of the billing service for all public accounts, (b) payroll management, and (c) provision of one integrated work-management system across all the city's divisions. Under the implementation, the Tacoma officials replaced 100 legacy systems with the ERP solution, and merged six major databases—including the (a) old customer information system, (b) human resources application (PeopleSoft), (c) financials, (d) permitting, (e) taxing, and (f) licensing. Taking advantage of the industry-best functionality of the ERP system, the city leaders also streamlined the city business processes, reducing from 650 individual processes (some of which were used by multiple departments) to only 350 processes overall (PR Newswire, 2003).

Issues, Controversies, and Problems

Citywide the transition to standardized technology had proven more difficult than was planned. A year after the city went live, concerns persisted that city officials had gone too fast in trying to implement new Enterprise Resource Planning (ERP) functionality without a clear understanding of the impact on business processes. The press reported that city staff members needed to plow through as many as five screens to access customer data. Frustrated city council members called for an audit because they were unable to determine if the significant gaps between expectations and actual operation were due to the software, the management of the city, or poor consulting (Songini, 2004).

In early 2005, the city officials contracted with IBM to audit the newly installed system. Completed in 2006 (IBM, 2006), findings from the audit included the following:

- Much difficulty had arisen from users' lack of awareness of standard processes. As a result, users executed processes in different ways.
- Departments with champions in embracing technology adjusted more quickly to the implementation of [new technology] than those departments that were resistant to change.
- In Tacoma government, technology generally has been viewed as a cost, not as an opportunity.
- Return On Investment (ROI) was not part of the rationale for a new system except in hindsight. The driver for change was the need to replace legacy systems that were no longer sustainable.
- The city officials had developed an expectation that the system would deliver functionality beyond what previously existed. In the near term since the implementation of the system, the city officials had to work to maintain the previous level of functionality within some business processes. In other areas, the extent of functionality had met or had exceeded previous levels.

As difficult as the citywide transformation to standardized technology had been, the impact to service levels was even more pronounced in BLUS, the division of the city charged with administering development regulation. The primary mission of BLUS is to oversee development permitting, which is the practice of regulating the built environment to ensure community standards are met. This practice is related to important public values such as (a) human health and safety, (b) protection of natural and cultural resources, (d) infrastructure, (e) economic development, and (f) emergency response.

Development codes have been considered a fundamental responsibility of government, dating back to the Code of Hammurabi circa 1700 BC, which stated that "if a builder builds a house and does not construct it properly, and the house falls in and kills its owner, then that builder shall be put to death" (Johns, 1904). Modern development codes are less onerous. Over time, however, they had become increasingly complex as developers recognized various hazards and ways to address them. Public expectations have also changed, which has broadened the scope of development regulations well beyond basic public safety to include factors such as (a) environmental protection, (b) growth management, (c) accessibility, (d) sustainability, and (e) other complex issues. Development permitting also has been subject to market conditions with large swings in permit volumes during economic booms and busts, and seasonal variations in weather. To manage the ever-increasing complexity in codes and maintain service levels through market ups and downs, the integration of technology with the permitting process has been essential.

BLUS was an integral part of the "America's #1 wired city" advertising campaign that came with the development of the Click! Network in the late 1990s. The two key elements promoted with the ad campaign were superior service and technical prowess. First, advertisers spread the word on the eight-weeks-or-less guarantee for commercial building permits: "If your building permit doesn't arrive in eight weeks or less, you don't pay!" (Reid, 2002). Second, the city leaders wanted businesses to be aware of its citywide fiber-optic and cable infrastructure, which allowed inexpensive, easy access to high-speed Internet and telecommunications (Click! Network, 2007). Other jurisdictions reacted with surprise. City leaders and building department members from throughout the region all came to Tacoma to learn about the permitting process and see how they might be able to reproduce it in their own communities (Natt Worth, 2003).

Before the city transition to standardized technology, BLUS was providing a high level of service, including online permitting for over the counter permits and online permit status checking (Demarche Consulting Group, 2006). Both services were a significant benefit to permitting customers in comparison to services in surrounding jurisdictions. The Internet services had been developed using specialized permitting software, which had been purchased through a permit fee surcharge following a stakeholder outreach effort. The specialized permitting software had resulted in significant service improvements across the permitting system and served as the cornerstone of the eight-week-service guarantee. Without the standardized software, however, the online feature to check permits would be lost when transitioning to standard technology, as would many other recently added services. The reluctance to eliminate this software had complicated matters as the final decision to eliminate the specialized permitting software was made late in the planning for the citywide transition to standardized technology (Demarche Consulting Group, 2006).

BLUS staff members were concerned that the implementation team, working under the "no best of breed" mantra, had no real understanding of the permitting process. The implementation plan was to "flip a switch" to immediately transition from legacy systems to the new enterprise system. In an attempt to motivate the organization's members and create a sense of anticipation, clocks were placed at various locations showing the countdown to "go live." In BLUS, whose staff members knew the change would result in a loss of service and a failure to meet expectations, the desired effect of the transition team's efforts to create a sense of anticipation had the counter-effect of creating apprehension (Demarche Consulting Group, 2006).

The impact on morale within BLUS persisted well after "go live," as teamwork and trust between

the business unit and the IT unit suffered while turf issues became more pronounced (Demarche Consulting Group, 2009). Although the implementation team trumpeted the transition, BLUS permitting staff was lamenting the loss of online services and permit tracking, the increase in customer dissatisfaction, and the workload necessary to manage the new system.

The findings of the IBM audit helped leaders chart an overall path toward successful implementation of standardized technology (IBM, 2006), but little resulted from the audit to resolve the issues in BLUS due to the loss of integrated technology with the permitting process. Impacts to production were significant: (a) staff training in the new system was intensified, (b) key functionality to support reporting of process performance was lost, (c) Interactive Voice Response (IVR) interface for inspections management was lost, (d) future Web access capabilities were sacrificed, and (e) capacity to use the technology system as a coordinating mechanism across and within the permitting process was reduced. The most dramatic impact on productivity was the cycle time to process new construction projects, which had increased from 56 days per project in 2002, to 108 days per project in 2003, and remained at a level of 90 days in 2006. Target performance was 60 days (Demarche Consulting Group, 2006).

Within BLUS, the land use section was particularly hard hit with a 70% increase in staff turnover between 2006 and 2008. By 2007, with challenges such as (a) the development bubble in the mid 2000s, (b) the loss of institutional knowledge through staff turnover, (c) the increase in permit volumes, and (d) increasing code complexity, the land use staff found it impossible to meet customer expectations (Demarche Consulting Group, 2009). An assessment of the BLUS operating model showed that even with increased volumes of new construction projects, staff members were able to improve services post-ERP implementation through (a) the development of over 200 system workarounds, (b) staff overtime, (c) the addition of duplicate tracking and management systems (Microsoft Excel and Word), and (d) process changes (Demarche Consulting Group, 2009).

After implementation, the ERP system was well utilized as a powerful enterprise-wide financial management system, serving the City of Tacoma well in terms of fee collection and financial management services. As a work management tool for customer interface, Web access, and a coordinating mechanism for permit tracking and reporting, the ERP system failed each of the permitting processes in most aspects of performance. The unintended or unanticipated, but notable consequences of implementation in a peak period of development were reported (Demarche Consulting Group, 2006, p. 4):

- After the loss of the legacy permits management system, no solid systems were in place to provide reporting about workload management or performance management. Additionally, the actual volume of work was great enough that the level of effort required to generate the work management reports manually was not typically done. So, 'seat of the pants' assessments of system performance related to service level targets was about all managers had time to complete. This disconnect from organization-wide performance measures or dashboards has been demoralizing and has not served the organization well in (a) managing the staffing needs, (b) obtaining additional staffing, or (c) in demonstrating to council members and others the real performance and workload of permitting employees.

Along with intense regulatory changes, other consequences were reported (Demarche Consulting Group, 2006, p. 4) and included:

- A loss of ability to track cycle times by permit to understand how long review was actually taking.
- When workloads exceeded capacity, employees had no systematic, dependable approach for training that kept pace with the changing regulations, further exacerbating the complexity of the workload.
- Code complexity (i.e., a growing number of regulatory constraints that affected workload) was an issue to be understood in terms of (a) its impact on the type of subject-matter experts required to accomplish the work; (b) the number of staff needed to review applications consistent with those regulations; and (c) the time required to understand, train workers, and implement regulations as they are published. Although the majority of regulatory changes were about Land Use, and the impact would be felt most significantly in the Land Use Section of BLUS, the impact would not be limited to that department.
- As each new regulation was adopted, further challenges included the agency's responsibility to educate the citizens and applicants. Developing and implementing effective education and outreach was the managers' way to navigate the increasingly complicated nature of the regulatory scheme. Applicants would need more information either by Web, phone, or in person. The need for a Web access information portal and education access was essential.
- The use of duplicate or auxiliary tools, such as a manual logbook or Excel spreadsheet by specific work groups, was a common means to accomplish workload management. In interviews, Subject Matter Experts (SMEs) indicated that, although the same or similar data were entered in ERP system, it was "impossible" to query, print, or publish reports from the ERP system in a way that made the ERP system

useful for work management (Demarche Consulting Group, 2006, p. 11).

- In 2006, the 51 BLUS staff members all interfaced in some way with the ERP system if they worked in the permitting process (Demarche Consulting Group, 2006). For example, the commercial permits process has approximately 262 steps mapped in detail. Approximately 45 of those process steps involved data entry to the ERP system. From none of those documented steps could be generated (a) an automatic report of activity, (b) a dashboard of process performance, (c) a project status, (d) a "mayday" on a SME's electronic calendar, or (e) any other performance-assisting tool. All 45 data entries resulted in zero automatic aids generated by the ERP system; however, out of those 45 data entry steps into the ERP system in the commercial process, both formal and routine manual queries were made to the ERP system for information. All these inquiries were for specific project status, project content notes, or project data. None of these queries for data was considered "dashboard" data, or process related information (e.g., performance of service levels). Staff members had indicated the ERP system was inordinately unfriendly to such queries; thus, it was unusable as a management and information tool (Demarche Consulting Group, 2006, p. 21).

- The inability for customers to "see into" the status of review was a problem (Demarche Consulting Group, 2006). As staff members had no such tracking system, customers could not access one; hence, no online access to permit status was available. Critical to any permitting organization in today's world is the ability to provide to customers real-time information about the status of their project. This is not a convenience, but a critical management and economic

imperative. Without it, staff spent more time on the phone with applicants or avoiding phone calls (Demarche Consulting Group, 2006). Builders and developers had depended on the ability of the agency to deliver a permit on time, when promised. The online ability to track the progress of a permit and the issues associated with its approval had become a service customers depended on, rather than become a professional "phone pest." Although repeated phone queries would be understandable from the applicant's perspective, answering calls reduced the reviewer's time and ability to accomplish the review, which became self-defeating. Adding the capability for the applicant to monitor permit progress through the review via Web access had reduced much of the need for applicants to call for status. With the new ERP implementation, the lack of this online status access (a) had increased the cost of a permit for applicants, (b) had extended the time to conduct a review, and (c) had reduced service levels and customer satisfaction (Demarche Consulting Group, 2006).

The 2003 ERP system implementation was the beginning of the standardized technology phase for the City of Tacoma. The 2009 BLUS Strategic Plan was used to move BLUS into rationalized data use and applications by identifying existing interoperable technology for optimization and by committing to an implementation schedule of outcomes for service improvements. At this time—in 2011 and 2012—BLUS has been moving into the business modularity phase while the rest of the city government has remained in transition from standardized technology to rationalized data and applications. Cultural change and coherence is a major issue when an organization is in transition from one phase to the next because the enterprise architecture is challenged and adjusted (structure, coordination, rules, silos, turf, etc.). In the City of Tacoma, different parts of the organization have been in different phases, making coherence particularly challenging.

Shortly after the 2003 ERP system implementation, significant changes were taking place in the city's senior management. Under the leadership of a new city manager in 2005, increased focus was placed on culture changes to transform the city into a high-performing, open, and engaged government. The city manager introduced ideas, challenges, and language to suggest innovation in the way the city services would be provided (CIPFA, 2009). One measure of high performance was based upon the development of a citizen-employee combined service provision and the reinforcement of partnerships among service providers in the community (City of Tacoma, 2009a). To meet these goals, cross-functional teams of employees and citizens were developed to improve the services and outcomes created for and by the citizens. Service-level agreements were developed for departments such as permitting and IT services to improve teamwork, trust, and transparency, while reducing turf-protection actions or the organizational tendency to re-form silos. The agreements also were used in the establishment of performance measures to gauge cost effectiveness and guide decision-making. Strategic organizational changes were made. In 2009, BLUS was moved out of the Public Works Department and placed under the Community and Economic Development Department of the city. Closer teamwork between the long-range planning team and the development permitting team was facilitated with this strategic change.

The new city manager placed emphasis on understanding and applying the approaches in the Viable System Model (VSM), appreciating that the internal complexity of an organization needs to be coequal to the external complexity of the environment it serves (Beer, 1972). For BLUS, that meant the organizational design (a) had to consist of complex technical subsystems, such as specialty code review areas; (b) would

be composed of a social network of individuals who each have their own value systems, such as planners, environmentalists, construction inspectors, and engineers; and (c) would be comprised of individuals who interacted with and adapted to a dynamic environment (Stich, Schmidt, Meyer, & Wienholdt, 2009). Some of this alignment has been realized in stronger partnerships between employees in environmental services, traffic engineering, current planning, and building plan review in the permit center. In all these disciplines, employees have provided increasingly better feedback on the work of long-range planning and code development/revision.

Solutions and Recommendations

The transformations from technology silos to technology standardization and the beginnings of process modularity have been challenging. By comparison, construction of the citywide broadband system was straightforward. Both projects have been early steps in the transformation to e-governance, but the comparison ends there. The construction of the broadband network required little detailed knowledge of financial, organizational, or regulatory mandates of the served customer population; however, the transformation from technology silos to standardized technology required all that detailed knowledge, plus an understanding of organizational behavior and motivations underlying change (MIT Sloan Management, 2006). The change in technology could be treated like a traditional capital project, but a successful organizational transformation requires deep understanding of people and process, coupled with a thoughtful implementation plan.

At first, during the transformation from technology silos to standardized technology, the city leaders did not have an overarching transformation plan or a structured approach to align software and data services directly with business processes. The steps after standardization to enable process optimization and business-technology alignment were not part of the strategic planning. An incomplete process was employed: standard platform and database were established, but the leaders' goals for standardization did not reflect an understanding of how optimizing and aligning the technologies with the business process would be crucial to achieving efficiencies. The first phase of the city process—the transformation from technology silos to standardized technology—was characterized by the lack of understanding (a) of processes, (b) of the high expectations for vastly improved services, and (c) of the interplay with organizational morale and behavior. The city officials' audit of the ERP implementation was the first in a series of steps to improve coherence and alignment between business processes and standardized technology (IBM, 2006).

As a result of the IBM audit in 2006, the following "course corrections" were made according to the Demarche Consulting Group's final report (2006):

- Revised the governance model for ongoing support of the ERP implementation.
- Established a "best business practice" committee that would be responsible for issue resolution.
- Restructured the ERP support organization.
- Assigned resources to certain quick-hit changes.
- Provided users with ongoing education and references.
- Improved reporting capabilities to enable decision-making.
- Applied best practices for upgrading to subsequent versions of ERP and/or adding functionality.
- Provided for the accuracy and integrity of all master data by creating an ownership structure and rules.
- Implemented more robust system control (p. 12).

These improvements, although helpful, did not address fully those issues that were affecting the permitting system, nor was a conceptual framework established that BLUS leaders could use to move the permit-system operating model and service innovation beyond standardized technology into data and process optimization. The system-wide improvements were a beginning in addressing technology support, governance, and documentation issues, but were not effective for addressing people and process concerns in BLUS (Demarche Consulting Group, 2006).

The operating model for permitting has changed little over the past 20 years; however, the integration of technology in the permitting process and the increasing code complexity have affected the performance of the model. Figure 1 shows a strategic schematic of the relationship between the review authorities and the service times for commercial project reviews that were the basis of the eight-week guarantee promoted in the advertising campaign during the City's broadband network development in the late 1990s.

The workflow through the model has annual variance with summer peaks in development activity and winter activity lows. The activity also has varied over multiple years with the ebb and flow of the economy. Adjustments to the model and process improvements typically have been made during periods of low workflow because during peak workflow all employee resources would be focused on meeting service levels.

Depending on the scope of a given project, the number of review authorities would increase or decrease. Review authorities requirements have been established in the Tacoma Municipal Code (TMC) under various chapters within code titles. The basic model has a nodal architecture that includes both sequential and concurrent activities. As shown in Figure 1, the critical path to meet the eight-week or 56-day plan-review guarantee was through the top branch of the model, in which the six days for permit setup and document routing and the six days for permit issuance were summed

Figure 1. Commercial plan review process–LOS 56 days (© 2011, C. Solverson, Building and Land Use Services, City of Tacoma)

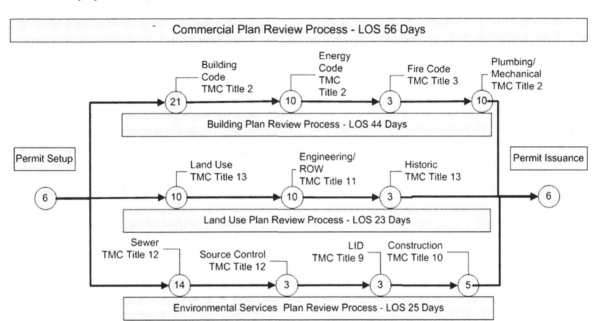

with the 44-day building plan review. A similar branching nodal architecture exists in other phases of project development such as pre-application services and inspection. The overall process is sequential; that is, permit setup must occur before permit issuance. However, the process between nodes is concurrent with multiple, simultaneous operations on multiple branches.

The Tacoma standardization project coincided with a prolonged, multiyear upturn in market activity that preceded the 2007 financial crisis. The period between the first phase of standardized technology (2003) and the start of the recent economic downturn (2008) could be characterized as a period of increasing incoherence in the standardization model caused by (a) the loss of technology and process alignment, (b) increasing code complexity, and (c) record-high permit volumes. These multiple factors were contributions to high staff turnover, which resulted in the loss of institutional knowledge. The combined effect was a severe drop in efficiency across the model. Coherence and performance of the system had

been severely degraded. The 56-day customer guarantee for commercial projects at the beginning of 2003 was replaced by a new normal in 2008, closer to 100 days.

Detailed mapping and assessment of the model had begun in 2006, in which a number of problem areas in need of solutions were identified (Demarche Consulting Group, 2006). These included issues that were captured under categories of technology, process, and people, as listed.

Technology:

- Customers lost the ability to "see into" the status of review, which resulted in increased customer information requests and added staff workload.
- Managers lost the ability to adequately track cycle times by permit and, hence, inability to assess how long review was taking actually on any given branch.
- An inability to communicate across the model existed. If one review authority rejected certain documents, no means exist-

ed to effectively communicate a stop-work order to other review authorities.

- Separate work tracking by individual review authorities was lost because the level of effort to generate the work management reports was so high that standardized reporting was inefficient.

Process:

- Specific groups' use of duplicate or auxiliary tools, such as a manual logbooks or Excel spreadsheets as a means to accomplish workload management, was eroding standardization.
- No systematic method existed to understand, train, or implement new regulations without performance reporting on the model, which was increasing the complexity, gaps, and overlaps in the system.
- From staff and management perspectives, technology transitions had an enormous impact in reduced productivity.
- From an organizational perspective, the code authorities, process design, and technology integration were poorly structured and were not keeping pace with changing regulations.

People:

- Turnover rates for both employees and customers have been very high, which has affected staff and institutional knowledge.
- From the stakeholder's perspective, permitting services had radically deteriorated in recent years (e.g., 56-day process became 100-day process).
- The degradation of the system had fostered a dynamic of (a) decreasing transparency, teamwork, and trust; and (b) increasing turf-protection (or fragmentation), which was self-reinforcing.

- The compounding effects of increasing code complexity, increasing permit request volume, loss of permit system coherence, and loss of trust was demoralizing to BLUS employees.

Concurrent with the mapping and analysis of the permitting operating model, BLUS managers undertook a cultural assessment to identify the elements that were influential on the commitment of staff to stay and elements that were influential on their motivation to leave. Since the move to standardization, staff turnover had been high; this was due to a number of factors, including some demographic and some inherent to the stress of a system in which performance routinely fell short of customer expectations. For the period between 2003 and 2010, based on a review of city records, years of service per employee in BLUS dropped 33%, from 15 years to 10 years.

Findings from both the cultural assessment and the analysis of the operating model were incorporated into the 2009 Permitting System Strategic Plan that led to the reorganization of BLUS and the redesign of the permitting system. The goal of the strategic plan was to redesign the system to improve service times and satisfaction levels with input from stakeholders.

FUTURE DIRECTIONS

Technology

The determination from the technology assessment was that although the transformation to standardized technology had severely affected the permitting system, the functionality of the new enterprise systems within the city could be optimized with respect to the permitting process to allow service innovation that was not achievable with the legacy systems. The initial transformation to standardized technology had been focused on ERP, but by the time the strategic plan for the permitting system

Figure 2. Enterprise software (© 2011, C. Solverson, Building and Land Use Services, City of Tacoma)

Enterprise Software					
Business Function	Technology Function	IVR	ERP	Website/ Collaboration	ECMS
Permit Setup	Web Access Portal			√	
	Form Creation				√
	Account Management		√		
	Document Ingestion				√
	Work Flow Routing				√
Plan Review	Online Collaboration			√	
	Document Editing				√
	Notifications				√
Permit Issuance	Form Creation				√
	Notifications				√
	Document Storage				√
Inspection	Call in scheduling	√			
	Work Flow Routing		√		
	Document Routing				√
	Form Creation				√

was completed, the city leaders had invested in enterprise technology with capabilities for on-line collaboration, document management, and workflow routing of large electronic documents.

A key outcome of the technology assessment was to change the permitting technology business model, which had been established during the ERP system implementation. The model was changed from relying primarily on the ERP system to a plan in which all enterprise-wide software would be optimized with respect to the permit system, based on the core functionality of the software. Before this change, customization of the ERP system to meet the needs of permitting had become increasingly complicated. In addition, with future upgrades to the ERP system already planned, customization work would need to start from scratch with each new ERP system upgrade. Instead of contorting the ERP system through customization, and to provide functionality outside of its core use, the focus was redirected to developing interoperability within the enterprise-wide software to meet the needs of the permitting system (see Figure 2).

In the core functionality assessment of enterprise-wide software, it became apparent that the document creation and workflow routing software, which had been incorporated into the city Electronic Content Management (ECM) system, would play a key role in the transition from a paper-based plan review process to an electronic plan review process. In the electronic plan review process currently being implemented in BLUS, the ECM system serves as a hub, into which data can be incorporated from other sources to auto-fill forms and initiate workflow (see Figure 3).

In 2009, when the strategic plan for BLUS was completed, the city was still in the early stages of procurement and implementation of the ECM system. BLUS worked with the city technology engineers to become an early adopter of the ECM system and had a staff member that served as a co-leader in the citywide implementation, which was completed in early 2011. BLUS developers understood the principle Hoverstadt (2008) described as the strong inverse correlation between involvement in a change program and

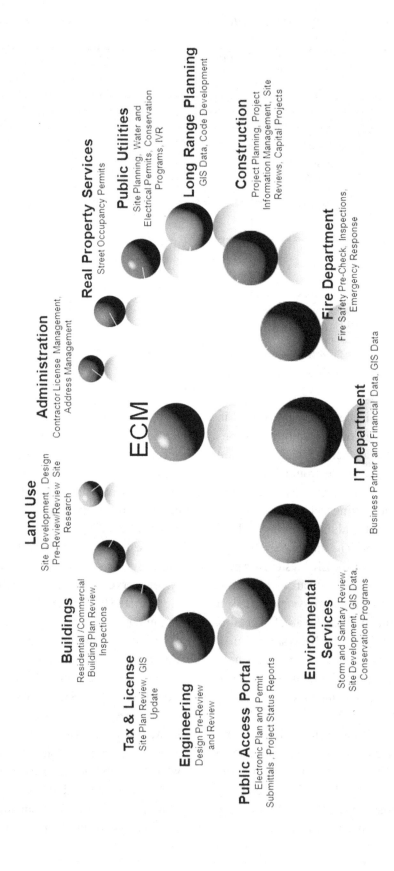

Figure 3. ECM hub (© 2011, C. Solverson, Building and Land Use Services, City of Tacoma)

resistance to it. People do not resist what they have a hand in designing; instead, they actively work to make it happen. As an early adopter of the ECM system, BLUS members showed little resistance to its implementation.

For BLUS, the implementation of the ERP system starting in 2002 and the implementation of the ECM system in 2010 were bookends on the transformation from business silo architecture to standardized technology architecture. The process is representative of a cultural transformation in the acceptance of change. The resistance to the implementation of the ERP system in 2002 gave way to support and advocacy for the implementation of the ECM system in 2010. With participation in the change-design process came a broader awareness among BLUS employees of the need for individual sacrifices for the greater good and awareness of a larger context for the evolution of EA within the City of Tacoma. Although implementation of the ECM system has been viewed as a final phase in the transformation to standardized technology architecture, the work that has been done to optimize enterprise software with respect to the permitting process has been viewed as the first phase of optimized core architecture. City leaders with a clearer understanding of the maturation of EA will enable a smooth transition to subsequent stages of EA and a sooner graduation to e-government.

Process and Financial Policy

The implementation of the ERP system was notable for the lack of collaboration between IT and BLUS. Moving into core optimization architecture has enabled the opposite process. Technology experts are being integrated more often into the work centers of permitting experts. The current organizational structure consists of work centers with cross-functional team members. This is a key element of the BLUS service delivery model, which helps to centralize intake, routing, issuance, tracking, and reporting of performance. By

ensuring that each center's employees have a clear mission and authority to deliver the services and service levels for its customers and stakeholders, and by tracking and assessing costs associated with permit activities, BLUS employees will continue to build robust platforms for improved service.

Essential to supporting these platforms of service will be appropriately matched technologies and processes for each center according to risk management and decision models (Demarche Consulting Group, 2009). Significant shifts in culture toward greater acceptance and aptitude among our SMEs have become apparent in the use of electronic tools to aid coordination, decision-making, transparency, and document management. The BLUS directors expect that, as they continue to engage the customer in the design of service models and service delivery for the future (e.g., fee-for-service and enterprise-service models); they will continue to realize iterative improvements.

Having identified that the limiting factor in e-government for BLUS has been the departments' capacity for organizational and cultural change rather than computer systems or software, the city leaders' focus will include long-term, sustainable training and development targeted at supporting the cross-functional team concept. The emerging trend in all the BLUS iterative work is a better understanding of what it means to become a learning organization. The challenges will continue to be acquiring knowledge and innovating fast enough to survive and thrive in the constraints and changes of the public sector environment. Members of learning organizations exhibit the following traits: (a) create a culture that encourages and supports continuous employee learning, critical thinking, and risk taking with new ideas; (b) allow mistakes and value both employee and stakeholder contributions; (c) learn from experience and experiment; and (d) disseminate the new knowledge throughout the organization for incorporation into day-to-day activities. The learning process requires intense collaboration between the technology staff and the business unit, requires on-going metrics, and requires governance policies for both specific business and technology processes.

Optimization and business-technology alignment are critical aspects of high performance, as the IT focus has shifted from managing technology to contributing to businesses' operational excellence. Close cooperation between IT staff and other department staff will be necessary to meet future challenges. The need will increase for the EA of the permitting system to co-evolve with the regulatory system in order to manage the complexity inherent in the collective decision-making process. The maturing and co-evolution of permit services' EA will be essential for the department to (a) remain financially sustainable, (b) manage knowledge for informed decision-making, and (c) transition to a systems approach.

A deepening recession has increased pressure on all parts of government to deliver significantly better outcomes for significantly lower costs (Parker, 2009). To provide financial sustainability, the Tacoma City Council restructured the permitting functions into an enterprise fund in 2010, with the intention of achieving full-cost recovery for fee-funded permitting activities. Since this restructuring, a financial management plan has been developed (Demarche Consulting Group, 2011) to accompany formal adoption of the enterprise fund in support of the building and land use permitting activities and functions. Policy issues and choices for setting fees (fee recovery rates) will be addressed in the financial plan, and hence, the need for general fund support or subsidy, grant funding, or other special reserve fund contributions will be determined. The permitting services' overall level of funding must also be balanced against the public expectation for a desired level of service and the city's economic development, historical preservation, and other strategic comprehensive plans. As part of this financial plan, the city leaders are concerned with understanding and developing a method of recovering costs of service over time to sustain the capacity of the city to serve both the customers and the stakeholders of the permitting process. Sustainability is especially important because the building and land use permitting process is notoriously cyclical, necessitating the ability to staff and structure for both "peak" and "slow" periods.

Secondly, the City of Tacoma leaders must be concerned about the balance between the public and private benefits of development regulation, and set cost-recovery targets as a part of a policy framework that is aligned with (a) financial objectives, (b) comprehensive plan strategies and policies, and (c) economic development drivers. In setting fees for development services, city officials have the latitude to consider public and private benefits and to establish cost-recovery targets for individual approval processes or for a class of activities (permit types). Online access to staff, to permits, and to permit submission will significantly reduce the impact of travel and costs on customers and stakeholders who do business with the government, and thus reduce operating costs for both the city and its customers. As part of the strategic planning for long-term financial sustainability, Tacoma city leaders are looking to EA and e-government to provide the return on investment that will allow fees to stay at a minimum, but keep service levels high, in an increasingly complex regulatory environment. Managing complexity in the regulatory environment will become increasingly important as the trend toward a systems approach to managing the built environment evolves. This trend is embodied in the new International Green Construction Code (IGCC).

Sustainability

The new IGCC is under development currently by the International Code Council (ICC). The first version of the code will be published in 2012 (International Code Council, 2010a). The new code is a systems approach to reduce the negative impacts of the built environment on the natural environment. As an example, the IGCC includes

Figure 4. Risks to future generations (© 2011, D. Eisenberg. Used with permission from D. Eisenberg, Development Center for Appropriate Technology)

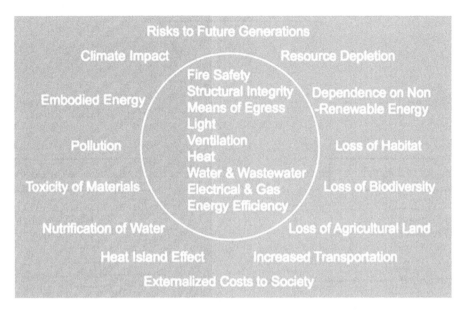

provisions for (a) the life-cycle assessment of fossil fuel depletion; (b) global warming potential; (c) ozone depletion; (d) acid rain; and (e) toxic releases to air, water, and land over the lifetime of a building (International Code Council, 2011c).

A direct relationship exists between the development of codes and complexity in regulating the built environment. Each code change requires new processes, forms, workflow, and public outreach. The building code evolution has meant also that instead of having a single codebook, separate building codes are used for fire, plumbing, mechanical systems, electrical systems, and others; communities now have model codes. Model codes have been extremely effective as a national standard for protection from fire, structural collapse, general deterioration, and extreme loads related to human-made and natural hazards. Model codes also have standards to protect natural resources, owner costs, and the environment through improved minimum building standards (American Society of Civil Engineers, 2011).

Builders also have to follow U.S. national, regional, state, and municipal codes. Uniformity has become an ongoing challenge. Simply because building codes are effectively used to manage specific hazards, the assumption is all the risks associated with development have been eliminated or greatly reduced. Growing awareness of the systemic effects of development regulations has become important from a cumulative harm or risk to future generations' perspective. Figure 4 shows the larger risks that are associated with the built environment. The risks within the circle are currently addressed under codes that are updated on a predictable cycle, in which changes to existing practices are incremental. The risks outside the circle are areas in which regulations are rapidly evolving.

The IGCC leaders have begun to address the issue of single-subject regulations by taking a systems approach to manage cumulative harm or risk from a future generations' perspective. Green development is only one stage of sustainable development (Eisenberg, 2011). Although the IGCC was established to "raise the floor" of green building, other efforts have been made to "raise the ceiling" to eliminate the negative impacts of

Figure 5. Enterprise architecture and sustainability (© 2011. Modified from PowerPoint presentation, D. Eisenberg. Used with permission from D. Eisenberg, Development Center for Appropriate Technology.)

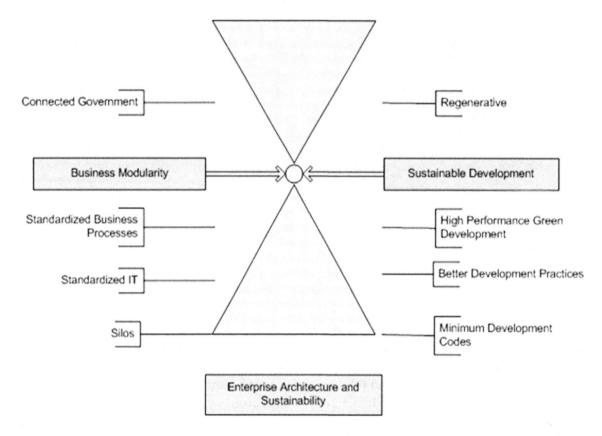

the built environment on the natural environment (International Code Council, 2010b). The stages of development regulation, which would be the process to move from the existing minimum codes to regenerative development, are shown in Figure 5. The left side of the figure shows a possible relationship between the stages leading to connected government and regenerative development.

Increasing awareness around sustainability is a driving force behind the systems approach for development regulation (International Code Council, 2010b). To meet this challenge, the development of EA and e-government will need to go hand-in-hand with the development of sustainability codes to provide the sophistication in operations and knowledge management required for transformation. EA is a potential approach to

provide the sustainable processes necessary for sustainable development.

Even with efforts such as the development of the IGCC to bring a systems approach to development regulation, single-subject codes will continue to be an on going source of complexity in the permitting process. Single-subject codes are an outcome of the common practice of single-subject rule making. The legislative process for code development has historically adhered to single-subject rule making, in which each code has its own legislative number, to avoid complexity in legislation and to avoid passing unfavorable legislation that is proposed within favorable legislation (US Legal, 2011).

This piece meal approach to regulating, although simplifying the legislative process, adds complexity to enterprise architecture because the number of codes and lack of uniformity between them has increased. An awareness has been growing that regulations for the built environment are frequently so narrow in focus and scope that huge impacts and consequences that lay outside the field of view are overlooked (Eisenberg, Done, & Ishida, 2002; Orien, 2011).

New legislation invariably adds new review requirements and new review authorities who require the creation of new business processes, routing, forms, and notifications. BLUS managers recognized that a system of coherency management must be implemented to provide logical, orderly, and consistent systems for incorporating new legislation into the business practice. Coherency management is necessary to reduce additional staffing needs caused by silos, turf, and segmented regulatory approaches that result from single-subject rule making.

Coherence is critical for advancing organizational alignment, agility, and assurance. These organizational characteristics are essential for the development of sustainable practices that reduce operating and capital costs of government. As costs are reduced, the government becomes more fiscally sound, thus increasing its capacity to provide necessary services with reduced error and risk (Doucet, Gøtze, Saha, & Bernard, 2009; Jordan, 2008). Economic development potential and viability will be increased as the regulatory environment becomes more coherent vertically and horizontally, and the cost of compliance is aligned with the benefits.

Service level agreements are one of the tools that BLUS have relied on for management of organizational drift, vertical and horizontal coherence, and maintaining a fiscally sound operating model (City of Tacoma, 2011a). Service level agreements are a means to consolidate, simplify, and standardize permitting processes between multiple authorities and a means to delegate authority for routine transactions. These agreements set expectations for the delivery of internal services as well as the role both service provider and recipient play in delivering those services. Service level agreements could be used to counteract the fragmentation and complexity introduced into the permitting process through single-subject legislation. Customers benefit from a more standardized, predictable process and procedure across authorities. The experience in BLUS has indicated that service level agreements are necessary to maintain and evolve EA.

Members of Tacoma's BLUS department believe that EA and sustainable development regulations are linked by the need to co-evolve. With this recognition, BLUS has incorporated the operationalization of sustainable development into its work with the Sustainable Tacoma Commission. The commission is an appointed body charged with oversight of implementation of Tacoma's Climate Action Plan (Green Ribbon Climate Action Task Force, 2009b). The plan contains a series of strategies to guide the city and community in reducing greenhouse gas emissions and curbing global warming.

BLUS is using process automation to help implement climate action plan strategies. As an example, automatic notifications are now provided to the Tacoma Recycling Center whenever a demolition permit has been issued. Based on studies by the recycling center, construction waste is 7% of the overall city waste stream (City of Tacoma, 2011b). Closer coordination between development permitting and the recycling center will decrease the amount of construction waste over time. In similar fashion, BLUS staff members are working to automate notifications for awareness in the permitting process for clean air, water, and renewable energy opportunities. The evolution of EA and e-government will increase developers' abilities to move beyond regulation and into the promotion of voluntary best practices.

People and Physical Improvements

The redesign of the permitting system has reinforced the belief that the knowledge of individuals within the permitting system is its greatest resource, and trust in the system by all stakeholders is critical to success in adoption of the redesign. The large drop in service levels in the permitting system during the transformation from business silo architecture to standardized technology architecture was due in part to the loss of institutional knowledge as the average years of service per employee dropped by more than 30% and many employees left their BLUS positions (Demarche Consulting Group, 2009). To manage institutional knowledge, the knowledge of individual members of an organization needs to be transformed into a collective organizational knowledge base. Collective knowledge is accumulated through communication, and can be a complement to the further development of individual knowledge. The amount of information needed to make informed decisions is not possible without technical support. Shared information needs to be accurate, timely, and comprehensive to support informed decision-making. Consistency in informed decision-making builds trust in the organization.

During the implementation of the ERP system in 2003, BLUS resistance to give up the legacy permitting system had an influence on departmental preparedness to transition to the new system. Staff mourned the old system long after the transition and felt that the city leaders had "betrayed" them in the decision to move to a standardized system. The sense of betrayal and loss of trust was reinforced by the loss of consistency in making informed decisions as institutional knowledge eroded through staff turnover and communication was compromised by poor integration of the ERP system with the permitting process (Demarche Consulting Group, 2006).

The BLUS 2009 Strategic Plan was the initial structure for a plan to address these issues (Demarche Consulting Group, 2009). Specific steps were aimed at increasing teamwork, trust, and transparency, while reducing turf protection associated with the traditional silos of government authority. A strategic plan and conceptual frame-

work for the future of the organization, coupled with effective communication, was deemed essential to motivate change.

A talent infrastructure that is representative of best practices for a learning organization is a necessary component in an overall knowledge and change management system (American Society of Civil Engineers, 2003). To become an organization that is defined by continuous improvement, employees' continuous learning becomes inseparable from acquiring new knowledge and knowing though experience. Continuous learning has the implication of incremental change as a strategy to implement behavioral change, which would be considered a structured approach to cultural shift (Chong & Choi, 2005).

A successful means to attain cultural shift in an organization is to strategically embed and link individuals within working groups who possess the necessary technical and organizational change talents, and holding these individuals accountable for being responsive to the work group members' needs. The desired shift from individual to group ownership and group commitment to achieving results has been emerging. This change has been called a shift to a matrix or cross-functional team structure. Transitions are more likely to have success when the affected individuals have a sense of control of the outcome and when the affected individuals see a model of the desired behavior. Affected individuals who are engaged in the development of new communication tools and processes in work groups are prepared better to accept the product of their own design (Mecca, 2004). As such, the team's confidence in the leadership and the leaders' confidence in the team co-exist and evolve.

The change process of an organizational system requires a series of transitions between three different states: unfreezing-transition-refreezing (Lewin, 1958). No change will occur unless the system is unfrozen, and no change will last unless the system is refrozen. Physical changes within the organization help in the communication of change and can help with breaking down traditional silos and improving teamwork. The City of Tacoma leaders have taken actions to increase teamwork, trust, and transparency, and simultaneously taken actions to reduce turf associations with the traditional silos of government authority. BLUS has placed emphasis on the design of physical improvements in multiple ways. Since 2009, a customer service (intake/permit) center has been operating, which is essential to the service delivery model for customer access. The City of Tacoma operations have been housed in a beautiful, yet somewhat antiquated facility that does not have an ideal configuration for customer service, for technology enhancement, or for workflow design (Demarche Consulting Group, 2009). These deficits have to be overcome, while taking advantage of an historic building, utilizing existing space well, and modernizing an otherwise poorly performing space; the effort will be made in concert with both the process changes and with the technology enhancements.

Workspace was improved to allow for the formation of cross-functional teams and transition from a paper-based review process to an electronic review process. Training resources were directed for the development of staff within the permitting system that had expertise in enterprise software and applications, so they could work alongside experts in permitting, such as structural engineers, land use planners, and environmental scientists. Emphasis was placed on increasing trust, transparency, and teamwork, while simultaneously reducing turf.

In making these physical structure changes, all intake and permit issuance services were consolidated into one customer service center. The customer service center had a single point-of-contact person for complex projects who would coordinate services across organizational boundaries and agencies and provide the customer with a well-managed experience (National Research Center, 2011). This change enabled better project tracking, more consistent decision-making, and routine feedback about code implementation.

Physical change also has been used to support the investment in greater teamwork across organizational silos as SMEs from the various permit review authorities are co-located in the permit center and work collaboratively to simplify the customers' experience. This collaboration has helped (a) to build relationships, (b) to improve and simplify the review process, (c) to streamline decision-making, (d) to identify those areas in which code reform and revision are most needed, and (e) to create cost benefits for both the customer and the city. The introduction and implementation of the electronic plan review created the need for larger cubicle workstations with large, dual monitors. Cross-functional teams demanded the creation of more technologically equipped conference space to operate at peak efficiency. All these investments in physical space are considered tools to assist the new worker and the new technology of the era. None of these additions is exceptional or extraordinary additions in a modern workplace.

Changing organizational culture requires leaders that will mobilize employees and stakeholders to view change as an exciting opportunity and that will provide holistic governance so internal members, as well as external stakeholders, are viewed as vital parts of an interdependent system (Doppelt, 2010). Communication strategies around new or evolving regulations must be considered to inspire the necessary cultural shift and to develop organizational members' support as the new regulations are operationalized.

CONCLUSION

For the successful transition from unconnected to connected government a change management strategy sophisticated enough to match the complex nature of social networks is necessary. Government networks are part of the larger social network and have a unique responsibility in the implementation of public policy.

The collective decision making process used in rule making to codify policy is limited to a single subject. Single-subject rule making is used to maintain order in the legislative process, but the effect of introducing disorder to good EA has been seen as it creates a piecemeal structure. The piecemeal nature of legislative action is challenging for the coherent integration and alignment of new rules with existing business processes. As complex issues are considered one subject at a time, inconsistencies within the whole will occur and will require reconciliation through the additional development of administrative policies and interpretations. In the parts of the organization where the regulatory framework shifts rapidly, technology standardization, process standardization, and business modularity are all made more difficult and can fall behind parts of the organization less impacted by shifts in public policy.

BLUS employees made a strategic mistake by trying to retain their legacy system and not become an early supporter in initial city officials' efforts to transition to standardized technology. In part, BLUS had a limited capacity to change at the time because of managing both regulatory and technology shifts in business process simultaneously. In terms of priority, regulatory changes take precedence over technology changes. The timeframe in which the city began to standardize technology in 2003 coincided with a period of significant regulatory change that affected BLUS business processes and high service demands from economic development activity. Given limited resources, the initial BLUS strategy was to try to keep the legacy system and focus on near-term challenges of implementing regulatory changes and maintaining service levels. Ultimately, long term enterprise demands to standardize technology prevailed and BLUS was added to the standardization project late in the planning phase. This led to a poor integration of the BLUS business process with supporting technology, and consequently, a significant drop in service levels.

In general, the early stages of the BLUS transition to standardized technology were hampered by (a) the lack of a conceptual framework for EA, (b) an under appreciation of the need to manage the change holistically, and (c) the absence of an endpoint vision sufficient to motivate change. Citywide problems with implementing technology standardization were identified as a shortcoming in the 2005 performance audit following implementation of Enterprise Resource Planning (ERP) software. The auditors noted that much difficulty had arisen from users' lack of awareness of standard processes and that, as a result, they executed processes in different ways. Departments with champions in embracing technology adjust more quickly to the implementation of [new technology] than those departments that resist change (IBM, 2006).

Although a lack of awareness of standard process and resistance to change were identified as barriers in the overall audit, the auditors did not recognize that for BLUS, the capacity for overall organizational change was far exceeded. The barriers and the additional strain of rapidly changing codes and regulations, tied to shifts in public policy, along with the change in technology were not conducive to BLUS employees accepting change. BLUS mangers did not resist change as much as they could not keep up with it. The technology implementation plan for the ERP and the subsequent audit assumed a homogenous capacity for change across the organization for IT standardization. Real capacity varies in relationship to the overall change occurring within the organization.

Within the parts of the city where organizational members are narrowly focused on commodity transactions for basic services, such as selling energy and assuring the supply water the regulatory environment is stable, a compelling vision of increased efficiency, agility, flexibility, and higher return on investment was a compelling motivator for change. In these parts of the organization, the transformation to standardized technology and the implementation of the ERP system were the most successful. In the broader parts of the organization, in which the regulatory environment has more flux and services are not defined or thought of as "commodity transactions," transformation has proved most difficult.

Over time, the idea that implementation across the organization needed to be applied in a deliberate and incremental fashion has emerged. A cross-functional change leadership team has been integrated into the permitting business model, which has facilitated steady, staff-generated solutions to digest changes for the business process. This aggregation of a team specifically was focused on integration of new codes, technologies, and other business impacts with the result of a positive impact on employee morale. The teams are cross-functional in every aspect (specialty area, seniority, and administrative to management roles). BLUS has also embedded IT specialists in the cross-functional teams as well. These IT specialists have learned the business process and have become essential contributors for integrating technology solutions to the business process.

Recognition of the value of every staff member in implementing change has become an essential part of moving into the business modularity phase. BLUS managers were not in a rush to implement change all at once. The leadership model is not temporary, but represents a permanent structural shift in support of delivery of sustainable change. Change also is celebrated and recognized at every level, so that staff members know that their contributions, whether large or small, have an important impact.

For the parts of the organization with focus on broader topics, such as sustainable or economic development, an endpoint vision with a broader sense of purpose is necessary to motivate the cultural change toward the maturity of EA. The imperatives of time to market, responsiveness, agility, flexibility, and return on investment may resonate in those the parts of the organization in which the regulatory framework is stable and services are delivered as if they are a commodity. These imperatives, however, are not sufficient to motivate cultural change in portions of government that have a broader and less easily defined duty. A well-conceived endpoint vision that is resonant with the core values of the community is the inspiration for cultural change. In our experience in Tacoma, cultural change, not IT systems and software, is what has limited the evolution of enterprise architecture. Re-visioning the endpoint of EA as a means to e-government and a sustainable future is more appropriate for the broader purpose of public enterprise than for the more commonly held vision of EA as a means to a competitive edge.

As the culture in BLUS has evolved to a more holistic approach to operation and regulation, a more coherent integration of technology into our services has been developed. Coherence has emerged within BLUS as process automation efforts have produced tangible benefit and a shift in attitudes. Consistent with findings noted by Jun and Weare (2011), City of Tacoma leaders have found that external drivers—customer and stakeholder expectations—are the more influential motivators to overcoming internal bureaucratic inertia. Change has become so internalized that were it not delivered in such regular and consistent intervals as in the past, questions, and concerns would arise about its delivery. This is a paradigm shift—change does not have to be pushed because both staff and customers want it and expect it—enabling and supporting an enhanced partnership between government and the community it serves.

As we look to the future, the phrase "chance favors the connected mind" (Johnson, 2010) seems to apply equally well to communities as to individuals. As we in the City of Tacoma transform to more open, transparent, and innovative practices, we are optimistic that chance will favor the connected community.

REFERENCES

Albert, S., Flournoy, D. M., & LeBrasseur, R. (2009). *Networked communities: Strategies for digital collaboration*. Hershey, PA: IGI Global. doi:10.4018/978-1-59904-771-3

American Society of Civil Engineers. (2003). Learning organization doctrine - Roadmap for transformation. Retrieved from http://www.au.af.mil/au/awc/awcgate/army/learning_org_doctrine.pdf.

American Society of Civil Engineers. (2011). Policy statement 525 -- Model building codes. Retrieved from http://www.asce.org/Public-Policies-and-Priorities/Public-Policy-Statements/Policy-Statement-525---Model-Building-Codes/.

Beer, S. (1972). *Brain of the firm: A development in management cybernetics*. New York, NY: Herder and Herder.

Chong, S. C., & Choi, Y. S. (2005). Critical factors in the successful implementation of knowledge management. Journal of Knowledge Management Practice. Retrieved from http://www.tlainc.com/articl90.htm.

CIPFA. (2009). New ways of working and innovation in local government. London, UK: CIPFA. Retrieved from http://www.improvementnetwork.gov.uk/imp/aio/1119705.

City of Tacoma. (2006). Deploying SAP® solutions optimizes and consolidates city service processes. Retrieved from http://www.sap.com/portugal/industries/publicsector/pdf/50078756_City_of_Tacoma.pdf.

City of Tacoma. (2009a). City managers evaluation form. Retrieved from http://cms.cityoftacoma.org/CRO/councileval.pdf.

City of Tacoma. (2009b). Green ribbon climate action task force. Retrieved from http://www.cityoftacoma.org/Page.aspx?nid=674.

City of Tacoma. (2011a). *Request for proposal*. Retrieved from http://cms.cityoftacoma.org/Purchasing/FormalBids/HR11-0452F.pdf.

City of Tacoma. (2011b). *Service level agreements*. Retrieved from http://www.cityoftacoma.org/Page.aspx?cid=12951.

City of Tacoma. (2011c). *Waste reduction strategies & residential food waste*. Retrieved from http://cms.cityoftacoma.org/cityclerk/Files/CouncilCommittees/Handouts/2011/EPWHandouts/EPW_20110511handouts.pdf.

Click! Network. (2007). Welcome to click! network, a division of Tacoma power. Retrieved from http://www.clickcabletv.com/AboutUs.aspx.

Demarche Consulting Group. (2006). *Final report to the city of Tacoma public works department: Building and land use division permit process documentation, analysis and resource assessment*. Retrieved from http://www.demarcheconsulting.com.

Demarche Consulting Group. (2009). *Strategic assessment and plan: City of Tacoma permitting*. Retrieved from http://www.demarcheconsulting.com.

Demarche Consulting Group. (2011). *Permitting cost recovery – A comparative investigation of structure and policy*. Retrieved from http://www.demarcheconsulting.com.

Doppelt, B. (2010). *Leading change toward sustainability: A change-management guide for business, government and civil society* (2nd ed.). Sheffield, UK: Greenleaf.

Doucet, G., Gøtze, J., Saha, P., & Bernard, S. (Eds.). (2009). *Coherency management: Architecting the enterprise for alignment, agility and assurance*. Bloomington, IN: AuthorHouse.

Eger, J. M., & Becker, A. M. (2000). *Telecommunications and municipal utilities: Cooperation and competition in the new economy*. Special Report Prepared for the American Public Power Association. Retrieved from http://www.smartcommunities.org/APPA_special_report.pdf.

Eisenberg, D. (2011). Building sustainability into codes: The evolution of building regulation. Paper presented at APEC Green Building Conference. Washington, DC.

Eisenberg, D., Done, R., & Ishida, L. (2002). *Breaking down the barrier: Challenges and solutions to code approval of green buildings*. Tucson, AZ: Development Center for Appropriate Technology.

Gruman, G. (2006). *The four stages of enterprise architecture*. Retrieved from http://www.cio.com/article/27079/The_Four_Stages_of_Enterprise_Architecture.

Hoverstadt, P. (2008). *The fractal organization: Creating sustainable organizations with the viable system model*. Hoboken, NJ: John Wiley & Sons.

IBM. (2006). City of Tacoma: Performance audit services for SAP functionality and departmental operations. Proposal No. IS05-0053F. Retrieved from http://www.ci.tacoma.wa.us/cronews/TacomaSAPAudit.pdf.

International Code Council. (2010a). 2010 report of the public hearing on public version 1.0 of the international green construction code. Retrieved from http://www.iccsafe.org/cs/IGCC/Documents/PublicComments0810/IGCC2010ROH.pdf.

International Code Council. (2010b). IGCC: A new approach for safe & sustainable construction. Retrieved from http://www.iccsafe.org/cs/IGCC/Documents/Media/IGCC_Flyer.pdf.

International Code Council. (2010c). IGCC public version 2.0 synopsis - International code council. Retrieved from http://www.iccsafe.org/cs/IGCC/Documents/PublicVersion/IGCC_PV2_Synopsis.pdf.

Johns, C. H. W. (1904). *Babylonian and Assyrian Laws, contracts and letters*. New York, NY: Charles Scribner's Sons.

Johnson, S. (2010). Where good ideas come. Paper presented at TED Conference. Long Beach, CA.

Jordan, A. (2008). The governance of sustainable development: Taking stock and looking forwards. *Environment and Planning. C, Government & Policy, 26*(1), 17–33. doi:10.1068/cav6

Jun, K.-N., & Weare, C. (2010). Institutional motivations in the adoption of innovations: The case of e-government. *Journal of Public Administration: Research and Theory, 21*(3), 495–519. doi:10.1093/jopart/muq020

Lewin, K. (1958). Group decision and social change. In Maccoby, E. E., Newcomb, T. N., & Hartley, E. L. (Eds.), *Readings in Social Psychology* (pp. 213–246). New York, NY: Holt, Rinehart, and Winston.

Mecca, T. (2004). Basic concepts for organizational change for administrative leaders. Retrieved from http://www.pcrest.com/PC/FacDev/2010/FI_reading.htm.

National Research Center. (2011). *BLUS customer satisfaction survey, summary report*. Washington, DC: National Research Center.

Net, A. W. C. (2003). Natt Worth & Mr. North: A Tacoma-style ad campaign. 2003 AWC Municipal Achievement Awards. Retrieved from http://www.awcnet.org/Apps/ma/projects/2003tacoma.pdf.

Newswire, P. R. (2003). City of Tacoma successfully launches most diverse SAP solution worldwide: Improved customer service, more efficient operation expected. Goliath: Business Knowledge on Demand. Retrieved from http://goliath.ecnext.com/coms2/gi_0199-3324000/City-of-Tacoma-Successfully-Launches.html.

NUS Institute of Systems Science. (2010). *Enterprise architecture as a platform for connection government*. NUS Government Enterprise Architecture Research Project, Phase 1 Report. Retrieved from http://unpan1.un.org/intradoc/groups/public/documents/unpan/unpan039390.pdf.

Orien, M. A. (2011). Green building: Growing from voluntary to mandatory. Nevada Business Journal Online. Retrieved from http://www.nbj.com/issue/0711/24/2438.

Parker, S. (Ed.). (2009). More than good ideas: The power of innovation in local government. London, UK: IDeA (Improvement and Development Agency). Retrieved from http://www.idea.gov.uk/idk/aio/9524940.

Reddick, C. G. (2011). Citizen interaction and e-government: Evidence for the managerial, consultative, and participatory models. Transforming Government: People. *Process and Policy*, 5(2), 167–184.

Reid, S. (2002). Tacoma, ho! Billboards in Seattle encourage business to move south. The Stranger. Retrieved from http://www.thestranger.com/seattle/tacoma-ho/Content?oid=12663.

Ross, J., Weill, P., & Robertson, D. (2006). *Enterprise architecture as strategy: Creating a foundation for business execution*. Boston, MA: Harvard Business School Press.

Schein, E. H. (1996). Three cultures of management: The key to organizational learning. *Sloan Management Review*, 38(1), 9. Retrieved from http://www.harvardmacy.org/Upload/pdf/Schein%20artilce.pdf

Sloan Management, M. I. T. (2006). Enterprise architecture: Driving business benefits from IT. Retrieved from http://cisr.mit.edu/blog/documents/2006/04/19/mit_cisrwp359_entarchslctdrsrchbriefs.pdf/.

Songini, M. L. (2004). $50M SAP rollout runs into trouble in Tacoma. Computerworld. Retrieved from http://www.computerworld.com/s/article/97690/_50M_SAP_Rollout_Runs_Into_Trouble_in_Tacoma.

Stich, V., Schmidt, C., Meyer, J. C., & Wienholdt, H. (2009). Viable production system for adaptable and flexible production planning and control processes. Paper presented at the POMS Twentieth Annual Conference. Orlando, FL. Retrieved from http://www.pomsmeetings.org/ConfProceedings/011/FullPapers/011-0269.pdf.

Tacoma Municipal Code. (2011). Title 1: Administration and personnel. Retrieved from http://www.cityoftacoma.org/Page.aspx?hid=1946.

United Nations. (2008). UN e-government survey 2008: From e-government to connected governance. New York, NY: UN. Retrieved from http://unpan1.un.org/intradoc/groups/ public/documents/un/unpan028607.pdf.

US Government Accountability Office. (2006). *Enterprise architecture: Leadership remains key to establishing and leveraging architectures for organizational transformation*. Retrieved from http://www.gao.gov/new.items/d06831.pdf.

US Legal. (2011). *One-subject rule law and legal definition*. Retrieved from http://definitions.uslegal.com/o/one-subject-rule/.

Washington City Managers Association Awards. (2002). *Website*. Retrieved from http://www.wc-cma.org/newsletter/0210wcmanews.pdf.

Washington State Constitution. (2011). *Website*. Retrieved from http://www.leg.wa.gov/LAWSANDAGENCYRULES/Pages/constitution.aspx.

Wilson, E. O. (1998). *Consilience: The unity of knowledge*. New York, NY: Knopf.

World, C. I. S. (2002). The "wired city" selects SAP for business systems improvement project. Retrieved from http://www.cisworld.com/news/2002/0916_sap.htm.

ADDITIONAL READING

Bekkers, V., & Homburg, V. (Eds.). (2005). *The information ecology of e-government: E-government as institutional and technological innovation in public administration*. Washington, DC: IOS Press.

Bernus, P., Nemes, L., & Schmidt, G. (Eds.). (2003). *Handbook on enterprise architecture*. Berlin, Germany: Springer.

Dunphy, S. H. (2002). City of destiny? Tacoma's nickname is starting to fit. Seattle Times. Retrieved from http://seattletimes.nwsource.com/news/business/washecon2002/tacoma.html.

Eisenberg, D. (1997). Sustainability and the building codes. The Last Straw. Retrieved from http://www.thelaststraw.org/history/eisenberg.html.

Fraser, K. L. (2003). Method, procedure, means, and manner: Washington's law of law-making. *Gonzaga Law Review, 39*(3), 447–494. Retrieved from http://blogs.gonzaga.edu/gulawreview/files/2011/01/Fraser.pdf

Giachetti, R. E. (2010). *Design of enterprise systems: Theory, architecture, and methods*. Boca Raton, FL: CRC Press.

Gilbert, M. D. (2006). Single subject rules and the legislative process. University of Pittsburgh Law Review, 67, 803–870. Retrieved from http://lawreview.law.pitt.edu/issues/67/67.4/Gilbert.pdf.

Goldsmith, S., & Kettl, D. F. (Eds.). (2009). *Unlocking the power of networks: Keys to high-performance government*. Washington, DC: Brookings Institution Press.

Golinelli, G. M. (2010). *Viable systems approach (VSA): Governing business dynamics*. Padova, Italy: CEDAM.

Hoogervorst, J. (2003). Enterprise architecture: Enabling integration, agility and change. *International Journal of Cooperative Information Systems, 13*(3), 213–234. Retrieved from http://www.lac2003.nl/academic_papers/J.Hoogervorst.pdf doi:10.1142/S021884300400095X

Kemp, R. L. (Ed.). (2007). *Regional government innovations: A handbook for citizens and public officials*. Jefferson, NC: McFarland.

Ross, J. W. (2003). Creating a strategic IT architecture competency: Learning in stages. MIT Sloan Working Paper No. 4314-03. Cambridge, MA: MIT Press.

KEY TERMS AND DEFINITIONS

Business Modularity Architecture: An organizations management and reuse of loosely coupled, IT-enabled business process components to preserve global standards but also enable local differences.

Business Silos Architecture: Organizational structure to maximize individual business unit needs or functional needs.

Coherence: A logical, orderly, and aesthetically consistent relationship of parts.

Consilience: A "jumping together" of knowledge by the linking of facts and fact-based theory across disciplines to create a common groundwork of explanation

Enterprise Architecture (EA): Enterprise Architecture (EA) is a blueprint for organizational change as defined in models (i.e., words, graphics, and other depictions) to describe in both business and technology terms how the organization is operating currently and how it will operate in the future.

E-Government: The utilization of the Internet and the world-wide-web for delivering government information and services to the citizens.

Optimized Core Architecture: Provides organization-wide data and process standardization as appropriate for the operating model.

Service Level Agreement: Agreement that sets expectations for the delivery of internal services and the role both service provider and recipient play in delivering those services.

Single-Subject Rule Making: A practice used to avoid complexity in legislation and the "piggybacking" of unfavorable legislation onto favorable legislation, which results in numerous individual codes that can lack of uniformity among the body of codes.

Standardized Technology Architecture: Provides IT efficiencies through streamlined technology uses, and in most cases, increased centralization of technology management.

Chapter 10
Whole-of-Enterprise Approach to Government Architecture Applied for Implementing a Directive of EU

Ivo Velitchkov
European Commission, Belgium

ABSTRACT

Sustainable benefits of EA efforts could only be realised if all structures and behaviour are taken into account together with their drivers and controls. This chapter tells the story of an e-Government project in Bulgaria where a whole-of-enterprise approach was applied to identify together legal, organizational, and technological measures related to achieving compliance with a new regulation and improvement of a set of e-Government services. One of the main objectives of the project was to discover the potential for simplification of administrative procedures for authorisation of service providers in line with a new regulation in the European Union supporting realisation of a single market of services. The obtained analytical results and the defined target state were not limited to improvement of online services but included pertinent legislation harmonisation and other non-IT related changes. The applied agile EA approach helped with completing the project within 6 months and realising results exceeding its scope.

DOI: 10.4018/978-1-4666-1824-4.ch010

INTRODUCTION

Enterprise Architecture (EA) is supposed to be a holistic approach. However, the predominant practice so far is still IT- and organisation-centric (Velitchkov, 2011). So are most of the frameworks. EA is not viewed as the architecture of the enterprise but rather as a business-conscious IT architecture.

Another approach that narrows the benefits of EA is related to scope. The frequent occurrence of it is when boundaries of 'the enterprise' are perceived as those of the organisation that is the main beneficiary of an EA effort. The negative consequences of such approach have been shown in the works of Tom Graves (2010, p. 13) and Chris Potts et al. (2010). The organisation-centric approach does not just limit the return on enterprise architecture management. When applied in a Government context it also supports the application of entrained intuitional patterns in decision-making.

There are a growing number of researchers and practitioners realising that if EA is IT-centric or organisation-centric it could not just have difficulties proving its value. The disillusionment of the EA (Gartner, Inc, 2010) will at best allot a marginal role for it in the business management. Thus it will not be able to even realise its potential as an IT-centric discipline aiming business-IT alignment.

The whole-of-enterprise approach is not an alternative approach. It is not called just "EA" only because, owing to its origin, "EA" is currently used to label something that is less than 'enterprise' and its architecture management, and the IT- and organizational-centrism are not the only issues. Information-centrism is just another limitation, albeit a less harmful one.

The chasm between business and IT is one of the drivers for the development of most of the EA frameworks, but it is sometimes overrated, leaving less attention to other chasms like the one between business strategy and execution, or

that between formal and informal architecture. A whole-of-enterprise approach would not just help to bring into EA scope elements like objectives, internal and external influencers, non-information technologies, knowledge, and trust. It would also mean keeping it coherent, not allowing new chasms to open, like the one between enterprise and solution architecture or the one between structured and unstructured processes.

This chapter tells the story of an e-Government project in Bulgaria. The project had so much weight of the legal analysis that it did not really prompt the usage of an EA approach and tooling, and as there have been many similar projects in the other countries of the European Union, it really turned out that doing it this way was more or less exotic.

The project was on one hand one of the many local measures supporting the realisation of a single internal European market for services. On the other hand, as it aimed to improve the Government and public services for authorisation of service providers, it was part of the further development of the Bulgarian e-Government. The scope of the project included analysis and identification of the needed legislation harmonisation as well as legal analysis relating to improvement of some administrative services provided by Government and non-Government institutions. One of its main objectives was to discover the potential for simplification of administrative procedures for authorisation of service providers in line with a new Directive of European Union supporting realisation of a single market for services. The obtained analytical results and the defined target state were not limited to improvement of online services but included pertinent legislation harmonisation and other non-IT related changes.

A whole-of-enterprise approach was applied to support together legislation harmonization, compliance, and e-Government efforts. The main benefits were realized through re-use of business objects in different views while ensuring coherence and unambiguity with a repository-based EA tool. A flexible architecture method was used to support handling of emergent patterns. The method implied but did not impose service orientation. Last but not least, the project success was due to the lean and agile project organisation.

The scope of the 'enterprise' included about 50 central and local Government agencies, other public service providers, businesses, and citizens. The project was realised in less than 6 months, achieving all objectives and realising additional benefits.

BACKGROUND

Services are very important for the economy of the European Union (EU). They represent 70% of the Gross Domestic Product (GDP) and employment in EU (European Parliament, 2006, p. 36). At the same time they are only 20% of the intra-EU trade, and the intended single market of services is happening much slower than expected. One of the main reasons is that services are much more prone to barriers than goods because of the little EU harmonization, luck of trust, protectionist tendencies, and cultural factors.

The Global Driver

One of the instruments to address this problem is the Directive 2006/123/EC (called "Services Directive" or just "The Directive" further in this chapter). It aims to modernise and simplify Member States' regulatory frameworks and to lift barriers to the functioning of the Internal Market for services. Lifting of barriers should be achieved by harmonisation of the Member State pertinent legislation, simplification of the administrative procedures and modernisation of administrative services. The latter includes ensuring their access online from "points of single contact" at national and EU-level.

The Directive is based on two basic rights established by the EC Treaty (which in terms of EA could be regarded as fundamental principles). These are the freedom of establishment (Article 43) and the freedom to provide services (Article 49) (European Union, 2006, pp. 31, 34). The latter implies four modes of temporary movement. These could be well illustrated with tourist services: 1) provider moves (tourist guide), 2) recipient moves (tourists), 3) both provider and recipient move (excursions), and 4) service moves (on-line sale of holiday package). The main objective of the Services Directive is to facilitate application of Arts. 43 and 49 by removing legal and administrative barriers.

The implementation efforts of the Services Directive affect all stakeholders: businesses (both providers and customers), citizens (both providers and customers), Government agencies and other public service providers and the legislative bodies.

The benefits for service providers are related to removal of unjustified and disproportionate burdens for business establishment in Member States and cross-border provision of services. All this should be not just possible but also made easy by simplification of bureaucracy and online single-point provision of the related public services.

The benefits for customers include prohibition of discriminatory conditions based on the nationality or residence of the service recipient, such as discriminatory tariffs. Additional benefits for customers are related to service quality. The Directive lays down a set of measures to promote high quality of services and to enhance information and transparency relating to service providers and their services.

The providers and customers of the services in the scope of the Directive are not the only beneficiaries of its implementation. It could positively affect the entire society at local and EU level. One way it could do that is by boosting the development of e-Government. The Directive is quite explicit on the use of on-line administrative procedures in relation to registration and other compulsorily requirements for service providers:

The setting up, in the reasonably near future, of electronic means of completing procedures and formalities will be vital for administrative simplification in the field of service activities, for the benefit of providers, recipients, and competent authorities (European Parliament, 2006, p. 43).

Simplification and modernization of Member States' regulatory frameworks is yet another benefit.

Finally, at EU level, the implementation of The Directive should increase and equalise the access to new jobs, increase competition among small and medium-size businesses and eventually the competitiveness of the European economy.

The Local Driver

The Services Directive was adopted by the European Parliament and the Council on 12th December 2006. The plan was to have it fully transposed by Member States into their national systems by 28 December 2009.

"The Act for Activities Related to Provision of Services" (Services Act, SA) came into effect in the beginning of 2010 in Bulgaria. It was the horizontal law implementing the Service Directive in the country.

The Ministry of Economy, Energy, and Tourism (MEET) initiated a project for identification of services that were within the scope of the Directive and the analysis of the corresponding pubic services, related to licensing etc. The objective was to document and analyse all those services provided by Central, Local Government and other public organisations in order to identify legislation gaps, optimisation opportunities and design transformation to a higher degree of e-service sophistication. Another objective was to ensure the required compliance and standardisation for realising access from a "Point of Single Contact" (PSC). The natural choice for the PSC in Bulgarian was the already launched e-Government portal.

THE PROJECT

The scope of the project was determined by the number of public services to be documented and analysed. However, this was not known, being in fact one of the deliverables. The number of public service providers that had to be contacted was not known for the same reason. Some additional constraints like the very short time frame—6 months—and the small project budget only made its objectives more difficult to achieve. This all was quite a challenge for our team of consultants, being less than 10 with the legal experts working part time.

Approach, Tool, and Methods

Our vision for the project was quite different from that of the other bidders in the tender. We regarded it as an Enterprise Architecture work. We based our estimation accordingly, which allowed us to bid at half the budget.

Determined to apply an EA-approach, we had several options for choice of tools. The first one, which we call "office," is the common approach applied by many consultants utilising MS Office products like Word, Excel, Visio and PowerPoint for both input and output when documenting and analysing artifacts. Such choice of tooling is one of the reasons for many EA failures but it was especially inappropriate in this case. There was a requirement to implement a mechanism for maintenance of the information about administrative services, which would allow keeping it up to date with legislative and procedural changes. That directed towards a repository-based tooling. One option was to design a database to serve as service register. However, we could not afford to postpone the actual work with the time to design and develop such an application. Moreover, it was far from clear which entities would be maintained, with what attributes and relations.

What we needed was a good, repository-based, and highly customisable EA tool. The team had experience with one of the leading EA suits in the market, so that determined the choice. We evaluated existing methods supported by the tool and designed a meta-model extending some of them to match the structures envisaged at the outset.

The choice of technical methods, tools and their adaptation was important but not as much as the agile approach applied for managing the whole project. One of the most popular EA methodologies TOGAF ADM (The Open Group, 2009, pp. 49-357) is a classical waterfall model. It could be applied successfully in controlled environments but normally requires a lot of time. Going through all phases in the cycle would take a year or two, sometimes more. For EA projects with high level of uncertainty and/or very short timeframe, such approaches with well prescribed processes could not be applied successfully even if scaled down. More flexible and adaptive ones should be used instead, and such was the one we applied in our project. We tried to be as lean and agile as possible. However, there were some governance mechanisms requiring overhead, which, although minimised, could not be spared. Examples of those were the meta-models and the modelling conventions.

The meta-model used in our project relied in the most part on what was existing in the EA tool. The extensions and modifications were related to specific interpretation or changing elements such as objects, connections, views, attributes and symbols. The 'interpretation' was a way to utilise as much as possible of the existing meta-model by just changing the meaning of certain elements that could well represent the analysed aspects of the reality but needed some tuning and agreement on the new semantics and syntax. The 'extension' included new object and attribute types, symbols, markers and connection types. The main viewpoints of the extended meta-model are shown in Figure 1.

Service Categorisation Viewpoint type was the one used initially for identification of economic classes that fell outside the scope of the directive. Public Service Viewpoint type included views used for documenting the relation between private and public services, their providers and legal grounds. The Administrative Procedures Viewpoint type was the one used for documenting and analysing procedures and their requirements to private service providers applying for licensing of their services so that they could be offered on the local market. The important viewpoint was used for documenting, analysis, and optimisation of the processes realising the public services related to private services included in the scope of the Directive. The target state of those processes incorporated changes needed to comply with the new legislation, simplify procedures, and ensure the capabilities required for online provision of the public services or improving online experience of those that already had some online implementation. The actual way the extended meta-model was used is described in the section "Project Realisation."

The initially created meta-model was based on the experience of the team with similar projects, the gathered information at the outset and many assumptions. It was discussed at weekly meetings where EA-method related issues were brought in for finding solutions. Normally those were some specific kind of relations or important patterns that were not supported by the current meta-model and conventions. The general approach was very conservative. Initially elaboration of applications and modification of conventions were attempted. In cases that could not resolve the issue and a pattern of the reported problems was recurring, we had to see how to support that pattern again with minimum changes in the meta-model. Once the changes were agreed upon, what followed was a quick impact analysis and in some cases regression tests. We had to keep re-work close to zero. If the impact analysis showed a need for non-value added changes, we had to look for an alternative way to modify the meta-model or a different solution.

Figure 1. The meta-model used in the project (main viewpoints)

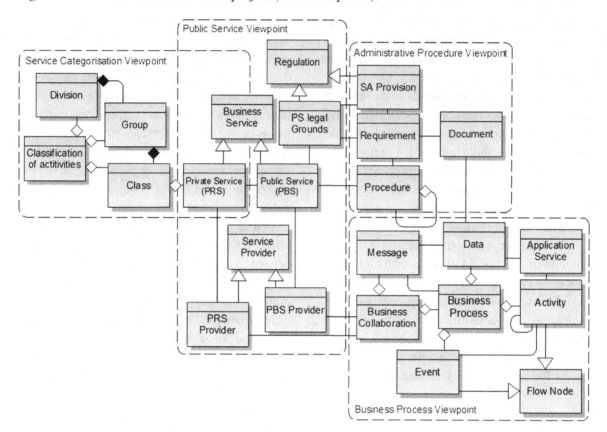

Modelling conventions are vital in any EA or BPM effort. Normally they are part of one or two documents that specify all agreed rules and provide guidelines how to apply them. EA modelling conventions should specify models, domains, views, viewpoints and level of modelling. They should include description of all objects used, their attributes, and symbols, what they represent and in which views are included. Other important conventions are those for naming, structure, and graphical representation.

Our project was not labelled as an EA effort and documenting modelling conventions was not required by the client. Nevertheless, they were needed for several reasons. Those that were configured in the tool had to be documented to ensure common understanding and standardised usage by the modellers. Others that were not

enforced by the tool and were a matter of compliance ensured by each team member, relied only on good elaboration, adequate communication, and discipline. Needless to say, the conventions had to be produced in a very short time and in a form that allowed access of all team members to the latest release and automatic notification in the event of modification. Meeting all those requirements with a dispersed team, working from seven different locations, demanded maintaining conventions, and similar content in a collaborative environment. We used a popular cloud service for that. The EA tool configuration specification, reports specification, guidelines, project schedule, visualisation of the artifacts production flow, projects logs and other project controls were all managed using that service.

Figure 2. Excerpt of NACE Rev.2

Division	Group	Class	
			SECTION H — TRANSPORTATION AND STORAGE
49			Land transport and transport via pipelines
	49.1		Passenger rail transport, interurban
		49.10	Passenger rail transport, interurban
	49.2		Freight rail transport
		49.20	Freight rail transport
	49.3		Other passenger land transport
		49.31	Urban and suburban passenger land transport
		49.32	Taxi operation
		49.39	Other passenger land transport n.e.c.
	49.4		Freight transport by road and removal services
		49.41	Freight transport by road
		49.42	Removal services
	49.5		Transport via pipeline
		49.50	Transport via pipeline
50			Water transport
	50.1		Sea and coastal passenger water transport
		50.10	Sea and coastal passenger water transport
	50.2		Sea and coastal freight water transport
		50.20	Sea and coastal freight water transport

The meta-model and the modelling conventions were created quite quickly, leaving sometimes room for interpretation. For such cases as well as other issues a collaborative FAQ[1]-like knowledge place was maintained utilising the same environment used for other project logs and control documents. The solutions/answers served as sort of elaboration of the method and conventions, and standardised the way specific patterns were handled by the team.

Project Realisation

The first challenge was to find out which were the services in the scope of the Directive. As there was no international classification of services, we had to use another standard classification. The only one that turned out to be appropriate was the standard EC (European Community) classification of economic activities NACE (Nomenclature statistique des Activités économiques dans la Communauté Européenne).

This classification has almost one thousand items in a three-lever hierarchy, the highest level being 'division' and the lowest 'class' (Figure 2). Each class has properties such as 'code,' 'description' and others clarifying its scope, namely 'includes' and 'excludes.'

What we had to do was import all data of the Bulgarian version of the classification (NACE.BG) in the architecture repository, but that would still mean a lot of manual work for modelling. That is why we used an import mechanism that created also relations between items. The whole model of the classifier was not modelled but automatically generated. It was visualised by one view per each division represented as tree structure (Figure 3, the main hierarchy with the darker symbols) following the rules of the Service Categorisation Viewpoint (Figure 1).

The Directive defines no criteria for inclusion, only for exclusion from the scope. That is why we had two additional attribute types for each entity of the classification, one Boolean to be set as "True" when an entity is excluded and one Text to reference the respective grounds for exclusion. The instances of the latter were in fact pointers to articles from the Services Act. There was a marker, which was set to appear in the symbol of the economic activity if the 'OutOfScope' attribute

Figure 3. Identified private services and their relations to economic activities and public services

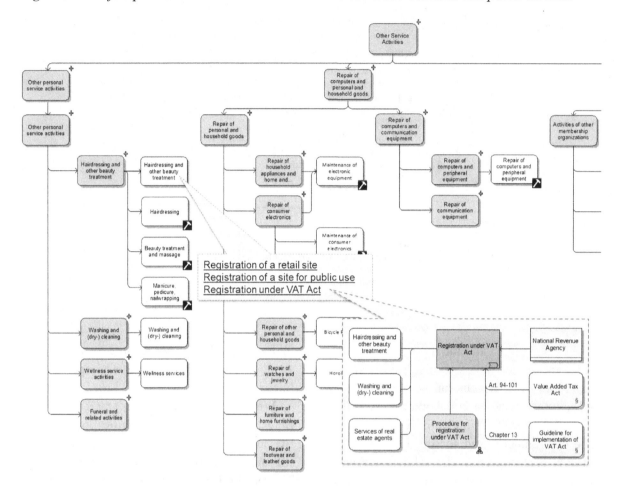

is "False." That visualisation was very useful for the business analysts working with the NACE. BG model, after the legal experts "filtered" that part of the classification, which was in the scope of the Directive.

The scope of the Directive based on the Services Act was determined by a small team of legal consultants. After a short training, they accessed the EA system with privileges set according to their responsibilities. Those privileges were part of the project governance rules which were defined and implemented following similar approach to the one applied for modelling conventions.

Once the scope defined, the business consultants, each responsible for a set of economic divisions, identified (groups of) services as fourth level of hierarchy by adding specific objects to the pertinent economic classes. At this level it was no more a pure hierarchy but one with cross-links, as there were cases with one service group belonging to more than one economic class (Figure 3, Example: "Maintenance of electronic equipment"). This new object also had specific attributes, including those with capability of controlling markers on the object symbol. One such example was to indicate if a service represented a craft, as crafts were subject to some specific regulation (Figure 3, Example: "Hairdressing").

We had to determine for each private service, which were the administrative services its provider had to use to attain the required license and other documents needed at specific stages of the service lifecycle. That required a lot of input from the team of legal experts. First it was identified what was required by law to allow provision of each service, then which institution issued the needed license and other compulsorily documents. Most of the institutions were Government agencies and municipalities but in some cases the service provision was mainly or additionally regulated by non-government institutions. Typical examples of the latter were related to services provided by architects, engineers, and craftsmen. All in all around 50 (types of) institutions turned out to be responsible for authorisation of services in the scope of the Directive. The selection included ministries, agencies, courts, municipalities, councils, notaries, chambers, and even museums.

When choosing a method for service design we presumed that at some stage the e-Government strategy may turn more seriously towards service-oriented computing. That was the reason public services were modelled using the business service object type which was central in the tool's SOA (service-oriented architecture) methods. The public services were first linked to the business processes that realised them at the time of the project. Then the target state of the public e-services was linked with optimised business process where for most of the process steps all needed capabilities were subsequently defined. That level of abstraction was important in order to separate the global need for certain realisation (mainly automation) with the local decision for building such capabilities or re-using active structures that already had them. The use of capability concepts is discussed further in the chapter.

When identifying the needed administrative and public services we faced serious standardisation issues. Sometimes the name of the service was one in the respective regulation, another on the website of the institution and yet another in the national register of the administrative services and on the e-Government portal.

That missing convention on the naming of services is just one example of the consequences of the technology-focused standardisation efforts. Some countries, when developing their e-Government Interoperability Frameworks (e-GIF), narrow their scope and/or start from the means-side. The interoperability is commonly regarded as having three levels, namely: semantic, organisational and technical (WP4, 2005). The focus on the technical part followed by organisational one sometimes leaves little attention to the semantic. Additional damages are caused by the fact that quite often technical interoperability is the starting point. This unfortunately was the case in Bulgaria, and having different nomenclatures of administrative services is just one of the consequences.

The views created for each administrative service included relations to all pertinent private services, legal grounds, procedures, and provider (Figure 1). Thus, apart from the visualisation, the model allowed for maintaining the relations between each private service to the economic classes it belongs to on one side and to related administrative services from another.

Each administrative service had one or—more often—a family of scenarios depending on the type of applicant or a specific set of options. There was a need for a simple solution that would make the work of business and legal consultants easier and at the same time provide means for rigorous description. Each scenario had a particular set of requirements, which the service applicants needed to meet and prove with substantiating documents, and each requirement was based on certain legal grounds. According to our EA method and conventions, that had to be modelled as a connection to the particular regulation specifying the exact paragraph as an attribute of that connection.

As the input had a lot of manual, although tool-supported work, keeping it simple was very important. There was almost no method extension created there, the weight being shifted towards analytical mechanisms to extract the information in the required format.

Some of the procedure families were simple, just one or two-level hierarchy with 'children'

Figure 4. View of the procedure for registration of European cooperative society

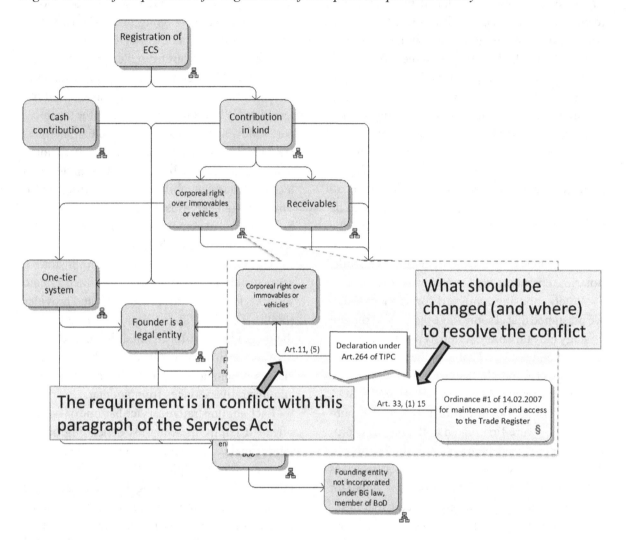

inheriting requirements of the 'parents,' but there were other cases where each service application case was represented by some complicated combination. Nevertheless, we kept the procedure view as hierarchy with cross-links allowing 'children' to have more than one 'parent' thus reusing the view type used for economic activities. Then it was the job of the analytical mechanism to determine each case, based on the view and a set of rules.

An example of such a complicated procedure is the Registration of European Cooperative Society (Figure 4). If the founder is a legal entity, the specific requirements are combined with those

inherited from one-tier and two-tier systems and then depending on whether the contribution is in cash or in kind. Thus the node 'Founder is a legal entity' represents four different case types depending on the combination of 'parents' and 'grandparents.' The fact that a simple recursive mechanism would not extract correctly each case but a bit more complicated one is needed, was a fair trade-off for the assured simplicity and hence high speed of the input. Using some business rule designer may seem a more elegant solution, but that's only if that particular part is regarded in isolation. All objects take part in different views where their relations with other objects are modelled according to the rules of the meta-model. Then different analytical results can be generated using the created structures and the maintained attributes.

Each member of the procedure family represented a set of terms and conditions. And there were specific requirements for each set. Those were modelled in separate views. The important relations and objects in those views were the representations of the legal grounds for each requirement. They supported two objectives. One was the identification of changes in vertical regulations needed in order to harmonise the existing legislation with the new Services Act. That was mainly related to demanding some information to be provided by the applicant that is obtainable from another agency or requiring original of certain document or to imposing some discriminatory conditions.

The second reason why these relations were important was connected to the online provision of the administrative services. The objective was to provide all services electronically and improve those that had already some online implementation. For example if only information about an administrative service was provided via internet, to enhance the service to one or two-way interaction. If it was already at the stage of two-way interaction, to further develop it to a full electronic case handling.

Meeting this objective faced technical, operational, and legal obstacles. Some of them at agency level, some at Government level. Identifying the legal obstacles was quite important. It helped allocation of issues to the appropriate place and level and development of a realistic transition plan.

The next step in our work was to carry out a detailed analysis of the business processes realising each administrative service. The objective was to propose target state model for each process, based on a set of principles and requirements. The requirements were directly derived from the Services Act and some were related to pure compliance. Others were a matter of application of principles for simplification of procedures, reducing the number of points and frequency of contacts between the public service providers and their clients.

There were several principles we followed when designing the target processes supporting e-services at higher stage of online sophistication. One such principle was to first optimise the processes and then design change of their structure to enable automation. It is common knowledge that automating a bad process just makes it produce bad results faster. Still, quite often that is exactly the case.

What we found is no surprise in any Government administration: long approval cycles, bottlenecks, too many organisational and system breaks, having more than one 'master'-data registers, too much data requested from the service applicant that is obtainable from other Government agencies and suchlike. A big part of them were caused by bad operational management but by compliance with legally fixed business rules that were either not changed after their rationale ceased to exist, or they were not harmonised with the new EC legislation.

Another principle we followed was to keep the target state at the level of 'what' avoiding the all too common deviation to 'how.' Normally that level of abstraction requires the models to be kept at conceptual level. We needed to go lower, to logical structures but still not prompting technologies or even specific solution architecture.

The process models had two groups of objects. One comprising events, activities, and gateways was used to model the sequence flow, or the behaviour. The other was used to describe the active (organisational units, application systems) and passive structures (documents, data). Usually the target state of business processes included changes of both structures. One new element in the target state was the 'capability' object.

Capabilities are typically expressed in general and high-level terms and typically require a combination of organization, people, processes, and technology to achieve (The Open Group, 2009, p. 28).

The view of capabilities as a crosscutting concept has its merits and it's a proven strategic approach to Enterprise Architecture. It has been long time used in DoDAF (USA Department of Defence, 2009) and appeared in the latest release of TOGAF (The Open Group, 2009). Business capability maps and other artefacts serve well to distinguish what is needed to achieve some strategic objective with how it is realised as a specific combination of process, people, systems, knowledge, etc.

We did not use capability objects as business capability but as a technical sub-type. Capabilities could be specialised in the similar manner services are sub-typed as technology, application, and business services to have additional layers abstracting the functionality exposed to external environment from mechanisms of its realisation (Lankhorst, 2004, p. 3). When using 'application capability' object to describe the required automation of certain step in a business process, there are several important benefits from both enterprise architecture and implementation viewpoint. Capabilities (from now one referring only to application capabilities) are defined at global level. Each activity in a process that needs automation is supported by one or more capabilities. These capabilities could have some local match of existing capability of an application system or service, or in cases no such active structure is existing, a requirement for its development had to be created.

The link between requirements and technical capabilities is very important but may be confusing. Requirements are temporary in nature, projects-based, while capabilities have much longer life cycle. Capabilities play an important role in both enterprise and solution architecture, while requirement are only pertinent to the latter.

Capabilities were identified in our project for most of the activities in the target business processes. This approach had several advantages over direct elicitation of requirements. First, it gave better visibility of repeatable capabilities needed by different business processes within one administration as well as in many administrations. Making such capabilities transparent provided good opportunity to look for cost savings and better flexibility realised through utilisation of shared services and standardisation. Second, it gave more freedom for decisions on utilisation of existing resources and acquisition of new capabilities. One and the same capability could be provided in one situation by an existing functionality of a certain module of an operational information system, in another—by some Web service or a reusable block. When nothing can be reused, such approach of documenting the target state could well support buy-or-build decisions. It's also in line with the best practices for service-orientated design (Erl, 2009).

As the EA tool allowed automatic comparison between current and target state, we used this feature to provide it in graphical and tabular form. This was accompanied by information about the changes of the internal procedures and the national legislation as one of the prerequisites for realisation of the target state. In some cases, more than one target state was designed, usually when certain circumstances necessitated a more gradual transition. For example, business processes behind some services that were at stage 2 of online sophistication, had one target design for stage 3 and another for stage 4.

G2G Services

Government to Government (G2G) electronic services are of primary importance for improvement of administrative services. The client-oriented Governments try to reduce the number of contacts with different institutions and the time spent by the clients when serving as intermediary between agencies.

Most of the public services in Bulgaria at the time of the project imposed a lot of requirements to the applicants. Each private service provider had to substantiate certain facts with documents issued by other agencies. Thus, even if all of them were provided online, the client had to submit applications for a number of administrative services, sometimes over twenty, to obtain certain certified information needed by the agency, giving authorisation for a particular service provision. Requesting information that had already been provided by the service applicant was prohibited by the Act for Electronic Government, which came into effect in 2008. The new Services Act included this in the list of things that the institutions had no longer the right to require from service providers applying for authorisation:

When certain circumstances are certified by another authority in the territory of the Republic of Bulgaria, the competent authority may not require proof by the service supplier, but is obliged to gather them directly from that authority (The Act for Activities Related to Provision of Services, Art 11, Par 5).

It was in the scope of the project to identify such requirements and link the procedure in which they appeared with the paragraphs of the respective legal act as part of the harmonisation analysis. The way this was done was explained earlier in this chapter. What the project scope did not explicitly include but was obviously a valuable output, was the identification of those G2G services that had to be realised to support compliance with the new regulation. As it turned out no additional modelling effort was needed. Using an EA repository-based tool, obtaining such information was a matter of having just another view showing a set of relations already existing in the model. As each procedure to be followed by applicants of public services was linked to the required documents certifying certain circumstances, occurrences of the same objects represented the same documents

identified as output of other public services. This directly provided the chain of relations between one authority, the service it provides, the required documents of proof, the services those appeared as a result of, and authorities providing those services.

The information from such views as well as most of the output delivered to the client was not in form of graphics but rather in tabular or text form. The information about administrative services followed a standardised form with sections such as:

- Name
- Institution, Address
- Description
- Legal grounds
- Applicants
- Fee
- Period
- Terms and Required Documents
- Procedure
- Stage of online sophistication
- Current realisation

Having all business objects documented in a repository-based EA tool gave a lot of analytical opportunities. It was easy to see all administrative services certain type of provider had to apply for to authorise its trade in the country. Then which were the institutions that most of the service providers depended on. Which agencies had the biggest number of procedure incompliant with the new law, or which laws needed to undergo most serious modifications to be harmonised with the Services Act.

Most of the results were delivered to the client in a tabular form. To make it as readable as possible the columns were constructed so that they formed a logically coherent sentence. For example the automatically generated report for identification of the needed G2G services had the following columns: 'competent authority'; 'to provide its administrative service'; 'requires document'; 'which is the result of'; 'administrative service'; 'of competent authority.' This table was populated with the values of attributes <agency name>, <administrative service>, <document>, <administrative service>, <agency name> following the relation where the document is input of the first and output of the second administrative service.

During the course of the project, there were a lot of changes in the legislation, but it was not a big effort to generate again all reports delivered in the earlier stages once the updates were made in the repository. There were thousands of pages delivered and it all contained correct, actual and coherent information.

It is worth noting that in this project, the phrase 'enterprise architecture' was not present in any report nor was it mentioned during meetings with the client and other beneficiaries.

FUTURE DIRECTIONS

A change of the paradigm of Enterprise Architecture is needed to unleash its true potential, and that starts with the answer of the question "What constitutes an enterprise?" If the European Union is regarded as one then the scope of the enterprise includes all that is in as well as relations with non-EU stakeholders. Then all articles in the Treaty should be regarded as architecture principles and the paragraphs of the European legislation as business rules. By applying EA and systems thinking to drivers and structures, a lot of complex situations could be managed more efficiently.

CONCLUSION

In such agile EA projects, it is important to start with an adaptive modelling method, especially when none is in existence and when there is a complex set of relations within the enterprise. The first version of the method should contain a good set of rules taken from best practice, the

enterprise architecture vision, and all information gathered before and during the first stage of the project. Then it should be flexible enough to accommodate new, conservatively but quickly, or change existing rules when there is no provision for the emerging patterns or a conflict with existing rules. The lifecycle management of the method should be a part of the project governance and enterprise architecture governance.

Enterprise Architecture management should be enterprise-wide. It should especially be non-IT centric. IT provides support in Government, it's just an enabler. IT is not part of the mission nor is it a core function, but Enterprise Architecture should not be EA-centric as well. It should speak the language of the enterprise, not the language for some EA framework, at least in the beginning. Having successful projects with tangible results first would credit EA with more trust than campaigns for ensuring stakeholders' buy-in with the promise for future benefits.

Using office tools or a diagram-drawing software for managing business objects is a common practice and one with little chance of success. Business objects have complicated relations and many important attributes worth documenting, analysing and maintaining. This could be achieved only with a good repository-based tool, supporting EA and business process standards and notations and capable of extending its meta-model to fit the needs the EA effort.

There is EA everywhere in the enterprise, and there was EA before the term was coined. When a formal EA-approach is used it should be aligned with the existing understanding of structures and their relations with objectives and factors. The actual EA work should be done, where possible, by the subject-matter experts, after their view is accommodated in the architecture method. In this case an important part of the work was done by lawyers, linking legal grounds with administrative procedures and marking discrepancies between the new and existing legislation, having all relevant documents already in the architecture repository.

Enterprise Architecture approaches can be applied in many situations so far not envisaged as part of this field, and deliver the results with better quality and speed than using other methods. To see these opportunities it is vital to regard Enterprise Architecture as the architecture of the whole enterprise, not just as business-conscious IT architecture or as architecture of one organisation. This is especially relevant in Government sector. A Whole-of-Government approach should not just regard all agencies as a whole but include all stakeholders—citizens, businesses, non-government organizations, and where relevant—as in the case of this chapter—other governments. The usual objects of EA such as actors, processes, systems, and data should live together with paragraphs from the legislation, other rules and controls as well as drivers and objectives.

REFERENCES

Erl, T. (2009). *SOA design paterns*. Upper Saddle River, NJ: Prentice Hall.

European Parliament. (2006). *Directive 2006/123/EC of the European parliament and of the council of 12 December 2006 on services in the internal market. Official Journal of the European Union*. Geneva, Switzerland: European Union.

European Union. (2006). Consolidated version of the treaty on European Union and of the treaty establishing the European Community. *Official Journal of the European Union*. Geneva, Switzerland: European Union.

Gartner, Inc. (2010). *Gartner's enterprise architecture hype cycle reveals two generations of enterprise architecture*. Retrieved 08 14, 2011, from http://www.gartner.com/it/page.jsp?id=1417513.

Graves, T. (2010). *Everyday enterprise architecture*. Colchester, UK: Tetradian Books.

Lankhorst, M. (2004). *ArchiMate language primer*. Enschede, The Netherlands: Telematica Instituut.

Potts, C. (2010). *recrEAtion*. Denville, NJ: Technics Publications.

The Open Group. (2009). *TOGAF version 9*. Reading, UK: The Open Group.

USA Department of Defence. (2009). DoD architecture framework, version 2.0: *Vol. 1. Introduction, overview and concepts*. Washington, DC: Department of Defence.

Velitchkov, I. (2011). *All-inclusive enterprise architecture*. Retrieved 08 15, 2011, from http://www.strategicstructures.com/?p=4.

WP4. (2005). *D4.2: Set of requirements for interoperability of identity management systems*. Retrieved from http://www.fidis.com.

ENDNOTE

[1]   FAQ – Frequently Asked Questions

Chapter 11
The Role of Services in Governmental Enterprise Architectures:
The Case of the German Federal Government

Dominik Birkmeier
University of Augsburg, Germany

Christian Neubert
Technische Universität München, Germany

Sabine Buckl
Technische Universität München, Germany

Sven Overhage
University of Augsburg, Germany

Andreas Gehlert
Federal Ministry of the Interior, Germany

Sascha Roth
Technische Universität München, Germany

Florian Matthes
Technische Universität München, Germany

Christian M. Schweda
Technische Universität München, Germany

Klaus Turowski
University of Augsburg, Germany

ABSTRACT

In the public sector, Information Technology (IT) as a means to support governmental processes is as important as in industry today. Delivering high quality eGovernment services requires an efficient and effective IT support. This IT support can only be provided if the requirements specified in the processes are correctly and completely transformed into IT solutions. Services are seen as major means to support this transformation. In this chapter, the authors propose a method which systematically translates business processes into services. The method contains 1) a data model describing the structure of the work products of the method, 2) a technique for emergent data modeling, which allows its users to customize the data model according to the government's needs, 3) a role model describing the required competen-

DOI: 10.4018/978-1-4666-1824-4.ch011

cies for each step, and 4) a process model describing the required steps to derive services from business processes. To succeed in a governmental context with diverse, federative organizational structures, the method needs a high degree of flexibility. In particular, the proposed method has been designed to be compatible with different process modeling techniques.

1. INTRODUCTION

Electronic Government (eGovernment) has a long tradition in Europe. This long tradition was recently underlined by the Ministerial Declaration on eGovernment (Ministers of the European Union, 2009). Among others, this so-called Malmö declaration strives for designing eGovernment services around the needs of the users, to reduce the effort for using these services and to increase the availability of public sector information (p. 2f).

The Malmö declaration was also influenced by Europe's Digital Agenda (European Commission, 2010c). The Digital Agenda describes problem areas, political goals, and actions for the development of Europe's IT. The major elements of Europe's Digital Agenda are the notions of business process orientation and service orientation (p. 15). Business process orientation as well as service orientation have been refined in more technical terms in the European Interoperability Strategy (EIS, European Commission, 2010a) and the European Interoperability Architecture (EIF 2.0, European Commission, 2010b).

Especially the EIF emphasizes the fact that eGovernment is more than the communication between administrations and citizens (A2C) or the communication between administrations and businesses (A2B). It particularly includes the communication between different administrative bodies (A2A). Although this communication is "invisible" to the citizen and the business, it directly supports the goals of increasing the efficiency and effectiveness of public services as expressed in the Malmö Declaration and the EIS (European Commission, 2010a; Ministers of the European Union, 2009). Therefore, we understand eGovernment as follows:

eGovernment is the IT-supported exchange of services between public administrations and citizens (A2C), between public administrations and industry (A2B), and between different public administrations (A2A).

Providing such administrative services efficiently requires that these services are supported by IT. The IT support, however, is only effective if the requirements of the business processes are correctly and completely translated into IT solutions. In this chapter, we cover the first step of this translation: We propose a method to systematically derive services from business processes.

Research Question: How can services systematically be derived from business processes?

Thereby, we understand the term *service* as follows:

A service is a set of requirements, which is already supported by IT solutions or will be realized by IT solutions in the future. By IT solutions we mean any software, or component thereof, which is capable to realize a service.

Given this definition, services are the crucial link between business and IT. On the one hand, services are extracted from business processes and are directly linked to them. On the other hand, IT solutions may implement one or more services so that these IT solutions are also linked to services. Services enable the business process engineer to support his/her processes with IT without any knowledge of the internal structure of the IT solutions. In the other direction, the solution owner does not need to have complete knowledge of the business processes to provide IT solutions, which are useful for the business.

Although a sound method is required to derive services from business processes systematically, such a method needs to respect the organizational settings of government agencies. The German Constitution for instance prescribes that every federal ministry is independent (Grundgesetz für die Bundesrepublik Deutschland, 1949). Consequently, it is very difficult to establish a certain technique in the entire German Federal Government. Therefore, a sound method needs to be flexible enough to respect a divergent degree of formalism as input. In our case, it means that the proposed method should be compatible with many process-modeling techniques and it should be possible to tailor the method according to the needs of the government agency.

We follow a design science research approach to provide the depicted method. The method is described in seven sections: In Section 2 we elicit requirements for the envisioned method. Based on these requirements, we discuss related work in the area of service identification and knowledge management via Web 2.0 and Enterprise 2.0 tools in Section 3. The method itself is introduced in Section 4. Thereby, we demonstrate how the "wisdom of the crowds" (Surowiecki, 2004) can be used to enable Enterprise Architecture (EA) management. By using Web 2.0 techniques, wikis, and an open templating mechanism, we show how the ivory tower syndrome can be cured, typical pitfalls are avoided, and employees are empowered to contribute their expert knowledge. Section 5 applies the method to an example from the governmental domain. It serves as an evaluation of the proposed method. Section 6 describes future directions that we see for the proposed method, and Section 7 summarizes our findings.

2. REQUIREMENTS

Industry trends such as globalization, rapid economic change, and the necessity to foster an organization's sustainable competitive advantage (Wagter, van den Berg, Luijpers, & van Steenbergen, 2005) have also reached public administrations today. One of the main drivers for innovation in public administrations is the need to provide governmental services in a digital form across different government agencies and different countries at low costs and without barriers (IT Planning Council, 2010). This requires on the one hand interoperable systems and on the other hand systems that can be modified quickly to comply with future jurisdiction.

A method for systematically deriving services is a key prerequisite for realizing eGovernment. This method should contain all constituents of a method as defined in the method engineering discipline (Brinkkemper, Saeki, & Harmsen, 1999):

Req1 The method for deriving services from business processes must contain a *process model* explaining important activities on how services should be derived; a *role model* explaining the roles, their competencies and responsibilities for certain activities in the process model; and a *data model* explaining how services are described.

Since the method should be applicable to many governmental agencies, the envisioned method especially cannot be based on a specific process modeling technique such as the Business Process Modeling Notation (BPMN). Therefore, we assume:

A1 The method for deriving services from business processes cannot rely on a single business process modeling technique.

Assumption A1, however, does not exclude the possibility to use conceptualizations common to many process modeling techniques such as activity or control flows in the envisioned method.

Governments usually have a strong separation of business and IT units. People working in these units have also very different backgrounds and qualifications. It is unlikely to find people with a strong IT background in a business unit; or people with a strong business background in the IT units (Frederiksa & van der Weideb, 2006). Since services are meant to be mediators between business and IT, the proposed method must be easily understood by business and IT experts. If the method is too complicated and cannot be communicated to both business and IT-experts, the method might not come into use:

Req2 The envisioned method must be designed in a way so that it can be easily understood by business and IT experts, i.e. it must build on a common terminology.

To reduce costs and to enhance the quality of IT assets, the method needs to support reuse. Therefore, the envisioned method has to provide support for cataloguing IT services and for managing this catalogue:

Req3 The envisioned method allows adding services to a service catalogue and supports re-shaping those services according to already existing services in the catalogue.

To link the different data sources within the organization, a common description for services has to be developed. This development often suffers from the 'ivory-tower syndrome,' i.e. leads to the creation of a wish list in which each stakeholder asks for the bits and pieces of data s/he is interested in. This results in an unmaintainable large model describing a service.

Req4 The envisioned method has to develop and/or provide a common service description

model understood by stakeholders with different backgrounds.

Information on processes and services has to be maintained on a regular basis to be useful for governing the IT. Accordingly, the documentation process must be conducted in a way, which is on the one hand feasible for stakeholders with various backgrounds (e.g. process or application owners), and on the other hand shows the benefits of their time spent on sharing knowledge. A concept for information maintenance requires motivating mechanisms for the information providers. Such mechanisms may be managerial orders or financial rewards. Such reward mechanisms are usually not available in the decentralized environment of interoperating administration bodies. In this light, "soft" incentive mechanisms are required, making the utility of the shared information visible to the corresponding provider.

Req5 Information providers must receive feedback on the utility and the appropriateness of the shared information.

In our context, service design targets the reuse of existing services on the basis of functional requirements. Thereby, the functional requirements may be provided in one department and be required in another one at a different location. Hence, it is crucial that different departments immediately are enabled 1) to share information about a service and 2) to discover already maintained services. Ideally, so-called base-services are identified which can be provided in a central manner, since those services provide functionality frequently used by multiple departments.

Req6 The envisioned method has to involve stakeholders of different departments distributed over several locations to assure service reusability.

Although we have motivated our requirements from the governmental domain, we believe that these requirements are equally applicable in other industries. The proposed method bridges the gap between business and IT and has only limited requirements on the needed inputs. Therefore, we believe that our chapter is not specific to the governmental domain and contributes also to the knowledge body of EA management where business-IT-alignment and service-orientation is a central topic of interest (Aier, Gleichauf, & Winter, 2011; Buckl, Marliani, Matthes, & Schweda, 2011).

3. BACKGROUND

There are many approaches addressing the topics of deriving services or of using the wisdom of the crowds to gather information. However, an approach to combine these two perspectives on information gathering in the context of service modeling is missing. Subsequently, we prepare our solution by investigating the existing knowledge base with respect to different methods and techniques that can be used to derive services (Section 3.1) and by revisiting typical functionality provided by Enterprise 2.0 platforms that has been proven to be useful to gather information from stakeholders with different backgrounds (Section 3.2).

3.1. Approaches for Deriving Services

Besides service-oriented design in general, especially the derivation of services has frequently been addressed in literature. The existing approaches, however, differ in their support for a systematic procedure. They range from general recommendations that should be considered during the derivation process (SAP, 2005) to approaches which cover at least some or ideally all parts of a comprehensive method as postulated in *Req1*

(Aier & Winter, 2009; Azevedo, et al., 2009; Erl, 2005; Erradi, Anand, & Kulkarni, 2006; Klose, Knackstedt, & Beverungen, 2007; Winkler, 2007), whereas the latter is not achieved yet. The service derivation approaches found in literature consider different aspects of information for the derivation process (such as activities, data, control flows, data flows, etc.). While similar approaches for older paradigms such as component-based development are sometimes dependent on specific modeling techniques (Jain, Chalimeda, Ivaturi, & Reddy, 2001), we found none of the examined service-oriented approaches to be that restrictive (*A1*).

Some approaches build upon a purely technical view of services and consequently apply an analysis of source-code and database schemes to derive services (Erradi, et al., 2006). Others aim at involving both business and IT experts into the process and, hence, provide a common terminology which can be equally understood by both sides (Azevedo, et al., 2009; Winkler, 2007). However, most approaches fail to address this requirement (*Req2*). With respect to the necessary input, the proposed approaches vary in their consideration of existing services (*Req3*). Only some are able to include existing structures during the derivation process (Erradi, et al., 2006; Klose, et al., 2007; SAP, 2005), while the others lack such possibilities so far.

With respect to the model used for service description (*Req4*), the proposed approaches range from domain-oriented to technically oriented solutions. None of the approaches aims at defining a common model that is understood by stakeholders with different backgrounds. The understanding of services is a key influence factor on the results of an approach, however (Birkmeier, Klöckner, & Overhage, 2009). To the best of our knowledge, none of the service derivation approaches proposed envisions an incentive mechanism for sharing information (*Req5*) or an explicit integration of stakeholders from different locations, departments, etc. to foster the reuse of services (*Req6*).

Table 1. Summary of related approaches in service derivation

	SAP (2005)	Erl (2005)	Erradi et al. (2006)	Winkler (2007)	Klose et al. (2007)	Azevedo et al. (2009)	Aier & Winter (2009)
Provisioning of process, role, and data models (*Req1*)	(✗,✗,✗)	(✓,✗,✓)	(✓,✗,✓)	(✓,✗,✗)	(✓,✗,✗)	(✓,✗,✗)	(✓,✗,✓)
Independency from modeling techniques (*A1*)	✓	✓	✓	✓	✓	✓	✓
Common terminology for business and IT (*Req2*)	✗	✗	✗	✓	✗	✓	✗
Consideration of existing services (*Req3*)	✓	✗	✓	✗	✓	✗	✗
Common model (*Req4*)	Technically-oriented	Technically-oriented	Domain-oriented	Domain-oriented	Domain-oriented	Domain-oriented	Domain-oriented
Information provider feed-back (*Req5*)	✗	✗	✗	✗	✗	✗	✗
Stakeholder involvement (*Req6*)	✗	✗	✗	✗	✗	✗	✗

A detailed comparison of the different approaches is summarized in Table 1. As it turns out, none of the approaches is able to fulfill all requirements. This observation is also supported by extensive literature studies on the state of the art in service derivation, which draw similar conclusions and attest that additional research effort is required to create more mature approaches (Birkmeier, et al., 2009; Dietz, Juhrisch, & Grossmann, 2011; Kohlborn, Korthaus, Chan, & Rosemann, 2009).

3.2. Web 2.0 and Enterprise 2.0

The term Web 2.0 has increasingly gained attention in the last years. In Tim O'Reilly's definition, Web 2.0 terms modern applications facilitating interactive collaboration and communication via the Internet (O'Reilly, 2008). He puts emphasis on Web 2.0 as applications which enable users to immediately share and reuse information. Since Web 2.0 applications primarily focus on users' personal reputation and expertise, the term is often used as a synonym for active user participation in the Internet. Objects in Web 2.0 applications which are primarily created by the users themselves and not statically given by a web provider

(e.g., media objects such as videos) are termed as "user-generated content" (O'Reilly, 2008).

Surowiecki (2004) introduces the term "the wisdom of crowds." This principle means that the quality of decisions conjointly taken by a group is often better than the one of those taken by particular persons. This phenomenon especially applies to Web 2.0 applications since they mainly support collaboration and communication tasks in teams and groups.

Today's most prominent Web 2.0 application in which the principles "the wisdom of crowd" and "user-generated content" (O'Reilly, 2008) are successfully applied, is the Wikipedia Encyclopedia (Leuf, 2001). This project aims to collect the world's knowledge, whereby everyone can contribute. A wiki is a "website" that allows the creation and editing of any number of interlinked web pages via a web browser using a simplified markup language or a WYSIWYG text editor (Wiki, 2011). In contrast to a classical content management system, where changes of the content must go through an editorial process before they are shown on the website, changes in wikis are immediately visible. An information consumer can thus instantly switch to information provisioning, making him or her effectively what is called a "prosumer" (Chang, 2006).

McAfee (2005) describes the application of Web 2.0 techniques in enterprises as so-called Enterprise 2.0 techniques. A great number of software vendors combine different individual Web 2.0 solutions to integrated Enterprise 2.0 platforms. Besides delivering the advantages of classical Web 2.0 applications, e.g. ease of use, these platforms are especially optimized for the deployment in enterprises, e.g. by means of advanced access control lists and desktop-oriented user interfaces.

In Büchner et al. (2009), the platforms of leading Enterprise 2.0 vendors are compared to each other. The authors provide a detailed functional analysis of the platforms and describe the:

- supported *content objects* which contain user generated content, e.g., wikis and blogs, and the
- provided *Enterprise 2.0 services* which are operations on the content objects, e.g., tagging.

In the following, we discuss selected Enterprise 2.0 services applied to wiki-based content and detail their usability in our application context:

S1: Authoring services support the users during the collaborative creation and manipulation of wiki-pages. These pages combine unstructured information, e.g. plain text, links, and images, with semi-structured content, e.g., attribute-value pairs. Semi-structured content can further be organized into *templates* that define the attributes for a more specific type of content, e.g. a wiki-page describing a business process.

S2: Tagging services support the collaborative categorization of content objects. A tag is a keyword that categorizes a content object against one or more user-created classification schemas (Golder & Huberman, 2005). More sophisticated implementations of tagging services facilitate to link certain tags, called "type tags," to templates for semi-structured content.

S3: Search services can be used to find content objects fulfilling specified criteria. These criteria can target the full text of the wiki-pages and can access semi-structured content as well. In particular, the user can specify searches that find pages, which supply a specific value for a chosen attribute. Furthermore, the searches can be restricted to deliver only wiki-pages tagged with selected keywords.

S4: Link Management services support the users in creating and maintaining references between wiki-pages. Internal links, i.e., links to content objects managed by the platform itself, are updated by the link management, whenever the link target is re-named. Thereby, consistency of the references is ensured. Link management services further highlight links that reference no longer existing content objects. Further, link management can be used to restrict the valid values for an attribute-value pair to wiki-pages that supply a specific type-tag.

S5: Awareness & Feedback services help the users to follow the activities of other users. Users can define watch-lists in order to get informed, when the content of selected wiki-pages is changed. Change feeds provide an overview of the ongoing editing activities in the wiki. View trackers anonymously log the visits of selected wiki-pages. Feedback mechanisms, such as comments and ratings, supply means to express the opinion on selected content objects.

In Section 4.2 we apply the aforementioned Enterprise 2.0 services in a technique for emergent data modeling.

3.3. Conclusions from the Literature Analysis

From the literature we reviewed we can conclude that no method exists that fulfills our requirements completely. The strengths of the service-oriented approaches are their level of completeness and their formality. For instance, all reviewed approaches are independent from the modeling language used for process modeling and most approaches have at least two of the required parts of a modeling method. However, the service-oriented approaches lack the collaboration aspect. None of the analyzed approaches supports feedback to the information provider or fosters the involvement of stakeholders with different backgrounds in the service identification task. The Web 2.0 and Enterprise 2.0 approaches focus mainly on collaboration but do not provide us with (semi-) formal methods on how to derive services from business processes.

The results of the literature analysis mean that the enterprise architect has either well-defined methods available that come with the risk of not being used in the enterprise since they lack appropriate collaboration techniques; or s/he uses well-established collaboration techniques without the necessary tools and guidance on how to derive services from business processes. Therefore, the method developed in Section 4 combines these two approaches:

- the proposed method is formal enough to allow the enterprise architect to derive services from business processes;
- the proposed method has very low requirements for its inputs and is, therefore, easy to use;
- the proposed method incorporates Web 2.0 techniques to foster collaboration; and
- the proposed method ensures feedback to the information provider to motivate him/her to provide accurate and up-to-date information in the future.

4. A METHOD FOR DERIVING SERVICES FROM BUSINESS PROCESSES

This section describes a method for deriving services from business processes along the following method constituents:

- *Data Model*: The data model describes the structure of the documentation (Section 4.1).
- *Technique for Emergent Data Modeling*: The technique describes how to adapt and extend the data model based on information gathered from different stakeholders (Section 4.2).
- *Role Model*: The role model describes the roles with their competencies and responsibilities for the activities in the process (Section 4.3).
- *Process Model*: The process model describes the relevant activities of the method (Section 4.4).

Each of the following subsections may contain specific assumptions, which restrict the design space (Gehlert, Schermann, Pohl, & Krcmar, 2009; Schermann, Gehlert, Krcmar, & Pohl, 2009). These assumptions and their implications are discussed in Section 6.

4.1. Data Model

The data model describes the general structure of the work-products of the method. It is depicted in Figure 1. Key elements of the data model belong to the business or the IT side or bridge both sides (cf. *Req2*) and are: *business process* and *activity* (on the business side) and *services* (on the IT side). The *function* is the linking element between the two worlds.

Assumption A1 prescribes that the method cannot rely on a concrete modeling technique. However, for the data model we need to assume

Figure 1. Data model of the proposed method (modeled as UML class diagram)

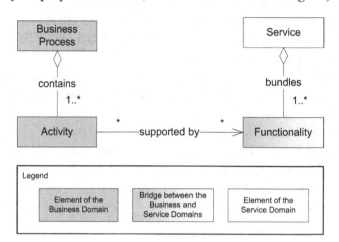

that business processes do exist and that these business processes consist of activities. Thus, we can formulate the following assumption:

A2 The results of the business process analysis are business processes, which consist of activities.

Assumption A2 means that the proposed method can only be applied *after* a business process analysis (or during its later phases). It also decouples the application of the method from business process modeling and particularly from a concrete process modeling technique. Activities are central concepts of many process modeling techniques, e.g. the Event-Driven Process Chain (EPC), the Activity Diagrams (AD), and the Business Process Modeling Notation (BPMN, Patig & Casanova-Brito, 2011). Therefore, assumption A2 is suitable for a governmental setting without a prevalent process modeling technique.

Activities are the basis for functions. A *function* represents a functional requirement described in the language of the process modeling expert. It is the bridge between the business and the IT worlds. Activities and functions share a many-to-many relationship. This many-to-many relationship decouples the structures of the business processes from the services and fosters a loose coupling

between those two elements. The relationship between activity and function can be described as follows:

- An activity may be *manual* and may not need IT support. Therefore, the activity may not have any function assigned.
- An activity may have exactly one function assigned. The activity is *automated*.
- An activity may have more than one function assigned. There are two reasons for this situation: either the business process is more coarse-grained than the functions or there is the need for an additional IT support for this activity. We call the functions of the latter case *implicit functions*. They result from the fact that not all IT-related aspects are reflected in the business process. For example, login or security functions are usually not modeled in business processes.
- A function may be assigned to more than on activity. This indicates that the business process is more fine-grained than the functions. This is typically the case when data objects are created, modified or quality-assured. These activities may well be represented separately in a business process. In IT, this situation may just be represented

as one function, which modifies a set of attributes of a particular data object.

Services bundle similar functional requirements and thus functions, which are or should be implemented in IT. As a service should fulfill a purpose, it contains at least one function. The collection of all services is called *service catalogue*.

4.2. A Technique to Emergent Data Modeling

For refining the model discussed above, we introduce a technique that builds upon Enterprise 2.0 services (cf. Section 3.2) to create data models over time using structured content in an Enterprise 2.0 platform incorporating basic thoughts of wiki-based systems. While the common process for developing models is based on "schema first," data second, our approach focuses on "data first, schema second." The technique is facilitated by the principles "the wisdom of crowds," "active participation," and "user-generated content" as introduced in Section 3.2.

The Enterprise 2.0 service S1 provides a mechanism known as *auto-completion*, which recommends values and names already used for the corresponding attribute in the semi-structured content. This mechanism is a key component for the technique to emergent data modeling, as the recommendations facilitate the development of a consistent terminology. In particular, the accidental introduction of new concepts and terms by occasional typographic errors is avoided.

Moreover S1 additionally provides mechanisms to explicitly specify the type of a wiki page, e.g. by means of wiki templates or tags. The type of a page indicates the class of the object being described in the content of the wiki page. A great number of wiki-based systems are using types (or concepts which are similar to types, e.g. templates) to enable authors to reuse often needed structures as well as to define specific integrity constraints. For example, a wiki template for a town could specify

that all town instances (i.e., pages that are using the template "town") should provide an attribute 'Population.' In the context of data modeling, the wiki templates can be regarded as instantiations of the 'construct templates' introduced in the ISO Standard 19440 (ISO/IEC, 2007). Such templates supply the name of a modeling type, describe the properties as well as relationships of this type, and textually define the semantics of the type. Multiple wiki-based systems offer functions to provide textual descriptions along the templates, which can be used to supply a semantics definition. In Matthes et al. (2011), so-called type tags are used for typing a wiki page instead of using templates. Furthermore, this approach introduces mechanisms providing a smooth transition from unstructured textual content to more structured wiki pages.

Besides the auto-completion mechanism for attribute names and attribute values, S1 provides a further recommendation technique, namely *attribute suggestions*. Attribute suggestions are generated based on a statistical analysis (cf. S3) of frequently used combinations of tags (cf. S2) and attributes in wiki-based systems. The name of the recommended attribute is shown with an empty value field (i.e. an attribute stub) on similar wiki pages to urge the wiki authors to provide a value for this empty field. For instance, if a particular wiki page is tagged with the keyword 'business process' and additionally provides an attribute "acronym" on other wiki pages also tagged as 'business process' a stub (attribute suggestion) for the attribute "acronym" is shown. On the one hand, attribute suggestions facilitate a data-driven evolution of the data model, on the other hand they contribute to a consistent terminology and a uniform data model, similar to the auto-completion mechanism.

In some wiki-based systems, types have an impact on both the auto-completion as well as on the attribute suggestions. For instance, if it is specified (in the type or template) that the aforementioned attribute 'Population' may only consist of integer values, the auto-completion control can provide input support optimized for integers. Furthermore, constraints can also have an impact on the ranking of auto-completion result lists. For instance, if an attribute (e.g. constituent country) is constrained to link values referencing wiki pages with a specific type (e.g. country) the auto-completion mechanism prefers pages fulfilling this constraint.

Changes to the type may also influence the attribute suggestion mechanism. For example, in case of the definition of an additional attribute-e.g. an attribute which is not yet used on any wiki page-on the type level, an attribute suggestion is provided on pages according to this type. By doing so, decisions made by a schema designer (data model designer) are immediately visible for the wiki page authors. Thus, the designers and authors enter into dialog and the evolution of the data model is facilitated and the set of terms converges to a commonly accepted terminology.

Kurpjuweit and Winter (2007) explain that the relations between objects are more important than the particular properties of the object itself. Wiki-based systems implement these findings and commonly provide services (cf. S4) to create (hyper-)links to other wikis pages as quickly and efficiently as possible. For instance, in some wikis a service is provided to transfer plain attribute text values to hyperlinks with little effort (i.e. with on-click). Since in this case plain text is transferred to an object having an individual identity (URL), we call this mechanism *objectification*. For users, optimized objectification mechanisms are very powerful to facilitate the evolution of the data model.

The introduced technique (mechanisms and services) enables data modeling from two perspectives:

- Bottom-up, i.e. the data model emerges spontaneously due to the interplay of particular wiki pages and their structured elements.

- Top-down, i.e. the definition of the data model takes place on a meta-level independent of the particular wiki pages.

In Section 5, we explain how this technique brings benefits to our project context and contributes to the fulfillment of the requirements as specified in Section 2. Furthermore, we describe how both methods (bottom-up and top-down data modeling) interlock and thereby benefit from each other.

4.3. Role Model

The method operates at the junction of the business and IT worlds. The role model reflects this fact and introduces roles with dedicated responsibilities in each world:

- *Process Engineer*: The Process Engineer is responsible for designing business processes. S/he knows the processes of the organizational unit in focus and is able to express those processes in a modeling language, which distinguishes at least processes and activities (cf. A2). Additionally, the role includes the rights to (re-)design the business processes of the organizational unit and to decide, which activities should be supported by IT. Furthermore, the Process Engineer is knowledgeable about organizational aspects, which are not covered in the business process and which may lead to implicit functions.

- *Service Engineer*: The Service Engineer is responsible for the service catalogue. S/he knows the structure and the content of the services in the service catalogue. In particular, the Service Engineer should know which services are already realized by IT. Furthermore, the Service Engineer is empowered to decide, which services may be added to the service catalogue and has experience in identifying implicit functions and in identifying services. S/he has in-depth knowledge of the proposed method for deriving services from business processes.

- *Stakeholders*: The Stakeholders may be different groups of professionals actually executing an activity of a process. They have insights regarding these activities and the corresponding functions from day-to-day application thereof in their professional occupations.
- *Solution Owners*: The Solution Owners host implemented service realizations, e.g. a running business application offering electronic publishing services.

In addition to the roles described before, it would be desirable that the Process Engineer has some knowledge of the principle of service-orientation and the method for deriving services. Furthermore, the Service Engineer should have some knowledge of business process modeling and the domain of the project. This additional knowledge will ease the communication between the two worlds.

4.4. Process Model

The presented method derives services from business processes, which may be—according to assumption A1—described in an arbitrary format. This format can range from formal process modeling techniques to informal textual descriptions. As a consequence, the business process descriptions may not state the information and data on which the processes operate. Therefore, many existing service identification approaches cannot be applied in such a setting.

A key complexity in the process-based identification approach is the consequence of the level of abstraction on which the activities constituting the business processes are documented. This level of abstraction is determined by the Stakeholders' understanding of the business and does not nec-

essarily match the level of abstraction, on which discussions on functions take place. In particular, two types of mismatch have to be distinguished:

- Process abstractions, where relevant IT functions, such as authentication or encryption, are only implicitly alluded to.
- Functional abstractions, where different activities can be supported by the same underlying function, e.g. apply this function only on different information.

The method for deriving services from business processes has to account for these types of mismatches. Figure 2 gives an overview on the method's underlying process.

In the first step of the method (step ❶ in Figure 2), the Process Engineer identifies the activities and decides which activities should be supported by IT. The Service Engineer may support the Process Engineer with information about already existing services, which may completely or partially satisfy the business needs. In addition, the Service Engineer may explain to the Process Engineer that the realization of certain function is not yet feasible. In this situation, Process Engineer and Service Engineer may discuss a compromise solution.

In the next step (step ❷ in Figure 2) the Process and Service Engineers jointly identify implicit functions, which are not described in the activities of the business process. This is the case when the business process is more abstract than the functions. This situation also covers functions needed for an IT support of the process (e.g. authentication, authorization, encryption, etc.) which are usually not modeled during the business process analysis. The Service Engineer contributes these functions based on the experiences of frequently used implicit functions.

During the identification of the implicit functions, the Process and the Service Engineers rely on the knowledge of the professionals, i.e. stakeholders, actually using the explicit function.

Figure 2. A process for deriving services from business processes

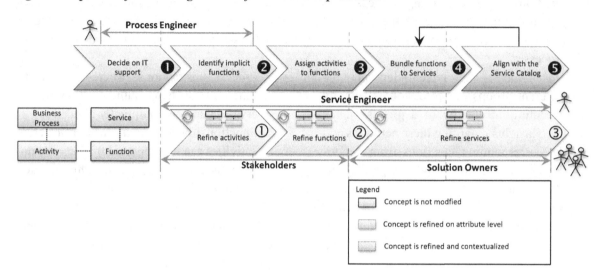

These stakeholders are involved and collaboratively refine the description of both explicit and implicit functions using the technique for emergent data modeling (*Req4*). In particular, new attributes are defined (*Req6*) and corresponding values are supplied, further specifying the nature of the discussed activities (supporting activity ① in Figure 2).

In the subsequent step (step ❸ in Figure 2), activities which require the same function are linked to the same functional requirement. This is the case when the business process is less abstract than the functions. An example of this situation is the creation, modification, authorization, and submission of a document. These activities may be relevant from a business process perspective. However, in IT these processes may modify only a set of attributes of a document in a document management system. Therefore, there is only one functional requirement "change attributes of a document" needed to support this activity. Step ❸ is also relevant for implicit functions. It may, for instance, be necessary that the user of the later system is authorized to execute a particular step in the business process. Again, the "authorization" function is assigned to more than one activity in this case.

After the execution of step ❸ of the proposed method, the Service and Process Engineers have identified a set of functions and have assigned those functions to the activities of the business process. Therefore, we need to assume:

A3 All implicit functions are known or can be identified when deriving services from processes.

Assumption A3 says that implicit functions are an additional input to the proposed method.

The process and service engineers involved in steps ❷ and ❸ need to understand the functions and activities in the business process correctly. If different interpretations of functions and/or activities persist, the resulting functions may not be correctly assigned to activities and, therefore, the support for the business process may not be optimal. Therefore, steps ❷ and ❸ should be supported by a collaboration tool, which facilitates the development of a concise and consistent understanding of the documented functions and activities. In such a tool, the Service Engineer can propose an assignment of the different activities to corresponding functions and therein refine the description of the function appropriately.

The stakeholders performing the corresponding activities receive notifications on the assignment of "their" activities (*Req6*). They can subsequently provide additional information on the nature of the activity. Further, they may relate standardization documents, relevant guidelines or white-papers to the function and detail the function specification as required (supporting activity ② in Figure 2). Feedback mechanisms facilitate stakeholder discussions on the details of the function (*Req5*). In case of an erroneous assignment, the stakeholders may enter direct interaction with the Service Engineer.

Steps ❹ and ❺, see Figure 2, are executed iteratively. They both target the bundling, i.e. the aggregation, of technically related functions to services. The bundling of related functions to services creates service demands which have to be aligned with an existing service catalogue. This catalogue contains initial descriptions of the available services. Comparing the service demands resulting from the bundling of functions with the available services, the Service Engineer may identify the following types of alignment:

1. *Full service alignment*: The identified service demand fits exactly with an existing service of the service catalogue. Existing IT solutions assigned to that service can directly be reused.

2. *Full function alignment*: In this case, all functions of the identified service demand are represented in the service catalogue but the functions may belong to different services. To foster reuse, the service demand should be re-organized according to the services of the service catalogue. As in situation 1), existing IT solutions can be directly reused.

3. *Partial function alignment:* In this case, only parts of the functions of the identified service demand are represented by services in the catalogue. The recommendation in this situation would be to re-organize the service demand: the set of functions covered by the service catalogue should be bundled to one service while the rest of the functions should be bundled to another service. In this way, existing IT solutions can be partially reused while the missing functions need to be implemented separately.

4. *Complete function mismatch:* In this case, none of the functions are covered by services in the catalogue. A decision must be made, whether the service should be added to the service catalogue or not. This situation will most likely appear during the initial set-up of the service catalogue.

The relevant analysis is supported by Enterprise 2.0 techniques, especially the *Search* service allowing to identify possibly matching services based on attributes but also based on full-text descriptions.

Situations 2) and 3) require splitting an already defined service. This may indicate that the service catalogue and the identified services are structured differently. Therefore, the identification of services (step ❹ in Figure 2) should be repeated iteratively. Additionally, in situation 3), the functions, which are not supported by a service of the catalogue, need to be bundled and new services need to be identified. This will most likely lead to situation 4) in the next iteration of the service identification process. During the analysis of the alignment of the service demands with the services in the catalogue, the Service Engineer may refine the description of the demanded service as well as that of an existing service (supporting activity ③ in Figure 2). In particular, new characterizations for non-functional requirements, e.g. security requirements, may be added to the service description template. The Solution Owners of the services' underlying IT solutions are in turn notified about the changes and refinements in "their" service descriptions. In case a novel characterization of the services does not match the characterization of the underlying IT solution, the Solution Owners can raise objections to the Service Engineer. In a subsequent iteration of the step, the Service Engineer can then re-align the functions according to the mismatch in non-functional characterizations.

5. ILLUSTRATIVE EXAMPLE SUPPORTED BY ENTERPRISE 2.0 SERVICES

In the following, the proposed method is applied to a typical example of the public sector: the procurement of goods and services. The method steps (steps ❶ to ❺ in Figure 2) will be exemplified. Concurrently to those method steps, Stakeholders, Service Engineer, and Solution Owners work on a close basis in an iterative manner addressing *Req6*. In addition to the example, the interplay of this cooperative work illustrated in Figure 2 (sub-method steps ① to ③ in Figure 2) will be described subsequently highlighting how concrete Enterprise 2.0 services of the Tricia platform are employed, to support and facilitate a technique for emergent data modeling (cf. Section 4.2).

The business process can be described as follows:

The business process starts with a request for goods or services. More specific requirements of these goods or services are formulated and a call for bids is issued. The bids are collected and evaluated according to the given requirements. Once the decision is made, one of the bids is accepted and a contract is issued. The goods or services are bought based on this contract. Finally, all relevant documents are archived. Figure 3 shows the resulting process on the left.

The Process Engineer decides on the IT support of the activities in the business process: The activities "publish call for bids," "receive bid," "accept bid and sign contract," and "archive relevant documents" should be automated. IT support is not required for all remaining activities.

According to our process and role models (cf. step ❶ in Figure 2), the Process and the Service Engineers need to agree on the functions behind those activities, which should be automated. The Process Engineer knows that bids are typically received as paper documents. Therefore, s/he proposes to scan those documents so that the documents can be handled electronically. The Service Engineer introduces an Optical Character Recognition (OCR) function to make the documents searchable to ease the evaluation of the bids in the next step. Both the Process and the Service Engineers have to ensure that *implicit functions are identified* and made explicit (cf. step ❷ in Figure 2). The Process Engineer identifies an implicit function: the notification of the bidders once the bid was received. This function should also be supported by IT.

Based on the activity descriptions of Stakeholders, which may be provided in full text, the Process and Service Engineers are provided with an information base for deciding whether certain functions may be supported by IT. These method steps (cf. steps ❷ and ① in Figure 2) can be executed concurrently, due to the employment of an Enterprise 2.0 platform (cf. *Authoring* in Section 3.2). This means: while the Stakeholders and Service Engineer *refine activities*, the Service and Process Engineers jointly identify potential implicitly described functions and make them explicit. In addition, the emergent data modeling technique introduced in Section 4.2 enables the Service Engineer to iteratively extend the model by attributes without explicitly changing the model, e.g. an attribute called *IT-supported* indicating whether or not a certain kind of function can be supported by IT (cf. Section 4.2).

The Process and Service Engineers identify the need for an authorization for the activities "publish call for bids"; "receive bid" and "accept bid and sign contract" (implicit functions; cf. step ❷ in Figure 2). However, both parties agree that the authentication and authorization required in these three activities are identical. Thus, the

Figure 3. Procurement process with functions and services

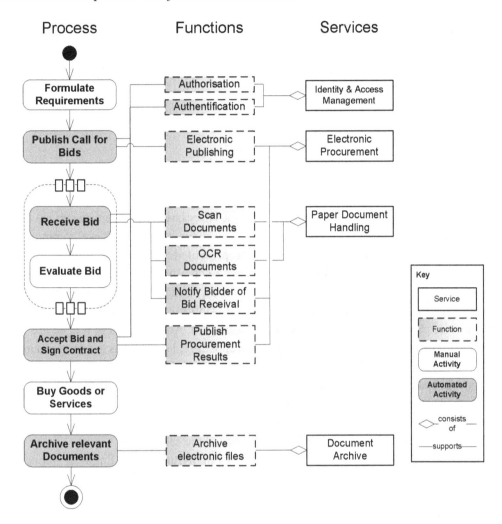

Service Engineer decides to assign these three activities to the authentication and authorization functions (step ❸ in Figure 2). While the Service Engineer is concerned with the method step *assign activities to functions* (cf. step ❸ in Figure 2), the Stakeholders are enabled to refine 1) the description of functions and 2) the structure of the functions (cf. step ② in Figure 2). Thereby, Stakeholders can describe functions in full-text, or attribute value pairs employing techniques like e.g. auto-completion with attribute suggestion (cf. Section 4.2 and Figure 4).

In the next step (cf. step ❹ in Figure 2), the Service Engineer bundles the six functions to services. The Service Engineer knows that there are already services in place, which allow handling paper documents. So the functions "Scan Documents" and "OCR documents" are bundled to one service. The same holds true for the function "Archive Electronic Files." The Service Engineer is not aware of an existing service for the remaining functions. However, the Service Engineer concludes that the remaining functions logically belong together and bundles them to the "Electronic Procurement" service. Figure 4 illustrates how the Enterprise 2.0 platform Tricia supports *bundling of functions to a service* via the Enterprise 2.0 service *Authoring* with auto-completion.

Figure 4. Bundling functions to a service using auto completion

Within the service description (Figure 5), Stakeholders and Service Engineers may specify Tags (cf. S2 in Section 3.2) for a particular service (cf. ① in Figure 5), so that a service: 1) can be specified, and 2) may be easily found. A full-text description (cf. ② in Figure 5) can be used to describe the service. Solution Owners can also contribute their knowledge on services already realized by IT (cf. ③ in Figure 2). Thereby, the Authoring concept ensures that common understanding evolves over time. Moreover, structured information can also be captured, such that explicitly known functions can be referenced and refined, if needed. Therefore, so-called Type-Tags (cf. ③ in Figure 5) can be used to specify, which concept is described. In this particular case, referencing functions is technically speaking a multi-value attribute (cf. ④ in Figure 5). Thereby, attributes can be hyperlinks referencing (cf. S4 in Section 3.2) other concepts or plaintext. As illustrated, these attributes can also be used to reference a concept of a certain type (cf. ⑤ in Figure 5), in this case a person or group.

Specifying additional attributes changes the model behind a concept immediately. On the basis of existing and already structured data, a model emerges. Based on this model and previously stored data, recommendations for attributes can be made to encourage users to use this particular attribute (cf. ⑥ in Figure 5). The platform also empowers stakeholders to leave comments on the page (cf. ⑦ in Figure 5) for discussing is-

sues they have with a certain service description, a used function, etc. These comments are then represented with the additional information of who actually wrote the comment (cf. ⑧ in Figure 5), so that a discussion about an issue in the description can be started instantly (cf. *S5* in Section 3.2). Any changes to a page are stored in a repository, i.e. versions are captured and are easily accessible (cf. ⑨ in Figure 5). For each version, it is marked *who* changed *what*, *when*. Finally, the last editor is shown on the page (cf. ⑩ in Figure 5) so that the Service Engineer sees *who* edited the service last.

Finally, the Service Engineer is concerned with *aligning the service with the service catalogue* (cf. step ❺ in Figure 2). Therefore, the Service Engineer compares the identified services with the existing service catalogue in more detail.

Using aforementioned full-text descriptions and attribute-value pairs (cf. *S1* in Section 3.2) enables the Service Engineer to employ another Enterprise 2.0 service artifact, i.e. using a full-text and faceted searches (cf. *S3* in Section 3.2). Thereby, full-text searches (cf. ① in Figure 6) can be combined with faceted searches. In this example, the facet selected refers to the concept of function (cf. ② in Figure 6), so that the functions are filtered according a certain attribute value (cf. ③ in Figure 6). The *auto-completion* feature will suggest only attributes that are relevant for the selected concept.

Figure 5. Service description example using hybrid-wiki concepts

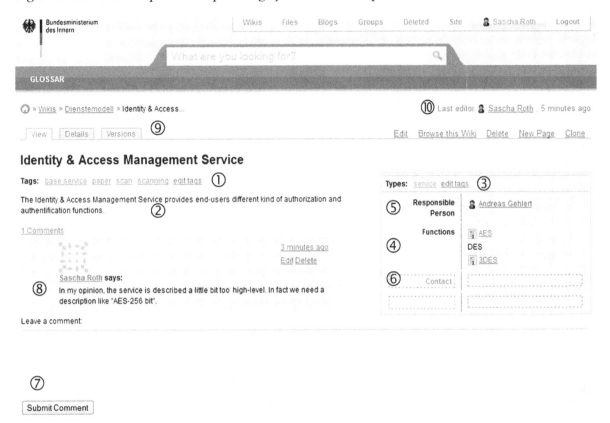

Simultaneously, Solutions Owners can help to contribute their knowledge to complete the service description (cf. step ③ in Figure 2). For instance, they could have objections against the usage of DES encryption. In turn, Solution Owners are notified if changes to subscribed services occur, i.e. if the Service Engineer removes DES encryption from the service's description.

Employing such techniques, the Service Engineer finds that the "Paper Document Handling" service also supports e-mail that can be used to notify the bidders once their bid is received. Reusing this function comes with the advantage, that an existing IT solution can also be reused and that the effort to realize the "electronic procurement" service can be reduced. By a comment of a Solution Owner, the Service Engineer finds out that there is a customer relationship management system in use, which provides a service with the same name. A detailed analysis of this service reveals that it contains a function "Contract Management," which could support the activity "Buy Goods or Services" partially. In this way, the Service Engineer contributes to the business by automating activities of the business process, which were not selected for automation by the business. Figure 7 represents the result of this analysis. All elements are highlighted, which are modified in the final step of the method.

6. FUTURE DIRECTIONS

The introduced method to derive services from business processes contributes to a closure of research gaps discussed before (cf. Section 3). In

Figure 6. Full-text search combined with an attribute filter

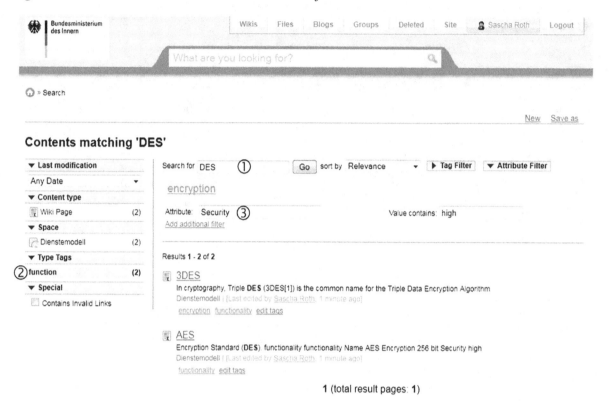

this section, we discuss the underlying assumptions (A1-A3) to draw conclusions about the generalizability of the method. This discussion also provides insights into future research.

According to assumption A1 (cf. Section 2), the method cannot rely on a single business process modeling technique. On the one hand, this ensures its applicability in many different projects with varying prerequisites. Additionally, it fits well to the situation found in practice, where modeling techniques are commonly adapted instead of being used by the book. However, the core set of elements (e.g. activities, control flow) is the same for most modeling notations so that the method is suitable for most process modeling notations. On the other hand, each modeling notation also has specific characteristics, such as e.g. different types of actions or events. A method which utilizes such characteristics during the derivation of services might, therefore, be able to achieve better results,

but it is then also fully dependent on a specific language. Whether this might be an advantage or in fact turn out as a drawback in practice remains to be examined more closely.

According to assumption A2 (cf. Section 4.1), the presented method only uses activities to derive services from business process models. As a consequence, it disregards the analysis of data structures, which generally form an important aspect during the modularization of systems (Parnas, 1972). In practice, however, business process modeling activities oftentimes do not encompass the documentation of processed data items. Our method thus is applicable even in such scenarios where many other proposed approaches cannot be used anymore. We will need to examine whether the proposed method can be extended in a way that it can also analyze data structures when present in business process models.

Figure 7. Process, functions, and services after comparison with the service catalogue

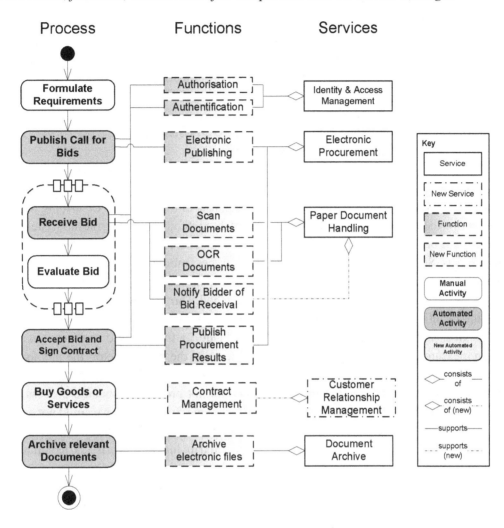

Assumption A2 also implies that a business process model is required before the proposed method can be used. This means that the proposed method cannot directly be applied to unstructured or ill-structured processes, which usually cannot be expressed as process models. An interesting approach to tackle this problem would be to allow hybrid wiki pages as inputs of the method. As wiki pages can be generally used to describe unstructured data and, therefore, also unstructured processes, it is sensible to assume that the hybrid wiki approach can be used to describe unstructured and ill-structured business processes. Nevertheless, the proposed method needs then to be extended to accept a business process description from a wiki page as input. The evaluation of this idea is subject to future research.

Assumption A3 (cf. Section 4.4) requires that implicit functions can be identified by the Service and Process Engineers. This is an essential requirement, as different processes include different implicit functions which have to be incorporated in services. However, no general rule for a systematic identification of implicit functions can be stated. Hence, we will need to further examine the application of the proposed method in order to determine how reliable the identification of implicit functions is in practice. Additionally, suggestions of common implicit functions should be provided to support the Service and Process Engineers.

Furthermore, it has to be evaluated in how far the current method that has been created for the German Federal Government can be seamlessly applied to equal problems in industry. Hence, the question whether all underlying assumptions are endurable in industrial practice as well has to be examined. Another key factor for its applicability is the acceptance of the method by all involved stakeholders. We therefore intend to further examine the users' commitment to the method once it has been applied in a significant number of projects. So far, the method proposed in this chapter has repeatedly produced usable services from a business perspective. We will have to examine the resulting service landscape with respect to design characteristics such as coupling and cohesion measures, though.

While the presented approach offers a high degree of flexibility, it also could lead to conflicts, e.g. disagreements on certain attribute names. The presented approach could also lead to a 'huge model,' i.e. a tremendous level of detail and detail imbalances in the model could occur since people differ in the way they abstract. Merging and gardening mechanisms have to be developed and applied so that unnecessary details can be abstracted. The application of Enterprise 2.0 techniques often relies on single entities, i.e. a driver. Put in other words, it is crucial that such a driver is within the project, since emergent data modeling relies on contributors to reach a critical mass. It is yet to prove, whether or not emergent data models reach higher user acceptance rates than traditional models.

Moreover, it will be interesting to see if the introduced approach scales in the context of the public sector, especially with a large number of contributing stakeholders, which are widely scattered across several departments. However, we are confident that this will be rather uncritical since Web 2.0 technologies successfully apply in many different large-scale projects, e.g., in Bachmann and Merson (2005), the authors describe their experiences made with a wiki used to create architecture documentation in a collaborative environment.

7. CONCLUSION

In this chapter, we proposed a method to derive services from business processes. The method consists of a data model describing the structure of the method's results, a role model describing the competencies needed to execute the method, and a process model describing the required activities and their sequence to produce the results of the method. The proposed method takes business processes as inputs and produces services as outputs.

Due to the specific organizational requirements of the public sector, the method needs to be generic regarding its inputs. Therefore, we could not presume a specific process modeling technique. In addition, we could not assume that the method has a fixed data model. Therefore, the method includes Enterprise 2.0 techniques, wikis, and an *open templating* mechanism, which link different data sources in socio-technical systems.

We see future work in the following fields:

- *Evaluation*: The method should be evaluated in a project applying a case study or action research method. We expect valuable insights from such an evaluation regarding the suitability, understandability, and usefulness of the proposed method. It would especially be interesting to examine whether the connection between process modeling, service engineering and Web 2.0 techniques works as expected in practice.
- *Extension*: The method should be prepared for more specific inputs. Especially, process modeling became very popular in the public administration over the last five years. Once the process modeling tech-

nique matures in public administrations, more advanced modeling techniques are being used. Therefore, it is very likely that the additional information codified in those process models lead to better services. In addition, there may be a potential to automate the process of deriving services from business processes.

- *Guidelines*: When applying the method in different organizational units, e.g. in different public administrations, it is very likely that modelers of those units apply different conceptualizations to produce the models. This may lead to incompatible models. Therefore, the method should be extended by guidelines to achieve a higher degree of consistency.

REFERENCES

Aier, S., Gleichauf, B., & Winter, R. (2011). *Understanding enterprise architecture management design - An empirical analysis.* Paper presented at the 10th International Conference on Wirtschaftsinformatik. Zurich, Switzerland.

Aier, S., & Winter, R. (2009). Virtual decoupling for IT/business alignment – Conceptual foundations, architecture design and implementation example. *Business & Information Systems Engineering, 1*(2), 150–163. doi:10.1007/s12599-008-0010-7

Azevedo, L. G., Santoro, F., Baião, F., Souza, J., Revoredo, K., Pereira, V., et al. (2009). *A method for service identification from business process models in a SOA approach.* Paper presented at the Enterprise, Business-Process and Information Systems Modeling. Amsterdam, The Netherlands.

Bachmann, F., & Merson, P. (2005). *Experience using the web-based tool wiki for architecture documentation.* Pittsburgh, PA: Carnegie Mellon University.

Birkmeier, D. Q., Klöckner, S., & Overhage, S. (2009). A survey of service identification approaches: classification framework, state of the art, and comparison. *Enterprise Modelling and Information Systems Architectures, 4*(2), 20–36.

Brinkkemper, S., Saeki, M., & Harmsen, F. (1999). Meta-modelling based assembly techniques for situational method engineering. *Information Systems, 24*(3), 209–228. doi:10.1016/S0306-4379(99)00016-2

Büchner, T., Matthes, F., & Neubert, C. (2009). *A concept and service based analysis of commercial and open.* Paper presented at the International Conference on Knowledge Management and Information Sharing. Madeira, Portugal.

Buckl, S., Marliani, R., Matthes, F., & Schweda, C. M. (2011). *Dynamic virtual enterprises - The challenges of the utility industry.* Paper presented at the International IFIP WG5.8 Working Conference on Enterprise Interoperability. Stockholm, Sweden.

Chang, S. (2006). *Are they willing to contribute? Prosumer characteristics among the Australian youth.* Paper presented at the Digital Natives in Australia and Korea, Conference at the University of Melbourne. Melbourne, Australia.

Dietz, G., Juhrisch, M., & Grossmann, K. (2011). *Inherence of ratios for service identification and evaluation.* Paper presented at the 17th Americas Conference on Information Systems. Detroit, MI.

Erl, T. (2005). *Service-oriented architecture - Concepts, technology, and design.* Upper Saddle River, NJ: Prentice Hall.

Erradi, A., Anand, S., & Kulkarni, N. (2006). *SOAF: An architectural framework for service definition and realization.* Paper presented at the IEEE International Conference on Services Computing 2006. New York, NY.

European Commission. (2010a). *Communication from the commission to the European parliament, the council, the European economic and social committee and the committee of regions 'towards interoperability for european public services': Annex I - European interoperability strategy (EIS) for European public services.* Geneva, Switzerland: European Commission.

European Commission. (2010b). *Communication from the commission to the European parliament, the council, the European economic and social committee and the committee of regions 'towards interoperability for European public services': Annex II - European interoperability framework (EIF) for European public services.* Geneva, Switzerland: European Commission.

European Commission. (2010c). *Communication from the commission to the European parliament, the council, the European economic and social committee and the committee of regions: A digital agenda for Europe.* Geneva, Switzerland: European Commission.

Frederiksa, P. J. M., & van der Weideb, T. P. (2006). Information modeling: The process and the required competencies of its participants. *Data & Knowledge Engineering, 58*(1), 4–20. doi:10.1016/j.datak.2005.05.007

Gehlert, A., Schermann, M., Pohl, K., & Krcmar, H. (2009). *Towards a research method for theory-driven design research.* Paper presented at the 9th International Conference on Wirtschaftsinformatik. Wien, Austria.

Golder, S. A., & Huberman, B. A. (2005). *The structure of collaborative tagging systems.* Retrieved May 17, 2011, from http://arxiv.org/abs/cs.DL/0508082.

Grundgesetz für die Bundesrepublik Deutschland 65. (1949). *Paper.* Berlin, Germany: Publisher.

ISO/IEC. (2007). *Enterprise integration - Constructs for enterprise modelling. No. ISO/IEC Standard 19440.* Geneva, Switzerland: International Organization for Standardization.

IT Planning Council. (2010). *National e-government strategy.* Washington, DC: IT Planning Council.

Jain, H., Chalimeda, N., Ivaturi, N., & Reddy, B. (2001). *Business component identification - A formal approach.* Paper presented at the 5th IEEE International Conference on Enterprise Distributed Object Computing. Seattle, WA.

Klose, K., Knackstedt, R., & Beverungen, D. (2007). *A stakeholder-based approach to SOA development and its application in the area of production planning.* Paper presented at the European Conference on Information Systems. St. Gallen, Switzerland.

Kohlborn, T., Korthaus, A., Chan, T., & Rosemann, M. (2009). Identification and analysis of business and software services - A consolidated approach. *IEEE Transactions on Services Computing, 2*(1), 50–64. doi:10.1109/TSC.2009.6

Kurpjuweit, S., & Winter, R. (2007). *Viewpoint-based meta model engineering.* Paper presented at the 2nd International Workshop on Enterprise Modelling and Information Systems Architectures. St. Goar, Germany.

Leuf, B. C. (2001). *The wiki way: Quick collaboration on the web.* Reading, MA: Addison-Wesley.

Matthes, F., Neubert, C., & Steinhoff, A. (2011). *Hybrid wikis: Empowering users to collaboratively structure information.* Paper presented at the 6th International Conference on Software and Data Technologies. Seville, Spain.

McAfee, A. P. (2005). Enterprise 2.0: The dawn of emergent collaboration. *MIT Sloan Management Review, 47,* 21–28.

Ministers of the European Union. (2009). *Ministerial declaration on egovernment.* Geneva, Switzerland: European Union.

O'Reilly, T. (2008). *What is web 2.0: Design patterns and business models for the next generation of software.* New York, NY: O'Reilly Media.

Parnas, D. L. (1972). On the criteria to be used in decomposing systems into modules. *Communications of the ACM, 15*(12), 1053–1058. doi:10.1145/361598.361623

Patig, S., & Casanova-Brito, V. (2011). *Requirements of process modeling languages – Results from an empirical investigation.* Paper presented at the 10th International Conference on Wirtschaftsinformatik. Zurich, Switzerland.

SAP. (2005). *Enterprise services architecture: Enterprise services design guide.* New York, NY: SAP AG.

Schermann, M., Gehlert, A., Krcmar, H., & Pohl, K. (2009). *Justifying design decisions with theory-based design principles.* Paper presented at the 17th European Conference on Information Systems. Verona, Italy.

Surowiecki, J. (2004). *The wisdom of crowds.* New York, NY: Random House.

Wagter, R., van den Berg, M., Luijpers, J., & van Steenbergen, M. (2005). *Dynamic enterprise architecture: How to make it work.* New York, NY: John Wiley.

Wiki. (2011). *Wikipedia.* Retrieved 10 May 2011, from http://en.wikipedia.org.

Winkler, V. (2007). Identifikation und gestaltung von services - Vorgehen und beispielhafte anwendung im finanzdienstleistungsbereich. *Wirtschaftsinformatik, 49*(4), 257–266. doi:10.1007/s11576-007-0062-1

ADDITIONAL READING

Birkmeier, D. Q., Klöckner, S., & Overhage, S. (2009). A survey of service identification approaches: Classification framework, state of the art, and comparison. *Enterprise Modelling and Information Systems Architectures, 4*(2), 20–36.

Buckl, S., Matthes, F., Neubert, C., & Schweda, C. M. (2010). *A lightweight approach to enterprise architecture modeling and documentation.* Paper presented at the 22nd International Conference on Advanced Information Systems Engineering. Hammamet, Tunisia.

Bughin, J. (2008). The rise of enterprise 2.0. *Journal of Direct. Data and Digital Marketing Practice, 9*(3), 251. doi:10.1057/palgrave.dddmp.4350100

Cook, N. (2008). *Enterprise 2.0: How social software will change the future of work.* Aldershot, UK: Gower Publishing Ltd.

Corporation, I. B. M. (1984). *Business systems planning: Information systems planning guide.* Washington, DC: Internationl Business Machines Corporation.

Drakos, N. (2007). *Magic quadrant for team collaboration and social software. Gartner Research, ID Number: G00151493.* Washington, DC: Gartner Research.

Edmunds, A., & Morris, A. (2000). The problem of information overload in business organisations: A review of the literature. *International Journal of Information Management, 20*(1), 17–28. doi:10.1016/S0268-4012(99)00051-1

Erl, T. (2005). *Service-oriented architecture - Concepts, technology, and design.* Upper Saddle River, NJ: Prentice Hall.

European Commission. (2010a). *Communication from the commission to the European parliament, the council, the European economic and social committee and the committee of regions 'towards interoperability for European public services': Annex I - European interoperability strategy (EIS) for European public services.* Geneva, Switzerland: European Commission.

European Commission. (2010b). *Communication from the commission to the European parliament, the council, the European economic and social committee and the committee of regions 'towards interoperability for European public services': Annex II - European interoperability framework (EIF) for European public services.* Geneva, Switzerland: European Commission.

European Commission. (2010c). *Communication from the commission to the European parliament, the council, the European economic and social committee and the committee of regions: A digital agenda for Europe.* Geneva, Switzerland: European Commission.

Koch, M. (2008). *CSCW and enterprise 2.0 - Towards an integrated perspective.* Paper presented at the Bled eConference. New York, NY.

Kohlborn, T., Korthaus, A., Chan, T., & Rosemann, M. (2009). Identification and analysis of business and software services - A consolidated approach. *IEEE Transactions on Services Computing, 2*(1), 50–64. doi:10.1109/TSC.2009.6

Matthes, F., Neubert, C., & Steinhoff, A. (2011). *Hybrid wikis: Empowering users to collaboratively structure information.* Paper presented at the 6th International Conference on Software and Data Technologies. Seville, Spain.

McAfee, A. (2009). *Enterprise 2.0: New collaborative tools for your organization's toughest challenges.* Boston, MA: Harvard Business Press.

Ministers of the European Union. (2009). *Ministerial declaration on egovernment.* Geneva, Switzerland: European Union.

Parnas, D. L. (1972). On the criteria to be used in decomposing systems into modules. *Communications of the ACM, 15*(12), 1053–1058. doi:10.1145/361598.361623

SAP. (2005). *Enterprise services architecture: Enterprise services design guide.* New York, NY: SAP AG.

Stocker, A., & Tochtermann, K. (2009). *Exploring the value of enterprise wikis: A multiple-case study.* Paper presented at the International Conference on Knowledge Management and Information Sharing. New York, NY.

Szyperski, C., Gruntz, D., & Murer, S. (2002). *Component software - Beyond object-oriented programming* (Vol. 2). New York, NY: ACM Press.

KEY TERMS AND DEFINITIONS

Activity: An activity is the core element of a *process*. It describes one step of that process. An activity is also the basic element to derive functions.

Emergent Data Modeling: In contrast to traditional database systems following a schema first, data second approach, emergent data modeling follows the principle of data first, schema second. After collaboratively collecting data in a non-rigidly typed system, a schema emerges (over time with rising data) and can be extracted based on instance data.

Function: A function represents a functional requirement. Functions are always assigned to *activities*. A many-to-many relationship between functions and *activities* decouple the granularity of the *processes* from the granularity of the *services*. Functions result either from a functional requirement from *activities* which should be automated or a requirement which results from the IT support of an activity (implicit function). Examples of the latter case are login or encryption functions.

Process: A process is a set of *activities* connected by a control flow. The control flow describes the logical sequence of the *activities*. Please note that many process modeling techniques may include other elements such as organizational roles, data or events in processes. This additional information, however, is not needed for our method.

Process Engineer: The Process Engineer is responsible for designing business *processes*. S/he knows the processes of the organizational unit in focus and is able to express those processes in a modeling language, which distinguishes at least processes and activities (cf. Assumption A2). Additionally, the role includes the rights to (re-) design the business processes of the organizational unit and to decide, which *activities* should be supported by IT. Furthermore, the Process Engineer is knowledgeable about organizational aspects, which are not covered in the business process and which may lead to implicit *functions*.

Service: A service is a set of requirements, which is already supported by IT solutions or will be realized by IT solutions in the future. By IT solutions, we mean any software, or component

thereof, which may realize a service. A service is made of *functions*.

Service Catalogue: The service catalogue contains all *services* of a public administration. It is the major means to foster reuse and to avoid the duplicate implementation of the *functions*.

Service Engineer: The Service Engineer is responsible for the *service catalogue*. S/he knows the structure and the content of the *services* in the service *catalogue*. In particular the Service Engineer should know which *services* are already realized by IT. Furthermore, the Service Engineer is empowered to decide, which *services* may be added to the *service catalogue* and has experience in identifying implicit *functions* and in identifying *services*. S/he has in-depth knowledge of the proposed method for deriving services from business processes.

Stakeholders: Stakeholders are represented by the different groups of professionals actually executing functions of a *process*. They have insights into the *process* steps, i.e. *activities* and corresponding *functions* from day-to-day application thereof in their professional occupations.

Solution Owners: Solution Owners are responsible for service realizations, e.g. a running business application offering electronic publishing.

Chapter 12
An Investigative Assessment of the Role of Enterprise Architecture in Realizing E–Government Transformation

Leonidas Anthopoulos
Technological Education Institute (TEI) of Larissa, Greece

ABSTRACT

Major e-strategies around the world have been implemented for more than a decade, and they have resulted in digital public service delivery and in internal efficiency for further transformation. Most of these strategies have been or are being updated, and their current versions focus on cross-departmental service delivery and on Connected Government. Enterprise Architecture (EA) offers the ability to determine and close departmental gaps, and in this context, it can support the migration to Connected Government.

In this chapter, some important e-strategies are investigated concerning the existence and the contribution of an EA to strategic implementation and transformation. Different EAs are compared, and architectures are aligned to strategic and to transformation objectives, via Connected Government. Moreover, the necessity of the alignment of an EA to the strategic update is underlined, and an EA maturity roadmap to Connected Government is considered.

DOI: 10.4018/978-1-4666-1824-4.ch012

1. INTRODUCTION

Ambitious e-strategies have led e-Government development around the world for more than a decade. Major e-strategies share common challenges and difficulties in the delivery of online public services, and on the implementation of a friendlier, more effective, and more efficient public administration. Most of the major e-strategies have closed their initial life cycles, and after review processes, they updated their targets or kept some for further improvement. Strategic visions were updated too, while strategic missions were reconsidered before re-launching.

Most of the updated e-strategies were *incremental* (Lysons & Farrington, 2006) or followed *forward integration* (Lysons & Farrington, 2006) to define their new targets without documenting or determining the reasons of success or failures of their previous versions. They all realize that the future of e-Government concerns cross-departmental service delivery, citizen satisfaction, social inclusion, and participation; perspectives that put "openness" and "connected" at the centre of the strategic vision. With respect to "openness," Obama (US OMB, 2009) envisioned an accountable and open public administration, where all citizens have access to well organized public information. Concerning "connected," Saha (2009) described United Nations' (UN) vision for the Connected Government as a networked approach to operations and structure: *the concept of connected government is derived from the Whole-Of-Government* (WOG) *approach which is increasingly looking towards technology as a strategic tool and as an enabler for public service innovation and productivity growth.*

On the other hand, the Enterprise Architecture (EA) standardizes and aligns e-Government projects to strategic vision (Anthopoulos, 2009; FEA Group, 2005), and encodes e-Government elements in a form that can be understood by its stakeholders (for example politicians, political parties, councils, heads of departments, etc.)

(Adigun & Biyela, 2003). All major e-strategies are accompanied by centrally defined EAs that can supply e-Government projects with common standards and operation principles. However, central EA has to deal with problems similar to the ones that central strategic planning faces (Anthopoulos, et al., 2007): "smooth transition" of the public Agencies from traditional procedures to e-Government, change acceptance by all target groups, and the treatment of individual, local, and peripheral needs.

Major e-Strategies seek their updated forms after more than a decade of implementation. Most of them present different review results, and are being directed mainly on citizen satisfaction and on service simplification (Fitsilis, et al., 2009), while the cross-departmental service execution is becoming a common pillar of their transformation. The demand for Business Process Reengineering (BPR) and Management (BPM) in order to align business processes to IT implementation for cross-departmental service delivery, suggests the existence of an architecture framework (Embrahim & Irani, 2005). In this context, it is questioned whether a close connection exists between the WOG approach and the availability of an architecture framework.

In this chapter the existence and the contribution of an EA to e-strategic implementation and transformation is investigated. Different EAs are compared, and architectures are aligned to strategic and to transformation objectives that relate to Connected Government. Moreover, the necessity of the alignment of an EA to the strategic update is underlined, and an EA maturity roadmap to Connected Government is considered.

This chapter is structured in four sections. In the primary section 2, various transformed e-strategies are briefly presented and compared to Connected Government vision. In the following, section 3, the main thrust of this chapter is presented according to the key findings from section 2: the existence and of an EA in all the examined e-strategies is concluded, and the particular role that the EA played in the strategic transformation to the principles of the Connected Government is justified. Moreover, an EA roadmap to the Connected Government is proposed, which consists of the alignment degree of an EA to the transformation requirements and of the maturity level of the EA. Finally, in section 4, the conclusions of this chapter are discussed.

2. BACKGROUND

Various strategic analysis methods such as the strategy map (Barrows & Frigo, 2008), the strategic life cycle (Lysons & Farrington, 2006), and the balanced scorecard (Creamer & Freund, 2010; Huang, 2009; Kaplan & Norton, 1996) are used for understanding, communicating, and visualizing a strategic plan, and making decisions for planning. For the purposes of this chapter, the strategic life cycle is used for the analysis of the investigated e-strategies. The strategic life cycle consists of the following phases: a) analysis, b) composition, c) evaluation of alternatives, d) implementation, and e) control and review. Each of the strategic phases provides useful information about the strategic priorities and the implementation methodology that was followed. For the purposes of this chapter, we analyze some important e-Strategies in order to identify the existence of an EA and the particular role that EA plays in strategic transformation to Connected Government. The strategic life cycle was applied in this analysis: the *composition* phase provides the vision and mission statements, and the Critical Success Factors (CSFs) of the e-Strategy. The *control and review* phase returns the updated vision and mission statements of the transformed e-Strategy. The investigation was performed geographically and approached the United States (U.S.) from North America; the British, the German, and the European Union's strategies from Europe; the Japanese, the Australian, the South Korean, and the Indian e-strategies from Asia

and the Pacific areas. The outcomes of the above analysis / assessment are summarized in Table 1.

2.1. Key Findings from Major e-Strategies

2.1.1. North America

United States (U.S.) Federal Government identified e-Government challenges early, it developed several action plans by 1993, and it composed its initial e-Government strategy in 2002 entitled "Expanding Government" (US OMB, 2002; US Congress, 2002). The strategic vision prioritized the development of a citizen-centered and results oriented public administration, which could be achieved by (1) capital planning and investment control for Information Technology (IT); (2) the development of enterprise architectures; (3) information security; (4) privacy; (5) access to, dissemination of, and preservation of Government information; and (6) accessibility. The U.S. strategy has delivered some important e-Government systems such as the one-stop e-Government portal (www.usa.gov), the e-Authentication system for secure public transactions, the ezTaxFilling for tax form submission, the Integrated Acquisition Environment (IAE) (www.acquisition.gov), and the smartBUY initiatives for public procurement services etc., which cover all the individual priorities of the strategy. The U.S. strategic mission has been implemented under the supervision of the Office of Electronic Government, established in the Office of Management and Budget (OMB), headed by an Administrator appointed by the U.S. President. The mission requires an amount of $71 billion (US OMB, 2009) annually, strategic progress was monitored annually with reports published by the supervisor. A clear organizational chart (US OMB, 2002) allocated duties at various managerial levels in order to lead and manage implementation and change. In this context, EA development had a leading role in organizing and

Table 1. Analysis of some important e-strategies with their updated versions

Strategy	Vision Statement	Mission Statement
USA - 2002: Expanding Government	Citizen centered, results oriented and market based public administration	Supervisor: Office of Electronic Government CSFs: a. capital planning / investment control: Integrated Acquisition Environment (IAE), SmartBUY b. service integration: Federal Enterprise Architecture (FEA) c. information security d. privacy e. Accessibility: usa.gov
Update: 2009 Open Government Initiative	Updated vision statement: transparency, participation, and collaboration Cost: $71 billion/year	Updated CSFs: a. best practices from the private sector to increase productivity; b. managerial methods: Open Government Directive, RIN c. public service transformation: Paper Reduction Act (PRA), customer satisfaction d. Government accountability: Federal IT Dashboard
UK - 1999: Modernizing Government	Improvement of citizens' and enterprises' everyday life via digital services, inclusive and integrated Government Cost: £1.7 billion	Supervisor: the Modernizing Government Secretariat, Office of the e-Envoy, Cabinet Office CSFs: a. high quality and efficient public services: directgov.uk b. citizen-centered services c. strategic policy making d. Joined up delivery of services: Government Secure Intranet (GSI) e. Interoperability: e-GIF interoperability framework f. Standardization: xGEA Enterprise Architecture
Update:2007 Transformational Government Enabled by Technology	Updated vision statement: accountability, economic productivity, social justice and public service reform, UK's leading role in Globalized Economy Updated Cost: £1.4 billion	Updated CSFs: a. service design around citizens and businesses b. shared services c. professionalism in terms of planning, delivery, management skills and governance of IT enabled change d. Public involvement e. Cost savings
Germany – 2001: Bund Online 2005	Citizen-centered and open environment	Supervisor: Federal Ministry of Interior, IT Planning council (2010)
Update: 2006 - Deutschland Online Update: 2007 – Federal IT Strategy Update: 2009 - Broadband Strategy of the Federal Government	Updated vision statement: inter-departmental service delivery and IT innovation's promotion	CSFs: a. Service digitization and availability b. Common basic components for payment transactions, data security, content management as well as workflow management, processes and organization c. Central coordination for service transformation: SAGA Enterprise Architecture d. Fifteen (15) One For All (OFA) services Updated CSFs: a. One-for-all (OFA) services b. Broadband diffusion c. Cross-agency service delivery
Europe - 1998, 2003: e-Europe 2002, e-Europe+, e-Europe 2005	Europe's transition towards a knowledge based economy, and the capitalization of the internet and of the ICT for better jobs and for quality public services	Supervisor: DG of the Information Society CSFs: a. Broadband diffusion, b. communication markets' deliberation c. ICT skills d. twenty (20) public services e. interoperable processes

continued on following page

Table 1. Continued

Strategy	Vision Statement	Mission Statement
Update: 2005 i2010 Update: 2010 - Digital Agenda	Updated vision statement: Common information space; Inclusive Information Society, ICT Innovation and Investment, effective, efficient, and transparent public administration, a flavor environment for communication between citizens and politicians, cross European services	Updated CSFs: a. digital convergence, b. digital single market, c. interoperability and standardization, d. trust and security, e. ultra-fast networks, f. research and innovation g. digital literacy and social challenges, h. digital e-identity, i. e-authentication, j. rights management, k. open source software
Australia-2000: Government Online	Better services for citizens and enterprises	Supervisor: National Office for the Information Economy of the Australian Government (NOIE) CSFs: a. 400 digital services online b. Enterprise Architecture (AGA) c. Government-wide Intranet d. Electronic payments
Update:2002: Better Services, Better Government	Updated vision statement: e-Government for economic growth	Updated CSFs: a. greater administrative efficiency, b. convenient access to information and services, c. responsive public services d. service integration e. user trust f. citizen engagement
Japan-2001: e-Japan 2003: e-Japan II	"knowledge-emergent society" with ICT	Supervisor: Prime Minister Office, IT Strategy Headquarters CSFs: a. ultra-high-speed networks b. e-commerce c. service and information provision d. information literacy e. enterprise architecture program (2004)
Update: 2006 - New IT Reform Strategy Update: 2009 i-Japan 2015	Updated vision statement: Inclusive and Innovative Society	Updated CSFs: a. citizen satisfaction b. e-local Government and standardization c. health and environmental challenges d. IT contribution to a decreasing and ageing society e. 50 percent of form applications by 2010 f. Elimination of paper certificate by 2020 g. multi-channel and via three-"mouse clicks" services h. Government offices i. e-PO box j. Digital ID
South Korea – 1987: Cyber Korea	Leading role in ICT industry	Supervisor: Headquarters in MOGAHA CSFs: a. Government Information Digitization b. Networking c. cross departmental service delivery
Update: 2003 e-Korea	Updated vision statement: leading role in global information society	Updated CSFs: a. national 'Broadband convergence Network,' b. educational programs on ICT c. promotion of e-business, d. Government transparency and productivity e. National Enterprise Architecture (GEAF) (2003)

continued on following page

Table 1. Continued

Strategy	Vision Statement	Mission Statement
India: 2006 National e-Governance Plan (NeGP)	Integration of Governance initiatives across the country, e-Governance acceleration	Supervisor: Department of Information Technology (DIT) of the Indian Ministry for Communications and Information Technology CSFs: 21 Mission Mode Projects (MMPs) and 8 components that deliver massive countrywide infrastructure and large-scale digitization of public records in order to bring public services closer to citizens

standardizing projects' portfolios for the various U.S. strategic priorities.

Annual reports underline good and less performances in strategic progress, both at federal and at departmental levels. However, without the declaration of a particular failure but with a cue for transparency and accountability by the Government, the U.S. Federal Government updated its strategy in 2009 to the one entitled the "Open Government Initiative," which was launched in 2009 (US OMB, 2010). The updated vision statement declared transparency, participation, and collaboration as the primary objectives, and organized its mission in a number of areas of precedence: (a) cost savings and avoidance, (b) transparency, participation, and collaboration, and (c) information and IT management. Various actions supported the strategic mission: the Open Government Directive (US OMB, 2009) provided guidelines for action concerning public sector's "openness"; the Regulation Identifier Number (RIN) tracks the regulation life cycle and support openness in the rulemaking; the Paperwork Reduction Act (PRA) provides instructions to the civil servants to eliminate paper use; Social media use is encouraged, and it is associated with the PRA. Moreover, the IT Dashboard (http://www.itdashboard.gov) offers public information about IT spending by the Governmental Agencies, and it is used both for making Government accountant and as a tool to control and to enhance IT spending management.

The CSFs for the new mission statement define a roadmap until 2015, and they were declared by the Forum on Modernizing Government (White House, 2010): a) best practices from the private sector will improve productivity; b) effective managerial methods such as visionary leadership, strong day-to-day management, detailed reporting, thorough evaluation of processes, and ongoing review of customer needs will guarantee project implementation and the maximization of return of investment; c) public customer service transformation is required, in terms of improving customer satisfaction measuring and monitoring, and in terms of better delivery of citizen-facing services; d) Government accountability will support large-scale project success and public trust. The U.S. e-strategic update aims in service transformation under a customer service culture (White House, 2010). However, it did not focus on a WOG environment, and the Federal Enterprise Architecture Framework (FEAF) has been used to provide with shared target architectures among Federal agencies (US OMB, 2010). Shared target segment architectures are used as alignment targets, and they provide agencies with detailed guidance to implement their investments and their IT projects. The development of the "Segment Architecture" as an extension of the FEAF has been observed, in order to manage various segment architectures' deployment and to create linkages from agency strategies to EA to segment architecture to IT investment.

2.1.2. Europe

The British Government developed its Modernizing Government strategy in 1999 (UK Modernizing Government Secretariat Cabinet Office, 1999), which is one of the most important European e-strategies. It envisioned the improvement of citizens' and businesses' life via public services' digitization, and it had to ensure that Government is both inclusive and integrated. British CSFs concerned the delivery of high quality and efficient public services; the alignment of services to citizens' needs; the development of joined up and strategic policymaking. A total spending of £1.7 billion was put on ICT infrastructures and on literature, in order to simplify citizen access to public information and services.

It is supervised by the Modernizing Government Secretariat in the Cabinet Office and by the Office of the e-Envoy. British Government launched a set of national, group-focused and area-based programs—with cross-departmental budgets—to improve delivery of services. Moreover, e-GIF (e-Government Interoperability Framework) provides a range of standards for data formats and protocols, in order to establish interoperability between different ICT solutions in British public Administration. By complying with the technical standards, all public Agencies access central solutions and principles. Moreover, the British Government developed its EA on 2005 (UK CIO, 2005) called the "cross-Government Enterprise Architecture (xGEA)," describing the common "business-led vision" and procedures for British Administration.

The British Government updated its strategy in 2005, entitled "Transformational Government Enabled by Technology" (UK Cabinet Office, 2005), which envisioned economic productivity, social justice, and public service reform as asset tools against globalization challenges. Both the transformation of public services and the efficiency of the corporate services were CSFs of the updated strategy, where service transformation led the quality services to personalized ones, and efficiency freed resources for the front line. Effective policymaking was another CSF, and it focused on the development and delivery of innovative

policy outcomes—inspired by technology—that affect citizens' daily lives.

"Transformational Government" visionary targets were approached with three key transformations (UK Cabinet Office, 2005; Irani, et al., 2007): service design around citizens and businesses against design around the provider; shared services' development with standardization and with the support of the xGEA, simplification and sharing across the public sector; professionalism in terms of planning, delivery, management skills, and governance of IT enabled change. These activities were funded by an unlocking of a 10 percent (£1.4 billion) from the annual spending for legacy systems, for investments on new technology enabled reforms in public services, and they have a timetable of completion by 2011. Today, UK e-strategy shifts towards personalized services versus the "one-fits-for all services." This modern vision is called "MyGov" (Brown, 2010) and also promises more public involvement and cost savings for the Government.

Germany launched its BundOnline 2005 strategic plan (German Federal Government, 2003) for its Information Society framework program, which was aligned to the European strategies and identified specific targets for e-government, such as the delivery of more than 400 different public services from more than 100 agencies via the portal Bund (www.bund.de). German Federal Government envisioned a citizen-centered and open environment, and its strategic mission was based on common basis components for service and information delivery (payment transactions, content and workflow management, etc.), on fifteen (15) One-For-All (OFA) services and on central coordination for service transformation. Central coordination used the SAGA EA Framework (KBSt Publication Series, 2003), that contains—centrally selected—common solutions and standards for ICT projects in the German Administration. Furthermore, the framework presents different perspectives that the ICT architecture designers in public Administration must follow for e-Government projects.

German e-strategy was updated in 2006 to the "Deutschland Online" and in 2007 to the "Federal IT strategy" (ePractice, 2011). Both of them envisioned the optimization of inter-departmental service delivery and IT innovation's promotion, and they prioritized infrastructure development and delivery of specific public services. This updated strategy was extended by 2009 when the "Broadband Strategy of the Federal Government" was adopted.

At a supranational level across Europe, European member states agreed on a common strategy for a European Information Society in 1998, called the eEurope 2002 (Commission of the European Communities, 2000). This e-strategy was launched on 2000, and it envisioned a knowledge-based economy, and the capitalization of the internet and of the ICT for better jobs and for quality public services. The eEurope 2002 was followed by the eEurope+ for the candidate countries (Commission of the European Communities, 2001), and by the eEurope 2005 (Commission of the European Communities, 2003). All of them allocated funds and obliged European Governments to achieve common CSFs on specific timetables: broadband use growth and national communication markets' deliberation across Europe; ICT skills for students and civil servants; twenty (20) common primary public services' delivery online and interoperable processes' deployment across Europe. Lots of deliverables were implemented by strategic deadlines by most of the European countries, while supranational projects were launched such as the Europa (http://europa.eu) portal, the Interchange of Data between Administrations (IDABC) framework for interoperable services across Europe, etc.

The e-Europe strategies ended in 2005, when the European Committee launched the i2010 strategy for an Information Society for growth and employment (Commission of the European Communities, 2005), which envisioned a) a common European information space; b) an Inclusive European Information Society; c) Innovation and Investment in ICT research for growth and for more and better jobs. The strategic mission focused on common CSFs for member states. The Digital convergence across Europe until 2010 was aimed by the i2010 strategy, an amount of €728 million was allocated (according to http://www.2007-2013.eu/by_scope_ict.php), and a number of key objectives—similar to the e-Europe ones—were funded concerning broadband diffusion, the reach of digital content creation, interoperability, and security. E-Government was related with the priority of the improvement of "Quality of Life." Specific key enablers for digital public services were identified and promoted: citizen common digital identity, rights management, ease of use, interoperability, and open source software. The i2010 strategy was co-funded with an amount of €1.8 billion annually by the Seventh European Research Framework Programme (FP7).

"The Digital Agenda for a flourish digital economy by 2020" (European Commission, 2010) is the current updated European Strategy. The Digital Agenda has prioritized the development of a European digital single market, interoperability and standardization, trust and security, the development of ultra fast networks, research, and innovation on the ICT, digital literacy, and the contribution of the ICT to various social challenges. It is obvious that the current European strategy follows the objectives of its previous ones, with the recognition of the economic crisis, the ageing society, the global competition and of the evolutions on the ICT. E-Government lies under the "ICT-enabled benefits for the European Society" priority, and it tries to commit Member States' to increase service penetration by deploying user-centric, personalized, multiplatform services until 2015 (European Union Member States' Ministers, 2009). CSFs for e-Government in the Digital Agenda concern common e-identification and e-authentication across the European countries, the definition of White Paper for common interconnected procurement services by the Member

States deployed via the Pan-European Public Procurement Online (PEPPOL) environment (http://www.peppol.eu), and a common list of key cross-border public services available online by 2015.

2.1.3 Asia and the Pacific

Asia has attracted international attention steadily over the last decade, due to its continuous economic and demographic growth. Asian countries perform significantly in IT too, and important e-Government cases have or are being developed, delivering useful outcomes and experiences.

The Australian Government released its first e-Government Strategy in 2000 with "Government Online" (Australian Government, 2000), which envisioned a friendly and efficient Government. Government Online declared clear CSFs concerning 400 digital public services' and public information delivery by 2001, electronic payments' establishment by 2000, and a government-wide intranet installation for secure online communications. These objectives were achieved in only a two-year period, by 2002, when the Australian Government proceeded to its updated strategy entitled "Better Services, Better Government." The National Office for the Information Economy of the Australian Government (NOIE) defined the strategic key objectives for public service transformation concerning greater administrative efficiency; convenient access to information and services; responsive public services; related service integration; strengthening user trust; and enhancing citizen engagement. The Australian Government Architecture (AGA) -based on U.S. EA- supports the delivery of more consistent and cohesive cross-agency services to citizens (AGIMO, 2007).

In Japan the Prime Minister Office launched the national e-strategy on 2001 called e-Japan (Japanese Government, 2001), which envisioned a "knowledge-emergent society" in Japan. The Japanese strategic mission concerned the establishment of ultra high-speed networks and of

relative competition policies; the facilitation of e-commerce; the realization of e-Government in means of service and information provision by 2003; the improvement of information literacy in order to capitalize national human resources. E-Japan succeeded in increasing broadband penetration and in Government reform; it was updated to the "e-Japan II" strategy in 2003 and defined its IT policy in 2005 (Japanese Government, 2005). These two structural documents gave priority to citizen satisfaction, to e-local Government with shared outsourcing efforts, and to standardization.

By 2006 (Japanese Government, 2006) a strategic reform was launched, which provided updated priorities and a modern implementation framework. In this new framework, a panel of IT Strategic Headquarters was structured under the Prime Minister that designed and coordinated the strategy, and cooperated with other national councils, while an assessment model was established for strategic progress measurement. Concerning e-Government, focus moved to a smaller and more effective administration, to e-Government penetration. In order to achieve these targets, more than 50 percent of form applications should be filled electronically by 2010. Moreover, activities were undertaken in respect to interoperability and standardization, since most of the previous programs ran autonomously. In this context, Japanese Enterprise Architecture (JEA) was structured to lead cross-organizational initiatives and service deployment, and public process re-engineering (Hashimoto, et al., 2007; Finnish Ministry of Finance, 2007; ICA, 2006; Ganesan & Paturi, 2008).

Two recent updates have been applied to Japanese e-Strategy, in 2009 with the "i-Japan 2015" and in 2010 with the "New Strategy in Information and Communications Technology (IT)." The "i-Japan 2015" (Japanese Government, 2009) envisioned an inclusive and innovative society, which is being approached with user-centric design and ease of use, while innovation in IT will support social cohesion, growth, and business competitiveness. Three groups of e-Government reforming activities are included in this strategy, concerning a) points-of-contact to administration via multi-channel and via three-"mouse clicks" services, b) government offices in order to oblige paperless transactions—the national e-Post Office (e-PO) box is another leading initiative of this reform, and it is planned to be implemented by 2013—and, c) transparency with service execution tracking.

In only one year, the "i-Japan 2015" was updated—not extended—to the "New Strategy in Information and Communications Technology (IT)" (Japanese Government, 2010), which envisions the potential contribution of IT to the Japanese society and growth by 2020 and contains e-Government, IT for local communities, and innovative new market areas of objectives. E-Government mission statement suggests the elimination of paper certificate issuing for citizens by 2020, the launching of administrating booths for service execution by 2013—with a target of installation in 50 percent of local administrations by 2020—while digital identities, service tracking and multi-channel services will be enabled by 2013.

In South Korea (Hwang, 2005; Yoon, 2007; Kim, 2010) IT investment has been increased from 2.4 percent to 6.1 percent of the Gross Domestic Product (GDP) during the last 20 years, while IT spending rose from 3.9 percent to 11.7 percent during the same period. Moreover, the average annual IT spending was estimated to $2 billion during the past decade, from which the 20 percent referred to e-Government activities. E-Government evolution in Korea passed from three different phases: the first during 1987 and 1995 with Government information digitization and networking. The second phase was executed during 1995 and 2001, and emphasized digital public service deployment across the administration. In this period it developed its EA framework called Government Enterprise Architecture Framework (GEAF) (National Computerization Agency, 2006; Schekkerman, 2005) to standardize cross-

agency service deployment. The third that was launched on 2001 and contains 11 key activities for administration's reform—lots of which were funded under Public-Private-Partnership (PPP) contracts—for transparency, for service quality, for integrated procurement, for advanced infrastructures, for social participation, and for ubiquitous data collection and services. Strategic planning and implementation is being supervised by the e-government Headquarters in MOGAHA, which consists of seven teams for various supervision areas, and the e-Government Learning Center. Korea's fourth e-Strategy was launched in 2003, called "e-Korea Vision 2006" (Lallana, 2004), which envisioned national productivity and quality of life growth, and doubling Korea's IT exports to $100 billion by 2007. CSFs in Korea mission statement concerned the national 'Broadband convergence Network' (BcN), the educational programmes on ICT in order to maximize the ability of citizens to actively participate in the information society, the promotion of e-business, the government transparency and productivity, a leading role in global information society.

The case of South Korea is the most well focused and well-organized among the analyzed strategies, and it appears as an ongoing long-term strategy with clear phases and clear objectives. In South Korea, each strategic update appears to be a sequence to the previous versions, without tremendous political differences and priorities' rearrangement. Although it followed U.S., Japan, and Europe in recognizing its Information Society challenges, it moved rapidly and on 2010 it was ranked 1st by the United Nations e-Government Development and the e-Participation indexes (Korean National Society Agency, 2010a), (Korean National Society Agency, 2010b). In spite of the huge funding for IT and e-Government—a phenomenon that appears in all the analyzed cases—the most significant factors that support this continuous IT evolution are the leading role of the Information and Communications Ministry, together with the strategy's supervising

Headquarters team, which consists of several task groups of experts with discrete authorities and areas of actions.

According to the World Bank, India holds a huge IT service industry, where many national and international IT vendors occupy a significant number of employees, while it is a leading software exporter among all developing countries (Cieslikowski, et al., 2009). India agreed on a specific strategy called the "National e-Governance Plan (NeGP)" in 2006, in order to structure a holistic view of e-Governance initiatives across the country, to integrate these initiatives into a collective vision, and to realize the Prime Minister's Announcement of 2002 for e-Governance acceleration. Previous approaches included various projects that tried to digitize Government procedures. The NeGP demands a $750 million annual funding, and consists of 21 Mission Mode Projects (MMPs) and 8 components that deliver massive countrywide infrastructure and large-scale digitization of public records in order to bring public services closer to citizens. Leading role of the strategic implementation has the Department of Information Technology (DIT) of the Indian Ministry for Communications and Information Technology (www.mit.gov.in), while the strategic coordination and management is assigned to the apex Committee who has the Cabinet Secretary as a chairman.

Useful information about the NeGP is given by Mathur et al. (2009), who present the mission priorities: efficiency, transparency, and accountability for public administration, together with the key strategic objectives as e-procurement, e-government adoption by citizens and businesses, common service centers for service delivery, service development outsourcing, private investments, connectivity, and research projects for Government systems. Digital public services approach the Indian citizen as a "common man" at his locality, and aim to be efficient and reliable at a low cost. Strategic implementation is based on a three tier e-Governance Framework (front-

end, middleware, back-end layers), and on the MMPs that secure ubiquitous connectivity at a state-level; nine departmental national services one of which is the implementation of the national identity (ID); eleven state area services; and seven cross-departmental projects, one of which is the one-stop e-Government portal (www.india.gov.in). India appears active in EA area (Schekkerman, 2005; Mahapatra & Perumal, 2007), and its EA framework is based on Zachman's and leads standardization in key projects. The MMPs leading role, together with the selection criteria that defined them, and with the organizational structures for strategic management suggest a unique managerial approach compared to the other cases.

2.2 Key Findings from the Investigated Cases

According to Schekkermann (2004), the EA is a collaborative force between business planning, aspects of business operations, aspects of automation, and the enabling technologies. Frameworks define architectures that support the EA to capture the strategic vision in all its dimension and complexity, while according to Handley (2008), they act as the roadmap to transition from current to strategic state.

EA is a "tool" that supports the central implementation of a Strategic Plan, by setting targets, principles, and methods able to be followed by all public agencies. According to CIO (2001), *"Enterprise Architecture (EA) is a strategic information asset base, which defines the mission, the information necessary to perform the mission, and the technologies necessary to perform the mission, and the transitional processes for implementing new technologies in response to the changing mission needs. EA includes baseline architecture, target architecture and a sequence plan."* EA is accompanied with a specific framework (CIO, 1999) containing the proper procedures, that each public Agency has to follow in order to implement the EA.

Moreover, various vendors have developed and deployed architecture frameworks, which have been associated with a holistic view on Connected and Transformational Government. Microsoft (2011), for instance, approaches the Connected Government issue with a four layer architecture framework that contains key challenges, people and processes, application capabilities, and technologies, as the appropriate architectures that can deal with recent e-Government missions. OASIS (2011) proposes a framework for the Transformational Government with four components: guiding principles, CSFs, service delivery processes, and benefit realization framework. CISCO (2007) realizes a three-stage maturity model from basic capability to transforming Government, and proposes a framework for next generation public services that relates change drivers with key-enablers. All of the abovementioned frameworks consider an ecosystem for the public administration, where citizens and enterprises cooperate and participate in the Connected Government.

Our investigation describes the e-strategic evolution across different continents and public administrations. Strategic priorities and CSFs show that digital public service delivery and infrastructure deployment were aimed under the first phase of the strategic implementation. During this initial period of all cases, the EA was applied for business process mapping and for IT project standardization. The European Union did not adopt EA and instead it used e-Government Interoperability Frameworks (e-GIFs) to standardize service deployment in member states. Additionally, India implements mission-mode projects in order to establish standardization.

On the contrary, the updated e-strategies prioritized different pillars: U.S. and U.K. paid significant attention on accountability, while U.S. approached it with openness and U.K. via service transformation and simplification. European e-Strategy mainly "re-arranged" its priorities after 2007, while Australia relates IT with economic growth, and Japan and Korea with innovation

and inclusion. Moreover, the WOG vision is not clearly adopted by the U.S. and the Japanese cases, while the other strategies approached it with different means: U.K., South Korea, and European Union talked about shared, cross-departmental, and cross-country service deployment, Germany considers the one-for-all services, and Australia, the integrated services.

Our analysis in combination with Schekkermann (2004), Saha (2007), and the Finnish Ministry of Finance (2007) determine many similarities regarding the existing applied EA frameworks: the U.S. FEAF, the South Korean, and the Indian frameworks follow Zachman's one, while the Japanese and the Australian follow the U.S. FEAF. Moreover, similarities in architectures and perspectives are observed among the investigated EAs, and their impact in strategic review is considered for the purposes of this chapter (Table 2). The investigation's findings determine a strong relation between the existence of an EA and the strategic mission's objectives, especially where cross-agency service delivery and standardization is required.

3. MAIN THRUST OF THIS CHAPTER

This chapter looks for a "strong relation" between transforming e-strategies—in means of Connected Government—and EA. It expects that strategic transformation would lead to appropriate alignments of the EA, and this chapter investigates architectural or perspective changes in EAs that are being performed coincidently to the transformational efforts.

The analysis that was performed under the above investigation of the particular cases delivers some important outcomes: a) it is proved that all major e-strategies have closed their initial life cycles, and most of them have been or are being transformed with means that can deploy cross-agency public services. b) Most of the examined cases focus on the WOG vision, and they

Table 2. EAs and strategic review

EA	Architectures / Perspectives	Updates related to the Connected Government	Related Architecture/ Perspective	Effect on Transformation
USA - FEA (follows Zachman's Framework)	Architectures: data/application/technology Perspectives: Planner/owner/designer/builder/subcontractor	a. capital planning / investment control: Integrated Acquisition Environment (IAE) b. service integration: Federal Enterprise Architecture (FEA)	Segment Architecture	Effective managerial methods
UK – xGEA	Architectures (Domains): Strategy/channel/business process/business information/application/infrastructure/service management/integration/security Perspectives: Business function / exemplar / EA landscape	Joined-up service delivery	Integration Architecture	Shared Services deployment
Germany – SAGA	Architectures: process/data/infrastructure/modules/standards Perspectives (viewpoints): Enterprise/computational/technology/engineering/information	Central coordination for service transformation		
Europe – no EA available		a. Cross-European services b. Standardization	e-GIF interoperability framework	
Australia-AGA (follows FEAF)	Reference Models: Performance/Business/Service/Data/Technical	Service Integration	Business Reference Model	Service Integration
Japan- enterprise architecture program (JEA)	Architectures: Business/ data/ application/ technical Perspectives: Policy, objective, function, operation, boundary, environment, information store and flow/wok-flow/BPR/resource	e-local Government and standardization		Optimization Plans for re-engineered services
South Korea – GEAF	Architectures: Business/data/application/infrastructure Perspectives: Planner/owner/designer/builder	cross departmental service delivery		
India – EA Framework (follows Zachman's Framework)	Architectures: data/application/technology Perspectives: Planner/owner/designer/builder/subcontractor	Integration of Governance initiatives across the country		21 Mission Mode Projects (MMPs) and 8 components

Table 3. EA maturity roadmap to connected government

	Prior	2004	2005	2006	2007	2008	2009	2010	2011
Embedded (*suitable for productivity growth*)									
Extended (suitable for integrated services)	Australia				UK		USA		
Foundation (suitable for information capitalization)	USA, UK, Australia, S. Korea, Germany	Japan		India					

approach shared services, integrated services, or cross-agency service delivery. c) All the examined cases—except from the European supranational strategies—incorporated and applied EA frameworks. d) Existing frameworks are mostly inspired by the Zachman's, and they try to define architectures and perspectives to lead strategic missions, and to introduce reference models for standardization in project implementation.

However, although an EA has its own life cycle that consists of separate phases (e.g. planning, developing, use, and maintenance) (National Computerization Agency, 2006), this life-cycle is not executed simultaneously to the strategic life-cycle. On the other hand, the Australian AGA moved to Service Oriented Architecture (SOA) early, while the U.S. FEAF and the British xGEA have later been updated properly to integrated services: they incorporated particular architectures—the *segment* and the *integration* architectures, respectively—in order to streamline integrated services.

The alignment of an EA to the e-strategic updates could be necessary for further evolution and guidance. Inspired from the private sector, an Enterprise Architecture Roadmap (Kawakami, 2005) seems to be useful for Governments. This roadmap is different for each strategy, and must present the maturity level of an EA. Nissan, for instance (Kawakami, 2005), defines the migration from the initial EA level where information is capitalized, to the optimized EA level where common services are managed and software is capitalized across the enterprise. In Government cases, EA maturity could be measured in means of coherency and agility (Doucet, Gøtze, Saha, & Bernard, 2008), and its roadmap to Connected Government could be defined (Table 3) by allocating cross-departmental service delivery to "extended EA," and productivity growth to the "embedded EA" where close collaboration between EA and daily operation is observed. In Table 3, the investigation outcomes were assigned to particular cells and to EA maturity levels, in order to visualize the international Government EA progress. It is proved that a lot of work has to be done in means of EA migration to support the productivity growth.

4. CONCLUSION

In this chapter, a strong relation between EA and strategic transformation was determined. The strategic migration to Connected Government is investigated, in terms of strong contribution by an EA, and in this context, some significant e-strategies from different continents were analyzed. Particular roadmaps were extracted as a means to show the underlying maturity and willing for cross-departmental service delivery and for productivity growth in public administration. The investigation's outcomes show that e-strategies have completed their initial life cycles, and they have updated both their vision and mission statements in forms with many similarities amongst each other. EA appears to play a leading role in most of the examined cases, but only some architectures from the investigated cases have been updated and aligned to the transformed mission. This observation led authors to use a roadmap tool to visualize the EA progress to maturity levels that align to the Connected Government principles.

REFERENCES

Adigun, M. O., & Biyela, D. P. (2003). Modelling and enterprise for re-engineering: A case study. In *Proceedings of the 2003 Annual Research Conference of the South African Institute of Computer Scientists and Information Technologists on Enablement through Technology (SAICSIT 2003)*. ACM Press.

AGIMO. (2007). *Cross-agency services architecture principles*. Retrieved, May 2011 from http://www.finance.gov.au/publications/cross-agency-services-architecture-principles/ docs/ CAS_Architecture_Principles.pdf.

Anthopoulos, L. (2009). Applying enterprise architecture for crisis management: A case of hellenic ministry of foreign affairs. In *Coherency Management: Architecting the Enterprise for Alignment, Agility and Assurance*. AuthorHouse Publishing.

Anthopoulos, L., Siozos, P., & Tsoukalas, I. A. (2007). Applying participatory design and collaboration in digital public services for discovering and re-designing e-government services. *Government Information Quarterly, 24*(2), 353–376. doi:10.1016/j.giq.2006.07.018

Australian Government. (2000). *Government online*. Retrieved, January 2011 from http://www.agimo.gov.au/archive/publications_noie/2000/04/govonline.html.

Australian Government. (2002). *Better services, better government*. Retrieved, January 2011 from http://www.agimo.gov.au/archive/__data/assets/pdf_file/0016/35503/Better_ Services-Better_Gov.pdf.

Australian Government. (2006). *Responsive government: A new service agenda*. Retrieved, January 2011 from, http://www.finance.gov.au/publications/2006-e-government-strategy/docs/e-gov_strategy.pdf.

Barrows, E. A., & Frigo, M. L. (2008). *Using the strategy map for competitor analysis*. Retrieved, August 2011 from http://hbr.org/product/using-the-strategy-map-for-competitor-analysis/an/B0807E-PDF-ENG.

CISCO. (2007). *Connected government: Creating a springboard for transformation and innovation*. Retrieved, August 2011 from http://www.cisco.com/web/about/ ac79/docs/wp/ctd/Connected_Govt_PoV_1030_finalCB.pdf.

Council, C. I. O. (1999). *Federal enterprise architecture framework*. Retrieved, May 2011 from http://www.cio.gov/Documents/fedarch1.pdf.

Council, C. I. O. (2001). *A practical guide to federal enterprise architecture*. Retrieved, May 2011 from http://www.gao.gov/bestpractices/bpeaguide.pdf.

Creamer, G., & Freund, Y. (2010). Learning a board balanced scorecard to improve corporate performance. *Decision Support Systems, 49*, 365–385. doi:10.1016/j.dss.2010.04.004

Doucet, G., Gøtze, J., Saha, P., & Bernard, S. (2008). *Coherency management: Using enterprise architecture for alignment, agility and assurance*. New York, NY: AuthorHouse.

Ebrahim, Z., & Irani, Z. (2005). E-government adoption: Architecture and barriers. *Business Process Management Journal, 11*(5), 589–611. doi:10.1108/14637150510619902 ePractice.eu. (2011). *eGovernment factsheet – Germany – Strategy*. Retrieved, May 2011 from http://www.epractice.eu/en/document/288242.

European Commission. (2010). *A digital agenda for Europe*. Retrieved, January 2011 from http://eur-lex.europa.eu/LexUriServ/LexUriServ.do?uri=COM:2010:0245:FIN:EN:PDF.

FEA Working Group. (2002). *E-gov enterprise architecture guidance (common reference model)*. Retrieved, January 2011 from http://www.feapmo.gov/resources/E-Gov_Guidance_Final_Draft_v2.0.pdf.

FEA Working Group. (2005). *Enabling citizen-centered electronic government: 2005-2006 FEA-PMO action plan*. Retrieved, January 2011 from http://www.whitehouse.gov/omb/egov/documents/2005_FEA_PMO_Action_Plan_FINAL.pdf.

Federal Statistical Office. Germany. (2002). *E-strategy, process analysis and design at the federal statistical office: A practical example*. Retrieved, May 2011 from https://www.bsi.bund.de/SharedDocs/Downloads/EN/BSI/Egovernment/5_StBA_en_pdf.pdf?__blob=publicationFile.

Finnish Ministry of Finance. (2007). *Overview of enterprise architecture work in 15 countries: Finnish enterprise architecture research project*. Retrieved, May 2011 from http://www.vm.fi/vm/en/04_publications_and_documents/01_publications/04_public_management/20071102Overvi/name.jsp.

Fitsilis, P., Anthopoulos, L., & Gerogiannis, V. (2009). An evaluation framework for e-government projects. In *Citizens and E-Government: Evaluating Policy and Management*. Hershey, PA: IGI Global.

Ganesan, E., & Paturi, R. (2008). A unified meta-model for elements can lead to effective business analysis. *Infosys Technologies Limited*. Retrieved, May 2011 from http://www.infosys.com/offerings/IT-services/architecture-services/white-papers/ Documents/enterprise-business-architecture.pdf.

German Federal Government. (2003). *BundOnline 2005: 2003 implementation plan*. Retrieved, May 2011 from http://www.epractice.eu/files/media/media_266.pdf.

Handley, J. (2008). *Enterprise architecture best practice handbook: Building, running and managing effective enterprise architecture programs - Ready to use supporting documents bringing enterprise architecture theory into practice*. Brisbane, Australia: Emereo Pty Ltd.

Hashimoto, D., Tanaka, A., & Yokoyama, M. (2007). Case study on RM-ODP and enterprise architecture. In *Proceedings of the Eleventh International IEEE EDOC Conference Workshop*, (pp. 216-223). IEEE Press.

Huang, H. C. (2009). Designing a knowledge-based system for strategic planning: A balanced scorecard perspective. *Expert Systems with Applications*, 36, 209–218. doi:10.1016/j.eswa.2007.09.046

Hwang, J. S. (2005). *e-Government in Korea*. Retrieved, January 2011 from http://www.apiicc.org/apiicc/Lecture/Special/IT_Study_Visit_Program_for_Vietnam/020103.pdf.

ICA. (2006). *Country report - Japan's e-Government*. Retrieved, May 2011 from http://unpan1.un.org/intradoc/groups/public/documents/apcity/unpan027268.pdf.

Japanese Government. (2010). *A new strategy in information and communications technology (IT)*. Retrieved, January 2011 from http://www.kantei.go.jp/foreign/policy/it/100511_full.pdf.

Kaplan, S. R., & Norton, P. D. (1996). *Translating strategy into action: The balanced scorecard.* Boston, MA: Harvard University Press.

Kawakami, T. (2005). *Direction of global enterprise architecture.* Retrieved, May 2011 from http://www.n2services.net/Local/Files/4_File_DirectionofGlobalEnterpriseArchitecture_Kawakami.pdf.

KBSt Publication Series. (2003). *SAGA: Standards and architectures for e-government applications, version 2.0.* Retrieved, January 2011 from http://egovstandards.gov.in/egs/eswg5/ enterprise-architecture-working-group-folder/standards-and-architectures-v2.pdf/ download.

Lallana, C. E. (2004). *An overview of ICT policies and e-strategies of select Asian economies.* Retrieved, May 2011 from http://www.apdip.net/publications/ict4d/ict4dlallana.pdf.

Lysons, K., & Farrington, B. (2006). *Purchasing and supply chain management.* Upper Saddle River, NJ: Prentice Hall Publishing.

Mahapatra, R., & Perumal, S. (2007). Enterprise architecture as an enabler for e-governance: An Indian perspective. In Saha, P. (Ed.), *Handbook of Enterprise Systems Architecture in Practice.* Hershey, PA: IGI Global. doi:10.4018/978-1-59904-189-6.ch016

Microsoft. (2011). *Connected government framework: Strategies to transform government in the 2.0 world.* Retrieved, August 2011 from http://www.microsoft.com/ download/en/details.aspx?displaylang=en&id=8295.

National Computerization Agency. (2006). *Government-wide enterprise architecture in Korea.* Retrieved, May 2011 from http://www.opengroup.org/architecture/ 0310wash/presents/ SungBum_Park_GEAF.pdf.

OASIS. (2011). *Transformational government framework, primer version 1.0.* Retrieved, August 2011 from http://www.oasis-open.org/committees/tgf/.

Saha, P. (2007). *Handbook of enterprise systems architecture in practice.* Hershey, PA: IGI Global. doi:10.4018/978-1-59904-189-6

Saha, P. (2009). Architecting the connected government: Practices and innovations in Singapore. In *Proceedings of the ICEGOV 2009.* ACM Press.

Schekkerman, J. (2004). *How to survive in the jungle of enterprise architecture frameworks: Creating or choosing an enterprise architecture framework* (2nd ed.). Victoria, Canada: Trafford Publishing.

Schekkerman, J. (2005). *Trends in enterprise architecture 2005: How are organizations progressing?* Retrieved, May 2011 from http://www.ea-consulting.com/Reports/ Enterprise%20Architecture%20Survey%202005%20IFEAD%20v10.pdf.

UK Cabinet Office. (2002). *e-Government interoperability framework (e-GIF), part two: Technical policies and specifications.* Retrieved, January 2011 from http://www.govtalk.gov.uk/documents/e-GIF4Pt2_2002-04-25.pdf.

UK Cabinet Office. (2005). *Transformational government enabled by technology.* Retrieved, September 2010 from http://archive.cabinetoffice.gov.uk/e-government/strategy/.

UK CIO. (2005). *Enterprise architecture for UK government: An overview of the process and deliverables for release 1.* Retrieved, May 2011 from http://tna.europarchive.org/20080727001118/http:/www.cio.gov.uk/documents/cto/pdf/enterprise_architecture_uk.pdf.

United Nations. (2008). *Connected government survey 2008*. Retrieved, May 2011 from http://unpan1.un.org/intradoc/groups/public/documents/un/unpan028607.pdf.

US OMB. (2009). *Open government directive*. Retrieved, December 2010 from http://www.whitehouse.gov/omb/assets/memoranda_2010/m10-06.pdf.

US OMB. (2010). *FY 2009 report to congress on the implementation of the e-government act of 2002*. Retrieved, August 2011 from http://www.whitehouse.gov/sites/default/files/omb/assets/egov_docs/2009_egov_report.pdf.

White House. (2010). *White house forum on modernizing government overview and next steps*. Retrieved, August 2011 from http://www.whitehouse.gov/sites/ default/files/omb/assets/modernizing_government/ModernizingGovernmentOverview.pdf.

Zachman, J. A. (1987). A framework for information systems architecture. *IBM Systems Journal, 26*(3). Retrieved, January 2011 from http://www.research.ibm.com/journal/sj/263/ibmsj2603E.pdf.

Chapter 13
Architecting for Connected Healthcare:
A Case of Telehomecare and Hypertension

Torben Tambo
Aarhus University, Denmark

Nikolai Hoffmann-Petersen
Regional Hospital Holstebro, Denmark

Karsten Bejder
Aarhus University, Denmark

ABSTRACT

The healthcare system is in many countries operated by the governments, and interaction with the healthcare system is one of the most frequent interactions between citizen and government. Demographic, medical, and technological changes are likely to bring new aspects of connectedness into the everyday life of people and place healthcare and homecare professionals in new roles. A transformation is taking place where hospital best practices are constantly reducing patient's in-hospital stays to alternative, less-costly care—notably at home. Telemedicine, telehealth, eHealth, home monitoring, and self-care are essential aspects of this transformation. Many issues are influencing this transformation, and new barriers are showing up where others are removed. A broadly oriented enterprise architecture effort is presented for the underpinning of the change process. The architectural approach encompasses views of the citizen, the healthcare system, the information infrastructure, and the citizen-oriented technology. A case of telemonitoring and self-care is presented using mobile hypertension measurement on a large-scale population cohort. Evaluation of the acceptance and success of the solutions is done within a combined understanding including technology, economy, organization, and culture.

DOI: 10.4018/978-1-4666-1824-4.ch013

INTRODUCTION

Telemedicine, TeleHealth, eHealth, telehomecare, and similar ICT-based systems are assumed to be critical in providing healthcare solutions in the future with ageing population, healthcare system under financial pressure, and with the "epidemic" in life-style chronic diseases (Kun, 2001). Traditionally, healthcare in industrialized societies has been built upon a physical, direct contact between healthcare professional and the citizen (patient). Physical interaction has put a linear-to-exponential load on the healthcare system. With new, smart electronic solutions, it is the belief that home-monitoring and self-care solutions will reduce the load by the individual patient with the distinct medical conditions on the healthcare system (Bellazzi, 2001). Interhuman interaction within the physical rooms of the healthcare system could be shifted into virtual rooms where none of the parties are limited in space and—in some case—also time. The logistics of patients, nurses, and doctors could be replaced by a logistics of information.

Many projects in this area are, however, still at an experimental level and narrowly technologically focused projects tend to overlook economic, social, and organizational issues like cases found in Savel et al. (2010) and MacFarlane et al. (2006). Even technologically oriented projects tend to focus on patients and "gadgets" and overlook infrastructure, and infrastructure might relate to hosts of new issues such as repositories, communication protocols, equipment, patient-doctor information logistics, embedding of new data into existing hospital systems, etc. This chapter is based on two case studies aimed at creating benefits of telemedicine both at the local and national level with a critical focus on the cross-organizational collaboration and communication. The chapter argues from the first of the projects that are looking at founding telehomecare as a cross-organizational phenomenon and the establishing of organizational constructs as the key transitional element from having experimental telehomecare and into operational telehomecare.

The lens used for this chapter is the investigation of the prerequisites in obtaining valuable connectedness between citizen and government, the technological, social, economic and organizational architecting necessary to make such a connection meaningful and create sound (business) cases. The disciplines of enterprise architecture and partially information systems are the bearing theoretical viewpoints each having its embedded paradoxes. Even if new public management strongly influences in governmental healthcare services, and a regime of business terminology is widespread, then medicine, people, and politics dominate are the main driving forces. Consequently, the strategic management objectives driving enterprise architectures might come from anything else than traditional market-driven profit-potentials.

The aim of the chapter is to illustrate a requirement for a flexible, well-defined architectural approach with a strong focus on engineering of organization, professional and clinical acceptance, user orientation, intra-/inter-organizational interfaces, and infrastructure more than technology itself.

BACKGROUND

This chapter has its background in the Danish healthcare system (Dinesen, et al., 2007; Strandberg-Larsen, et al., 2010; Pedersen, et al., 2011) that consists of the primary care mainly General Practitioners (GPs), but also groups like dentists, therapists, and various medical specialists. All act as self-employed despite being largely governmentally funded. The secondary care consists of hospitals, clinics, and various care and rehabilitation centers; most are governmentally run enterprises; a few are privately held. The tertiary sector is municipal or private care in form of homecare or nursing homes. Almost all revenues in all the sectors are funded by the government in form of taxes. In the understanding of a healthcare system, the responsibility for innovation and development of technology is interesting to identify and bodies of such must be seen in their ability to promote the necessary results within single domains as well as adequate interoperability and collaboration whether in single GP offices or large hospitals. Fragmentation is dominant between 5 hospital operating units. GPs use around 21 different systems but have extensive access to hospital system via integration or direct access. Basically, the healthcare system is organized after the principles of Beveridge (Health Consumer Powerhouse, 2009)—here it is also described that these principles seem to work in smaller, highly developed countries, but face problems in larger countries.

Data sharing and integration is largely regarded as the single key factor in the internationally recognized success of implementing and harvesting of benefits of the digitizing of the healthcare system in Denmark (Protti & Johansen, 2010; Wanscher, et al., 2006; Medcom, 2010). The success has partially been on the sacrifice of standards. More than 50 key documents and supporting coding systems and master data have been implemented and are in full operation. The documents cover a host of inter- and intraorganizational interoperability messages both with patients medical data, treatment logistics and billing. In general, E-health Denmark is regarded in the European top 5 (Health Consumer Powerhouse, 2009).

Basically, enterprise architectures exist per organizational entity, i.e. the national government is issuing EA to be followed by all hospital operators and joint systems, the association of hospital operators is to a certain extent converting this EA into suggestions for the 5 hospital operators, but it is eventually up to the hospital operators to ensure implementation. Most EA work is on voluntary basis, if a hospital operator does not follow national guidelines for EA in certain areas, no sanctions exist. Each hospital operator has also to struggle with EA issues founded in

numerous different standards and legacy systems combined with different business processes based on size, tradition, and interdependencies. EA should ideally secure proper links between operational and clinical systems, however this is often not the case, and clinical specializations tend to focus on non-connected systems is areas like radiology/oncology, cardio-vascular, medicine, or pulmonary. When hospital operators lack ability to exploit EA across organizational boundaries and to achieve sufficient internal architectural alignment, it becomes also difficult to connect with citizens in healthcare offerings in the home and daily environment of the citizen. This chapter is further on discussing the architectural issues that must be dealt with in the desire for telehomecare.

Methodological Approach

The changes in demography have for a long time been recognized in industrialized countries, new industrialized countries, and the middle-class of developing countries. The stress on governmental spending is many-fold with decreasing taxation options, attrition among healthcare professionals, ageing population and the 'epidemic' of life-style related—often chronic—health problems. A key methodological approach is to look away from patients in various silos and switch attention to engaging citizens in their own health situation.

The methodology of this study is inspired from classic, qualitative information systems case study methodology (Klein & Myers, 1999; Baskerville & Wood-Harper, 1998; Mathiassen & Nielsen, 2008) observing systems, processes, actors and having strong interaction with professionals. The group of authors acts within the projects described and has been engaged with telehomecare in various projects since 2004.

The case studies have the weakness of being on a more architectural level and are largely forward looking. However, a good deal of the technological artefacts exists or is to be made under all circumstances, and this should support the conclusions optimally. An element of mixed methods, however, exists when it comes to the quantitative survey and numerical processing of the interaction with patients (Bryman & Bell, 2007). Enterprise Architecture is also placed methodologically between the quantitative and the interpretive approaches when it comes to decision-making and analysis of strategic directives.

Telemedicine as Enabling Technology

Telemedicine includes a host of mobile and remote technologies connecting healthcare professional with each other or connecting patients and healthcare professionals. Only the latter is of focus in this contribution. The remote place can be the patient's home or—in case of mobility and adequate roaming—anywhere. Various taxonomical approaches have been proposed, which basically include:

- Active or "passive" two-way communication, e.g. using voice or video links (Chae, et al., 2001) between doctor and patient.
- Enabling the patient's personal ability—self-care (Juhl, 2007; Rahimpour, et al., 2008; Newbold, 2004)—or linking healthcare professional and patient, also known as store-and-forward or monitoring.
- More complex solutions using oxygen, intravenous injections, etc.

In the current context, telemedicine will be regarded as equipment performing physical measurements on the patient's body and/or questionnaire-based data-collection, intelligently interacting and supporting the patient, supporting remoteness and potentially mobility, a level of synchronous or asynchronous interaction with the healthcare and homecare system (Cegarra-Navarroa & Sánchez-Polo, 2010). The proposed term is telehomecare (Nourizadeh, et al., 2009;

Dinesen, et al., 2007; Essen & Conrick, 2008; Bellazzi, et al., 2010).

Early concerns on telehomecare were user and professional acceptance (Or & Karsch, 2009; Kim, et al., 2009; Rahimpour, et al., 2008; Garshnek, et al., 1997); if systems provided credible and social/cultural matching reflection of the user's need. Loebbecke (2009) calls for a participative approach to the design and construction of equipment and work situations. Comprehensible protocols, clear text/voice/video explanations, fail-safe product design are parts of this issue. Deeper reflection on patient's emotional and intellectual state and momentary mental capability is also adding to the acceptance issue. Moreover, supporting ICT-processes must have a fair level of quality to support credibility. This goes from decent cellular phone coverage of mobile systems and to well-functioning infrastructure forwarding data to appropriate receivers. On the professional side numerous issues might occur, from over-complex user authentication to lack of appropriate data-integration. Acceptance thus addresses not only cultural validity of telehomecare equipment as such but also broader infrastructural and organizational matters potentially related to completely different systems. At least one of the professional areas of critical concern is the linkage to GPs systems (Flett, et al., 2008; Thornett, 2001). In the current national context 8 GP-systems exists in 13 versions. GPs are generally regarded as the key 'coordinator' of most people's health and treatment and thus need working integrations. All in all, acceptance relates to persons with a certain level of skills and mental capability; in the study below, potential users were defined as 'the able,' excluding patients with concerns about technology; on the longer term, the limit of ability might shift due to engagement of home-care professionals, relatives, and the general increasing acceptance in the population of mobile, personal technology associated with cellphones, etc. (May, et al., 2003).

A certain area of telehomecare is vital signs (Ashraf, et al., 2008; Nourizadeh, et al., 2009) where patient monitoring extends into real time connectedness in cases in immediate danger, thus providing a certain degree of comfort to patients and relatives and replacing physical monitoring. Dinesen et al. (2008) discuss this as 'under surveillance and yet looked after.'

Critical to telemedicine is the fact that it only yields a meaningful value proposition to the health care system when it is integrated and showing certain degree of interoperability with other healthcare information systems (Kuusik, et al., 2011; Savel, et al., 2010; Tsiknakis, et al., 2002). Data from telemedicine must exhibit a flow to the right systems and actors and be available at the right time. All three major pillars in the healthcare system are potential stakeholders.

No generalized standards seem to dominate for ensuring interoperability from the equipment in the home to national infrastructures. Equipment providers, however, provide management systems with underlying databases that seem as workable integration points. The rapid development in smartphones and other networked technologies seems ideal, but they do not currently offer linkage to breadth of the professional healthcare system.

A strong requirement for highly explicit architectural approaches including repositories, messaging, document infrastructure and distribution of technology component responsibilities exists to make telehomecare successful (Lin, et al., 2007; Martin, et al., 2010; Alemdar & Ersoy, 2010).

Enterprise Architecture

Enterprise Architecture (EA) is the discipline of establishing clear relationships between corporate requirements and the associated or existing IT systems including infrastructure, interfaces, data, networks, functions, and processes (Bernard, 2005). EA is occasionally mixed with strategic IT (Ross, et al., 2008; Broadbent, et al., 1999) but has generally a different purpose. Other authors

underline the requirement for not only observing IT systems but looking at the enterprise in a much broader context including organization, HR, potential outsourcing, and elaborate business engagement and justification (Doucet, et al., 2009). Some authors see the EA as the prime result of the role of the enterprise architect (van den Berg & van Steenbergen, 2010) where others see the enterprise architect in a more facilitating role.

20 years of effort of IT in healthcare has not yet led to strong and convincing results: Different systems not sharing data in identical formats, doctors having to spend up to 37 minutes per day in signing-in, IT-policies blocking staff access to external systems, constant threats on information security violations, and infrastructures not ready for connecting patients at home to hospital core systems. EA is facing a tremendous task in healthcare. In discussions in the national project mentioned below, individual and idiosyncratic requirements of doctors, again, come from different traditions in specialized medical fields. Organizational issues also have an important role with different systems in the three different pillars of the healthcare systems, again meeting specialized requirements of each field. Under the category of chronic, it was suggested to add pregnant women knowing that the chronic state would come to an end.

EA is basically indifferent to whether it is dealing with private or governmental enterprises (Hjort-Madsen, 2009). However, some issues make governmental enterprises different: Politicians are the strategists but have far less integrity than business managers; the demand for services is infinite, but the supply of funding is finite; popular and pragmatic purposes might be as critical as objective criterions leaving business cases a matter of belief. There are few publications on specific frameworks for EA in healthcare (Ahsan, et al., 2009). Saha (2011) reflects on a stakeholder view from WHO including medicine, technology, governance, information, finance, service delivery, HR, and people. Several authors present views on strategic application of technology in healthcare as information architecture (Kuusik, et al., 2011; Martin, et al., 2010; Savel, et al., 2010; Alemdar & Ersoy, 2010; Lin, et al., 2007). Caro (2008) points to the study socio-political elements in driving forces of inter-sectorial ICT in healthcare. EHR is in most cases the fulcrum of the EA in healthcare discussions (De Toledo, et al., 2006). Fundamental to EA is the issue of organizational readiness (Jahani, et al., 2010).

EA in its core should provide enterprise—here societies—with guidance in understanding the requirements for improving the healthcare system by system-based understanding of all attributing factors, providing models, and suggesting implementation and change processes. Holt and Perry (2010) suggest to base EA projects on four viewpoints: The business context view, the competency view, the project life-cycle model view, and the infrastructure life cycle view. In respect to connected healthcare, all of these views include the perspectives of both healthcare professional and the citizen, e.g. the professional's business context is perhaps to provide simple services more effectively, whereas the citizen has a business context to receive services without having to travel to the doctor's office and wait to be serviced. EA might identify "secondary" benefits and risks in understanding peripheral factors of influence, e.g. a new medicine might make a certain treatment obsolete.

EA is generally accepted as a necessary element in re-architecting healthcare systems to adapt to a stronger degree of connection with the citizens. This requires a detailed understanding of typical basic elements of EA, such as given by Lankhorst et al. (2009) or Bernard (2005). With Bernard (2005) such an understanding could be elaborated as Table 1.

Ahsan et al. (2009) argue that EA in healthcare is one of more safeguards to tackle failing IT projects, furthermore is argued the importance of selecting the right EA framework, and Lankhorst et al. (2009)'s ArchiMate framework is used ex-

emplary. With Ashraf et al. (2008) global ID's on patients might significantly fight confusion and secure foreign keys to all digital data. In the cases below parts of the infrastructure exists where citizens and healthcare data are connected through global ID with these also managing the desired level of security.

Changing technological potentials, straight focus on architecture, and an orientation towards people—users and professionals—is the offset for looking at how to move citizens and government closer using smart ICT. Thereby, this chapter is following Nicolini (2008) in the suggestion for making telemedicine work by understanding people and respectfully making them articulate practice versus requirements.

MAIN FOCUS

This chapter has it offset in two concrete projects and a portfolio of projects under development in Denmark. The first concrete project works on several approaches to employing large and regular scale of telemonitoring of blood pressure related to patients with hypertension and patients with serious kidney problems. The second concrete project is going to strengthen the coherency among telehomecare projects in Denmark by creating a more generalized infrastructure and a temporary set of interfaces between telehomecare equipment and a messaging infrastructure.

The Hypertension Project

Hypertension is the most prevalent chronic condition within the population (Bobrie, et al., 2007). 17% of the population are diagnosed with hypertension and are receiving antihypertensive drugs. At least 6% are assumed to suffer from hypertension without having been diagnosed. Another part of the population is in the grey zone of prehypertension of 120-139/80-89 mmHg. Yet another group of mainly elderly has once been

Table 1. Connected healthcare analytical concepts inspired by Bernard (2005)

Connected healthcare analytic concept	
Goals and initiatives	Relevant healthcare segments, technological maturity of hardware and clinical processes Degree of citizens connectedness – uni-, bi- or omni-directional Organizational and inter-organizational relations
Products and services	Single or combined connections. Expectations on professional engagement. Contingencies. Responsibilities
Data and information	Availability. Delays. Degree of detail. Quantitative vs. qualitative. Information logistics
Systems and applications	Distributed vs central systems Reusability Interoperability
Network and infrastructure	Access and gateways, bandwidth Repositories Message brokering and service orientation
Cross cutting concepts	
Strategy	National vs local health prioritizations Adaption of clinical practices Business cases
Lines of business	Primary, secondary and tertiary healthcare Multiple doctor relations, cross-clinical issues Self-helped vs assisted patients
Security	Transparency vs privacy Supported infrastructures
Standards	Ad hoc efficiency vs standards regimes Interoperability in clinical collaboration

diagnosed wrongly or suffer from so-called white coat hypertension only found in GPs office, and experience dizziness and risk of physical injuries.

It is well-established that blood pressure is best measured at home. It is also well established that patients might bias their values in one or the other direction if they have to deliver these results to the GP by themselves (Logan, et al., 2007). Furthermore, data acquired by a measurement run initiated by the GP will not port itself to the hospital even if necessary.

To add further complexity, persons not in treatment for hypertension or anything else are system-wise not patients as they do not have Electronic Health Records (EHR) (Saha, 2011; Juhl, 2007; Jähn, et al., 2005). In this project, these persons remain citizens. Persons with severe chronic conditions might be under treatment for

this at a hospital, leaving out the GP. Thus, silos of dis-integrated data might exist.

A project has been designed to encompass the different silos of measurement, diagnosis, and monitoring of hypertension in a random set of the population in a municipality of 57,000 citizens. 6,000 citizens between 55 and 64 years are offered 3 days of use of a telemedical kit (Tambo, et al., 2010; ABT-fonden, 2010). The kit consists of an A & D 767BT blood pressure monitor and a Tunstall RTX3371 Telehealth Monitor with GSM/GPRS communication (Tunstall, 2011; Hoffmann-Petersen, et al., 2009). The findings on effect and potential positive outcome are based on a former project among other verifying quality of life aspects using the standardized SF36 health survey methodology (Madsen, et al., 2008a, 2008b).

The project has had the following phases:

1. Pilot run of the telehealth kit in a hospital outpatient clinic with 102 patients and a consecutive implementation of the telehealth kit as standard operating procedure.
2. A large-scale test with 6,000 invited citizens between 55 and 64 years of age with the aim of creating collaboration between GPs, municipal preventive medical effort and potentially specialized staff within the hospital.
3. A randomized run out of the large scale test, where persons with hitherto unrecognized hypertension are divided into two groups, one for telemedically supported treatment and one for traditional.

The pilot runs with 100 patients in a hospital renal outpatient clinic. The patients all suffering from severe kidney issues had been frequent visitors at the clinic for years. Hypertension is critical to their condition. The patients were called in and able patients were explained about the telehealth kit. Upon acceptance of use, they were given an instruction of use of 15 – 20 minutes. The case has shown viable application of Telehomecare (THC) in the field of hypertension not only measurement, but also monitoring and treatment. A survey was conducted along the pilot run. N=100. Age 56.5 years (17 – 81). 96 – 98% state that despite reservations to new technology the equipment was easy or fairly easy to use. 82 – 88% found information good, informative, and relevant. 80% found the home monitoring acceptable or quick and easy. Few want more functionality. Few discovered lack of GSM/GPRS coverage while travelling.

The large-scale project seems to have a good popular reception. GPs and their associated cohort of patients are informed, one office at the time. Briefing is given individually but is later on considered to be in groups. The municipal preventive care center manages all the equipment logistics. Furthermore, it gets an excellent opportunity to interact with a broader part of the population on additional and general health issues. No negative

response is received from included citizens. Upon returning of equipment, the citizen is briefed on findings and in case of elevated blood pressure, the doctor and the patient are informed. The telehomecare kit continues to follow the patient in case of hypertension, and it has been found that the telehomecare approach has a far more engaging role of the patients than a control group who received traditional GPs office feedback on treatment.

Mentioned above is a question upon finding secondary effects of initiatives and make these primary through EA considerations. One observation in the project has been that patients under telemedical monitoring tend to reach a higher compliance in taking his medicine; this has also a stabilizing effect on his general health. Furthermore does it seem like doctor's and patient extends their collaboration in trying to reach the desired target of blood pressure level, where as conventional treatment and monitoring seem to stop prematurely in the blood pressure reduction.

As an ongoing project, full integration of data, equipment, and 'business' processes in the general healthcare system are not fully accomplished. Funding of the preventive care unit, telehomecare equipment and GPs work are still matters under negotiation. The project, however, is through an easily accessible website able to connect citizens and all three pillars of the healthcare system. The equipment side of telehomecare is generally regarded as 'commodities,' but the organizational and economical side still remains complex.

Architectural considerations in this project relate to connectedness in general and the different stakeholder's integration barriers to access a central repository specifically. So far, equipment and management infrastructure reside with the equipment supplier, but the project has proven obvious barriers in accessing a joint telemedical system from both citizens, GPs, municipal actors and hospital. At least with the municipal and hospitals information infrastructure, security has been more dominating than other respects in the information systems architecture. As all other project throughout the country is facing the same issues, the Ministry of Finance requested the following project:

The National Telemedical Coherency Project

The above-mentioned project has several times applied (ABT Fonden, 2010) for national funding at a centrally placed fund (ABT) with the purpose of promoting technological development at all governmental levels. Advisers to the fund (Pedersen, 2008; Pedersen, 2010) have also several times pointed out that all of the telemedical projects gave individual meaning, but they also severely lacked internal coherency and coordination. Each project operated with its own database and with management systems requiring stand-alone logins, lacking security around patient's data, unable to scale, etc. For that reason, representatives of most applied-for projects and national enterprise architects were asked to envision a common framework for a national telemedical infrastructure. This includes discussions and definitions of process flow, interface descriptions, inclusion of already done projects, equipment and information logistics, and organizational responsibilities. The project agenda was:

- Ensuring avoidance of information silos in the healthcare system.
- Further development of the (existing) common information infrastructure.
- Enable access to data across the three main pillars of the healthcare systems.
- Enable citizens' and employees' access to one coherent e-health system.
- As much as possible use general technological infrastructure and standards.
- Secure a phase-divided expansion for new health areas (besides the 5 – 7 health conditions included in the project).

The Coherency Project has taken its offset in a series of existing hospital systems mainly EHR systems.

The project is suggesting to separate tele-homecare solutions from the general healthcare infrastructure through a Vendor Neutral Archieve (VNA) (Hilbel, et al., 2007). Microsoft HealthVault™, Google Health™, and Oracle's™ personalized healthcare products were also considered but rejected due to the risk of dependency of a single vendor. Likewise with Microsoft's ™ Connected Health Framework where vendor dependency is regarded as a serious drawback: Implementation any vendor-dependent technology will create a 15 – 25 years obligation to existing and future taxpayers in paying bills to a specific company. Vendor independency and use of open standards has been made a key issue.

The leading argument is that all cases show a heavy reliance between the technological artifact dedicated to the home and the attached, central management system. The management system manages data, personalizes the equipment (protocol, language, special needs), controls the "fleet" of equipment, intelligent agent and 'business intelligence' is also seen as a part of management systems. Following the argument, it is assumed that major players in the market are better to compete on combined patients- and professionals-systems and the wider use of data must be kept at a single entry point.

The VNA is to index and store data using the Cross-Enterprise Document Sharing (XDS) from the 'Integrating the Healthcare Enterprise' (IHE) initiative. Despite the former success of nationally adapted XML-exchange documents, a part of the developed proposal is to continue with the internationally recognized formats of HL7 CDA 2.0 (Health Language 7 Clinical Document Architecture) as the messaging format (Benson, 2010; Huang, 2010; HL7, 2011). CDA drivers an architectural reference model increasingly being used in most new projects in many countries. Subscribing to emerging standards should create

Figure 1. Conceptual chart of two hospital operators with a national platform in the center

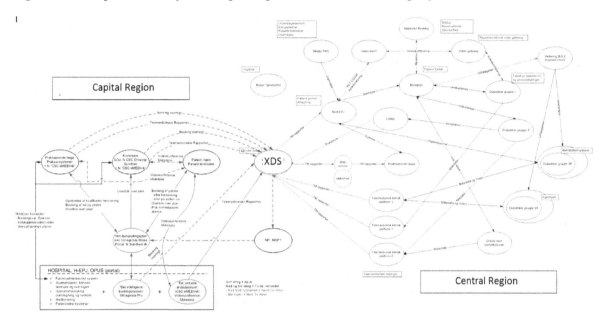

an easier way of integrating future products and platforms.

The developed framework is schematically shown below with XDS in the center, two hospital operators, and their respective technology stacks. Additionally each hospital operator is assumed to maintain his stocks of telemedical equipment, although citizen's access via Web-portals is mainly to be organized at national levels or on national platforms issuing Web-service invocation to each regional operator for data. Characteristically is also the split between operational and clinical systems in the hospital domain, and also the split of systems between the three sectors (see Figure 1).

The issue of telehomecare on individuals not being patients and not being registered in EHR-systems has been addressed. A common portal for government-citizens connectedness www.borger.dk has a section for basic health information www.sundhed.dk (Pedersen, 2010b). This portal can e.g. provide hospital laboratory test results directly to the patient, but is does not make up a repository of its own for measurements. This

extension is regarded as useful and forward-looking and is going to be implemented.

Several other issues need elaboration, particularly on logistics of patients, equipment, data, and professionals. Which citizens should have which equipment at what time, and who is responsible for observing the data when they arrive, if they arrive? Equipment booking systems can support this, also association of citizens IDs to all data support appropriate flow of data. The use of local health centers and of 'commodity' view on equipment can support flexibility in the solution.

Issues

For more than 10 years telehomecare has been touted as the easy win in managing large groups of mainly elderly citizens at home, and providing them with professional monitoring and assistance on an as-needed basis. Several issues remain, however. Equipment for telehomecare is evolving from un-intelligent measurement equipment, to equipment with data-collection readable in GPs office, to wired, internet-connected equipment

Figure 2. Success factors and risks of telehomecare

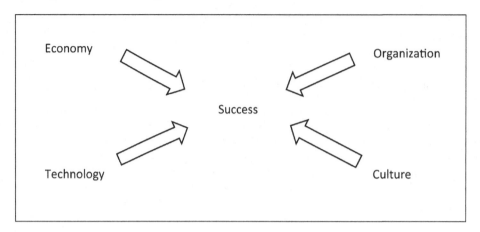

and now mobile, internetworked, interactive platforms. Lack of technology does not seem to be the problem – more the complexity and management of it. Neither does acceptance of the basic artefacts seem a problem from the patients' view. The case studies above indicate a host of non-technological issues influencing the possibilities and success of telehomecare.

Organization has been addressed by making a project that by design bypasses all sectorial boundaries. The authors are aware that collaboration is not coming from design but from clear awareness at each organizational level (silo) of the potential positive outcome of the joint work. Contractual agreements with GPs also remain even if contracts have already included electronic consultations as billable, but responsibility between equipment-owners and equipment-"actors" likewise remains open.

The lack of common architecture raised the initial criticism. A common "frontend" architecture has been developed. 5 different hospital-clusters in a small country with 5 different EHR-systems impose strong issues with the backend where also different business processes seem to exist. The "frontend" architecture will ensure data transfer between patients and central management systems and further on to citizens' portal and GPs systems.

The internal dataflow among all relevant hospital systems remains unsolved.

Controversies, Problems

It is suggested that the balance between success factors and risks of telehomecare solutions and projects should be viewed as Figure 2.

Despite obvious organizational conflicts, the empirical interactions associated with the current studies have had little resistance. Strong barrier has been the concerns of IT implementation costs and the concerns of effectiveness of implementation IT integrations. Acceptance of medical data flowing between governmental organizations has raised certain ethical concerns, but unavailability of data can also give ethical concerns in other contexts. The current approach is that optimal flow of data is critical for the development of the healthcare system.

Vendor roles are still not sufficiently clear—the area is not yet sufficiently standardized between hardware, software, infrastructure, and there are little signs that it will be. The design based on 'encapsulation' of the telemedical trail from probe to database including (mobile) communication could be regarded as a bankruptcy statement for interoperability in healthcare, but such must be accepted in most large technical installations e.g.

MR-scanners. The pragmatism in this area is a key success factor.

Isolating suitable business cases seem hard and include far more than techno-economical factors. The chronic issue is gaining grounds with the good justification that chronic diseases are said to provide around 80% of the load on the healthcare system most authors agree on this (RegionH, 2011; Saha, 2011; Flett, 2008; Rahimpour, et al., 2008). Prioritization of chronic patients raises ethical considerations on the remainder of the patients where causes might be more abrupt. Even this can be highlighted in sound business case modeling.

Solutions and Recommendations

Telehomecare seems to call for bridging a number of gaps in the organization of existing healthcare services by introducing the home as a safer platform for the patient, provide semi-real-time data to the healthcare professionals, and create transparency in data both in its raw form and with higher-level data, e.g. including doctor's comments.

A potential shortcoming in traditional enterprise architecture is the requirement for strategic management directives and business objectives. Given that politicians might be the 'strategic managers' they would normally delegate directives and actual policy formulation to chief doctors and healthcare directors. These, however, tend to represent the hospital-silo of the healthcare system and less the primary and tertiary sectors. Business cases and business objectives are likewise difficult to extract within the fragmentation; extension of life expectancy is contradictory with traditional business case thinking as it probably increase society's cost to retirement and other care services. Both social and ethical aspects influence along with political considerations. In the above-mentioned hypertension project the short term business case is argued as:

- Better measurements.
- Improved healthcare-to-patient interaction due to home-monitoring.
- Flow of information between sectorial actors.
- Shifts in tasks from more expensive to less expensive personnel.
- Deeper engagement of the patient in own treatment.

Long-term business case considerations have not been welcomed by most funding authorities, but lie objectively within:

- Avoidance of serious effects of hypertension such as strokes and cerebral hemorrhage.
- Cost savings due to massive care cost in patients hit by such effects.
- Avoiding fall-accidents from dizziness due to over-medication.
- Avoidance of dialysis or transplantation from kidney diseases caused by hypertension.
- Attribution to the already declining mortality from cardio-vascular diseases.

A schematic for the evaluation of potential might be suggested as Table 2 using data from the actual case of hypertension.

The schematic could be added with axis for considerations on politics, economy, culture, and technology. Furthermore, it would describe the human life cycle in its interaction with services of the healthcare system.

Connectedness between citizen and government is highly a matter of organizational engineering: Cost-optimization, shifts in responsibilities, community care center's role, GPs role, "ownership," and responsibilities regarding data, monitoring of failing health conditions, etc. The actual case has shown that hospitals, GPs, municipal care and preventive medicine can act positively

Table 2. Evaluation considerations for connect healthcare: a sectorial approach

	Preventive healthcare	Primary healthcare	Secondary healthcare	Tertiary healthcare
Users (patients, citizens)	Avoid health problems	Faster and easier adjustment of blood pressure	Faster treatment, engagement, qualitative self-care	Safety from technology
Professionals	Highlight issues	Less workload	Qualified data	Interaction among professionals
ICT	Support flow of information	Collaboration between GP and patient	Cross-sectorial interaction	Supporting patients during life cycle

Figure 3. Principles of connected e-health

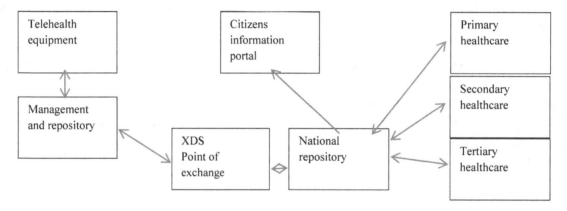

together obtaining mutual benefits on behalf of the patient and the funding organizations.

Connectedness can be illustrated by Figure 3.

The number of double arrows reflecting data sends both forth and back might look complex, but e.g. the telehealth equipment need language and specific patient information, the management system should retrieve basic patient data from the national systems, etc. Worth noticing is the apparent double connection to citizens. The citizen needs both specific equipment but do also need a consolidated view. The more 'gadget' view might claim that e.g. an iPhone was capable of both, but the obligation to use proven equipment contradicts with the desire for novel, personal solutions. This paradox is also an EA paradox: Why having to establish two or more channels of communication with the citizen, when one could do?

FUTURE DIRECTIONS

A popular interpretation of the male Danish population stated that the life expectancy will rise 6 hours per day, meaning that over a 10 year period the governmental healthcare system and the general change in lifestyles have increased male life expectancy with 2.5 years. With the shrinking productive workforce, all sails must be set to develop new "smart" methods to shift healthcare effort from governmental manpower to attracting and including elderly and involve citizens in self-care.

Architecture is highly a matter of "talking the same language," e.g. with DICOM and HL7 CDA, but also far more organizational and 'business oriented' methodologies understand the role and assignments of the stakeholders. Danish e-health success has—put simply—been built not adhering to international standards, but more using common sense. Now adherence to standards should allow utilization of standard equipment and systems. The architectural approach as outlined in the national project, encapsulate each individual telemedical vendor with his equipment, network, management system and repository, only the VNA integration point is shared among healthcare systems and the citizen-oriented system. This is still not ideal, and the long-term direction is to call for open interface were healthcare services and 'gadgets' are linked with direct connections to both patient and healthcare professional.

Even if the national project above was asked to adapt the national architecture to contain 7 telehomecare projects, it was also assumed that these projects all together were sufficiently representative for create a de facto general national architecture. This applies mostly to the technical subsystem of the telehomecare complex, leaving the economical, organizational, and cultural issues in the hands to local project makers. It is recommended to consider embed an EA practice at local levels on project basis to ensure the fullest inclusion of relevant factors in the project design. The EA practice can link national and local requirements and link the technical construct with the organizational (business) construct and widen out project from 'gadgets' to inclusion in operational and clinical practice.

Based on the previous observations a broad inclusion-based transition view is made on the telemedical development encompassing not only primary, secondary, and tertiary healthcare but also preventive healthcare focused on lifestyle and 'early warnings.' Strandberg-Larsen et al. (2008) suggest looking at some of the best US healthcare organizations where strict financial controlling mechanisms are governing.

Expected growth in 'smart devices' is assumed to have a strong impact: From electronic patches, to smartphones employing various vital sign monitors, and to traditional medical equipment designed for the home—all connected and with expectations that governmentally operated healthcare services are ready to support all of these data. Our studies indicate that it will take years before expectations can be met, and benefits can be reaped. Immense specialization of physicians and surgeons in all countries is weighting in on this, where doctors have difficulties in sponsoring systems outside his core competencies. The connectedness of the citizen needs realistic piecemeal approaches no matter if regarded wasteful.

As telehomecare is expected to solve economic burdens on the healthcare systems, telehomecare is not inexpensive. In the hypertension case, cost of apparatus plus infrastructure operations is around €150 per month. Nurse hours spend on instruction, doctor's review of measurements, and logistics accounts for a factor 2 – 4 on the top of this.

Issues on privacy, ethics, and responsibilities can change the technological promises. Although it falls out of scope in this study, the dimension of social acceptance must never be overlooked.

CONCLUSION

Connected healthcare is highly attractive in moving from externalized healthcare to self-care yielding not only almost real-time patient monitoring and protocol-bound interaction, but also an inclusion of able and increasingly knowledgeable patients in actions and consequences upon health. The connectedness is in contrast to Nicolini (2007) not so much a matter of sealing the relationship between the center and the remote, but far more a point in establishing a technological and organizational network-based mesh of relationships between the citizen-patient and the multitude of professionals in care with due respect to plenty of local practices for different medical conditions.

Whether governments are engaged directly in healthcare maintenance or have indirect roles as policy makers the financial and manpower problems of changed demographics call for solutions. The case studies of this chapter display that elaborate engagement of government driven enterprise architectures is fundamental for the transition from high cost (and low quality) and into low cost (and improved quality) solutions and the transition from physical to virtual/digital connections between citizen and government.

Wider architectural models encompassing issues of organization, technology, economy and culture will be beneficial to achieving the long-term targets of utilizing technology for the best of all.

REFERENCES

ABT-Fonden. (2010). *Telemedical blood pressure diagnostic, treatment and monitoring – Final application.* Copenhagen, Denmark: ABT-Fonden.

Ahsan, K., Shah, H., & Kingston, P. (2009). The role of enterprise architecture in healthcare-IT. In *Proceedings of the 2009 Sixth International Conference on Information Technology: New Generations*, (pp. 1462-1467). IEEE.

Alemdar, H., & Ersoy, C. (2010). Wireless sensor networks for healthcare: A survey. *Computer Networks, 54*(15), 2688–2710. doi:10.1016/j.comnet.2010.05.003

Ashraf, A., Chowdry, B. S., Mustafa, G., & Hashmani, M. A. (2008). Unified application of tele-healthcare architecture and globalized patient IDs. In *Proceedings of the International Conference on Applied Computer Science*. Applied Computer Science.

Baskerville, R., & Wood-Harper, A. T. (1998). Diversity in information systems action research methods. *European Journal of Information Systems, 7*, 90–107. doi:10.1057/palgrave.ejis.3000298

Bellazzi, R., Montani, S., Riva, A., & Stefanelli, M. (2010). Web-based telemedicine systems for home-care: Technical issues and experiences. *Computer Methods and Programs in Biomedicine, 64*, 175–187. doi:10.1016/S0169-2607(00)00137-1

Benson, T. (2010). *Principles of health interoperability HL7 and SNOMED.* London, UK: Springer.

Berg, V. D. M., & Steenbergen, V. M. (2010). *Building an enterprise architecture practice.* Berlin, Germany: Springer.

Bernard, S. (2005). *Enterprise architecture.* Bloomington, IN: AuthorHouse.

Bobrie, G., Postel-Vinay, N., Delonca, J., & Corvol, P. (2007). Self-measurement and self-titration in hypertension A pilot telemedicine study. *American Journal of Hypertension, 20*, 1314–1320. doi:10.1016/j.amjhyper.2007.08.011

Broadbent, M., Weill, P., & Neo, B. S. (1999). Strategic context and patterns of IT infrastructure capability. *The Journal of Strategic Information Systems, 8*, 157–187. doi:10.1016/S0963-8687(99)00022-0

Bryman, A., & Bell, E. (2007). *Business research strategy* (2nd ed.). Oxford, UK: Oxford University Press.

Caro, D. H. J. (2008). Deconstructing symbiotic dyadic e-health networks: Transnational and transgenic perspectives. *International Journal of Information Management, 28*, 94–101. doi:10.1016/j.ijinfomgt.2007.12.002

Cegarra-Navarroa, J.-G., & Sánchez-Polo, M. T. (2010). Implementing telemedicine through eListening in hospital-in-the-home units. *International Journal of Information Management, 48*(10), 895–918.

Chae, Y. M., Lee, J. H., Ho, S. H., Kim, H. J., Jun, K. H., & Won, J. U. (2001). Patient satisfaction with telemedicine in home health services for the elderly. *International Journal of Medical Informatics, 61*, 167–173. doi:10.1016/S1386-5056(01)00139-3

De Toledo, P., Lalinde, W., del Pozo, F., Thurber, D., & Jimenez-Fernandez, S. (2006). Interoperability of a mobile health care solution with electronic healthcare record systems. In *Proceedings of the Engineering in Medicine and Biology Society Conference*. IEEE.

Digital Sundhed. (2010). *Sammenhængende digital sundhed i Danmark*. Retrieved November 12, 2010, from http://sdsd.dk/.

Dinesen, B., Gustafsson, J., Nøhr, C., Andersen, S. K., Sejersen, H., & Toft, E. (2007). Telehomecare technology across sectors: claims of jurisdiction and emerging controversies. *International Journal of Integrated Care, 7*(21), 1–11.

Dinesen, B., Nøhr, C., Andersen, S. K., Sejersen, H., & Toft, E. (2008). Under surveillance, yet looked after: Telehomecare as viewed by patients and their spouse/partners. *European Journal of Cardiovascular Nursing, 7*, 239–246. doi:10.1016/j.ejcnurse.2007.11.004

Doucet, G., Gøtze, J., Saha, P., & Bernard, S. (2009). *Coherency management – Architecting the enterprise for alignment, agility and assurance*. Bloomington, IN: AuthorHouse.

Essén, A., & Conrick, M. (2008). New e-service development in the homecare sector: Beyond implementing a radical technology. *International Journal of Medical Informatics, 77*(7), 679–688. doi:10.1016/j.ijmedinf.2008.02.001

Flett, P., Curry, A., & Peat, A. (2008). Reengineering systems in general practice—A case study review. *International Journal of Information Management, 28*, 83–93. doi:10.1016/j.ijinfomgt.2007.06.001

Garshnek, V., Logan, J. S., & Hassell, L. H. (1997). The telemedicine frontier: Going the extra mile. *Space Policy, 13*(1), 37–46. doi:10.1016/S0265-9646(96)00036-7

HL7. (2011). *Health level seven international*. Retrieved from http://www.hl7.org/index.cfm.

Health Consumer Powerhouse. (2009). *Euro health consumer index 2009 report*. Danderyd, Sweden: Health Consumer Powerhouse AB.

Hilbel, T., Brown, B. D., de Bie, J., Lux, R. L., & Katus, H. L. (2007). Innovation and advantage of the DICOM ECG standard for viewing, interchange and permanent archiving of the diagnostic electrocardiogram. *Computers in Cardiology, 34*, 633–636.

Hjort-Madsen, K. (2009). *Architecting Government understanding enterprise architecture adoption in the public sector*. PhD Thesis. Copenhagen, Denmark: The IT University.

Hoffmann-Petersen, N., Pedersen, E. B., Bech, J., & Mikkelsen, L. (2009). *Telemedinsk hjemme BT måling: Regionshospitalet holstebro*. Unpublished.

Holt, J., & Perry, S. (2010). *Modelling enterprise architectures*. New York, NY: The Institution of Engineering and Technology.

Huang, H. K. (2010). Industrial standards (HL7 and DICOM) and integrating the healthcare enterprise (IHE). In *PACS and imaging informatics: Basic principles and applications* (2nd ed.). Hoboken, NJ: John Wiley & Sons, Inc.

Jahani, B. S., Javadein, & Jafari, H. (2010). Measurement of enterprise architecture readiness within organizations. *Business Strategy Series, 11*(3), 177–191. doi:10.1108/17515631011043840

Jähn, K., Reiher, T. M., & Stuhl, T. (2005). Telemedical projects in Bavaria—What is the current position and what needs to be done? *International Congress Series, 1281*, 180–185. doi:10.1016/j.ics.2005.03.296

Juhl, A. (2007). *E-health in Denmark*. Conference presentation. New York, NY.

Kim, Y. J., Chun, J. U., & Song, J. (2009). Investigating the role of attitude in technology acceptance from an attitude strength perspective. *International Journal of Information Management, 29*, 67–77. doi:10.1016/j.ijinfomgt.2008.01.011

Klein, H. K., & Myers, M. (1999). A set of principles for conducting and evaluating interpretive field studies in information systems. *Management Information Systems Quarterly, 23*(1), 67–97. doi:10.2307/249410

Kun, L. G. (2001). Telehealth and the global health network in the 21st century: From homecare to public health informatics. *Computer Methods and Programs in Biomedicine, 64*, 155–167. doi:10.1016/S0169-2607(00)00135-8

Kuusik, A., Reilent, E., Loobas, I., & Parve, M. (2011). Software architecture for modern telehealth care systems. *Advances on Information Sciences and Service Sciences, 3*(2).

Lankhorst, M. (Eds.). (2009). *Enterprise architecture at work*. Berlin, Germany: Springer Verlag. doi:10.1007/978-3-642-01310-2

Lin, C.-H., Young, S.-T., & Kuo, T.-S. (2007). A remote data access architecture for home-monitoring health-care applications. *Medical Engineering & Physics, 29*, 199–204. doi:10.1016/j.medengphy.2006.03.002

Loebbecke, C. (2009). Furthering distributed participative design - Unlocking the walled gardens. *Scandinavian Journal of Information Systems, 21*(1), 77–106.

Logan, A. G. (2007). Mobile phone-based remote patient monitoring system for management of hypertension in diabetic patients. *American Journal of Hypertension, 20*, 942–948. doi:10.1016/j.amjhyper.2007.03.020

MacFarlane, A., Murphy, A. W., & Clerkin, P. (2006). Telemedicine services in the Republic of Ireland: An evolving policy context. *Health Policy (Amsterdam), 76*, 245–258. doi:10.1016/j.healthpol.2005.06.006

Madsen, L. B., Kirkegaard, P., & Pedersen, E. B. (2008a). Blood pressure control during telemonitoring of home blood pressure: A randomized controlled trial during 6 months. *Blood Pressure, 17*, 78–86. doi:10.1080/08037050801915468

Madsen, L. B., Kirkegaard, P., & Pedersen, E. B. (2008b). Health-related quality of life (SF-36) during telemonitoring of home blood pressure in hypertensive patients: A randomized, controlled study. *Blood Pressure, 17*, 227–232. doi:10.1080/08037050802433701

Martin, A., Dimitriev, D., & Akeroyd, J. (2010). A resurgence of interest in information architecture. *International Journal of Information Management, 30*, 6–12. doi:10.1016/j.ijinfomgt.2009.11.008

Mathiassen, L., & Nielsen, P. A. (2008). Engaged scholarship in IS research. *Scandinavian Journal of Information Systems, 20*(2), 3–20.

May, C., Harrison, R., Finch, T., MacFarlane, A., Mair, F., & Wallace, P. (2003). Understanding the normalization of telemedicine services through qualitative evaluation. *Journal of the American Medical Informatics Association, 10*(6), 596–604. doi:10.1197/jamia.M1145

Medcom. (2010). *Det danske sundhedsdatanet*. Retrieved April 1, 2011, from http://medcom.dk/wm1.

Medcom. (2011). *Lægesystemer, sende/modtage*. Retrieved April 1, 2011, from http://medcom.dk/wm110032.

Microsoft. (2011). *Connected health framework architecture and design blueprint, part 1 - 5*. Retrieved July, 15, 2011 from http://www.microsoft.com/health/ww/ict/Pages/Connected-Health-Framework.aspx.

Nicolini, D. (2008). The work to make tele-medicine work: A social and articulative view. *Social Science & Medicine, 62,* 2754–2767. doi:10.1016/j.socscimed.2005.11.001

Nourizadeh, S., Deroussent, C., Song, Y. Q., & Thomesse, J. P. (2009). Medical and home automation sensor networks for senior citizens telehomecare. In *Proceedings of the First International Workshop on Medical Applications Networking.* IEEE Press.

Or, C. K. L., & Karsh, B.-T. (2009). A systematic review of patient acceptance of consumer health information technology. *Journal of the American Medical Informatics Association, 16*(4), 550–560. doi:10.1197/jamia.M2888

Pedersen, I. L. (2008). *Hvordan kan sundheds-væsenets digitalisering styres.* Paper presented at EHR Observers Annual Meeting. Retrieved from http://www.epj-observatoriet.dk/konference2008/sli-des/P2/Pedersen-IvanLund.pdf.

Pedersen, I. L. (2010). *Erfaringer og barrierer ifm: Implementering af tværsektorielle IT-projekter, fx medicinkortet.* Paper presented at Danish Quality Unit in General Practice. Retrieved from http://www.dak-e.dk/files/157/erfaringer_og_barrierer_ifm_im-plementering_af_tvaer-sektorielle_it-projekter_digital_sundhed.pdf.

Pedersen, K. M., Bech, M., & Vrangbæk, K. (2011). *The Danish health care system: An analysis of strengths, weaknesses, opportunities and threats.* Copenhagen, Denmark: Copenhagen Consensus Center.

Pedersen, M. E. (2010). *The Danish national e-health portal.* Paper presented at Health 2.0 Europe. Retrieved from http://www.slideshare.net/Health2con/health-20-europe-keynote-the-danish-national-ehealth-portal.

Petersen, J. (2011). *ABT koordineringsprojekt - Teknisk delprojekt.* Odense, Denmark: MedCom.

Protti, D., & Johansen, I. (2010). Widespread adoption of information technology in primary care physician offices in Denmark: A case study. *Commonwealth Fund, 1379*(80).

Rahimpoura, M., Lovell, N. H., Celler, B. G., & McCormick, J. (2008). Patients' perceptions of a home telecare system. *International Journal of Medical Informatics, 77*(7), 486–498. doi:10.1016/j.ijmedinf.2007.10.006

Region, H. (2011). *Demonstrationsprojekt til it-understøttelse af forløbsprogrammer.* Copenhagen, Denmark: Region Hovedstaden.

Ross, J. W., Weill, P., & Robertson, D. C. (2008). *Enterprise architecture as strategy.* Boston, MA: Harvard Business School Press.

Saha, P. (2011). *Architecting for business insight and strategic foresight: A systems approach to management of chronic diseases in Singapore.* Singapore, Singapore: Research Publication of National University of Singapore.

Savel, T. (2010). A public health grid (PHGrid): Architecture and value proposition for 21st century public health. *International Journal of Medical Informatics, 79*(7), 523–529. doi:10.1016/j.ijmedinf.2010.04.002

Strandberg-Larsen, M., Schiøtz, M. L., Silver, J. D., Andersen, J. S., Frølich, A., & Krasnik, A. (2010). Is the Kaiser permanente model superior in terms of clinical integration: A comparative study of Kaiser permanente, northern California and the Danish healthcare system. *BMC Health Services Research, 10*(91), 1–13.

Sundhed.dk. (2010a). *Website.* Retrieved from https://www.sundhed.dk/.

Sundhed.dk. (2010b). *Min e-journal.* Retrieved from https://www.sund-hed.dk/profil-.aspx?id=29462.852.

Tambo, T. N., Hoffmann-Petersen, E. B., & Bejder, K. (2010). Coherent national IT infrastructure for telehomecare - A case of hypertension measurement, treatment and monitoring. *World Academy of Science. Engineering and Technology, 6*(71), 757–764.

Thornett, A. M. (2001). Computer decision support systems in general practice. *International Journal of Information Management, 21,* 39–47. doi:10.1016/S0268-4012(00)00049-9

Tsiknakis, M., Katehakis, D. G., & Orphanoudakis, S. C. (2002). An open, component-based information infrastructure for integrated health information networks. *International Journal of Medical Informatics, 68,* 3–26. doi:10.1016/S1386-5056(02)00060-6

Tunstall. (2011). *Technical specifications: RTX3371 telehealth monitor, GSM/GPRS.* Retrieved from http://www.tunstall healthcare.com/Spec._RTX 3371_(GSM/GPRS)-2144.aspx.

Wanscher, C., Pederson, C. D., & Jones, T. (2006). *Medcom, Denmark: Danish health data network.* Bonn, Germany: Empirica.

ADDITIONAL READING

Alter, S. (2008). Defining information systems as work systems: Implications for the IS field. *European Journal of Information Systems, 17,* 448–469. doi:10.1057/ejis.2008.37

Coulouris, G., Dollimore, J., & Kindberg, T. (2009). *Distributed systems: Concepts and design* (4th ed.). Reading, MA: Addison-Wesley.

Duggala, V. G., Saltzman, C., & Klein, L. R. (2007). Infrastructure and productivity: An extension to private infrastructure and IT productivity. *Journal of Econometrics, 140,* 485–502. doi:10.1016/j.jeconom.2006.07.010

Fink, L., & Neumann, S. (2009). Exploring the perceived business value of the flexibility enabled by information technology infrastructure. *Information & Management, 46,* 90–99. doi:10.1016/j.im.2008.11.007

Ghaye, T. (2006). *Building the reflective healthcare organisation.* Oxford, UK: Blackwell.

Hoyt, R. E. (2010). *Medical informatics: Practical guide for healthcare and information technology professionals* (4th ed). Retrieved from http://www.Lulu.com.

Kakabadse, A., Abdulla, M. O., Abouchakra, R., & Jawad, A. (2011). *Leading smart transformation: A roadmap for world class government.* Basingstoke, UK: Palgrave MacMillan. doi:10.1057/9780230306493

Kazorowski, W. (Ed.). (2004). *Connected government: Cisco series on thought leaders.* London, UK: Premium Publishing.

Lindberg, D. A. B. (1994). Global information infrastructure. *International Journal of Bio-Medical Computing, 34,* 13–19. doi:10.1016/0020-7101(94)90006-X

Newbold, S. K. (2004). Information technology as an infrastructure for patient safety: Nursing research needs. *International Journal of Medical Informatics, 73,* 657–662. doi:10.1016/j.ijmedinf.2004.04.016

Norris, A. C. (2001). *Essentials of telemedicine and telecare.* Chichester, UK: Wiley. doi:10.1002/0470846348

O'Brien, J. A., & Marakas, G. M. (2009). *Management information systems.* New York, NY: McGraw-Hill.

Wootton, R., Craig, J., & Patterson, V. (2006). *Introduction to telemedicine.* London, UK: Royal Society of Medicine.

Wootton, R., Dimmick, S. L., & Kvedar, J. C. (2006). *Home telehealth: Connecting care with community*. London, UK: Royal Society of Medicine Press.

Yogesan, K., Bos, L., Brett, P., & Gibbons, M. C. (2009). *Handbook of digital homecare*. Berlin, Germany: Springer.

KEY TERMS AND DEFINITIONS

Chronic: A persistent, normally irreversible, sometimes deteriorating health condition requiring recurring medical attention and specialized precautions not progress further.

Coherency (business): (Well-) organized interrelation among systems, processes, information, infrastructure and people typically focused on achieving common objectives. Literally coherency is thought as 'going in parallel in the same direction.' Ideally (good) coherency is underpinning business activities optimally and (lack of) coherency is no relatedness between key components of the business.

Continua Health Alliance: Continua Health Alliance is a non-profit, open industry organization of healthcare and technology companies aimed at improving the quality of personal healthcare. It has 200+ member companies around the world, and is looking at establishing a system of interoperable personal connected health solutions with the knowledge that extending those solutions into the home provides independence, helps individuals and offer opportunity for personalized health and wellness management.

HL7-CDA: HL7's Clinical Document Architecture describing key process XML-documents for the health care industry such as referrals, orders, discharges, etc.

HL7-RIM: HL7's Reference Information Model for the health care information modeling and standardization effort. RIM provides succes-sively enhancing precision in medical information modeling and collects international initiatives on harmonizing of health care data representation. Also known as ANSI/HL7 RIM R3-2010 and ISO 21731.

Mobility: The ability to physically move around in smaller or larger spaces with a purpose or with the opportunity to use the same services at almost identical quality levels no matter where to be positioned. In healthcare it can relate to patients using equipment non-stationary at home, locally, or at large distances from home or central hubs.

Self-care: The concept of have patients and citizens caring for themselves in their own home typically under monitoring or advice from hospital or GP. The term reflects some degree of medical history for suggesting a necessity for care. A care plan or prescriptions might be associated with self-care.

Telehomecare: Information and medical technologies aimed at providing self-care and assisted care in the patient's home. Associated with communication technologies and integration technologies telehomecare can provide networked care services and monitoring. With wireless—narrow or wide area types—telehomecare can furthermore be mobile and support the patient out of home in surroundings of the patient's preference.

VNA: Vendor Neutral Archive – a software system for indexing and archiving documents of different actors in the healthcare system. It aims at bypassing critical barriers of past/present healthcare informatics characterized by informational silos connected to systems rather than organizations and patients.

XDS: Cross Enterprise Document Sharing – a framework for (secure) exchange of clinical documents between relevant actors ideally an underlying layer for electronic health records (EHR). XDS include main components of document source, consumer, registry and repository and also include the patient as bearing id for activities.

Chapter 14
An Approach to Multi-Agency and Intra-Agency Unification with Enterprise Architecture Driven e-Government in South Africa

R. Benjamin
Nanograte Knowledge Technologies, South Africa

ABSTRACT

This chapter introduces an emerging EA (Enterprise Architecture) approach to e-government. Within the South African reality, it would be fair to expect an adequate level of e-governance to achieve a minimum level of standardized data-administration practices. For purposes of this chapter, this level of governance would be viewed as the desired strategic objective for e-government. For the past 4 years, an approach for engaging with government was prototyped and tested. Its intent was to deliver governance-oriented ICT (Information and Communication Technology) solutions. Its main objective was to provide data integrity to multi-agency requirements and help design solutions aimed at satisfying those requirements.

The diplomatic path towards standardizing data-administration practices within government is not always direct. Due consideration was given to technology, organization, people and process aspects. It would seem that the outcomes, which resulted from employing the ontology, addressed an underlying need of governmental agencies across the board, namely the need for unification. This chapter explains how multi-agency and intra-agency unification was facilitated.

DOI: 10.4018/978-1-4666-1824-4.ch014

INTRODUCTION

EA represents a systemic framework, incorporating design principles, which govern the evolutionary design of an enterprise.

To understand the general perspective of this chapter, it is important to understand the general condition of the IT (Information Technology) industry and e-government within a post 27 April, 1994, South Africa – the day a new democracy was born.

While certain day-to-day realities of e-government are going to be mentioned in this chapter, which may at first seem less flattering, such inclusion would be justified on the hand of setting and maintaining an appropriate context for this chapter.

Whilst readers from developing economies may be able to relate more easily to many aspects being depicted as the business-as-usual environment, readers from developed economies may become challenged by this worldview. To help explain the general reasoning behind the business-as-usual environment, additional detail and explanations would be provided.

In order to understand e-government and EA within a developing economy, a degree of understanding of the strategic realities within South Africa should first have to be constructed. To the relative stability of a mature (developed) economy, the true machinations of a new democracy and developing economy could almost be fantastically unimaginable. However, the high impact, which e-government practices typically have on the performance of national economics, would probably justify the inclusion of such a perspective.

References exist for most of the anecdotal statements and examples. However, these references are either constrained via NDAs (Non Disclosure Agreements), or deemed to be sensitive information pertaining to government. As such, it would seem contrary to the spirit of this chapter to include any of them.

Within a "new" South Africa, it is not deemed to be politically correct to conduct empirical research into any administrative failures. Criticism of the majority party is generally regarded as a hostile act, instead of a rightful act of democracy. The recent failed attempt by government to muzzle the media should suffice to illustrate the point (Langeni, 2010).

Commenting on the efficacy of e-government activities has to be approached with much discretion so as to avoid it appearing to be offensive, ignorant, and arrogant. When EA engages with the softer underbelly of the South-African administration, via e-government projects, diplomatic prowess becomes a critical success factor.

It follows that any EA competency in South Africa should definitely include diplomacy as a standard tool. Without diplomatic competency, EA cannot be effective in South Africa. However, too often diplomatic competency becomes confused with socio-cultural fit as opposed to political correctness. EA is required to collaborate effectively with all government employees, and not merely mingle in select groupings. As such, the general notion of diplomacy referred to herein should be considered in its widest sense, and not be constrained to concepts of 'etiquette', 'professionalism' and 'ethics' alone.

Specifically, this EA diplomacy would refer to an ability to engage with government in a manner, which would:

1. Further mutual respect for person, groups of persons, and profession.
2. Facilitate consensus amongst stakeholders.
3. Deliver progress to e-government initiatives.

This author's view is that EA in South Africa has for the most part become ineffective. It has mainly been supplanted by a form of "insider" function, unrelated to the practical skills EA should bring to the table. EA may have lost its strategic teeth, and hence its ability to influence e-government policy, as a function of governance.

In the absence of core skills, EA have become no more than credible, window dressing.

It would be possible to find many "causes" for this state of EA affairs. For example the continued brain drain of migrating professionals, cultural changes within government itself, and so on. However, the author would rather assert how it might be EA itself, as a professional practice, that may have failed e-government in its strategic obligation to lead policy integration and compliance practices.

This assertion is similar to the notion that management science may have failed business-systems engineering by not developing IT-industry competency tools to manage exponential complexity with. It would follow that failure in existing approaches and methods necessitated exploratory changes in practice, giving rise to emerging approaches (Curtis & Cobham, 2002).

This chapter could be viewed in the light of a field report in the area of EA and e-government. On the one hand, this researcher's position as an independent practitioner provides the unique opportunity to be left with somewhat more latitude to introduce this perspective on EA and e-government. While on the other hand, the absence of a substantial, researched body of knowledge tends to hamper the structure and the availability of reliable data on the subject.

Within the context of South-African, e-government projects, typical project-performance metrics may not always be 100% applicable. Some metrics must needs be adapted in order to enable the measurement of project results. Further, in the absence of structured, academic research on projects, it would take a very-long time to establish a useful body of knowledge. Such a collection of data has been established over the past 4 years, and it is from this store that a selection was made for inclusion in this chapter.

It is vital to the interests of the IT industry, EA, and the e-government sector to submit this selection of data (as published measurements, observations, reports, anecdotes, and experiences)

to a recognized academic body for review and critique, such as what is being done with this chapter. In this sense this chapter would help to formalize the EA industry's body of knowledge.

Given the organizational sensitivities that EA generally have to operate within, the introduction and presence of large teams of observers, interviewers, and so on would not be tolerated by political sponsors of projects and stakeholders alike. As a means of collecting vital group data on trends and so on, the author has discovered a seemingly high tolerance for "pop quizzes" during workshops.

Once assembled as a valid and reliable knowledge sample of an organisational domain, the before-mentioned "pop quiz" may be used with high effect. For example, a question such as: "How many in this room would be willing to participate in a data-administration workshop?" may help determine the level of interest and tolerance for data administration in general, and so on.

For research purposes, the EA approach employed used a standard, data-capturing method, which also doubles as a design tool (Benjamin, 2008). During the test period resistance to using this combination of approach and tool, for facilitating e-government work sessions, was found to be insignificant. Work sessions were highly structured, well attended, productive, and generally positive. This was mainly due to the principles embedded in the approach and method. However, as indicated before, the diplomatic role of the session facilitator did play a vital role as well.

For performance purposes, the actual value of the contribution made by participants would be assessed in-situ and transparently so. The "metric" used for gauging adoption of the results was based on the collective approval rating given by all. If they were all willing to sign off on the results, and provide permission for those results to go "public" within their departments, then the conclusion was drawn that the session was 100% successful.

Experience showed that if group consensus could be reached, then the results could be regarded as probably (60%) good enough in terms of validity and reliability. Although the probability seems quite low, it could be considered adequate for complex, adaptive systems, such as the combination of Technology, Organisation, People and Process encountered within e-government scenarios.

Further, testing the results with different decision makers from the same department over time found that results remained relevant to the organisation for periods of up to 12 months. In terms of cost benefit and sustainability this turned out to be a significant finding. For one, it would minimise the political risk of departmental consensus changing whenever staff changed positions (a high incidence being found within those levels of governmental decision makers). Second, it minimised losses typically incurred by the effects of strategic drift and on-going projects.

In rare instances where consensus was not reached during a work session, it would be concluded that the data-gathering session had failed in its entirety. Such results would be analysed and reported against to the session sponsor, typically a departmental director.

It seems to be within the reality of an e-government context that the South-African EA industry finds itself at a loss to effect the practical changes espoused by the discipline's accepted, theoretical norms. Even though EA certification within South Africa for TOGAF (The Open Group Architecture Forum) and COBiT (Control Objectives for Information and Related Technology) resembles 10% of global EA certification, it is more a reflection of job requirements for skills development, than a true reflection of an increase in the leadership role EA plays within e-government (RealiRM, 2011).

Notwithstanding its own performance, EA is still being presented with an opportunity to prove its own worth to e-government and enabling service delivery. To achieve this objective, the South-African EA industry would clearly have

to re-invent itself considerably, "grow up" and start earning its keep.

In keeping with the above-mentioned opportunity, this chapter would show the following:

1. The relevance of a post-modern EA ontology to the South African e-government context.
2. The relative ease with which mainstream EA could be introduced into a developing economy.
3. The significance of the results achieved within challenging, sociological conditions.

BACKGROUND

The discussion in this chapter is primarily supported by 3 items of practical research spanning a period of more than 12 years. Within these documents, credit is given to the body of knowledge preceding it. The SE (Systems Engineering) ontology, which later became an EA approach, was conceptualized in 1998. This was at a time when the dotcom bubble was about to burst, when global IT project failures became an economic force to be reckoned with (Charette, 2004). It was also a time of mergers and acquisitions, a time where globalization was fast maturing, warts and all (Johnson & Turner, 2003).

The fundamental theory for this approach was developed and implemented in test form within the telecoms systems-engineering domain. As part of a formalization process, it was later encapsulated in an unpublished dissertation (Benjamin, 2006).

A tested version of the systems-engineering ontology was first introduced to the world in 2008 as a white paper for the PICMET '08 conference (Benjamin, 2008). As subject, it used a real e-government project.

The following year a further development in the form of an EA framework was submitted for review to the IEEE's PICMET '09 conference (Benjamin, 2009). These white papers resembled the backbone of an emerging, hybrid EA methodology, later proving suitable for supporting e-government initiatives. In 2002, emerging, hybrid methodologies constituted 5% of mainstream project methodologies (Curtis & Cobham, 2002).

Further development has been on going to find the most-acceptable recipe for engaging with government via this ontology. In 2009 the importance of enterprise data administration escalated with the establishment of the DAMA (data administration association) and its various chapters all over the world (DAMA, 2011).

The author's work resonated with the concepts of DAMA. A proposal for "grassroots" data-administration practices was drafted and indirectly introduced to government agencies in various provinces to be tested for acceptance. In all cases the indication was that the acceptance level was probably high.

Further project work in 2010 and 2011 included the first, solution-based introduction of a formal version of the data-administration guidelines and procedures to Ekurhuleni Municipality in Gauteng. This introduction saw the start of a "standard" model for operationalizing e-government in terms of data administration.

The proposed EA model is still progressing in its practical value, focussed on becoming a standardized, e-government model for developing economies.

MAIN FOCUS OF THE CHAPTER

An EA Approach to the South African Government

The EA approach in this chapter adopts the view where organizational decision making flows within a five-level, organizational decision hierarchy (refer to Figure 4). Whereas Curtis & Cobham (2002) suggested the much-used 3-level triangle, the 5-level decision hierarchy seemingly increases the granularity and accuracy of enterprise function,

and decision making. It is likely to encourage an increase in data granularity and accuracy.

It is asserted how an increase in the efficacy of EA data-administration practices, would probably lead to an improvement of e-governance, and thus e-government practices (see Figure 1).

South Africa has a highly-complex, e-government environment. The democratically-elected government has become the largest enterprise in South Africa to be administered and managed by persons who are undergoing a steep learning curve. Its adoption of the developmental concept of PPP (Public Private Partnership) has produced hybridized enterprises, meaning private enterprises tightly coupled with government (Bender & Gibson, 2010).

This author worked closely with a group of EAs from IBM, South Africa. EA encapsulates numerous disciplines and specialities. During work sessions to specify a collective view on EA, no less that 50 knowledge components were discovered within the EA system. Each one of these components represented a fully-fledged subject within either IT, or Business Administration. For the 1st time, the enormous extent of EA was visualized. Further, it became clear how EA could only be engineered as a systemic solution, or as a service to enterprise, and not implemented as a job performed by individuals and small bands of consultants.

It is this large-scaled systemic expertise, which seems to be lacking within the industry. It takes many years' of experience before systemic competency is developed. Given that B-BBEE (Broad-Based Black Economic Empowerment) was enacted in 2003, and mainstreamed around 2008, it could be asserted how the South African government has been offered relatively little time for any form of EA expertise to develop within its midst (BUSA, 2008).

The service economy in South Africa may have regressed to a hybrid service/production economy. When dealing with e-government officials, it is more common to encounter a "production" mind

Figure 1. E-governance life cycle

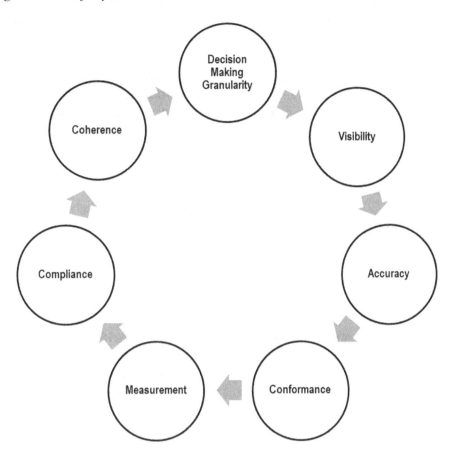

set, as opposed to a "services" mind set. In general, officials seemingly expect "tangible" results in the form of diagrams, reports, project plans, meetings, facts and figures.

Given such operational-level results, it could well be argued that little creative room has been left for e-government EAs to engage in product and service solution design, or for assisting with medium-to-long term enterprise strategies. This does not mean that no room has been allowed for this EA role at all. Rather, it is suggested how the required application of "EA-type" of roles fall outside the provisioned scope of, commonly-accepted EA theory.

Theoretical EA may have become misaligned with the needs of e-organizational realities. In general, EA seemingly contain skill sets, which

are best suited to mature environments. As such, "traditional" EA would seem more suited to developed economies where enterprise and systems maturity are well advanced and where investment funds are generally more accessible.

When dealing with economies exhibiting low levels of maturity, it may become appropriate for the theoretical context of EA to be re-established. A more-relevant EA context would surely have to be specified for South Africa and other developing economies. It is asserted how the global, IE (Information Engineering) fraternity would find such a mind shift very difficult to accept. IE theory was mainly founded on theoretical development and practical cases within developed economies. Further, EA did not originate from Africa, or developing economies. For the most part, it is a product of the Western world, of developed economies. If such a mind shift was possible and a theoretical EA standard for developing economies could be developed, then global EA relevance could be scaled exponentially.

EA has extensive methodologies and a significant knowledge toolset to deal with environmental complexities. Therefore, the EA mind-set holds tremendous value to e-government, even beyond IT solutions. Following are a few examples within the South African government where such value was indeed realised:

- A multi-national vendor alleged how an e-government deputy director had signed a technical change order on the rollout of a multi-million Euro IT project. This change order would've generated much revenue for this multi-national, at the expense of business continuity for this critical, e-government area of business. When an EA mind-set was applied, it enabled the parties to come to understanding of how the relevant document was technically incorrect, morally unfair, and unlawful. The multi-national vendor was tasked to fix the problem at own cost and to bring business back on line again.
- In another instance a name-brand auditing house's subsidiary wanted to charge an e-government department more than Euro 60,000 for critical software to support their proprietary computer program used by the client. This e-government agency requested the support of EA and on recommendation the "lock-in" strategy of the vendor was negated, the contract was not renewed, and a better technological solution was installed at an estimated cost of Euro 2,000.

Unfortunately, many more costly examples exist where e-government agencies would not seek EA assistance, or did not know enough about technology and process to realise assistance had

to be sought from EA. Such instances point to a likely gap in understanding the role and application of EA services.

Understanding the Current Operational Environment of EA-Influence and e-Governance Frameworks within South Africa

During the years spent with various governmental agencies and departments, it was observed that a high degree of sensitivity existed around aspects of autonomy and jurisdiction.

In this context, autonomy is referred to as the right to decide over a specific area of operations. Further, jurisdiction would be viewed as the legal (mandated) right to say what an autonomous area of operation should be, what it should do, and even how it should perform its operations. It is quite understandable why government departments would have sensitivities over such areas, especially when they are mandated to implement acts of law and overarching policies.

Based on briefings by government officials during IT requirements work sessions, it has become apparent how "IT" has increasingly been drawn into areas of service conflict to help bring about changes at socio-political level. Within South Africa, e-government IT projects often harbour explicit political agendas. For example, a particular project plan addressed the administration of fresh water as a resource, whilst secretively following a forensics design to identify a suspected stream of corruption.

Adaptive skills are required for EA efficacy in South Africa. Whilst general EA skills have seemingly fallen into low demand, they may have been offset by a significant increase in the demand for skills supporting political processes within governmental organizations. In the absence of adaptive EA practices, such fundamental changes in the demand for EA services may have impacted negatively on the national EA industry, and the development of a reputable, South-African EA workforce.

Service delivery has become a key political issue in South Africa (South African Government Information, 2009). Whilst it seems that advisers to e-government may be advocating a single, e-service product suite as the solution to all service woes, it remains unclear how this would be done via a technology products alone. Further, it is asserted that if EA were to "come down to earth" to engage with community and all the stakeholders, it may just find a collection of solution components in unlikely places, such as within e-governance itself. Such engagement would require a different skill set, not currently espoused by theoretical EA.

Lack of Service Delivery: A Different Perspective

It was observed how trust issues seemingly existed between government and the private sector. From an EA perspective, it would seem that such sensitivities may often have been purposely initiated and furthered by unscrupulous, private enterprises trying to embed themselves into the governmental system, some perhaps via PPP arrangements. The net result seems to be that EA opportunities to influence e-government decision making have become increasingly exclusive.

For example, let's consider the case against point solutions. A point solution is deemed to be a stand-alone technical solution, or one which does not integrate with, or enhance the existing IT infrastructure of a department, or technology configuration. By design, a point solution would not be able to positively affect e-government in any true sense. It exists, and works, in relative isolation. E-government cannot function publicly in isolation, yet isolation is the state that is seemingly emerging.

In the main, it has seemingly become acceptable for commercial suppliers to deliver point ICT solutions in "support" of e-government. These

solutions are often sold with highly cryptic, and politically correct "safe" statements of value, in order to not be found wanting. For example, many products promised to save money and time, to transfer knowledge and to create employment. On assessment, if these products delivered as promised, why would service delivery still be lacking?

A point solution would typically not be deemed to conform to holistic EA standards of any kind. If by some chance it did manage to satisfy clear EA standards, it would not be deemed to fit within EA's holistic systems philosophy and practices. It seems reasonable to ask the question: who sets these standards within e-government? Are they set by the trusted few within PPPs, or based on the EA industry as a whole?

It has already been suggested that South Africa may have lost most of its EA prowess at a mature level. This could mean that few, institutionalized e-government frameworks remain to filter proposed technology-related solutions of any kind. The EA shields seem to be down and without those EA shields, e-government and citizens could be left widely exposed to disruptive, state-of-the-art technologies. It seems an opportune moment to restate a rhetorical question: Why do the public really have such a negative experience with most e-government services in South Africa?

Modern technology has seemingly obscured the point-solution argument. By probably using EA thinking, marketing experts have been able to repackage point solutions as solution platforms offering end-to-end "services." As with the origin of most EA theory, such platforms originate from the developed economies of the Western world. Once these "offshore" platforms are contracted into a developing economy, they effectively prescribe the direction of e-government practices via its embedded software processes.

It could be asserted how such "platform management tools" mostly contain the equivalent of "stealth" technology, which provide technical managers with eyes and ears on e-government practices – all in the name of systems and data administration. In many instances, access to sensitive information is acquired, which may not have been specifically granted via the spirit or intent of commercial agreements. In addition, such management processes often do not synchronize with the environmental realities of developing economies and the practical demand for basic services.

In keeping with its origins, packaged platform solutions are typically presented to government via multinational enterprises, which may often be bundled into strategic alliances with PPPs. Invariably, they are aimed at penetrating provincial, or national e-government levels. These "solutions" also typically come replete with EAs and a host of other consulting staff, conveniently trained in the delivery of such platforms.

EAs in the know would recognize this trend as a fragmentation effect, as one where multiple point solutions would add up to an exponential diminishing of value inherent in tightly-integrated ICT environments. Some may even view this as a hostile takeover of sorts. By no means could such practices be in the strategic interests of the Republic of South Africa and its citizens.

e-Government and the multinationals. Most multinational enterprises reserve their best talent for the developed economies, which often means they rely on the same diffused, local talent within a restricted pool of skills for developing economies. These skills are often offered at triple its value to government and the tax payer. In one such a case, it was observed how a prominent multinational was allegedly being paid Euros 1,000 per hour for such a "specialist." To put it into a proper, economic perspective, this 1 **hour** approximates twice the per capita **monthly** personal income of South Africans.

Somehow, multinationals still tend to get major contracts within South Africa, almost always accompanied by some obscure B-BBEE newcomer, or one who barely has any credentials of delivering e-government solutions. Multinationals have seemingly learned to "partner" with a preferred B-BBEE, or fund a new one, and in that way get access to lucrative business deals, which would exclusively favour their "EA" views, their products, and their offerings. For the time being, there seems to be no industry balancing factor at all.

It is asserted how such an exclusivity economy, or monopoly, may neither be healthy for the Southern-African EA industry, nor the South-African economy as a whole.

The dreaded "C" word. Corruption has absolute relevance to EA, in the sense that EA may find itself implicated, challenged and compromised by inappropriate requests. EA practitioners may also be requested to draft and present solutions in a biased manner to favour particular outcomes.

It is of grave concern to notice how previously-professional EA practitioners have been willing to compromise their profession for the sake of personal benefits. These persons know how to write up the EA documentation to pass the government processes, to circumvent checks and balances, and position solutions in a jargon and manner to pass initial reviews. They are the deal makers in the background, the silent attendees making notes at briefings holding great value, or the authoritative presenters at steering-committee meetings.

Activities of corruption are a travesty to the trusting public, and to the many, sincere e-government officials who are intent on service delivery as their mandate. Corruption destroys budgets, stops progress, and undermines law and order. In addition, it places the government and the nation at considerable risk.

In the absence of objective, EA-driven auditing systems, reports may easily disappear, or even be altered at will. Opposing stakeholders could be re-arranged (the sideways promotion thing), and "solution" presentations could easily be made repeatedly until the desired outcomes are achieved. Under such conditions, people tend to lose hope, and start accepting the status quo.

Clearly, "corruption-related" *opportunities* need to exist first before government officials could become part of them, even if they existed from within the ranks of government. The contention is made that the ones who corrupt at scale may not necessarily be *in* government. Even though they might be holding official positions, they may not qualify as civil servants at all.

Many ex senior officials of government have seemingly been employed into decision-making positions within private enterprises. It has almost become a who's who of industry decision making. Once the loop between such a private placement and e-government has been closed, especially within a context of PPP jurisdiction, then free-market competition evaporates. Public "service" then becomes a cloak word for political agenda. No room is left for an inclusive, EA-industry perspective.

Many e-government "officials" who enriched themselves have long left government. Some were never listed as government officials, yet enjoyed full government privileges. Others still could be found appointed to senior, decision making positions within existing, or new e-government-friendly enterprises. To them, their sense of "entitlement" to public funds does not pass as corruption.

Regardless of motive or opinion, such a failure in promised services to the people is a failure in e-government obligation. Where such failures include non-South African decision makers in any form, it could easily become a matter of national security.

The dire need for EA to deliver a critical road-map towards policy-driven practices to secure and manage government data cannot be stressed enough. National treasures should not be left in the hands of individuals, but should be dealt with as a transparent system of management, of checks and balances. Similar to the dreaded "C" word, surfaced the dreaded "T" word, namely Transparency.

According to KPMG (2011), in their advisory to India, e-governance transparency may be enabled via a technological approach. It is interesting to note that their EA perspective assumed the need for government business processes to be re-engi-

neered. Whilst the inclusion of a BPM (Business Process Management) competency is regarded as a plus, their implication that the client-engagement life cycle had to include process re-engineering as a "standard" KPMG e-government practice remains questionable.

In general, the EA industry has not stated an observation, or considered any client engagement norm where e–government business processes are necessarily in error, or in need of re-engineering rescue efforts. A qualified EA mind-set would suppose that any change to an enterprise, especially at governance level, would constitute significant risk to service delivery.

Further, such changes, when scaled to exponential level, would in all probability reduce the economic growth of such an enterprise due to the instability it might introduce at the macro-economic level. As such, a sound EA approach would be at great pains not to exceed the thresholds of change tolerance inherent in organizational systems, as purely theoretical systems. This is the main argument in favour of a scientific vs populist-based EA approach for developing economies.

Barroso (2011) included stability as a key concern for a growing the European market. Fiscal discipline at local level and efficient competition were two other main issues to complement the economic effects of stability. From an EA perspective, such issues should be taken note of and supportive architectures implemented for the benefit of South Africa, Africa, and the global partner nations to its economy. Perhaps, this view flies in the face of the existing status quo within South Africa?

This author would like to issue a constant challenge to pre-judicial "assumptions" within EA frameworks from developed economies, regarding e-governance business processes within developing economies.

Government data is by default regarded as a national asset, similar to a nuclear power station, or a national airline. In a developed economy, would foreign national and private persons be allowed to access such facilities at will, to affect it at will? Is this perhaps the real state of corruption within South Africa, the complete compromise of national assets, and in doing so, putting the unknowing, ever-believing public at considerable risk?

It is at this level of impact where commercial activities, as economic activities of monetary profit and loss, take on a more-threatening tone, where profit and loss may be extended to risk human lives, property, and the environment.

Considering the risk associated with global warming, and the incidence of global social unrest, would non-transparent practices not indirectly be putting nations, or continents at risk? Further, would it not negate potential returns on appropriate investment in those countries?

In summary, the line between fair economic activity and corruption is simultaneously both clear and fuzzy. The notion of any PPP being in competition with a large portion of the private sector is a disturbing one. How would one appease the emerging paradox of e-government, economic growth, profit, corruption, and service delivery?

What do Government Agencies Demand from EA?

On analysis, the primary justification for e-government projects seemed to be the enablement of enterprise-information coherence and data integrity. It seems the previously-observed barrier of inaccessibility to Technology has gradually shifted to issues of Organization, People, and Processes, and in that order.

Whilst dealing with the socio-technical issues affecting e-government, requests seem to focus around the need to help deliver socio-political and socio-economical solutions to the public. This is far more complex than administrative, service delivery would be. To complicate matters even further, service providers are seemingly expected to manage the political complexity as part and parcel of a project. Such an expectation may have given rise to an emerging pattern of choosing mono-cultural solution providers for delivering services to e-government.

How would multi-nationals possibly relate to an emerging, mono-cultural commercial preference within e-government? It is suspected that multi-national service providers who thus form part of PPPs could well be fulfilling the roles of 3rd-party product suppliers, transformational funders, and possibly even the façade of fair competition. On analysis, the same names, in different commercial "clothing," could be repeatedly associated with mega projects.

Due to perceived political sensitivities, street-wise officials have learned to be very careful about exposing their careers by introducing initiatives into e-government. To many e-government officials, the concept of EA is at once both foreign and new. It is unlikely that most would adopt an approach, which did not receive the official "nod" of approval. This would be the case even if it was an internationally-recognized EA practice.

Senior officials are usually pleased to discover the existence of local content and examples of ready success within the proposed approach to e-government solutions. The more the successes, the easier it would become to justify the benefits of the approach. With published successes, it would also become less risky to politicians who need to sponsor and/or request this e-government approach. However, few successes exist.

In summary, the positive reception thus far, to the EA approach proposed herein, could be regarded as excellent news for perhaps a fledgling, South-African EA role. Where such qualities are valued, the approach's tenets of **inclusion, transparency, auditability, and respect** have slowly been able to overcome much scepticism and mistrust towards such practices. Access to industry acceptance, government recognition, and development funding is expected to remain the primary, future challenge. There seems to be very-little demand from e-government for "mainstream" EA as we know it.

E-GOVERNMENT ISSUES

In the light of this example of tentative, EA progress, let us consider a few stark issues, which might still be facing EA and e-government.

Failure to deliver e-government solutions would always have a significant internal cost. Such costs do not pertain to money alone. In financial terms though, one could think of this cost as opportunity cost. Sometimes the demand for services is met and exceeded, but most often the e-government demand remains undiscovered, ill-specified via tenders, hidden, and ill supplied.

e-Government failure erodes organizational trust. From an EA perspective, inappropriate practices by officials and vendors eventually degrade e-government gains and capabilities. Even where e-government failure occurred for genuine operational reasons, diminished organizational trust has been observed, cynicism crept in, and finger pointing resulted.

Essential services are non-negotiable services. Essential services are matters of life and death, and pertain to the overall value government places on its own abilities and society as a whole. By way of its essential services, government has to answer to the public on its stance to the environment, safety, security, property, and life. It becomes a national issue with far-reaching consequences. It is in the arena of essential services where EA has a significant e-government role to play, to enable enterprise-wide services via core designs and integrated synergy.

Expertise to engineer policies into operational procedures is in short supply. EA expertise would often require a minimum of postgraduate qualification and many years' of practical experience. The financial cost of paying for specialised, policy-engineering services are often not adequately described within the WBS (Work Breakdown Structure) of programme/project planning – and therefore deemed superfluous, or viewed with suspicion. When EA services are not transpar-

ently institutionalized, the benefits of systems-engineering continuity may not be maintained.

Reckless control of budgets. Government officials are not the owners of the budgets they are meant to administer. It is not their money per se and they ought to give an account for every cent spent. Many officials have seemingly failed to accept this basic fact. Education and certification on a best-fit, EA mind-set regarding e-governance might encourage sustainable, results-oriented budgeting. This would do away with innovative budgeting practices.

Exploitation of EA services. A trend has been observed where EA service providers are expected to bear upfront solution requirements and design costs in order to submit proposals in response for possible projects. Increasingly, it has been noted how officials would use submitted proposals unethically to do insider trading with, or to play one supplier off against another. Further, loyalty has its price, meaning that once a service provider was engaged, government officials might expect frequent visitations and costly presentations for free.

The absence of a respectable EA competency for e-government is a growing issue for the EA industry. It is suggested how a seeming lack of intra-governmental buy in to help establish their EA competency could eventually minimize the EA industry considerably.

A few, rotten eggs. Fortunately, it seems to be more a case of the few, ethically-challenged officials giving the conscientious ones a bad name, than a general demise in administrative responsibility. It has been noticed how, with a proper marketing approach and presentation of value, government officials would generally be content to pay for controlled EA services, even if the demand for such services remained relatively low. While many decision makers may not be practicing corruption, the possibility does exist that "e-government culture" may have conditioned them to turn a blind eye to questionable activities.

Impractical EA processes. EA services need to be presented at a practical level where it would make sense to e-government officials and staff. No fancy jargon or abstract diagrams. When EA was made practical via the approach in this chapter, a "standard" process for engaging with e-government emerged. This high-level process would work as follows:

1. A proposal would be submitted to conduct a phase of the EA SDLC (Systems Development Life Cycle), for example requirements engineering.
2. If the client would not approve the proposal, thus allocate budgets to this project phase, then no further work would be performed, no designs have been submitted, and no IP (Intellectual Property) would be lost.
3. However, if the requirements phase was approved, project work would commence.
4. Once the initial phase of work was completed, a proposal for the design phase would be forwarded for approval. It would be made transparently clear to the client how the requirements phase of the project would inform the solution phase.
5. Again, if the proposal for a design phase was not approved, no design work would be done and no IP would be lost.
6. The net value would be that the client would still have received a complete requirements specification which could then be used for internal communication, or to plan further projects from. Tangible value was delivered at every step of the process.
7. If the proposed solution design was approved, the phases for building and commissioning the product would be proposed.
8. At times, it would be deemed appropriate to include an additional proposal for support services for the product, so as to be transparent about the total estimated cost of services.
9. Again, no further project work would be conducted until the building and commis-

sioning proposal has been approved. Due to the cost-implication of lapsed time, the addendum for support could still be left open for negotiations later on.

No governance-driven EA model. On the one hand, the absence of any "standard" solution process seemingly provided vendors with an opportunity to bypass policy-alignment aspects and to proceed directly to rolling out computer applications at their lowest cost. On the other hand, e-government officials have seemingly shown scant regard for proposal validity periods and efforts to offer best-in-class for the best price. The solution-acceptance criteria have seemingly become non-EA based, subjective and biased.

It was observed how service providers had to maintain the pricing and specification of a proposal for months on end, and to continually absorb all costs and technology changes. A governance-driven EA model would have ensured that tender proposals remained strategically and commercially relevant.

It is estimated that less than 5% of South-African municipalities would be able to show a relevant, EA practice. They would probably refer such queries to IT. It has been found that municipal IT departments remain heavily focussed on products and embroiled in a substantial Business/IT tug-of-war. EA's ability to help bring synergy to these organizational divisions is much needed.

Lack of data administration standards. As a general rule, the SABS (South African Bureau of Standards) language is hardly ever heard within government departments. Many SANS (South African National Standard) requirements have not been made compulsory, which enables provincial government to implement frameworks of data-quality management as they see fit.

To date, no practical, e-government framework for data administration has been found to be in use for guiding provincial-level standards and practices and for establishing data-auditing policies and compliance. Many ICT officials within the South-African government would disagree vehemently with the previous statement, but the point of the statement is not to suggest that frameworks, and even standards, may not exist in written form, somewhere.

Rather, a categorical statement is being made how such policies may not be readily observed, nor made available in practice, and could thus be deemed immature for ISO9001 certification. The knock-on effect of flexible e-government "standards" becomes apparent when considering the relationship between ICT infrastructure and business processes.

It is asserted how conformance to ITIL3, as ISO20000, would simply not be possible if ISO9001 was not operational in the first instance. ICT infrastructure, as an enabler of business process, would fail in part due to the absence of non-standardised business processes and data artefacts (documentation). This is an enterprise issue.

Where such frameworks and standards might exist in a mature, operational form, it would primarily be within respective IT departments, or within the office of the CIO (Chief Information Officer) via outsourced, commercial data centres and so on, and more as a symbol of "individual" competence rather than of an explicit, national, e-government policy.

SOLUTIONS AND RECOMMENDATIONS

The EA activities discussed in this chapter typically occurred under trying and even hostile conditions. Often, they had to be adapted to the environment in order to be allowed the opportunity and influence they have wielded.

In gratitude for the opportunities within e-government thus far, the proposed approach has been tried and tested for flexibility, economy, timeliness, and delivery. It delivered agreed and measurable e-government value. Most impor-

tantly, it has managed to survive various tests on its integrity.

This approach is not fool proof. As long as it remains in manual form, it would be exposed to human motives. Thus far, it has passed in every instance of deployment, on merit alone. Following are suggestions for increasing the probability of EA and e-government success:

Automate EA-Driven, Data-Administration Standards

Within the South African context, it seems desirable to eliminate opportunities for human error. Computerized automation of the proposed, data-administration practice is relatively easy to achieve. It would take the form of "hook-ups" to data-administration within centralized, database-driven applications, culminating in a specialized data-administration centre. Unified, data-administration centres would provide e-government information pertaining to the e-governance lifecycle functionality as suggested in Figure 1.

Some would be specialized in governance functions. Others would be scaled centres, where data gets rolled up as would be the case in data marts, or MIS (Management Information System) and BIS (Business Information System) solutions. Data unification and explicit data-administration practices are primary objectives of this design. For purposes of national security, centres should not be outsourced, but developed as in-house, e-government competencies.

Further, as a protection against abuse, function-oriented centres should be jointly-managed by a federation of representative e-government officials. For example, all the relevant agencies for joint operations around traffic management would form a federation to manage that specific data centre.

Activate the National EA Function within E-Government

SETA's (Sector Education and Training Authority) contribution has seen no practical value at municipal level. e-Government projects often end up being no more than vendor-product implementations at a local level, or stepping stones for selling and promoting more products and services from.

To protect e-government and effective service delivery, government agencies should set up a competent, national-EA function which is tightly integrated with, and operationally correlated to EA activities at provincial and municipal levels. This national EA function should open itself up to an annual independent audit by a respected body of continental and inter-continental EA practitioners and standards.

It should be willing to research and develop, as well as subscribe to best EA practices for developing economies within agreed curricula and standards of certified education. It would benefit from this global association via access to EA practitioner training, common EA models, skills and competency support and professional services

Activate EA within the municipalities.

In order to act, municipalities do not have to wait for national, or provincial government agencies to give them permission. They are mandated and empowered within the various Acts to implement e-government data governance. This chapter recommends a sustainable approach as a 1st step to e-government success. All government agencies, at any level, could kick off with the business process in "Getting Started: The Data Administration Business Process."

Set Compulsory Data-Administration Standards, SOGs and SOPs

Data-administration standards should clearly specify how data should be managed within e-

government, at any level of government. These standards should be specified as SOGs (Standard Operational Guidelines) and SOPs (Standard Operational Procedures), to ISO9001 level, audited, and enforced.

Use EA Competency to the Maximum

EA has a highly-specialized mind set for assisting with e-government projects. Enlist EA services to assess the long-term cost and service-delivery implications of e-government contracts pertaining to **Technology, Organization, People, Process**.

Incorporate EA services as standard packages of work within e-government projects. Where budgets should limit the appointment of full-time EA's, the project office should set a standard to ensure all projects include this aspect of audit and quality control within their project plans, and justify the payment of supervisory EA services on the hand of the e-government objectives and measurable data-administration deliverables.

Keep EA Practical and Deliver Justifiable Value

This is a large area of practitioner application. Start by using the suggested business process for data-administration.

Fight E-Government Non-Compliance and Corruption

Standardized, data-administration practices would detect and highlight anomalies and potential abuses. E-Government officials could learn and adapt as they progress.

FUTURE DIRECTIONS

Based on the emergence of virtualization technologies, the future for human-driven data administration within organizations is looking bleak. The reason for this is that technology is increasingly separating human decision making from data-administration automation, embedding it at a level of complexity, which most persons could not suitably comprehend.

Complexity within computerized solutions is fast reaching exponential levels resembling black-box technologies. This is the critical reason why the data-administration aspect of business solutions has to be de-coupled from the computer programs, and placed back into the hands of e-government decision makers. This may also be the justification for the suggested e-government approach and process. It has proven its ability to function well within areas of exponential complexity.

The trends of technology convergence and increased complexity would probably escalate within the next 3-5 years. Technological control over enterprises would therefore increase significantly at the expense of human control. e-Government functionality could become de-humanized and clinical, dealing with masses of the public as statistics, mere blips on a screen or a number of calls, and so on.

Is it perhaps true that the few who would control the technologies would be able to control the business environment? Unless the People aspect of the equation could learn and adapt to this necessary change in scaled service delivery, e-governance could soon be taking on a singular tone.

Within developed economies, it seems likely that EA would be able to increase its influence and decision-making power over enterprise and e-government governance. It would probably do so via its influence on Technology, Process, and Organization. The People would have to follow along.

Within developing nations, a real risk of *total government outsourcing* exists. While this may bode well for multinationals in service of foreign governments, it would have vastly destructive impacts on local economies and social stability. The basic reason for concluding as such is: where technology rules people, it is actually the

motives and will of the designers and owners of the technology which rule the people. Even if nationally-outsourced service delivery to the people should be improved considerably, it would be at the expense of their democratic liberties. The "computer" would become the boss.

The global need for technology is increasing in proportion with the needs and wants of the world's population. Mega factories have become the norm. The road to a mega-everything is seen by post-modernists as the only sensible way to meet the insatiable demand of consumers and populations. Even if this approach seems questionable, it resembles a status quo for ensuring a form of economic and social stability. EAs could play a significant role in this regard, to design and roll out People-focussed, mega programs in support of world health, world economies, world peace, and so on.

The question we need to ask is whether or not it makes intellectual sense, or whether it is academically sound, to place countries in the same category of demand, which might actually be lagging in the technology curve by 5 years and more? Would treating all countries equally in technological terms not be destroying the very essence of global diversity required for the evolution - and thus survival - of mankind?

There are many forms of technology, computers being but one of them. When a particular technology is appointed as a dominant technology, it seems likely to be at the expense of another technology, for example by appointing computers as a dominant technology over societal coherence. What about service delivery?

Following is a practical suggestion for a low-cost, easy-and-simple future EA role within South Africa, and developing economies all over the world. It also offers an e-government approach, which could be used as an alternative by developed nations, to offset the dehumanizing nature of exponential technologies and to increase service delivery.

Figure 2. The policy paradigm

Getting Started: The Data Administration Business Process

Definition: Data administration could be said to be the formal orchestration of Technology, Organization, People, and Process as an enabler of enterprise data.

Higher-Strategic Role

Data Administration would drive the formulation and establishment of data and information standardization within operations, for example SOGs (Standard Operating Guidelines) and SOPs (Standard operating Procedures).

SOGs specify guidelines, which is applicable to the operational use of data resources. SOPs define the step-by-step procedures to be followed operationally in support of the SOGs.

SOGs could be regarded as the operational laws for effectively using e-government data resources and SOPs could be seen as the application of the business rules in support of those laws (See Figure 2).

Over the lifetime of a system, business rules would probably change to accommodate the needs of an Organization. When such business-rule changes occur, a data-administration Process would have to ensure that:

1. The changes in the organizational business processes, and their impact on the associated databases and operational practices, happen in a controlled, consultative, and transparent manner.
2. All changes are properly authorized by all the stakeholders who rely on the e-government system for service delivery.
3. The changes do not conflict with the strategic intent of the policy statements within the collective SOGs.

The adoption and application of a data-administration business process would ensure that a "standard" approach to managing e-government data resources would support the unification and integrity of the information presented within any

Figure 3 - Data Administration Components

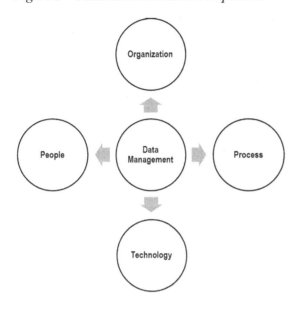

rollup of data, and/or information, in the form of an e-government MIS, or BIS.

Data administration is a critical component in the interactive system, which comprises e-government. It affects, and is affected by Technology, Organization, People, and Process (See Figure 3). These are the primary architectural aspects, which should be addressed by EA and operations managers alike.

Benefits

The 5 main benefits of using an e-governance data-administration business process are:

1. It would provide a first step of compliance towards enabling the e-government lifecycle, namely by establishing the proper handling of government-related data and information.
2. It would help with enabling the Organization towards benefiting further from enterprise-wide archiving, backup and recovery, and disaster-management policies and procedures.
3. It would unify the management aspects of Technology, Organization, People, and

Process – thereby enhancing the overall efficacy of document and information management and e-government service delivery.
4. It would enhance service delivery by providing the correct data in the correct format to the correct systems and persons at the correct location and time for the correct purposes.
5. It would prevent unauthorized impacts on operational data and bring transparency to the impacts business decisions might have on data administration.

People

The 'People' component of data administration represents the decision structure, its user base, and those who interact with Process, via computer-based application, or a manual system.

Data owners within a department would typically decide which documents would be linked to which business activities. Further, they would also determine what data would be required by whom, when, where, how often, and in which format. 'People' also decide how data should be unified and presented as information via reports. In other words, *'People' decide the meaningfulness of data*.

'People' are also one of the main contributors to change within any system. With this change comes the risk of affecting the trustworthiness of the data within a data centre. This effect is often brought about via changes in policy and processes, requests for non-standard reports, and so on.

'People' may also request functional enhancements to an existing system, or training for additional users. All these requests may result in change effects to an MIS, and should therefore be formally managed via a dedicated, enterprise change-management process, which should support the e-government data-administration business process.

As such, a representative group of stakeholders (data administration forum) should probably be established at every level of the decision-making hierarchy to own the e-government, data-administration business process and to ensure its functionality and operational conformance, and compliance.

The following functions have been identified as guidelines for establishing the 'People' component of e-government data administration within a business-unit environment.

- Identifying the appropriate data representatives in each business area.
- Agreeing people roles and responsibilities with their business managers.
- Providing the required training and certification programs to ensure appointees are able to fulfil their roles.
- Ensuring regular management meetings are held to deal pro-actively with all e-government, data-administration requests and issues.
- Ensuring that e-government data administration fulfils its intended function and delivers the expected value to the operational departments.
- Ensuring enhancements, or technical projects, are formally assessed for its potential impact on the data centre.
- Overseeing the timeous, overall, and accurate establishment of training and communication initiatives to ensure all associated persons are able to perform their duties equally.

Process

While Technology and ICT practices are generally owned by the office of the CIO, business processes and their associated data and information are owned by the e-government business departments. This data is typically generated and utilized during departmental workflow activities.

Useful information is produced via value-adding processes and delivered via technological channels in meaningful format and structure.

Policy and operational requirements define the functional value of business processes. They also have a direct influence on the definition of the core, e-government data being utilized by business processes. In general, policies and operational requirements would be encapsulated in written SOGs and SOPs for a particular area.

Once a mature, e-government process foundation has been put into operation via ISO9001 certification, more cost-effective vehicles for representing SOGs and SOPs could be designed. Such advances could range from automatically formatting SOGs and SOPs from an e-government database perspective, or employing AI (Artificial Intelligence) to instantiate the most-current SOGs and SOPs on a JIT (Just In Time) demand basis, as an event-driven system.

The following functions are proposed as guidelines for establishing the Process component of data administration within the e-government data administration services:

- Specifying the ingredients of a data centre's SOGs and SOPs.
- Ensuring SOGs and SOPs are properly documented and distributed to all users for operational use to ISO9001 standard.
- Ensuring policies and procedures exist for managing stakeholders and stakeholder requests.
- Ensuring policies and procedures are put in place for ensuring the trustworthiness of a data centre's source data.
- Ensuring policies and procedures are in place for encouraging conformance and measurement of the operational compliance to SOGs and SOPs.
- Ensuring policies and procedures are in place for linking the compliance results to functional and departmental scorecards. This practice would ensure a sustainable demand for a data-administration service exists.

Figure 4. Data administration decision structure

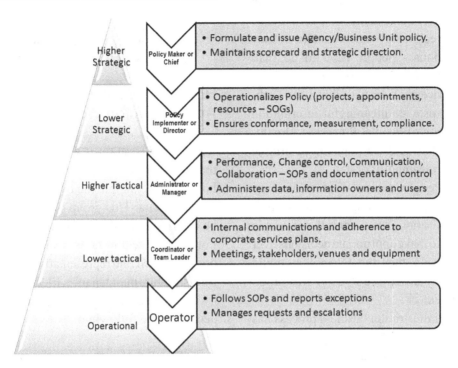

Organization

Organization is the ability to structure people, equipment, knowhow, money, and processes in order to do a particular job. The ability to organise has a direct effect on how a job performs, and thus the ability of work to comply with SOPs and SOGS (as policies and rules). Due to its influence on every aspect of e-government, data administration is regarded as one of those high-level functions, which require a lot of organisation to succeed.

The following functions are proposed as guidelines for establishing the 'Organization' component of data administration.

- Identifying the required resources to per-form data administration with.
- Placing the resources within a decision structure where they could perform (See Figure 4).

- Enabling this structure with People, Process, Technology, and performance criteria.
- Regularly assessing organizational competency, training, mentorship and certification.
- Standardizing best practices at all levels of the data-administration decision hierarchy.
- Institutionalizing best practices for each data centre.

Technology

Technology is the enabler of the combination of Process, Organisation and People. It has the ability to unify data across various departments, and to show data that is usually invisible to the human eye. Technology has the amazing ability to flow across functional departments without having to upset the organisation in any way. It has the power to process volumes of data and to put collected data together in such a way as to show rolled-up views of distributed data centres.

However, Technology cannot make agency business decisions - people need to do that. Technology cannot guarantee quality data either – people and processes need to do that. Last, Technology cannot provide meaningful information - the combination of People, Processes, Organisation, and the business environment determine what would be meaningful or not.

However, People decide what technology should do, and how technology should perform within an organisation. The point is that if people are not enabled to make appropriate decisions over data administration, then the Technology could become a mainly disruptive force of frustration and disappointed.

The data-administration business process has as objective to ensure that the Technology part of the equation performs according to requirements and expectations. This is the EA mind set in action. Technology must do the job it was intended to do and deliver the specified value to the business.

The following functions are proposed as guidelines for establishing the 'Technology' component of data administration:

- Ensuring the data and information requirements are concrete and clearly specified.
- Ensuring the chosen technology can adequately satisfy the data requirements.
- Ensuring the chosen technology can access the business data, safely collect the data, and flow it throughout the business, according to the business process rules.
- Ensuring the technology can communicate with other existing technologies within the business environment.
- Ensuring that business departments remain completely in control of their data and processes.
- Ensuring that business departments do not become IT departments.

- Ensuring that the technology supports data integrity, decision support, information trustworthiness, the people who rely upon it, and departmental scorecards.

How Does Data Administration Work?

Data Administration is a People-driven process that is administered by a collective of data stakeholders, for example the owners of different domains of data. This group of stakeholders could be referred to as the data-administration forum. For example, within the data-administration forum one could well find representatives from Revenue, Infrastructure maintenance, Electricity, and so on.

The data administration forum would jointly decide on the following:

1. The People, Process, Organization and Technology aspects for their domain data.
2. How the forum would handle changes to all their domain data.
3. How data security and access to sensitive data would be handled within their respective domains.

It is suggested that data-administration forum representatives take quarterly turns to chair the forum, and to ensure attendance registers, minutes of meeting, and progress reports are being completed and properly archived for auditing purposes.

Further, the data-administration forum would ensure that the right data would be available to the right person at the right time. To enable this, the forum would have jurisdiction over:

- The ICT architecture and tools required.
- Appropriate Standards, Policies and Procedures for good governance and compliance.
- The establishment of a culture of data quality.

- How communication is established at all decision levels.
- Adequate education for all end users of systems, or creators of data.
- Data-administration role players receiving certified training.
- How data administration would be incorporated in a policy-enabled performance management process.

Lower-Strategic Role

In order to implement the required data-administration component, the following high-level activities would have to be performed:

- Incorporating data quality principles into 'People' roles and responsibilities, and into job descriptions, to ensure all stakeholders practice avoidance of poor data.
- Ensuring that 'People' who act on behalf of their business areas are capable of fulfilling their data-administration roles.
- Ensuring that 'People' have the authority to act on behalf of data and processes within their areas of business.
- Setting up a federal forum where all stakeholder agencies, and other 3rd parties, are represented in decision making pertaining to the operational use and management of an operational database.
- Encouraging the establishment of Data Forums to address data issues throughout the 'Organization'. Data Stewards/ Operators should have the respect of the business users who will then report data issues at the earliest point of intervention.

Tactical Role

Training in data-administration policies and practices should be administered to all persons who contribute to, or access a data centre. Most errors in data quality could be eliminated during the ETL (Extract, Transform, Load) process. Re-training of administration staff may be indicated where significant changes have been made to a data centre, for example adding new fields for recording data in, or altering business processes using the data, and so on.

Every attempt should be made to achieve a standard level of approved data-administration certification for each member of the federated decision-making team. This certification could be an in-house, e-government certification. It is **not recommended** to follow the DAMA route of data-administration certification.

The main reason for this is that it does not appear to be **suitable for current, South African conditions** and could disrupt the practical value a "grassroots" approach would bring. Once the maturity level of data administration has been established to ISO9001 and level 3 of business processes, then selective DAMA certification of technically-oriented supervisors could be implemented. At current levels of federated maturity, such certification could be considered to be imprudent and wasteful expenditure.

This is an area where EA could currently have a significant impact on People and Organizational aspects of e-government. Data-quality awareness pertains to the accounting principle of GIGO (Garbage In, Garbage Out). This means that if rubbish data is fed into a database, then nonsensical information would show up in reports. The level of quality of a database could be vastly improved by carefully managing the quality of the source data as well as the integrity of the data.

Data quality awareness also has to do with awareness of the e-government data lifecycle. Changes to any database's source, or database itself, would directly affect the capabilities of agency decision making. Therefore, all changes to data must be closely managed to achieve the best possible data-quality effect on service delivery.

Functional rollout of data administration would require a degree of "hand-holding" by EA consultants. All fresh beginnings need maximum support. EA services should include mentorship on federated data administration.

Once established, further services could be designed and rolled out without compromising the data integrity of, what should become "business as usual." Autonomy and jurisdiction of all stake-holders should be guaranteed throughout the value chain. Cross-functional synthesis would probably ensue via data-administration workflow across the various EA components for each instance of an EA application, or service (Benjamin, 2009).

CONCLUSION

This chapter focused on the essence of e-government services, on the issues of quality of life and the retention of societal values. It suggested how in order to move faster people may have to slow down a little. It attempted to show how a global EA mind-set could be utilized to enable everyday benefits to the masses, in the form of re-humanized Technology, Organization, People and Process activities.

Further, it was suggested how the same change-inducing technology could by choice be used differently, in a way where less would be more, where the runaway train of technological progress would not necessarily have to be adopted, especially in developing economies.

There are alternatives to technological dominance, to building empires via technology. These alternatives reside in the faith and hope in People, in the essential good of man. It is strange how technological progress has seemingly brought about a situation where the Freudian Soul of Man must again be addressed, and this, via the Soul of a Machine.

REFERENCES

Barroso, J. M. D. (2011). *President of the European Commission Press conference in advance of the European Council Brussels, 21 June 2011*. Retrieved September 4, 2011, from http://europa.eu/rapid/pressReleasesAction.do?reference=SPEECH/11/459

Bender, P., & Gibson, S. (2010). *Mbombela (Nelspruit) water and sanitation concession South Africa*. Retrieved September 4, 2011, from http://www.ppp.gov.za/documents/casestudies/Nelspruit%20Case%20Study%20Final%2029%20May%202010.pdf

Benjamin, R. (2006). *Project success as a function of project management methodology: An emergent systems approach*. Unpublished Master's thesis, University of Hull, UK.

Benjamin, R. (2008). *Last-mile knowledge engineering: Quest for the Holy Grail? An emergence-based approach to complex systems engineering (forward, reverse, and re-engineering)*. Management of Engineering & Technology, 2008. Retrieved May 25, 2011, from http://ieeexplore.ieee.org/xpl/freeabs_all.jsp?arnumber=4599702

Benjamin, R. (2009). *Project success and the component architecture management framework (CAMF)*. Retrieved May 25, 2011, from http://www.nanogr8.com/37201/39501.html

BUSA. (2008). *A practitioner's guide to the codes of good conduct on broad-based economic empowerment.*

Charette, R. (2004). *IT project failures or blunders?* Retrieved November 11, 2004, from www.cutter.com/research/2004/edge040427.html

Curtis, G., & Cobham, D. (2002). *Business information systems: Analysis, design and practice* (4th ed.). Harlow, UK: Prentice Hall.

DAMA. (2011). *Website*. Retrieved May 25, 2011, from http://www.dama.org/i4a/pages/index.cfm?pageid=1

Johnson, D., & Turner, C. (2003). *International business: Themes and issues in the modern global economy*. New York, NY: Routledge. doi:10.4324/9780203634141

KPMG. (2011). *E-Governance: Enabling transparency and efficiency in government*. Retrieved September 4, 2011, from http://www.kpmg.com/IN/en/WhatWeDo/Advisory/Performance-Technology/ITAS/eG_Links/eGovernance.pdf

Langeni, L. (2010, August 19). Ambassador warns SA over media tribunal. *Business Day*. Retrieved May 25, 2011, from http://www.businessday.co.za/articles/Content.aspx?id=118388

Reali, R. M. (2011). *EA forum - Cape Town*. The Vines Sanlam Head Office, 2011/09/30: 10:00 AM

South African Government Information. (2009). *Key issues*. Retrieved May 25, 2011, from http://www.info.gov.za/issues/index.htm

KEY TERMS AND DEFINITIONS

Automation: The optimal application of computer-enabled processing power and logic to repeatable packages of organizational work with the intent to minimize the need for human intervention.

Components: Components are part of a system, which collaborate within a system context to achieve a common goal.

Data Administration: The business aspect of managing data.

Design: A specification of components and functional ingredients, which collaborate over particular logic to satisfy a model of principles.

EA (Enterprise Architecture): The design principles governing an enterprise in terms of standard systems components, which include at least decision structure, governance, data, information, function, business process, business rules, application, and technology infrastructure.

EA Diplomacy: A demeanour and approach best suited for achieving mutual respect, consensus, and progress within e-government initiatives

e-Government: Is a policy-driven, computerized version of mega-scale services to be managed and administered by government agencies in compliance with a country's constitution and acts.

Governance: A system of laws and rules which relate to a desired state of activity within organizations.

Requirements: A specified structure of a problem's needs, which define functionality to form the shape of a particular solution for that problem.

Transparency: The e-government process for allowing objective EA auditing of all governance-related compliance, policies, practices, projects, processes, procedures, data, systems, and results to forensic level.

Chapter 15

An Architecture Driven Methodology for Transforming from Fragmented to Connected Government:
A Case of a Local Government in Italy

Walter Castelnovo
University of Insubria, Italy

ABSTRACT

Connected government implies that citizens and enterprises can interact with government as with a single entity rather than with a number of different public authorities. In countries characterized by a highly fragmented system of Local Government, connected government at the local level can be achieved only through a process of progressive integration on a wider area of systems of local government already integrated at the local level. In the chapter, the author argues that this process should be based on a maturity model and a reference model that define the technological and organizational conditions that allow the establishment of more and more integrated aggregations of municipalities. With reference to a study funded by the Region Lombardia (Italy), the chapter introduces the concept of Integrated System of Local Government (ISLG) and describes the process that leads to the establishment of ISLGs as an intermediate step toward connected government at the local level. Moreover, the chapter discusses the conditions that can induce different aggregations of municipalities to comply with a set of standard requirements in the implementation of their integration processes.

DOI: 10.4018/978-1-4666-1824-4.ch015

FROM E-GOVERNMENT TO CONNECTED LOCAL GOVERNMENT

During the past years, a transformation in the concept of E-Government has been observed worldwide, at the point that a discussion was started concerning whether "E-Government is dead." Be this true or not, what is certain is that the high emphasis put on online services as the fundamental goal of E-Government has been constantly lowering in the past years and a new emphasis has been put on the transformational potential of ICTs for public sector transformation.

What such transformation amounts to is:

(...) a continuous process of changing the features of the public sector towards a desired set of features typically defined politically. These features are often service delivery features (e.g. choice of and access to services, speed of service delivery, responsiveness, etc.) or organisational features (e.g. institutional boundaries and responsibilities, cross-organisational collaboration and co-operation, collaboration and co-operation across levels of government, etc.) (OECD, 2007, p. 12).

Public sector transformation concerns both service delivery and organizational transformation. However, ICT enabled service delivery transformation and organizational transformation are strictly related. On the one hand, service delivery cannot be improved without transforming the way in which Government organizations operate to produce and deliver services to citizens and enterprises. As observed in the 2008 United Nations E-Government Survey "an increase in the value of services is not possible without consolidating the way the back-end systems and processes work to bring about the front-end of service delivery" (UNDESA, 2008, p. 5). On the other hand, organizational transformation cannot be considered as a value in itself; actually, Government organizations should transform themselves only insofar this allows them to deliver greater value to citizens.

Focusing on both service delivery transformation and organizational transformation leads to the so-called "Second Generation e-Government Paradigm" that according to the 2008 UN report can be considered as "an emerging paradigm that maintains that to achieve greater value in service delivery and reduce costs, integration and redesign of government organization and processes is a necessity" (UNDESA 2008, p. 5).

This paradigm characterizes the connected/ networked government that "enables governments to connect seamlessly across functions, agencies, and jurisdictions to deliver effective and efficient services to citizens and businesses" (Pallab, 2010, p. 8).

Connected government is usually considered to be a multi-dimensional construct (Kaczorowski, 2004; Pallab, 2010), including dimensions such as:

- Citizen centricity as the guiding principle for the public sector transformation processes, whose goal is to create greater value for citizens, not only for citizens as users/consumers or beneficiaries, but also for citizens as taxpayers, as participants in the democratic processes, as policy makers and employees in public administration agencies and as suppliers and entrepreneurs as well (Castelnovo & Simonetta, 2007)
- Back-office reorganisation, to force the public administration agencies to "rethink their operations to move from being system-oriented to chain-oriented with respect to their structure, functioning, skills and capabilities, and culture and management" (UNDESA, 2008, p. 5)
- Networked organisational model, to transform a fragmented system of government agencies in a networked virtual organization that operates seamlessly toward a common mission, that is to deliver more

value to citizens and enterprises (Johnston, 2006)

- Standardized infrastructures and interoperability, to allow the vertical integration among different levels of Government as well as the horizontal integration among government organizations belonging to the same institutional level (Microsoft, 2011)
- Public sector governance, to guarantee the consistency of the transformation processes implemented both at the Central and the Local Government level, and to assure that all the transformation processes preserve the public interest and increase the value for citizens
- Social inclusion, as a way to bridging the gap between government and citizens, to building trust in government and to assure that no citizen is left behind

In the whole-of-government approach typical of connected government, the public sector transformation process leading to connected government must involve all the public agencies at all the levels comprised within an institutional system. Considering, for instance, the case of Italy this means that besides the Central Government (including all the Central Government agencies and bodies), the public sector transformation process should involve all the 8094 Italian municipalities, as well as the 110 provinces and the 20 regions that make up the Italian system of Local Government.

This raises the problem of how the horizontal and vertical integration among government bodies and agencies that is instrumental for connected government can be achieved within a so highly fragmented system of Local Government.

This problem does not concern only Italy, of course; as shown in Table 1, many European countries are characterized by a highly fragmented system of Local Government.

In a highly fragmented system of Local Government the horizontal and vertical integration

Table 1. The system of local government in the countries of the Europe of 27 (CEMR, 2010)

		1st tier	2nd tier	3rd tier
Federal states	Austria	2357	9	
	Belgium	589	10	6
	Germany	12104	301	16
	Cyprus	378		
	Czech Republic	6250	14	
	Denmark	98	5	
	Estonia	226		
	Finland	342	2	
	France	36682	100	26
	Greece	325	13	
	Hungary	3177	19	
	Ireland	114		
	Italy	8094	110	20
	Latvia	119		
	Lithuania	60		
	Luxembourg	105		
	Malta	68		
	Netherlands	430	12	
	Poland	2479	379	16
	Portugal	308	2	
	Romania	3180	41	
	Slovakia	2928	8	
	Slovenia	210		
	Spain	8116	52	17
	Sweden	290	20	
	United Kingdom	406	28	3
Total EU 27 - year 2009		89699	1125	104
Total EU 27 - year 2008		90782	1171	106

among government bodies and agencies can be better achieved by integrating on a wider territorial scale systems of government organizations already integrated at the local level. Of course, to be carried out effectively, such a process of progressive interorganisational integration requires the availability of a well-defined reference model and a clear roadmap defining the stages and the modalities for the integration, as well as a strong governance of the process. In the absence of these elements, it is not possible to guarantee the coherence of the integration processes carried out at the local level and their consistency with the public sector transformation objectives defined at the higher level.

Although without explicitly referring to the concept of connected government, the problem of how to define a process of progressive integration among Local Government organizations has been considered in a two years research project funded by the Regional Government of Lombardia (Italy) in 2008 and 2009, with the aim of:

- Defining a cooperation model among Local Government organizations that enables the establishment of long-term strategic public-public partnerships at the local level, with the aim of reducing the problems determined by administrative fragmentation through interorganisational cooperation
- Defining a standard process for the design and the establishment of public-public partnerships based on the cooperation model defined within the project
- Defining an interorganisational cooperation maturity model providing a framework for the progressive integration on a wider scale of systems of government organizations already integrated at the local level

This chapter will describe the results of the research project funded by the Region Lombardia, presenting them as an example of how the progressive integration among Local Government organizations could be achieved through a highly standardized transformation process based on:

- Back-office reorganisation, assuming inter-agency cooperation as the fundamental organizing principle and the networked

model as the organizational model to pursue in the public sector transformation
- The attainment of a high level of interoperability among Local Government organizations, not only at the technical level, but also at the operational, organizational and strategic level as well
- A strong governance of the integration process, in order to guarantee the consistency of the transformation processes implemented within a highly fragmented system of Local Government
- The exploitation of the results achieved through the programmes for the spreading of innovation at the local level implemented during the previous years

E-GOVERNMENT IN THE REGION LOMBARDIA (ITALY)

Starting from the year 2003, the development of E-Government in Italy has been based mostly on projects funded under the National Action Plan for E-Government, launched by the National Government with an announcement for the co-financing of ICT based projects with the aim of:

- Using ICTs to achieve a significant increase in quality and efficiency of the services delivered to citizens and enterprises;
- Promoting the creation, or the transformation, of the services delivered by Local Government into online services, or anyway services accessible through multiple channels.

The first announcement was followed by the presentation of 377 projects, whose overall value was 1200 Mln Euros. Out of these 377 projects, 134 have been co-financed with 120 Mln Euros (for an overall value of about 500 Mln Euros) (CNIPA, 2007). The funded projects involved about 3400 of the 8101 Italian municipalities (in

2003 the number of the Italian municipalities was greater than now), covering an overall population of about 38 million citizens. Out of the 134 projects which have been funded, 25 involved 628 municipalities of Lombardia (about 40% of the municipalities of Lombardia) for an overall value of 203 Mln Euros.

Besides the innovation projects funded under the National Action Plan, other specific programs for the inclusion of the municipalities of Lombardia in the spread of E-Government at the local level have been defined by the Regional Government, as shown in Table 2.

Among these programs, the most interesting one is the SISCoTEL (Interorganizational Information Systems for Local Government) program, that has been addressed exclusively to aggregations of municipalities (especially small municipalities, that is municipalities with less than 5000 inhabitants) with the aim of implementing a shared technological and organizational infrastructure allowing the members of the aggregations to share the management of services for citizens and enterprises.

Table 3 compares the National Action Plan for E-Government and the SISCoTEL program with respect to their main characteristics.

As a result of the innovation programmes implemented during the past years, the municipalities of Lombardia achieved a quite satisfactory state concerning the availability of technological infrastructures (see the indicators reported in Figure 1). The same cannot be said with respect to the level of the services delivered

online, especially concerning the transactional services and the services requiring the integration among different authorities. Actually, from the 2010 Report on E-Government in Italy (DigitPA & PCM, 2010) it resulted that only 6% of the Italian municipalities allows transactional services (two ways interactive services) on their websites, as shown in Table 4.

The data reported in Table 4 clearly show that the largest Italian regions (in terms of the number of their municipalities) scores under the average national value with respect to the transactional services offered. Actually, all the regions comprising more than 500 municipalities (Lombardia is among them) belong to this class. It can thus be concluded that a high administrative fragmentation, which in a country like Italy entails a large number of small municipalities, represents a critical element for the ICT enabled public sector transformation process, mainly due to the scarcity of the resources that small municipalities can usually devote to innovation.

The sharing of resources and competences within aggregations of municipalities represents a possible solution small local government organizations can pursue to overcome the scarcity of resources affecting them. This was the inspiring principle of the SISCoTEL programme that resulted in the establishment of 74 aggregations of municipalities, involving more than 900 municipalities of Lombardia, that share the management of services delivered to citizens and enterprises. However, the adhesion of the municipalities to an aggregation established under the SISCoTEL

Table 2. Regional programmes for the spreading of e-government at the local level

Funding Programme	Total amount of the funding	Period covered
Interorganizational Information Systems for Local Government (SISCoTEL)	76 Mln	2001-2005
One stop shop for enterprises (SUAP)	10 Mln	2001-2003
Diffusion of broadband infrastructures at the local level	5,6 Mln	2005
Intermunicipal Cooperation for service delivery	9 Mln	2005-2007

Table 3. Comparison between RP_SISCoTEL and NAP_E-Government (Castelnovo & Simonetta, 2007)

	SISCoTEL	**National Action Plan**
Supporting model	Co-financing addressed exclusively to aggregations of municipalities	Co-financing addressed to single organizations of Local Government or to their aggregations
Goals of the funding program	Technological and organizational integration among the members of an aggregation of municipalities	Implementing technological solutions for the online delivery of services to citizens and enterprises
Characteristics of the beneficiaries of the program	Small to medium size aggregations of small municipalities which are geographically contiguous and share the interest in the activation of a Shared Service Center	Large aggregations of municipalities without any constraints as to the modality of adhesion of the partners. The aggregations are not required to continue their collaboration after finishing the implementation of the funded project
Time span covered by the supporting actions	Repeated funding of aggregations for which it is possible to provide a six-year span of activity	Non-recurring funding. The time span of the collaboration corresponds to that of the project (2 years)
Municipalities of Lombardy covered by the programme	63,5% out of the 1546 municipalities of Lombardy	40,9% out of the 1546 municipalities of Lombardy

programme was voluntary; this allowed a municipality to adhere to an aggregation also on a temporary basis, thus possibly pursuing an immediate opportunistic goal instead of the strategic goal related to the reduction of the administrative fragmentation. Actually, there is no guarantee that a municipality will stay within an aggregation after the conclusion of a project funded under the programme, and this sensibly limited the possibility of reducing the problems determined by administrative fragmentation through the cooperation among municipalities.

In order to overcome the problems that limited the positive effect of the SISCoTEL programme the Regional Government of Lombardia funded a study with the aim of identifying the technological and organizational conditions that would make it possible to establish stable aggregations of cooperating municipalities, based on a standard reference model.

The conditions that have been identified by this study, that will be discussed in the next section, not only allow the establishment of stable aggregations but can also help them to activate processes of further strengthening of the interorganisational relationships, up to the establishment of systems of Local Government organizations that are strictly

integrated at the local level. The diffusion of such standardized and integrated aggregations across the whole territory of Lombardia represents an enabling condition toward the integration of the whole system of Local Government, one of the fundamental aspects of connected government. The study funded by the Regional Government described a process of progressive integration of the system of Local Government of Lombardia, represented graphically in Figure 2, that comprises the following stages:

- **Administrative fragmentation:** presence of completely independent organizations that have not defined any form of interorganisational cooperation
- **Episodic cooperation:** presence of different forms of intermunicipal cooperation, mostly established with the aim of taking advantage of favourable situations (such as funding programmes exclusively devoted to aggregations of municipalities). The cooperation is opportunistic; the same municipality can join different aggregations, even without territorial contiguity constraints

Figure 1. Some data concerning Lombardia

N° Inhabitants (31 Dec 2009): 9.826.100 (16,28 % of the Italian population)			
The system of Local Government in Lombardy and Italy (31 Dec 2009):			
N° inhabitants	N° of municipalities in Lombardia	N° of municipalities in Italy	%
0-5000	1153	5.836	19,76
5000-20000	333	1172	28,41
20000-100000	56	431	12,99
More that 100000	4	42	9,52
TOTAL	1546	8101	19,08

N° of Provinces in Lombardia	N° of Provinces in Italy	%
13	110	11,82

Some indicators of technological innovation in the municipalities (in Italy and in Lombardia) – 2009 - Source: Italian National Institute of Statistics)	Lombardia	Italy
Municipalities with an office devoted to the management of ICT (% of the total number of municipalities)	14,7	15,3
Employees devoted to the management of ICT (% of the total number of employees of the municipality)	1,6	1,6
N° of PCs available for 100 employees	92,2	84,8
Municipalities using LANs (% of the total number of municipalities)	95,4	95,5
N° of PCs connected to the LAN (% of the total number of PCs)	91,5	91,2
Municipalities with Internet access (% of the total number of municipalities)	99,8	99,9
Municipalities with a broadband Internet access (% of the total number of municipalities with Internet access)	74,9	74,7
Employees with Internet access (% of the total number of employees of the municipality)	74,6	71,3
Municipalities with a Web site (% of the total number of municipalities)	93,7	91,2
Municipalities that allow online payments (% of the total number of municipalities)	12,2	13,2

GDP per capita in Purchasing Power Standards (PPS) (EU-27 = 100) - Source: EUROSTAT												
	1997	1998	1999	2000	2001	2002	2003	2004	2005	2006	2007	2008
European Union (27 countries)	100	100	100	100	100	100	100	100	100	100	100	100
Euro area (17 countries)	113	113	113	112	112	111	110	109	109	109	109	109
Euro area (16 countries)	113	113	113	113	112	111	111	109	110	109	109	109
Italy	119	120	117	117	118	112	110	106	105	104	104	104
Lombardia	161	162	157	155	157	149	147	140	138	135	135	134

• **Stable aggregations:** establishment of stable and multifunctional aggregations, which implement long-term sharing of different kinds of resources. The cooperation is no more opportunistic: joining an aggregation is a strategic decision

• **Local integration:** stable aggregations involved in an integration process in terms

Table 4. Levels of online services in the Italian municipalities (DigitPA & PCM, 2010)

Italian Regions	Information	One way interaction	Two ways interaction	Complete transaction
Veneto	90%	70%	9%	1%
Basilicata	66%	43%	6%	2%
Umbria	96%	73%	12%	4%
Piemonte	87%	59%	11%	5%
Province of Bolzano	88%	63%	10%	5%
Lombardia	91%	72%	14%	6%
Sardegna	86%	62%	13%	6%
Campania	92%	66%	17%	7%
Toscana	96%	83%	22%	8%
Abruzzo	78%	53%	13%	8%
Puglia	91%	69%	18%	8%
Calabria	86%	54%	13%	8%
Sicilia	85%	55%	11%	8%
Valle d'Aosta	96%	78%	17%	9%
Lazio	86%	58%	15%	9%
Friuli Venezia Giulia	95%	86%	20%	10%
Molise	93%	61%	20%	10%
Emilia-Romagna	99%	86%	20%	11%
Province of Trento	97%	82%	30%	12%
Liguria	95%	79%	18%	12%
Marche	92%	71%	22%	13%
ITALY	90%	68%	15%	7%

of cooperability conditions (US-CREST, 2000; Stewart, Clarke, Goillau, Verrall, & Widdowson, 2004) setting up an integrated system. The interorganisational cooperation turns into systematic sharing of information, as well as of technological and human resources

- **Inter-system cooperation:** the cooperation is not anymore restrained to a local area; different interoperable integrated systems of Local Government cooperate within a wider context defined by regional bounds
- **Virtualization (connected government):** networked organisation that allows a multiplicity of different municipalities to oper-

ate seamlessly to deliver greater value to citizens (and enterprises)

STANDARDIZED/INTEGRATED SYSTEMS OF LOCAL GOVERNMENT

The cooperation model to be defined by the study funded by the Regional Government of Lombardia had to satisfy three requirements:

- It should allow the establishment of strategic aggregations of municipalities that would be stable in time
- The municipalities' adhesion to an aggregation should be on a voluntary basis, due

Figure 2. Stages of the integration process leading to connected government at the local level

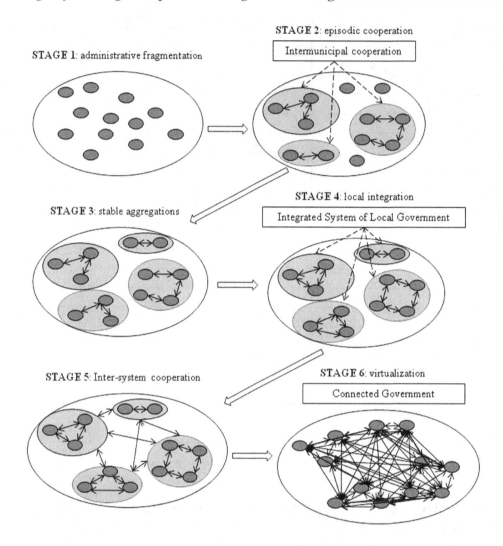

to the constitutionally guaranteed autonomy of the Italian municipalities

- The cooperation should not necessarily be of the institutionalized type (Council of Europe, 2007).

Based on these requirements, the result of the study has been the definition of the concepts of Standardized System of Local Government (SSLG) and Integrated System of Local Government (ISLG), as well as the detailed description of the steps of a standard process for the establish-

ment of aggregations of municipalities that would activate a SSLG and/or an ISLG.

Roughly speaking, a SSLG is an aggregation of municipalities whose members share a cooperation environment (Castelnovo, 2009) that makes the partners able to cooperate efficiently and effectively on a set of activities they agreed to perform jointly. The sharing of the cooperation environment makes the members of a SSLG strictly interoperable, not only at the technical level but also at the operational, organizational and strategic level as well (Tolk, 2003). This is due to the fact that the members of a SSLG could need to share resources of many different kinds, including human resources, and, consequently, different aspects of interoperability have to be considered in the definition of the cooperation environment, besides those usually related to information and systems interoperability (Castelnovo, 2007).

Given the variety of the resources that can be shared, in the definition of a cooperation environment organizational compatibility attributes referring to different domains should be included, as shown in Table 5 (Castelnovo & Simonetta, 2007):

With each of the conditions listed in Table 5 different levels have been associated, corresponding to more or less restrictive requirements that the members of a SSLG are required to satisfy, leading to more or less strict forms of compatibility among different organizations, similar to the integration levels described in C4ISR (1998) and Clark and Jones (1999).

The set of the interoperability conditions with the specification of the levels associated with them characterize a reference model that can be used to define, and compare, different cooperation environments. Actually, by selecting for each of the conditions comprised in the reference model the level that is more appropriate for the type of cooperation the partners are interested in, it is possible to define different cooperation profiles that specify different standards for the cooperation the members of a SSLG have to comply with.

The establishment of the appropriate cooperation environment (that means the establishment of a SSLG) can thus be considered as the transformation process that lead the partners to satisfy the conditions specified by the cooperation profile they defined. From this point of view, the members of a SSLG are standardized, although only with respect to the cooperation profile they agreed on.

Due to the sharing of a cooperation environment by all its members, a SSLG can be considered as a system of pre-qualified partners that, with respect to the specific cooperation profile they defined, are characterized by a high level of readiness for the cooperation and the sharing of resources. This makes it possible, when needed, to define a sharing of resources among the partners

Table 5. Conditions defining the cooperation environment

Domain	Interoperability Conditions
Strategic The conditions pertaining to the strategic domain concern the level of the partners' strategic commitment towards the interorganisational cooperation.	sharing the mission and the objectives of the cooperation
	degree of each partner's involvement in the cooperation
	sharing of a standard organizational structure
	sharing of a common organizational ontology and terminology
Organizational The conditions pertaining to the organizational domain concern the level of homogeneity among the partners with respect to the way they manage their business processes.	level of standardization of the business processes
	common management styles
	sharing of the resources
	dissemination of information
Operational The conditions pertaining to the operational domain concern the level of homogeneity among the partners with respect to their day to day operational activities.	homogeneity of working tools used by the partners
	sharing of the training activities
	availability of tools for interorganizational communication
	availability of tools for the monitoring of the cooperation
Technological The conditions pertaining to the technological domain concern the level of homogeneity among the partners with respect to their technological infrastructures.	sharing of infrastructures for connectivity
	homogeneity of the partners' IT application portfolio
	sharing of data among the partners
	sharing of the security policies

of the SSLG (even on a temporary basis) in a plug & play modality, that is without requiring any further adjustment to the partners in order to use efficiently and effectively the shared resources. Of course, this does not mean that the members of an SSLG should necessarily be involved in actual interorganisational activities. As a matter of fact, an SSLG simply defines and implements the conditions that make the member municipalities highly compatible, thus reducing the level of heterogeneity within a system of Local Government. This is a goal an aggregation of municipalities can pursue, even without considering the possibility of implementing an actual sharing of resources.

Although the standardization of the partners enables them to (makes it possible for them to) share resources also in a "just in time" modality, the members of an SSLG (not necessarily all of them) can decide to further strengthen their relationship and to stabilize the cooperation by transforming it in a long term day to day operating modality. This leads the SSLG (or part of it) to evolve into an Integrated System of Local Government (ISLG), that is an aggregations of municipalities that, being members of an SSLG, are strictly interoperable (up to cooperability [US-CREST, 2000; Stewart, Clarke, Goillau, Verrall, & Widdowson, 2004]) and that agree to share their activities (or at least a substantial part of them) with the partners, including the delivery of services to citizens and enterprises.

ISLG's members are not, strictly speaking, integrated in the system; actually, the establishment of an ISLG simply amounts to the adoption of a particular cooperation environment and to the systematic sharing of activities that its members would find difficult to perform individually. This allows the members of an ISLG to retain local democratic accountability and local decision making on policy and priority, whilst achieving efficiencies through a more coherent and joined up approach to the design and delivery of services.

Strictly speaking, the integration among the partners within an ISLG is only virtual. This has some particularly important consequences:

- Each member of the ISLG keeps its autonomy, though it agrees to coordinate its activities with that of its partners and to systematically share resources (of various sorts) with them;
- As the integration is exclusively determined by the adoption of a shared cooperation environment, the establishment of an ISLG does not necessarily require the definition of new levels of government and/or governance (as it happens in the case of institutionalized forms of integration, such as the Unions of Communes and the Mountain Communities (Council of Europe, 2007)

An ISLG determines a weak integration among its partners when the management of the cooperation is based on the definition of some shared coordination schemes (both at the decisional and operational level) and on the implementation of a soft managerial system to which only two functions are assigned:

- The management of the cooperation environment and of all the activities necessary for its maintenance and, possibly, evolution
- The coordination of the resources shared within the ISLG and that, nevertheless, still belong to the single members of the system which manage them according to policies and management styles shared with the partners

An ISLG determines a strong integration (although it still remains a virtual integration) of the partners when it is based on an unique interorganisational management system that completely manages all the resources involved in the activities shared within the system. Such resources can be either directly transferred to the ISLG or they can still belong to the single members of the system, with their management transferred to the ISLG.

In both cases, the ISLG determines a strict integration of the partners at the operational level so that from the point of view of an external observer the result would be indistinguishable from that which would be obtained with the fusion of the member municipalities.

For this characteristic, an ISLG whose members realize a strong integration, up to the virtual fusion of its members, could represent a possible solution to the problems related to administrative fragmentation. What makes this solution particularly attractive is the fact that it allows to achieve the same results that would be achieved through the merger of municipalities, while guaranteeing the preservation of the autonomy of local communities. As observed above, this is due to the fact that the members of an ISLG are integrated at the managerial and operational level, while maintaining their autonomy at the level of the definition of the policies. From this point of view, an ISLG should not be considered simply as a cooperative system; rather it is a coopetitive system (Brandenburger & Nalebuff, 1997), since it allows the cooperation among the partners at the managerial and operative level and the competition at the level of the policies.

THE STANDARDIZATION/ INTEGRATION PROCESS

The coopetitive model the concept of ISGL in based on should help avoiding some of the problems determined by administrative fragmentation through the establishment of long-term stable local public-public partnerships among municipalities (Castelnovo, 2011). However, the properties of a cooperation model, however good it would be, do not suffice by themselves to guarantee that the partners will avoid (or at least sensibly reduce) opportunistic behaviours, that is one of the main

causes of aggregation instability. Actually, the stability in time of aggregations of municipalities implementing an intermunicipal cooperation can be achieved only by maintaining a high level of involvement and commitment of the partners towards the cooperation. One way to accomplish this result is through a careful management of the process that leads to the establishment of the cooperation, starting from an accurate selection of the potential partners.

For this reason, the project funded by Region Lombardia (henceforth indicated as SSLG/ISLG project) devoted a particular attention to the description of a standard process for the establishment of stable aggregations of municipalities and for their possible evolution into a SSLG or in an ISLG. The process comprises the following steps:

- Call for interest
- Profiling of the potential partners
- Assessment of the networkability level of the potential partners
- Definition of the strategic goals of the cooperation
- Establishment of the aggregation

The Call for Interest

The first step of the process amounts to a subject launching a call for interest concerning the establishment of a partnership among municipalities, generally within the boundaries of a given administrative territory. Such a subject, that stimulates the formation of aggregations of municipalities, plays a catalyst role, partially analogous to the role of the net broker as described in Franke (2002) with respect to the establishment of virtual organizations. The catalyst role should normally be played by a public sector subject, since this guarantees a public sector governance of the whole process.

All the municipalities interested in some form of cooperation could answer the call. Since it could be based on very smooth requirements, the number of municipalities that initially answer the call can be quite large. The set of these municipalities represents the pool of the potential partners for the cooperation. The process leading to the setting up of a stable aggregation, one that will possibly implement a SSLG and that could evolve into an ISLG, can be considered as a refinement process that selects the appropriate partners from the set of all the potential partners that answered the call for interest.

During the refinement process some potential partners will be discarded; hence it is necessary to guarantee that the selection is fair and based exclusively on criteria related to the well functioning of the aggregation that will be set up. As in the case of the catalyst, also this guaranteeing role should be played by a public sector subject, one that has authority over the municipalities involved; in a constitutional arrangement like the Italian one, this role can be played by the Regional Government.

The guaranteeing role can be considered as an enabling role since it facilitates the establishment of an aggregation of municipalities by assuring the potential partners that in all the phases of the process the fairness and the equity requirements are satisfied. The subject that plays this role, as well as other facilitating functions such as the establishment of the appropriate legislative context and, possibly, the provision to the municipalities of infrastructures and services that can support intermunicipal cooperation, can be considered as the enabler of the standardization/integration process.

The Potential Partners' Profiling

The partners profiling amounts to a standardized description of each potential partner that is made available to all the members of the pool of the potential partners. The content of the partners profile, as well as the format of the information contained in it, can be defined in the call for interest launched by the catalyst.

The potential partners profile should include, at least, information concerning:

- Human resources
- Organizational resources
- Managerial resources
- Technological resources
- Financial resources

The profiling of the human resources, with particular concern to the kind and the level of the competencies available within each partner organization, is a critical element because, especially when the partners are small municipalities, the well-functioning of the cooperation mainly depends on the quality of the human resources involved (Koch & de Kok, 1999).

The organizational resources represent the organizational culture each partner contributes to the cooperation, both in terms of its previous experiences in interorganisational cooperation and in terms of its good internal organization and functioning. The profiling information concerning organizational resources include:

- The description and the evaluation of previous cooperation experiences the candidate municipalities have been involved in
- The description of all the contracts for service provision in force
- The description, for each service delivered to citizens and enterprises, of how it is managed and delivered
- The perceived elements of strength and weakness in the organization

The availability of adequate managerial resources within the members of the pool of the potential partners is crucial for the well functioning of the cooperation (Agranoff, 2003, 2006). However, small municipalities often lack managerial resources (as defined, for instance, in Castanias and Helfat [2001]). Actually, this is one of the reasons that forces small municipalities to enter

Table 6. Managerial roles within small municipalities

Managerial roles (based on the classification in Castanias and Helfat [2001])	Corresponding roles in small municipalities without specific managerial roles
Board of directors	Executive body
CEO	Major
Top Management team	n.a.
Upper level manager	employee that is responsible for the delivery of the services related to a given homogeneous area
Middle level manager	employee that is responsible for the delivery of single services
Lower level manager	

into an intermunicipal cooperation. From this point of view, the critical step for the profiling of the managerial resources concerns the identification of the managerial roles within a small municipality.

Given the regulation in force in Italy, in the case of small municipalities the managerial resources can be defined as in Table 6.

For each employee exerting a managerial role, the profile should describe the type of his competence, considering whether it is:

- A competence of a generic type (for instance the educational background)
- A competence acquired through previous experiences within public administration bodies
- A competence acquired through previous experiences within other Local Government bodies
- A competence acquired within the same municipality

The partners' profile should also provide a detailed description of the technological resources each partner has at his disposal. Actually, these resources represent both one of the objects of the standardization process related to the establish-

ment of a SSLG and a fundamental enabling element for intermunicipal cooperation. The profile should include information concerning:

- The number and the quality of the ICT devices/equipment in use
- A complete and detailed description of the application portfolio
- The security policies and the policies for the backup of information

The information concerning financial resources are included within the profile since they can give to the potential partners an insight concerning how well a municipality is being administered. Moreover, by considering a municipality's financial status the catalyst, as well as all the potential partners, could appreciate whether the possible inclusion of that municipality within the aggregation would constraint its functioning.

The Partners' Networkability Assessment

Once the pool of the potential partners has been established and its members have been profiled, the next step is the assessment of the networkability level of each potential partner, that is its capability to establish, maintain, and develop relationships with other organisations in order to pursue new common business opportunities or improve the results of an existing business through co-operation (Fleisch & Österle, 2000).

On the one hand, the assessment of the potential partners' networkability level allows to identify those potential partners that are more likely to form a stable and efficient aggregation. On the other hand, by considering the results of the assessment it is possible to evaluate how much the standardization/integration process will be difficult to implement as well as the type and the amount of the resources that will be necessary to support the process.

In the SSLG/ISLG project, the networkability assessment has been based on the reference model described in Table 5. This means that a potential partner's networkability level is determined by its cooperation profile, as defined in the section above. An organization's cooperation profile can be determined by considering the value a selected group of key stakeholders within that organization associate with the interoperability conditions comprised in the reference model.

The assessment process includes the following steps:

- Ientification of the key stakeholders within the organization and selection of the people to be involved in the assessment
- Evaluation of the interoperability conditions by the selected stakeholder
- Comparison and discussion among the stakeholders of the results of the evaluation
- Convergence of the stakeholders on a shared evaluation of the interoperability conditions

During the assessment, a twofold evaluation is required to the stakeholders. On the one hand, they are asked to evaluate the interoperability conditions with respect to the level they believe characterizes the current status of the organization (the current cooperation profile). On the other hand, they are asked to indicate what level they believe would be necessary in order to adequately support a stable and efficient cooperation (the required cooperation profile).

This determines two profiles that can (and usually are) different, as exemplified in Figure 3.

The level of networkability of an organization that will be used in the partners selection process is the one corresponding to the required profile, that represents the maximum amount of organizational change that a potential partner is willing to undertake to enter in an interorganisational cooperation.

However, by comparing the current and the required profiles it is possible to evaluate how much that organization can be expected to invest in change management in order achieve the networkability level it thinks is the one required for the establishment of a stable, efficient, and effective cooperation. Moreover, for each interoperability condition, the possible discrepancy between the current and the required values gives an indication concerning the most critical elements the change process should consider.

The Definition of the Strategic Goals of the Cooperation

The definition of the goals of the cooperation determines a further selection among the potential partners, since not all of them could be interested in the defined form of cooperation. The first element that can reduce the number of the potential partners concerns the decision whether to establish a stable aggregation with the aim of:

- Share a standardization process leading to a SSLG, that is a system of partners that are strictly interoperable, up to cooperability, without considering the opportunity of evolving the SSLG into an ISLG
- Implementing a SSLG as a preliminary step of a process that the partners already agree will lead at the end to an ISLG (this means that the partners agree on a two phases process: first standardization, then integration)
- Directly implement an ISLG, thus agreeing to run the standardization and integration processes in parallel.

The choice of one of these possibilities is the result of an agreement among the potential partners that, among other things, includes the specification of the interoperability level required for the planned form of cooperation. This specification can be obtained by setting the appropriate values

Figure 3. Example of an organization's current and required cooperation profiles

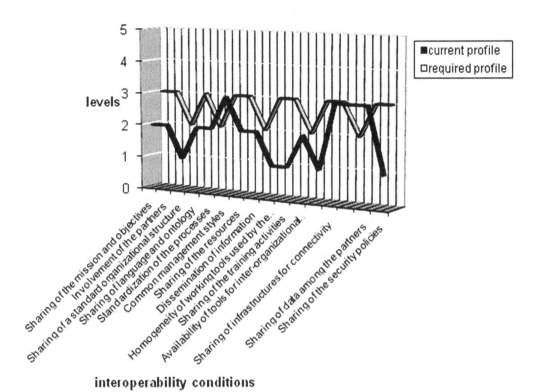

of the interoperability conditions defined by the reference model, thus defining a cooperation profile the partners agree to consider as the one required by the particular form of cooperation they agreed on.

By considering how much the cooperation requirements specified by the shared cooperation profile differ from those that characterize the cooperation profile it considers to be the required one, each candidate partner can evaluate the impact the planned form of cooperation would have on its own organization. Such impact evaluation could lead a potential partner to decide whether to adhere from the beginning to the standardization/integration process, to adhere to it only successively or not adhering to it at all.

The evaluation can be performed by the catalyst as well. Although some of the potential partners evaluate themselves as ready for the cooperation,

it could happen that their membership in the aggregation do not add any value to the cooperation. In this case, it could be more productive to delay the adhesion of those potential partners until the cooperation has been settled down and adequately enforced. Such an evaluation, that let alone the potential partners' desires only considers the possible advantages to the whole system, can be performed only by an external role that can guarantee the fairness of the evaluation. This is another reason why the whole process needs a public sector governance.

The Establishment of the Aggregation

The steps of the partner's selection process described so far determine a refinement of the set of the potential members of a SSLG and/or an ISLG.

However, as observed above, the aggregation of municipalities that will be established does not necessarily need to include from the beginning all the potential partners that have been qualified during the selection process. Actually, the standardization/integration process requires a high a level of commitment by the partners and the success probability of the process is higher if some further conditions are satisfied, concerning both properties of the aggregation and properties that characterize the selected partners.

Among the properties that can make an aggregation of municipalities more apt to implement a standardization/integration process the dimension, in terms of the number of the member municipalities, and the balancing of power among the partners are particularly relevant.

The number of the partners is a relevant element to consider, since it seems to be strictly related to the manageability of the aggregation; as observed in (ODPM, 2003):

It should always be borne in mind that the economic case for a partnership is strengthened when the processes are comparatively straightforward and the number of parties involved is manageable. The process costs increase significantly when the number of parties to a partnership is increased, along with the increased cost of developing and maintaining the partnership that could be disproportionate to the added value of the extra partner (ODPM, 2003, p. 47).

However, despite its seeming obviousness, the thesis according to which a small aggregation of municipalities can be managed more easily and can perform better than a bigger one is not so conclusive. On the one hand, it does not consider the intrinsic complexities of the activities in which the partners will be involved. Actually, some activities could be performed with higher efficiency and effectiveness when they are shared among a large number of partners, whereas other activities can be performed more efficiently and

effectively by a smaller aggregation. On the other hand, that thesis does not consider the properties that characterize the partners. Actually, it is quite obvious to expect that a large aggregation of partners characterized by a high organizational compatibility will be managed more easily and will perform better than a small aggregation of less compatible partners.

There are empirical data that clearly point out that the relation between the dimension of an aggregation and its manageability, efficiency and effectiveness is not so simple as it could seem. Indeed, by considering data concerning 1335 joint ventures involving Japanese firms, Beamish and Kachra (2004) show that there is an increasing in an alliance's productivity as the number of its partners grows. According to Beamish and Kachra this result depends on the fact that as the number of the partners grows, it also grows the probability that more resources, heterogeneous and complementary, become available for the alliance; this, if the alliance is correctly managed, represents a competitive advantage for the partners.

Although it is unreasonable to define an abstract criterion concerning the number of partners to be included within an aggregation, it is reasonable to assume that the number of the partners must be related to the number and nature of the functions that will be jointly managed by its members. This assumption is supported by empirical data. Actually, based on an empirical analysis of the formation of networks for social service delivery, Graddy and Chen (2006) concludes that:

The greater the number of potential partners in a service area, the greater the number of services required in a contract, and the more ethnically homogeneous the client population, the more organizations are included in the service delivery network (Graddy & Chen, 2006, p. 549).

Based on the observations above, in the establishment of an aggregation of municipalities that will implement a SSLG than can possibly evolve into an ISLG the number of the partners to be included (from the beginning) within the aggregation can be determined by considering criteria like the following:

- The (transactional) costs for the establishment and the management of the aggregation, that grow as the number of the partners grows
- The benefits that could derive from an increased availability of heterogeneous and complementary resources related to the rising of the number of the partners
- The number and type of the functions that will be jointly managed by the members municipalities, considering that the more these functions are, the more are the heterogeneous and complementary resources that will be needed to manage them

Besides the number of the partners, in the establishment of an aggregation also the relative dimension of the partners should be carefully considered, in order to avoid the establishment of aggregations that include partners that differ too much in dimension from one another. Actually, the inclusion within an aggregation of municipalities whose dimensions are sensibly different is very likely to determine the establishment of unbalanced power relationships among the partners that can ultimately undermine the same stability of the aggregation. This could happen because:

- The larger municipalities in the aggregation are those that are more likely to hold the resources, the skills and the competences needed for its well functioning. This can determine an asymmetry within the aggregation and thus the establishment of unbalanced power relationships among the partners that could lead the smaller municipalities to weaken their commitment
- If, as it often happens, the governance mechanisms of the aggregation are deter-

mined also considering the dimension of the partners involved, the inclusion within the aggregation of partners that differ too much in dimension from one another determines the establishment of uneven powers of control among the partners. This could lead the smaller municipalities to fear of loosing their autonomy and, consequently, to re-consider their membership
- If, as it often happens, the distribution of the costs for the functioning of the aggregation among the partners also considers their dimension, the inclusion within the aggregation of partners that differ too much in dimension from one another determines an uneven distribution of the costs. This could lead the larger municipalities to consider too expensive their membership

THE PATH TO CONNECTED GOVERNMENT THROUGH THE SSLG/ISLG MODEL

The fundamental thesis of this chapter has been the claim according to which the establishment of SSLGs and ISLGs at the local level can be considered as an intermediate step toward connected government in a highly fragmented system of Local Government. However, besides what argued in the preceding sections, two further problems must be considered to support this claim:

- Connected government implies that government agencies operate in a so seamlessly integrated way to be perceived as a single virtual and networked enterprise; if the goal is the complete virtualization of the whole system of Local Government, why should it be necessary to pass though the establishment of standardized/integrated systems of Local Government?
- Due to the constitutionally granted autonomy of the Italian municipality, the SSLG/ISLG model allows aggregation of munici-

palities to define and establish cooperation systems based on requirements defined locally; how could it be avoided the establishment of local systems whose properties would make it difficult to integrate them on a wider area?

The answer to the first question has already been anticipated and it is related to the inherent complexities of connected government. Connected government is the most sophisticated level of e-government initiatives and, as pointed out in UNDESA (2008):

As countries move upwards towards the stage of connected government, they pass through many thresholds in terms of infrastructure development, content delivery, business re-engineering, data management, security, and customer management (UNDESA, 2008, p. 15).

To achieve these intermediate goals at the local level, local government organizations are required to implement transformational processes, both at the technological and the organizational level, that necessitate those resources, skills and competences that small local government organizations are more likely to lack. From this point of view, the systematic sharing of resources among the members of an ISLG can be considered as one of the conditions that allow them to take part in the transformational process leading to connected government.

Moreover, as observed at the beginning of this chapter, given the high number of local government bodies that should be involved in it, the process toward connected government can be sensibly simplified if all the connections it requires (horizontal and vertical connections among government bodies, infrastructure connections, connections between governments and citizens, and connections among stakeholders) are firstly established on restricted local areas.

This is exactly what the SSLG/ISLG model is intended to achieve.

The second question above concerns the conditions that would make it possible to connect different SSLGs/ISLGs established locally through a system of systems integration. Such an integration would be easier if all the local systems have been based on the same principles and the same reference model. However, due to the legislation in force, the Italian municipalities cannot be forced by authority to adhere to a particular organizational model. For this reason, the SSLG/ISLG project also considered how an authority of a higher institutional level (the Regional Government in the case of Lombardia) could induce the municipalities to comply with the SSLG/ISLG model by offering them some incentives, advantages, and facilities. This can be done through the implementation of a system of supporting actions that besides through financial incentives also support aggregations of municipalities that agree to establish a SSLG and/or an ISLG through information, training, assistance as well as control and regulation actions.

Information actions are intended primarily for the dissemination of information concerning the SSLG/ISLG model at all the levels within the organizations that will be involved in the standardization/integration process. These actions aim to create within the organizations a shared knowledge concerning the standardization/integration process. This help reducing the risk of the rising of conflicts among people involved in the process, due to the presence of subcultures within the organization that can affect the success probability of the standardization/integration process (Schein, 1996).

The training actions aim at reducing the lack of skills and specialized competencies within Local Government organizations, especially in the case of small municipalities. As part of the supporting system the training activities are intended to achieve two goals. On the one hand, they contribute to spread a culture of innovation within small municipalities, thus improving their human capital. On the other hand, they give the people involved in the standardization/integration process the specific competencies required for carrying it out. Training actions thus differ from information actions because they aim at creating competencies within small municipalities, whereas information actions simply aim at the dissemination of information and knowledge, not necessarily of the operative kind.

The assistance actions amount to the delivering to small municipalities of professional and consulting services that can help them to manage all the activities related to the establishment of a SSLG and/or an ISLG.

Assistance services should be centralized; this not only guarantees the achievement of economies of scale but, more importantly, also helps guaranteeing that the standardization/integration processes implemented at the local level comply with the requirements defined by the SSLG/ISLG model.

The primary objective of the control and regulation actions is to determine the appropriate legal framework for the standardization/integration processes, concerning the matters on which the higher-level authority that implements the supporting system has power. However, the control and regulation actions can also help avoiding the rising of potential conflicts between different innovation projects involving small municipalities at the local level.

Financial support concerns the transfer of financial resources to the municipalities involved in the standardization/integration processes by funding all those activities small municipalities most often are not able to fund by themselves, due to the scarce resources at their disposal. Well-known examples of such activities include, for instance, the reengineering of the processes, the re-organization of the back-office and the training of the personnel.

The higher-level authority can support small municipalities also through constraints reduction (for instance by reducing some of the controls that it should perform on the activities of the municipalities) or the devolution of power to the local level (for instance the transfer to the municipali-

Figure 4. The supporting system

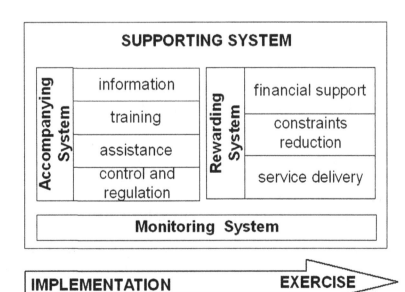

ties of the competence concerning some activities normally performed by the higher-level authority). These can be considered as supporting actions since they can help reducing the bureaucratic burden on small municipalities, thus allowing them to release resources that could be devoted to the standardization/integration process.

The same result can be achieved by means of service delivery actions. As a component of the rewarding system, service delivery amounts to the higher-level authority delivering services to the municipalities involved in the standardization/integration processes. Service delivery can be conceived as an element of the supporting system because it allows small municipalities to avoid managing on their own particularly complex activities or activities that might require resources that they could instead devote elsewhere.

Finally, the inclusion of rewarding actions within the supporting system allows the higher level authority to force the members of an SSLGs and/or an ISLGs to satisfy some quality requirements in order to access the benefits; this is why the supporting system includes a monitoring subsystem too, with the aim of allowing the continuous assessment of the SSLGs and the ISLGs that have been established.

Figure 4 summarizes the components of the supporting system defined within the SSLG/ISLG project.

The supporting system completes the SSLG/ISLG approach to connected government at the local level. The approach considers all the six pillars connected government is based on. Citizen centricity has been accounted for by defining the conditions that would allow small municipalities to deliver high quality services to citizens and enterprises through intermunicipal cooperation and the systematic sharing of resources among the partners of an integrated system. Indeed, a more efficient use of the scarce resources available not only entails the delivery of more "value for money," but also helps avoiding that citizens (and

enterprises) could experience differences in the quality of the services delivered by Local Government depending on whether they live and operate in a small municipality or in a larger one. This not only represents an aspect of citizen centricity but also accounts for one important aspect of social inclusion.

Back-office reorganisation and the assumption of a networked organisational model are at the core of the SSLG/ISLG model, as are standardization and interoperability, defined not only at the technological and infrastructural level, but at the organizational and strategic level as well. Thus, also these pillars of connected government have been taken into account by the SSLG/ISLG approach.

Finally, also the pillar of governance has been considered in the SSLG/ISLG approach. On the one hand, the coopetitive model the concept of ISLG has been based on allows to retain local democratic accountability and local decision making on policy and priority, that represent fundamental aspects of good governance. On the other hand, the SSLG/ISLG approach defines some roles that can facilitate the standardization/integration process, namely the role of the catalyst, that initiate the standardization/integration process, and the role of the enabler, that implements the supporting actions addressed to the municipalities involved in the process. Played by a higher-level authority, these roles allow a coordinated governance of the standardization/integration processes defined locally, thus avoiding the lack of coordination and consistency and the implementation of not interoperable solutions that would destroy the efforts toward connected government.

REFERENCES

C4ISR. (1998). *Levels of information systems interoperability (LISI)*. Washington, DC: Department of Defense.

Agranoff, R. (2003). *Leveraging networks: A guide for public managers working across organizations*. Washington, DC: IBM Center for the Business of Government.

Agranoff, R. (2006). Inside collaborative networks: Ten lessons for public managers. *Public Administration Review, 66*(1), 56–65. doi:10.1111/j.1540-6210.2006.00666.x

Beamish, P. W., & Kachra, A. (2004). Number of partners and JV performance. *Journal of World Business, 39*, 107–120. doi:10.1016/j.jwb.2003.08.013

Brandenburger, A. M., & Nalebuff, B. J. (1997). *Co-opetition: A revolution mindset that combines competition and cooperation: The game theory strategy that's changing the game of business*. New York, NY: Currency Doubleday.

Castanias, R. P., & Helfat, C. E. (2001). The managerial rents model: Theory and empirical analysis. *Journal of Management, 27*, 661–678. doi:10.1177/014920630102700604

Castelnovo, W. (2007). Interorganizational cooperation and cooperability. In *Proceedings of the EGov Interop 2007 Conference*. Retrieved April 12, 2011 from http://80.14.185.155/egovinterop/www.egovinterop.net/Res/10/T10C.pdf.

Castelnovo, W. (2009). Enhancing cooperation among small local government organizations. In A. Kaplan, A. Balci, C. Can Aktan, & O. Dalbay (Eds.), *Advances in eGovernment and eGovernance, Proceedings of ICEGOV 2009*. Ankara, Turkey: ICEGOV.

Castelnovo, W. (2011). The governance of partnerships in local government. In Piaggesi, D., Sund, K. J., & Castelnovo, W. (Eds.), *Global Strategy and Practice of E-Governance: Examples from Around the World* (pp. 83–101). Hershey, PA: IGI Global. doi:10.4018/978-1-60960-489-9.ch006

Castelnovo, W., & Simonetta, M. (2007). The evaluation of e-government projects for small local government organizations. *Electronic Journal of E-Government, 5*(1).

CEMR. (2010). EU subnational government – 2009 key figures. *Council of European Municipalities and Regions*. Retrieved April 12, 2011, from http://www.ccre.org/docs/chiffres_cles_2010_UK_bd.pdf.

Clark, T., & Jones, R. (1999). Organisational interoperability maturity model for C2. In *Proceedings of the Command and Control Research and Technology Symposium*. Retrieved April 12, 2011 from http://www.dodccrp.org/events/1999_CCRTS/pdf_files/track_5/049clark.pdf.

CNIPA. (2007). *Monitoraggio dei progetti di e-government - Fase 1: Rapporto finale*. Retrieved April 12, 2011, from http://archivio.cnipa.gov.it/site/_files/EG000_RP05_0007_V1_RapportoSintesiConclusivo.pdf.

Council of Europe. (2007). *Draft report on inter-municipal cooperation*. Geneva, Switzerland: Council of Europe.

Cresswell, A. M., Canestraro, D., & Pardo, T. A. (2008). *A multi-dimensional approach to digital government capability assessment*. CTG Working Paper No. 05-2008. Albany, NY: SUNY.

DigitPA, & PCM. (2010). *Rapporto e-gov Italia 2010, DigitPA and dipartimento per la digitalizzazione della PA e l'Innovazione tecnologica*. Retrieved April 12, 2011 from http://www.innovazionepa.gov.it/media/611301/rapporto_e-gov_italia_master.pdf.

Fleisch, E., & Österle, H. (2000). Business networking: A process-oriented framework. In Österle, H., Fleisch, E., & Alt, R. (Eds.), *Business Networking - Shaping Enterprise Relationships on the Internet* (pp. 55–91). Berlin, Germany: Springer.

Franke, U. J. (2002). The competence-based view on the management of virtual web organizations. In Franke, U. J. (Ed.), *Managing Virtual Web Organizations in the 21st Century: Issues and Challenges*. Hershey, PA: IGI Global. doi:10.4018/978-1-930708-24-2.ch001

Graddy, E., & Chen, B. (2006). Influences on the size and scope of networks for social service delivery. *Journal of Public Administration: Research and Theory, 16*(4), 533–552. doi:10.1093/jopart/muj005

Johnston, P. (2006). *21st century networked local government*. White Paper. Retrieved July 20, 2011, from http://www.cisco.com/web/about/ac79/docs/wp/21st_Century_Networked_Local_Government.pdf.

Kaczorowski, W. (Ed.). (2004). *Connected government*. London, UK: Premium Publishing.

Koch, C., & de Kok, J. (1999). *A human-resource-based theory of the small firm*. EIM Research Report 9906/E. Retrieved from http://www.ondernemerschap.nl/pdf-ez/H199906.pdf.

Microsoft. (2011). *Connected government in a connected world*. White Paper. Retrieved July 20, 2011, from http://www.microsoft.com/download/en/details.aspx?id=8295.

ODPM. (2003). *Rethinking service delivery, volume two - From vision to outline business case*. Office of the Deputy Prime Minister.

OECD. (2007). *E-government as a tool for transformation*. Retrieved April 12, 2011, from http://www.eurim.org.uk/activities/tgdialogues/E-Government_as_a_Tool_for_Transformation.pdf.

Pallab, S. (2010). *Understanding the impact of enterprise architecture on connected government*. Retrieved April 12, 2011, from http://unpan1.un.org/intradoc/groups/public/documents/unpan/unpan039390.pdf.

Schein, E. H. (1996). Three cultures of management: The key to organizational learning. *Sloan Management Review, 38*(1), 9–20.

Stewart, K., Clarke, H., Goillau, P., Verrall, N., & Widdowson, W. (2004). Non-technical interoperability in multinational forces. In *Proceedings of the 9th International Command and Control Research and Technology Symposium*. Copenhagen, Denmark: IEEE.

Tolk, A. (2003). Beyond technical interoperability - Introducing a reference model for measures of merit for coalition interoperability. In *Proceedings of the 8th International Command and Control Research and Technology Symposium (ICCRTS)*. Washington, DC: ICCRTS.

UNDESA. (2008). *e-Government survey 2008: From e-government to connected governance*. New York, NY: United Nations.

US-CREST. (2000). *Coalition military operations - The way ahead through cooperability*. Retrieved April 12, 2011, from http://www.uscrest.org/CMOfinalReport.pdf.

KEY TERMS AND DEFINITIONS

Architecture Driven Transformation: A transformational process based on a reference model that provides a comprehensive approach to the design, planning, implementation, and governance of an organizational system.

Administrative Fragmentation: Situation in which the system of Local Government is characterized by a high number of municipalities, most of which are small municipalities; administrative fragmentation can affect the efficiency and effectiveness of Local Government.

Cooperability: A form of non-technical interoperability that allows the successful bridging between partners of differences in vision, organization, operational processes, and culture.

Connected Local Government: The result of a transformational process that leads Local Government organizations to achieve a level of integration such that citizens and enterprises can interact with government as with a single entity rather than with a number of different public authorities.

Integrated System of Local Government: An aggregation of (Small) Local Government Organizations that on the basis of a preliminary sharing of interests jointly define systematic forms of cooperation based on a strict form of interoperability, up to cooperability.

Intermunicipal Cooperation: Cooperative or contractual arrangement between two or more municipalities for the sharing of resources and/or the delivery of services.

Small Local Government Organizations: Municipalities with less than 5000 inhabitants; Small Local Government Organizations often lack the resources and the specialized competencies required to manage innovation.

Chapter 16
Moving towards the Connected Transformational Government:
Perspectives from Malaysia and Beyond

Dzaharudin Mansor
Microsoft Corporation, Malaysia

Mohd. Rosmadi Mokhtar
National Universiti (UKM), Malaysia

Azlina Azman
Malaysian Administrative Modernisation and Management Planning Unit (MAMPU), Malaysia

ABSTRACT

Policy makers around the world today are quickly embracing ICT as an enabler to improve government service delivery. However, in trying to achieve this, they are faced with the challenge of how to deal with silos of core systems entrenched for many years and owned by different governmental departments. Given that a rip-and-replace approach is not practical, governments have become very interested in interoperable solutions.

This chapter provides insights into interoperability from the point of view of delivering government services. It shows that today, technology and the industry have progressed to such an extent that the technical barriers to interoperability can be overcome in many ways. The real challenge is to address business interoperability that involves the interplay of technical, architectural, strategic, organizational, policy, and legal dimensions. This, in turn, has influenced the evolution of government interoperability frameworks, where some governments have incorporated Enterprise Architecture approaches. Today, new socio-economic challenges require policy makers to rethink their approaches in ways that will enable them to constantly improve and evolve citizen-centric services powered by an ICT-enabled Connected Transformational Government.

DOI: 10.4018/978-1-4666-1824-4.ch016

INTRODUCTION

Governments have been one of the early adopters of computing technologies in the areas of research, military, and others. From these early days, systems and applications were typically purchased and managed by individual departments and organizations. Over the years, government systems are generally purchased on a solution-by-solution basis, and driven by the need to acquire the best solution for a specific purpose. The result of this is the creation of a wide range of separate information and data islands across Government with no easy way of unlocking the valuable information assets they collectively contain to support more useful and productive processes.

The increasing use of networks of computers and the explosion in the consumption of digital media content over the last twenty years have influenced government to rethink the way they interact with their citizens leveraging on the evolving technologies. This has led to the numerous "e-Government" initiatives that were seen across the globe. Starting with basic access to static government web sites, policy makers came to realize the potential cost savings and other advantages in moving traditional face-to-face transactions to the electronic form. This resulted in the shift towards e-Government applications that not only can respond to citizen requests dynamically with the most up-to-date information, but also able to support transactions such as information updates and payments.

More recently, governments around the world have been confronted with opposing challenges. The increasing pervasiveness of high technology within society demands that government meets the expectations of an IT-savvy society. On the other hand, Governments find the growing need to deal with the ever-increasing pressures of cut-backs and cost reduction while addressing ever rising public expectations. Consequently, public administrators are forced to rethink their strategy to create a more coherent e-Government landscape that leverages on interoperability across the organization. This typically involves the orchestration of a collection of sub-services that can span across multiple departments, which are delivered in an integrated manner using multiple channels and devices. Such successful initiatives not only simplify the way citizens and businesses interact with governments, but it can also enhance the effectiveness and productivity of the government machinery to power the national transformational agendas that many countries have. The "No Wrong Door" initiative in Malaysia is an example of an effort by a developing country.

Case Study: "No Wrong Door Initiative in Malaysia"

Malaysians today have very high expectations of the Government delivery system. They expect fast, efficient and quality service when dealing with the Government, regardless of time or place. Effective and optimum use of Information and Communication Technology (ICT) is the best means to boost the quality of the public service delivery system. In 2008, Malaysia's Chief Secretary to the Government outlined the definition of being customer-focused in public service delivery. The main goal here was to institutionalize the delivery of quality public services in Malaysia. In essence, the Malaysian Public Service was gearing itself to enable its citizens to easily access public services. This program was called the "One Service, One Delivery, No Wrong Door" that reflects the Government's aspiration to present a 'One Government, Many Agencies' identity when delivering services to the citizens. The program goals were to ascertain the following:

- Government agencies are viewed as an integrated entity, well coordinated, well informed, and customer friendly.

- Customers can deal with Government agencies in a fast, simple, and transparent manner using various service channels.
- Customer satisfaction through speedy action by Government personnel and agencies.

This is implemented via a number of channels:

- One-Stop Centers that facilitate access to a range of public services (post office, local authorities).
- A centralized portal called "myGovernment" that becomes a gateway to a diverse set of on-line services offered by agencies across the government.
- Supporting electronic payment for transactions requiring payments to the government when using e-service delivery channels.
- Case management systems to manage complaints raised by citizens or businesses.
- One number emergency call to streamline and simplify emergency calls.

Moving forward, all government agencies in Malaysia are required to embrace and work towards supporting this concept. As a matter of principle, an agency must expand its services channel and look at the possibilities in delivering its services via channels and interfaces provided by other agencies. It is envisioned that citizens will no longer be disappointed with the inability to complete a transaction just because it involves a process that is outside the jurisdiction of the agency they are interacting with. The sharing of information, resources, and technology is the enabler, which will provide seamless services to the citizens through a single door. That said, effective interoperability that encompass the business and technical aspects is the key enabler towards achieving these goals.

INTEROPERABILITY

Today, most governments would have an e-Government in one way or another. As discussed, the need for collaboration across the government becomes more and more important as the expected services become more advanced. For this reasons, it is not surprising that governments are very concerned about interoperability, which is considered to be a key requirement for the seamless delivery of complex services involving multiple agencies and systems to their citizens and businesses.

The industry has taken great strides in responding to demands and expectations for improved interoperability. Gone are the days where ICT systems exist in silos that locked customers into specific products. Today great strides have been made in ensuring interoperability between technology products from different vendors. The ability for customers to mix and match hardware and software at various levels of the computing stack demonstrates this high degree of technical interoperability, a remarkable achievement that has brought about many benefits to the consumers as well as industry.

Despite this, organizations are still challenged in delivering interoperable solutions effectively. There has been a realisation that technical interoperability is not sufficient by itself to achieve the "seamless administration" that governments seek. For this, they must also address their internal operations and remove barriers that block collaboration between agencies, departments, and ministries. Hence, the aspirations to delivery seamless citizen-centric services can only succeed if various agencies are "interoperable" whereby their systems and organizations work well together.

Defining Interoperability

The International Standards Organization (ISO), that many countries are members of, defines interoperability as "The capability to communicate, execute programs, or transfer data among various functional units in a manner that requires the user to have little or no knowledge of the unique characteristics of those units" (ISO/IEC 2382-1:1993, 1993). In ICT, the general understanding of interoperability is the ability to efficiently transfer and use information uniformly across organizations, heterogeneous systems, or components. It helps link systems, information and processes within and across enterprises.

Various sources worldwide are consistent with this definition. For example, MyGIF (Malaysia Administration Modernization and Management Planning Unit, 2003, p 5) explains that interoperability covers the areas of interconnection, data integration, information access, security and metadata that govern the communication of systems, flow of information, as well as the exchange of data and business processes that relates to Government Ministries, agencies and departments. The U.S. e-Government Act of 2002 (Library of Congress, 2002) defines interoperability as "the ability of different operating and software systems, applications, and services to communicate and exchange data in an accurate, effective, and consistent manner." Likewise, the European Interoperability Framework Version 2 (European Commission, 2010), an initiative to facilitate the interoperability of services and systems at a pan-European level, defines interoperability as "the ability of disparate and diverse organizations to interact towards mutually beneficial and agreed common goals, involving the sharing of information and knowledge between the organizations, through the business processes they support, by means of the exchange of data between their respective ICT systems."

Simply put, we can view interoperability as ensuring systems work together to meet some business objectives. To achieve this, there are two broad areas that need to be addressed namely interoperability from a technical perspective (Technical Interoperability), and secondly interoperability from a business perspective (Business or Non-Technical Interoperability). It turns out that the former of these two is easier to deal with given the state of the IT industry today where the market forces have led to IT products to being highly interoperable. Business interoperability require more focus (OASIS eGovernment Member Section, 2010) and expected to be the more challenging of the two because this involves and impacts people, organizations and governance.

Technical Interoperability

Technical interoperability relies upon solutions that enable information to move successfully between systems. This technical level of interoperability spans both infrastructure (such as network protocols) and system level interoperability (such as Web services).

We have pointed out earlier that the industry has achieved a high level of interoperability in their products and technology. So how have they done this? The industry has achieved this through a number of complementary approaches including:

- *Making their products inherently interoperable*: products such as operating systems, networking equipment, middleware and others are designed to be interoperable. Consequently, these technologies will typically integrate well with a wide variety of hardware and software by explicitly supporting the different types of protocols, products, and technologies that will provide a competitive edge.
- *Communities working together on interoperability for mutual benefit*: frequently business partners and even competitors cooperate in win-win arrangement to enable their products and technologies to work well together to provide interoperable solutions in a typically heterogeneous customer environment.
- *Access to underlying technologies*: some companies make their products interoperable with others though enabling access

to the underlying technologies through licensing and cross-licensing arrangements. In some cases, these licensing programs are designed to promote interoperability by removing associated barriers such as the Microsoft Open Specification Promise (Microsoft Open Specification, 2011) and others.

- *Complying with widely used Standards:* here, the products and technologies from different vendors interoperate by conforming to widely technical specifications that are widely adopted. These include Open Standards such as IEEE 802.11 (Wi-Fi), TCP/IP, GSM, HTTP, as well as many others that are developed by well-known standards-setting organizations such as IEEE, ISO/IEC, OASIS, W3C, ETSI, and ITU-T. Further, popular proprietary standards in the market such as Java, Adobe Flash Video format, Microsoft Word binary formats, and others have proven to contribute toward promoting real-world interoperability.

Open Standards

Standards play an important role in fostering interoperability. Whilst the term "Standard" within the context of technology widely accepted to mean a specification, there has been lack of clarity on what is an "Open Standard." Some would also confuse between Open Source and Open Standards, using these terms interchangeably. It is clear that Open Source relates to software that conforms to a class of licensing model, while Open Standards relates to specifications that incorporates characteristics related with openness.

Given the great interest in Open Standards and the lack of a widely accepted definition for this, at the 11th Global Standards Collaboration (GSC) meeting, leading Standards Setting Organizations (SSOs such as ETSI, ITU), national standards bodies (e.g. from China [CCSA], Japan [ARIB,

ATIS]) and industry organizations (ACIF [Australia], ATIS, etc.) have agreed that Open Standards are technical specifications that conform to key characteristics including the following (RESOLUTION GSC-11/4, 2006):

- The standard is developed and/or approved, and maintained by a collaborative consensus-based process;
- Such process is transparent;
- Materially affected and interested parties are not excluded from such process;
- The standard is subject to RAND/FRAND Intellectual Property Right (IPR) policies which do not mandate, but may permit, at the option of the IPR holder, licensing essential intellectual property without compensation; and
- The standard is published and made available to the general public under reasonable terms (including for reasonable fee or for free).

There are a number of other definitions subscribed by various organizations and companies, some being very similar to this, while others are understandably more restrictive to uphold specific interests they represent.

Business Interoperability

While technical interoperability helps to overcome the technical barriers that prevent the different systems from working together, alone, it is not sufficient to deliver interoperability solutions in the real world especially when this involves participation of systems that spans across different organizational boundaries. The term "Business Interoperability" used here is also referred to as "Non-technical interoperability" (Stewart, Cremin, Mills, & Phipps, 2004), "People Interoperability" (Tsilas, 2007), and other similar terms in literature. Some of the elements of business interoperability that has been highlighted in literature include:

- Semantic interoperability.
- Cultural interoperability.
- Organizational interoperability.
- Privacy, confidentiality, security, and data protection.
- Accessibility.
- Governance.

Semantic Interoperability addresses the need to ensure that the data is represented and understood in a consistent way by the producers and consumers of the data. For example, the transport department may describe a citizen as a driver, while another system may interpret the information as an offender by the police, or a patient at a hospital. To allow these systems to interpret the information correctly, these different system owners need to work together and provide mechanisms (e.g. data catalogue and mapping) to ensure semantic equivalence.

Cultural Interoperability addresses people issues when establishing interoperable solutions. For example, enabling information to flow between systems in more successful and productive ways may expose duplication between and within government organizations. Further, there could be a perception of loss of control and ownership of data that traverses across to another agency. As in any transformation process, this requires effective change management is required to ensure a successful project.

Organizational Interoperability relates to the need to have the different entities involved to have an agreement and common understanding in resolving a set of interoperability issues. For example, one organization may have developed a set of standards internally that meets its own needs, but these may be different from another organization with which it wishes to collaborate. At a macro level, therefore, the same issues (technical, semantic, cultural) also need to be addressed.

Privacy, Confidentiality, Security, and Data Protection are important considerations that need to be addressed when systems exchange data across organizational boundaries. For example, a country's national registry may have strict privacy policies protecting citizens' personal information, while the human resource department may be less strict in providing the same information to potential employers. It is also possible that different jurisdictions may have different laws related to the privacy of individuals, the confidentiality of sensitive information, as well as the security framework between systems and organizations. An agreed framework that ensures a common set of privacy, confidentiality, security and data protection policies must exist, and implementation must uphold these requirements.

Accessibility is an important government concern and a number of countries have laws that ensure equal access and participation in e-services. In general, this needs to be catered for by presentation layer of interoperable solutions, but an agreement on the appropriate aspects of accessibility to be supported will require consensus across the different stakeholders and interested parties. Over-engineering accessibility features will be wasteful while under-delivering will result may lead to political and legal issues.

As in any cross-organization initiatives, a governance framework that is mutually agreed by all parties involved is important to ensure that there is overall alignment between systems and organizations to ensure success of the initiative. These include aspects such as prioritization, resource commitment, funding, conflict resolution/escalation procedures, and others.

GOVERNMENT INTEROPERABILITY FRAMEWORKS

With the increasing awareness of the importance of interoperability within governments, policy makers have started to see the need to develop

IT policies that facilitate interoperability between governments IT systems. The UK government e-Government Interoperability Framework (eGIF) that was published in 2000 was one of the earliest attempts to legislate interoperability. Subsequently, many other countries used the UK e-GIF as a benchmark, even as the basis for their own national Government Interoperability Framework (CS Transform, 2009) or GIF.

Challenges in Early Interoperability Frameworks

These early interoperability frameworks centred on defining technical and data interoperability. This included areas such as ICT standards, technical specifications, information flow, and metadata specifications that facilitate exchange of data across the different ministries. The UK e-GIF evolved from defining a set of standards for users of the UK government Gateway, to a full set of standards for Government to Government (G2G), Government to Citizen (G2C), and Government to Business (G2B) e-Services (CS Transform, 2009). Countries that started with interoperability frameworks similar to this include Australia, Denmark, Estonia, Germany, South Africa, Hong Kong, Malaysia, Mauritius, New Zealand and others.

In practice however, technical standards and specifications on technology and data were not sufficient to deliver interoperable e-Government solutions. Many of the standards listed in these GIFs were either irrelevant or became obsolete with the rapid changes in the ICT industry and market. Even if they had been relevant, they might not have necessarily addressed the business and organizational needs to enable collaboration between government agencies and departments, or "Business Interoperability."

Case Study: Interoperability Challenges for Public-Private E-Government Implementation

In order to increase the efficiency and effectiveness of the government services to the Malaysian public, the Electronic Government (EG) initiative were introduced in Malaysia as one of the seven flagships of the Multimedia Super Corridor (MSC) back in 1996. This policy, coordinative effort, and collective commitment that leverages on Information and Communications Technology (ICT) was viewed to be a means that will help propel Malaysia into the next millennium.

In one of the projects under the EG flagship referred to as "E-Services," three competing private consortiums were selected by the government to drive this project forward. The objective here was to provide Malaysians with online government services as an alternative to the existing over-the-counter services. It was the government aspiration that E-Services would be a catalyst for the growth of handling transactions across various service departments in a convenient and timely manner - be it at federal, state, or local level.

The major service departments involved in the initial e-services rollout were the Road Transport Department that is responsible for road tax renewal and application of learners' driving licence, the Police Department that handles the payment of traffic summonses and utility companies that provide billing inquiry and payment services.

Nevertheless, the implementation process of such concepts, that can be considered advanced at that point of time, was not all plain sailing. There were instances where the whole predicament could have been avoided if the business interoperability issues had been better understood and addressed beforehand. The following examples illustrate this.

- *Disjointed Learners' Driving License Permit Test Process.* An E-Service for processing the theory portion of the driver's licence test was considered to be a good starting point given the high number of applicants for the learners' driving permit which was a pre-requisite to taking the driver's license test. The learner's driving licence test is divided into two parts, the theoretical part and the practical part. The solution just focused on the first part where applicants will go to the service centres of their choice to take their test. Only when they have passed this theory test will they be able to proceed to the next practical part. For a number of reasons, the results from each test centres were manually delivered on diskettes at the end of each day to the data centres for updating. Hence it did not cater for the scenario where the applicant would take their practical test on the same day as the theoretical part. As a result, until these results are updated at the Road Transport Department end, successful and eager candidates were unable to proceed with the subsequent part. The issue was subsequently resolved when additional measures (that involved infrastructure, cost, and SLAs) were taken to ensure that the information related to the results of the theory part of the test was updated in a timely manner into the system.

- *Inconsistent Handling of Data Representation across Different Organizations.* Another service that was offered was the handling of traffic summonses of the Police Department. Communications between these different agencies were typically handled by a central gateway shown in Figure 1 which serves as the "middleman" to relay the communication between the related parties. In the case of the Police Department, they appointed another private company to do this on their behalf. Problems appeared when the number of characters supported for vehicle registration was found to be inadequate to take into account all scenarios. For example, when a new special vehicle registration format such as the "Putrajaya" plate registration was endorsed by the Road Transport Department, the Police Department would remove some unexpected trailing characters and concatenated the resulting truncated string with the following numeric digit(s). Addressing business interoperability issues between the Police Department and Road Transport Department was clearly needed here.

Figure 1. Communication flow between service agencies, gateway provider, and e-service consortiums

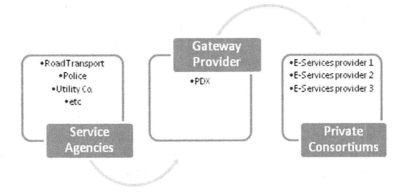

These are just some of the many examples of unforeseen business interoperability issues faced in real e-Government implementations. In the first case, the tight coupling of two sub-processes had not taken into account that the bulk update approach taken by the service provider for the first process due to cost pressures led to failure to support key scenarios until it was subsequently resolved. Meanwhile in the second example, there was no proper governance platform between related departments that could avoid and quickly resolve semantic interoperability issues such issue such as this. There are also many examples including those arising due to minimal involvement by key stakeholders and the governance model to actually plan and address infrastructure strategic direction. Therefore, the obstacles that prevent rapid development and deployment of electronic government services in practice clearly involved 'non-technical' challenges which can be more difficult to address than the technical ones (Scholl & Klischewski, 2007).

Evolution of Government Interoperability Frameworks

The early GIFs that were technology focused fell short in meeting real-world interoperability requirements for e-Government. This led to a number of attempts to broaden the scope of these frameworks that takes into account business interoperability. Some countries chose to adopt Enterprise Architecture methodologies that were used by large companies, as a means to address the limitation of early GIFs, while others took the approach of evolving their early GIFs to expand the scope to incorporate a broad range of business interoperability issues.

Enterprise Architecture

Enterprise Architecture (EA) defines the main components of an organization and how the functions in the core systems in the organization work together to achieve a defined business objective (McGovern, et al., 2004). Well known EA methodologies include Zachman Framework and The Open Group Architecture Framework (TOGAF). These methodologies adopt a top down approach in system design, and models views in a number of dimensions that include business, information, operational, organizational, and architectural and infrastructure hence addressing both technical and business interoperability. EA was considered by IT professionals as a methodology to enable enterprises develop interoperable solutions that meets the business needs of the organization.

Given that the EA addresses similar technical and business issues faced when implementing interoperable government services, it is natural for some governments to take the opportunity in leveraging on the existing body of knowledge, experience, and expertise in this field. Amongst the many countries embracing EA, USA has been most notable with its Federal Enterprise Architecture Program (Federal Enterprise Architecture Program, 2007). Over time, many EA methodologies and practices in governments evolved to become flexible frameworks that were more practical and effective as the adopters addressed the challenges over time, which resulted in producing better results. For example, although Federal Enterprise Architecture Program (FEAP) emphasises delivering business value to the stakeholders leveraging on EA principles, it does not prescribe the adoption of any specific EA methodologies or technologies. Instead, FEAP enriches EA by providing overarching guidelines when applying the selected EA approach in projects undertaken by a government agency.

Whilst EA methodology has a track record in addressing interoperability challenges within an enterprise, it can be argued that more guidance is needed when implementing interoperable solutions across different autonomous entities, especially those that may even span cross political boundaries.

The European Union (EU) Interoperability Framework

Some governments have taken the approach to continue evolve their early GIFs to address the shortcomings of the preceding version(s). A well-known example of this is the European Union Interoperability Framework (EIF). Initially, in 2004, an EU funded agency published an EU document of a working group that is referred to as EIF 1.0 (Interoperable Delivery of European E-Government Services to public Administrations, Businesses, and Citizens, 2004). A unique challenge that EU has compared to other governments is the need to cater for the additional complexity of taking into account the different laws and regulations of the independent EU member countries and still provide a practical and seamless interoperability approach between the member states.

EIF 1.0 is a report that was an initial attempt to provide a common framework to promote interoperability for developing cross-national e-Government services. EIF 1.0 provided recommendations that attempts to cover both technical and business interoperability (organizational and semantic) and invited member states to apply these guidelines for providing user-centred e-Services at a pan-European level. To facilitate internal and external interoperability, it recommended that member states develop local GIF consistent with EIF 1.0 to enable this. It should be noted that being a report, the contents were not legally binding for EU member states or any European Institution as indicated by the disclaimer in the EIF 1.0 document.

Using EIF 1.0 as the basis, a comprehensive revision was subsequently initiated with broad consultations from multiple stakeholders and primarily driven by an expert group of member states officials. EIF 2.0 was published in 2010 and had a number of significant changes to further improve the framework in the context of the European Union. Based on the Lisbon Treaty (2009), the European Commission published December 2010 the European Interoperability Communication with 2 annexes, namely the European Interoperability Strategy and European Interoperability Framework 2.0. A Communication is a legal instrument in Europe, which is legally binding for European Institutions. Hence, this European Interoperability Communication is seen as an impetus (see European Digital Agenda and European eGovernment Action Plan) for the member states to use EIF 2.0 to promote interoperability while accommodating for the continued co-existence of different e-Government frameworks in Europe – one of the biggest barriers towards the vision of an EU digital single market.

EIF 2.0 moves away from providing the prescriptive guidance on technology, and instead focuses on processes and governance of the interoperability framework. To further improve practicality, it allows for each participating government in a pan-European e-Services project to have its own specification for technical and business interoperability policies, while working on a governance model that is agreed to by all participating parties. This is referred to as an Interoperability Agreement that also includes legal dimensions to cater for interoperability between the different laws of the member states.

It is our opinion that EIF 2.0 represents an interesting evolution from the earlier GIF. Consistent with the view that technical interoperability is less of an issue, EIF 2.0 has moved away from its earlier focus on technical interoperability, and strives to address those higher layers of the interoperability model, where the core competence of governments is available and most beneficial to the overall objective to improve its services effectively.

Transformational Government Framework

Based on the experiences of many countries over the years, it has become clear that technology itself is not a silver bullet for implementing interoperable government services. Further, many of these initiatives are challenged with the need to minimize duplicated IT expenses, maximize use of the investments and most importantly, achieving the core public policy objectives set out in the first place (OASIS TGF Technical Committee, 2011). This has led to standards organization such as OASIS (Organization for the Advancement of Structured Information Standards—www.oasis-open.org) towards embarking on initiatives to help advance a framework for using ICT to improve the delivery of public services. Platforms such as this represent an interesting approach that will foster pooling of the wealth of experience from experts and practitioners from all over the world.

The OASIS Transformational Government Framework (TGF) can be considered as a meta-framework for citizen-centric service delivery that recognizes that these needs would differ from one country to another, and avoids a "one-size-fits-all" approach by providing a broad set of universally applicable rules, principles, and processes for delivering a successful program. Central to the approach promoted by OASIS TGF is a service delivery business model that is referred to as the "Franchise Marketplace" where:

- The Citizens and/or Businesses users are central to driving the requirements for a service.
- The existing government entities become supplier of a set of clearly defined services.
- An intermediate agile "virtual" business layer is then built around the customers' needs that are made up by joining up the disparate services provided by the required government entities to provide a service for this set of users (known as the "franchise business").

To support this business model, OASIS TGF recommends the adoption of Service Oriented Architecture (SOA) it is broadest sense. This provides a mechanism that enables the delivery of a diverse set of citizen centric services without the need for restructuring participating parts of the government. The approach is technology and methodology neutral, and calls for the use of interoperable open standards, which are well supported in the market place where possible to ensure that the solutions are future proof. Further, this promotes the reuse of existing investments in infrastructure, application, resources and know-how, hence minimizes the costs and risks associated with changes in people, technology and processes.

OASIS TGF provides a holistic set of guidelines to develop citizen centric services and is made up of the following four main components:

1. **Guiding Principles:** these are enduring statement and values that steer the business decisions over the long term. The framework emphasises on transforming the whole relationship between the government and users of public services. Hence, the TGF guiding principles encourages governments to better understand the citizens and business customers, and then build services around customer needs rather than organizational structure. These services should focus on what is done with citizens rather than to them. Success of these services requires initiatives that grow the market to include all parts of the society leveraging on partnerships with other market players.

2. **Critical Success Factors:** these are factors that any government embarking on a TGF program need to address to maximize success of the investments and effort. These factors include:
   a. Strategic clarity.
   b. Leadership.
   c. User focus.
   d. Stakeholder engagement.
   e. Skills.
   f. Supplier partnership.
   g. Future proofing.

h. Achievable delivery.

i. Benefit realization.

3. **Service Delivery Frameworks** – TGF provides a reference model for delivering services in a citizen centric way to deliver transformational impact. The model defines a number of key processes which are:

   a. **Business Management Framework:** includes leadership, stakeholder governance model, as well as policies related to development and management of the program. This process requires a business model to be defined, where the "Franchise Marketplace" model explained above is recommended. Business management process also calls for the need for establishing common terminologies, reference architecture, and a clear delivery roadmap for the program.

   b. **Customer Management Framework:** provides guidelines for citizen centric service design and delivery process is holistic and market driven. This requires a "Brand-led Service Delivery" which drives deep understanding of the citizens and business customers that improves relevance of the services. Effective Identity Management and Citizen Empowerment component(s) are required to enable secure citizen participation to stimulate on-going service innovation.

   c. **Channel Management Framework:** this requires a TGF program to acquire insights into the combination of channels that are being used by citizens and business users when accessing the services. Together with a good understanding on the owners of each of these channels, this will facilitate a "Channel Transformation Strategy" that optimizes cost while improving user experience through appropriate shifting of traffic as well as cross-channel management.

   d. **Technology Management Framework:** this concerns the delivery of services that leverages on ICT that is based on a general Service Oriented Architecture (SOA) paradigm. This involves the identification and effective management of resources that include technology and information, which are building blocks for service implementation. To ensure that these services meet the requirements of citizens, there must be clear models and deep understanding of the stakeholders, actors, and systems that form the overall ecosystems. On-going changes in the ecosystem must be captured, which in turn trigger revisions that evolve the services in accordance to the changing needs. Concerns such as SOA technical architecture, reuse, service policies, identity management, cloud computing and others required to implement and govern SOA based systems are to be addressed as part of this process.

4. **Benefit realization Framework:** a process that incorporates activities that will ensure that TGF program delivers benefits and impacts in practice. This includes mapping the intended beneficial outcomes of the transformation program to specific activities and investments. The framework then requires measuring and comparing actual performance against target output and outcomes. Further, there should be governance arrangements that ensures the benefits will continue to be delivered.

OASIS TGF proposes an approach that moves away from just e-enabling existing transactional services, and instead puts the needs of citizens and businesses at the heart of the process of an

ICT-enabled change in the public sector in order to achieve significant and transformational impact on the efficiency and effectiveness of government (OASIS, 2011).

It is also worth noting that whilst OASIS TGF addresses a broader set of policy issues and is more holistic compared to most GIFs and EA, it is general enough to accommodate for the different types of EA and GIFs that countries may already have in place. Further, it allows services to be composed of a combination of different governments and TGF programs, hence enabling services delivery to be driven by wide ranging citizen needs rather than policy.

MOVING FORWARD

Governments all around the world recognize ICT as a key enabler towards government service delivery. The specific agenda may vary for country to country, but delivering the required services to the citizens and businesses in a seamless, frictionless, and cost-effective manner in a rapidly changing environment is considered to be the main goal to their efforts and investments. ICT enabled delivery of citizen centric-services are able:

- To deliver citizen centric-services: ensuring the provision of public services and information in ways that make sense to citizens
- To improve operational efficiency: enabling Government to streamline business and technology processes and work more effectively as a collective organization rather than a set of separate silos
- To maximize return on investment: interoperability between new environments and existing systems enables any move to new platforms to be gradual, efficient and evolutionary

We have seen that governments have initially adopted a bottom-up approach to interoperability by defining technical interoperability frameworks that were expected to solve the interoperability problem. Over the years, it became quite clear that standards and technical solutions have not been silver bullets that enable interoperability. Experience has shown that the complex business issues involving people, culture and organizations needed to be addressed in practice.

Later versions of the frameworks address business interoperability more comprehensively and emphasise less on technical issues. These may be in the form of new versions of GIFs or frameworks that leverages on Enterprise Architecture. However, further improvement was required as it falls short in addressing the on-going changes in socio-economic requirements and expectations faced by governments.

Hence, more recently, approaches such as the CSTransform's "Citizen Service Transformation" (CS Transform, 2009) and the OASIS Transformational Government Framework (OASIS, 2011) offer over-arching framework for developing citizen-centric services. These meta-frameworks provide a holistic guideline for developing government citizen centric services. It then suggests a Service Oriented business approach that is supported by the appropriate guidance on areas that need to be addressed by the program without being specific neither on methodology nor technology. With this, existing approaches and investments can be reused with minimal changes in the participating organizations, hence reducing risks and costs.

One could argue that a policy-centric approach in delivering interoperable government services diverts the focus away from the major goal of achieving the national objectives. Instead, the national needs should be central in driving their implementation, enabled by interoperable technologies and the appropriate organizational transformations. This is appearing to be more like a typical development and deployment of any software based solution that the ICT industry is familiar with. It is our opinion that this area is still evolving and requires further research and sharing of experiences.

REFERENCES

European Commission. (2010). *European interoperability framework (EIF) for European public services, version 2.0*. Brussels, Belgium: European Commission. Retrieved from http://ec.europa.eu/isa/strategy/doc/annex_ii_eif_en.pdf.

Federal Enterprise Architecture Program. (2007). *FEA practice guidance*. Retrieved from http://www.whitehouse.gov/sites/default/files/omb/assets/fea_docs/FEA_Practice_Guidance_Nov_2007.pdf.

IDABC. (2004). *European interoperability framework for pan-European egovernment services, version 1.0*. Retrieved from http://ec.europa.eu/idabc/en/document/3473/5585.html#top.

ISO. (1993). *ISO/IEC 2382-1:1993: Information technology – Vocabulary – Part 1: Fundamental terms*. New York, NY: International Organization For Standardization.

ITU. (2006). *Resolution GSC-11/4*. Retrieved from http://www.itu.int/ITU-T/gsc/gsc11/documents/GSC-11_Resolutions_IndexR3.doc.

Library of Congress. (2002). *E-government act of 2002: Title II: Federal management and promotion of electronic government services*. Washington, DC: Library of Congress. Retrieved from http://thomas.loc.gov/cgi-bin/bdquery/z?d107:HR02458:@@@L&summ2=m&|TOM:/bss/d107query.html|.

MAMPU. (2003). *Standards, policies and guidelines - Malaysian government interoperability framework (MyGIF) version 1.0*. Kuala Lumpur, Malaysia: MAMPU.

MAMPU. (2008). *Towards one service delivery no wrong door*. Kuala Lumpur, Malaysia: MAMPU.

McGovern, J., Ambler, S. W., Stevens, M. E., Linn, J., Sharan, V., & Jo, E. K. (2004). *A practical guide to enterprise architecture*. Upper Saddle River, NJ: Prentice Hall.

Microsoft Open Specifications. (2011). *Microsoft open specification promise (OSP)*. Retrieved from http://www.microsoft.com/openspecifications/en/us/programs/osp/default.aspx.

O'Toole, L. J., Jr., Brown, M. M., & Brundey, L. J. (1998). Implementing information technology in government: An empirical assessment of the role of local partnerships. *Journal of Public Administration Research And Theory, 8*(4), 499-525. Retrieved May 1, 2011 from http://www.highbeam.com/doc/1G1-53383712.html.

OASIS. (2011). *Transformational government framework (TGF) primer version 1.0*. Committee Note Draft 01 (CND01). Retrieved from http://docs.oasis-open.org/tgf/TGF-Primer/v1.0/TGF-Primer-v1.0.docx.

OASIS eGovernment Member Section. (2010). *Avoiding the pitfalls of egovernment - 10 lessons learnt from egovernment deployments*. Retrieved from http://www.oasis-egov.org/sites/oasis-egov.org/files/eGov_Pitfalls_Guidance%20Doc_v1.pdf.

OASIS TGF Technical Committee. (2011). *OASIS TGF technical committee, statement of purpose*. Retrieved from https://www.oasis-open.org/committees/tgf/charter.php.

Scholl, H. J., & Klischewski, R. (2007). E-government integration and interoperability: Framing the research agenda. *International Journal of Public Administration, 30*(8), 889–920. doi:10.1080/01900690701402668

Stewart, K., Cremin, D., Mills, M., & Phipps, D. (2004). *Non-technical interoperability: The challenge of command leadership in multinational operations.* Paper presented at the 10th International Command and Control Research and Technology Symposium: The Future of C2. Retrieved from http://www.dodccrp.org/events/10th_ICCRTS/ CD/papers/298.pdf.

Transform, C. S. (2009). *Beyond interoperability – A new policy framework for e-government.* CS Transform White Papers. London, UK: CS Transform Limited. Retrieved on May 4th from http://www.cstransform.com/resources/white_papers/ BeyondInteropV1.0.pdf.

Tsilas, N. L. (2007). Enabling open innovation and interoperability: Recommendations for policy makers. In *Proceedings of the 1st International Conference on Theory and Practice of Electronic Governance.* New York, NY: ACM Press.

KEY TERMS AND DEFINITIONS

Business Interoperability: Also known as "Non-technical interoperability" enables the required information to be exchanged and used effectively across different systems and organizations through addressing non-technical barriers such as those involving people, process, and policies.

Enterprise Architecture (EA): An approach to designing systems for an enterprise through defining the main components of an organization, and how functions in the organization core systems work together to achieve a defined business objective.

Government Interoperability Framework (GIF): Are government policies that are meant to enable interoperability in intra-government and inter-government ICT initiatives.

Interoperability: The capability to communicate, execute programs, or transfer data among various functional units in a manner that requires the user to have little or no knowledge of the unique characteristics of those units (ISO/IEC 2382-1:1993, 1993).

Open Standards: Are standards that incorporate elements of openness such as collaborative development, non-exclusive, reasonable, and non-discriminatory intellectual property terms, accessible and others.

Standard: In the context of this topic is widely accepted as a technology specification that enables interoperability.

Technical Interoperability: The ability for information to move successfully between systems.

Chapter 17
Enterprise Architecture for Personalization of e-Government Services:
Reflections from Turkey

Alpay Erdem
Middle East Technical University (METU), Turkey

İhsan Tolga Medeni
Middle East Technical University (METU), Turkey & Turksat, Turkey & Çankaya University, Turkey

Tunç D. Medeni
Turksat, Turkey & Middle East Technical University (METU), Turkey & Yildirim Beyazit University (YBU), Turkey

ABSTRACT

As there has not yet been enough work on enterprise architectures for fully integrated knowledge-based, highly-sophisticated (citizen-oriented) personalized services, this chapter aims to articulate a perspective to design architectures for the development and provision of sophisticated, personalized services. Doing so, the authors benefit from their knowledge and experience in the Turkish e-Government Gateway (eGG) and general e-Government services development and provision. First providing an introduction and background information, the chapter discusses the development of eGG services in Turkey, and then provides a visionary suggestion for knowledge-based personalized, citizen-centric e-Government. Among the suggested perspectives, an E-Citizen Decision Support System, and Entity-Utility and Information Flow Model could be useful for eGG development in Turkey and elsewhere.

DOI: 10.4018/978-1-4666-1824-4.ch017

INTRODUCTION

According to the UN report (2008), in recent years e-government services have brought about a more collaborative mindset, owing to the tremendous opportunities for sharing information and aligning (if not integrating) service offerings across different providers. Then, a core challenge for e-government's enterprise architecture is that a more seamless governance be nurtured through collaborative opportunities between units (i.e. departments and agencies), or more aggressively pursued through a single, central service provider. One centralizing force is the pursuit of greater interoperability across enterprise-wide architectures (important elements of a platform for service delivery) for the public sector as a whole. Yet the manner in which centralization and collaboration are viewed as complementary is a significant novelty in this digital environment.

Meanwhile based upon the Swedish Administrative Development Agency (VERVA)'s previous work, Vinnova (2009, pp. 77-80) report four basic scenarios of e-Government development according to these two criteria:

1. *degree of central coordination by the state*: what the state should organize and what should be organized by municipalities and county councils, the market and trade organizations, as well as ways for steering and financing public services. With a low degree of central coordination, conditions for developing different forms of market solutions will be more favorable.
2. *degree of central integration of public agencies' systems and processes:* how well systems, processes and financing are integrated between the public agencies. With a high degree of integration, the various systems in public administration are linked together by automate communication and exchange systems.

With respect to these two criteria, there are four scenarios:

1. Information Chaos (decentralised coordination, low integration)
2. Guide (centralised coordination, low integration)
3. Clusters (decentralised coordination, high integration)
4. One-stop-shop (centralised coordination, high integration)

Capgemini (2007) also specifically evaluates the services of EU countries and suggests the user challenge benchmarking for the provision of online public services. Starting with basic informational, one or two-way interactional levels of provision, the services advance towards fully transactional and personalized provisions.

In accordance with these challenges and scenarios, Turkey aims to develop and sophisticate its e-Government Gateway (eGG) as the user-oriented one-stop-shop with fully personalized and orchestrated services for its citizens, as well as businesses and government agencies. eGG currently provides (as of June 2011) around 260 e-services integrated into e-Government Gateway with more than 8,000,000 registered/regular users, as well as thousands of content pages with guiding links to related agencies for further info or service.

Providing a common framework for the governments to achieve e-government transformation is a desired but hard-to-achieve goal for not only Turkey but most of the well-known Information Technology (IT) leaders of the globe, as well. The supplied services mostly are defined by the demographic characteristics of the country; for instance, a country with a young population would probably prioritize the services that are appealing for the younger people, however, a country with an older population would choose another approach. For this reason, we can assume that IT companies with a high-level of expertise in different countries could be able to provide a more flexible framework. To test this assumption it can be useful to look at some of these companies' product white papers and Web pages, from the perspectives of personalization and privacy.

For instance, Microsoft's "Connected Framework" concentrates on providing e-government services with secure interconnected systems and applications (Microsoft Corporation, 2007). This model seems to look at the government as an IT structure; however, it does not put a proper life cycle concept into its framework, which is an important part for the personal user activities. However, giving identity and access is probably an important part of the privacy. Next, Oracle's iGovernment foundation (Oracle, 2011) framework brings innovation, integration, and intelligent operations to life through a Service Oriented Architecture (SOA) and a decision support mechanism. However, for personalization and privacy issues, it does not provide much more information. Meanwhile, another framework is presented with the collaborative work of the IBM and Government Interoperability Framework (GIF) is prepared. Under IBM's Web page, e-Government Interoperability Guide is reachable (United Nations, 2007). This document mainly concentrates on interoperability between the government agencies. GIF presents a set of standards and guidelines, including technical perspective with respect to its process documentation, implementation, and compliance regimes. Rather than Microsoft's and Oracle's view point, this is mainly based on the policy part of the system. Finally, OASIS eGov is an organization to serve governmental and public administration requirements for standardization. The Transformational Government framework concentrates on citizen engagement to the e-Government activities (OASIS, 2011). This framework includes a reference model, definition of a series of policy products, a value chain for citizen service transformation, guiding principles, business model, a delivery roadmap, and a checklist of critical success factors.

As it can be seen from the above examples, although there are various works on enterprise architectures, up to authors' best knowledge, there has not been enough attention given for a perspective on developing enterprise architecture for fully integrated knowledge-based, highly-sophisticated (citizen-oriented) personalized services yet. This chapter thus aims to elaborate further upon a guiding perspective for design of architectures for development and provision of sophisticated, personalized services, benefiting from authors' Turkish eGG and general e-Government experience. After this introductory, background information, the chapter continues with a discussion on development of eGG services in Turkey, and finally provides a visionary suggestion for knowledge-based personalized, citizen-centric e-government.

DEVELOPMENT OF EGG SERVICES IN TURKEY

In Turkey, Turksat develops and operates the eGG. Based upon available maturity and sophistication frameworks, the below maturity levels have been considered for a citizen-oriented evaluation of available e-government services at Turksat (CEES, 2010).

- **Maturity Level 1, Information:** General information services (categorised content, announcements, daily-updated info on exchange rate or weather conditions) that can be accessed without authentication and authorization
- **Maturity Level 2, Interaction:** General e-services that can be accessed with authentication and authorization, and that rely on simple data exchange
- **Maturity Level 3, Transaction:** More sophisticated services that have, for instance, financial transactions, value-added information processing, etc.

- **Maturity Level 4, Personalization:** Services that can be personalized by citizens on their personal pages

Later the merging of levels 2 and 3 into one level was tried (Osman, et al., 2011). Meanwhile, Personalization has been taken as the last stage of maturity with respect to the Capgemini (2007) framework.

General Infrastructure and Philosophy of eGG

e-Government Gateway infrastructure has been developed, as in Figure 1, to support high transactional ratios of Web service usage. A basic representation of the Turkish eGG architecture can be found in this figure.

According to this figure, one group of related e-government operations is the Government-to-

Citizen services. The citizen users can reach the services they desire via internet browsers. In the e-Government portal called e-Devlet Kapısı, the services are published via a portlet server. This portlet server is directly connected to the Enterprise Service Bus (ESB) of e-Devlet Kapısı, which orchestrates the connections and transactions between e-Devlet Kapısı and Web service publishers or Web service clients. Meanwhile, to establish interoperability between different government organizations, e-Devlet Kapısı functions in the middle to establish communication lines. For transactions and processes concerning Web Service (WS) usage, ESB offers services like those it offers to citizens. While technology independence is an important factor for global markets, Java- and .Net-based technologies are the most dominant ones in the Turkish market, and this dominance is also reflected in government organizations' technology usage habits. WS and e-

Figure 1. Summarized web service architecture of e-devlet kapisi (e-government gateway) in Turkey

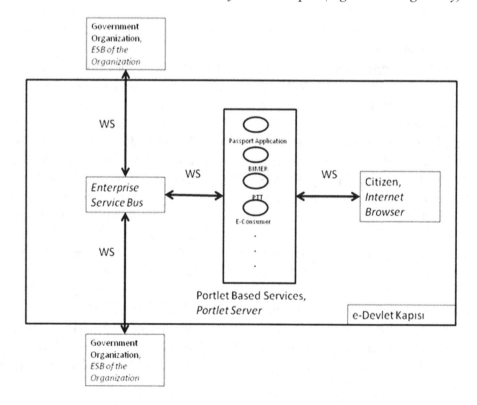

Devlet Kapısı thus have an important role to provide interoperability not only for intra-government but also inter-government operations (government-to-government). As explained in Yildirim et al. (2010), to be more specific, eGG is formed of three main layers that are both separated and collaborating;

1. the gateway layer
2. the backbone-repository layer and
3. the presentation layer (a combination of view and controller layers consumes the related Web services on the gateway layer, called as eGG ESB) (p 55).

Accordingly:

The modules of presentation layer do involve minimum number of business rules so that injecting a different kind of presentation domain into this layer such as WAP or mobile java applications reside as an easy task in terms of development. The modules of this layer are mainly the portlet applications for Web and jsp/servlet applications for mobile implementations. The aim of ESB of e-Government Gateway is to orchestrate the connections and transactions between e-Government Gateway, and Web service publishers or Web service clients. These clients are government organizations. The main purpose of this orchestration is to connect necessary Web services of the government organizations to another one. With this approach, when Web services of the organizations will be used as associated around one certain result and the users will get the information they need without witnessing the complexity of the system behind. To establish interoperability between different government organizations, e-Government Gateway functions in the middle to establish communication lines. For transactions and processes concerning Web service usage, ESB offers services like those it offers to citizens. At this point, the ESB is also used to connect the repository layer which consists of the database and the e-mail servers of

e-Government Gateway to the presentation layer so that the full orchestration of the infra-structure is completed (p. 55).

Identity management using personal password (citizens can apply to widespread Postal Offices to get one) and e-signature are integrated into the system, and limited financial transactions and higher levels of personalization are also currently available. While before Turkey was considered to have an ad-hoc approach for e-Government applications using electronic signatures (IDABC, 2007), the 2008 launch of eGG that implements unified access and centralized authentication module, enables a shared service to represent the national framework. Thanks to this approach, issues of security, the management of sign-up mechanisms, back office management, handling of user problems, addressing back up could be solved more easily and adequately in a unified way by the eGG.

eGG was officially launched in December 2008 with 20 services in Ankara, as a major milestone for transforming into a sophisticated Information/Knowledge Society for and achieving the related Strategic Goals set by Turkey (DPT, 2006). Although the 5-year strategy is completed, the eGG project will also be under continuous development in response to the arising needs of integration and interoperability from citizens, business enterprises and public institutions, which could also be resembled with a spiral model for project management. Accordingly, the project can be divided into phases (Analysis, Design, Implementation, Testing) that build upon the previous one and with a running release of software produced at the end (Ariadne Training, 2001). In collaboration with front office, the back office can then work on the entire lifecycle, within which testing and learning from experience is embedded. First, the main modules are developed together with a limited number of services available, upon which new modules and services are integrated in time. Meanwhile, continuous, incremental improvements on available services with respect to user feedback are utilized. The logo of eGG also reflects this spiral model (Figure 2).

From a system's perspective, this spiral model can also be considered the results of reflective and refractive interactions within and across different cultural entities such as various governmental institutions, citizens and other stakeholders. While reflection can be understood as seeing reality as it is, refraction complements this understanding as reconceiving and changing reality (Wankel & DeFillippi, 2006). The importance of reflection and refraction for boundary-crossing interactions can then be argued (Medeni, Cook, & Elwell, 2007; Medeni, Iwatsuki, & Cook, 2008). Cross-cultural refraction and cross-cultural reflection occur, when and where two or more knowledge systems encounter so that their living entities initiate a knowledge-creating process. Within this process, knowledge creation is initiated by the acquisition of not only extant but also new knowledge through cross-cultural reflection and cross-cultural refraction. The cross-cultural reflection for the acquisition of extant knowledge addresses the reflective learning and practice that generate apparently new understandings that are not immediately related to specific existing knowledge although clearly they are based on what we know (Moon, 2004). The cross-cultural

refraction for the acquisition of new knowledge, addresses a more critical and creative type of reflection, for experiential learning and practice that facilitate emergent thinking to cross the boundary between different episteme as reflection and new mindsets (Moon, 2004; Uno, 1999; Medeni, Medeni, Balcı, & Dalbay, 2009).

Selected Interactions with Citizens, Demands for More Personalized Information and Services

According to such continuous interactions and improvements with respect to using citizens' feedback so far, certain operational examples can be given. For instance, regarding single sign-in (identification and authentication) module, # button has been added to the virtual keyboard, and automatic log-out has been extended, following user feedback. Moreover, it has become possible for users to choose the default location for weather forecast information, while it used to be Ankara, as the political capital city, by default, at the beginning. Again, thanks to citizen feedback and demands, it has also become possible to expand the operations to the citizens living abroad. Finally, adding necessary parameters to print-outs as confirmations of the information transactions conducted via e-Government Gateway has been

Figure 2. Spiral model and the logo of e-government gateway, Turkey (Adapted from Ariadne Training, 2001, p. 12)

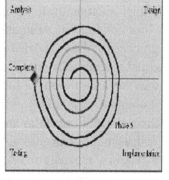

done for certain services. (Citizens request these hard copies to be recognized as official document, even if the whole concept of the eGG aims to eliminate the need for citizens to provide these hard copies to public institutions, enabling flow of information virtually among the public institutions themselves). Another example of ongoing development and sophistication with respect to input from user experience can also be given as the case of Service for Inquiring for Social Security Premium.

Before eGG, the Social Security Agency was providing the Social Security Inquiry service. It was open to any third parties, as soon as they know the related personal information—which was also not so hard to find. In this way, for instance, lawyers were able to trace the accounts for salary or retirement payments of people without their consent. This was common in such cases that, as an example scenario, these people borrow money from a legal entity such as a bank, but do not pay it back, so the entity asks its lawyer to search for other accounts of these people so that it can block (if there is) any transaction such as the salary or retirement payments as a pressure tool to receive its money back. Meanwhile, the inquiry service was open to any other misuse—to get access to private data without the consent of citizens.

Almost from the beginning of its launch, eGG provided this Social Security Premium Inquiry Service, while the service was still available from the related government agency website. However, the users need to authenticate themselves, if they want to use this service via eGG. The registered users were around 2 million. After the second year, however, the service provision from the Agency website was ceased, and the service became available only via eGG. This caused enormous resentment and complaints from the users, even blaming eGG for preventing citizens' receiving what they need/want. Some of these complaints were indeed fair and true, as initially the transition to a more secure system that requires use of authentication mechanisms and prior cumbersome

application procedures caused real operational problems. Some patients had to be carried from hospital to application offices, as they needed to show evidence of their social security payments and the public servants were not yet aware/capable of using any procedure for appointing legal representatives who can deal with the application procedures, or blind people had difficulty getting the identity password for the authentication, even if they applied for one, because the actual contract stated that "it must be read by the applicant," and there was no preparation for enabling blind citizens to read the contract. Some other complaints, however, were unfair, such as those who criticized that ordinary citizens were not yet familiar enough with Internet to use this eGG e-service, ignoring the fact that this service had actually been provided via internet @ the agency website in the first place. It was also clear that this take-over by eGG ended an old era where citizens' personal data could have been accessed by third parties, and these third parties would not be that happy about this new situation. Majority of the complaints were however due to the enormous demand that overloaded the administrative procedures and electronic service system in the beginning. Specifically, this system overload also caused unwanted delays in the other related public administrative affairs. As a consequence, the levels of satisfaction from the related electronic services were very low in contrast to high levels from other frequently used services. However, in general these operational issues were sorted out reasonably well. Finally, as of December 2011, a recent decision was made so that the related services will have been provided again at the website of the Social Security Agency, as well.

At the moment, the eGG has more than 11 million users and one of the biggest registered user groups is elderly people who are mostly using services such as these social security premium inquiry services. This is more striking, when the fact is recalled that Turkey's population is not an aging but a young one. It is clear that the service take-over by eGG has enormously increased and continues to increase the usage rates. Meanwhile, a new personalized feature has been added to eGG so that users can allow specific entities to access their information. Only these entities for which the users give their consent can access and in this way the related administrative and public affairs can proceed efficiently, addressing the major source of citizen dis/satisfaction.

A project on measuring citizen satisfaction with the "Citizen Satisfaction Index" has also been initiated in 2008 (T-VOHSU Project) as a collaboration between Türksat and Kahramanmaraş Sütçü İmam Üniversitesi. (Bakan, Aydın, Kar, and Öz 2008, 2009). As a part of the T-VOHSU project, a pilot survey to measure citizen satisfaction was also implemented at the eGG. Certain initial qualitative results of this pilot survey are available (CEES Workshop, ICEGEG conference, Antalya, 2010), in which a citizen demand for more personalized information and service provision can be highlighted as a result of our analysis.

To contribute to these initial findings, another research based on user feedback as citizen suggestions and complaints that reached the eGG call center for seven-month period (from June to December 2009) was conducted. As the result of the data collection and analysis, 95 citizen feedbacks were categorized. The most significant of the feedback categories incorporate requests for new specific processes and information to be included in the future system developments. (Çetin et. al. 2010)

An EU-funded international project for citizen-oriented evaluation of e-Government services (C.E.E.S.) has also been initiated in 2009 in collaboration with Brunel University, UK and American University of Beirut, Lebanon. The project aims to develop a reference process model that will allow the application of findings to Turkey as well as to other EU countries (Lee, et al., 2009). Results from an initial analysis of the citizen comments that are incidentally collected for four months can further elicit and update user

perspectives (on newer services). (Medeni et al 2011).

Additional Service Request category includes suggestions about other services that may be part of the future development of the gateway. (Example: "I want more information about services." "More information needed on military services section." "I want a new section about my education information." "Current services are not enough, more services needed" (p. 9).

In general these qualitative results underline the demands of citizens for more personalized information and services to be provided at the eGG. In addition to these initial qualitative results, more quantitative results are also available elsewhere (Osman et al 2011). Starting from Summer 2011, however, a new concept is being applied into the provision of eGG services, based upon citizen feedback as well as benchmarking studies. Measurement of citizen evaluation and satisfaction continues accordingly.

Interactions among Public Institutions

Meanwhile, it is also important to look at the implementation of citizen-centric and transformative e-government from a policy and governance perspective. The most recent implementation interactions among governmental agencies and other stakeholders' policy levels are based upon Information Society Strategy document that specifically emphasize citizen focused service transformation and modernization in public administration.

In 2006, the Information Society Strategy document published by the State Planning Organization (Devlet Planlanma Teşkilatı, DPT, currently has become the Ministry of Development) continued the development of e-Government services for transforming Turkey into an information society (DPT, 2006). In the 2008 Progress Report by DPT (2008), nevertheless, it is noted that among the 111 actions defined in the strategy document, only 3 are concluded, 51 are works-in-progress, 34 are in their infancy, and 23 are yet to start. In the report, DPT (2008) highlights the idea that the priorities and objectives of the Strategy still need to be appreciated and owned by all stakeholders, and other responsible and interested entities in the society. Problems experienced in the implementation of the strategy are described in the report under the headings of Legislation (and Legal) Issues, Financial Issues, Personnel (and Human Resources) Issues, Issues of Intra-Institutional Coordination, Issues of Inter-Institutional Coordination, and Other Issues (DPT, 2008).

Our analysis show that Legislation Issues and Issues of Inter-Institutional Coordination are evaluated to have the highest (negative) impact (21%), followed by Personnel Issues (19%), Financial Issues (16%), Issues of Intra-Institutional Coordination (13%) and Other Issues (%10), which also include coordination issues, in the implementation of the Strategy. Similarly for the implementation of the individual action points/ projects to pave the way for reaching Information Society within the overall strategy; Legislation Issues and Issues of Inter-Institutional Coordination are highlighted the most (19%) followed by Personnel and Financial Issues (18%), Issues of Intra-Institutional Coordination (17%) and Other Issues (9%).

Recently, a new progress report has also been issued (DPT, 2010). Accordingly, by 2009 22 actions have been completed, 62 actions have recorded significant progress, 19 actions are at initial stage, 8 actions are yet-to-start. Information on problems based on the same categories is also presented.

According to our comparative analysis of the 2008 and 2010 reports, it is worth noting that from 2008 to 2010, intra-institutional, internal coordination problems have a relative decrease, while inter-institutional, external coordination problems have increased. Besides, legislative problems increasingly continue and their relative percentage also rises respectively. Personnel

problems also increase, although their relative percentage remains constant or becomes lower. Financial problems, meanwhile, does not record such an increase, on the contrary have a tendency to remain constant or become lower.

Overall, these analyses underline the vivid existence and/but difficult nature of myriad cross-cultural interactions among various societal entities for the integration and interoperability of e-Government services in Turkey. The difficulties experienced at the individual actions cause a significant policy resistance on aggregate, hindering the successful implementation of the e-government projects.

Examples from the Current State of eGG

Nevertheless, as a result of all these developments, research and implementation work, continuous improvement of e-Government services, and transformation of public services on the supply side and personalization of them on the demand side is the ultimate aim. With respect to the ultimate aim, one of the latest developments, for instance, is an integrated municipality tax payment service. This online municipal tax payment operates according to service orchestration principles and integrates municipalities with governmental institutions for citizens' payment via authorized banks (Figure 3). This integrated service is provided as an embedded aspect of personalized "my page." While currently the service is finalizing its pilot application, it aims to be fully operational soon (Figure 4). In addition to this pilot work on tax payment, citizen can currently access various personal information and services on their personalized page such as school information of their kids, information on traffic fines or legal cases, among others.

Furthermore, the recent developments in cloud computing can provide useful solutions for developing more citizen-oriented systems. Turkey also tries to catch-up-with these recent developments in clouds.

Figure 3. The structure of online payment of municipal taxes (Adapted from Kahramaner, 2010)

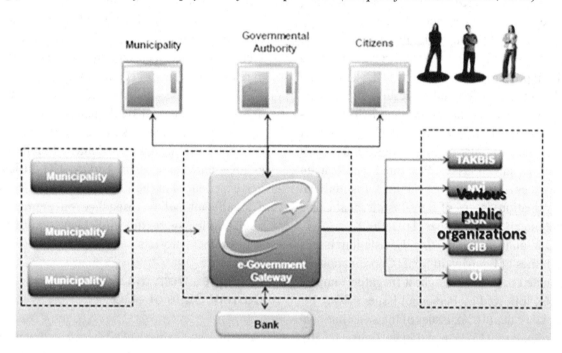

For instance, with respect to a latest research in the USA that reflects 30 cloud cases in central and local government institutions, Citizen Relationship Management, central e-mail applications, and application and data servings are among the major uses of cloud computing. For instance, The Social Security Administration (SSA) handles millions of questions and inquiries from citizens every year such as what they can do online, or how to get a social security number, file for benefits, locate a field office, get a retirement estimate, or request a proof of income letter. In order to provide the public with a convenient means to answer their questions anytime and anywhere, Internet access is available; the agency provides an online database of Frequently Asked Questions, leveraging a cloud-based solution. Accordingly, visitors to socialsecurity.gov can search for answers by category, keyword, or phrase, which helps them quickly find the information they are looking for. Over a thousand questions and answers are included up in the knowledge base. In 2009, the number of answers provided through

SSA's Frequently Asked Questions grew to over 34 million, which would not have been normally possible for office staff and 800-number agents (Kundra, 2010).

Accordingly, in Turkey, Turksat envisions development and use of cloud computing applications and solutions for central e-mail, Citizen Relationship Management that can include social media, inter-institutional legal communications and documentations, common/shared data and application (budget, accounting, personnel) serving. In addition to the suggested benefits to everyone, generally cloud architecture can also improve user satisfaction in public agencies whose changing needs cannot be met by package-ICT solutions.

As a pioneering institution in the public and business area, Turksat specifically suggests a cloud solution for local agencies in collaboration with a national municipalities agency. Accordingly, a database layer, application layer, and user interface layer can be suggested: While each agency can keep their own data, the data will be standardized in the database layer. There are many com-

Figure 4. The operation of online payment of municipal taxes (Adapted from Yılmaz & Yıldırım, 2010)

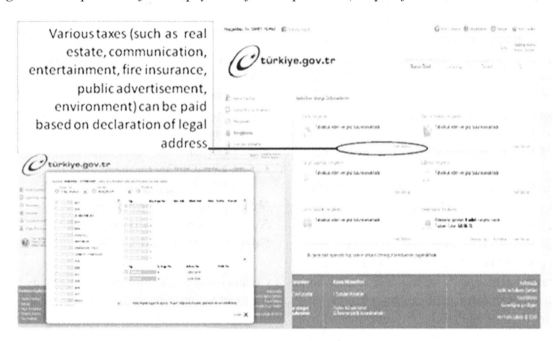

monalities in the used data and, if there are any differences, these can be acknowledged. While all the applications can be hosted freely, the used applications should ensure the standardization of the data. Meanwhile a pricing scheme can be established with respect to the use of Web services that establish the link between the applications and user interface. No interface elements will be included in the application layer, while all specific, ever-changing user needs with respect to usability, reporting, and business intelligence tools can be addressed agilely in the interface layer. In this way, it is aimed that new business sectors for ICT companies, and satisfaction of end users will be developed together with common benefits of cloud such as effectiveness and environment-friendliness.

A SUGGESTION FOR KNOWLEDGE-BASED PERSONALIZED, CITIZEN-CENTRIC E-GOVERNMENT ENTERPRISE

In the previous section, we discussed the recent eGG services developments in Turkey. In this section, personalization of services and related citizen-centric e-Government concepts within an enterprise and Enterprise Architecture (EA) perspective are explained in more detail.

In simple terms, EA can guarantee service and data availability through all of the enterprise divisions. Here, we assume enterprise as the social institution of e-government. For comprehending e-Government Enterprise (eGE), however, it is first good to explain the traditional approach.

Traditional Approach

The traditional approach considers government agencies as service providers and citizens as service consumers. Accordingly, typical e-services are provided for each citizen independent of its profile or any other proprietary characteristics. Government agencies have mostly unprocessed data piles about each individual, which are neither unified nor interpreted. That means valuable data resources are partially used and not available through the enterprise.

Furthermore, in traditional service provision, only citizens asks for service and get results. Government has goals about health sector, finance sector, and so on. Government provides the service access point and makes it easy to access those services.

The current level of e-services also benefits from personal knowledge and knowledge shared by government agency operations. In conventional e-government applications, citizens can also try to mine and reach services provided by e-government. This process obviously is limited to the services provided by e-services and to the usage level by citizen. Typically, for realizing an operation, a citizen searches for corresponding available services, and in the case of an existing service, he/she then proceeds toward completing the process. In this case, at the level of society, aka enterprise, knowledge is not shared and used for any knowledge construction process. Meanwhile, a government actor is also able to inform each individual about legal responsibilities like income tax, building tax, among others. E-government may also be considered as a portal for making public announcements, policies, and so on.

Accordingly, even if we consider each citizen as a part of the eGG, knowledge about rest of the enterprise is not used for any specific citizen by government authorities. Knowledge about each citizen remains unused for others. Nevertheless, a personalized, citizen-centric approach suggests unification of knowledge for each individual and utilization of merged data at society level, making it available through eGG.

In conventional e-government approaches, government agencies can provide e-services through the e-Government portal shorten the wait and ease citizen access services to achieve social responsibilities (ECeGov, 2011). In this way, government can, for instance, access citizens' cloud for announcements, policies, regularities, deadlines—i.e. share public news, but does not offer personalized services for citizens. Meanwhile, certain level of service customization is achieved by existing e-government approaches in the sense that citizens can follow their taxes, electricity bills, and make payments for them.

Motivation for Proposed System: Personalization of Services can Add Value

Certain personalization approaches already exist (European Commission, 2011; Kautz, Selman, & Shah, 1997; Balabanovic, Shoham, & Fab, 1997). Accordingly, a citizen tries to access services and knowledge, learns his/her responsibilities from e-government portal, which helps to define business processes, and makes them available to be accessed from a well-known point, one-stop-shop. Increased availableness of government services enables citizens accessing these services in a 7*24 manner, and also provides ease of access from every edge point of internet where internet availability has been dramatically increased. This conventional approach defines and makes available services and waits for citizens to discover and use right ones for managing government services in context of social responsibility. This direction of interaction between government and citizens is in a passive manner, and becomes useful when discovered by citizens. However, in cased where the proper services are not discovered by citizens, usage percentage of these services decreases. In this case of service provision, proper matching of service supply and demand is out of consideration, as finding out the proper service is up to the individual efforts of the citizen. What is generally happening in the current situation of e-Government policy is that an individual tries to identify and make use of e-services within his/her limited perspective and tries to make life easier, aiming to create value for him/herself on his/her own. Still, there are newly emerging perspectives such as providing complementary channels of call centers for not only enabling citizens' access to the public institutions but also proactively enabling these institutions' access to the individuals they serve.

Existing works related with personalization and citizen-centric services also typically concentrate on best matching mechanisms for profile of citizen and service recommendation (Guo & Lu, 2007; Amoroso, 2004; Riecken, 2000; Resnick, 1997). This aspect deals with presenting related service content to target citizen profile. Our personalized services approach, however, considers the social institution of e-government as an enterprise and tries to extract knowledge through this enterprise, making it a useful service for each citizen rather than letting citizens explore services beneficial for themselves.

Personalized e-government services can make use of data resources from a very wide range of government agencies, private sector, citizen and others; mine enterprise data for individual feature vector, and extract similarities with enterprise profiles. Although these services may seem outside the scope of direct e-government goals, in fact it is not. Providing better life conditions through availability of personalized services would contribute much to enterprise level welfare status. A citizen-centric government service approach shifts the paradigm of providing government related services through more effective ways. Adding value to each citizen would mean adding value to society, which is the enterprise itself. More than a simple service provision, it can turn out to provide a more interactive content. The system, for instance, can fuse all health data of individuals, analyse genetic and environmental conditions, utilize past knowledge for similar cases, and detect and alert for potential health problems.

Accordingly, activities like consolidating all the health data of each individual and being able to access through enterprise have been successful pioneering ideas (ECeGov, 2011). Mining this data at society level such as embedding genetic and environmental factors for diseases and correlating these ones from mined data would be a critical step for becoming a real enterprise government. For being able to enterprise, however, common knowledge obtained again from enterprise elements should also be shared by all elements of enterprise, where elements here may indicate each citizen.

From the policy makers and governance aspect, citizen centric eGG may then function as a tool providing alignment for long term policy determination process, since system will be supplying clear figures and empirical measurements for existing situation and estimations for future, based on enterprise-level fused knowledge. Policy makers and governors will then have chance of being aligned about how to improve existing society welfare, how to explore deficiencies, and what are potential remedy steps to take. This alignment covers health, finance, education, employment areas in a basic approach. The system lets focusing on more strategic points, covering long-term plans. This gives opportunity of selecting investment areas, assigning proper weight for each focus area, and making schedules for projects. At this point, however, the fundamental target should be increasing the welfare of society and the welfare of each individual, which is the most crucial goal of citizen-centric eGG.

One of the critical targets of e-government applications can actually be considered to be knowledge dissemination at society level. Although e-government applications are considered as speeding up processes and leveraging government services, knowledge sharing via e-government is another rising aspect of the issue.

One of important advantage of citizen-centric eGG can be that citizens will be benefiting eGG services and so share knowledge by requesting services from agencies or personalized services suggested from system. Another motivation of proposed e-citizen centric approach is increased maturity level of provided services by government. Citizen centric eGG has the chance of supplying more sophisticated and useful services to citizens such as related to their academic and industrial careers, health issues, environmental ones, and so on.

E-Government could also remove limitations over integrated services for following and paying taxes. In this way, quality of provided services by government would increase. Although certain level of service customization is achieved by existing e-government approaches, there certainly exists the need of further customization for specific individuals and groups, and even for each individual—where level of customization could be relatively increased by the application of the proposed approach.

Personalization and Citizen-Centric Services for e-Government Enterprise

At this point, an analogy about search approaches over the Internet may be a useful example. Preferring Google search over other search approaches is possibly due to the fact that more personalized and relevant results related to the given keywords by Google. Sharing worldwide knowledge by considering the keywords entered, users are more likely to be happy for getting most relevant pages that are reaching specific knowledge cloud in a fast way. The idea is very basic: nobody likes to read hundreds of Web pages, among which they have to select one. It has certain costs such as time and energy. Similarly, conventional e-government approach may provide many services for benefit of citizens but it is a somewhat time-consuming process—to waste time to find and access appropriate service. It is like reading hundreds of Web pages for getting specific information.

Due to reasons and motivations stated above, personalized services can be developed by using unified/fused information about each individual.

Since in conventional approaches dissemination of knowledge is limited to individuals' personal efforts, government provides services and waits for access of citizens to those utilities. In this proposed system, government makes effort to push more customized, critical, value-added services to citizens. With personalized, citizen-centric services, e-Government may not remain as one-way communication, it may propose two-way interactions, adding value to the welfare of each individual and so to the total welfare of society.

In this proposed personalized citizen-centric service provision, government could have the duty of collecting detailed information about each citizen and sharing this knowledge across society—by all means considering all the related privacy, security, and trustworthiness issues. Abuse of personal information is also possible as a side effect but proper privacy policies may be enforced, ensuring usage of collected personal information for only well defined target areas. As an example, disability information of an individual may be a critical symptom for health issues; meanwhile issues that could lead to discrimination should be prevented. Thus, privacy issue is important aspect of this approach. Whether each citizen would allow his/her personal data to be collected, used, traced is among the questions to be addressed.

In order to realize this system, nevertheless, collecting and consolidating data for each citizen can be proposed to make use of inferences for the benefit of the citizen. Adding, creating value for individual is the process of utilizing common knowledge of society for that particular individual. The other side of creating value for individual is exactly creating value for government, society, common goals, and values of the country. An example can be given as analyzing health status, checking for potentially serious diseases beforehand, and directing individuals for solutions, which contributes to health strategies, policies, and applications of government. Preventing a cancer case by early diagnosis this way saves life of citizen and also contributes to health budget by not spending effort and money for that particular case. Another example is that government always has a goal for reducing unemployment rates. Analyzing qualifications of individuals by using their e-citizen portal and matching these features with potential employment industry or companies that look for employees, and as a result providing connective information to both individual and employer is an efficient way of policy implementation of reducing unemployment. For this purpose, an e-citizen portal having consolidated data, or enhancing access to personal data and a decision support system, which makes inferences based on consolidated data of individuals for offering personalized services to related stakeholders, could be useful.

Government should thus offer more customized/specialized services for individuals depending on their data. E-government concept should be extended to this scope rather than just easing administration, gaining time, and so on. In this way, government also has a more sophisticated way of reaching citizen that is a rather efficient and interactive way compared to conventional methods. Government may then alert citizen for his/her responsibilities, give clear schedules for due dates of certain tasks which are obligatory. In the citizen portal, government can add a personalized schedule so that clear understanding of responsibilities can be established.

In summary, our personalized, citizen-centric e-Government approach is set up over the idea of using society level knowledge reachable by government for again the benefit of each citizen individually. In this concept, government can be accessed via Web or other digital channels by citizens but also citizens should be accessed digitally by government to sustain better customized set of services. In conventional e-Government approaches, government collects certain amount of data/information, but makes limited use of them for e-services. Our proposed personalized

citizen-centric approach utilizes social level knowledge for the benefit of the citizen in the form of e-service. For this purpose, government collects, consolidates, and analyzes information for each citizen to provide customized services.

Citizen-Centric e-Government Enterprise Structure: Possible Scenarios

In this suggested approach, government, as an active actor, constructs citizen data warehouse regarding all digital information about each citizen. For instance, health history of each citizen could be collected through health institutions and used as a base for mining and inferences for e-services. Academic background and job skills and experience again can be obtained through related institutions. All dimensions are merged at each citizen base to supply citizen data warehouse (Figure 5). In this way, namely E-Citizen Decision Support System (DSS), government has capability to mine patterns over all citizens, obtain patterns and behaviors, and make some inferences according to rules and goals of e-Government approach.

This decision support system aims to provide citizens more personalized content about their conditions, and make them aware of related utilities/opportunities and facilities provided by government, making them accessible through e-services in a quick manner. Citizen data warehouse may become accessible through personal portal of each citizen by considering privacy issues and getting permissions of citizen. That is to say, health records, taxes, social security information, education career, business track, personal capabilities, languages and skills of citizen may be provided over personal portal for benefit of other government institutions (health sector) or companies (job skills and experience for employment purpose). E-Citizen portal owns consolidated information about citizen, collected from e-Government agencies, private sector and personal

Figure 5. E-citizen data warehouse: collecting data about each citizen

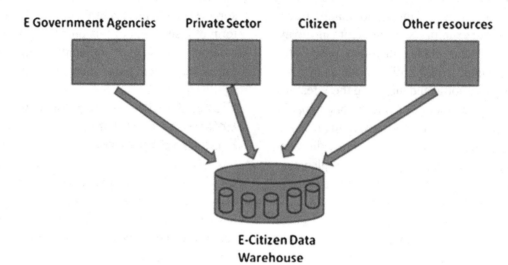

Figure 6. Citizen DSS, mining and producing recommendations via inference engine

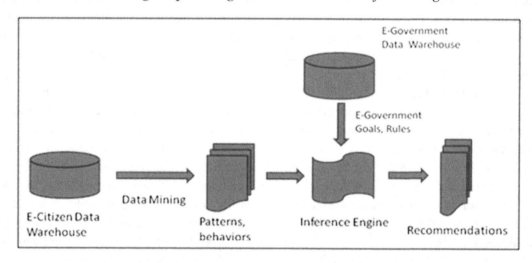

information entered by the citizens themselves (Figure 6).

Information about education, career, business experience, health, and many other domains of citizen life can then be made available to government for mining purposes to be used with the permission of citizen. Government utilizes this digitalized information for analysis and mining operations to provide more customized services and to give better direction to citizens. Citizen DSS analyzes and mines Citizen Data Warehouse

and makes inferences about citizen, and prepares analysis reports, recommendations, schedules, potential e-services that citizen can use. Meanwhile the system customizes e-services, i.e. making use of e-services on behalf of users to increase conditions of citizens.

For instance, as a scenario, health services may detect potential cancer inference of a citizen, based on personal health information collected from all public and private hospitals. Citizen can then be invited to enter a detailed check-up. System can then make use of common medical knowledge to infer potential signs and symptoms based on consolidated health information of citizen. Accordingly, some criteria for system use can be:

- Using or having used tobacco products
- Drinking alcohol
- Being exposed to chemicals that may cause cancer
- Being at risk of skin cancer

Accordingly, the system warns the citizen and may alert his/her family doctor and assigns monitoring of that citizen. System also lists available hospitals/doctors for cancer. Early detection of cancer may save the life of the citizen and add value to health level of society. That could become a successful and practical usage of available knowledge about each citizen and direct him/her to possible solutions.

As another example, for a jobless citizen, government tries to match features and potential positions, and recommends individual a job list. Job search of system may lead to a very quick job finding on behalf of citizen. System gets criteria from citizen, such as salary range, working conditions, office placement, then constructs a feature vector for citizen and computes match ratios with required skills/professions, returning then a match list to citizen starting with highest match score. System may also enable companies searching employees from this information pool. Citizen indicates his/her status as jobless, enters job criteria. Company searches and gives proper list of citizens, and makes its proposal to citizen.

For a university student citizen, system can also propose available training programs from universities and companies, student exchange programs, inform about practical fields of interests. For a graduate student, academic career positions in faculties can be offered or announcement of conferences and seminars that is related to his/her subject are forwarded.

Social and Cloud Computing: Meta-Knowledge Visualization (and Related Newly Emerging Issues)

While all of these scenarios can lead to sharing knowledge of society for wellness of citizens, enterprise architectures disseminate knowledge, guaranteeing data availability through whole enterprise divisions with proper authorization. E-government enterprise architecture collects valuable information, merges, and shares the knowledge of every citizen, where maintaining privacy rises as a crucial issue at every step. Sharing common knowledge of society through e-governance enterprise seems a useful and critical activity for achieving better vision, although ensuring privacy of data during processing steps should be ensured. Keeping privacy of data/information means for every piece of data or information, ensuring relevance of personal information and personal identity could not be obtainable from any citizen or government institutes except the legal process coverage. That means no citizen would be subjected to especially negative attitude by institutes in relevance due to private information of that citizen. Very basic level information privacy means that no citizen would be able to access another citizen's private information. However, preventing government agencies and also private sector agencies from using individual specific information is another important issue. At this point defining "authority" and "authorization coverage" must be supported by legal regulations. Information is to be used only for constructing the enterprise e-government warehouse level.

Having much experience in cyber domain, Web 2.0 has added significant value for the communication area. Social networks have become the dominant platform for connectivity. Critical part of society has experienced having identity (ECeG Project 2003) and establishing virtual relations with other identities where those identities may reflect real identities, filtered ones, or totally irrelevant ones. Many companies searched and employed people from social networks.

Critical components are identity and connectivity. Easing accessibility of each citizen by other ones has dramatically increased the connectivity of people. For Enterprise e-Government, each citizen would be unique and have an official identity for being able to access or accessed by Government Enterprise divisions, namely government agencies. Within enterprise government, citizen may ask for services to government agencies, and these agencies may convey service results to citizen, also important deadlines, responsibilities, legislative regularities, and so on. For example government may be considered to have fulfilled its own responsibility when it declares legal responsibility, such as "invitation to court" through enterprise e-government by using citizens' unique identity, with an electronic mail posted to citizen's portal mail. This will soon become possible in Turkey, thanks to the completion of Registered e-Mail Project and the related legislations.

For case of business or academic position applications, in conventional way, institutes ask for application documents to be collected from different places. As formal Web portal of individual, e-Citizen can provide all documents such as diploma, graduate certificate, business experience, other certificates from conferences and trainings attended. Applied institute can also access and ask e-Citizen for citizen's confirmation of required documents and those are sent by using digital signature of citizen.

In addition, considering the increasingly-becoming-global health issues and work forces, cross-border interactions for even non-citizens should also be taken into account for fulfilling the related services. New cross-border project frameworks such as EU ICT Policy Support Programme (PSP) also now aim to address the related issue of providing user-centric services for not only citizens but also non-citizens.

When we consider the available EA frameworks and models, we should also acknowledge

that they remain at a too high and abstract level for total transformation of the whole government to the proposed frameworks and models. From the IT perspective, however, to realize such transformation, it would first be required to visualize the common stakeholders of the system, and what they use to communicate and interact with each other. This is especially required for the SOA-based architecture.

Accordingly, a candidate framework, called Entity-Utility and Information Flow Model, could be suggested (Figure 7). In this framework, two critical concepts are given, entities and their utilities. Entities are the system stakeholders. Utilities are the potential gadgets for the entities. Two main entities are defined for this framework, user and the government.

User is the stakeholder of the eGG system, i.e. citizen, business, governmental user, and non-citizen. For the user utility part, a cloud for these user groups could be defined. When a human being is taken into the account, more than one user entity definition could be given. For instance, a government officer could not only be a citizen but also a governmental user. Also, this person may need to use another country's eGG; thus, this user will be a non-citizen for that system. The utilities defined for each group would change according to entity. To manage entity utilizes a single sign-on mechanism that will dynamically control authorization rights according to the current service in use. For providing currently available services, a cloud utility system for the entities is required. This cloud will also provide information of service consumption and service mapping of the specified services (In here complex, orchestration required services are not included). For the government part, to show which part of the government is responsible for the given part and define the complex and orchestration required services, and to utilize the heavily required SOA activities, government utility cloud is required. To create the connection of user utility to government utility and government utility to user utility,

Figure 7. Entity-utility and information flow model

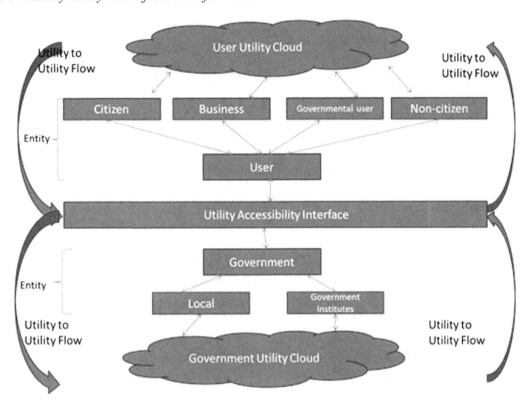

as well as the user to government and government to user interaction, a middle layer is required, as well. Utility accessibility interface actually brings the technological requirements that were given in the e-government frameworks. Actually the wired and wireless devices, privacy related single sign on gadgets, the used ESB servers, even the used programming languages could be included into this part (Meanwhile, here, the definition, concepts, technologies, and the policies related with the eGG are not given-up. Actually, because they are already integrated with the given entity parts, it is not required to reflect them in this model.).

The entity-utility concept can also be associated with the economic utility function of societal entities, as another note. Meanwhile, this framework can also be integrated with the meta-knowledge engine to support knowledge visualization require-

ments. Accordingly, a visualization engine can also enhance the suggested DSS.

Under a knowledge management approach, a model with three-tier structure could give a general structure for the meta model for knowledge visualization. This structure model works in two directions: top to bottom and bottom to top. In each direction, the responsibility and the epistemic meanings are changing. From the perspective of top-down direction, the model's primary aim is to transform knowledge and information to the Meta data. However, the primary perspective for this purpose is the bottom to top direction. The bottom to top direction finds its meaning when the visualization of the specific information and knowledge is required.

- *Knowledge Visualization Layer:* This layer is an external interface between system and external environment. Knowledge and information received in this layer. Mostly, system users are responsible for gathering new knowledge and information. This part is also responsible for filtering knowledge and information before sending it to the knowledge logic layer. The requested knowledge and information are also visualized in this layer. This layer also presents the information and knowledge clusters as relations with respect to the given requirements.

- *Core Knowledge Layer:* This part is the memory of the model. The transformed knowledge and information kept as data under this layer. Information and knowledge are kept as knowledge parameters and these parameters kept as weighted values. As a secondary purpose, this perspective also takes visualization requirements and directs it to the lower levels. When the core knowledge level received the required visualization, in a given requirement, this layer defines parameters, and calculates possible relations in each parameter. Then it sends possible relations to the upper level as data segments.
- *Knowledge Logic Layer:* After filtered knowledge and information received from upper layer, this layer is responsible for forming, teaching, and updating the system through self-learning mechanism. A fuzzy-neural network is responsible for each sub-steps of the system. The new knowledge and information send to the core knowledge layer as data. The received data segments also turns into information and knowledge clusters in this layer and then it sends them to the visualization layer.

There is of course a long and thin way towards such sophisticated, personalized, knowledge-based formal eGG. Still these related examples and scenarios exemplify our vision and suggestions for future, concluding this section as well as our chapter.

CONCLUSION

The outline of this chapter has been first introductory background information, then discussion on development of eGG services in Turkey, and finally a visionary suggestion for personalized, citizen-centric e-government. Addressing a gap of not having enough work on enterprise architecture for knowledge-based, highly-sophisticated, and citizen-oriented personalized services, the chapter has articulated a perspective for the design of architectures for development and provision of such knowledge-based, sophisticated, personalized services. The authors have benefited from their experience in Turkey eGG, aiming to provide guidance to other examples and cases in the world. E-Citizen Decision Support System, and Entity-Utility and Information Flow Model are among the suggested approaches for such dependable guidance for eGG and other initiatives.

A major assumption of the chapter, however, is that for gateway development and provision it assumes the scenario of one-stop shop to have personalized services as the highest maturity level. For different assumptions based upon other scenarios and maturities, different conclusions can be reached, limiting the impact of this chapter. For instance, as an extreme case presented at the Introduction, with respect to the Information Chaos (decentralized coordination, low integration) scenario of Vinnova (2009) a whole different set of parameters need to be considered.

ACKNOWLEDGMENT

We would like to thank Turksat, and METU, Turkey; Brunel University, UK, and AUB, Lebanon for supporting this work. The ongoing work resulted in this paper is partially supported by T-VOHSU (Turkish Project for measuring satisfaction from provision of citizen-oriented e-Government services); and CEES (Citizen-oriented Evaluation of E-Government Services: A Reference Process Model), EU FP7 IAPP PEOPLE (Industry Academia Partnerships and Pathways) project. Some part of this work is accordingly adapted from previously presented works of co-authors such as the work presented in tGov Workshop in West London '11. (Medeni et al. 2011)

REFERENCES

Amoroso, D. L., & Reinig, B. A. (2004). Personalization management systems: Minitrack introduction. In *Proceedings of the 37th Annual Hawaii International Conference on System Sciences (HICSS 2004)*, (vol 7). Big Island, HI: HICSS.

Ariadne Training Limited. (2001). *Engineering software –Applied object oriented analysis and design using the UML*. Wincanton, UK: Ariadne Training Limited.

Bakan, I. A., Aydın Kar, H. M., & Öz, B. (2008). *T-VOHSU project phase 1 report*. Turkey: Türksat.

Bakan, I. A., Aydın Kar, H. M., & Öz, B. (2009). *T-VOHSU project phase 2 report*. Turkey: Türksat.

Balabanovic, M., & Shoham, Y. (1997). Fab: Content-based collaborative recommendation. *Communications of the ACM, 40*, 66–72. doi:10.1145/245108.245124

Capgemini. (2007). *The user challenge benchmarking: The supply of online public services, 7th measurement*. Retrieved Jan 28, 2011, from http://ec.europa.eu/information_society/eeurope/i2010/docs/benchmarking/egov_benchmark_2007.pdf.

CEES. (2009). Citizen-oriented evaluation of e-government services. *EU Marie Curie IAPP Funded Project*. Retrieved from http://www.iapp-cees.eu.

Çetin, Y., Medeni, T. D., Özkan, S., Balcı, A., & Dalbay, Ö. (2010). *Improving e-government from citizens' perspectives: An analysis of suggestions for e-government gateway in Turkey*. Paper presented at the ICEGEG 2010 Conference. Antalya, Turkey.

DPT. (2006). *Bilgi toplumu stratejisi ve eylem plani*. Wincanton, UK: Ariadne Training.

DPT. (2008). *Bilgi toplumu stratejisi ve eylem plan: 1: Değerlendirme raporu*. Wincanton, UK: Ariadne Training.

DPT. (2010). *Bilgi toplumu stratejisi ve eylem plan: 2: Değerlendirme raporu*. Wincanton, UK: Ariadne Training.

ECeG Project. (2003). The semantic web techniques for the management of digital identity and the access to norms. *PRIN Project Home Page*. Retrieved January 15, 2008, from http://www.cirsfid.unibo.it/eGov03/.

ECeGov. (2011). *The European commission e-government home page*. Retrieved from http://europa.eu.int/information_society/eeurope/2005/all_about/egovernment/index_en.htm.

EU ICT. (2011). *Policy support programme*. Retrieved from http://ec.europa.eu/information_society/activities/ict_psp/about/index_en.htm.

Event, I. D. C. (2011). *Webpage*. Retrieved from http://www.idc-cema.com/?showproduct=40681&content_lang=ENG&action=Presentations.

Good, N., Schafer, J. B., Konstan, J. A., Borchers, A., Sarwar, B., Herlocker, J., & Riedl, J. (1999). Combining collaborative filtering with personal agents for better recommendations. In *Proceedings of the 16th National Conference on Artificial Intelligence*, (pp. 439-446). Orlando, FL: ACM.

Guo, X., & Lu, J. (2007). Intelligent e-government services with personalized recommendation techniques. *International Journal of Intelligent Systems, 22*, 401–417. doi:10.1002/int.20206

IDABC. (2007). *Preliminary study on mutual recognition of esignatures for egovernment applications*. Brussels, Belgium: IDABC.

Kautz, H., Selman, B., & Shah, M. (1997). Referral web: Combining social networks and collaborative filtering. *Communications of the ACM, 40*, 63–65. doi:10.1145/245108.245123

Kundra, V. (2010). *State of public sector cloud computing*. Washington, DC: CIO Council.

Lee, H., Irani, Z., Osman, I., Balcı, A., Özkan, S., & Medeni, T. (2008). Research note: Toward a reference process model for citizen-oriented evaluation of e-government services. *Transforming Government: People, Process and Policy, 2*(4), 297-310.

Medeni, T., Elwell, M., & Cook, S. (2007). Digitally deaf into games for learning: Towards a theory of reflective and refractive space-time for knowledge management. In *Proceedings of BEYKON 2007*. Turkey: Immersing.

Medeni, T., Iwatsuki, S., & Cook, S. (2008). Reflective ba and refractive ma in cross-cultural learning. In Putnik, G. D., & Cunha, M. M. (Eds.), *Encyclopedia of Networked and Virtual Organizations*. Hershey, PA: IGI Global. doi:10.4018/978-1-59904-885-7.ch178

Medeni, T., Medeni, I. T., Balci, A., & Dalbay, Ö. (2009). *Suggesting a framework for transition towards more interoperable e-government in Turkey: A nautilus model of cross-cultural knowledge creation and organizational learning*. Ankara, Turkey: ICEGOV.

Medeni, T., Erdem, A., Osman, I., Anouze, A, Irani, Z., Lee, H., Balcı, A, Weerakkody, V. (2011) *Information Society Strategy & E-Government Gateway Development In Turkey: Moving Towards Integrated Processes And Personalized Services*. West London, UK. tGov Workshop http://www.iseing.org/tgovwebsite/tGovWorkshop2011/CRCPDF/tGOV-20/Paper%2020.pdf

Microsoft Corporation. (2007). *Solutions for connected government*. Seattle, WA: Microsoft.

Moon, J. (2004). *A handbook of reflective and experiential learning: Theory and practice*. London, UK: RoutledgeFalmer.

Oasis. (2011). *Oasis transformational government web page*. Retrieved from http://www.oasis-open.org/committees/tgf/charter.php#item-4.

Oracle. (2011). *Oracle igovernment*. Retrieved from http://www.oracle.com.

Osman, I., Anouze, A., Irani, Z., Lee, H., Balcı, A., Medeni, T., & Weerakkody, V. (2011). *A new cobras framework to evaluate e-government services: A citizen centric perspective*. Paper presented at the Tgovernment workshop. London, UK.

Resnick, P., & Varian, H. R. (1997). Recommender systems. *Communications of the ACM, 40*, 56–58. doi:10.1145/245108.245121

Riecken, D. (2000). Personalized views of personalization. *Communications of the ACM, 43*, 26–28. doi:10.1145/345124.345133

United Nations. (2007). *UNDEP e-government interoperability guide: United Nations development programme with the support of IBM, Oracle*. New York, NY: United Nations.

United Nations. (2008). *E-government survey 2008 - From e-government to connected governance*. New York, NY: United Nations.

Uno, Y. (1999). Why the concept of trans-cultural refraction necessary. *Intercultural Communication, 35*.

Vinnova. (2009). *eGovernment of tomorrow: Future scenarios for 2020*. Retrieved Jan 28, 2011, from http://www.vinnova.se/upload/EPiStorePDF/vr-09-28.pdf.

Wankel, C., & DeFillippi, R. (2006). *New visions of graduate management education*. New Haven, CT: Information Age Publishing.

Yildirim, G., Medeni, T., Aktaş, M., Kutluoğlu, U., & Kahramaner, Y. (2010). *M-government as an extension of e-government gateway: A case study*. Antalya, Turkey: ICEGEG.

KEY TERMS AND DEFINITIONS

Cloud: A general unification of epistemological or ontological entities as in citizen cloud, knowledge cloud, utility cloud.

E-Citizen Decision Support System: E-government service system recommendation system that makes inferences based on citizen data warehouse.

eGG: e-Government Gateway/portal in Turkey that aims to enable citizens (as well as businesses & state institutions) securely and conveniently reaching all electronic government services and essential information at one single access point.

Enterprise: The social institution of e-government within a visionary perspective

Entity-Utility and Information Flow: The framework to visualize the common stakeholders of the IT system, and what they use to communicate and interact with each other. Entities are the system stakeholders, and utilities are the potential gadgets for the entities.

Social Responsibility: A combined expression for citizens' responsibility towards society and/or state's responsibility towards citizens and society.

Chapter 18

IT and Enterprise Architecture in US Public Sector Reform:
Issues and Recommendations

Terry F. Buss
Carnegie Mellon University, USA

Anna Shillabeer
Griffin Information Solutions, Australia

ABSTRACT

This chapter looks at public sector whole-of-government reform from an Information Technology (IT) focused Enterprise Architecture (EA) perspective. The chapter summarizes reforms undertaken under three US presidents—Clinton, Bush, and Obama—and discusses how they have too frequently failed to meet expectations of policy makers, public servants, the public, and other stakeholders. We find that IT reforms in support of larger public sector reform have been ineffective and unsustainable, although many IT reforms have been successful in a narrower context. EA has suffered as a once promising methodology: it has not become the "silver bullet" in managing the IT and information infrastructure to support reform, knowledge management, and decision making. It was also seen as an important tool for reducing information management silos that successive governments have unsuccessfully tried to reduce. This chapter raises the spectre of endemic barriers to reform that must be overcome if EA and IT reform are to realize their potential, and offers recommendations for overcoming these hurdles in the context of whole-of-government public sector reforms.

INTRODUCTION

Over the past two decades, presidents Bill Clinton, George W. Bush, and Barack Obama have launched one major whole-of-government public sector reform after another in an effort to make government more effective, efficient, economic, and perhaps equitable (the four E's)[1], focusing on performance management and budgeting, and citizen services, engagement, and participation (for an overview, see, especially: Kettl, 2005; Redburn, Shea, & Buss, 2007; Bouchaert &

DOI: 10.4018/978-1-4666-1824-4.ch018

Halligan, 2007; Frederickson, Smith, Larimer, & Licari, 2011). Policy makers soon latched on to the potential of IT to serve as the platform upon which to build, develop and maintain the four E's, in the process making government more transparent and accountable. Over this period as new technologies evolved, many believed that: automation would improve overall government efficiency, improve quality of services, and reduce service delivery costs; E-government would improve government-citizen, government-business, government-government transactions, and public service delivery; and social media would facilitate and foster intra-governmental collaboration and communication and enhanced citizen engagement and participation. EA would provide the platform to better link IT to policy, planning, management, strategy, information, and process. Many even claimed that this reform agenda would enhance democracy, as well as good governance (Gerson, 2006; Buss, Redburn, & Guo, 2006; Kamarck & Nye, 2002).

In spite of successes here and there[2] in the context of whole-of-government reforms, many believe that public sector IT reforms have not lived up to the expectations upon which policy makers placed so much hope, and EA has yet to fully take hold across government and where EA has diffused widely, it has been problematic. IT and EA may have fallen victim to the failure of the public sector reform agenda's problems, rather than its own shortcomings. Perhaps, though, both are at fault. In any case, this is distressing to critics who point out that over the past decade alone, the federal government has spent more than $600 billion on IT, and EA has been around for more than 25 years but is still yet to deliver the benefits promised, again in the context of public sector reforms[3].

Using the US federal government as a case study, this chapter looks at public sector and IT reforms primarily in the context of EA and addresses the following questions: What have been the driving forces in public sector reform? Why are public sector IT reform initiatives so ineffective and how does this relate to public sector reform across the whole of government? Why have EA efforts not realised their potential? And, What can be done to make public sector reform through IT and EA implementation more effective?

PUBLIC SECTOR REFORM INITIATIVES

Public sector reform undertaken in a whole-of-government framework has featured in the agendas of most presidents over the past 120 years, but it is only in the last 20 or so that reform initiatives have become a high priority and expected to engender massive changes in governance (see Buss & Buss, 2011, for a review). Policy makers understood that they could not accomplish missions, attain policy goals, and deliver quality public services unless government could achieve the four E's. The public, empowered by unprecedented access to information and greater transparency in government operations, also began to expect much more value in return for the taxes paid or fees charged, and demand more input into, and responsiveness from, political processes affecting their lives. Social media enabled a move towards "people power" as an unavoidable influence on government decision making and processes and provided a unique motivation for reform and a new era of government responsiveness. With perpetual burgeoning budget deficits, out of control long-term debt, and increased demand for public services, government would have to do much more for much less (Balutis, Buss, & Ink, 2011).

Two trends provide a context for reform, one attempted to make government operate more like a business (Osborn & Gaebler, 1992), the other broke down formal, hierarchical command and control structures of government into informal networks (Goldsmith & Eggers, 2004; Kettl, 2009).

The New Public Management

Many credit David Osborne with auguring in a new movement, the *New Public Management* (NPM), which forms the intellectual undergirding for performance management, the corner stone of contemporary public sector reform. In 1992, Osborne and Ted Gaebler described innovative state and local government efforts to become more efficient and effective in *Reinventing Government*. A House of Lords Report, *The Public Service* (1997-8), summed up the movement well:

The doctrines of NPM involve a focus on management, performance appraisal and efficiency; the use of agencies which deal with each other on a user-pays basis; the use of quasi-markets and contracting out to foster competition; cost-cutting; and a style of management which emphasizes, among other things, output targets, limited term contracts, monetary incentives and freedom to manage.

In addition to furthering public sector reform, the New Public Management seemed to comport well with potential gains expected to be realized through IT and EA as an approaches. After all, if the private sector gained from IT and EA, then so should government if it became market-driven and adopted private sector practices. Our contention here is that this has not been the case.

Networked Government

While policy makers were trying to operate government more like a business under New Public Management, governance itself was undergoing profound change (Balutis, Buss, & Ink, 2011), including the rise of informal networks in paralleling and often displacing more traditional, formal, hierarchical systems (Goldsmith & Eggers, 2004). Informal networks are both a solution and a problem for reform. Informal networks are non-hierarchical, self-organizing, transitory, collaborative, and fragile. So, for example, during the Hurricane Katrina disaster, there was a formal hierarchical system of governance in place that botched the initial response to this mega-disaster, and an informal one—involving the private sector, non profits, citizens and extra-governmental collaborations—that was much more effective.

There is little in the literature on the potential usefulness of IT and EA in an informal networked government. One might hypothesize that the informal, unstructured aspects of networked government might defy IT and EA solutions, or in some cases thwart them as system engineers try to model them. We believe this to be the case.

THE CONTEXT FOR PUBLIC SECTOR REFORM

For many critics, public sector reforms were frequent, massive, complex, inadequately thought through, unsustainable, ineffective and did not generally succeed (critical works include: Frederickson & Frederickson, 2006; Radin, 2006; Denhardt & Denhardt, 2007; Frederickson, Smith, Larimer, & Licari, 2011; while de Vries, 2010; Redburn, Shea, & Buss 2008; Sistare, Shiplett, & Buss, 2008 effectively provides an alternative argument). Regardless of whether one agrees or disagrees about the success of reforms working toward the four Es, here are some facts on which nearly all would agree...

- The country now has an annual budget deficit of $1.4 trillion that will recur at comparably high levels for a decade or more to come, and it is currently in debt for a staggering $14 trillion (Committee on the Fiscal Future of the United States, 2011).
- Governance failure—gridlock, extreme partisanship, and animosity—as witnessed in unsuccessful efforts to reduce the US

deficit and debt, and in most other policy areas, is worsening (Mann & Ornstein, 2008). In July 2011, according to the Rasmussen tracking poll, only 5% of likely voters rate Congress as doing an "excellent or good" job. In August 2011, according to a Gallop poll, President Obama enjoys only a 41% positive approval rating.

- Federal government employment, rather than decreasing, has exponentially grown when outsourced federal functions are taken into account (Frederickson & Frederickson, 2006; Light, 1999).
- Citizen satisfaction with government services is not terribly high and declining (Johnson, 2011). The vast majority of Americans are dissatisfied with the direction the country is taking.
- Federal government regulation is growing dramatically, adding tens of billions to the cost of doing business (Gattuso & Katz, 2011). The Obama Administration added $40 billion in costs over its first two years in office, an amount that can be added to Bush's $60 billion. Obama has re-regulated deregulation under Bush.
- At the policy level, macro-economic, health, education, transportation and economic development are in dire straits. There are, for example, more than 80 economic development programs and 100 surface transportation programs that are duplicative and unable to demonstrate that they are efficient and effective (Government Accountability Office, 2011a).
- Most importantly, each successive presidential administration has abandoned or overturned reform efforts of the previous administration creating waste and havoc (see below).

AN OVERVIEW OF PUBLIC SECTOR REFORM

Clinton, Bush, and Obama have taken whole-of-government reforms in very different directions.

The Bill Clinton Era

Immediately upon taking office in 1993, President Clinton began implementing the National Performance Review (NPR), describing his platform as a call for "reinventing government." National Performance Review tried to reduce red tape by streamlining processes and eliminating unnecessary regulatory overkill, improving customer service by creating more market-like dynamics, decentralizing decision-making processes to empower public managers, and reducing the federal workforce. National Performance Review's organizing principle was attainment of efficient, effective, and economical customer service, in this case, three of the four Es. The three Es were to be achieved through business practices such as Total Quality Management (TQM), Management by Objectives (MBO), and Business Process Re-Engineering (BPR).

It was Congress, in passing the *Chief Financial Officers (CFO) Act* (PL 101-576) in 1990, followed by the *Government Performance and Results Act* (GPRA) (PL 103-62) in 1993, that took a rare active role in performance management. The Chief Financial Officers Act created a Deputy Director of Management position at the Office of Management and Budget, essentially making the appointee responsible for information policy, procurement, and productivity improvement across the federal government. This Act promulgated the first whole-of-government approach.

The Government Performance and Results Act shifted "the focus of federal management and accountability from what federal agencies are doing to what they are accomplishing," noting that:

1. Waste and inefficiency in Federal programs undermined the confidence of the American people in the Government and reduced the Federal Government's ability to adequately address vital public needs.
2. Federal managers were seriously disadvantaged in their efforts to improve program efficiency and effectiveness due to insufficient articulation of program goals and inadequate information on program performance.
3. Congressional policymaking, spending decisions, and program oversight were seriously handicapped by insufficient attention to program performance and results.

The National Performance Review, steeped in and modelled after the New Public Management philosophy, had some mixed success (Moe, 1994; Kettl & DiLulio, 1995; Nesterczuk, 1996; Shillabeer, Buss, & Rousseau, 2011). Citizen satisfaction with services seemed to improve. Decentralization in decision-making increased. Federal employment fell, but this resulted largely by cutting the armed forces. Regulatory promulgation continued to grow. Many of the reforms may have worked well, but the initiative overall did not produce adequate performance information to make such an assessment. Most importantly, the approach failed to develop a management capacity to sustain reforms (Kettl & DiLulio, 1995).

The Government Performance and Results Act was a definite milestone in reform compared to past initiatives (Ellig, McTigue, & Wray, 2011), but it failed to realize enough reforms to radically change government operations. Many agencies treated the Act's requirements as a compliance exercise rather than a way to work toward the four Es. In fairness, the notion of measuring performance against a set of goals and objectives was in its infancy, focusing on inputs and in some cases outputs, rather than on outcomes (did services accomplish what they were intended to accomplish?) and efficiency (Hatry, 2007). To this

day, most federal programs still assess themselves against outputs, rather than outcomes.

The Bush Administration, seemingly having learned lessons from Clinton and espousing its own market-driven approach, tried its hand at reform on an unprecedented, massive scale.

The George W. Bush Era

Upon taking office in 2001, George W. Bush, being dissatisfied with the progress made under the Clinton Administration's reinventing government scheme overall and the Government Performance and Results Act's focus on agencies rather than programs, launched the President's Management Agenda (PMA), a whole-of-government, evidence-driven approach explicitly linking program performance, evaluation, strategic and human capital management, and budgeting in the same system and making government "citizen centric" both in terms of participation but also service delivery (Office of Management and Budget, 2002; Redburn, Shea, & Buss, 2008; Shillabeer, Buss, & Rousseau, 2011). Policy makers grounded the President's Management Agenda in the following principles:

- *Shift the burden of proof.* Those who propose to shift priorities or adjust funding levels are expected to demonstrate that a program or activity should be changed.
- *Focus on the "base" not the "increment."* This requirement reverses the presumption that this year's funding level is the starting point for considering next year's funding level.
- *Focus on results.* Performance-based budgeting means that money is allocated not just on the basis of perceived needs, but also on the basis of what is actually being accomplished.
- *Impose consequences.* Wasteful or duplicative government programs *are* identified, with an eye to cutting their funding,

redesigning them, or eliminating them altogether.

- *Demand evidence.* Many agencies and programs lack rigorous data or evaluations to show that they work. Such evidence should be a prerequisite to continued funding.

For our purposes, the President's Management Agenda had several major components:

1. Outsourcing federal employment to the private sector, including Non-Governmental Organizations (NGOs).
2. The Budget and Program Integration initiative built on the Program Assessment Rating Tool (PART).
3. The *Human Capital Assessment and Accountability Framework* (HCAAF), a system that builds capacity in the public service to undertake "results-oriented management and culture" to further the performance agenda.
4. Creation of new or reorganization of existing agencies to enhance performance.

Outsourcing

Contracting out every activity "not inherently governmental" allowed the Bush Administration to gain control of government by transferring much of what the public sector did to private sector contractors. This not only imposed market discipline on government, but it also bypassed the civil service who were often seen as a barrier to achieving good governance. This created a murky sector—"the third sector"—that clouded transparency and accountability, not to mention masking the operations of government from the public scrutiny (Frederickson & Frederickson, 2006). Everything from counterintelligence through issuing visa to delivering mail was privatized. It was impossible even to discover how many contractors there were, let alone determine exactly what they did (Light, 1999). Paul Light credibly estimates

that the federal government was 10 times larger than official statistics suggested, once outsourced employment was taken into account. Additionally, the Bush Administration downsized its procurement capacity, then outsourced that function, causing havoc as agencies struggled to make the procurement process work. For example, Bush created the Millennium Challenge Corporation (see below) that awarded billions in funding in foreign aid to developing countries, but manned its procurement office with only a handful of staff (Buss & Gardner, 2008). As a consequence, billions lay unspent for several years. Similarly, the Defence Department, which now employs a staggering 118,000 civil servants in its procurement office, is actually short 20,000 workers, not only precipitating delays but also fostering waste, fraud and abuse.

PART

In 2002, the Bush administration rolled out its PART program in *Rating the Performance of Federal Programs*. PART evaluation proceeded through four critical areas of assessment—purpose and design, strategic planning, management, and results and accountability. PART also required agencies to establish and report performance measure data on outcomes, outputs, and efficiency and defines targets the program intended to meet on an annual basis. Programs also reported management plans they had in place to correct deficiencies in program management, and actions they had completed to improve performance. Finally, programs published budget data in the annual report and on the Web[4]. Many analysts considered it the "gold standard" in performance management. In the end, PART was roundly criticised, rightly or wrongly, by the Obama Administration (as discussed below) and then abandoned. But most informed observers agree that a major problem with PART was senior public managers and policy makers did not use performance information to manage programs (Government Accountability Office, 2005), and often decision makers failed to use the information in making budget decisions about programs (Redburn, Shea, & Buss, 2008).

HCAAF

HCAAF supported the President's Management Agenda by requiring agencies to have in place strategic human capital management systems that realized the following[5]:

- *Strategic Alignment*—aligns human capital management strategies with an agency's mission, goals, and objectives through analysis, planning, investment, measurement, and management of human capital programs.
- *Leadership and Knowledge Management*—ensures continuity of leadership developing and maintaining organizational knowledge and learning.
- *Results-Oriented Performance Culture*—promotes high-performing workforce through effective performance management systems.
- *Talent Management*—establishes a system to attract, acquire, develop, promote and retain quality talent in workforce.
- *Accountability*—monitors and evaluates the results of human capital management policies, programs, and activities against merit system principles.

The Office of Personnel Management (OPM) directed policy makers and agency heads to evaluate their agency against a set of standards deemed to be state-of-the-art in human capital management. Each standard included a set of metrics, critical success factors, and expected results. Performance indicators provided evidence that the agency meets acceptable standards. HCAAF combined performance management and good management practice in one instrument. HCAAF, unlike the PART, has received little criticism and

has been little studied. The failure of the PART to fulfill expectations suggests that the HCAAF was also ineffective because it remained a separate initiative from the PART which it was supposed to support. In some ways, this management failure was also characteristic of the earlier National Performance Review.

New Agencies and Reorganizations

Following from the terrorist attacks of September 11, 2001, in the national defence and security arena, the Bush Administration created the Department of Homeland Security (DHS), the Office of the Director of National Intelligence (ODNI), and Millennium Challenge Corporation (MCC), and reorganized the Department of Defence (DOD) and Federal Bureau of Investigation (FBI). These interventions were unprecedented in scope in federal government as policy makers pursued the four Es. They also were guided by the principles embodied in the President's Management Agenda and the New Public Management.

DHS

The Bush Administration created the DHS in 2002 by folding 22 separate agencies and around 200,000 employees into one department, most notably among them the Federal Emergency Management Agency (FEMA), the Coast Guard, the Customs Bureau, the Immigration and Naturalization Service, and the Transportation Security Administration. This became by far the largest organizational reengineering effort since the formation of the Defence Department, National Security Council (NSC), and Central Intelligence Agency (CIA) under the *National Security Act* of 1947 (PL 80-235) and it took five years to get the agency up and running (see National Academy of Public Administration, 2003). Bush attempted to breakdown the cumbersome legacy civil service structures of the new agency, but a federal court nullified the effort leaving in place an overly complex environment in which to communicate and effect reform (Sistare, Shiplett, & Buss, 2008). From an IT/EA perspective, imagine developing architecture for each separate agency and program, then have them merged together, only to be reorganized again. This was a reengineering nightmare for IT departments, which themselves were also engaged in the reorganizations.

ODNI

The *Intelligence Reform and Terrorism Prevention Act* of 2004 (PL 108-458) created ODNI to head the nation's intelligence agencies and oversee implementation of the National Intelligence Program. There are more than 20 intelligence agencies in the U.S. government. The various departmental organizations with intelligence missions must retain relative autonomy from a central authority to serve their unique missions to maintain security and independence. Consequently, proprietary agencies have been reluctant to surrender resources, information collection and reporting procedures even when directed to do so by the President. To make matters worse, ODNI is underfunded and unable to break down intelligence silos even if it wanted to. As might be imagined, intelligence organizations remain stove-piped and unable to exploit fully the IT solutions that might be available to them. Integrating these systems is almost an unfathomable task given the overlay of politics on the agencies.

MCC

The Millennium Challenge Act of 2003 (PL 108-199) launched the new, independent, performance-based agency—MCC (Picard & Buss, 2009; Buss & Gardner, 2008). Its main point of differentiation from other agencies was that it was intentionally designed from its inception to run like a business. The Bush Administration believed aid allocated under the U.S. Agency for International Development (USAID) was ineffective, and aid tended to wind up in the hands of those who were

problematic for US foreign and security policy. Because USAID proved difficult to either reform or terminate, policy makers created MCC to work in parallel with it or against it, depending on your perspective. At the same time, USAID was folded into the State Department, losing much of its independence. The MCC was charged with increasing foreign assistance, and investing it in countries that seemed to be making progress in their own governance. Possibly due to this new model of operation, during its first three years of operation, MCC had to be reorganized several times and put under new leadership, before it became well-functioning. Management capacity, as with so many initiatives, was an issue. Procurement was especially ill-conceived as noted above: policy makers assumed that less staff was, by definition, better. From an IT/EA perspective, systems in the agency were not well developed and were under-staffed, making it difficult to employ an effective IT strategy.

FBI

Since September 11, 2001, the FBI has come under pressure to transform its operations from traditional criminal investigation and law enforcement to a new focus on counterterrorism (National Academy of Public Administration, 2006). To critics, this transformation proved problematic, but not nearly on the scale of the DHS transformation. The FBI had a specialized workforce, neither hired nor trained for counterterrorism, and their information systems were not designed for work in the new field (see section below). Its working relationships with the intelligence community were also hopelessly stove-piped. The FBI's transformation took several years and required engagement in new hiring, training, career development, IT, and management initiatives on a large scale. It has only recently become well-functioning. The FBI transformation has taken years and is still not complete. As such, it makes it difficult to deploy IT solutions that are sustainable.

Defence

The Defence Department is the largest agency in the federal system. Its employees are not only military personnel, but many are also civilians and contractors. The Bush Administration adjudged Defence civilian personnel to be inefficient, ineffective and uneconomical, and therefore in need of reorganization. Bush tried to break down civil service protections that posed barriers to good management (see the *Defence Authorization Act* of 2004[PL 108-375]). Bush almost succeeded, but his efforts were overturned by the Obama Administration, ostensibly in support of civil service labour unions. No matter, systems work on one HR system had to be redone yet again. Defence is still struggling to accommodate the uncertainties.

The Barack Obama Era

Just as George W. Bush faced the herculean tasks of reorganizing the government and fighting wars in Iraq and Afghanistan (to name a few), Barack Obama found himself faced not only with the Bush challenges, but also with a deep recession and the global financial crisis, along with a complex domestic policy agenda that included health care, energy, climate change, bank regulation and numerous other initiatives. Obama rejected some of Bush's efforts and replaced them with his own policies, but in many cases he simply allowed them to fade away.

Performance Management

Under public sector reform, the Obama Administration undid Bush's PART performance management system, announcing *A New Era of Responsibility: Renewing America's Promise* (2009, p. 1) that:

The Administration will fundamentally reconfigure the PART. We will open up the insular performance measurement process to the public, the Congress and outside experts. The Administration will eliminate ideological performance goals and replace them with goals Americans care about and that are based on congressional intent and feedback from the people served by Government programs. Programs will not be measured in isolation, but assessed in the context of other programs that are serving the same population or meeting the same goals.

According to *Government Executive* magazine, the Obama administration originally suggested that it would "replace the Bush administration's PART with a new performance improvement and analysis framework. The focus will shift from grading programs as successful or unsuccessful to requiring agency leaders to set priorities, demonstrate progress in achieving defined goals and explain performance trends. In an attempt to break down inter- and intra-agency silos, the performance model will give cross-program and cross-agency goals at least as much attention as program-specific ones" (*Government Executive,* 2009, p. 1). As of April 2011, the Obama Administration had not articulated the specifics of its performance agenda, and PART lapsed into oblivion.

The Government Performance and Results Act Reengineered. With so little specificity in public sector reform, Congress once again launched its own performance management agenda in enacting the *GPRA Modernization Act* of 2010 (PL 111-352). The legislation passed with little opposition. The Act imposes substantially more performance information reporting on agencies, creates positions in government to monitor and promote performance, and requires agencies to post more data on websites. The Act offers little specificity on what these initiatives would actually look like but it mandates[6]:

- Revised agency strategic planning requirements.

- Revised agency annual performance planning requirements.
- Revised agency performance reporting requirements.
- New requirements to designate crosscutting federal priority goals and agency-level priority goals.
- New requirements for quarterly reviews and reporting of government-wide and agency-level priority goals.
- Codification of the existing governance framework that had evolved over the past 15 years.

Specifically, it legislatively creates:

- Chief operating officers,
- Program improvement officers,
- A government-wide performance improvement council, and
- A government-wide performance website.
- Other new implementation actions, including better training for program managers and a timetable for action.

From an IT perspective, some systems have been abandoned, others are on hold and still others are not specific. This is a poor environment in which to pursue a performance agenda applied across the government.

Sustainability

The Obama Administration continued support for MCC downplayed reforms in the FBI and intelligence community, and restored funding to USAID, but undid the reorganization of the Pentagon's civilian workforce. Obama launched a reengineered health care system in 2010, but now being unravelled by a Republican Congress. Climate change, energy, and infrastructure policy are failing or abandoned, not to mention economic policy, which appears to be in free fall. Importantly, Obama announced that the federal government

would engage in massive (re)hiring as it attempted to claw back as many of the previously outsourced jobs as it could. Then, with the July 2011 budget/debt reduction agreements with Congress, Obama has launched a massive federal employee layoff scheme that could affect 500,000 workers. IT workers will also be targets of layoffs.

Next we look at how each administration used IT reform and EA to further its public service reform agendas.

IT INITIATIVES IN THE FEDERAL GOVERNMENT

IT initiatives in the federal government in part grew out of the recognition that if public sector reform was to succeed, then it would need a substantial IT infrastructure. E-government became a mechanism for improving transactions between citizens, businesses, and government services. With the rise of the social media—Web 2.0 and its public sector counterpart, Government 2.0—modes of citizen engagement greatly expanded (Balutis, Buss, & Ink, 2011). Collaboration within and across federal agencies blossomed and government began to share data across agencies and make them available to the public. All of this called for a more collaborative information and policy environment and the requirement for consistency across agencies to ensure success. It was a natural progression towards an interest in the potential offered by EA, which seemed the perfect tool to help build and sustain such an environment.

We begin this discussion with an overview of IT reforms across the period of interest then define the role of EA within this context.

IT Reforms

An overview of IT solutions and EA applications across the three presidencies shows that both became increasingly more sophisticated as technology and software development advanced, and became seemingly able to conquer any challenge. However, as time moved on, evidence showed that these innovations were often poorly realized, systems continued to fail, procurement and acquisition were problematic, and large portions of government were left in the dark ages.

IT reforms were developed to alleviate public sector reform issues as defined above, and create an environment in which public sector reform, could be achieved and sustained. There were two overarching IT reforms released in the mid 1990's that both provided an impetus for public sector reform generally and an increase in the application of unified IT systems and structures across the whole of government.

The innocuously-sounding *Paperwork Reduction Act* of 1995 (PRA)(PL 96-511), required agencies to perform information resource management activities in an efficient, effective, and economical manner. PRA was taken to be grounded in IT due to the promise of a paperless office if nothing else. By reducing the reliance on hardcopy information and developing a government wide information repository the potential for more effective, evidence-based decision making and improved knowledge management and analytical capacity were the obvious benefits. These processes and outputs clearly aligned with a number of public sector reforms discussed earlier including:

- The call for decentralised decision-making process by the Clinton era National Performance Review that could have been facilitated by access to up to date, whole of government information.
- Facilitating the Government Performance and Results Act through being able to rapidly analyse large amounts of data collected across many agencies to provide evidence for policy development and spending decisions; and by providing a medium for collaborative information policy and program development, management and dissemination.

- The requirement by the Bush Administration's President's Management Agenda to demonstrate with evidence that a program, activity, or budget should be changed and the focus on performance metrics as the driver for all funding decisions.
- The focus on knowledge management, strategic alignment of programs across agencies and evaluation across a defined set of national performance indicators as the core to human capital management.
- Prevent loss of information due to major restructuring.

The *Information Technology Management Reform Act* of 1996 (also known as the Clinger-Cohen Act) (PL 104-106) helped take the New Public Management to new levels under Clinton. The Clinger-Cohen Act sought to improve IT planning and procurement, and created Chief Information Officer (CIO) positions in agencies. The Act required agencies to use a disciplined Capital Planning and Investment Control (CPIC) process to acquire, use, maintain and dispose of IT. A CIO Council was created and charged with oversight responsibility for implementation of the Act. Management of the CIO Council became the responsibility of the Chief Information Officer in the Office of Management and Budget (see E-Government Act below). The Act directs CIOs of "major departments and agencies to develop, maintain, and facilitate the implementation of IT architectures as a means of integrating agency goals and business processes." The clear interface between Clinger-Cohen and the Government Performance and Results Acts show that IT is to support performance management across government.

In sections below, we look more specifically at E-government, Web 2.0/Government 2.0 and open government initiatives. In a separate section we examine EA, which both encompasses public sector and IT reform, and is greatly impacted by them.

E-Government

The *E-Government Act* of 2002 (PL 107-347) sought to improve the management and promotion of electronic government primarily through the Internet. The Act created the Chief Information Officer position within OMB and also established an E-government fund to pay for special initiatives. A cumulative minimum of $345 million for 2003 to 2007 was authorised and placed under the management of the Government Services Agency (GSA).

The Bush President's Management Agenda fully embraced E-government as a major goal of the administration, allocating some $100 million from 2002 to 2004. The President's Management Agenda mandated easy-to-find access points on the Web for citizens—for example, www.FirstGov.gov—better collaboration across agencies, automation of internal processes, digital signatures, single procurement portals—for example, www.FedBizOpps.gov—online grant applications and use of the Web to inform citizens about regulatory actions.

In 2007, the E-Government Act became due for reauthorization (Seifert, 2008). Congress, concerned about oversight of the fund, reduced the annual expenditure to no more than $5 million annually. This significantly impacted the capacity of government to deliver effective reform.

E-Government has become the latest casualty in the power struggle in Washington. Obama tried to continue funding E-government following on the Bush Administration, but when Republicans took over the House of Representatives in 2010, budget cuts reduced E-government programs funding from $34 million down to $2 million. Data.gov and the IT Dashboard (see sections below) will most likely be casualties.

Web 2.0/Government 2.0

Web 2.0 was born in 2004 after a conference brainstorming session between Tim O'Reilly of O'Reilly Communications and Web Pioneer, Dale Dougherty. Its focus is on "harnessing collective intelligence" and encouraging informal networks to develop around Web interactions including personal social media sites such as Twitter and Facebook and open social media sites for text, image, and video based information sharing such as YouTube, Flickr, blogs including communities of practice forums and Wikis (O'Reilly & Battelle, 2009).

Under the Bush Administration, Web 2.0 took off as public managers began to exploit the emerging social media both as a way to interface with citizens, and to improve workflows within government. The potential for improved information sharing to meet many of the requirements of general public sector reform as outlined earlier was obvious. The U.S. Coast Guard (USCG) offers an early example:

Faced with a coming "revolution" in information management and social networking, the USGC, under former Commandant Thad Allen, began a service-wide initiative to utilize technologies such as YouTube, Facebook, and blogs, to adapt to accelerating change and improve communication processes within the service. Just months into the initiative, thousands of visitors to the Commandant's daily blog, thousands of "fans" on the Facebook pages of the USCG and Commandant and many followers of the Coast Guard's YouTube channel are enabling the Coast guard to interact on a more collaborative level than ever before[7].

Open Government/Open Data

Opening up government data holdings to be shared within government and the public is characterized by fits and starts and changes in direction. Under the Clinton and Bush Administrations, intelligence data on terrorists was siloed in agencies and not shared, then de-siloed to facilitate intelligence sharing, then re-siloed again; but even this pattern was uneven across agencies.

Social media opened up data and information sharing—mostly in the non-security arena—to unprecedented levels, breaking down barriers erected by government. Frequent compromises of data held by the government including Internal Revenue Service, Social Security, and Veteran's data lead to tightening again. Guidelines for data gathering on private citizens and foreigners under the Patriot Act loosened sharing in some areas and simultaneously tightened others. All along, agencies and programs resisted posting data on websites that would have enabled the public to monitor how their tax dollars were spent.

The Obama Administration made open government and open data a high priority for his administration. His first official act as president was to direct agencies to release massive amounts of data to the public! Obama's open government framework is as follows (Ginsberg, 2010):

Goal:

- To strengthen democracy and improve efficiency and effectiveness of government

Guiding Principles:

- Transparency to foster accountability
- Public participation through social media and "crowd sourcing"
- Collaboration across and within agencies, and externally with citizens

Data availability:

- Render data into machine readable form
- Promote accessibility
- Declassify

Accountability:

- Creation of dashboard to monitor initiative progress

- Post open data plans on Web for public comment
- Form transparency working group to promote accountability and implementation

Best Practices:

Post best practices at a central website: www.challenge.gov.

Exploit IT:

- Provide leadership through OMB Chief Information Officer
- Create new Chief Technology Officer
- Create new open data Task Force
- Assign responsible officers at program and agency level to implement initiative

Web based:

- Move from Web 2.0 to Web 3.0, the semantic Web
- Impose cloud first computing policy
- Infuse social media everywhere
- Use open source software to save money
- Promote use of third party websites and applications
- Promote communities of interest and best practices

Data.gov

In May 2009, the Obama Administration launched www.Data.gov, a central repository of federal data sets. As of September 2011, www.Data.gov hosted 389.915 datasets, 1,071 government applications, and 236 citizen applications. The website promotes use of Web 3.0 (the semantic Web) applications, which allow users to perform some analysis, merge datasets, and convert them into graphics. Unfortunately, budget cuts in Congress will likely eliminate this program.

IT Dashboard

In an effort to improve federal government development, acquisition, and implementation of IT systems, the Obama Administration created the IT Dashboard in 2009[8]. The dashboard quantifies and reports on the high level status of around 7000 IT projects across 27 agencies at any given time. Detailed data are provided on 800 projects classified as 'major.' These data are then fed into the annual budget cycle to be used in decision making on future IT funding for each project. The IT Dashboard is currently scheduled for defunding under the current round of budget cuts.

In January 2010, the Obama Administration created TechStat, a "face-to-face, evidence-based review of any IT program with OMB and agency leadership, enabling the government to turnaround, halt or terminate IT investments that are not paying dividends." More specifically, "improve line-of-sight between project teams and senior executives, increase the precision of ongoing measurement of IT program health, and boost the quality and timing of interventions to keep projects on track TechStat has remained in place even after budget cuts[9].

Many believe that the open government initiative, as of July 2011, is in serious trouble (Wadhwa, 2011). Under budget cuts in 2011, Obama agreed to cut the $35 million E-government initiative to $8 million, effectively gutting the program. The CIO, Vivek Kundra, architect and evangelist of the initiative, promptly resigned. Only time will tell whether the open government initiative succeeds. Many are doubtful.

Cloud First

The Obama Administration now requires that all agencies employ cloud computing as a first resort, and if they do not, they must justify why not. Cloud computing is adjudged to be more cost effective and better facilitates collaboration within and across agencies[10]. The switch to the cloud has apparently been successful after encountering some resistance from agencies. Why? The Office of Management and Budget informed them that they would not receive funding for future IT projects. The cloud presents a dilemma for achieving efficiencies: the cloud is less expensive to operate than in-house systems, yet layoffs in IT and reduced IT budgets will make it difficult to migrate systems to the cloud.

Consolidated Data Centres

In 1998, there were about 432 federal data centres; by 2010 there were 2,094. By 2015, the Obama Administration wants to reduce them by about half. They are duplicative and not cost effective. They also might be better served in a cloud computing environment. This seems to be an unqualified success in IT reform.

Open Source Software

The Obama Administration does not require agencies to look for open source software opportunities to save money, but neither does it discourage the practice. GSA, whose mission is to procure or consult on software products, offers agencies a website where they can find information on free and open source software applications. In 2011, the government released its own IT Dashboard as an open source application[11], but this initiative is meagre. The federal government could save billions were it to transition to open source, but there is no impetus to do so.

Possible Setbacks for Open Government Initiatives

Just as Obama's open government initiative was in full swing, the Wikileaks scandal broke. A rogue anarchist computer hacker, Julian Assange allowed hundreds of thousands of classified documents from the Defence Department and State Departments to be published to his website,

Wikileaks. This act caused turmoil in governments around the world, and according to some, potential deaths among sympathizers, informants, clandestine operators and spies. With computer security concerns already looming over cloud computing, open source software, social media, incompetence in handling public data, Wikileaks has the potential to single-handedly reverse gains in policies opening up data to the public.

Congressional initiatives to reduce America's unsustainable budget deficits and national debt pose another threat. Budgeters are targeting IT initiatives for reduction or elimination (Johnson, 2011). Rather than expanding IT in government, the country has entered entering an era of "cutback management." What advances in reform have been achieved may well retrench, but, the extent of the cutbacks is yet to be known.

So, enter enterprise architecture in the context of public sector and IT reform.

ENTERPRISE ARCHITECTURE

EA is intended to be the glue that holds together and guides the implementation of public sector reform and IT advances across the whole-of-government. It provides a layered structure that gives a strong framework upon which to build broad reform at an intra- or inter- agency level while ensuring conformation to national requirements. While grounded in information and IT management, it also provides structure to project management, enables integration of reform or policy across agency operations and facilitates informed collaboration between all stakeholders thus reducing the potential for error and misinterpretation. Although the approach has now been in place for about two decades, it continues to change fairly dramatically, as specialists develop new tools and applications, frameworks become more sophisticated, and policy makers learn what works and what does not. Agencies and programs are expected to adopt EA frameworks, but much

remains to be done and there is resistance in some quarters, and this presents barriers in the current environment.

Brief Historical Background

Building on John Zachman's original EA framework published in 1987 (Zachman, 1987), the National Institute of Standards and Technology (NIST), under its legislative mandate, issued the first guidance on EA for federal agencies in 1989 (NIST, 1989). In 1992, the Government Accountability Office (GAO) published a more comprehensive guide for federal agencies (GAO, 1992) followed by a research report on best practices drawn primarily from the private sector (GAO, 1994). None of this was mandatory.

The Defence Department became one of the first federal agencies to more widely employ EA in 1994, under the *Architecture Framework for Information Management* (TAFIM), various versions of which had been developed several years earlier in the 1980s. In addition to laying out general guidelines, TAFIM called for the use of segmented architecture approaches that would simplify the design of large complex systems by breaking them into modules. Defence has since published frequent revisions of the initial framework (Department of Defence, 2009).

As noted above, the Clinger-Cohen Act of 1996 mandated that CIOs across government implement EA frameworks in their agencies. In 1999, the CIO Council produced the *Federal Enterprise Architecture Framework* (FEAF) as the first whole-of-government guidance to agencies (CIOC, 2000, 2001). In 2000, the Department of Treasury published the *Treasury EA Framework*, suggesting that some agencies, as was the case with Defence, wanted to retain control of their own IT (Department of Treasury, 2000). The *Federal Information Security Management Act* of 2002 (FISMA) (PL 107-37) required agencies to integrate IT security into their capital planning and EA processes, conduct annual IT security reviews of all programs and systems, and report the results.

In 2002, OMB established the *Federal Enterprise Architecture Program Management Office* (FEAPMO), and issued the revised *Federal Enterprise Architecture* (FEA) guidance, which fleshed out five reference models that guide all architecture initiatives today: business, performance, data and information, service, and technical, intended to capture the architecture of what agencies do (OMB, 1997).

In 2003, GAO issued its own guidance to agencies on EA which more or less paralleled guidance by other government agencies (GAO, 2003). In 2002-3, GAO promoted the *EA Management Maturity Framework* (EAMMF) which is used to assess agency development against seven stages: (1) creating EA awareness, (2) establishing EA institutional commitment and direction, (3) creating the management foundation for EA development and use, (4) developing initial EA versions, (5) completing and using an initial EA version for targeted results, (6) expanding and evolving the EA and its use for institutional transformation, and (7) continuously improving the EA and its use to achieve corporate optimization (GAO, 2002, 2003, 2010). EAMMF is a model similar to the widely-employed Capability Maturity Model (CMM) which helps organizations reduce errors in software development and makes organizations more efficient, effective and economical (Humphrey, 2002).

The synthesis between EA and IT Project Management is obvious. Neither can be successful without integration of the other where both exist.

Current State of Play in EA and IT Project Management

In 2004, OMB issued the first version of the *Enterprise Architecture Assessment Framework* (EAAF), frequently revised and now in Version 3.1 (OMB, 2008, 2009). This is the standard framework against which agency EA is evaluated.

EAAF recognizes that EA must link strategic planning, Capital Planning and Investment Control (CPIC) and performance based management and budgeting. EAAF is template based. EAAF also aligns with the *Federal Transition Framework* (FTF), *Enterprise Transition Plan* (ETP), *Federal Segment Architecture Methodology* (FSAM), and *Visualization to Understand Expenditures in IT framework* (VUE-IT). FTF uses the five reference models above to segment the model into component parts—mission, business services, and enterprise services. ETP is the plan detailing how an enterprise will transition from a baseline state to a desired future state. FSAM details segment architecture and fleshes out the ETP. The CPIC framework refers to capital programming as a decision-making process for ensuring IT investments integrate strategic planning, budgeting, procurement, and the management of IT in support of agency missions and business needs. VUE-IT is a graphics tool allowing policymakers to see expenditure data more clearly. GAO continues to assess EA schemes using its EAMMF model.

OMB launched two approaches to mitigate risks in IT projects in 2005: watch lists and Earned Value Management (EVM). The watch lists include the Management Watch List, based on an assessment of planning documents, and the High Risk List, based on an actual assessment of projects (OMB, 2005a, 2005b). Under the Obama Administration, IT projects may be terminated if they fail to score well on either list. In June 2009, OMB replaced the Management Watch List and High Risk List initiatives with the IT Dashboard and the TechStat process (Kundra, 2010) putting project management into the public domain.

EVM is "intended to identify project status, schedule delays, cost overruns and unbiased estimates of total costs, demonstrate government and contractor costs for all major IT projects, as well as to show how close projects are to meeting approved cost, schedule and performance goals. EVM is a structured method for integrating technical, schedule and cost performance that has long proven effective in managing performance of complex government projects" (Gartner, 2006, p. 1; see also, GAO, 2009). EVM undergirds the high-risk lists and IT Dashboard.

NIST, in 2010, supplemented OMB's guidance applying risk management to the FEA lists (NIST, 2010). The NIST guidance helps agencies meet responsibilities under FISMA, in the process stressing security from an information system's initial design through implementation and daily operations. This provides an extra layer throughout the project management lifecycle that would be developed from whole of government requirements and would feed into a consolidated EA approach after delivery.

The frameworks outlined above are combined into an overall assessment by OMB to determine what IT programs will be developed, terminated, or revised and how they will be assessed, especially in terms of allocation of the president's budget.

The EA approach aligns well with public sector reforms, because it provides a framework in which to apply and measure quality standards and outlines intra- and inter- agency data management and sharing guidelines, including with outside parties. This offers an enabling environment in which reporting, quality assurance, performance measurement, and evidence-based decision making processes can be realised. Accepting that EA produces many benefits, the question becomes: What are the barriers impeding progress in realizing public sector and IT reform and how could EA be applied to alleviate these issues?

BARRIERS

At Risk IT

IT has remained on the "high risk list" of whole-of-government initiatives for the past 20 years and the GAO (2011a) continues to place IT on its list of initiatives at risk of failure or operate in highly dysfunctional ways. From its website:

The federal government relies on information management systems and networks to help carry out vital missions and public services, but its management and use of IT are not always effective. Improvements are necessary to ensure that taxpayer money is not ill spent and vital government missions are not compromised. Agencies have spent billions of dollars on developing systems and processes that are not cost effective, fail to deliver expected results, and do not provide the best solutions to agencies' needs. Not all agencies are taking full advantage of the opportunities provided by technological change and innovation, including opportunities to make dramatic improvements in customer service and drive down administrative costs. In an era of rapidly changing technology, agencies are challenged not only in managing information systems but also in the collection, use, and dissemination of information. Managing these systems and information requires agencies, among other things, to provide adequate security and privacy protections[12].

Accountability systems including the Management Watch Lists for IT are working quite well: bad IT projects are being identified, managed, or terminated, but the number of bad projects is disturbing to many critics because management systems are not correcting many of the weaknesses and shortcomings in IT projects as they progress and are not learning from mistakes of the past. In short, critics demand more and faster progress. From 2004 to 2008, GAO reviewed all projects placed on the Management Watch List based on OMB assessments (GAO, 2009). In 2008, alone, there were 352 projects, totalling $23.4 billion in costs, published on the Watch List because they had cost, schedule, performance, security, privacy and/or acquisition weaknesses[13].

Consider an example: The FBI, realizing that its antiquated IT systems would greatly impede its effectiveness in becoming a counter terrorism focused organization, launched the Trilogy Program to replace computer equipment, develop better networks, and improve IT case management systems. The FBI, just after September 11, tried to develop a new IT system, a Virtual Case File that would transform the agency from a paper-based system (in line with the PRA) to one that would allow intelligence officers and investigators to share information and conduct analyses. In 2005, the new system, costing over $100 million to develop, had to be abandoned because it did not work. The inspector general at the Justice Department found that this, the most publicized IT system failure in history, resulted from: "poorly defined and slowly evolving design requirements; overly ambitious schedules; and the lack of a plan to guide hardware purchases, network deployments, and software development for the bureau" (Goldstein, 2005). A private IT vendor and the FBI, according to the FBI's inspector general, shared the blame.

Should there be any doubt about the state of IT in government, the Obama Administration itself includes on the OMB website the following statement[14]:

IT advancements have been at the center of a transformation in how the private sector operates—and revolutionized the efficiency, convenience, and effectiveness with which it serves its customers. The federal government largely has missed out on that transformation due to poor management of technology investments, with IT projects too often costing hundreds of millions of dollars more than they should, taking years longer than necessary to deploy, and delivering technologies that are obsolete by the time they are completed. We are working to close the resulting gap between the best performing private sector organizations and the federal government.

Finally, compliance and accountability are sorely lacking in federal agencies. Consider information security. In the past five years, security breaches, both from outside and inside agencies, has risen 650%. In 2009-2010, the government took steps to improve the security of its data across

the board. The Government Accountability Office (2011i) found that information security initiatives were not pursued as they should have been, and that much more needed to be done.

EA resides in this broader IT context, and hence may be unable to realize its potential: guilt by association.

EA Problems

EA has not been rigorously studied in the federal system, so it is difficult to assess how well it is working. One exception is an evaluation by the Government Accountability Office (2011h) which reported that EA appeared to be fostering a great deal of duplication across government rather than reducing it. GAO has placed EA on its list of targets that could lead to major cost savings over time.

Outsourcing Limitations

Any EA should reflect the current state of play if it is to be of any value so any delays as suggested above, in such a rapidly changing environment are critical to success. EA should also reflect the desirable state of play and this requires an intimate knowledge of the agency processes, structures and interactions it is trying to document. Federal agencies, let alone programs, often have neither sufficient staff, nor expertise, nor in-house resources to take on public sector reform challenges in an EA compatible context as defined above. This will worsen as layoffs in federal government proceed. As a result, EA projects are predominantly outsourced. This exacerbates barriers further by not meeting these two critical requirements due to knowledge gaps and delays in understanding and consequently delivery of a late, low quality product. Additionally, in spite of attempts to correct the problem, there is still a huge gap between agency and program staff and IT staff: neither particularly understands one another. This means that by definition, there will be a gap between government IT and non-IT staff and government staff and outside, private sector vendors. Because of these disconnects, there often are other entities, systems integrators or project managers, who attempt to intermediate trying to integrate the whole process together. For critics, is it any wonder why something as complicated as EA, especially in a whole-of-government approach has a high risk of failure or cost overruns in both its development and implementation phases?

Flawed Management and Policy Processes

Either because IT and non-IT staff do not understand one another, or because they have agendas that do not support EA initiatives, it is likely that EA frameworks will simply replicate or capture all of the existing problems in management and policy processes rather than looking to reflect solutions. As mentioned above, any EA framework should reflect the best scenario for the current environment, that is, the one that if followed would provide the best outcome. For example, we know that the lion's share of civil servants will be retiring over the next few years—the so-called retirement tsunami. Critics ask, are we to believe that they will want to devote several years to working on a whole-of-government public sector and IT reform initiatives that will very likely be undone by next the new administration? Probably not. It is easier just to model the existing system warts and all, rather than completely rethink it leading to further instances of poor EA for the record.

Consider another example. Under Bush, PART, the greatest public service reform ever, never clearly spelled out the explicit relationship between the Government Performance and Results Act's five year *Strategic Plan*, annual *Performance and Accountability Report*, and *Annual Performance Plan* requirements. Even the PART's relationship to the President's Management Agenda scorecard assessments on whole-of-government initiatives was never articulated. Management components of the HCAAF were never tied into the manage-

ment components of the PART. Importantly, the PART and Performance Assessment Report (PAR) were to be folded into an EA but this was never completed, especially in the ETP. As noted earlier in this chapter, PART was discontinued in 2008.

Now under Obama, the entire PART has been abandoned. And true to form according to detractors, the Obama Administration has not articulated in detail what its reform agenda will look like, let alone lay out detailed specifics that can be used by enterprise architects, after more than two years in office. This makes creating an enterprise wide architecture that will meet the reform agenda near impossible. It also reduces the ability to develop, meet, and report on performance indicators making anything other than failure unlikely.

Erroneous or Misleading Data

GAO reports that data about the performance of EA initiatives are often deeply flawed, so much so that making management or policy decisions about them is risky business (GAO, 2009, 2011a, 2011c, 2011d, 2011e, 2011f). To the optimist, this means that the process is good at identifying issues that in the past may have been masked. To the pessimist, this means that the process is likely creating errors not reducing them.

Databases housed in EA infrastructure are also flawed in the minds of critics, because they can be used to misrepresent government performance under public sector reform. Capturing data through EA platforms in many cases does not make these data any more intelligible to the public under IT and public sector reforms. Consider this example. In 2009, the Obama Administration launched the *American Recovery and Reinvestment Act*, an $800 billion stimulus package to jump start the economy during the recession. Only three Republicans voted for the measure in Congress, making the program politically contentious. The Obama Administration tried to sell the unprecedented expenditure arguing that it would create jobs. In a few short months of its launch, it became clear that jobs were not being created. Therefore, the administration revised the definition to "jobs created or retained." This soon had to be abandoned once it became clear that jobs were not likely to disappear in the absence of stimulus funding. Finally, the administration began reporting hours worked under stimulus funding. This did the trick, now they could claim 586,000 jobs on their impact website. The EA capturing these data could be easily modified to account for definitional changes, but, to critics, EA also made it much easier to mislead citizens about the policy underpinnings and its impact on the economy. Citizens logging into the government's www.Recovery.gov website could "drill down" to find jobs in their neighbourhood associated with Recovery Act funding thus potentially revealing the previously hidden 'truth.'

Legacy System Impediments

The dogged persistence of legacy systems—hardware and software—in place in federal agencies thwart advances promised by EA approaches. Consider this. On January 27, 2010, President Obama held a forum on "Modernizing Government," a key theme of which was the promotion of IT (Obama, 2010). In an opening speech at the forum he observed, the best efforts of government employees "are thwarted because the technological revolution that has transformed our society over the past two decades has yet to reach many parts of government. Many [government employees] will tell you that their kids have better technology in their backpacks and in their bedrooms than they have at the desks at their work." He goes on to note the situation at the US Patent and Trademark Office (PTO). Patents are the driver of economic development in western countries. Without patents, few would bother to produce goods and services. PTO receives about 80 percent of patent applications online, but then it manually prints them out, scans them, and enters them into an outdated case management system.

As a consequence, patent processing times average three years. EA does little to resolve these performance issues that are all too common across the federal system.

Dysfunctional Organizational Culture

The GAO and numerous others have observed that there are major organizational barriers in getting agency or program buy-in to implement EA initiatives. As noted above, some of this is generational: older workers may not be interested in devoting the time necessary to implement public sector reform projects before they leave public service, but, even in the IT community, many practitioners still do not support EA: the "old ways are the best ways." Even knowing that organizational culture impedes progress, policy makers tend not to fund organizational change schemes to help build the culture necessary to achieve intended reform results. Such initiatives are considered expensive and do not have tangible, directly measurable returns. Many others consider them a waste of time given the workload they already have and most probably do not want to be told what to do especially in their own area of perceived expertise.

A corollary point is that those who are not committed to reform nevertheless likely will try to appear to be in support and compliance. Obama's open government initiative that encourages citizen engagement is a case in point for critics. A review of government websites revealed the following shortcomings (see OMB Watch, 2010, and see also, Lukensmeyer, Goldman, & Stern, 2011):

- Great deal of variation in what agencies accomplished, ranging from very little to a great deal.
- The worse rated agency was the Office of Management and Budget, the office responsible for overseeing the open government initiative.
- The open government initiative performance dashboard was compliance based,

with no concern for quality, relevance, or efficiency.

- Limited guidance and standards were offered to guide agencies in preparing open government websites.
- Inspector General reports—that heavily criticize agencies and programs—tended to be buried in difficult to find places on agency websites.
- Budget justifications were difficult to find on websites.
- Designated responsible officers were not listed or links to them were inoperable.
- Open government Web pages were not integrated into general agency Web pages.
- Websites lacked public participation—social media—tools linked to open government initiatives.
- Data on websites tended to be outdated.

Additionally, a study of federal websites by NextGov found that fully one-fourth are unreachable (Marks, 2011).

Organizational culture as a barrier to change was recently illustrated in a study of federal managers conducted by NextGov and the Government Business Council (NextGov, 2011): most federal managers felt that with respect to Obama's Open Government Initiative, they were already posting all the data that needed to be posted on the Web. More than half also believed that transparency was not their job!

Low Returns on Investment

Given the expense of implementing EA schemes in a whole-of-government framework, many critics are questioning whether this even makes sense. Some agencies have developed websites that incorporate EA and open data principles. Yet many programs and agencies are finding that no one accesses them. Originally, policy makers recognized that this could be a problem

and required that open data apply to "high value data" rather than all data, but many in their haste to open up, are opening up everything possible, even though demand is not there. For example, the Government Services Administration created a Twitter account to announce Government 2.0 news to vendors, stakeholders and other agencies. Shortly thereafter, they shut it down due to lack of interest.

Lack of Application

With the Bush Administration out of office, PART has attracted much criticism. Barack Obama's head of management at OMB, Jeffrey Zients (2009), summed up the problems on PART in testimony before Congress on October 29, 2009:

The test of a performance management system is whether it is used. Despite the extent and breadth of these historic efforts, the current approach fails this test. Congress doesn't use it. Agencies don't use it. And it doesn't produce meaningful information for the public. Most metrics are process-oriented and not outcomes-based. We do not track progress on goals that cut across agencies. Overall, too much emphasis has been placed on producing performance information to comply with a checklist of requirements instead of using it to drive change.

In addition, the Bush Administration had originally hoped that analysis of data collected by the PART would provide convincing evidence upon which to build a case for increasing or decreasing budget based on performance. The large number of mandatory spending programs and the political protections for many discretionary programs greatly dampened this expectation and linking budgets to performance and management was all but abandoned.

Periodic surveys of federal managers on their use of performance information under The

Government Performance and Results Act shows that "while significantly more federal managers reported having performance measures for their programs than they did 10 years ago, their reported use of performance information to make management decisions has not changed significantly" (GAO, 2009). Critics therefore view expensive EA initiatives as a waste of time.

Inadequate Development Processes

According to detractors, governments frequently launch initiatives before they are ready for "prime time." In so doing, the initiatives often underperform and fail, and the credibility of approaches is undermined. Consider the www.Recovery.gov website mentioned above. The website was hastily rolled out in 2008 in a highly publicized launch to promote the Obama Administration's commitment to transparency and accountability. The site was live for months but the data posted was so meagre that it was of no use to the public. In spite of being billed as a state of the art approach to accountability, it was not appropriately implemented for the time or the user base and hence could be considered just too clever for its own good. After two years and an avalanche of criticism, the website had to be rebuilt and now is probably as good an example of Web 3.0 in action as there is in government. It has been able to effectively incorporate leading technologies such as:

- MS Sharepoint, FAST Search and SQL Server,
- Web 2.0 and 3.0 features: wikis, podcasts, blogs, widgets, gadgets, pipes, and microblogs,
- Open source components, and
- Amazon cloud.

The reengineered website was created in a few weeks. Had the administration taken time to research best practice and acquire evidence for what users really want to see when they developed the website originally, it could have avoided a great deal of criticism.

Ineffective Leadership

Without top-level management and policy maker support for initiatives like the EA, they tend to be highly uneven in execution. Some managers pursue them vigorously while others do not. Consider the US Department of Housing and Urban Development's EA scheme. Looking at the HUD CIO website, one discovers numerous EA strategies, plans, standards, templates and the like[15]. The CIO published a strategic plan for IT that appears to integrate IT into the broader strategies for the agencies. The problem is that all of the documents that promise regular and frequent updates, along with measurable goals and objects, end in 2008 when President George Bush left and Barack Obama took office and are no longer applied or updated. At best, this shows a lack of commitment to transparency and accountability; while at worst, it shows a lack of progress.

Federal Planning Cycles Misaligned

Even though many recurring processes like budgeting and strategic planning are established in law, policy, regulation and custom, they often do not align well. The budget process, which drives much planning and certainly nearly all financing is perpetually out of alignment with strategic planning, human capital management, capital planning, performance management and IT. This is the kind of thing EA was expected to address. Obama's CIO, Vivek Kundra, for example, notes, that IT acquisition and procurement is woefully out of alignment with the budget process, not to mention the other processes mentioned (Kundra, 2010). This implies that attempts to get a handle on IT development, spending, and implementation regardless of the frameworks available, ranging from dashboards to reviews, are likely to lead to risk of failure. In the context of EA, this means that developers will face great uncertainty about what they are to develop and when, how to report and when, and when to apply for budget consideration to ensure timely procurement.

Informal Networks Capture

We observed above that informal networks, although not new to governance, have only been recently "discovered" and are only now being seriously studied. Even given their omnipresence in the political landscape, relatively little is known about them, especially regarding their potential in this context. At the same time, it may be that EA frameworks are not yet sophisticated enough to capture them. Consider the coordinated government response to the series of killer tornados, which swept through Orlando, Florida, in 2007. The government was unable to get food to first responders, was greatly delayed in getting rebuilding underway, and was unable to forward disaster loan applications to central processing centers in a timely fashion. Yet these things were all achieved with relative ease by the private sector. A Starbucks Coffee truck provided coffee and food to workers, church groups came on the scene with volunteer builders and materials and began repairing homes. Federal Express in spite of being in the middle of a disaster, picked up loan packages and delivered the next day to federal processing centres in Texas. EA should be able to capture this networking and apply it as a blueprint for improved government services in the future if it was known to exist, but federal IT workers were unaware of it.

SOLUTIONS AND OPPORTUNITIES

Those who are interested in public sector and IT reform, and realizing the promise of EA, would do well to devise strategies to overcome the barriers enumerated above. This will not be easy, and it may not be possible.

The recommendations provided below will help create an environment in which public sector IT reform and EA can be sustained, but they are probably not sufficient if applied in isolation.

Promote Sustainability across Administrations

Massive transformation following each change in administration (or in mid-term changes within government) particularly in whole-of-government policies involving IT and EA plays havoc with systems. This is even more problematic when change is chaotic as it usually is in this context. Before whole-of-government IT approaches are launched, policy advocates need to build consensus across party lines, within the bureaucracy, and across powerful stakeholders, all of which can sustain or terminate an initiative. Although difficult, consensus can be achieved. Health care policies under presidents Clinton and Obama either failed or are floundering because a baseline consensus was not developed. But Medicare, one of the largest federal programs, has thrived and survived for more than 50 years because various stakeholders came together to make it work (Balutis, Buss, & Ink, 2011).

Appoint Management and Policy Makers (IT and Non-IT) Who Know What to Do and Want to Do It, and Get Buy-In from Civil Servants

It goes without saying that the president and cabinet officers must show leadership if reform is to be successful, but a perpetual problem with federal government is that top policy makers and managers often do not have the skills, expertise, or desire to make major initiatives succeed. They obtained their positions for political reasons, not because of competency or commitment. In about two years, they leave to pursue other careers or opportunities. Initiatives languish. At the same time, civil servants do not necessarily buy-in to every new administration's agenda. As such, they may not pursue policies, programs, and initiatives in support of a new administration or a "lame duck" administration that is powerless. Because administrations and political appointees quickly come and go, the civil service often finds it easier to outwait their political masters, knowing full well that a new batch will soon arrive and change everything around once again. For IT and public service reforms to succeed, political appointees, and senior civil servants must cooperate. For reforms to gain traction, civil servants and policy makers must buy-in to the agenda and make it work. For all of its faults, the Bush Administration's PART initiative, which had major IT and EA components, not to mention public service reforms, was a master stroke in that the president gained support of the senior civil service to design and implement PART, and assigned political appointees to manage the initiative as their major responsibility in government. The president made it a centrepiece against which he and his managers were to be held accountable. The fact that PART was terminated, illustrates that buy-in and commitment alone are not sufficient to make reforms sustainable.

Change Organizational Culture

The federal government has a rare opportunity to replace its aging civil servants with younger talent who might be better suited for work in the "information age." Human resource management, as directed by policy makers and managers, need to promote hiring of new professionals who can straddle both IT and general management. This will be difficult as these skill sets are uncommon. As a long-term strategy, it would be good practice for universities to add management to IT programs and IT to management programs, at least for those students who aspire to employment in the field. The massive, and heavily resourced, training

system in the federal government could also be reengineered to better fuse management and IT. Finally, high quality organizational transformation programs in federal agencies or programs that are critical to public sector and IT reform need to be an integral part of any reform effort.

Rather than Seeking Massive Reform, Focus much more on Small Incremental Change

In reviewing much of the documentation of successful public sector and IT reform, it becomes apparent that success occurred because an initiative was undertaken in a rather narrow arena where managers and political appointees were in agreement and committed, where resources were sufficient to achieve results, where the initiative could be pursued in relative isolation from other initiatives, where the initiative produced results that were valued because they improved efficiency, effectiveness and economy, and where civil servants and political appointees realized personal rewards and credit. If initiatives in public sector and IT reforms were pursued in this way, rather than in a whole-of-government framework, then enterprise architecture can become a fine tool for sticking together these components into something larger. This approach seems achievable, where large-scale systems pose extraordinary risks.

ACKNOWLEDGMENT

This work is dedicated to Elmer Staats, former controller general of the United States, who passed away in August 2011. His contribution to public management was unprecedented.

REFERENCES

Apps. (2011a). *Cloud*. Retrieved from https://www.apps.gov/cloud/main/start_page.do.

Apps. (2011b). *Cloud.* Retrieved from https://www.apps.gov/cloud/cloud/category_home.do?&c=SA.

Balutis, A., Buss, T. F., & Ink, D. (Eds.). (2011). *American governance 3.0: Rebooting the public square.* Armonk, NY: ME Sharpe.

Bouchaert, G., & Halligan, J. (2007). *Managing performance: International comparisons.* London, UK: Routledge.

Buss, T. F., & Gardner, A. (2008). The millennium challenge account: An early appraisal. In Picard, L., Groelsema, R., & Buss, T. F. (Eds.), *Foreign Aid and Foreign Policy* (pp. 329–355). Armonk, NY: ME Sharpe.

Buss, T. F., & Picard, L. (Eds.). (2011). *African security and the Africa command.* Sterling, VA: Kumarian Press.

Buss, T. F., Redburn, F. S., & Guo, C. (2006). *Modernizing democracy.* Armonk, NY: ME Sharpe.

Chief Information Officer. (2008). *Enterprise modernization plan: EA transition strategy, v.3.* Washington, DC: US Department of Housing and Urban Development. Retrieved from www.hud.gov/offices/cio/ea/newea/resources/eatpv2.pdf.

Chief Information Officers Council. (2000). *Architecture alignment and assessment guide.* Washington, DC: CIOC.

Chief Information Officers Council. (2001). *A practice guide to federal enterprise architecture, version 1.0.* Washington, DC: CIOC.

Chief Information Officers Council. (2007). *Architecture principles for the US government.* Washington, DC: CIOC.

Chief Information Officers Council. (2008). *Improving agency performance using information and IT: Enterprise architecture assessment framework, version 3.* Washington, DC: CIOC.

CIO. (2011). *Techstat.* Retrieved from http://www.cio.gov/techstat/.

Collaboration Project. (2011). *Website.* Retrieved from http://www.collaborationproject.org/display/home/Home.

Committee on Fiscal Futures for the US. (2011). *Choosing the nation's fiscal future.* Washington, DC: National Research Council and National Academy of Public Administration.

De Vries, J. (2010). Is the new public management really dead? *OECD Journal on Budgeting, 1,* 1–5. doi:10.1787/budget-10-5km8xx3mp60n

Denhardt, J. V., & Denhardt, R. B. (2007). *The new public service: Serving not steering.* Armonk, NY: ME Sharpe.

Department of Defense. (2009). *Department of Defense architecture framework, version 2.0 (Vol. I-III).* Washington, DC: DOD.

Expect More. (2011). *Website.* Retrieved from http://www.expectmore.gov.

Figliola, P. M. (2010). *The federal networking and IT research and development program.* Washington, DC: Congressional Research Service.

Frederickson, D. G., & Frederickson, H. G. (2006). *Measuring performance of the hollow state.* Washington, DC: Georgetown University Press.

Frederickson, H. G., Smith, K. B., Larimer, C. W., & Licari, M. (2011). *The PA theory primer.* Boulder, CO: Westwood Press.

GAO. (2011). *Information technology.* Retrieved from Http://www.gao.gov/highrisk/challenges/information_technology/home_information_technology.php.

Gattuso, J., & Katz, D. (2011). *Red tape rising.* Washington, DC: Heritage Foundation. Retrieved from http://www.heritage.org/research/reports/2011/07/red-tape-rising-a-2011-mid-year-report.

Gerson, D. (2006). *Pubic information technology and e-governance: Managing the virtual state.* New York, NY: Jones and Bartlett Learning.

Ginsberg, W. (2010). *The Obama administration's OGI.* Washington, DC: Congressional Research Service.

Goldsmith, S., & Eggers, W. (2004). *Governing by network: The new shape of the public sector.* Washington, DC: Brookings Institution Press.

Goldstein, H. (2005). Who killed the virtual case file? *IEEE Spectrum Magazine.* Retrieved from http://spectrum.ieee.org/computing/software/who-killed-the-virtual-case-file.

Government Accountability Office. (1992). *Strategic information planning: Framework for designing and developing system architectures.* Washington, DC: GAO.

Government Accountability Office. (1994). *Executive guide: Improving mission performance through strategic information management and technology.* Washington, DC: GAO.

Government Accountability Office. (2002). *Information technology: Enterprise architecture use across the Federal government can be improved.* Washington, DC: GAO.

Government Accountability Office. (2003). *Information technology: A framework for assessing and improving enterprise architecture management.* Washington, DC: GAO.

Government Accountability Office. (2005). *Managing for results: Enhancing agency use of performance information for management decision making.* Washington, DC: GAO.

Government Accountability Office. (2008). *Military departments need to strengthen management of EA programs.* Washington, DC: GAO.

Government Accountability Office. (2009). *Information technology: Management and oversight of projects totalling billions of dollars need attention.* Washington, DC: GAO.

Government Accountability Office. (2010). *Organizational transformation: A framework for assessing and improving enterprise architecture management (version 2.0).* Washington, DC: GAO.

Government Accountability Office. (2011a). *High risk list.* Washington, DC: GAO. Retrieved from http://www.gao.gov/highrisk/challenges/information_technology/home_information_technology.php.

Government Accountability Office. (2011b). *Information technology: Investment oversight and management have improved but continued attention is needed.* Washington, DC: GAO.

Government Accountability Office. (2011c). *OMB has made improvements to its dashboard, but further work is needed to ensure data accuracy.* Washington, DC: GAO.

Government Accountability Office. (2011d). *DOD and VA should remove barriers and improve efforts to meet their common system needs.* Washington, DC: GAO.

Government Accountability Office. (2011e). *Better informed decision making needed on Navy's next generation enterprise network acquisition.* Washington, DC: GAO.

Government Accountability Office. (2011f). *Information technology: Continued improvements in investment oversight and management can yield billions in savings.* Washington, DC: GAO.

Government Accountability Office. (2011g). *Information technology: Continued attention needed to accurately report federal spending and improve management.* Washington, DC: GAO.

Government Accountability Office. (2011h). *Opportunities to reduce potential duplication.* Washington, DC: GAO. Retrieved from http://www.gao.gov/ereport/GAO-11-318SP/overview.

Government Accountability Office. (2011i). *Information security: Weaknesses continue amid new federal efforts to implement requirements.* Washington, DC: GAO.

Government Executive Magazine. (2009). Obama team outlines its performance agenda. *GovExec.* Retrieved from http://www.govexec.com/dailyfed/0509/051109e1.htm.

Hatry, H. (2007). *Performance measurement.* Washington, DC: Urban Institute Press.

House of Lords. (1997). *Report on the public service.* London, UK: House of Lords.

HUD. (2011). *Website.* Retrieved from http://www.hud.gov/offices/cio/ea/newea/index.cfm.

Humphrey, W. S. (2002). *Winning with software: An executive strategy.* Pittsburgh, PA: Carnegie Mellon University.

Johnson, N., & Svara, J. (2011). *Justice for all: Promoting social equity in public administration.* Armonk, NY: ME Sharpe.

Johnson, N. B. (2011). Citizens less satisfied with government services. *Federal Times.* Retrieved from http://www.federaltimes.com/article/20110125/AGENCY02/101250302/1055/AGENCY.

Johnson, N. B. (2011). Tight budgets prompt IT cutbacks. *Federal Times.* Retrieved from http://www.federaltimes.com/article/20110814/IT03/108140303.

Kamarck, E., & Nye, J. S. (2002). *Governance. com: Democracy in the information age.* Washington, DC: Brookings Institute Press.

Kettl, D., & Dilulio, J. J. (1995). *Inside the reinvention machine.* Washington, DC: Brookings Institute Press.

Kettle, D. (2005). *The global public management review.* Washington, DC: Brookings Institute Press.

Kettle, D. (2009). *The next government of the United States.* New York, NY: WW Norton.

Kundra, V. (2010). *25 point implementation plan to reform federal IT management.* Washington, DC: Office of CIO.

Light, P. C. (1999). *The true size of government.* Washington, DC: Brookings Institution.

Lukensmeyer, C. J., Goldman, J., & Stern, D. (2011). *Assessing public participation in an open government era: A review of federal agency plans.* Washington, DC: IBM Center for the Business of Government. Retrieved from http://www.federaltimes.com/article/20110814/IT03/108140303.

Marks, J. (2011). *Nearly a quarter of dot-gov domains don't work.* Washington, DC: NextGov. Retrieved from http://www.nextgov.com.

Moe, R. (1994). The reinventing government exercise. *Public Administration Review, 54*(2), 111–122. doi:10.2307/976519

National Academy of Public Administration. (2003). *Homeland security: Lessons learned from prior government reorganizations.* Washington, DC: NAPA.

National Academy of Public Administration. (2006). *Transforming the FBI.* Washington, DC: NAPA.

National Institute of Standards and Technology. (1989). *Information management directions: The integration challenge.* Washington, DC: NIST.

National Institute of Standards and Technology. (2010). *Guide for applying the risk management framework to federal information systems*. Washington, DC: NIST.

Nesterczuk, G. (1996). Reviewing the national performance review. *Regulation, 3*, 31–39.

NextGov. (2011). *What transparency means to feds*. Washington, DC: NextGov/Government Business Council. Retrieved from http://www.nextgov.com.

O'Reilly, T., & Battelle, J. (2009). *Web squared: Web 2.0 five years on*. Retrieved from http://assets.en.oreilly.com/1/event/28/web2009_websquared-whitepaper.pdf.

Obama, B. (2010). *President's position on modernizing government: Remarks at the forum on modernizing government*. Washington, DC: The White House.

Office of Management and Budget. (1997). *Information technology architectures, memorandum M-97-16*. Washington, DC: OMB.

Office of Management and Budget. (2002a). *The president's management agenda*. Washington, DC: OMB.

Office of Management and Budget. (2002b). *Expanded electronic government in the President's management agenda*. Washington, DC: OMB.

Office of Management and Budget. (2002c). *Rating the performance of federal programs*. Washington, DC: OMB.

Office of Management and Budget. (2005a). *OMB memorandum M-05-23, improving IT project planning and execution*. Washington, DC: OMB.

Office of Management and Budget. (2005b). *OMB memorandum M-06-02, improving public access to and dissemination of government information and using the federal EA data reference model*. Washington, DC: OMB.

Office of Management and Budget. (2009a). *A new era of responsibility: Renewing America's promise*. Washington, DC: OMB.

Office of Management and Budget. (2009b). *Improving agency performance using information and information technology, version 3.1*. Washington, DC: OMB.

Office of Management and Budget. (2010). *OMB circular A-11, preparation, execution and submission of the budget*. Washington, DC: OMB.

OPM. (2011). *HCAAF resource center*. Retrieved from http://www.opm.gov/hcaaf_resource_center/.

Osborne, D. (1988). *Laboratories of democracy*. Cambridge, MA: Harvard Business School Press.

Osborne, D., & Gaebler, T. (1992). *Reinventing government*. Cambridge, MA: Harvard Business School Press.

Picard, L., & Buss, T. F. (2009). *A fragile balance: Re-examining the history of foreign aid, security and diplomacy*. Sterling, VA: Kumarian Press.

Radin, B. (2006). *Challenging the performance movement*. Washington, DC: Georgetown University Press.

Redburn, F. S., Shea, S., & Buss, T. F. (Eds.). (2008). *Performance based management and budgeting*. Armonk, NY: ME Sharpe.

Scribd. (2011). *GPRA modernization act of 2010*. Retrieved from http://www.scribd.com/doc/47464749/GPRA-Modernization-Act-of-2010-Explained.

Seifert, J. W. (2008). *Reauthorization of the e-government act*. Washington, DC: Congressional Research Service.

Shillabeer, A., Buss, T. F., & Rousseau, D. (Eds.). (2011). *Evidence based public management*. Armonk, NY: ME Sharpe.

Sistare, H. S., Shiplett, M. H., & Buss, T. (2008). *Innovations in human service management: Getting the public's work done in the 21st century*. Armonk, NY: ME Sharpe.

Spending, U. S. A. (2011). *Website*. Retrieved from http://it.usaspending.gov/.

Wadhwa, V. (2011). The death of open government. *Washington Post*. Retrieved from http://www.transparency-initiative.org/news/kundra-resignation.

Watch, O. M. B. (2010). *Leaders and laggards in agency open government web pages*. Washington, DC: OMB Watch. Retrieved from http://www.ombwatch.org/node/10785.

White House. (2011). *OMB*. Retrieved from http://www.whitehouse.gov/omb/egov.

Zachman, J. (1987). A framework for information systems architecture. *IBM Systems Journal, 26*(3). doi:10.1147/sj.263.0276

ENDNOTES

[1]   The inclusion of social equity was added not so long ago by the US National Academy of Public Administration (see Johnson & Svara, 2011).

[2]   We acknowledge that there are successes everywhere in government, but they tend to be agency and/or program specific, rather than applicable across government.

[3]   To our knowledge, no one has estimated the cost of whole-of-government reforms.

[4]   See Expect More (2011).

[5]   See OPM (2011).

[6]   See Scribd (2011).

[7]   See Collaboration Project (2011).

[8]   See USA Spending (2011).

[9]   See CIO (2011).

[10]   See Apps (2011a).

[11]   See Apps (2011b).

[12]   See GAO (2011).

[13]   See Government Accountability Office reports offering analysis of IT management issues (Government Accountability Office, 2011b, 2011c, 2011d, 2011e, 2011f).

[14]   See White House (2011).

[15]   See HUD (2011).

Section 5
Public Value Management in Connected Government

Chapter 19
Assessing the Value of Investments in Government Interoperability

Anthony M. Cresswell
SUNY Albany, USA

Djoko Sigit Sayogo
SUNY Albany, USA

Lorenzo Madrid
Microsoft Corporation, USA

ABSTRACT

Government investments in enhancing the interoperability of ICT systems have the potential to improve services and help governments respond to the diverse and often incompatible needs and interests of individual citizens, organizations, and society at large. These diverse needs and interests encompass a broad range of value propositions and demands that can seldom be met by single programs or assessed by simple metrics. The diversity of stakeholder needs and the complexity inherent in interoperable systems for connected government require an architecture that is up to the task. Such an architecture must include the reference models and components that can accommodate and integrate large portfolios of applications and support multiple kinds of performance assessments. The value propositions that underlie the architecture's performance assessment or reference model are fundamental. The propositions must be broad enough to span the full scope of the government program's goals, a substantial challenge. In recognition of that challenge, this chapter puts forward two perspectives for assessing the value of interoperable ICT investments, incorporating outcomes beyond financial metrics. The first is the network value approach to assessment of investments in interoperable ICT systems for government. The second is the public value framework developed by the Center for Technology in Government, which expands on the network value approach to include a broader range of public value outcomes. These approaches are illustrated in two case studies: the I-Choose project designed to produce interoperable government and private sector data about a specific agricultural market and the government of Colombia's interoperability efforts with expanded metrics based on the expansion of interoperability networks.

DOI: 10.4018/978-1-4666-1824-4.ch019

INTRODUCTION

Assessing the value expected from increased interoperability in government presents policy makers, managers, and analysts with a difficult and multifaceted problem. The high-level goal of increasing government interoperability is to better serve the citizens and society at large. The demands and interests of citizens are diverse and often incompatible, reflecting the complexity of modern societies. Thus, there is no simple value proposition. Methods to assess returns on investments in ICT interoperability should therefore incorporate a broad sense of public value that goes well beyond the traditional financial or program performance metrics. Such a broad value proposition is necessary to direct decision-makers' attention to the full range of benefits possible from increased interoperability, and thereby improve the design and implementation of enhanced interoperability into existing and new systems.

This chapter presents a perspective on assessing the value of interoperability that includes a broad public value proposition. Such a value proposition reflects the complexity of an enterprise architecture that encompasses the range of applications needed for interoperability in a connected government context. This chapter outlines strategies and recommendations for policy makers to enhance the assessment of government investments in ICTs to include returns to both the direct and indirect beneficiaries of government activities, and to society at large through such outcomes as gains in per capita GDP.

The chapter presents two approaches to assessing value that go beyond traditional Return On Investment (ROI) analyses. The first is an analysis of societal-level economic returns from expanding government network interoperability based on a review of a white paper, "The Economic Impact of Interoperability" (Madrid, 2008). The second, based on the public value framework developed by the Center for Technology in Government (CTG),

looks at a broad set of values that governments can potentially deliver through interoperable ICT investments to include financial, political, social, strategic, ideological, quality of life, and stewardship. With these examples, this chapter illustrates how a more comprehensive understanding of the values of interoperable ICT investment can yield more comprehensive and effective justification to support large portfolios of applications and investments in connected government.

The value of increased interoperability can accrue from a great variety of ICT investments and government programs. The chapter briefly addresses the general idea of interoperability to set the context for the specific cases and assessment approaches to be presented. This context setting discussion includes some attention to current shortcomings and inadequacies of the typical financial ROI measurement for assessing the value of government interoperability-related ICT projects. The discussion includes particular attention to the more macroeconomic returns on government ICT investments in terms of increases in economic activity as reflected in national Gross Domestic Product (GDP). Section 4 describes the public value framework for assessing government interoperability projects that consider broader stakeholders' perspectives. Finally, section 5 illustrates the application of these approaches to two cases. The first is a proposed data interoperability framework to support the provision of a wide range of information for sustainable agricultural products, initially focused on fair trade coffee. This initiative, known as I-Choose, will aggregate information on fair trade certification above the national level in the areas of product classifications and government standards, government labeling schemes, and third party certification systems. The second case will focus on government ICTs in Colombia, where the government has been able to provide data on the economic impact of government interoperability efforts.

BACKGROUND

The Development of ICT Investment in the Public Sector

Government services continue to evolve along with the ongoing development and increasing availability of ICT systems. Increasing familiarity with ICT resources has encouraged citizens to pressure government agencies to accelerate the offering of online services (Madrid, 2008). In addition, the development of government ICT investments and new projects internal to government drive change within agencies. However the transformation of government services and operations through ICT and interoperability projects is typically a gradual process rather than a revolutionary one (West, 2004). The adoption of a more sophisticated design develops over time as government program managers and developers gains more experience (Ho, 2002).

One line of research on e-government development in US cities and municipalities represents e-government capabilities as developing through a series of stages (Moon, 2002; West, 2004). There are various studies proposing e-government development in terms of stages or maturity models (Karokola & Yngstrom, 2009). This chapter is based in part on this approach: the UN1 (2002) and Gartner2 e-government maturity models (Baum & Di Maio, 2000). Both of these models propose a four or five-stage progression of increasing capability to describe and rank how countries compare on e-government services deployment. Stages one and two in the UN model both refer to the "Web presence stage." The sequence of e-government progression in both the UN and Gartner models is based on similar stages or phases: the Web presence/emerging phase, the interaction/enhanced phase, the transaction/interactive phase, and the standardization/transactional phase (United Nations, 2001; Baum & Di Maio, 2000).

The idea of progressive stages of maturity in e-government systems should be taken as a metaphor to describe variations in capability across settings, not as a literal description of development that follows a fixed sequence of events. At any time, different governments will display varying levels of capability that can be described as more or less mature. However, two governments that display similar levels of capability have not necessarily achieved those levels through the same sequence of development. According to the United Nations (2002):

The stages are a method for quantifying progress. They are representative of the governments level of development based primarily on the content and deliverable services available through official websites. This is not to suggest, however, that in order to achieve immediate success; a country must follow this linear path, but rather reflects the type of analysis and standards used in 2001 (p. 11).

The main differences among the stages are based on the interdependence of action and systems integration. In the first and second stages, agencies take action independently, without connecting or integrating efforts with other agencies. In the third stage, the transaction/interactive phase, actors begin to recognize the need to have an integrated system between agencies. This phase signifies the first recognition by agencies of the need for interoperable systems. In practice, many government agencies initially overlook the need for interoperability and instead develop their separate systems and solutions independently (Madrid, 2008). The development of interoperability, i.e., the effort to integrate various applications among different agencies, emerges as a necessity in the last stage: standardization/transactional. In this last phase, government agencies integrate separate information systems across organizational boundaries, jurisdictions, and levels. Hence, the interoperability of information systems in government is a natural expansion of efforts to add value and improve performance from the point of view of their stakeholders (Pardo & Burke, 2009).

The interoperable government information system will simplify the transactions and relationships between government and their stakeholders (Madrid, 2008). The interoperable system also allows for identification and reduction of redundant and non-value added activities. A number of studies argue that as a result, interoperability will generate an overall increase in productivity and improvement of data and information quality (Madrid, 2008; Pardo & Burke, 2009). The task is not simple. Generating new levels of interoperability across the boundaries of government agencies, across different levels, and with other non-governmental institutions requires sustained effort at coordination and collaboration (Pardo & Burke, 2009). These coordination and collaboration efforts must account for and overcome differences in systems, procedures, information sharing mechanism, and stakeholder interests across different agencies, levels, and non-governmental entities.

Interoperability and Enterprise Architecture (EA) in Connected Government

A number of studies argue that the adoption of an enterprise architecture model for IT development and operation as a strategy for interoperability provides better planning and coordination in government (Hjort-Madsen, 2009). Enterprise architecture in this sense is a rigorous model or description of an organization that includes the business components and how they are linked to each other and to the other components of the organization's IT systems and infrastructure components. In their research, Pardo and Burke (2009) pointed at the emergence of a new governance model where autonomous government agencies and non-governmental institutions need to work as coherent network to accommodate the needs of their constituents and to deliver value (Pardo & Burke, 2009). The United Nations coined this as "connected government," in which agencies transcend the functional, organizational, and jurisdictional boundaries to provide value for their constituents (Saha, 2010). This governance model includes sustained effort for coordination and collaboration to mitigate the complexity of the networked system (Pardo & Burke, 2009). The implementation and achievement of these tasks are challenging and complicated. Saha (2010) calls for the use of enterprise architecture as a necessary strategy to mitigate the complexity of interoperable systems in the connected government. Enterprise architecture is regarded as a useful tool for transformational government (Hjort-Madsen, 2009; Hjort-Madsen & Pries-Heje, 2009) and effective for facilitating interoperability and handling interoperability conflict (Schekkerman, 2006; Janssen & Kuk, 2006).

Saha (2010) further argues the importance of a close fit between interoperability, connected government, and enterprise architecture. An enterprise architecture model can enable effective strategic planning to improve interoperability and connections among government agencies (Saha, 2010). Enterprise architecture as an organizing and structuring framework has higher potential to yield more efficient coordination and extend interoperability among government agencies, particularly in the higher levels such as federal agencies (Guijarro, 2007). Saha (2010) also points out the possible correlation between the maturity levels of e-government and the implementation of enterprise architecture methods. Each level of the e-government maturity index correlates positively with an enterprise architecture maturity level. For instance, the transformational and connected e-government level that promotes interoperability correlates with levels 3 and 4 of enterprise architecture—namely, rationalized data and modular architecture (Saha, 2010). Rationalized data architecture refers to the standardization of data and process in the architecture, while modular architecture provides flexible modules that incorporate and enable both global standards and local differences (Ross, 2003). Arguably, successful government service delivery in a network of connected agencies and interoperability requires an IT infrastructure that facilitates, at the very least, standardization of data and processes or a more flexible modular architecture.

However, the adoption and implementation of enterprise architecture to support interoperable IT investment in government are contingent on at least two conditions: 1) EA is embedded within contextual elements (Janssen & Hjort-Mardsen, 2007; Hjort-Mardsen, 2009) and 2) EA is influenced by the social interactions and diverse needs of the stakeholders (Janssen, 2011). The culture, history, and standard practices of government agencies and the national government determine the adoption of enterprise architecture in public sector (Hjort-Mardsen, 2009). The implementation of enterprise architecture also needs to account for the interactions and social interdependencies among constituents or stakeholders (Janssen, 2011). As a result, effective adoption and implementation of enterprise architecture in the public sector demands understanding and reengineering of the public sector structure (Janssen & Cresswell, 2005).

Evaluating the effectiveness of network government is very complex and has been mostly neglected in the public administration literature (Provan & Milward, 2001). In a similar manner, the complexity of enterprise architecture has led to a challenge in understanding the value of enterprise architecture applications (Tamm, Seddon, Shanks, & Reynolds, 2011). Tamm et al. (2011) point to the fragmented and incomplete explanations on the value of enterprise architecture adoption and implementation. They call for future research to advance the understanding of the value of enterprise architecture. The subject of the Tamm et al. (2011) study was private institutions. Applying the value assessment in the public sector context will add additional challenges.

Government, as opposed to private institutions, has more diverse stakeholders and constituents, such as individual citizens, organizations, and society at large. These constituents might have varied and often discordant and conflicting needs and interests (Creswell et al., 2006). Diversity of needs and interests makes the assessment of stakeholder commitments and involvements a crucial determinant for successful enterprise architecture implementation (Janssen & Cresswell, 2005). This chapter argues that for such a wide transformation in assessing the value of interoperable projects in a connected government, the typical financial ROI methods for assessing overall value are inadequate. Instead, this chapter proposes and outlines two approaches that recognize a much broader range of values as potential returns from interoperable systems. These are 1) the network values on economic productivity approach and 2) the public value framework to assess interoperable government ICT investment projects.

The Shortcomings of Traditional Return On Investment (ROI) Analysis

In the simplest definition of Return On Investment (ROI) in public sector accounting terms, the return is the simple ratio of excess profit to investment, in terms of either past performance or future expectations (McNulty & Tharenou, 2005; Purser, 2004; Schachner, 1973). This basic idea is typically the way ROI is considered in ICT projects, with a consistent focus on the financial returns, though the financial metrics may differ in the public sector where profit accounting does not apply. However, some analysts argue that ROI in interoperability-related ICT projects is more complicated (Carrata, et al., 2006) because of the variety of their purpose and the nature of information technology investment (Rastrick & Corner, 2010). As result, a single measurement might not be adequate (Rastrick & Corner, 2010; Weill & Olson, 1989). The typical financial ROI measurement has been extensively criticized for its inadequacy (Richard, Devinney, Yip, & Johnson, 2009) due to distortion through accounting policies, human error, and deception (Jacobson, 1987), especially in relation to government ICT projects

(Dadayan, 2006; Cresswell, 2010). Building on the literature in economics, public administration, and information science, this chapter will describe specific shortcomings of the narrow, financial approaches to ROI analysis for investments to enhance government interoperability.

Discussions of these shortcomings by Dadayan (2006) and Markov (2006) point to three limitations of the financial ROI model for ICT: 1) the inaccuracy of the model to predict the actual return due to complexity in ICT investment; 2) the assumption of a high degree of certainty of the cost and benefit measures in traditional ROI; 3) the exclusion of political dynamics underlying ICT investment decisions. Similar criticisms and objections to the validity of strictly financial ROI measurement have a long standing in economics and finance analysis (Jacobson, 1987). The critiques by Fisher and McGowan (1983) on the misuse of ROI measurement pointed to the inaccuracy of the model for predicting financial performance. The measurement of ROI by relating profit fractions to capitalization of investment is also prone to error (Fisher & McGowan, 1983; Moorthy & Polley, 2010). The ratio does not necessarily properly link profit generation to the characteristics and performance of the investment (Fisher & McGowan, 1983; Fisher, 1984; Jacobson, 1987; Richard, et al., 2009). The ratio may be further misleading because the profits as a numerator signify a result of past performance, while the denominator (capitalization of investments) reflects both past and potential future revenue/profit streams (Fisher & McGowan, 1983; Fisher, 1984; Jacobson, 1987; Richard, et al., 2009). Further problems result from the possibility of accounting measurement error affecting both the numerator and denominator (Salamon, 1985).

These criticisms of the validity of financial ROI, specifically in term of proper measurement of the returns in relation to costs and risks, also apply to public sector ICT investments (Cresswell, 2004, 2010; Cresswell, et al., 2006). A study by Cresswell et al. (2006) indicates three significant

shortcomings of the existing methods and models of public returns assessment for government ICT and interoperability projects. First is the narrow scope in defining the returns, which leads to incomplete analysis of public value and fails to incorporate the way political factors can affect the returns (Keefer & Knack, 2007). A second shortcoming relates to the lack of systematic attention to public perspectives when identifying value from government investments (Lamore, Link, & Blackmond, 2006). A third shortcoming is the inadequacy or unavailability of methods to fit the public ROI assessment to the specificity of government ICT investments, both in terms of context and goals (Cresswell, et al., 2006). In sum, the first two shortcomings can be combined into a more general critique of financial ROI: financial-only calculations ignore the importance of non-financial returns and their differential impacts across a variety of stakeholders (Epstein & Mealem, 2009). In addition, ROI does not typically take into account the important influences of specific ICT investment contexts.

The first flaw reflects an underestimation of the significant influence from the political process, the functioning of government organizations, and the diversity of goals in ICT investment projects in the public sector. ICT initiatives in government can vary from system-wide transformations to narrowly defined projects focused on a single program or service (Cresswell, et al., 2006). The time span of complex government ICT and interoperability projects could challenge the capability of classic evaluation approaches such as ROI (Markov, 2006). The stakeholders of government are varied and potential returns to the stakeholders can be direct and easily observable or indirect, obscure, and extended over long time periods (Dadayan, 2006; Cresswell, et al., 2006). Project goals and related returns may shift over the life of a project because highly complex government ICT and interoperability projects can be much more vulnerable to political dynamics. Government failure related to any ICT project can lead to serious political consequences for both sponsors and developers (Cresswell, 2010).

The second flaw relates to the problems of measuring the public value of ICT and interoperability projects. Cresswell et al. (2006) argue that the measurement of returns in public sector investments should consider financial and non-financial returns to direct and indirect beneficiaries and also to the society at large (Cresswell, et al., 2006). Building on this argument, this chapter will show two approaches to measuring returns from interoperable ICT investment projects. The first examines the network value of interoperable ICT investment and how it can influence economic productivity of the society at large. The second approach, the public value framework (Cresswell, et al., 2006), expands the network value approach to include additional variables that reflect a broader public perspective. The next section will describe and outline the network value approach and illustrate the impact of government investments in interoperability-related ICT projects on the economic returns to the society at large based on Madrid's (2008) white paper, "The Economic Impact of Interoperability."

MAIN FOCUS OF THE CHAPTER

The Network Value Approach: Economic Returns on Government Investments in Interoperability-Related ICT Projects

A number of studies point at the significant impact of ICT investment on a country's economic development. An ongoing study by WITSA3 has always found that ICT expenditure is a critically important element of the global economy. Their study found that the ICT industry is among the most significant drivers of the global economy, accounting for US $1.8 trillion in spending in 1997, approximately 6 percent of the global GDP (WITSA, 1999). Their study also suggests that

national GDP grows when ICT spending increases. In addition, the productivity gains will increase subsequent to the investment in digital technology (Bernasek, 2002). Research by Waverman et al. (2005) found a significant GDP growth rate of 0.59 percentage points annually with an increase of 10 mobile phones per 100 people from 1996 to 2003 (Waverman, et al., 2005). These studies provide strong indications of the economic impact of ICT investment, particularly in GDP development.

A study by Madrid (2008) points to the duality of citizen needs for government service provision. Citizens, as the major stakeholder of government, have vertical needs as well as horizontal needs (Madrid, 2008). Vertical need refers to the reliance of citizens on separate services provided by single agencies. Madrid (2008) further argues that these vertical needs shape the basic design of conventional government ICT projects. For these projects, the initial goal of e-government is usually to find and develop customized solutions to address specific internal government agency workflows to provide better services, agency by agency, to fulfill specific citizen needs. This stand-alone design of e-government development is referred to here as the vertical approach (Madrid, 2008). As a result of this vertical approach, each government system is disconnected from one another, which results in independent legacy systems. The vertical approach to systems may work well for some internal agency process issues, but it can overlook public value returns that are indirect or collateral with the nominal goals of the program or service and may ignore significant stakeholders.

Citizens also have horizontal needs. These are needs met by services that cross agency boundaries and involve inter-agency processes, such as passport applications that may involve multiple agencies. However, the vertical orientation of most e-government development has forced citizens to transact and interact with independent and non-integrated processes in separate government agencies. These multiple transactions not only inconvenience citizens, but also add costs and affect overall economic productivity. This section presents a network value approach to show how integrated and interoperable government information systems could provide value to the society at large in terms of economic productivity.

The Network Value Impact of Interoperability

The last stage of many e-government maturity models point to the standardization/transactional phase, which provides the setting for a great variety of transactions to be integrated. Such a level of interconnection and integration of information systems among government agencies will result in highly networked systems. In line with Metcalfe's network effect law (Shapiro & Varian, 1998), Madrid's (2008) study revealed that increasing the integration of e-government system networks could produce a huge impact in improving the economic productivity of a country. Metcalfe's Law asserts that networks become more valuable as they reach more users. Hence, when government systems become more interoperable and better connected with one another, the resulting systems will provide higher overall value for the society.

The potential magnitude of the added value of a more integrated network can be measured or correlated to the number of possible connections with other actors in the network. Allee (2003) proposed that "the value and capability of a network expands with the numbers of connections...when a certain level of connectivity is reached in a complex system, the capabilities that are being unleashed may be far greater than the sum of the parts" (Allee, 2003, p. 78). Similarly, as pointed at in Metcalfe's Law, the number of unique connections in the network of n number of actors is equal to n(n-1)/2 (Shapiro & Varian, 1998). Hence, leveraging the network effect, the value of interoperable (networked) government information systems can also be estimated mathematically as a function of the number of connected

transactions (Madrid, 2008). In his study, Madrid (2008) represented this function as:

$$value = \sum_{i=1}^{m} \lambda^i \left(\frac{t!1}{(t-n)!\,n!} \right)$$

where:

t is the total number of transactions to interoperate
n is the number of transactions that need to be combined to complete a process
m is the number of sub-systems
λ is the correlation factor

The formula indicates that an increased number of connections in the network will also increase the efficiency of the system and value. The following illustration for N=2 shows how significant the increase is on the network value as we increase the number of transactions that interconnect or interoperate. Mathematically speaking, this is a factorial progression (Figure 1).

Network Value and Economic Productivity

Considering the potentially significant impact of the network's value, the adoption of a fully interoperable government system can create enormous returns. For instance, applying this logic to economic growth, greater interoperability of government information systems can result in a huge increase in economic productivity overtime. The analysis presented here builds on Madrid's (2008) white paper on "The Economic Impact of Interoperability." To provide a better understanding of the network value of interoperability, this chapter will apply the logic of network value impacts on productivity in terms of GDP. Consider the condition where a citizen needs to wait in line for a government service due to disconnected government systems. Time wasted while waiting in line is reduced opportunity to

Figure 1. Network value of interoperability

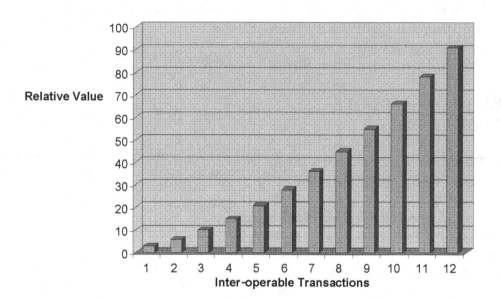

produce economic value. The longer the time a citizen needs to wait in line or to travel to different agencies, the greater the potential for the loss of that citizen's opportunity to work productively and produce economic benefits.

To apply this logic, first we need to measure the contribution of one working hour to increase economic productivity in terms of GDP. The citizen's contribution to GDP per working hour can be calculated by dividing a country's GDP in one year by the population by annual working hours. This function can be represented as:

$$GDP_{/workinghours} = \left[\frac{(GDP_{t_i} / Population_{t_i}}{Workinghours_{t_i}} \right]$$

Assuming that the citizen waiting on line is employed and in a country with a developed or emerging economy, he or she will average 2,000 working hours per year. GDP per working hour can then be calculated by dividing GDP by the product of the number in a country's full time labor force, multiplied by 2,000 working hours per year. Table 1 represents the working hours

of citizens for the year of 2006 in developed and emerging economy countries.

Based on Table 1, presumably, if a citizen of the United States is wasting time available for paid work while waiting in line or traveling to different agencies, this citizen will lose the opportunity to contribute to GDP by $21.86 per hour.

The variation in the number of possible time-wasting activities and how long they will take can have a major effect on the results of this kind of calculation. To account for some of these variations, the original study included a sensitivity analysis. This sensitivity analysis is used to adjust for the impact on the analysis of variation in type of activities and time to accomplish them. Table 2 shows that increased variations in the disconnected number of activities and in the times require to fulfill each activity have an inverse relation with the effects on GDP (refer to Table 2). Arguably, this finding provides suggestive evidence about the influence of an interoperable system on the economic productivity of a country in terms of GDP.

It seems clear that government investments in interoperability-related ICT projects have the

Table 1. GDP per working hour

Country	GDP (millions of USD)	Population	GDP / cap	GDP / Working Hour
World	48,244,879	6,671,226,000	7,232	3.62
Australia	768,178	20,850,000	36,843	18.42
Belgium	392,001	10,457,000	37,487	18.74
Brazil	1,067,962	186,500,000	5,726	2.86
Canada	1,251,463	32,990,000	37,935	18.97
China	2,668,071	1,319,000,000	2,023	1.01
France	2,230,721	64,102,140	34,799	17.40
Germany	2,906,681	82,310,000	35,314	17.66
India	906,268	1,169,016,000	775	0.39
Italy	1,844,749	58,883,958	31,329	15.66
Japan	4,340,133	127,720,000	33,982	16.99
Mexico	839,182	103,263,388	8,127	4.06
Netherlands	657,590	16,390,000	40,121	20.06
Russia	986,940	142,499,000	6,926	3.46
South Korea	888,024	48,224,000	18,415	9.21
Spain	1,223,988	44,708,964	27,377	13.69
Sweden	384,927	9,150,000	42,069	21.03
Switzerland	379,758	7,484,000	50,743	25.37
Turkey	402,710	74,877,000	5,378	2.69
United Kingdom	2,345,015	60,209,500	38,948	19.47
United States	13,201,819	301,950,000	43,722	21.86

Source: Adapted from Madrid (2008)

Table 2. Normalized impact on GDP

Number of activities per year										
10	15	20	25	30	35	40	45	50	55	60
0.04%	0.06%	0.08%	0.10%	0.13%	0.15%	0.17%	0.19%	0.21%	0.23%	0.25%
0.08%	0.13%	0.17%	0.21%	0.25%	0.29%	0.33%	0.38%	0.42%	0.46%	0.50%
0.13%	0.19%	0.25%	0.31%	0.38%	0.44%	0.50%	0.56%	0.63%	0.69%	0.75%
0.17%	0.25%	0.33%	0.42%	0.50%	0.58%	0.67%	0.75%	0.83%	0.92%	1.00%
0.21%	0.31%	0.42%	0.52%	0.63%	0.73%	0.83%	0.94%	1.04%	1.15%	1.25%
0.25%	0.38%	0.50%	0.63%	0.75%	0.88%	1.00%	1.13%	1.25%	1.38%	1.50%
0.29%	0.44%	0.58%	0.73%	0.88%	1.02%	1.17%	1.31%	1.46%	1.60%	1.75%
0.33%	0.50%	0.67%	0.83%	1.00%	1.17%	1.33%	1.50%	1.67%	1.83%	2.00%
0.38%	0.56%	0.75%	0.94%	1.13%	1.31%	1.50%	1.69%	1.88%	2.06%	2.25%
0.42%	0.63%	0.83%	1.04%	1.25%	1.46%	1.67%	1.88%	2.08%	2.29%	2.50%
0.46%	0.69%	0.92%	1.15%	1.38%	1.60%	1.83%	2.06%	2.29%	2.52%	2.75%
0.50%	0.75%	1.00%	1.25%	1.50%	1.75%	2.00%	2.25%	2.50%	2.75%	3.00%

Source: Adopted from Madrid (2008)

potential to provide value beyond internal agency efficiencies or other financial returns. E-government initiatives that work primarily on diminishing the time to process each transaction (vertical approach) overlook the larger potential of network values in providing greater value to the public (Madrid, 2008). Those e-government initiatives that integrate various disparate government information systems have an impact value similar to the network effect perspective. This network effect of interoperability-related ICT projects could generate enormous returns and value to the society. As previously demonstrated, the network combinatorial effect of interoperable government systems translates into a positive-leverage impact on GDP growth.

ROI in interoperability-related ICT projects can be enlarged, including more diverse values than the financial (GDP) results shown above. Cresswell et al. (2006) point out that measuring the returns on public sector investments should consider the value to direct and indirect beneficiaries and also to the society at large. These returns encompass both tangible and non-tangible outcomes. Furthermore, Cresswell et al. (2006, 2010) posit two ways in which government ICT investments generate value: 1) by improving the intrinsic value of government as an asset to the community and 2) by providing direct specific benefits to stakeholders (persons, groups, or organizations). The first is value resulting from internal improvements to government for the benefit of the society at large. The second one manifest in multiple forms: a combination of financial, political, and social returns. Positive economic advantage is part of the social returns on government ICT projects (Cresswell, et al., 2006). The next section will outline the public value framework as an alternative for government ICT project assessment that expands the network value approach and incorporates broader public value perspectives at large.

The Public Value Approach: An Assessment Framework

This section extends the discussion by presenting a framework for incorporating a wider public value perspective in the analysis of returns on government ICT investments. That framework shows how to assess interoperability-related ICT projects in terms of delivering value4 to citizens and to the society as a whole. To do so, the framework illustrates how to answer basic assessment questions, such as what is the nature of the value produced? who are the beneficiaries? what is the value generating mechanism? What are the necessary conditions for value generation? A full description of the framework and its use is too long for this section, but can be found in the public value framework report from the Center for Technology in Government (Cresswell, 2006).

The Concept and Application of the Public Value Framework

The CTG framework (Cresswell, 2006, 2010) defines public value in terms of how an investment in government information technology can affect the individual, collective, or societal interests of stakeholders. Such an investment can produce results that have either a positive or negative impact on one or more stakeholder groups. This general definition of public value emphasizes the variety of interests to be accounted for in describing public value. This approach is in direct contrast with the utilitarian view that considers value in the aggregate—the greatest good for the greatest number—in ways that can obscure important variations in the distribution of results in a society.

In this regard, a framework to assess the public value of government interoperability-related ICT investments must acknowledge and provide ways to deal with diverse stakeholder interests. Cresswell et al. (2006) emphasize the three main elements in a public value assessment: the nature of the technology investment, the related interests of stakeholders, and the government programs and operations affected by the investment. Public value is located in the intersection of these three elements (Figure 2). Identifying and documenting public value necessitates examination of the interactions among these three elements. The methods presented for public value assessment depend on understanding and specifying the relationships among these elements.

That is, the public value assessment treats value creation as a result of complex nonlinear interactions among the operation of government programs and operations, the technology investment, and how that affects stakeholders. The effects include both positive and negative impacts on stakeholder interests, along with their support for and trust in the government generally (Cresswell, et al., 2006).

A simplified description of those relationships is represented in Figure 3. This schematic shows the connections between changes in the business process and goals in government agencies with regard to the new ICT investment (on the left) and the impact on the stakeholders (on the right).[5] The activities in the left side of the framework connect the goals of government ICT and interoperability projects with the related business processes and how they generate public value. These activities have consequences for stakeholders' interests and risks on the right side of the framework.

Figure 2. The basic elements in the public value framework

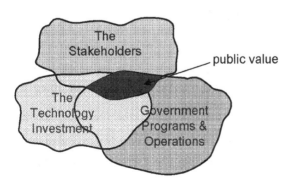

This analysis is not conceived as a linear process, but rather one that allows for learning and adjustments at each step, with possible returns to preceding steps with new information or insights. Therefore the arrows in Figure 3 represent the flow of results from one step to another and possibly looping back to preceding steps as needed. When the assessment is finished, the report of results can be combined with risk analysis and mitigation strategies.

The Public Value Generators and Impact

Each mechanism in the public value framework could generate more than one kind of public value depending on the nature of the ICT investment. To allow for this kind of variability, the framework identifies four basic public value generators that can apply to a wide range of particular ICT initiatives. Each of these generators entails different measurements and implications for assessment. The four public value generators are:

- Increase in Efficiency: gaining higher output or other goals using same amount of resources or consuming less resources to maintaining existing level of output or goals.
- Increase in Effectiveness: improving the quality or quantity of a desirable outcome (e.g., service transaction, policy, etc.).
- Intrinsic Enhancement: changing the environment or circumstances of a stakeholder in ways that the stakeholder values for their own sake.
- Enablement: providing means or allowing otherwise infeasible or prohibited desired activity, or preventing or reducing undesirable events or outcomes.

For any given ICT investment, these four public value generators can act independently or in consort to influence the overall return to the stake-

Figure 3. The public value framework

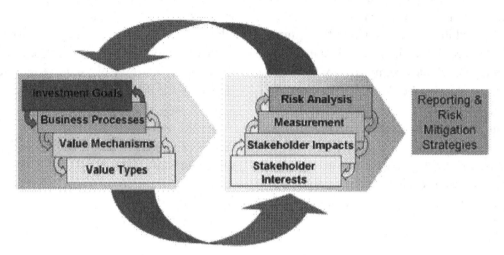

holders. An interoperability-related ICT project can incorporate, in principle, all four generators: 1) interoperability increases efficiency by reducing the redundant activities across government agencies, 2) interoperability improves the quality of government service delivery to the stakeholders, 3) interoperability changes the environment in which citizens interact with government that led to improve economic productivity, and 4) interoperability increases citizens' convenience in interacting with or in requesting government services by enabling integrated services across agencies boundaries and levels.

Likewise, considering that investments in interoperability-related government ICT projects involve various stakeholders, each of these value generators can be linked to a variety of interests. This public value framework employs seven basic types of value as a way to analyze how the investments may affect stakeholder interests. The basic public value types are:

- **Financial**: impacts on current or anticipated income, asset values, liabilities, entitlements, and other aspects of wealth or risks to any of the above.

- **Political**: impacts on personal or corporate influence on government actions or policy, role in political affairs, or influence in political parties or prospects for current of future public office.

- **Social**: impacts on family or community relationships, social mobility, status, and identity.

- **Strategic**: impacts on person's or groups economic or political advantage or opportunities, goals, and resources for innovation or planning.

- **Quality of Life**: impacts on individual and household health, security, satisfaction, and general well-being.

- **Ideological**: impacts on beliefs, moral or ethical commitments, alignment of government actions or policies or social outcomes with beliefs, or moral or ethical positions.

- **Stewardship**: impacts on the public's view of government officials as faithful stewards or guardians of the value of the government in terms of public trust, integrity, and legitimacy.

This way of describing public value is intended as an extension of the current method used by governments to assess the internal efficiency gains or savings returns on particular investments or performance evaluations (Cresswell, et al., 2006). In this way, the framework can serve to supplement the current internally focused assessment method by uncovering broader potential values of government ICT investment.

The Stakeholders of Government Interoperability-Related ICT Investments

As depicted in Figure 3, assessments employing this public value framework require identification of government programs, business processes, and the associated stakeholders. The process to identify those who have an interest in the value generation of a government ICT investment project is half of the public value framework process. Cresswell et al. (2006) describe this stakeholder analysis as consisting of three parts:

- Identifying the individuals or groups who have interest in the investment project.
- Identifying the specific interests of the stakeholders.
- Assessing the role and potential influence of the stakeholders in the delivery of public value.

A thorough and systematic stakeholder analysis is important to identify the linkages that connect the ICT investment with business processes and value creation for various stakeholders. Identification of stakeholders should include those internal to the ICT project, those in related government agencies across different levels, and possible external parties affected by or who have an interest in this project.

There are no rigid formulas for this form of stakeholder analysis, dependent as it is on the context of the ICT project and the agencies involved. In this sense, the crucial resource for effective stakeholder identification is in-depth knowledge

of the operational and broader context of the ICT investment. To assemble this knowledge, stakeholder analysis generally engages a group of participants with extensive knowledge of the political and organizational setting of the investment. Despite much room for variation, there are four common consistencies found among different methods of stakeholder analysis:

- Involvement of multiple analysts with in-depth knowledge of the stakeholder environment.
- Use of brainstorming or other related method to identify all possible relevant stakeholders in the broader perspectives.
- Identification of multiple stakeholder roles, internal and external to the organization setting.
- Identification of potential stakeholder expectations, influence potential, past and future participation possibilities, and level of interest.

Cross referencing the stakeholders with the potential value identifies impacts on interests and the kinds of evidence that can reveal value outcomes. For a more detailed discussion on the application of the framework, refer to the Center for Technology in Government (CTG) white paper on the public value framework (Cresswell, et al., 2006). The next section describes two instances of interoperable ICT investment and how they relate to public value assessment. The main focus is on stakeholder identification and the value impacts of the interoperable ICT investment.

I-Choose: An Interoperable Data Architecture to Support Full Information Product Pricing

The I-Choose project, a current activity at the Center for Technology in Government (funded by the US National Science Foundation), can provide useful illustrations of how the framework can support a public value assessment. The goal of this project is to develop and test a data sharing architecture to provide a wide range of trusted product information to assist consumer choices in purchasing food products, in particular sustainable coffee that is "Fair Trade" certified. The project, known as "Building Information Sharing Networks to Support Consumer Choice (I-Choose)," will focus on the development of an information architecture for interoperability among stakeholders for coffee grown in Mexico and distributed and consumed in Canada and the United States. I-Choose will use emerging Semantic Web technologies to create a new generation of "linked data" mash ups connecting actors who have interests linked to the fair-trade coffee product supply-chain. To achieve their vision, a collaborative network of international researchers from three countries in North America will focus

on developing an interoperable data architecture of full product information necessary for a sustainable coffee supply chain.

The I-Choose Vision

The I-Choose interoperable data architecture will facilitate consumer queries submitted through an application on the consumer's mobile device (smartphones). When in use, the consumer will be able to employ the I-Choose application to find more information on a coffee product in the sustainable coffee supply chain. The consumer can simply scan the product's UPC code (or other type of barcode) readable by camera phones. The information will come from supply chain operators and third party certifiers who will create and maintain interoperable data networks through their compliance with the I-Choose RDF-based

Figure 4. The vision of i-choose interoperable data architecture

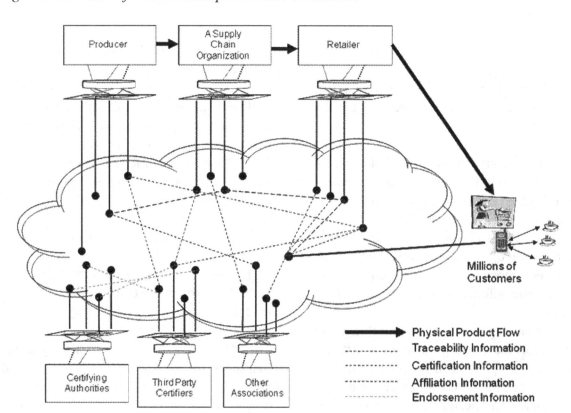

specialty coffee supply chain ontology. As shown in Figure 4, once the consumer scans the UPC code (or other type of barcode), the application will start composing information about the sustainable supply chain. For instance, the consumer could discover that the coffee was shade grown at the Velasquez Coffee Cooperative in Mexico that has been certified by the United Fair Trade Association (UFTA), and is well-rated by the Consumer Value Institute. Thus, consumers can make purchasing decisions that better reflect their personal commitments to environment sustainability.

The I-Choose application will provide additional information on particular coffee products to assist the consumer in making buying decisions and checking the trustworthiness of the information (Figure 4). The I-Choose approach to developing an interoperable data architecture begins with a network of diverse communities in the supply chain. The members of these communities will collaborate in creating an ontology of the necessary terms and concepts, then develop a hierarchical taxonomy of domains in the supply-chain. These will be the foundation of an interoperable data architecture.

Identification of Stakeholders and Network Formation

Building this interoperable data architecture will consist of a multi-stage iterative process of consensus building activities with actors from the supply-chain communities. The process begins with developing the network of diverse communities in the supply chain. The network acknowledges the roles of each stakeholder affected or having an interest in the I-Choose framework. The network will include various communities and stakeholders involved in the product supply-chains and external stakeholders with interests in the supply-chain. The stakeholder identification process in I-Choose incorporates brainstorming among actors with in-depth knowledge of the stakeholder environment. The group includes

researchers from three countries, gathered in two sets of different meetings (team and network meeting), in a two-stage process.

The first brainstorming session is to identify the impacted stakeholders, based on the researchers' background knowledge and experience in their previous collaborative project. The stakeholders identified in this first step are then invited to the second stage for more in-depth brainstorming with the research team to help expand the network further. In addition to the face-to-face meetings, regular online forums will be conducted through a variety of media (e.g., email, SharePoint, Skype, and teleconferences). These mechanisms are designed to ensure the involvement of all relevant stakeholders to ensure that the interoperable architecture will improve the quality of the deliverables.

Value Impact of I-Choose Interoperable Data Architecture

The I-Choose data architecture, incorporating network interoperability among the actors across the supply chain, is expected to produce value returns for all seven types of public value identified in the framework.

- **Financial returns**: One interoperability goal for I-Choose is to create value in improving the current and anticipated income of suppliers and distributers involved in fair-trade coffee produced in Mexico and consumed in the United States and Canada. Some early evidence suggests that this is a likely outcome. A fair-trade coffee producer member of the CESMACH cooperative in Chiapas, Raul Gutierrez expects positive results. In an email to a roaster in Canada, Raul said that support for fair-trade will improve the economic condition of his family and his community. Having I-Choose to provide trusted information to the United States and Canadian consumers that Raul is a real grower and that the coffee is indeed a fair-trade product could stimulate consumption and increase income for Raul and other growers like him. This can substantially improve the economic conditions of the region. Increasing the growers' income will arguably increase income tax revenue for the government to support development.

- **Political**: I-Choose's introduction of non-price product information that moves beyond a description of product features can alter how policy makers conceptualize trade and trade regulations. The public may increase pressure for environmentally friendly, socially responsible, and safer products. Current efforts to force compliance with legal standards to address environmental and labor issues lack the potential added force of consumer participation. The I-Choose interoperable architecture can open new venues for citizen participation in policy making on environmental issues.
- **Social**: In the example of Raul, I-Choose provides validation for his community, the Campesinos Ecologicos de la Sierra Madre de Chiappas (CESMACH), can help attract new members, and encourage the formation of similar co-ops.
- **Quality of Life**: Consumers will appreciate that I-Choose will allow them to create their own value profile so that product ratings provided by I-Choose can reflect their personal preferences. This creates a price-value rating that can be tailored to meet a consumer's budgets and enhance the consumer's satisfaction.
- **Strategic**: The ability of I-Choose to connect consumer preferences to actors in the supply chain will create economic advantage or opportunities for them, such as allowing retailers to tailor their products to consumer preferences, which could poten-

tially increase their sale or expand their market share.
- **Ideological**: I-Choose acknowledges and supports individuals with strong values and beliefs about the importance of environmental stewardship and avoiding the economic exploitation of coffee growers by choosing their consumption pattern accordingly.

If fully implemented to support trusted and full information interoperability, the I-Choose data architecture can generate a diverse mix of public values. These values affect stakeholders differently. In this regard, assessment of interoperable ICT investment should and could incorporate broader values than financial metrics. As the I-Choose case illustrates, focusing only on internal efficiency, savings, or other financial metrics alone will overlook other significant potential values to different stakeholders. The next section provides another case about the successful effort of the government of Colombia to provide metrics for measuring the impact of an interoperable project based on GDP.

Interoperable ICT in Colombia

Gobierno en Linea, or Government Online in Colombia, started with the enactment of Decree 1151 of 2008. This decree serves as the guideline for the implementation of an online government strategy (Murcia, et al., 2010). Maria Isabel Meija Jaramillo, the Chief Director for the Connectivity Agenda Agency, asserted in 2010 that "government on-line is a national Colombian Strategy, leaded by the Ministry of Communications, to build a more transparent and efficient Government to provide better services to the citizens and business through the use of ICT" (Meija-Jaramillo, 2010). The key message to be delivered to the citizens is, "Making easier your relationship with the Government" (Meija-Jaramillo, 2010).

The objectives of the Colombian Online Government strategies include rendering better services by saving money and time and also promoting citizen access to multiple channels (Murcia, et al., 2009). A major challenge that Maria Isabel Meija pointed out is the massive number of services that the Colombian public administration offered to the citizens. There are more than two thousand services in Colombia, which makes it impractical to offer each of them online (Meija-Jaramillo, 2010). Meija pointed out that the government of Colombia has attempted three transformation efforts. First, to provide services and organize the procedures around user needs. Second is developing a "cluster service model" by organizing the procedures based on the user needs. Finally, the government identifies, prioritizes, and optimizes clusters of procedures prior to the introduction of the new technology (Meija-Jaramillo, 2010).

Three examples within the Gobierno en Linea strategy are outlined in this section: the certificado judicial en linea, the Procuraduria General de la Nacion, and the Movil Social en Accion. The certificado judicial en linea, or online judicial certificate, is the certificate to record criminal records based on the data collected and reported by the judicial branch. In the online system, the patron only need to go through two steps, enter the application online, follow the instructions, and make an appointment by phone for the next day between 7:00 am and 4:00 pm to complete their transaction. The processes for the other two examples are basically similar. This interoperable gateway that the Colombian government is offering to their citizens results in increased public value.

- **Financial return**: The portal of Gobierno en Linea (http://www.gobiernoenlinea. gov.co) provides an interoperable gateway where citizens can find various government services in one place. This service provision results in time and money sav-

ings for citizens and public agencies. The certificado judicial en linea processes 371,079 certificates from November 2008 through August 2009, reducing the transaction time from two hours to ten minutes, saving US $ 4.54 in indirect costs for users/citizens. The Procuraduria General de la Nacion processed 3,407,047 certificates from November 2008 to August 2009, reducing the transaction time from 1.3 hours to five minutes and saving the users/citizens US $ 3.48 in indirect costs. Finally, the Movil Social en Accion was used by 960,487 people from October 2008 to August 2009, reducing the transaction time from four hours to fifteen minutes and saving the public agency US $ 2.02 in delivery costs.

- **Political**: The Gobierno en Linea portal also encourages citizen participation through wikis, blogs, and forums. This portal enables a novel form of citizen participation that could influence government actions or policies for citizen services.

- **Social**: One example of the social impact of Gobierno en Linea is the recognition and balancing of national identity and multiculturalism. The basic language of Gobierno en Linea is Spanish, as their national identity. However, this portal also provides English as an alternative presentation. This bilingual offering serves to preserve the national identity of Columbia and at the same time provides broader service offerings to others with different nationalities.

- **Quality of Life**: The Gobierno en Linea provides total convenience to the citizens. This portal allows citizens the freedom to access government on their own time by liberating or lessening the obligation and hassle of getting public services, which also contributes to quality of life.

- **Strategic value:** refers to the condition of improved opportunity beyond what is immediately available. The Gobierno en Linea provides various features that stimulate citizen creativity and innovation. For instance: the opinion survey in the Gobierno en Linea website indicates that 63% of citizens will seek help from the website either through email, chat, or the contact mailbox. Citizens also indicate that 46% will check online if they have subpoenas or traffic fines. These are two examples of improved opportunity through the offering of an interoperability gateway.

- **Ideological value:** results when government actions or policies align with stakeholder beliefs, morals, or ethical positions. The Gobierno en Linea provides a forum where citizens and users can present and discuss social issues for the consideration of the Colombian government. The feedback loop enables citizens to raise issues pertaining to their ideology, beliefs, or moral values. For instance, in January of 2010, one citizen raised the issue of regulation applicable to bikers and called for change in the National Traffic Code.

- **Stewardship**: The Gobierno en Linea has the potential to improve citizen trust, and enhance the integrity, accountability, and legitimacy of the Colombian government. Citizens could directly measure the performance of government through this online offering. In addition, the citizen participation feature afforded by this portal could induce increased public trust in the government as an effective steward of the society.

The Colombian case demonstrates the combination of the network value effect and the public value framework. The time and money savings generated from the Gobierno en linea project clearly illustrate the network value effect of interoperable ICT investment. At the same time, this case also demonstrates the diverse public values from interoperable government ICT investment.

FUTURE DIRECTIONS

Finding the best ways to build and improve government IT systems will depend more and more on being able to assess the performance of interoperable systems, especially where government agencies and non-government institutions need to work as an effective network. In an interoperable system for connected government, supported with architecture that encompasses a large portfolio of applications, complex and multiple assessment approaches are necessary. This study provides alternative methods and frameworks that complement the usual financial metrics employed in assessing the value of government IT investments, in particular by incorporating a broader perspective in term of public and network value. In this way, this study shows a path for validation and development in future research on value assessment. Future studies could ascertain the generalizability of the propositions outlined here to other contexts and cases. As a preliminary study of the value assessment framework for interoperable IT investment, this research also provides a foundation for further empirical testing.

CONCLUSION

This chapter addresses the challenge of expanding the definition of value for ICT projects, particularly those dealing with government interoperability. The chapter argues for a broader public value proposition as the basis for assessment, a value proposition that goes beyond the usual financial metrics used to examine return on investment. This chapter shows specifically that investing in interoperable government ICT systems has the potential to provide value beyond internal agency efficiencies and other financial returns. That value includes returns to both the direct and indirect beneficiaries of interoperable ICT systems, i.e., stakeholders, and returns to the society at large.

The value returns for enhanced interoperability are largely a result of network effects. We therefore employed the network value approach to show ways interoperable ICT systems create interrelated service offerings. The value of a network will be manifested in an increased number of connections. The returns are a result of how an expanded network can yield combinatorial effects that generate large returns, as in the example of a substantial boost to GDP growth. Similarly, the case of Gobierno en Linea in Colombia shows the significant amount of money and time savings and improvement in quality of life that emerge from an interoperable e-government investment.

In the second approach, this chapter has shown that the ROI in interoperability-related government ICT projects includes a diverse set of benefits. The public value framework acknowledges the diversity and incompatibility of the demands and interests of multiple stakeholder groups. This framework employs an iterative process of assessing the mechanisms and results of value generation based on an analysis of government stakeholders. The framework treats public value in terms of seven value types that can result from e-government investments. These seven public value types are financial, political, social, ideological, stewardship, strategic, and quality of life. The assessment framework provides a way to link the characteristics of an interoperability-related ICT project to the value types of interest to stakeholders. By expanding the value proposition beyond financial metrics, this approach provides a more robust way to justify and evaluate investments in government interoperability.

Applications of the public value framework to two case studies illustrate the kinds of results that can be produced. Through the cases, the chapter shows the diverse values that can result from interoperable e-government investment initiatives. These examples are offered to assist public officials and policy makers in considering the full range of benefits possible from increased interoperability efforts, and thereby improve the overall design strategies for ICT investment and interoperability implementation.

ACKNOWLEDGMENT

The authors wish to acknowledge the generous support for this work by Microsoft and the leaders of the I-Choose project for their permission to use their project data in this study. The I-Choose project is funded by the US National Science Foundation, Grant No. 0955935. The opinions and findings represented here are those of the authors alone and do not reflect the views of the Microsoft Corporation or the policies or views of the National Science Foundation.

REFERENCES

Allee, V. (2003). *The future of knowledge, increasing prosperity through value networks*. London, UK: Elsevier Science.

Andersen, D. F., Andersen, D. L., Jarman, H., Whitmore, A., Luna-Reyes, L., & Zhang, J. … Tayi, G. (2011). *Case study*. Paper presented at I-Choose Network Meeting. Albany, NY.

Baum, C., & Maio, D. (2000). *Gartner's four phases of e-government model*. Gartner's Group White Paper. Retrieved from http://www.gartner.com/DisplayDocument?id=317292.

Bernasek, A. (2002). The productivity miracle is for real. *Fortune, 145*(6), 84.

Carratta, T., Dadayan, L., & Ferro, E. (2006). Electronic government ROI analysis in e-government assessment trials: The case of sistema piemonte. *Lecture Notes in Computer Science, 4084*, 329–340. doi:10.1007/11823100_29

Cresswell, A. M. (2004). *Return on investment in information technology: A guide for managers*. Retrieved from http://www.ctg.albany.edu/publications/reports/advancing_roi.

Cresswell, A. M. (2010). *Public value and government ICT investment*. Paper presented at the Second International Conference on eGovernment and eGovernance. Antalya, Turkey.

Cresswell, A. M., Burke, G. B., & Pardo, T. A. (2006). *Advancing return on investment analysis for government IT - A public value framework*. Retrieved from http://www.ctg.albany.edu/publications/reports/advancing_roi/advancing_roi.pdf.

Dadayan, L. (2006). *Measuring return on government IT investments*. Paper presented at the 13th European Conference on Information Technology Evaluation. Genoa, Italy.

Epstein, G., & Mealem, Y. (2009). Group specific public goods, orchestration of interest groups with free riding. *Public Choice, 139*(3/4), 357–369. doi:10.1007/s11127-009-9398-y

Fisher, F. M. (1984). The misuse of accounting rates of return. *The American Economic Review, 74*(3), 509–517.

Fisher, F. M., & McGowan, J. J. (1983). On the misuse of accounting rates of return to infer monopoly profits. *The American Economic Review, 73*(1), 82–97.

Guijarro, L. (2010). Frameworks for fostering cross-agency interoperability in e-government initiatives. *Advances in Management Information Systems, 17*, 280–300.

Hjort-Madsen, K. (2009). *Architecting government: Understanding enterprise architecture adoption in the public sector*. Doctoral Dissertation. Copenhagen, Denmark: IT University of Copenhagen. Retrieved from http://www.eagov.com/archives/Hjort-MadsenK_March09.pdf.

Hjort-Madsen, K., & Pries-Heje, J. (2009). *Enterprise architecture in government: Fad or future?* Paper presented at the 42th Hawaii International Conference on System Sciences. Hawaii, HI.

Ho, A. T. K. (2002). Reinventing local governments and the e-government initiative. *Public Administration Review, 62*(4), 434–444. doi:10.1111/0033-3352.00197

Jacobson, R. (1987). The validity of ROI as a measure of business performance. *The American Economic Review, 77*(3), 470–478.

Janssen, M. (2011). Sociopolitical aspects of interoperability and enterprise architecture in e-government. *Social Science Computer Review, 30*, 24–36. doi:10.1177/0894439310392187

Janssen, M., & Creswell, A. M. (2005). An enterprise application integration methodology for e-government. *The Journal of Enterprise Information Management, 18*(5), 531–547. doi:10.1108/17410390510623990

Janssen, M., & Hjort-Madsen, K. (2007). *Analyzing enterprise architecture in national governments: The cases of Denmark and the Netherlands*. Paper presented at the 40th Hawaii International Conference on System Sciences. Hawaii, HI.

Janssen, M., & Kuk, G. (2006). *A complex adaptive system perspective of enterprise architecture in electronic government*. Paper presented at the 39th Hawaii International Conference on System Sciences. Hawaii, HI.

Karokola, G., & Yngstrom, L. (2009). *Discussing e-government maturity models for developing world – Security view*. Paper presented at the 2009 Information Security South Africa (ISSA) Conference. Johannesburg, South Africa.

Keefer, P., & Knack, S. (2007). Boondoggles, rent-seeking, and political checks and balances: Public investment under unaccountable governments. *The Review of Economics and Statistics, 89*(3), 566–572. doi:10.1162/rest.89.3.566

Lamore, R., Link, T., & Blackmond, T. (2006). Renewing people and places: Institutional investment policies that enhance social capital and improve the built environment of distressed communities. *Journal of Urban Affairs, 28*(5), 429–442. doi:10.1111/j.1467-9906.2006.00308.x

Madhav, R. V., Stefan, R., & Soliman, M. T. (2007). Conservatism, growth, and return on investment. *Review of Accounting Studies, 12*, 325–370. doi:10.1007/s11142-007-9035-2

Madrid, L. (2008). *Measuring the returns from investments on e-government.* Microsoft White Paper. Seattle, WA: Microsoft.

Markov, R. (2006). *Economical impact of IT investments in the public sector: The case of local electronic government.* Paper presented at the Business Informatics Workshop. Dublin, Ireland.

McNulty, Y. M., & Tharenou, P. (2005). Expatriate return on investment: A definition and antecedents. *International Studies of Management and Organization, 34*(3), 68–95.

Moon, M. J. (2002). The evolution of e-government among municipalities: Rhetoric or reality? *Public Administration Review, 62*(4), 424–433. doi:10.1111/0033-3352.00196

Moorthy, S., & Polley, D. E. (2007). Technological knowledge breadth and depth: Performance impacts. *Journal of Knowledge Management, 14*(3), 359–377. doi:10.1108/13673271011050102

Pardo, T. A., & Burke, G. B. (2009). *IT governance capability: Laying the foundation for government interoperability.* Retrieved from http://www.ctg.albany.edu/publications.

Provan, K. G., & Milward, H. B. (2001). Do networks really work? A framework for evaluating public-sector organizational networks. *Public Administration Review, 61*(4), 414–423. doi:10.1111/0033-3352.00045

Purser, S. A. (2004). Improving the ROI of the security management process. *Computers & Security, 23*, 542–546. doi:10.1016/j.cose.2004.09.004

Richard, P. J., Devinney, T. M., Yip, G. S., & Jhonson, G. (2009). Measuring organizational performance: Towards methodological best practice. *Journal of Management, 35*(3), 718–804. doi:10.1177/0149206308330560

Ross, J. W. (2003). Creating a strategic IT architecture competency: Learning in stages. *MIS Quarterly Executive, 2*(1), 31–43.

Saha, P. (2010). *Enterprise architecture as platform for connected government: Advancing the whole-of-government enterprise architecture adoption with strategic (systems) thinking.* Retrieved from http://unpan1.un.org.

Salamon, G. L. (1985). Accounting rates of return. *The American Economic Review, 75*(3), 495–504.

Schachner, L. (1973). Return on investment: Its values, determination and uses. *The CPA Journal, 43*(4), 277–281.

Schekkerman, J. (2006). *How to survive in the jungle of enterprise architecture frameworks: Creating or choosing an enterprise architecture framework* (2nd ed.). Victoria, Canada: Trafford Publishing.

Shapiro, C., & Varian, H. R. (1998). *Information rules: A strategic guide to the network economy.* Watertown, MA: Harvard Business Press Books.

Tamm, T., Seddon, P. B., Shanks, G., & Reynolds, P. (2011). How does enterprise architecture add value to organisations? *Communications of the Association for Information Systems, 28*(1), 141–168.

United Nations Division for Public Economics and Public Administration and the American Society for Public Administration. (2002). *Benchmarking e-government: A global perspective --- Assessing the UN member states*. Retrieved from http://unpan1.un.org/intradoc/groups/public/documents/un/unpan021547.pdf.

Waverman, L., Meschi, M., & Fuss, M. (2005). *The impact of telecoms on economic growth in developing countries*. Paper presented at the Telecommunications Policy Research Conference. New York, NY.

Weill, P., & Olson, M. H. (1989). Managing investment in information technology: Mini case examples and implications. *Management Information Systems Quarterly*, *13*(1), 3–17. doi:10.2307/248694

West, D. M. (2004). E-government and the transformation of service delivery and citizen attitudes. *Public Administration Review*, *64*(1), 15–27. doi:10.1111/j.1540-6210.2004.00343.x

WITSA. (1999). *Critical information protection (CIP): A framework for government/industry dialogue*. Retrieved from http://www.witsa.org/papers/cip.htm.

ADDITIONAL READING

Alford, J. (2011). Public value from co-production by clients. In *Public Value: Theory and Practice* (pp. 196–219). Basingstoke, UK: Macmillan.

Alonso, J., Martínez de Soria, I., Orue-Echevarria, L., & Vergara, M. (2010). Enterprise collaboration maturity model (ECMM): Preliminary definition and future challenges. *Enterprise Interoperability*, *7*, 429–438.

Blau, B. S., Conte, T. D., & Weinhardt, C. (2010). *Incentives in service value networks–On truthfulness, sustainability, and interoperability*. Paper presented at the International Conferences of Information Systems (ICIS 2010). New York, NY.

Bovaird, T. (2005). Public governance: Balancing stakeholder power in a network society. *International Review of Administrative Sciences*, *71*(2), 217. doi:10.1177/0020852305053881

Bozeman, B. (2002). Public-value failure: When efficient markets may not do. *Public Administration Review*, *62*(2), 145–161. doi:10.1111/0033-3352.00165

Castelnovo, W., & Simonetta, M. (2007). The evaluation of e-government projects for small local government organisations. *The Electronic Journal of E-Government*, *5*(1), 21–28.

Cresswell, A. M., Burke, G. B., & Pardo, T. M. (2006). *Advancing return on investment analysis for government IT: A public value framework*. Retrieved from http://www.ctg.albany.edu/publications/reports/advancing_roi.

Criado, J. I. (2011). Interoperability of egovernment for building intergovernmental integration in the European Union. *Social Science Computer Review*. Retrieved from http://ssc.sagepub.com/content/early/2011/03/10/0894439310392189.abstract?rss=1.

Dawes, S. S., Cresswell, A. M., & Cahan, B. B. (2004). Learning From crisis. *Social Science Computer Review*, *22*(1), 52. doi:10.1177/0894439303259887

Diedrich, E., Schmidt, D., & Wimmer, M. (2006). *A three dimensional framework to realize interoperability in public administrations*. Paper presented at the workshop on Semantic Web for eGovernment. New York, NY.

dos Santos, E. M., & Reinhard, N. (2011). Electronic government interoperability: Identifying the barriers for frameworks adoption. *Social Science Computer Review*. Retrieved from http://ssc.sagepub.com/content/30/1/71.abstract.

Friesen, A. (2011). On challenges in enterprise systems management and engineering for the networked enterprise of the future. *Enterprise Interoperability-Lecture Notes in Business Information Processing, 76*(1-2).

Gil-Garcia, J. R., Chun, S. A., & Janssen, M. (2009). Government information sharing and integration: Combining the social and the technical. *Information Polity, 14*(1), 1–10.

Gottschalk, P. (2009). Maturity levels for interoperability in digital government. *Government Information Quarterly, 26*(1), 75–81. doi:10.1016/j.giq.2008.03.003

Gottschalk, P., & Solli-Saether, H. (2008). Stages of e-government interoperability. *Electronic Government: An International Journal, 5*(3), 310–320. doi:10.1504/EG.2008.018877

Grimsley, M., & Meehan, A. (2007). e-Government information systems: Evaluation-led design for public value and client trust. *European Journal of Information Systems, 16*(2), 134–148. doi:10.1057/palgrave.ejis.3000674

Guclu, A. N., & Bilgen, S. (2011). Modelling and assessment of the effectiveness of government information technologies-value space approach with a public sector case study in Turkey. *The Electronic Journal of Information Systems in Developing Countries, 45*.

Harrison, T. M., Guerrero, S., Burke, G. B., Cook, M., Cresswell, A., Helbig, N., et al. (2011). *Open government and e-government: Democratic challenges from a public value perspective*. Paper presented at the 12th Annual International Conference on Digital Government Research. New York, NY.

Klischewski, R., & Ukena, S. (2009). A value network analysis of automated access to e-government services. In *Proceedings of the Wirtschaftinformatik*. Wirtschaftinformatik.

Kubicek, H., & Cimander, R. (2009). Three dimensions of organizational interoperability. *European Journal of ePractice, 6*.

Kuehn, A., Kaschewsky, M., Kappeler, A., Spichiger, A., & Riedl, R. (2011). Interoperability and information brokers in public safety: an approach toward seamless emergency communications. *Journal of Theoretical and Applied Electronic Commerce Research, 6*(1), 43–60.

Mellouli, S., Gil-Garcia, J. R., Navarrete, C., Pardo, T. A., Cresswell, A., Zheng, L., & Scholl, H. J. (2010). *Integration and interoperability at the border in North America: A status report*. Paper presented at the 11th Annual International Digital Government Research Conference on Public Administration. New York, NY.

Misuraca, G., Alfano, G., & Viscusi, G. (2011). Interoperability challenges for ICT-enabled governance: Towards a pan-European conceptual framework. *Journal of Theoretical and Applied Electronic Commerce Research, 6*(1), 95–111.

Moore, M. H. (1995). *Creating public value: Strategic management in government*. Boston, MA: Harvard University Press.

Moore, M. H. (2000). Managing for value: Organizational strategy in for-profit, nonprofit, and governmental organizations. *Nonprofit and Voluntary Sector Quarterly, 29*(1), 183. doi:10.1177/089976400773746391

O'Flynn, J. (2007). From new public management to public value: Paradigmatic change and managerial implications. *Australian Journal of Public Administration, 66*(3), 353. doi:10.1111/j.1467-8500.2007.00545.x

Ojo, A., & Janowski, T. (2010). *A whole-of-government approach to information technology strategy management*. Paper presented at the 11th Annual International Digital Government Research Conference on Public Administration. New York, NY.

Sánchez-Nielsen, E., González-Morales, D., & Pena-Dorta, C. (2011). Architectural guidelines and practical experiences in the realization of e-gov employment services. *International Journal of E-Services and Mobile Applications*, *3*(3), 1–15. doi:10.4018/jesma.2011070101

Seltsikas, P., & O'Keefe, R. M. (2010). Expectations and outcomes in electronic identity management: The role of trust and public value. *European Journal of Information Systems*, *19*(1), 93–103. doi:10.1057/ejis.2009.51

Solli-Sather, H. (2011). A framework for analysing interoperability in electronic government. *International Journal of Electronic Finance*, *5*(1), 32–48. doi:10.1504/IJEF.2011.038221

Srivastava, S. C. (2011). Is e-government providing the promised returns? A value framework for assessing e-government impact. *Transforming Government: People, Process and Policy*, *5*(2), 107–113.

Witsa. (2011). *Website*. Retrieved from http://www.witsa.org/.

KEY TERMS AND DEFINITIONS

Economic Productivity: Increase in economic output and/or production of a nations due to the reduction in unnecessary costs.

Interoperability: Condition where the diverse and disconnected systems in organizations are able to inter-operate or work together.

Network Effects: The multiplying impact as result of connectivity among actors in a particular network.

Network Value Framework: Framework for assessing the value of government IT investment that takes into account the number of connections in the network of n numbers of actors.

Networked Government: Situation where autonomous government agencies and non-governmental institutions need to work as coherent network and inter-connected to one another to accommodate the needs of their constituents and to deliver values.

Public Value Framework: Framework for assessing the value of broad range of government IT investment that takes into account the diverse needs and interests of government constituents (individual citizen, organization, and society at large).

Return on Investment: Profit, or gain or benefit derived from investment, usually in the form of simple ratio of excess profit to investment.

Value Assessment: The approach for evaluating the worth and significance of investment that emphasize on broader scope.

ENDNOTES

1. The UN utilizes this model to publish its e-*Government Readiness Index*.
2. Gartner group (www.gartner.com).
3. See Witsa (2011).
4. Cresswell et al. (2006) use the term "value" in contrast to "return" to emphasize the broader scope of returns in government ICT investment.
5. A more complete description of the Public Value Framework and how it can be used can be found in Cresswell, Burke, and Pardo (2006).

Chapter 20

A Public Economics Approach to Enabling Enterprise Architecture with the Government Cloud in Belgium

Marc Rabaey
University of Hasselt, Belgium

ABSTRACT

Cloud computing is a very demanding technology regarding the level of maturity (stages) of Enterprise Architecture (EA), certainly when the business processes of the government are directly affected by the implementation of cloud computing. Therefore, an extra stage in EA and an extra service model are conceived to better map the opportunities and risks while investing in cloud computing.

A holistic investment framework (generic) is proposed to align the cloud computing and other investments with the higher strategy and operational strategies of the government. Real options and option games (along with classical investment techniques) are used to give the public management the flexibility to adjust the course of actions of the (investment) projects.

In this framework, the move of legacy systems to the Cloud and the overall risks related to the implementation of cloud computing are discussed. The main question is if a government can implement ambitious cloud computing projects without EA, and if not, which stage should be used?

INTRODUCTION: HOLISTIC APPROACH

A government is a collection of institutions that act with authority and create formal obligations. A Government may administer or supervise a state, a set group of people, or a collection of assets (UNU-IIST-SP, 2008). Therefore, it needs an information system to manage its functions and responsibilities, but a common characteristic for many governments is that the information systems of all the departments of the governments were in the beginning of Information Technology (IT) isolated. They look more like an archipelago with

DOI: 10.4018/978-1-4666-1824-4.ch020

a deep sea in-between than (inter)connected governmental departments, and although Enterprise Architecture (EA) has already been on the scene for many years, the smooth interfacing of all the different departments and their information systems remains a problematic area in need of further attention.

The Information Technology (IT) implemented by these departments was based on their needs and culture. In some departments, like Defense, multiple different, incompatible IT systems were implemented. From the government (business) unit's point of view, it looks to optimize its investment. However, at the level of the national government, there are often incompatibilities and vulnerabilities that result in serious expenses due to the inability to collaborate or communicate between the different governmental departments in an efficient and effective way, but worse, the citizen is suffering from this: less service, more tax, and thus a less productive government.

Luckily, we are observing that the IT industry is moving towards an (more) easy integration of technological solutions. This is not caused by an altruistic reflex of those companies, but by the Internet as the concept of interconnecting everything, everywhere at any time.

The newest trend (some call it hype) is cloud computing (pay per use IT-services), which uses models such as the public cloud (for everybody), private cloud (only for one organization), hybrid cloud (mixture of public and private), and community cloud. We will present GovCloud which is a form of community cloud specific for governments and how Enterprise Architecture is as a matter of fact, a conditio sine qua non, to succeed the implementation of cloud computing.

However, security issues are still very important. They need to be addressed by the government in order to protect the privacy of the citizen and the national (or regional) confidential information. So when investments in IT have to be made, not only the service (efficiency and effectiveness) have to be considered but also the risks. Classic investment techniques such as Return on Investment (ROI) or Net Present Value (NPV) do not implicitly consider these risks. Real Option Valuation (ROV) does and moreover it gives the organization the flexibility to decide to postpone, start, stop, exit projects, where ROI and NPV give only a decision for a project from start to end, without the possibility to handle uncertainty (lack of information, no information coming from pilot projects, market evolutions, etc.).

Of course, investments (in IT or other domains) should be aligned with the grand strategy and business strategy of an organization (or group of organizations). Starting from a study on the *Art of War*, Rabaey et al. (2005a, 2007) proposed a generic process of aligning investments with the higher strategy, whereby all resources (not only IT) are evaluated and decisions made based on ROV. As such, it is a holistic approach, because all aspects of business and resources are being brought into consideration in what they call Interdisciplinary Forum (IF). Besides portfolio management of projects and business processes, Steering Plans and Service Level Agreements (SLA) are established: the citizens are put in the spotlights. In addition, the links between the governmental departments are taken into account.

As already mentioned, the process is generic so that an instantiated process based on existing decision methods (except classic investment techniques) and frameworks like Enterprise Architecture (EA) can be designed in function of the culture of the organization.

From an e-Government perspective, we will show that IF provides a way to assess Cloud Computing as an enabler for a more integrated (connected) government(s) based on government EA. We will first discuss EA and Cloud Computing before handling the Interdisciplinary Forum (concept, ROA and processing). Before we conclude, we will bring all concepts together in the light of e-Gov in a Cloud Computing environment.

CLOUD COMPUTING

Since e-gov EA will be discussed in the context of Cloud Computing, some terms in the domain of cloud computing need to be defined. We will give an overview of the definitions and characteristics of cloud computing by the National Institute of Standards and Technology (NIST). The quoted parts are extracted from NIST (2011) (see Table 1).

Regarding "Broad network access," the network is the computer. On the one hand the governmental departments need quick and reliable access to the applications and/or data in the Cloud, and on the other hand the citizens should be able to use all communication devices. The network is an issue in cloud computing, and therefore the government should not only look at the internal communication but also approach it from the perspective of the citizen (see Table 2).

BPaaS is pre-assembled business processes which are provided via cloud application platforms to the consumers (Marks, et al., 2010). We are proposing BPaaS based on the concept of Business Process Embedded Information System (BPEIS), an additional stage in EA (Rabaey, et al., 2007). The principle is that organizations can use a standardized business process (BP) that contains a standardized, automated information system (see Table 3).

BPaaS in e-Government

A government consists of different departments and agencies. Some of them are the core business of the government; others support the core business, for example human resources, budgeting, which are led by resource managers. Every Government Organization (GO) organizes their core Business Processes (BP) and the support or Resources Processes (RP) (see Figure 1). These RP are particular (so therefore different) implementations of higher directives and procedures. So in every GO, we find experts of the different resource domains. If a change of directives has to be implemented, all those experts of every GO need to adapt processes and/or data in the local RP, which may prove problematic, demanding a lot of efforts for each individual GO.

In the context of connected government and Cloud Computing, the concept of BPEIS can be implemented by the respective competent resources-managers through BPaaS. The RP are nothing

Table 1. Characteristics of cloud computing

Characteristics	Description
On-demand self-service	"A consumer can unilaterally provision computing capabilities, such as server time and network storage, as needed automatically without requiring human interaction with each service's provider."
Broad network access	"Capabilities are available over the network and accessed through standard mechanisms that promote use by heterogeneous thin or thick client platforms (e.g., mobile phones, laptops, and PDAs)."
Resource pooling	"The provider's computing resources are pooled to serve multiple consumers using a multi-tenant model, with different physical and virtual resources dynamically assigned and reassigned according to consumer demand. There is a sense of location independence in that the customer generally has no control or knowledge over the exact location of the provided resources but may be able to specify location at a higher level of abstraction (e.g., country, state, or datacenter)."
Rapid elasticity	"Capabilities can be rapidly and elastically provisioned, in some cases automatically, to quickly scale out, and rapidly released to quickly scale in. To the consumer, the capabilities available for provisioning often appear to be unlimited and can be purchased in any quantity at any time."
Measured Service	"Cloud systems automatically control and optimize resource use by leveraging a metering capability at some level of abstraction appropriate to the type of service (e.g., storage, processing, bandwidth, and active user accounts). Resource usage can be monitored, controlled, and reported, providing transparency for both the provider and consumer of the utilized service."

Table 2. Service models of cloud computing

Service Model	Description
Cloud Software as a Service (SaaS).	"The capability provided to the consumer is to use the provider's applications running on a cloud infrastructure. The applications are accessible from various client devices through a thin client interface such as a Web browser."
Cloud Platform as a Service (PaaS)	"The capability provided to the consumer is to deploy onto the cloud infrastructure consumer-created or acquired applications created using programming languages and tools supported by the provider. The consumer does not manage or control the underlying cloud infrastructure including network, servers, operating systems, or storage, but has control over the deployed applications and possibly application hosting environment configurations."
Cloud Infrastructure as a Service (IaaS)	"The capability provided to the consumer is to provision processing, storage, networks, and other fundamental computing resources where the consumer is able to deploy and run arbitrary software, which can include operating systems and applications."
Cloud Business Process as a Service (BPaaS)	Business Process as a Service is not a standard Cloud Computing Service (see below).

more than BPaaS and one change of directives are directly implemented in every GO. GO can have temporary needs of capabilities to launch campaigns, surveys or tasks. An example of task or responsibility in the European Union is the half-yearly presidency of the EU by a member-state. Most of the processes are the same, but need to be, for the duration of the presidency, integrated with the administration of the member state.

In 2002, the Ministry of Defense of Belgium was transformed so that all the resource managers (like Human Resources [HR]) of every staff unit of the armed force and the Joint Staff was transferred to the respective resource domains (in the case of human resources to General Direction Human Resources [HR]). The Army has changed into Land Component, Air Force into Air Component, Navy into Naval Component and the Medical Service into Medical Component. Since there was no EA, the transformation took longer than foreseen, and the applications are still in transformation or ready to be replaced by another software. If an EA had existed, this could have been prevented.

Another issue was the culture change of the personnel working in the RP and of those who needed to leave his/her armed force to go to a newly formed resource domain. Although there is no explicit link between (the conventional) EA and the culture of an organization, every change

Table 3. Deployment models of cloud computing

Deployment model	Description
Private cloud	"The cloud infrastructure is operated solely for an organization. It may be managed by the organization or a third party and may exist on premise or off premise."
Community cloud	"The cloud infrastructure is shared by several organizations and supports a specific community that has shared concerns (e.g., mission, security requirements, policy, and compliance considerations). It may be managed by the organizations or a third party and may exist on premise or off premise." This is the model that we are using for government(s).
Public cloud	"The cloud infrastructure is made available to the general public or a large industry group and is owned by an organization selling cloud services."
Hybrid cloud	"The cloud infrastructure is a composition of two or more clouds (private, community, or public) that remain unique entities but are bound together by standardized or proprietary technology that enables data and application portability (e.g., cloud bursting for load balancing between clouds)."

Figure 1. Core and corporate processes

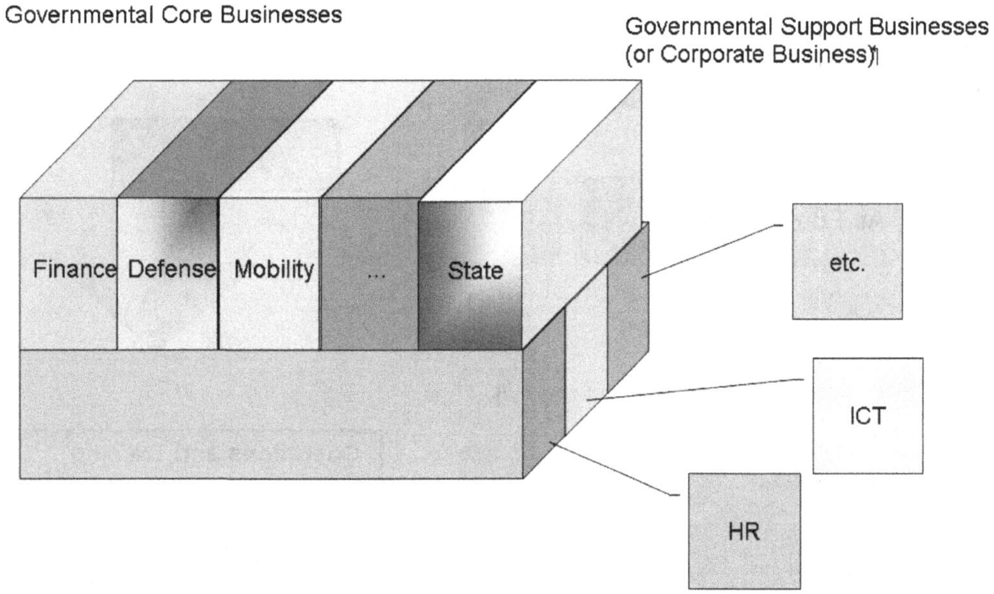

should take the resistance into account (Change management).

Culture however can be captured in the belief system of a department. This belief system is based on the experience of knowledge in the department. By implementing an additional (knowledge) architecture in EA, culture can be considered in EA (future research) (see Figure 2).

ENTERPRISE ARCHITECTURE

Overview

Lots of different interpretations of the term Enterprise Architecture (EA) exist (Rabaey, et al., 2007). Some hold lists of technological choices that an organization should make concerning infrastructure and application design. Others put these technological decisions into sets of guidelines to information architecture and business architecture.

We are proposing a holistic framework for investments based on the right balance of goals and means. Therefore, EA should be put in a broader context than merely infrastructure architecture and application architecture, because applications are built to support business processes and operate on information gathered through these business processes. Hence, architecture only concerned with infrastructure and application design is insufficient to support a business. The architecture of a building is based on the function that this building will have (store, house, manufacturing, etc.). So an Enterprise Architecture should consider the business and its dynamics so that it can take precautions for changing business requirements or the reuse of certain artifacts in other business domains.

The Enterprise Architecture Research Forum (EARF, 2011) defines Enterprise Architecture as "the continuous practice of describing the essential elements of a socio-technical organization, their relationships to each other and to the environment, in order to understand complexity and manage change." Therefore, Enterprise Architecture should consist of Table 4's levels.

The knowledge architecture is an extra level we are proposing to be inserted into EA. If Cloud

Figure 2. Belgian ministry of defense

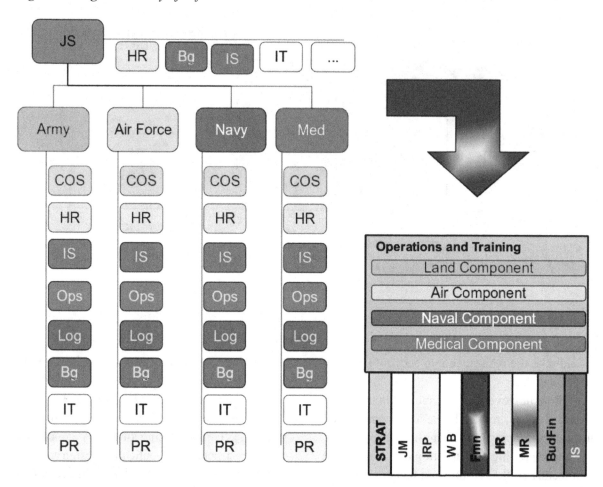

Computing will come up to the expectations of the market then IT will become a utility (commodity) and competitive/collaborative advantage will become almost fully dependent from the capability of producing intelligence for decision-making and knowledge management (in systems, processes and human resources). So the differentiation will be made on the level of knowledge assets and therefore knowledge has to be addressed in a specific architecture. That is why we are proposing this extra level.

In the part on Cloud Computing, services as Infrastructure, Platform and Software will be discussed. These three service models are more situated in the two lower EA layers (Application

and Infrastructure). However, in e-Government the difference between business process and Software is very small, so that Cloud Computing (Software as a Service) is also situated at the business architecture level. In this regard, BPaaS is a special form of SaaS, and by definition BPaaS is situated in the business part (Marks, et al., 2010; Rabaey, 2011).

Goal of EA

A well-developed and maintained Enterprise Architecture enables the organization to respond quickly and adequately to changes inside the organization and in the environment in which

Table 4. Levels of enterprise architecture

Level Architecture	Description
Business Architecture	Is about the description of the business processes as viewed from a business perspective. It should focus on the strategic environment and the business processes, which should attain the objectives.
Knowledge Architecture	Brings the asset of knowledge in chart.
Information Architecture	Describes the information the business is dependent on. This description must pay attention to where information enters the business processes, how this information enters the process, electronically, or by other means, who is the owner of the information, and by whom it is to be used.
Application Architecture	Is about how to implement the applications or IT systems in all of its aspects (programming, development environment, quality book of software, etc.).
Infrastructure Architecture	Deals with guidelines concerning hardware platforms, network infrastructure, operating systems.

the organization operates. In combination with the strategic interaction analysis (game theory) it serves as a base to create scenarios and to assess the impact of the changes on each of the EA-layers. These scenarios are the input of the investment process (interdisciplinary forum, see below).

Therefore one of the goals of EA is to assess, plan and implement changes in the organization so that they can respond with more agile responsiveness of the organization and this in an efficient (cost- and resources based) and effective (strategic and operational objectives) way, and thus improve respectively the overall performance and output (good and/or services).

Stages

Ross (2003) defines four stages: Application Silo Stage, Technology Standardization Stage, Data Rationalization Stage, and A Modular Architecture.

Application Silo Stage is about the archipelago we mentioned in the introduction. In this stage Enterprise Architecture is just the collection of the architectures of isolated applications, most of them implemented in different technologies.

Technology Standardization Stage is the first step towards an Enterprise Architecture in which technology gets standardized and often centralization is put in place. The deployment of

resources shifts from application development into the development of a shared infrastructure. This phase is further often characterized by the introduction of business intelligence and a first attempt to manage business processes.

Data Rationalization Stage consists of process and data standardization. The deployment of resources shifts from application development into data management and infrastructure development. The involvement of senior business managers becomes institutionalized by a common forum of IT and business managers. In this phase, we see a shift of data ownership from IT towards the business.

A Modular Architecture characterized by enterprise wide global standards with loosely coupled applications, information, and technology components to preserve the global standards while enabling local differences through modules extending the core processes.

Business Process Embedded Information System (BPEIS)

Rabaey et al. (2006, 2007) have added a fifth stage: business process embedded information systems. At that moment Grid Computing and Enterprise Application Integration (EAI) were known, but not yet Cloud Computing (as a reality). Cloud computing in combination with Service Oriented

Architecture (SOA) makes BPEIS technically possible.

Due to the ever faster changing environment of an organization and increasing interactions with it, a global and central "steering" becomes quite impossible, if the organization aims to have a flexible and rapid response. So the organization delegates to the business units and their processes. Therefore, the IT must be federated to obtain the necessary autonomy for the IT-applications. That is why the authors are proposing to embed information systems into business processes. In the context of cloud computing BPEIS can be considered as BPaaS (see above).

All aspects of the information system can be federated without losing the consistency of the information system of the highest governmental level. However, before going to the fifth stage, a government and its departments have to perform a knowledge and information model as described above. Knowledge becomes a belief system and merging or separating processes (or structures) should be assessed to determine if the cultures of the different parties fit the new organization. Thus at the same time, the structure of the government and its departments has to be defined, and the business processes have to be modeled in the Business Process Management tool, which is obviously managed at the level business level of EA.

Once the business model, knowledge model and the conceptual information model are defined, then they need to be merged into a global model (information, knowledge mapping, and business processes), where the departments should manage their own (embedded) information system, but as already mentioned, it has to start with a conceptual information model to solve the problems of information management. Following, the knowledge model should test the cultural compatibilities of the applications with the business.

Since the environment of the organization is permanently changing and thus the organization also, the information system of the organization has to be adapted to the new situation. This will reflect the most at the knowledge infrastructure, because information systems in the Cloud will become commodity.

If a business process could be fully automated and it holds itself the information, then a consistent part of the producible and needed information will be embedded in the business process, in accordance with the culture.

The concept of embedding is not new, Object-Oriented Programming (OOP) keeps methods and data private in objects. Those objects are interfacing with their environment through public functions and data. A step further is the Service Oriented Architecture (SOA) where services are delivered through the contract of the Web services, next to SaaS and BPaaS.

Gov-EA

Goal

Governments are organizations as any other business enterprise but they are more complex (different levels of government, political influences, etc.) and therefore frameworks as EA can put everything on a map and indicate solutions. Pallab Saha writes: "Most governments worldwide are in the midst of substantial public sector transformation activities. A majority of these initiatives are triggered by the need to have better and seamless government services delivered online. The focus on automating government services often is a largely limited to specific ministries and agencies. However, such initiatives lack the cross-ministry / agency viewpoint and coordination. This creates challenges in taking a whole-of-government (W-O-G) approach and concomitant benefits, which are much more than benefits derived by taking agency-centric viewpoints" (Saha, 2010a).

He defines three key goals of EA in government organizations: make them citizen-centered, results-oriented and market-based. One of the possible ways to achieve this is by introducing the concept of "Connected Government": "Connected government enables governments to connect seamlessly across functions, agencies, and jurisdictions to deliver effective and efficient services to citizens and businesses"(Saha, 2010a).

EA and Connected Government

The dimensions of Connected Government are:

- Citizen centricity;
- Common infrastructure and interoperability;
- Collaborative services and business operations;
- Public sector governance;
- Networked organizational model;
- Social inclusion;
- Transparent and open government.

Those dimensions can be drawn in a "cause-and-effect diagram" (based on the Balanced ScoreCard philosophy) and show in this way the interdependency of these dimensions of Connected Government (Figure 3). This interdependency will point to possible risks of failure if lower (causing) goals are not attained.

The public sector governance is the base of all and is derived from the EA. From the organizational view, the governments should business-wise already be connected (business, knowledge architecture), while more IT-bound information, application architecture should be compatible and interoperable. In the context of cloud computing, the infrastructure will also be taken into account. As we will see below in the discussion on the Interdisciplinary Forum, business and IT come (along with the other resources) together at the operational level: collaborative services and business operations. Combined with the citizen centricity and the social inclusion, it has the connected government as output and as outcome the open and transparent government.

This cause and effect diagram shows in another way the importance of EA. If EA is not present

or not fully developed then the operational level may suffer from inconsistencies in the allocation of resources or in the definition of operational objectives.

CLOUD COMPUTING: HYPE OR SURVIVAL?

Paradigm Shift

Cloud computing is a hot topic not to say a hype, amongst business and IT leaders today for its potential to transform IT service delivery and to galvanize Service-Oriented Architecture (SOA). Some people even state that just like electricity and telephone, IT will be transformed into a commodity or the fifth form of utility.

The technology of cloud computing forces the top management of organizations to think (more carefully) about competition and collaboration, be it now in relation to the customers, suppliers, government, or "traditional" competitors. Brandenburger et al. (1995) talk about "Co-opetition" a combination of Cooperation and Competition in the evolution of Game Theory, which through strategic games can be applied in the investment decision process in general and in IT in particular.

The US Office of E-Government and Information Technology states that IT advancements have been at the center of a transformation in how the private sector operates - and revolutionized the efficiency, convenience, and effectiveness with which it serves its customers. "The Federal Government largely has missed out on that transformation due to poor management of technology investments, with IT projects too often costing hundreds of millions of dollars more than they should, taking years longer than necessary to deploy, and delivering technologies that are obsolete by the time they are completed. We are working to close the resulting gap between the best performing private sector organizations and the federal government.

Figure 3. Cause and effect diagram for connected government

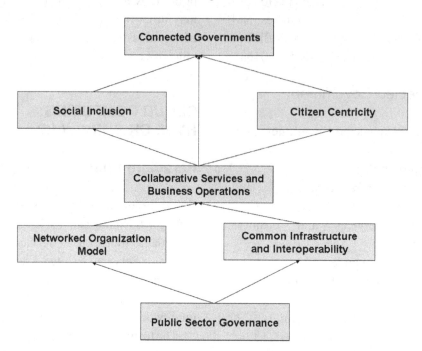

The Office of E-Government and Information Technology (E-Gov), headed by the Federal Government's Chief Information Officer, develops and provides direction in the use of Internet-based technologies to make it easier for citizens and businesses to interact with the Federal Government, save taxpayer dollars, and streamline citizen participation" (Whitehouse, 2011).

As a consequence, the Obama administration has enforced that for every new initiative in e-government, Cloud Computing solutions should be considered first (Spínola, 2009).

We will first discuss the types of e-Government.

Types of e-Government

Government-to-Government (G2G) can be national (amongst departments), intranational (higher and lower governmental authorities like provinces), or international (like the European Union [EU]). Collaboration is not always trivial.

Although SOA is at first glance the more obvious solution (interconnected with or without Enterprise Service Bus [ESB]), cloud computing in a community model may offer more secure and economical possibilities. It is at the political level that the commitment should be made, in conformity with the EA philosophy. It does not have to be fully integrated at the national level, because also special exclusive domains as Defense can be possible (NATO—European Union—Member state—Defense Department).

Government-to-Client (G2C) is client-oriented (citizens, companies). The time of information portal is over. Cloud computing is the enabler of knowledge portals in combination with services portals. One may argue that knowledge should be seen as an output of a service and that it can be incorporated in the service portal. However knowledge transfer should be so that the citizens and the companies can make better decisions by themselves, while services is more a product as an output of (virtual) processes.

A New Government Thinking Model?

Is there a need for a new Government Thinking Model? It may not only be technology driven (otherwise hype) but also citizen driven and company driven (both are clients of the government). As a matter of fact it should be a combination of both which should already be implemented in the development of the Grand Strategy. The Grand Strategy is the art of combining all resources of a nation or alliance into a dynamic adaptable plan to achieve its (political) goals (Rabaey, et al., 2007a). Since we want to integrate the cloud computing philosophy in the Enterprise Architecture, the whole way of planning and implementing IT-solutions has to change.

Only in this way the new paradigm can be proliferated into governmental business strategy and resources strategy (like IT-strategy), resulting in an awareness at the operational level (business processes and projects). Since the Grand Strategy is the result of the balance between goals and means, the business strategies (goals) and the resources strategies (like IT) are distinguished from each other and are derived from the Grand Strategy. IT will develop the mainstream use of IT in the organization, while the business strategy will define the environment in which they would like to attain the government objectives.

A consequence is that the investment methodology has to follow this new concept where adequate tools as game theory (strategic interaction) and real options valuation (uncertainty, risk, flexibility) can be implemented. Vendors of Cloud Computing do only use the classic investment techniques, such as ROI to show the economic benefits and refer to their own or third party consultants to assess the risks of their implementation of Cloud Computing.

Standardization and Virtualization

The main characteristic of cloud computing is standardization (of services). Through this standardization on every level, management becomes easier. Another advantage of standardization is the efficiency and therefore the reduction of costs in setting up and maintaining services. Mr. Peter Strickx, CTO of Federal ICT Agency (FedICT) said that not the cloud computing on itself will make IT more efficient but the way to get into the Cloud, the preparation, like standardization and virtualization makes IT more efficient (personal communication, March 23rd, 2011).

This standardization permits a better virtualization because it provides a whole set of processes, activities, and tools to support the virtualization and the on-demand-self-service, by providing standardized approval cycles, and even pre-approved services with special rules.

To enable the move to the Cloud for the Belgian federal departments, FedICT is implementing a DCaaS: Data Center as a Service. It is a community cloud with external and internal infrastructure. The main reason for keeping an internal infrastructure is security. More specifically the databases (with confidential information) will stay in hands of FedICT.

INTERDISCIPLINARY FORUM

The proposed investment methodology is used in a holistic framework called Interdisciplinary Forum (IF) (Rabaey, et al., 2004, 2005) based on their study of the Art of War. In the case of GovCloud IF defines the process "from Strategy to Service." The Grand Strategy of an organization determines the Business Strategy and Resources Strategy (as Human Resources and IT).

The first rule of the Art of War is the balance between goals and means, if goals are more demanding than the existing means then the effectiveness is jeopardized. In the opposite case, the organization is not efficient. That is why they split the influence of Grand Strategy into two parts: Business Strategy (goals), Resources Strategy (means). In function of the Grand Strategy, the resources managers will develop their own strategies.

The splitting is also advised by elements of Behavioral Economics that shows that the behavior and expressing of ideas during group discussions differ from what the participants originally were thinking (Ariely, 2009; Montier, 2010). It is better to present the solutions to problems and/or challenges in a later stage, more precisely the operational strategy.

Business processes and projects are then discussed in the Interdisciplinary Forum to determine the operational strategy (Figure 4). Different scenarios are presented to the decision-making unit of the government. Once the steering plans are decided and the Service Level Agreements (SLA) are adapted, then the new objectives are communicated to the business units and resources units.

Gartner presented in 2010 something similar "the hybrid thinking," although Gartner focuses more on business and IT, and not that much on the other resources. Therefore, it is less holistic.

The Interaction IF and EA

The blueprint of the organization is the EA. Combing the game theory with the strategic planning function of EA, different scenarios are developed based on this blueprint. It will show the advantages, disadvantages, and risks of any changes made to this blueprint, not only for the IT but also for the other resources.

With the introduction of SOA and Cloud Computing, the influence of IT on the way the organization is run, increases everyday. IT governance therefore is crucial for the success of the

Figure 4. System of interdisciplinary forum

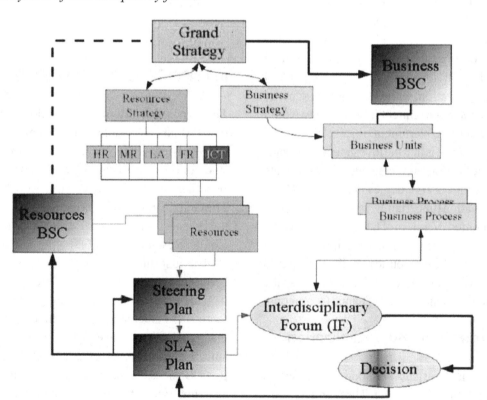

organization because IT interferes now in every level of EA (see Figure 5).

Now that we have discussed Cloud Computing and SOA and their relation to EA, we will extend the cause-and-effect diagram of the dimensions of Connected Government (see Figure 6), which becomes a crucial path scheme for implementing Cloud services.

The base stays more than ever the Public Sector Governance. With the introduction of Knowledge architecture in EA (knowledge becomes a belief system) where the citizen centricity is now part of the culture. Since its importance, we keep it separate in the diagram.

The infrastructure is replaced by IaaS and PaaS, because they enable the optimization and flexibility of the IT-resources. Probably a complete Cloud configuration will not exist; therefore, "legacy systems" can be moved on the IaaS and produce as before collaborative services.

BPaaS and SaaS are replacing for a part the collaborative services and business operations.

They are also connected with the "social networking on the Web." Nowadays governments are also making the move to the "Web social networking" as a hype because they want to use as much as possible the same tools as their citizens. However if this move is not covered by EA, then resources will probably wasted.

Finally, the connected government(s) driven by the cloud business layer (BPaaS, SaaS) in combination with the older legacy systems will have as outcome a transparent open government, but here, more than ever EA is of crucial importance to attain the objective of having a connected government(s).

Real Options

We will discuss how e-government can start or step into a Cloud-based architecture taken into account the Government EA. Most of the governments have legacy systems, so this is a topic that

Figure 5. IF-EA relationship for IT

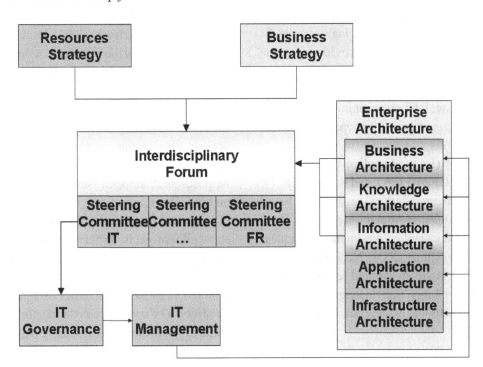

Figure 6. Dimensions of connected government and cloud computing

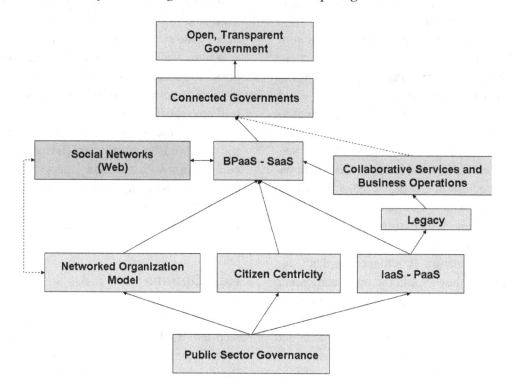

we will focus on, more than starting from scratch to move to the Cloud.

A preliminary remark is that governments are not obliged to follow a path from IaaS over PaaS to SaaS, as Cloud Computing providers appear to propose. We will show that with EA it is advisable to work with an Enterprise Service Bus (ESB) for an easier integration or interoperability of the different agencies and/or departments (see Figures 4 and 9).

Saha (2006) (EA), Mikaelian (2009) (EA), Rabaey et al. (2006a) (SOA), and Rabaey (2011) (government procurement), amongst others, have discussed the problems of making investment decisions based on the classic investment techniques as Return Of Investment (ROI), Net Present Value (NPV). These classic investment techniques are lacking the flexibility that management needs to be able to postpone, delay, start, and abandon projects.

Real Option Valuation (ROV) gives management this flexibility and it tackles the problem of uncertainty and risk related to each investment (Fichman, 2004; Brach, 2003; Mun, 2006). Financial options are the right but not the obligation to execute an action (sell or buy). Based upon the theory of financial options, we define real options as the right, not the obligation to adjust the course of actions regarding process and projects. So real options give management the possibility (right but no obligation) to decide if projects should be postponed, stopped, started, restarted, or put on hold. The reasons may be because of the lack of relevant information, or to wait for results of some pilot projects. Table 5 gives an overview of possible real options (Brach, 2003, p. 67).

The option's underlying is the project in question and is modeled in terms of spot price and volatility. The spot price is the starting or current value of the project and is usually based on management's best guess as to the gross value of the project's cash flows and resultant NPV. Volatility is the uncertainty as to the change in value over time is required (Wikipedia Real Options Valuation, 2011). Real option valuation sees volatility as a potential upside factor and ascribes value to it (Brach, 2003, p. 3).

Some characteristics are common to all real options (Brach, 2003, p. 48):

- The value of the option is the expected value of the asset minus the price of acquiring the option and minus the price of exercising the option.
- The correlation between asset value volatility and cost volatility defines the option value, not the absolute volatilities of either one.
- Taking maximum advantage from optionality requires that option holders be capable of exercising their option—financially and organizationally.
- Financial options do not discriminate: the same price and value is valid for every participant in the market. Real options, on the contrary, are individual. Acquiring the right on the same real asset will have different option values to different organizations, as skills, capabilities and, therefore, probability distributions and payoffs vary."

Be it real option valuation or other investment techniques, a problem for every non-profit organization is the expression of benefits or value of an investment. In the best case, this type of organization can define the costs but not the benefits. With Professor Housel, the Naval Postgraduate School has developed the concept of Knowledge Value Added (KVA) (Mun, et al., 2006, 2010). "KVA is a general theory for estimating the value added by knowledge assets, human and IT, using a methodology that is analytic and tautological. It is based on the premise that businesses and other organizations produce outputs (e.g., products and services) through a series of processes and subprocesses which change, in some manner, the raw inputs (i.e., labor into services, information into reports). KVA explains the changes made on the inputs by organizational processes to produce outputs in terms of the equivalent corresponding changes in entropy. The concept of entropy is defined in the American Heritage Dictionary as a 'measure of the degree of disorder [or change] in a closed system.' In the business context, it can be used as a surrogate for the amount of changes that a process makes to inputs to produce the resulting outputs" (Rios, 2005, p. 16).

The eventual introduction of KVA and ROV in Belgium is still in research (Rabaey, 2011).

Option Games

ROV however has a common drawback as like the classic investment techniques, being the lack of taking into account the interaction of the or-

Table 5. Types of real options

Option	Description
Defer	Wait to determine whether to implement certain modules (hardware, software, network...) without imperiling the potential benefits.
Abandon	Abandon the project (terminate at the current stage) (exit)
Switch	Re-arrange the sequence of installing/updating/finishing modules
Expand/contract	Add new modules not scheduled previously or increase quality / Remove already installed modules or reduce quality
Explore	Investing in a prototype to explore the possibilities
Stage	Flexibility to stop and resume modules in progress

ganization with its environment (market, citizen, companies, etc.) (Grenadier, 2000; Smit, et al., 2009; Ferreira, et al., 2009). The solution is to combine ROV with game theory, which results in the theory of option games.

Thus, option games are a combination of two complementary theories: real option valuation and game theory. Real Options is meant for "planning," therefore a set of chains of future decisions, while game theory is about actual "interactions." The former is conceived for flexibility of the management and for a better management of the uncertainties (in the future). As already mentioned above, real options express the value of waiting to decide: (defer, abandon, switch, etc.), but it is without considering the strategic interaction from the other market players. This is where game theory comes into the picture.

Game theory on its own analyzes complexities of the equilibriums and the payoffs into detail by determining players' utility functions without any relation to market values. Real options valuation places these payoff values under uncertainty, considering market values and the flexibility of response by the optimal exercise of the options.

A government is assessing situations at a moment in the future, but game options place them in a game theoretic context. Thus it is not only a chain of possible decisions (as in the non-interactive original version of real options), but it is also a chain of possible interactions (situations) represented by games.

Every decision node consists of two phases. The first is to assess the situation in which the decision has to be made, in other words the probable payoff matrix of the game. The second phase is to determine the value of the real option based on this payoff matrix.

If only one game is always considered, then this is a mono-game chain of options. A more complex version is to consider more than one game, and therefore determine the value of the real option for each game (and its corresponding payoff matrix). As a result, each node with multiple games (in the so called multi-game chain of options) will generate more branches than in the case of a mono-game chain of options (Rabaey, 2011).

Investment in Cloud Computing

General Considerations

The government can play three roles in investing in Cloud Computing. It can itself be a cloud service-provider, or it is a cloud customer (cloud service-consumer) or the government can be a mixture of both (hybrid situation). We make the assumption that the IT-resources are managed by one governmental organization, that we call GovIT. In Belgium the Federal Agency of Information and Communication Technology (FedICT) does not fulfill completely this role, but is instead an enabler and coordinator at federal level. As such, every federal public service also has an IT-department. However, in the context of cloud computing, FedICT is fulfilling the role.

The GovIT is the interface between the other governmental organizations, which are always cloud service consumers, and the cloud service-provider (itself or a third party).

Cloud computing gives the possibility to optimize the use of IT-resources, only the efficiency makes it such that IT-resources are delivered in a just-in-time philosophy. As a matter of fact, the IT-resources are kept scarce. Therefore, even as a cloud service consumer a capacity planning is in any case needed. This capacity planning is linked to the strategic planning (long term vision) and the business operational planning (short term vision, and present), formalized through the EA.

In both cases, GovIT will probably always have to acquire software from third party. The fact that GovIT represents the whole government, it can negotiate very good prices for the use of software. Since Cloud Computing is about standardization, the government has all interest to offer Open Source Software (OSS) as part of the services. Some examples in the infrastructure are Linux,

MariaDB, in the platform eclipse, in the software Alfresco, openoffice, and Intalio and Bonita for BPaaS. The costs of ownership can be reduced to the professional maintenance and consultancy for these OSS. By avoiding acquiring costs, GovIT can eventually invest in the OSS development in order to direct it more to the needs of the GO.

An example is the Public Federal Service Personnel and Organization in Belgium. It implemented Alfresco as content and community platform. Other public federal services can join the projects by adding (standardized) hardware (disks) in the IT-infrastructure.

Government as Cloud Provider

Unlike a commercial Cloud Data Center (CDC), the GovIT has a planning of the needed resources, thanks to the government EA. A commercial CDC has to invest in infrastructure, hardware and people for customers it does not know yet. They cannot wait for the customer to be known, because due to the short service delivery time demanded by the customer, it would be too late for the commercial CDC to acquire new resources.

As already mentioned a CDC has to make a trade-off between the number of offered standard services and the manageability of that number of services.

Besides the number of services (in the service catalog), it has to agree the service level for every offered service with the GO (Service Level Agreement) regarding Recovery Time and Recovery Point Objectives (See below the point on 'Disaster and Recovery').

The GovIT needs to foresee a backup site, it has the choice to keep a backup site alive, or itself can negotiate with a third party for a backup site. One may not forget that when the backup site has to take over from the main site, the backup site itself has no other backup site. So in the case that GovIT has its (second) own backup site, it will still have to negotiate a backup of that second CDC. Of course, GovIT can always keep a third CDC

alive, but this becomes very expensive, unless it sells its Cloud capacity to others. This is a typical growth option.

Government as Cloud Customer

It is possible that GovIT is abandoning the idea to be a CDC or to continue to be a CDC. This is only possible if all five levels of architecture in EA are well defined and understood. In general, GovIT will opt for a hybrid solution. Hybrid in two ways: integrating legacy systems with the Cloud and hybrid deployment model (public-private combination).

Legacy System

Regarding mainframes, the people who can work with them are retiring. However, there are still a lot of applications running on mainframes. The purpose is to virtualize these mainframes in a CDC. The maintenance of these is then outsourced to specialized groups of people.

In general, the goal is to connect parts of those applications in the cloud. Different strategies are possible like Enterprise Application Integration (EAI), but with the introduction of SOA, legacy systems can be wrapped into Web services. The next step is to wrap modules in Web services (SOA-components) and to migrate the different SOA-components to the Cloud (See Figure 7).

The message is not to convert all legacy systems into Cloud or SOA-components. If the legacy system performs well and at a reasonable price and acceptable service, these systems can stay (until signs of functional or technical obsolescence are spotted).

The reasons for moving towards the Cloud and/or SOA is that the legacy system is becoming economically, functionally or technically obsolete. Moving from legacy systems towards SaaS has to be carefully planned and for a government having only legacy systems, moving to the cloud is as a matter of fact a real option on itself (Spínola,

Figure 7. Legacy system, SOA, and cloud computing

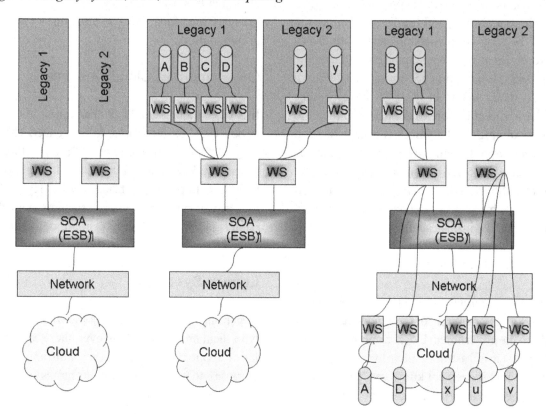

2009). It gives flexibility to the government and if successful the operational costs are reduced. In a growth scenario, pay per use becomes pay-as-you-grow.

Rabaey (2004a, 2005a, 2007) are proposing an assessment system for Enterprise Application Integration (EAI) based on the interdisciplinary forum, which can also be used for cloud computing.

Figure 8 (adapted from Rabaey, et al., 2007) shows the process to move applications to the cloud. First the department decides which processes should be migrated. The interdependency of all processes is mapped in the Process-Process (PP-) matrix, where in the rows and the columns the processes are listed. In the corresponding cell is mentioned what the relationships and relative relations are. The IT does a similar exercise but for the applications (AA-matrix). By merging both matrices into the PA-matrix, the IF can detect through the Enterprise Architecture which

processes are affected and which applications (or part of them) should be moved to the Cloud.

The following picture depicts the concept of a possible architecture combing legacy systems, SOA (ESB) and GovCloud.

Although SaaS can be directly presented to the clients (citizens, companies, other governments) (C2G, G2G) some softwares are better contained in Web services. Most of them are based on business processes which use confidential data (see also 'Risk Management Aspects' below).

If business oriented services would fail or be too risky, the department should consider moving the infrastructure of the legacy system anyway to the cloud technology (private, public, hybrid cloud). It will be at least flexible regarding security (disaster and recovery) and/or cost reduction (pay-per-use) and/or create the option to move faster from one service provider to another.

Based on the assessment of IF, the department will decide to move or not to move one or more applications to the cloud, and if so then in which deployment and/or service models. The go-decision will always be built on a Service Level Agreement (SLA) be it in the case of GovIT or a commercial cloud service provider. The choice of which financial technique (game option, real option, ROI) to be used depends if it is situated in the operational strategy (problems related to other resources domains and/or business) or if it is a more IT-related strategy (basically infrastructure).

An example can be that by implementing a SaaS, a reorganization has to be executed, in which people may have to move to other departments. Strikes may be more damaging for the department than the possible technological risks due to the introduction of cloud computing. In this case, the "uncertainty" captured in a real option has to be brought at a higher (department, operational) level, thus the assessment of the technical risks can be seriously influenced by the business (process) level, so that less complex financial techniques can be used at the IT level.

RISK MANAGEMENT ASPECTS

Cloud Cube Model

The Jericho Forum of the Open Group are proposing the Cloud Cube Model (Figure 10) as a framework to investigate the secure collaboration in cloud formations (models) (OG, 2009; Chang, 2010) and to define the best model for the business needs (Chang, 2010a), but it also can be used to assess the risks for the different service models and/or deployment models.

Following questions are examples of questions that can be assessed by the government with CCM, as long with issues around some possible solutions: "What are the risks (security) for Private and Public Clouds?" "How do you couple Public with Private (hybrid thus), and what are the right

reasons for it?" "A private cloud application using the corporate e-mail system in the public cloud," and "a public cloud application using resources from the private cloud."

As discussed above, the main issue to opt for a global cloud computing strategy in an organization or a government is certainly the interoperability of applications inside the organization (private cloud, legacy systems) and outside the organization (public cloud, non-cloud third party systems). This is more complex than implementing a hybrid cloud, or for that matter a community cloud. The cloud cube model gives a good framework to determine the risks, but also the opportunities (see Table 6).

Risk Categories

While CCM gives a good insight in how the cloud should be approached in the architectural domain, other kind of risks should also be considered. Triantis (2000) in his discussion on real option valuation gives a general classification of risks. For each risk category (first column) in Table 7, some examples can be found in the second column.

The technological risk category is fully covered by the CCM, but an additional point of interest is "Disaster and Recovery" (D&R) Two parameters are important to define the SLA of D&R:

- **Recovery Time Objectives (RTO):** what's the maximum downtime (for an application)
- **Recovery Point Objectives (RPO):** the amount of loss of data, or transactions

In function of these two parameters and the cost of each solution, two ways of D&R are possible: active-active and active-passive. Active-active means that the second site is receiving every change of state of the applications and their data (transactions), and vice verse. The benefits of active-active are quick recovery and take over, while the costs are keeping two CDC alive and of course the bandwidth use. With Active-Passive,

Figure 8. EA-IF decision process for legacy-2-cloud

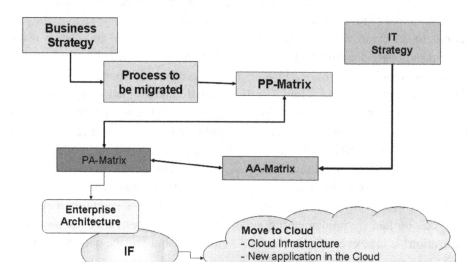

Figure 9. SOA and cloud computing

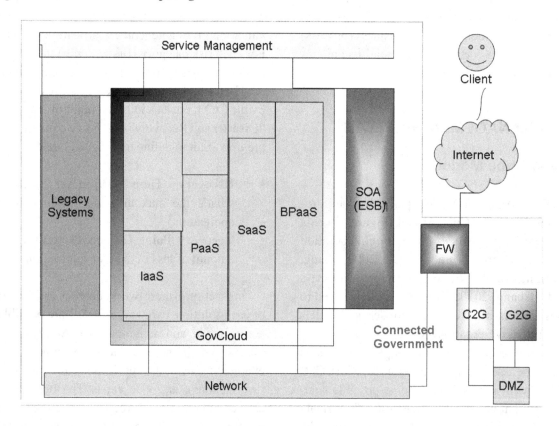

Figure 10. Cloud cube model (CCM)

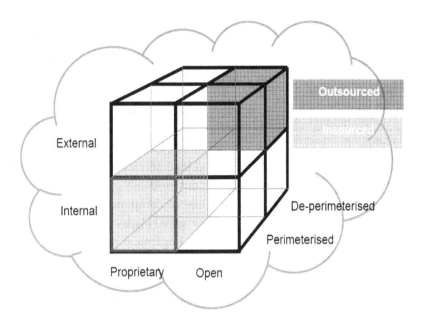

the second site is receiving everything, but it is not put on line. The benefits of active-passive are less demanding service to back up (so cheaper), but it takes more time to come back on line in the Cloud.

The technological risks are for a first implementation a considerable issue, particularly for the private cloud because all of the risks stays in the organization and it remains a capital investment (CAPEX), and not an operational cost (OPEX) (Marks, et al., 2010). Due to this, the private cloud is also more sensitive for economical fluctuations (negative). On the other hand, since public cloud is another form of outsourcing, the performance

Table 6. Dimensions of cloud cube model

Dimension	Description	Remarks
Internal and External	the type of deployment model (internal: private; external: public; both: hybrid)	
Open and Proprietary	defines the state of ownership of the cloud technology and indicates the degree of interoperability, as well as enabling "data/application transportability" between providers. It also indicates any constraints on being able to share applications.	the 'lock-in' with a provider
Perimeterised (Per) / De-perimeterised (D-p)	represents the architectural mindset if one is operating inside the traditional IT perimeter (with firewall) or outside	De-perimeterisation (OG, 2009, 2010) has always been related to the gradual failure / removal / shrinking / collapse of the traditional silo-based IT perimeter. It is about the way data can be accessed from a private cloud (like VPN) or from a public cloud (like data segregation, privileged user access).
Insourced and Out-sourced	is about respectively in-house development of clouds and the services provided by cloud service providers.	

Table 7. Types of risks of cloud computing

Risk Category	Example
Technological	Implementing new technology Production breakdown, operational risks
Economical	Material cost Macroeconomic conditions
Financial	CAPEX (Investment budget) OPEX (Budgets for Operational costs)
Legal/Regulatory	Political regime and legislation Environmental change
Performance	Subcontractor Judicial risk

of the cloud service provider is something that the organization does not control except through SLA and penalties (Spínola, 2009).

Therefore, the economical risks are for a government very important. Although it can have an impact on the macroeconomics conditions, some issues like the latest financial crisis are not under control. As a consequence, the economical risks may have an influence in the financial domain in casu the budgets for investments (CAPEX) and operational costs (OPEX), and vice verse. Cloud computing in a public or hybrid cloud gives the flexibility as like a real option. The same author Triantis (2000) defines real options as opportunities to delay and adjust investment and operating decisions over time in response to the resolution of uncertainty. Therefore, they not only protect a department from the adverse consequences of excess risk exposure, they also provide opportunities to exploit uncertainty.

One may ask if a pure private cloud can really save money (except for the operational cost savings due to standardization and virtualization. In this context, cloud service providers as IBM are proposing shared private cloud (computing) which is a public cloud but located in countries that GovIT agreed on. The term private indicates that the servers or services for one organization are protected from the rest of the servers in that particular cloud (this is a security issue, some

cloud service providers cannot guarantee this security service).

The fact that cloud service providers are giving choices where the data and/or applications are hosted is also linked with the legal and/or regulatory risk category. The legislation of the country where the cloud service provider has data centers or service centers, is applicable, not the legislation of the country of the customer or cloud service provider. The political or cultural environment at the possible locations of one or more components of service management (see Figure 11) may influence the decision about where to implement components.

China demands that every IT-communication crossing its border is unencrypted; therefore, for touchy information the CDC in a location in China, while interacting with customers outside China, may have a No-Go light.

Other issues that have to be taken into account are the tax regulation and the culture (attitude) of the local service managers to follow procedures (discipline, care, etc.).

Judicial risks lies more in the domain of confidentiality of the data, especially towards the customers of the organization (also linked with previous category) and the quality of service of the cloud service provider. Questions about the latter are: "What if the Cloud provider cannot fulfill his SLA?" "If the government ICT is itself responsible as Cloud provider then what are the risks and legal aspects of this failure?"

BRINGING THE PIECES TOGETHER: INTERDISCIPLINARY FORUM

Enterprise Architecture is the blueprint of the government's business and IT organization. Many stages (of maturity) are possible, but it is a condition sine qua non, if the government wants to implement SaaS on a large scale, that it has reached at least the level of modular architecture, and for BPaaS the level of BPEIS. For IaaS and

Figure 11. Service management model

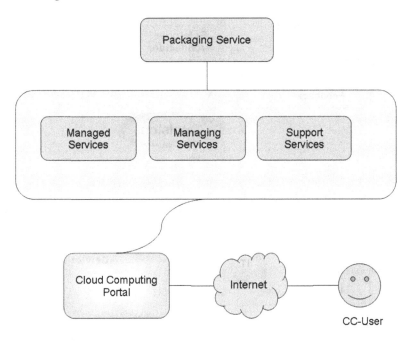

PaaS, respectively Technology Standardization and Data Rationalization should be implemented.

If the governments want to move the functionality of legacy systems to the Cloud, then the governments may use the migration system proposed in this chapter. Here also EA is important, because it will determine which processes will be affected and which applications should be focused on to move to the Cloud. The government has three choices: PaaS, SaaS, and BPaaS. As explained above the stage levels of EA will determine the ambition level of the migration (see Figure 12).

If the ambition level for the Cloud is not in balance with the stage level of EA, then the government should put first effort in EA. However, it is possible that it can acquire a more demanding service model, if and only if it can acquire the corresponding EA. Examples are ERP-packages, in this case ported to the Cloud. This is not without any risk, because of the knowledge architecture, which does not only represent the knowledge mapping but also the belief system of the department, phrased otherwise "the cultural shock."

All this is discussed and evaluated in the Interdisciplinary Forum. Since IF is holistic (therefore also other investment in resources than IT), the IT is capable to handle EA as reference for the investment proposals (Figure 12). Itself produces and updates SLA and Steering Plans, which should be integrated into EA.

IF will evaluate the investment proposals and projects on a continuous base, so that no opportunities are missed or no risk appears or increases without being noticed. The combination of CCM (OG, 2009, 2010) and the risk categorization of Triantis (2000) highlight the unhidden risks and uncertainties. In the context of finance and investment decisions, risk refers to the volatility of potential outcomes (Brach, 2003, p. 5). In function of the liberty of action of the IT manager and the volatility of expressed value, the IF will chose amongst ROV and classical investment techniques to assess the projects. In the case of BPaaS, it is possible to opt for option games.

It is a continuous cyclic process and because of the holistic character of IF business people and IT people are continuously informed about the

Figure 12. ROV and risk management

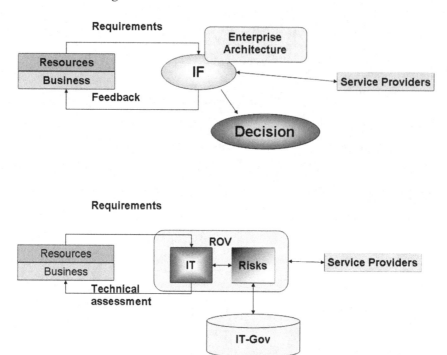

progress (and of course the changes in the environment of the department). This will encourage the government to keep its EA also up-to-date.

On the one hand, we can state that the philosophy of real options enforces the government to be better informed of what is going on inside and outside the organization and therefore will render more and/or better service to the citizen (and to the companies).

Cloud computing on the other hand enforces the government to attain and maintain high stages of EA, which will increase the efficiency and effectiveness of the information systems and therefore will do more for less, which the taxpayer will appreciate.

FUTURE DIRECTIONS

The main problem for non-profit organizations is the lack of revenues, which should exist for profit organizations. The fact that most investment

techniques are using revenues causes problems for non-profit organizations to apply properly these techniques.

Briefly, Knowledge Value Added (KVA) replaces monetary output units (revenues) by knowledge value output units. The internal resources are contributing relatively to this output and therefore their performance and added value can be determined in the non-monetary output units.

This technique has been successfully used in the US DOD, profit, and non-profit organizations. With Monte Carlo simulations, the volatility of the real options can be calculated. The further research is to examine if this technique KVA along with ROV can be used in the Belgian federal departments. Not only cultural but also legal issues have to be examined. A test case (simulation) will be studied.

Last but not least, the research should investigate if there is a link between KVA and EA, more precisely the knowledge architecture.

CONCLUSION

We came to the conclusion that the answer to the question in the beginning is "No": government, as any other organization, cannot have ambitious cloud computing projects without (a corresponding stage of) EA.

Already with SOA with permits loosely coupled applications to interact with each other, the minimum stage is the modular architecture, so the highest level in the classical scheme of EA. BPaaS and the corresponding EA stage BPEIS go beyond modular architecture and propose an autonomous (almost organic) information system. BPEIS reaches almost the domain of intelligent agents, see (Rabaey, et al., 2003, 2007a) for the concept of business intelligent agents.

Since public management is heavily involved with the concept of BPaaS and SaaS, a holistic investment framework is needed. Holistic because at this high level every aspect should be considered (not only IT). The IF handles strategy on three levels: the Grand Strategy derived from it the business and resources strategies and at the lowest level: the operational strategy where the business processes are defined and the resources like IT and HR are allocated.

Due to the fact that Cloud Computing may hold some serious risks real option valuation is most of the time used. ROV gives the public management the flexibility to adapt the course of actions in function of the environment (internal and external) and the encountered risks.

With EA as the blueprint of the department, IF formulates proposals amongst which the decision unit of the department and/or government will chose. The resulting decisions have as consequence that SLA- and Steering Plans need to be adapted and which should be added to the EA for updating the EA.

Cloud Computing is a technology, which is very complicated to implement in a department on a large scale in a consistent and integrated way. It demands a highly documented EA at the highest stage of EA. We can therefore conclude that Cloud Computing is an enabler of Government EA.

REFERENCES

Ariely, D. (2009). *Predictably irrational*. London, UK: Harper Collins.

Brach, M. (2003). *Real options in practice*. Hoboken, NJ: John Wiley & Sons.

Brandenburger, A., & Nalebuff, B. (1995). The right game: Use game theory to shape strategy. *Harvard Business Review*. Retrieved from http://hbr.org/1995/07/the-right-game-use-game-theory-to-shape-strategy/ar/1.

Chang, V., Bacigalupo, D., Wills, G., & De Roure, D. (2010a). *A categorisation of cloud computing business models*. Southampton, UK: University of Southampton.

Chang, V., Wills, G., & De Roure, D. (2010). *A review of cloud business models and sustainability*. Southampton, UK: University of Southampton.

EARF. (2011). *Website*. Retrieved April 11, 2001, from http://earf.meraka.org.za/earfhome/our-projects-1/completed-projects/.

Fereira, N., Kar, J., & Trigeorgis, L. (2009). Option games: The key to competing in capital-intensive industries. *Harvard Business Review*. Retrieved from http://hbr.org/product/option-games-the-key-to-competing-in-capital-inten/an/R0903H-PDF-ENG.

Fichman, R. (2004). Real options and IT platform adoption: Implications for theory and practice. *Information Systems Research*, *15*(2), 132–154. doi:10.1287/isre.1040.0021

Housel, T. J., & Bell, A. H. (2001). *Measuring and managing knowledge*. New York, NY: McGraw-Hill/Irwin. Grenadier, S. (200). Option exercise games: The intersection of real options and game theory. *Journal of Applied Corporate Finance, 13*(2), 99–107.

Marks, E., & Lozano, R. (2010). *Executive's guide to cloud computing*. Hoboken, NJ: John Wiley & Sons.

Montier, J. (2010). *The little book of behavioral investing*. Hoboken, NJ: John Wiley & Sons.

Mun, J. (2006). *Real options analysis versus traditional DCF valuation in layman's terms*. Retrieved April 09, 2011, from http://www.realoptionsvaluation.com/download.html#CASESTUDIES.

Mun, J., & Housel, T. (2006). *A primer on return on investment and real options for portfolio optimization*. Monterey, CA: Naval Postgraduate School.

Mun, J., & Housel, T. (2010). *A primer on applying Monte Carlo simulation, real options analysis, knowledge value added, forecasting, and portfolio optimization*. Monterey, CA: Naval Postgraduate School.

NIST. (2011). *National institute of standards and technology*. Retrieved March 25, 2011 from http://www.nist.gov/itl/csd/cloud-020111.cfm.

OG. (2009). *The open group cloud cube model: Selecting cloud formations for secure collaboration*. Retrieved April 9, 2011, from http://www.opengroup.org/jericho/publications.htm.

OG. (2010). *The open group building return on investment from cloud computing*. Retrieved April 9, 2011, from http://www.opengroup.org/cloud/whitepapers/ccroi/index.htm.

Rabaey, M. (2004a). *Decision process of enterprise application integration problems*. Paper presented at Enterprise Application Integration and Software Re-Engineering 2004. Ghent, Belgium.

Rabaey, M. (2011). *Game theoretic real option approach of the procurement of department of defense: Competition or collaboration*. Paper presented at the 8th Annual Acquisition Research Symposium. Monterey, CA.

Rabaey, M., Hoffman, G., & Vandenborre, K. (2004). *Aligning business- and resource-strategy: An interdisciplinary forum*. Paper presented at the 13th International Conference on Management Technology (IAMOT 2004). Washington, DC.

Rabaey, M., Leclercq, J.-M., Vandijck, E., Hoffman, G., & Timmerman, M. (2005a). *Intelligence base: Strategic instrument of an organization*. Paper presented at the Meeting of NATO IST-055 Specialist Meeting. The Hague, The Netherlands.

Rabaey, M., Tromp, H., & Vandenborre, K. (2007a). Holistic approach to align ICT capabilities with business integration. In Cunha, M., Cortes, B., & Putnik, G. (Eds.), *Adaptive Technologies and Business Integration: Social, Managerial, and Organizational Dimensions* (pp. 160–173). Hershey, PA: IGI Global. doi:10.4018/978-1-59904-048-6.ch008

Rabaey, M., Vandenborre, K., Vandijck, E., Timmerman, M., & Tromp, H. (2007b). Semantic web services and BPEL: Semantic service oriented architecture - Economical and philosophical issues. A. Salam & J. Stevens (Eds.), *Semantic Web Technologies and eBusiness: Toward the Integrated Virtual Organization and Business Process Automation*, (pp. 127-153). Hershey, PA: IGI Global.

Rabaey, M., Vandenborre, K., Vandijck, E., Tromp, H., & Timmerman, M. (2006a). *Business process embedded information systems - For flexibility and adaptability*. Paper presented at 8th International Conference on Enterprise Information Systems: Databases and Information Systems Integration. Paphos, Cyprus.

Rabaey, M., Vandenborre, K., Vandijck, E., Tromp, H., & Timmerman, M. (2006b). *Service oriented investments.* Paper presented at the 17th Information Resource Management Association International Conference. Washington, DC.

Rabaey, M., Vandijck, E., & Hoffman, G. (2005b). *An evaluation framework for enterprise application integration.* Paper presented at the 16th IRMA International Conference. San Diego, CA.

Rabaey, M., Vandijck, E., & Tromp, H. (2003). *Business intelligent agents for enterprise application integration: The link between business process management and web services.* Paper presented at the International Conference Software and Systems Engineering and their Applications 2003. Paris, France.

Real Options Valuation. (2011). *Wikipedia.* Retrieved March 24, 2011, from http://en.wikipedia. org/wiki/Real_options_valuation.

Ross, J. (2003). *Creating a strategic IT architecture competency: Learning in stages.* Working Paper. Cambridge, MA: Massachusetts Institute of Technology. Retrieved April 10, 2011 from http://ideas.repec.org/p/mit/sloanp/3526.html.

Smit, H., & Trigeorgis, L. (2009). Valuing infrastructure investment: An option game approach. *California Management Review, 51*(2), 79–100.

Spínola, M. (2009). *An essential guide to possibilities and risks of cloud computing.* Retrieved April 10, 2011, from http://www.mariaspinola. com/cloud-computing/.

UNU-IIST-SP. (2008). *15th UNeGov.net school on foundations of electronic governance.* Retrieved April 11, 2011, from http://www.egov. iist.unu.edu/.

Whitehouse. (2011). *Office of e-government & information technology.* Retrieved March 26, 2011, from http://www.whitehouse.gov/omb/e-gov/.

Chapter 21

Addressing the U.S. Federal Government Financial Crisis:
A Case for a U.S. Department of Defense Enterprise Architecture–Based Approach

William S. Boddie[1]

National Defense University iCollege, USA

ABSTRACT

The United States (U.S.) Federal Government is in an extreme financial crisis. The U.S. national debt is $14T and the national deficit is $1.3T. The U.S. Government seeks to improve government-wide performance, reduce operating costs, reduce the national debt, and reduce the national deficit. If the U.S. Government continues its current enterprise management approach, the national debt and national deficit could become greater and the Government could default on its debt. The DoD institutionalized a Business Mission Area Enterprise Architecture (EA) and improved performance and reduced operating costs. Leaders in the DoD leveraged an EA-based approach to improve department-wide performance and reduce costs in selected instances. This chapter proposes that the DoD institutionalize an EA-based approach to improve department-wide performance, reduce operating costs, reduce the national debt, and reduce the national deficit.

"As President Obama has said, our growing national debt, if not addressed, will imperil our prosperity, hurt our credibility and influence around the world, and ultimately put our national security at risk. As part of the nation's efforts to get its finances in order, defense spending will be—and i believe it must be—part of the solution."

Leon E. Panetta, Secretary, U.S. Department of Defense, August 3, 2011

DOI: 10.4018/978-1-4666-1824-4.ch021

INTRODUCTION

This chapter examines the current United States (U.S.) Federal Government financial crisis. The chapter reviews the current and anticipated impact of the crisis on the Government. The chapter examines the U.S. Department of Defense (DoD) and explores the impact of DoD operations and initiatives on the national debt and national deficit. The chapter proposes that the DoD institutionalize an EA-based approach to improve performance, reduce operating costs, reduce the U.S. national debt, and reduce the national deficit.

Although EA is rooted in Information Technology (IT) and IT-related areas in U.S. Government organizations, the concepts and principles of EA are not exclusive to IT and/or IT-related activities. The EA concepts and principles are applicable to the entire enterprise. Additionally, although EA has applicability to electronic government (e-Government) operations, EA is not limited exclusively to e-Government operations. The EA concepts and principles are applicable to the whole of government. Further, although the U.S. DoD implemented an EA for its business mission area and improved performance outcomes and reduced costs, the DoD could significantly improve performance, reduce operating costs, reduce the U.S. national debt, and reduce the national deficit by institutionalizing an EA-based approach for its department-wide enterprise management.

BACKGROUND

The U.S. national debt is approximately $14T. The national debt is the amount the U.S. Government owes to others including "individuals, corporations, state or local governments, foreign governments, and other entities outside the United States Government" (US Department of Treasury, 2011). The U.S. national deficit for Fiscal Year (FY) 2011 is projected to be $1.3T. The national deficit is "the fiscal year difference between what the United States Government (Government) takes in from taxes and other revenues, called receipts, and the amount of money the Government spends, called outlays. The items included in the deficit are considered either on-budget or off-budget" (US Department of Treasury, 2011).

Government debt has been a fact of the U.S. since the birth of the country. The U.S. incurred a national debt of $75M during the Revolutionary War. Alexander Hamilton, in the First Report of the Public Credit, in 1790, stated:

The United States debt, foreign and domestic, was the price of liberty. The faith of America has been repeatedly pledged for it... Among ourselves, the most enlightened friends of good government are those whose expectations of prompt payment are the highest. To justify and preserve their confidence; to promote the increasing respectability of the American name; to answer the calls of justice; to restore landed property to its due value; to furnish new resources, both to agriculture and commerce; to cement more closely the Union of the States; to add to their security against foreign attack; to establish public order on the basis of an upright and liberal policy; these are the great and invaluable ends to be secured by a proper and adequate provision, at the present period, for the support of public credit (Hamilton as cited in U.S. Bureau of Public Debt, Our History).

Except for a brief period in 1835, the U.S. national debt grew continually to its current level. Following the American Civil War the national debt was $2.7B. Following WWI the debt was $22B. Following WWII the debt was $260B. Between 1980 and 1990, the debt grew to more than triple its amount. By the end of FY 2008, the debt had grown to over $10T, more than 10 times the 1980 level. Several U.S. Presidents attempted to address the national debt.

U.S. President Ronald Reagan declared the national debt to be one of his key presidential initiatives. In his first presidential inaugural address Reagan stated:

For decades, we have piled deficit upon deficit, mortgaging our future and our children's future for the temporary convenience of the present.... You and I, as individuals, can, by borrowing, live beyond our means, but for only a limited period of time. Why, then, should we think that collectively, as a nation, we are not bound by that same limitation? (CNN, 2011, Ronald Reagan's First Inaugural Address).

U.S. President Bill Clinton led the U.S. to greater fiscal responsibility and, in 1998, presented to the U.S. Congress the first balanced budget since 1969 (Bureau of Public Debt, 2011). However, the terrorist attacks of September 11, 2001 adversely impacted the economic growth the U.S. experienced during the Clinton years. "To counter the effects of the economic slowdown and the increased expenditures on national security that followed the attacks, the new president, George W. Bush instituted tax cuts and refunds, but the deficit grew, and with it, the national debt" (Bureau of Public Debt, 2011).

The U.S. national debt was $10.6T when President Barack Obama was inaugurated in January, 2009 (CBS, 2011). As of this writing, the debt is approximately $14T and the national deficit is approximately $1.3T. According to CBS News (2010), the U.S. last had a balanced federal budget from 1998 to 2001. The ever-growing U.S. national debt and national deficit has produced an extreme sense of urgency throughout the nation. If the U.S. Government continues its current enterprise management approach, the Government could become bankrupt. U.S. Federal Government elected, appointed, and career officials are extremely concerned about improving Government performance, reducing operating costs, reducing the national debt, and reducing the national deficit.

AN EXTREME SENSE OF URGENCY TO IMPROVE U.S. FEDERAL GOVERNMENT PERFORMANCE, REDUCE OPERATING COSTS, REDUCE THE NATIONAL DEBT, AND REDUCE THE NATIONAL DEFICIT

The extreme sense of urgency to improve performance, reduce operating costs, reduce the national debt, and reduce the national deficit resonates across the U.S. Government including the U.S. Congress, U.S. President, Congressional Budget Office, the Office of Management and budget, and

the Department of Defense. As one significant response to the extreme sense of urgency, the U.S. Congress passed, and the U.S. President Barack Obama, signed into law, the Budget Control Act of 2011, on August 2, 2011. This Act, among various requirements, established U.S. Federal Government discretionary spending controls for fiscal years (FY) 2012 – 2021. The Act imposed a "cap on appropriations of new discretionary budget authority that start at $1,043 billion in 2012 and reach $1,234 billion in 2021" (US Congress, 2011, Section 101). The discretionary spending controls are not applicable to the funding for the current wars in Afghanistan and Iraq, for overseas contingency operations, or for national security funding appropriations. The national security funding appropriations categories include funding for the Department of Defense, Department of Homeland Security, Department of Veterans Affairs, National Nuclear Security Administration, and the Intelligence Community (Section 101).

The Congressional Budget Office (CBO, 2011) estimated the impact of the Budget Control Act of 2011. The CBO estimated that the caps on discretionary spending would reduce budget deficits by $917 billion between 2012 and 2021 (CBO, 2011, p. 1). Additionally, the CBO reported that automatic reductions in spending authority that would occur in the absence of the act "would reduce deficits by at least $1.2 trillion over the 10-year period. Therefore, the deficit reduction stemming from this legislation would total at least $2.1 trillion over the 2012 – 2021 period" (p. 1). The passage of this Act is a significant action taken by U.S. elected leaders and has the potential to significantly reduce the national debt and to reduce the national deficit. However, as discussed earlier, the Department of Defense's spending authority was specifically excluded from the spending caps mandated in this Act. As another example of the extreme sense of urgency felt by U.S. elected leaders, U.S. President Obama issued an executive order to improve U.S. Federal Government performance, reduce operating costs, reduce the national debt, and reduce the national deficit.

U.S. President Barack Obama signed into law the Executive Order for Delivering an Efficient, Effective, and Accountable Government on June 13, 2011 (US White House, 2011a). This Order is designed to identify Government reforms necessary to "eliminate wasteful, duplicative, or otherwise inefficient programs" (Section 1). The Order also directed the Chief Financial Officers at all Federal Government departments and agencies to deliver a combined $2.1B in administrative cost savings identified in the Fiscal Year 2012 (Section 2). Although this Order focused on administrative savings for FY 2012, the Order reinforced the extreme sense of urgency for U.S. Federal Government departments and agencies to improve performance, reduce operating costs, reduce the national debt, and reduce the national deficit. The CBO reported the projected FY 2011 U.S. Federal Government budget to be $1.3 trillion (CBO, 2011a). The CBO reported this budget deficit to be the "third-largest shortfall in the past 65 years (exceeded only by the deficits of the preceding two years)" (Summary). Elected U.S. officials have taken numerous actions, including the examples cited in this chapter and others not included to help improve U.S. Federal Government performance, reduce government operating costs, reduce the national debt, and reduce the national deficit. The Office of Management and Budget issued a Federal Government-wide memorandum to achieve these goals.

The Office of Management and Budget (OMB) issued a memorandum in August, 2011, regarding Fiscal Year 2013 Budget Guidance. This memorandum, OMB M-11-30, directed Federal Government departments and agencies to "provide options to support the President's commitment to cut waste and reorder priorities to achieve deficit reduction while investing in those areas critical to job creation and economic growth" (OMB, 2011, p. 1). OMB M-11-30 also directed that, "Unless your agency has been given explicit direction otherwise by OMB, your overall agency request for 2013 should be at least 5 percent below your 2011 enacted discretionary appropriation" (p. 1). OMB M-11-30 further directed that department and agency "2013 budget submission should also identify additional discretionary funding reductions that would bring your request to a level that is at least 10 percent below your 2011 enacted discretionary appropriation" (p. 1). Senior leaders in the DoD understood this extreme sense of urgency and initiated actions to improve performance, reduce operating costs, reduce the national debt, and reduce the national deficit.

Department of Defense Secretary Leon Panetta emphasized to DoD personnel (DoD, 2011) in August, 2011, that the DoD must be part of the solution to help reduce the national debt and reduce the national deficit. In his second month as the Secretary, Secretary Panetta stated:

The reductions in defense spending that will take place as a result of the debt ceiling agreement reached by Congress and the President are in line with what this Department's civilian and military leaders were anticipating, and I believe we can implement these reductions while maintaining the excellence of our military. But to do that, spending choices must be based on sound strategy and policy (para. 3).

Secretary Panetta stated the department must make spending choices "based on sound strategy and policy" (para. 3). Secretary Panetta further stated:

We are asking ourselves: What are the essential missions our military must do to protect America and our way of life? What are the risks of the strategic choices we make? And what are the financial costs? Achieving savings based on sound national security policy will serve our nation's interests, and will also prove more enforceable and sustainable over the long-term (para. 4).

In addition to Secretary Panetta, other senior leaders throughout the DoD acknowledged the extreme sense of urgency to improve performance, reduce operating costs, reduce the national debt, and reduce the national deficit.

Leaders in the U.S. Air Force understood the extreme sense of urgency and initiated actions to respond to the urgency. Air Force Chief of Staff General Norton Schwartz emphasized the urgency in his response to OMB's M-11-30 (Fiscal Year 2013 Budget Guidance). General Schwartz stated, in August, 2011, regarding the expected FY 2013 budget levels, "it requires choices, serious choices, and painful choices in some cases. The approach that we have taken is to preserve the readiness of our Air Force as a prime imperative - that whatever size we end up, that we are going to be a ready, well-trained, highly motivated and supremely capable force" (para. 3). As another example of the actions Air Force senior leaders took to address the extreme sense of urgency, Lieutenant General Darrell Jones, Air Force Deputy Chief of Staff for Manpower, Personnel, and Services, announced a civilian hiring freeze for the Air Force on August 9, 2011. The Air Force seeks to reduce its authorization of 146,000 full-time permanent civilians by approximately 4,000 (Government Executive, 2011, para. 2). Regarding the hiring freeze General Jones stated, "We are mindful of the potential impacts of budget constraints on our civilian force and their families, which is why we are seeking to reduce the need for involuntary measures" (para. 2). Senior Air Force Leaders recognized this extreme sense of urgency to improve Air Force performance and to reduce Air Force operating costs. Senior leaders throughout the U.S. Army felt this same extreme sense of urgency.

Responding to the extreme sense of urgency Department of the Army Secretary John McHugh created the Institutional Army Transformation Commission in August, 2011. The purpose of the commission was to transform the Army's "massive bureaucracy into a more agile and cost-effective organization" (National Journal, 2011, para. 1). McHugh, as cited in the National Journal, stated the commission would build on the work of a short-term task force he had earlier created. The earlier task force was established to:

root out overlap and redundancies in research and development, review temporary organizations and task forces to see if they are still needed, consolidate and streamline the requirements process, reform installations management, optimize Army acquisitions, and make changes in human capital management (para. 3).

However, McHugh recognized that large-scale institutional change can require years. McHugh commissioned the commission to function for three years to "implement changes already identified by the task force and identify new opportunities for cost savings" (para. 4). McHugh acknowledged the need for the Army to transform and stated, "We're not just asking people to change the way they budget," McHugh said. "We're asking them to change the way they think" (para. 5). In addition to seeking to change how Army employees think the U.S. Army plans to reduce its force by more than 8,700 civilians in FY 2012 to improve performance and reduce operating costs.

Assistant Secretary of the Army for Manpower and Reserve Affairs Thomas Lamont announced in July, 2011, that the reduction in employees was needed to meet President Obama's FY 2012 budget and to fulfill policies enacted earlier in 2012 by former Secretary Gates. Lamont stated:

We are in a very challenging fiscal environment and understand the impact these cuts will have on our civilians and their families," said Thomas R. Lamont, assistant secretary of the Army for manpower and reserve affairs. "Tough choices have to be made, but we'll make them in a thoughtful and deliberate manner that best supports the Army's mission" (Government Executive, 2011c, para. 3).

In another example of responding to the extreme sense of urgency, the U.S. Army Chief Information Officer (CIO) Lieutenant General Jeffrey Sorenson imposed a moratorium on new computer system server purchases Army-wide in August, 2011. The Army CIO issued this moratorium to stop "the proliferation of single-purpose physical servers while the Army begins consolidating data centers and creating compute clouds in select data centers" (InformationWeek, 2011, para. 2). The Army seeks to improve its information technology performance and reduce its IT operating costs. As cited in InformationWeek, "The Army wants to exert control over server deployments as it prepares to consolidate data centers and, in the process, convert designated data centers into cloud computing environments that provide shared services across its operations" (para. 3). The Army stated these moves are "consistent with the Obama administration policy requiring federal agencies to devise data center consolidation plans and encouraging the use of cloud computing as a potentially cheaper and more efficient way of providing IT services to government employees" (para. 4). Senior leaders in the U.S. Army, as with the U.S. Air Force, recognized the extreme sense of urgency to improve performance, reduce operating costs, and reduce the national debt, and reduce the national deficit. The extreme sense of urgency to improve performance and reduce operating costs did not escape senior leaders in the U.S. Department of the Navy.

Department of the Navy (DON) Chief Information Officer (CIO) Terry Halvorsen issued a memorandum in July, 2011, that directed the U.S. Navy and the U.S. Marine Corps to designate an Information Technology Expenditure Approval Authority (ITEAA) (Department of the Navy, 2011). The memorandum stated:

Under the Department of the Navy's (DON) current methods of operation, decentralized authority to initiate, develop and sustain IT projects enables DON commands and organizations to use Enterprise resources to develop or procure capabilities that tend to sub-optimize the Enterprise. Duplicative capabilities and projects that are not aligned with DON IT goals and objectives are not only inefficient uses of our dwindling resources; they render us less operationally effective by hampering interoperability, information sharing and security (para. 1).

The DON CIO memorandum stated that the ITEAA was needed to promote DON IT effectiveness and efficiency. The DON CIO memorandum further stated the ITEAA would be responsible to ensure that all IT projects undertaken by the Navy and Marine Corps were integral parts of rationalized Service portfolios, aligned with DON IT goals and conform to the DON and Department of Defense enterprise architectures. The DON CIO emphasized the extreme sense of urgency regarding the situation and the memorandum. The DON CIO further emphasized this sense of urgency regarding purchasing software licenses from Microsoft.

DON CIO Halvorsen envisioned that the DoD could drive economies of scale by negotiating a single license for Microsoft software products. Halvorsen believed the DoD to be one of the largest enterprises in the world and believed leveraging a single-license approach would enable the department to realize significant cost savings. Halvorsen stated, as cited in NextGov (2011), "Considering the Navy has more than 60 Microsoft contract vehicles, enterprise licenses will not only drive down purchase prices, but also will reduce the costs of contract administration" (para. 3). Halvorsen understood the extreme sense of urgency to improve DON performance and reduce operating costs. The DoD CIO also understood and emphasized this sense of urgency.

Department of Defense CIO Terry Takai, appointed to the position in October 2010, viewed the DoD from an enterprise perspective and advanced strategies from an enterprise perspective. Takai stated, as cited in Information Week (2011a), "There's a tremendous opportunity to look at the DOD as an enterprise," she said. "It's not something we've done very well, but the technology is pushing us to go there. While we've talked about the net-centric environment before this, now we're there" (para. 3). Takai's comments emphasized the criticality of viewing DoD programs, strategies, and related investments from an enterprise perspective rather than from a parochial military service, organization, or agency view. In addition to the U.S. President, the U.S. Congress, the CBO, OMB, and senior leaders in the DoD acknowledging the extreme sense of urgency, the U.S. Government Accountability Office published several reports warning of the impending national financial crisis.

U.S. Government Accountability Office Reports of the Impending U.S. Federal Government Financial Crisis

There exists an extreme sense of urgency for the U.S. Federal Government to improve performance, reduce operating costs, reduce the national debt, and reduce the national deficit. The Government Accountability Office (GAO), since 2005, published several reports warning of the impending financial crisis as a result of the growing national debt and growing national deficit. In a 2005 report the GAO (2005, p. 11) reported that the U.S. faced large and growing structural deficits and that tough choices would be needed be made to address this crisis. The GAO concluded that the U.S. needed a multi-faceted approach to close the long-term fiscal gap that included reassessing and revising how the government does business. The GAO identified national defense operations and management as an area that should be reexamined to help close the long-term fiscal gap.

The GAO, in a 2006 report, stated, "The federal government is on a "burning platform," and the status quo way of doing business is unacceptable for a variety of reasons, including," among other reasons, "Numerous government performance/accountability and high risk challenges" and "Outdated federal organizational structures, policies, and practices" (p. 2). Included in the GAO's recommendations to address this crisis were to expand scrutiny of all proposed new programs, policies, and activities and strengthen internal agency structure and processes. The GAO published numerous similar reports since 2007.

The GAO published a seminal report in 2011 that identified numerous opportunities for the Government to realize greater operating efficiency, reduce potential duplication in Government programs, save tax dollars, and increase revenue. This was the first of the GAO's congressionally mandated annual reports in which the GAO is required to "identify federal programs, agencies, offices, and initiatives, either within departments or governmentwide, which have duplicative goals or activities" (GAO, 2011, p. 1). The GAO stated, "This work will inform government policymakers as they address the rapidly building fiscal pressures facing our national government" (p. 1). The GAO's objectives in the report were to "(1) identify federal programs or functional areas where unnecessary duplication, overlap, or fragmentation exists, the actions needed to address such conditions, and the potential financial and other benefits of doing so; and (2) highlight other opportunities for potential cost savings or enhanced revenues" (p. 1).

In its 2011 report, the GAO identified 81 areas where Government organizations and programs could realize greater operating efficiency, reduce potential duplication in Government programs, save tax dollars, and increase revenue. More specifically, the GAO identified "34 areas where agencies, offices, or initiatives have similar or overlapping objectives or provide similar services to the same populations; or where government missions are fragmented across multiple agencies or programs" (p. 1). The GAO stated:

These areas span a range of government missions: agriculture, defense, economic development, energy, general government, health, homeland security, international affairs, and social services. Within and across these missions, this report touches on hundreds of federal programs, affecting virtually all major federal departments and agencies (p. 2).

Additionally, the GAO identified 47 additional areas, beyond the 34 areas, for the U.S. Congress and/or the Government to take action that could either "reduce the cost of government operations or enhance revenue collections for the Treasury. These costs-savings and revenue opportunities also span a wide range of federal government agencies and mission areas" (p. 2).

The GAO 2011 report included, in the 34 specific areas, six in which the DoD was exclusively identified as involving similar or overlapping objectives, providing similar services to the same populations, and/or fragmented department missions. These specific areas included medical service delivery, warfighter urgent needs, counter-improvised explosive device efforts, intelligence, surveillance, and reconnaissance capabilities, tactical wheeled vehicles, pre-positioning programs, and business systems modernization. Included in the 47 additional areas where cost-savings and/or revenue enhancement options might exist were six areas for which the DoD was identified as the owner. These areas included overseas military presence, military personnel costs, weapons systems acquisition programs, DoD spare parts programs, sustaining weapon systems, and corrosion prevention. The GAO was required to identify actions to address the opportunities it identified. The GAO, in its 2011 report, identified enterprise architecture as a key government-wide approach to identify potential capability overlap and duplications. The GAO did not identify any additional government-wide approach that could identify potential capability overlap and duplications and

that could be leveraged to improve performance, reduce operating costs, reduce the national debt, and reduce the national deficit.

ENTERPRISE ARCHITECTURE AS A STRATEGIC ORGANIZATIONAL PERFORMANCE ENABLER

Senior leaders in the U.S. Federal Government, including the U.S. Congress, President Obama, the Secretary of Defense, and senior leaders throughout the DoD acknowledged the extreme sense of urgency to improve U.S. Federal Government performance, reduce operating costs, reduce the national debt, and reduce the national deficit. These leaders enacted legislation, issued executive orders, implemented policies, issued memoranda, and initiated actions to realize these goals. However, the Department of Defense lacks an institutionalized approach for effective department-wide enterprise management. This chapter proposes that the DoD institutionalize an enterprise architecture-based approach to understand its current performance capabilities, to envision its desired performance capabilities, to articulate strategies and investments to advance toward its desired performance capabilities, and to understand the costs and benefits related to these strategies and expected investments. Institutionalizing a department-wide enterprise architecture-based approach could enable the department to improve performance, reduce costs, reduce the U.S. national debt, and reduce the national deficit.

Enterprise Architecture (EA) has been accepted in the U.S. Government for over a decade as an effective approach to enable government organizations to meet strategic performance goals and/or to transform. The U.S. Congress, in 1996, defined an Information Technology (IT) architecture as "an integrated framework for evolving or maintaining existing information technology or acquiring new information technology to achieve

501

the agency's strategic goals and information resources management goals" (p. 686). The U.S. Congress, in 2002, defined EA as "a strategic information asset base, which defines the mission; the information necessary to perform the mission; the technologies necessary to perform the mission; and the transitional processes for implementing new technologies in response to changing mission needs. An EA includes a baseline architecture, a target architecture; and a sequencing plan" (p. 4).

The U.S. Chief Information Officer's Council defined EA as "a strategic information asset base, which defines the mission, the information necessary to perform the mission and the technologies necessary to perform the mission, and the transitional processes for implementing new technologies in response to the changing mission needs. An enterprise architecture includes a baseline architecture, target architecture, and a sequencing plan" (2001, p. 5). OMB advanced EA as a critical management approach to enable Government organizations to realize strategic goals since 1996. OMB (2007) defined EA a "management practice for aligning resources to improve business performance and help agencies better execute their core missions. An EA describes the current and future state of the agency, and lays out a plan for transitioning from the current state to the desired future state" (p. A-1).

The U.S. GAO has been a very strong proponent of EA as a critical management approach to enable government organizations to transform. As of this writing, the GAO published over 240 reports regarding U.S. government EA programs since 1998. The GAO (2011) defined EA as "a modernization blueprint that is used by organizations to describe their current state and a desired future state and to leverage information technology (IT) to transform business and mission operations" (p. 62). The GAO identified EA as the key mechanism to identify potential capability duplication and overlap. Thus, enterprise architecture is the

single enterprise management approach that can enable an enterprise to effectively transform.

An enterprise is "an organization (or cross organizational entity) supporting a defined business scope and mission. An enterprise includes interdependent resources (people, organizations, and technology) who must coordinate their functions and share information in support of a common mission (or set of related missions)" (CIO Council, 2001, p. 5). The CIO Council further stated, "Although the term *enterprise* is defined in terms of an organization, it must be understood that in many cases, the enterprise may transcend established organizational boundaries (e.g., trade, grant management, financial management, logistics)" (p. 5). The U.S. DoD defined enterprise as "any collection of organizations that has a common set of goals and/or a single bottom line. An enterprise, by that definition, can encompass a Military Department, DoD as a whole, a division within an organization, an organization in a single location, or a chain of geographically distant organizations linked by a common management or purpose" (DoD, 2009, p. 8). The DoD institutionalized an EA-based approach for its business mission area enterprise management and improved performance and reduced operating costs. Institutionalizing an EA-based approach for its department-wide enterprise management could enable the DoD to improve performance, reduce operating costs, reduce the national debt, and reduce the national deficit.

THE U.S. DEPARTMENT OF DEFENSE BUSINESS MISSION AREA: ENTERPRISE ARCHITECTURE

The Department of Defense improved performance and reduced operating costs for its business mission area by institutionalizing an EA-based approach. Title 10 of the U.S. Code, Section 2222,

National Defense Authorization Act for FY 2005 (US Congress, 2005), required the DoD to develop an EA for its business systems area. Specifically, the Act stated:

(c) Enterprise Architecture for Defense Business Systems—not later than September 30, 2005, the Secretary of Defense, acting through the Defense Business Systems Management Committee, shall develop—(1) an enterprise architecture to cover all defense business systems, and the functions and activities supported by defense business systems, which shall be sufficiently defined to effectively guide, constrain, and permit implementation of interoperable defense business system solutions and consistent with the policies and procedures established by the Director of the Office of Management and Budget, and (2) a transition plan for implementing the enterprise architecture for defense business systems (Section 2222).

The National Defense Authorization Act for FY 2005 also established the DoD Business Transformation Agency (BTA). The BTA's mission is to "guide the transformation of business operations throughout the Department of Defense and to deliver Enterprise-level capabilities that align to warfighter needs" (BTA, 2011). The BTA delivered its initial Business Enterprise Architecture (BEA) to the U.S. Congress in 2006. The BEA is "the enterprise architecture for the DoD BMA and reflects the DoD business transformation priorities; the business capabilities required to support those priorities; and the combinations of enterprise systems and initiatives that enable those capabilities" (BTA, 2011a). The BTA purpose is to:

Provide a blueprint for DoD business transformation that helps ensure the right capabilities, resources and materiel are rapidly delivered to our warfighters—what they need, where they need it, when they need it, anywhere in the world. The BEA guides and constrains implementation of interoperable defense business system solutions

as required by the National Defense Authorization Act (NDAA). It also guides Information Technology (IT) investment management to align with strategic business capabilities as required by the Clinger-Cohen Act, and supporting Office of Management and Budget (OMB) and Government Accountability Office (GAO) policies (BTA, 2011a).

The BTA delivered BEA v8.0 to the U.S. Congress in 2011. The BEA v8.0 includes descriptions of the 15 business mission area End-to-End (E2E) processes. Table 1 identifies the 15 E2Es defined within the BEA (BTA, 2011a).

Although the DoD improved its business mission area performance and reduced operating costs by institutionalizing an EA-based approach, the department is greater than the confines of the business mission area. In addition to improving business mission area performance and reducing costs, the DoD improved performance and reduced operating costs in selected instances in other mission areas by leveraging an EA-based approach.

The U.S. Department of Defense's Selected Use of an Enterprise Architecture-Based Approach to Improve Performance and Reduce Costs

The DoD used an EA-based approach to improve department-wide performance and reduce operating in selected instances. Leveraging an EA-based approach enabled the DoD to understand its current performance capability, envision improved performance, and articulate strategies to improve performance. These three fundamental considerations are the essence of leveraging an EA-based approach to improve enterprise performance.

In 2010, former Department of Defense Secretary Robert Gates sought to realize improved performance and cost savings in the department's business operations. Secretary Gates stated, "To sustain necessary investment levels for Depart-

Table 1. Business enterprise architecture end-to-end processes

Acquire-to-Retire (A2R)	Market-to-Prospect (M2P)
Budget-to-Report (B2R)	Order-to-Cash (O2C)
Concept-to-Product (C2P)	Plan-to-Stock – Inventory Management (P2S)
Cost Management (CM)	Proposal-to-Reward (P2R)
Deployment-to-Redeployment/ Retrograde (D2RR)	Procure-to-Pay (P2P)
Environmental Liabilities (EL)	Prospect-to-Order (P2O)
Hire-to-Retire (H2R)	Service Request-to-Resolution (SR2R)
Service-to-Satisfaction (S2S)	

ment of Defense mission-essential activities, we must significantly improve the effectiveness and efficiency of our business operations. Doing so will increase funding available for our mission functions from efficiency savings in overhead, support and non-mission areas" (DoD, Personal Communication, June 4, 2010, p. 1). The DoD established a total cost savings expectation of $100B from FY 2012 through FY 2016.

Secretary Gates announced strategies to improve business operations performance and reduce operating costs and announced an expected cost savings of $150B in business operations efficiencies. The DoD announced it would realize these savings and gain the efficiencies by "reducing overhead costs, improving business practices and culling excess or troubled programs" (DoD, 2011, p. 2). The U.S. Navy used an EA-based approach and proposed a cost savings of more than $35B over five years through various strategies to gain business operations efficiencies. The Navy proposed the cost savings after understanding its current business operations performance capabilities, envisioning improved performance, and identifying strategies that would enable the Navy to improve performance (DoD, 2011, p. 2).

The U.S. Air Force used an EA-based approach (understanding its current business operations performance, envisioning improved performance, and articulating strategies to improve performance) and concluded it could save over $34B over five years (DoD, 2011, p. 3). The U.S. Army

used an EA-based approach and proposed costs savings of $29B (DoD, 2011, p. 3). Secretary Gates, in announcing these expected cost savings and efficiency gains stated, "This Department simply cannot risk continuing down the same path – where our investment priorities, bureaucratic habits, and lax attitudes towards costs are increasingly divorced from the real threats of today, the growing perils of tomorrow, and the nation's grim financial outlook" (DoD, 2011). Although Secretary Gates might not have explicitly leveraged a DoD business operations EA it is clear that Secretary Gates leveraged an EA-based approach to improve business operations performance and reduce operating costs.

The military services demonstrated using an EA-based approach to improve enterprise performance. Secretary Gates further stated:

Meeting real-world requirements. Doing right by our people. Reducing excess. Being more efficient. Squeezing costs. Setting priorities and sticking to them. Making tough choices. These are all things that we should do as a Department and as a military regardless of the time and circumstance. But they are more important than ever at a time of extreme fiscal duress, when budget pressures and scrutiny fall on all areas of government, including defense (DoD, 2011, p. 5).

In these selected instances, the DoD used an EA-based approach to improve business operations performance and reduce costs. Secretary Gates stated, "These times demand that all of our nation's leaders rise above the politics and parochialism that have too often plagued considerations of our nation's defense – whether from inside the Pentagon, from industry and interest groups, and from one end of Pennsylvania Avenue to the other" (p. 5). In addition to improving business operations performance and reducing operating costs by using an EA-based approach, Secretary Gates used an EA-based approach in other selected instances.

Secretary Gates used an EA-based approach to guide his termination of the U.S. Marine Corps Expeditionary Fighting Vehicle (EFV) Program. The EFV was designed to be an armored, high-speed amphibious assault weapon that had been planned since the 1980s. Secretary Gates cancelled the program as the $14B program experienced continued delays and cost increases, (Government Executive, 2011a). Secretary Gates noted that the DoD could not afford a program that would "essentially swallow the entire Marine vehicle budget" (Government Executive, 2011a, para. 3). Secretary Gates used an EA-based approach to this decision. He understood the current U.S. Marine Corps enterprise performance capability, envisioned improved performance, and articulated a strategy to realize improved performance.

Secretary Gates used an EA-based approach to improve department-wide performance when he proposed the dis-establishment of the U.S. Joint Forces Command (JFCOM). The JFCOM "provides mission-ready joint-capable forces and supports the development and integration of joint, interagency, and multinational capabilities to meet the present and future operational needs of the joint force" (JFCOM, 2011, Command Mission and Strategic Goals). The JFCOM is headquartered in Norfolk, VA, has approximately 5,800 military members, employs approximately 3,900 civilians, and has military and civilians located in Virginia, Nevada, and Florida (Government Executive, 2011b). Secretary Gates announced the proposed

disestablishment of the JFCOM after reviewing the department's current performance capability and envisioning improved performance. President Barack Obama approved the Secretary's recommendation and the JFCOM will be disestablished on September 30, 2012 (US White House, 2011).

Secretary Gates again used an EA-based approach to inform the planned closures of the Business Transformation Agency and the Office of the Assistant Secretary of Defense for Networks and Information Integration (NII) (DoD, 2010). Secretary Gates determined that these two organizations delivered unnecessarily duplicative capabilities that other existing DoD organizations could deliver. Secretary Gates concluded that the DoD could improve performance and reduce costs by closing these two organizations. Secretary Gates continued to demonstrate that the DoD could improve performance and reduce costs by leveraging an EA-based approach. Secretary Gates led the DoD to improved department-wide performance and reduced costs in many instances not specifically discussed in this chapter including but not limited to his decision to terminate the department's plan to develop an alternative engine for the F-35 Joint Strike Fighter aircraft, his decision regarding replacing U.S. Air Force refueling tankers, and his decision regarding modernizing the aging U.S. Navy Ohio-class ballistic missile submarine. Secretary Gates leveraged the EA-based construct of understanding the DoD current performance capability, envisioning improved performance, and articulating strategies to improve performance in these instances. Although the DoD institutionalized an EA-based approach to improve business mission area performance, the DoD has yet to institutionalize a department-wide EA-based approach to improve performance, reduce costs, reduce the national debt, and reduce the national deficit. The criticality of institutionalizing an EA-based approach to improve performance and reduce operating costs was emphasized in a separate GAO 2011 report regarding the U.S. military departments' enterprise architecture management maturity.

The GAO reported (2011a) that the military departments "have much to before their [EA management] efforts can be considered mature" (p. 1). The GAO reported that, based on the 59 elements in its Enterprise Architecture Management Maturity Framework, v2.0, that the Air Force had "fully satisfied 20 percent, partially satisfied 47 percent, and not satisfied 32 percent of GAO's framework elements" (p. 1); that the Army had "fully satisfied 12 percent and partially satisfied 42 percent of the elements, with the remaining 46 percent not satisfied" (p. 1); and that the Department of the Navy had "satisfied 27 percent, partially satisfied 41 percent, and had not satisfied 32 percent of the framework elements" (p. 1). The GAO recommended that the military departments develop plans to fully satisfy the elements of GAO's framework or provide the U.S. Congress their rationale for not developing such plans.

This chapter proposes that the DoD institutionalize a department-wide EA-based approach to improve performance, reduce costs, reduce the national debt, and reduce the national deficit. This chapter also proposes that the DoD leverage the Department of Defense Enterprise Management Integrated Framework (proposed) to improve performance and reduce operating costs.

The DoD Enterprise Management Integrated Framework (Proposed)

This chapter proposes that the DoD leverage the DoD Enterprise Management Integrated Framework (proposed) to improve performance, reduce costs, reduce the national debt, and reduce the national deficit. Figure 1, DoD Enterprise Management Integrated Framework (proposed), depicts an EA-based approach, within the construct of key integrated enterprise management functions, that the DoD could use to improve performance, reduce costs, reduce the national debt, and reduce the national deficit.

Key enterprise management functions include leadership, governance, strategic planning, enterprise architecture, portfolio management, and capital planning and investment control. These functions do not exist in isolation and should be performed in an integrated manner within the DoD enterprise management capability. As depicted in the DoD Enterprise Management Integrated Framework (proposed) the leader is accountable to establish a vision of the future that is shared by enterprise members. The leader is also accountable to lead with integrity, which means doing the right thing. Further, the leader is accountable for considering the enterprise goals and objectives rather than focusing exclusively on sub-enterprise and/or parochial interests. Secretary Gates consistently demonstrated this leadership orientation. For example, Secretary Gates led to the DoD to partner with the Veterans Affairs (VA) Department to develop an interoperable electronic health care records solution that supports the DoD and the VA (US Senate, 2011). Leaders in the DoD should lead similar to the orientation Secretary Gates demonstrated and should consistently lead with vision, integrity, and an enterprise focus.

Governance involves establishing the rules, roles, and responsibilities for enterprise decision-making. The governance capability is comprised of the decision-making bodies in the enterprise. For example, the Defense Business Systems Management Committee serves as the senior decision-making body for the DoD business mission area. Each DoD organization should establish a governance capability in which the senior most leaders are accountable to make enterprise decisions based on established rules, roles, and responsibilities.

DoD organizations should establish a strategic plan that provides an overarching enterprise direction and guides the enterprise activities. A strategic plan establishes "a comprehensive framework for considering organizational changes, making resource decisions, and holding key players ac-

Figure 1. DoD enterprise management integrated framework (proposed) Adapted from Boddie (2009)

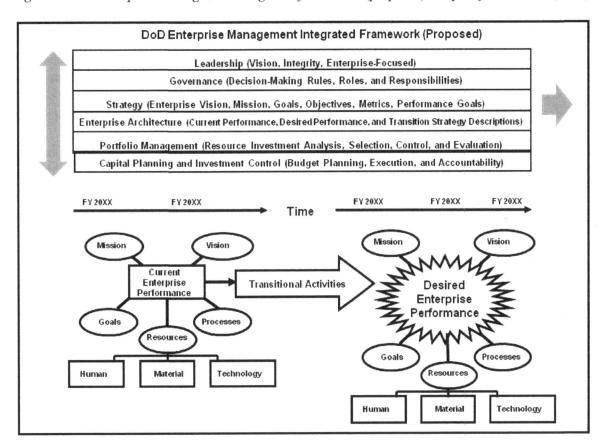

countable for achieving realize and sustainable results" (GAO, 2007, p. 15). The strategic plan should include a vision statement, mission statement, goals, objectives, performance metrics, and performance goals. Each DoD organization's major initiatives and investments should be based on the strategic plan. After establishing the strategic plan, the organization should establish an EA.

An EA describes the current performance capability, describes improved performance, and describes the strategies needed to improve performance. The DoD established an EA for its business mission area and realized improved performance and reduced costs. The DoD should institutionalize a department-wide EA-based approach to improve performance, reduce costs, reduce the national debt, and reduce the national deficit. Each DoD organization should understand its current

performance, describe improved performance, and articulate strategies to improve performance. Secretary Gates demonstrated using an EA-based approach in selected instances to improve DoD performance, reduce costs, reduce the national debt, and reduce the national deficit. The actionable EA enables the organization to make informed decisions regarding enterprise human, material, and technology resource portfolio investments.

Portfolio management is the process of understanding enterprise performance gaps, analyzing alternative solutions to close the gap, selecting an appropriate solution, implementing the solution, and evaluating the extent to which the implemented solution enabled improved performance. Enterprise portfolio assets include human, material, technology, and other resource categories. DoD organizations should describe the processes and resources supporting the enterprise and determine the extent to which the processes and resources enable the organization to meet strategic goals and objectives. If the processes and resources are insufficient to meet performance outcome goals, the organization should plan for improved processes and to acquire the resources needed to support the improved processes. Secretary Gates performed enterprise portfolio management in examples such as the dis-establishment of JFCOM, the BTA, and the NII.

DoD leaders should continually consult with organizational capital planning and investment management professionals to understand how enterprise funds can be planned and executed to support improved performance. Funding is a key fuel that drives enterprise activities. The DoD's management of its enterprise finances has been on the GAO's high-risk list since 1995 and remains on this list as of this writing. The GAO reported (2011b):

Pervasive deficiencies in financial management processes, systems, and controls, and the resulting lack of data reliability, continue to impair management's ability to assess the resources needed for DOD operations; track and control costs; ensure basic accountability; anticipate future costs; measure performance; maintain funds control; and reduce the risk of loss from fraud, waste, and abuse (p. 1).

DoD operational effectiveness and efficiency is severely hampered by pervasive enterprise financial management challenges. The GAO (2011b) reported "Other business operations, including the high-risk areas of contract management, supply chain management, support infrastructure management, and weapon systems acquisition are directly impacted by the problems in financial management" (p. 5). The GAO reported that committed and sustained leadership, effective planning to correct internal control weaknesses, competent financial management workforce, accountability

and effective oversight, a well-defined enterprise architecture, and successful implementation of the enterprise resource planning systems as challenges to improved DoD financial management (p. 10). DoD leaders should partner with enterprise capital planners to integrate capital planning and effective financial management into enterprise management.

Secretary Gates used an EA-based approach to lead the DoD to improved performance. Although not specifically codified, Secretary Gates leveraged leadership, governance, strategic planning, EA, portfolio management, and capital planning and investment management to improve department-wide performance, reduce costs, reduce the national debt, and reduce the national deficit. The DoD should institutionalize the DoD Enterprise Management Integration Framework (proposed) to realize these goals. Although leveraging this framework and institutionalizing an EA-based approach can enable the DoD to improve performance, challenges exist to implementing these strategies.

Challenges to Leveraging an EA-Based Approach to Improve Performance, Reduce Costs, Reduce the National Debt, and Reduce the National Deficit

Numerous challenges exist that can constrain and limit the DoD's use of an EA-based approach to improve performance, reduce costs, reduce the national debt, and reduce the national deficit. These challenges include, but are not limited to, cultural resistance and parochialism. The DoD, as with other large organizations, is deeply steeped in a culture involving accepted behaviors and norms. The DoD population includes career government employees who might remain DoD employees from the career cradle through retirement, which can easily span 30 years or longer. The DoD also includes military members who might spend 20 years or longer in the military.

Many DoD employees and military members will need to change their behaviors and norms to leverage an EA-based approach to improve performance, reduce costs, reduce the national debt, and reduce the national deficit. To effectively address this challenge, DoD employees and military members should consider John Kotter's seminal research. To lead organizational transformation and overcome cultural challenges adversely impacting organizational transformation, Kotter (1995) offered a well-researched and systematic approach.

Kotter researched over 100 organizations regarding leading organizational transformation. Kotter developed an eight-step model that enterprise members can use to effectively lead change. Kotter found that enterprises that followed the model's eight-steps, and followed them in the prescribed order, realized the desired organizational transformational outcomes far greater than organizations that did not. Kotter's eight-steps are:

- Establish a sense of urgency
- Form a powerful guiding coalition
- Create a clear and compelling vision
- Communicate the vision
- Empower others to act on the vision
- Plan for and create short-term wins
- Consolidate improvements and create still more change
- Institutionalize new approaches

Although the author was unable to determine if Secretary Gates was aware of Kotter's Model it is clear that Secretary Gates understood Kotter's Model and the eight-steps. DoD employees and military members should carefully consider Kotter's Model to overcome cultural resistance to change.

Many DoD civilian employees and senior military members are assigned to positions for three years or less. Occasionally some of these members might seek to enhance their promotion potential by enhancing their area of responsibility, which might sub-optimize the greater department enterprise needs and goals. Additionally, some employees and military members might seek to advance parochial organizational interests, which might compromise or impede realizing enterprise goals. DoD employees and military members should consider the department's Defense Senior Leadership Development Program to address some of the challenges to institutionalizing an EA-based approach.

The U.S. Department of Defense embraced an enterprise-wide perspective for its senior leaders. The DoD implemented a Defense Senior Leadership Development Program (DSLDP) in 2009. The purpose of this program is to "provide structured learning opportunities to enable the deliberate development of a diverse cadre of senior civilian leaders with the Enterprise-wide Perspective and competencies needed to lead organizations, programs and people and achieve results in the Joint, interagency, and multi-national environments" (DoD, 2010a, p. 2). The DSLDP is the "premier Department program for senior civilians and a critical part of leadership pipeline" (p. 3). The DoD's Civilian Leader Development Framework includes six primary competencies: Leading Change, Leading People, Results Driven, Business Acumen, Building Coalitions, and Enterprise-Wide Perspective. The Enterprise-Wide Perspective involves having:

a broad point of view of the DoD mission and an understanding of individual or organizational responsibilities in relation to the larger DoD strategic priorities. The perspective is shaped by experience and education and characterized by a strategic, top-level focus on broad requirements, joint experiences, fusion of information, collaboration, and vertical and horizontal integration of information (DoD, 2010a, p. 6).

The DoD is committed to developing leaders who focus on the greater enterprise goals. Focusing on enterprise goals can enable DoD senior civilians and military members to overcome parochialism. Although using Kotter's Model to lead organizational transformation and by focusing on the enterprise can help DoD leaders overcome some challenges to institutionalizing an EA approach to improve performance and reduce costs there is no prescriptive approach than can guarantee this outcome. DoD leaders will also need to be patient, persist, and persevere to institutionalize using an EA-based approach to improve enterprise performance, reduce costs, and reduce the national debt and national deficit.

FUTURE TRENDS

This chapter proposed that the DoD institutionalize an EA-based approach to improve performance, reduce costs, reduce the national debt, and reduce the national deficit. However, the DoD is but one of 27 U.S. Government departments and agencies. Most U.S. Government departments and agencies developed EA programs that focus on IT and/or IT-related activities. As this chapter proposed that the DoD institutionalize an EA-based approach to address the national sense of extreme urgency, other Government departments and agencies should also institutionalize an EA-based approach to address this extremely urgent situation. As discussed earlier in the chapter EA is applicable to all aspects of U.S. Federal Government departments and agencies. U.S. Federal Government departments and agencies can improve performance, reduce costs, reduce the national debt, and reduce the national deficit by institutionalizing an EA-based approach to enterprise management.

CONCLUSION

The U.S. Federal Government is in an extremely urgent financial crisis. The national debt is $14T and the national deficit is $1.3T. The U.S. Federal Government might become bankrupt if it unable

to pay this debt. EA is the single enterprise management approach that can enable an enterprise to effectively transform. An EA-based approach can enable Government leaders to identify unplanned capability duplication, overlap, and mission support fragmentation. Achieving these objectives can enable these leaders to improve performance and reduce operating costs.

The DoD institutionalized an EA-based approach for its business mission area and improved performance and reduced costs. Secretary Gates leveraged an EA-based approach in selected instances to improve department performance and reduce operating costs. The DoD should institutionalize an EA-based approach to improve performance, reduce costs, reduce the national debt, and reduce the national deficit.

The DoD has significant opportunities to improve performance, reduce costs, reduce the national debt, and reduce the national deficit. The DoD has various alternatives regarding enterprise management strategies. "Insanity is doing the same thing over and over again but expecting different results." If the DoD continues its current enterprise management approach it will miss significant opportunities to improve performance and reduce operating costs. However, if the DoD institutionalizes an EA-based approach it could improve department-wide performance, reduce costs, reduce the national debt, and reduce the national deficit.

REFERENCES

Boddie, W. S. (2009). The criticality of transformational leadership to advancing United States government enterprise architecture adoption. In Saha, P. (Ed.), *Advances in Government Enterprise Architecture*. Hershey, PA: IGI Global. doi:10.4018/978-1-60566-068-4.ch006

Bureau of the Public Debt. (2011). *Our history*. Retrieved on April 9, 2011, from http://www.publicdebt.treas.gov/history/history.htm.

Business Transformation Agency. (2011a). *Mission*. Retrieved on March 10, 2011, from http://www.bta.mil/about/mission.html.

Business Transformation Agency. (2011b). *Mission*. Retrieved on March 10, 2011, from http://www.bta.mil/products/bea.html.

Cable News Network. (2011). *Ronald Reagan's first inaugural address*. Retrieved on March 15, 2011, from http://articles.cnn.com/2011-01-20/politics/reagan.inaugural_1_tax-burden-tax-system-national-history?_s=PM:POLITICS.

CBS News. (2010). *National debt up $3 trillion on Obama's watch*. Retrieved on April 3, 2011, from http://www.cbsnews.com/8301-503544_162-20019931-503544.html.

Chief Information Officers Council. (2001). *A practical guide to federal enterprise architecture, version 1.0*. Retrieved on January 10, 2011, from http://www.cio.gov/documents/bpeaguide.pdf.

Congressional Budget Office. (2011a). *Budget control act of 2011*. Retrieved on August 5, 2011, from http://cbo.gov/ftpdocs/123xx/doc12357/BudgetControlActAug1.pdf.

Congressional Budget Office. (2011b). *The budget and economic outlook: An update*. Retrieved on August 22, 2011, from http://www.cbo.gov/ftpdocs/123xx/doc12316/08-24-BudgetEconUpdate.pdf.

Department of Defense. (2010a). *DOD news briefing with Secretary Gates from the Pentagon*. Retrieved February 7, 2011, from http://www.defense.gov/transcripts/transcript.aspx?transcriptid=4669.

Department of Defense. (2010b). *Defense senior leader development program*. Retrieved on April 25, 2011, from http://www.cpms.osd.mil/ASSETS/2F792DE33C9F4D1F9E51DE66AAD5F2FB/DSLDP%20Program%20Brief%20-%20June%202010.pdf.

Department of Defense. (2011). *Meeting our fiscal and national security responsibility*. Retrieved on August 6, 2011, from http://www.defense.gov/home/features/2011/0711_message1/.

Department of the Navy. (2011a). *Department of the Navy (DON) information technology expenditure approval authorities (ITEAA)*. Retrieved on July 24, 2011, from www.doncio.navy.mil/Download.aspx?AttachID=1756.

Department of the Navy. (2011b). *Department of the Navy (DON) data center consolidation (DCC) policy guidance*. Retrieved on July 24, 2011, from http://www.doncio.navy.mil/Download.aspx?AttachID=1751.

Department of Treasury. (2011). *Frequently asked questions about the public debt*. Retrieved on April 13, 2011, from http://www.treasurydirect.gov/govt/resources/faq/faq_publicdebt.htm.

Government Executive. (2011a). *Air Force announces civilian hiring freeze*. Retrieved on August 18, 2011, from http://www.govexec.com/story_page_pf.cfm?articleid=48544&printerfriendlyvers=1.

Government Executive. (2011b). *Gates takes ax to defense programs to end culture of endless money*. Retrieved on March 15, 2011, from http://www.govexec.com/story_page_pf.cfm?articleid=46833&printerfriendlyvers=1.

Government Executive. (2011c). *Plans for closing joint forces command likely ready next month*. Retrieved on March 15, 2011, from http://www.govexec.com/story_page_pf.cfm?articleid=46859&printerfriendlyvers=1.

Government Executive. (2011d). *Army sets stage to slash 8,700 civilian jobs*. Retrieved on August 8, 2011, from http://www.govexec.com/dailyfed/0811/080511cc1.htm.

InformationWeek Government. (2011). *Army suspends server buys amid cloud plans*. Retrieved on July 18, 2011, from http://www.informationweek.com/news/government/cloud-saas/225300325.

InformationWeek Government. (2011a). *DOD CIO driving enterprise IT structure across military*. Retrieved on August 22, 2011, from http://www.informationweek.com/news/government/policy/231500294.

Kotter, J. P. (1995). Leading change: Why transformation efforts fail. *Harvard Business Review*, *73*(2), 59–67.

National Journal. (2011). *Army secretary creates commission to simplify bureaucracy*. Retrieved on August 18, 2011, from http://www.nationaljournal.com/nationalsecurity/mchugh-creates-commission-to-streamline-army-bureaucracy-20110815?mrefid=site_search.

NextGov. (2011). *Navy CIO envisions defense wide software buys*. Retrieved on August 25, 2011, from http://www.nextgov.com/site_services/print_article.php?StoryID=ng_20110823_4178.

Office of Management and Budget. (2007). *FEA practice guidance*. Retrieved on January 13, 2011, from http://www.whitehouse.gov/sites/default/files/omb/assets/fea_docs/FEA_Practice_Guidance_Nov_2007.pdf.

Office of Management and Budget. (2011a). *Fiscal year 2013 budget guidance*. Retrieved on August 21, 2011, from http://www.whitehouse.gov/sites/default/files/omb/memoranda/2011/m11-30.pdf.

Office of Management and Budget. (2011b). *Delivering an efficient, effective, and accountable government*. Retrieved on August 21, 2011, from http://www.whitehouse.gov/sites/default/files/omb/memoranda/2011/m11-31.pdf.

Schwartz, N. (2011). *Gen. Norton Schwartz*. Retrieved on September 1, 2011, http://www.defensenews.com/story.php?i=7508661&c=FEA&s=INT.

US Congress. (1996). *Public law 104-106, 110 Stat. 186*. Washington, DC: US Congress.

US Congress. (2002). *Public law 107-002*. Retrieved on February 8, 2011, from http://www.gpo.gov/fdsys/pkg/BILLS-107hr2458enr/pdf/BILLS-107hr2458enr.pdf.

US Congress. (2011). *Budget control act of 2011*. Retrieved August 11, 2011, from http://www.gpo.gov/fdsys/pkg/BILLS-112s365eah/pdf/BILLS-112s365eah.pdf.

US Government Accountability Office. (2005). *Saving our future requires tough choices today*. Retrieved on March 10, 2011, from http://www.gao.gov/cghome/hrfn20050210/hrfn20050210.pdf.

US Government Accountability Office. (2006). *Saving our future requires tough choices today*. Retrieved on March 11, 2011, from http://www.gao.gov/cghome/d061084cg.pdf.

US Government Accountability Office. (2007). *A call for stewardship: Enhancing the federal government's ability to address key fiscal and other 21st century challenges*. Retrieved on January 6, 2011, from http://www.gao.gov/new.items/d0893sp.pdf.

US Government Accountability Office. (2011a). *Opportunities to reduce potential duplication in government programs, save tax dollars, and enhance revenue*. Retrieved on March 30, 2011, from http://www.gao.gov/new.items/d11318sp.pdf.

US Government Accountability Office. (2011b). *Organizational transformation: Military departments can improve their enterprise architecture programs*. Retrieved on September 24, 2011, from http://www.gao.gov/new.items/d11902.pdf.

US Government Accountability Office. (2011c). *DOD financial management: Improved controls, processes, and systems are needed for accurate and reliable financial information.* Retrieved on September 24, 2011, from http://www.gao.gov/new.items/d11933t.pdf.

US Senate. (2011). *Hearing on FY 2012 VA budget request.* Retrieved on April 13, 2011, from http://appropriations.senate.gov/ht-military.cfm?method=hearings.view&id=b8375dc5-1738-4279-bdb9-6670ae3a24d5.

US White House. (2011a). *Presidential memorandum – Disestablishment of the joint forces command.* Retrieved on March 3, 2011, from http://www.whitehouse.gov/the-press-office/2011/01/06/presidential-memorandum-disestablishment-united-states-joint-forces-comm.

US White House. (2011b). *Executive order--Delivering an efficient, effective, and accountable government.* Retrieved on June 18, 2011, from http://www.whitehouse.gov/the-press-office/2011/06/13/executive-order-delivering-efficient-effective-and-accountable-governmen.

ADDITIONAL READING

Allega, P. (2008). *First 100 days: The agenda for first-time enterprise architecture development efforts.* Stamford, CT: Gartner, Inc.

Bittler, R. S. (2009a). *Six best practices for enterprise architecture governance.* Stamford, CT: Gartner, Inc.

Bittler, R. S. (2009b). *Enterprise architecture research index: EA governance.* Stamford, CT: Gartner, Inc.

Bittler, R. S., & Short, J. (2010). *2010 enterprise architecture research index: EA governance.* Stamford, CT: Gartner, Inc.

Boddie, W. S. (2007). Is enterprise architecture an effective strategy to improve enterprise performance effectiveness? *Information Technology Standards Committee Synthesis Journal 2007,* 21-26. Retrieved from http://www.itsc.org.sg/pdf/synthesis07/Two_EA.pdf.

Boddie, W. S., & Newman, E. M. (2008). Enterprise architecture: Key to netcentricity. *Military Information Technology, 12*(1). Retrieved from http://www.kmimediagroup.com/mit-home/38-mit-2008-volume-12-issue-1/260-enterprise-architecture-key-to-netcentricity.html.

Burke, B. (2008). *Organize your enterprise architecture effort: Tips for game planning and launching the EA program.* Stamford, CT: Gartner, Inc.

Burke, B. (2009). *Enterprise architecture research index: EA organization and staffing.* Stamford, CT: Gartner, Inc.

Burton, B. (2008). *Communication is key to enterprise architecture success.* Stamford, CT: Gartner, Inc.

Chief Information Officers Council. (2001). *A practical guide to federal enterprise architecture, version 1.0.* Retrieved from http://www.cio.gov/documents/bpeaguide.pdf.

Chief Information Officers Council. (2009). *Federal segment architecture methodology website.* Retrieved from http://www.fsam.gov/.

Collins, J. (2001). *Level 5 leadership: The triumph of humility and fierce resolve.* Retrieved from http://www.ebscohost.com.

Handler, R. (2008). *The EA staffing conundrum.* Stamford, CT: Gartner, Inc.

Handler, R. A. (2008a). *Developing and using stakeholder analysis to build support for EA.* Stamford, CT: Gartner, Inc.

Handler, R. A. (2009). *Role definition and organization structure: Chief enterprise architect.* Stamford, CT: Gartner, Inc.

Lapkin, A. (2009). *Five best practices for improving EA communications.* Stamford, CT: Gartner, Inc.

US Department of Defense. (2009). *Department of defense architectural framework, version 2.0.* Retrieved from http://cio-nii.defense.gov/docs/DoDAF%20V2%20-%20Volume%202.pdf.

US Government Accountability Office. (2006). *Enterprise architecture: Leadership remains key to establishing and leveraging architectures for organizational transformation.* Retrieved from http://www.gao.gov/new.items/d06831.pdf.

US Government Accountability Office. (2008). *Military departments need to strengthen management of enterprise architecture programs.* Retrieved from http://www.gao.gov/new.items/d08519.pdf.

US Government Accountability Office. (2010). *Organizational transformation: A framework for assessing and improving enterprise architecture management (version 2.0).* Retrieved from http://www.gao.gov/new.items/d10846g.pdf.

US Office of Management and Budget. (2007). *FEA consolidated reference model document version 2.3.* Retrieved from http://www.whitehouse.gov/omb/assets/fea_docs/FEA_CRM_v23_Final_Oct_2007_Revised.pdf.

US Office of Management and Budget. (2009). *Improving agency performance using information and information technology (enterprise architecture assessment framework v3.1).* Retrieved from http://www.whitehouse.gov/sites/default/files/omb/assets/fea_docs/OMB_EA_Assessment_Framework_v3_1_June_2009.pdf.

KEY TERMS AND DEFINITIONS

Capital Planning and Investment Management: This is the process of planning for, executing, and reporting on capital investments.

Enterprise Architecture: This is a description of the current enterprise performance capability, the desired performance capability, and the strategies to transition from the current to the desired.

Governance: This is any formal body that is accountable to make decisions for an enterprise or a component of the enterprise based on rules, roles, and responsibilities.

Portfolio Management: This is the process of analyzing gaps in enterprise performance, determining alternatives that might close the gap, selecting a solution(s) to close the gap, controlling the implementation of the solution, and evaluating the extent to which the solution enable the enterprise to close the performance gap.

Strategic Plan: The is the instrument that documents the enterprise vision, mission, goals, objectives, performance management approach, and performance goals.

U.S. National Deficit: This is the condition in which the amount of financial outlays is greater than the income the U.S. Government receives on an annual basis.

U.S. National Debt: This is the aggregate of the annual deficits the U.S. Government accumulates over time.

ENDNOTE

[1] The views expressed in this chapter are those of the author and do not necessarily reflect the official policy or position of the National Defense University, the Department of Defense, or the U.S. Government.

Compilation of References

Aagesen, G., Veenstra, A. F., Janssen, M., & Krogstie, J. (2011). The entanglement of enterprise architecture and IT-governance: The cases of Norway and the Netherlands. In *Proceedings of the 44th Hawaii International Conference on System Sciences*. Hawaii, HI: System Sciences.

Abramson, M. A., Breul, J. D., & Kamensky, J. M. (2005). *Six trends transforming government*. IBM Center for the Business of Government Report. Retrieved from http://www.businessofgovernment.org/report/six-trends-transforming-government.

ABT-Fonden. (2010). *Telemedical blood pressure diagnostic, treatment and monitoring – Final application*. Copenhagen, Denmark: ABT-Fonden.

Ackoff, R. L. (1974). *Redesigning the future: A systems approach to societal problems*. New York, NY: John Wiley & Sons.

Adigun, M. O., & Biyela, D. P. (2003). Modelling and enterprise for re-engineering: A case study. In *Proceedings of the 2003 Annual Research Conference of the South African Institute of Computer Scientists and Information Technologists on Enablement through Technology (SAICSIT 2003)*. ACM Press.

AGIMO. (2007). *Cross-agency services architecture principles*. Retrieved, May 2011 from http://www.finance.gov.au/publications/cross-agency-services-architecture-principles/ docs/CAS_Architecture_Principles.pdf.

AGIMO. (2010). *Engage: Getting on with government 2.0. report of the government 2.0 taskforce*. Canberra, Australia: Government of Australia.

Agranoff, R. (2003). *Leveraging networks: A guide for public managers working across organizations*. Washington, DC: IBM Center for the Business of Government.

Agranoff, R. (2006). Inside collaborative networks: Ten lessons for public managers. *Public Administration Review*, *66*(1), 56–65. doi:10.1111/j.1540-6210.2006.00666.x

Ahsan, K., Shah, H., & Kingston, P. (2009). The role of enterprise architecture in healthcare-IT. In *Proceedings of the 2009 Sixth International Conference on Information Technology: New Generations*, (pp. 1462-1467). IEEE.

Aier, S., Gleichauf, B., & Winter, R. (2011). *Understanding enterprise architecture management design - An empirical analysis*. Paper presented at the 10th International Conference on Wirtschaftsinformatik. Zurich, Switzerland.

Aier, S., & Winter, R. (2009). Virtual decoupling for IT/business alignment – Conceptual foundations, architecture design and implementation example. *Business & Information Systems Engineering*, *1*(2), 150–163. doi:10.1007/s12599-008-0010-7

Albert, S., Flournoy, D. M., & LeBrasseur, R. (2009). *Networked communities: Strategies for digital collaboration*. Hershey, PA: IGI Global. doi:10.4018/978-1-59904-771-3

Alemdar, H., & Ersoy, C. (2010). Wireless sensor networks for healthcare: A survey. *Computer Networks*, *54*(15), 2688–2710. doi:10.1016/j.comnet.2010.05.003

Allee, V. (2003). *The future of knowledge, increasing prosperity through value networks*. London, UK: Elsevier Science.

American Society of Civil Engineers. (2003). Learning organization doctrine - Roadmap for transformation. Retrieved from http://www.au.af.mil/au/awc/awcgate/army/learning_org_doctrine.pdf.

American Society of Civil Engineers. (2011). Policy statement 525 -- Model building codes. Retrieved from http://www.asce.org/Public-Policies-and-Priorities/Public-Policy-Statements/Policy-Statement-525---Model-Building-Codes/.

Amoroso, D. L., & Reinig, B. A. (2004). Personalization management systems: Minitrack introduction. In *Proceedings of the 37th Annual Hawaii International Conference on System Sciences (HICSS 2004)*, (vol 7). Big Island, HI: HICSS.

Andersen, D. F., Andersen, D. L., Jarman, H., Whitmore, A., Luna-Reyes, L., & Zhang, J. … Tayi, G. (2011). *Case study.* Paper presented at I-Choose Network Meeting. Albany, NY.

Anthopoulos, L. (2009). Applying enterprise architecture for crisis management: A case of hellenic ministry of foreign affairs. In *Coherency Management: Architecting the Enterprise for Alignment, Agility and Assurance.* AuthorHouse Publishing.

Anthopoulos, L., Siozos, P., & Tsoukalas, I. A. (2007). Applying participatory design and collaboration in digital public services for discovering and re-designing e-government services. *Government Information Quarterly*, *24*(2), 353–376. doi:10.1016/j.giq.2006.07.018

APDIP. (2007a). *E-government interoperability: A review of government interoperability frameworks in selected countries.* Bangkok, Thailand: United Nations Development Program Regional Center.

APDIP. (2007b). *E-government interoperability guide.* Bangkok, Thailand: United Nations Development Program Regional Center.

Apps. (2011a). *Cloud.* Retrieved from https://www.apps.gov/cloud/main/start_page.do.

Apps. (2011b). *Cloud.* Retrieved from https://www.apps.gov/cloud/cloud/category_home.do?&c=SA.

Ariadne Training Limited. (2001). *Engineering software –Applied object oriented analysis and design using the UML.* Wincanton, UK: Ariadne Training Limited.

Ariely, D. (2009). *Predictably irrational.* London, UK: Harper Collins.

Armour, F. (2003). A UML-driven enterprise architecture case study. In *Proceedings of the 36th Hawaii International Conference on System Sciences.* Hawaii, HI: System Sciences.

Ashraf, A., Chowdry, B. S., Mustafa, G., & Hashmani, M. A. (2008). Unified application of tele-healthcare architecture and globalized patient IDs. In *Proceedings of the International Conference on Applied Computer Science.* Applied Computer Science.

Atkinson, R. D., & McKay, A. S. (2007). *Digital prosperity – Understanding the economic benefits of information technology revolution.* Washington, DC: The Information Technology & Innovation Foundation.

Aurenmalik. (2010). Core concepts of TOGAF. *Architect's Journal.* Retrieved from http://archjournal.wordpress.com/tag/core-concepts-of-togaf.

Australian Government Information Management Office. (2009). *Australian government architecture reference models.* Retrieved March 3, 2011, from http://www.finance.gov.au/e-government/strategy-and-governance/aga-rm/AGA-RM.html.

Australian Government. (2000). *Government online.* Retrieved, January 2011 from http://www.agimo.gov.au/archive/publications_noie/2000/04/govonline.html.

Australian Government. (2002). *Better services, better government.* Retrieved, January 2011 from http://www.agimo.gov.au/archive/__data/assets/pdf_file/0016/35503/Better_Services-Better_Gov.pdf.

Australian Government. (2006). *Responsive government: A new service agenda.* Retrieved, January 2011 from, http://www.finance.gov.au/publications/2006-e-government-strategy/docs/e-gov_strategy.pdf.

Azevedo, L. G., Santoro, F., Baião, F., Souza, J., Revoredo, K., Pereira, V., et al. (2009). *A method for service identification from business process models in a SOA approach.* Paper presented at the Enterprise, Business-Process and Information Systems Modeling. Amsterdam, The Netherlands.

Bachmann, F., & Merson, P. (2005). *Experience using the web-based tool wiki for architecture documentation.* Pittsburgh, PA: Carnegie Mellon University.

Bakan, I. A., Aydın Kar, H. M., & Öz, B. (2008). *T-VOHSU project phase 1 report*. Turkey: Türksat.

Bakan, I. A., Aydın Kar, H. M., & Öz, B. (2009). *T-VOHSU project phase 2 report*. Turkey: Türksat.

Balabanovic, M., & Shoham, Y. (1997). Fab: Content-based collaborative recommendation. *Communications of the ACM, 40*, 66–72. doi:10.1145/245108.245124

Balutis, A., Buss, T. F., & Ink, D. (Eds.). (2011). *American governance 3.0: Rebooting the public square*. Armonk, NY: ME Sharpe.

Barroso, J. M. D. (2011). *President of the European commission press conference in advance of the European council, Brussels, 21 June 2011*. Retrieved 4 September, 2011, from http://europa.eu/rapid/pressReleasesAction. do?reference=SPEECH/11/459.

Barrows, E. A., & Frigo, M. L. (2008). *Using the strategy map for competitor analysis*. Retrieved, August 2011 from http://hbr.org/product/using-the-strategy-map-for-competitor-analysis/an/B0807E-PDF-ENG.

Baskerville, R., & Wood-Harper, A. T. (1998). Diversity in information systems action research methods. *European Journal of Information Systems, 7*, 90–107. doi:10.1057/palgrave.ejis.3000298

Baum, C., & Maio, D. (2000). *Gartner's four phases of e-government model*. Gartner's Group White Paper. Retrieved from http://www.gartner.com/DisplayDocument?id=317292.

Beamish, P. W., & Kachra, A. (2004). Number of partners and JV performance. *Journal of World Business, 39*, 107–120. doi:10.1016/j.jwb.2003.08.013

Beer, S. (1972). *Brain of the firm: A development in management cybernetics*. New York, NY: Herder and Herder.

Bellazzi, R., Montani, S., Riva, A., & Stefanelli, M. (2010). Web-based telemedicine systems for home-care: Technical issues and experiences. *Computer Methods and Programs in Biomedicine, 64*, 175–187. doi:10.1016/S0169-2607(00)00137-1

Bender, P., & Gibson, S. (2010). *Mbombela (Nelspruit) water and sanitation concession South Africa*. Retrieved 4 September, 2011, from http://www.ppp.gov.za/documents/casestudies/Nelspruit%20Case%20Study%20Final%2029%20May%202010.pdf.

Benjamin, R. (2006). *Project success as a function of project management methodology: An emergent systems approach*. Unpublished Master's Thesis. Hull, UK: University of Hull.

Benjamin, R. (2008). Last-mile knowledge engineering: Quest for the holy grail? An emergence-based approach to complex systems engineering (forward, reverse, and re-engineering). *Management of Engineering & Technology*. Retrieved May 25, 2011, from http://ieeexplore.ieee.org/xpl/freeabs_all.jsp?arnumber=4599702.

Benjamin, R. (2009). *Project success and the component architecture management framework (CAMF)*. Retrieved May 25, 2011, from http://www.nanogr8.com/37201/39501.html.

Bennett, S. G., Carrato, T., Dico, A., Gejnevall, M., Harrington, E., & Hornford, D. (2011). Using TOGAF to define and govern service-oriented architectures. *The Open Group*. Retrieved from https://www2.open-group.org/ogsys/jsp/publications/PublicationDetails.jsp?publicationid=12390.

Benson, T. (2010). *Principles of health interoperability HL7 and SNOMED*. London, UK: Springer.

Berg, V. D. M., & Steenbergen, V. M. (2010). *Building an enterprise architecture practice*. Berlin, Germany: Springer.

Bernard, S. (2005). *Enterprise architecture*. Bloomington, IN: AuthorHouse.

Bernasek, A. (2002). The productivity miracle is for real. *Fortune, 145*(6), 84.

Biggert, T., & Suryavanshi, K. (2008). Using enterprise architecture to transform service delivery: The U.S. federal government's human resources line of business. In Saha, P. (Ed.), *Advances in Government Enterprise Architecture*. Hershey, PA: IGI Global. doi:10.4018/978-1-60566-068-4.ch014

Biological Classification. (2011). *Wikipedia.* Retrieved May 1, 2011, from http://en.wikipedia.org/wiki/Biological_classification.

Birkmeier, D. Q., Klöckner, S., & Overhage, S. (2009). A survey of service identification approaches: classification framework, state of the art, and comparison. *Enterprise Modelling and Information Systems Architectures, 4*(2), 20–36.

Bittinger, S. (2011). *Hype cycle for government transformation 2011.* Gartner Industry Research ID Number: G00214747. Retrieved from http://www.gartner.com.

Blevins, T., Dandashi, F., & Tolbert, M. (2010). *The open group architecture framework (TOGAF™ 9) and the US department of defense architecture framework 2.0 (DoDAF 2.0).* Retrieved from https://www2.opengroup.org/ogsys/jsp/publications/PublicationDetails.jsp?catalogno=w105.

Bobrie, G., Postel-Vinay, N., Delonca, J., & Corvol, P. (2007). Self-measurement and self-titration in hypertension A pilot telemedicine study. *American Journal of Hypertension, 20,* 1314–1320. doi:10.1016/j.amjhyper.2007.08.011

Boddie, W. S. (2009). The criticality of transformational leadership to advancing United States government enterprise architecture adoption. In Saha, P. (Ed.), *Advances in Government Enterprise Architecture.* Hershey, PA: IGI Global. doi:10.4018/978-1-60566-068-4.ch006

Boh, W., & Yellin, D. (2007). Using enterprise architecture standards in managing information technology. *Journal of Management Information Systems, 23,* 163–207. doi:10.2753/MIS0742-1222230307

Bouchaert, G., & Halligan, J. (2007). *Managing performance: International comparisons.* London, UK: Routledge.

Brach, M. (2003). *Real options in practice.* Hoboken, NJ: John Wiley & Sons.

Brandenburger, A., & Nalebuff, B. (1995). The right game: Use game theory to shape strategy. *Harvard Business Review.* Retrieved from http://hbr.org/1995/07/the-right-game-use-game-theory-to-shape-strategy/ar/1.

Brandenburger, A. M., & Nalebuff, B. J. (1997). *Co-opetition: A revolution mindset that combines competition and cooperation: The game theory strategy that's changing the game of business.* New York, NY: Currency Doubleday.

Brinkkemper, S., Saeki, M., & Harmsen, F. (1999). Meta-modelling based assembly techniques for situational method engineering. *Information Systems, 24*(3), 209–228. doi:10.1016/S0306-4379(99)00016-2

Broadbent, M., Weill, P., & Neo, B. S. (1999). Strategic context and patterns of IT infrastructure capability. *The Journal of Strategic Information Systems, 8,* 157–187. doi:10.1016/S0963-8687(99)00022-0

Bryman, A., & Bell, E. (2007). *Business research strategy* (2nd ed.). Oxford, UK: Oxford University Press.

Bryson, R., & Perry, A. (2009). *Government of Canada enterprise architecture- A collaborative practice.* Retrieved from https://www.opengroup.org/conference-live/uploads/40/20078/Mon_-_am_-_2_-_Perry.pdf.

Büchner, T., Matthes, F., & Neubert, C. (2009). *A concept and service based analysis of commercial and open.* Paper presented at the International Conference on Knowledge Management and Information Sharing. Madeira, Portugal.

Buckl, S., Marliani, R., Matthes, F., & Schweda, C. M. (2011). *Dynamic virtual enterprises - The challenges of the utility industry.* Paper presented at the International IFIP WG5.8 Working Conference on Enterprise Interoperability. Stockholm, Sweden.

Bureau of the Public Debt. (2011). *Our history.* Retrieved on April 9, 2011, from http://www.publicdebt.treas.gov/history/history.htm.

Burns, P., Neutens, M., Newman, D., & Power, T. (2009). Building value through enterprise architecture: A global study. *Booz & Company Perspective.* Retrieved from http://www.booz.com/media/file/Building_Value_through_Enterprise_Architecture.pdf.

Burton, B., & Allega, P. (2011). *Hype cycle for enterprise architecture 2011.* Gartner Industry Research ID Number: G00214756. Retrieved from http://www.gartner.com.

BUSA. (2008). *A practitioner's guide to the codes of good conduct on broad-based economic empowerment.* Johannesburg, South Africa: BUSA.

Business Transformation Agency. (2011a). *Mission.* Retrieved on March 10, 2011, from http://www.bta.mil/about/mission.html.

Business Transformation Agency. (2011b). *Mission.* Retrieved on March 10, 2011, from http://www.bta.mil/products/bea.html.

Buss, T. F., & Gardner, A. (2008). The millennium challenge account: An early appraisal. In Picard, L., Groelsema, R., & Buss, T. F. (Eds.), *Foreign Aid and Foreign Policy* (pp. 329–355). Armonk, NY: ME Sharpe.

Buss, T. F., & Picard, L. (Eds.). (2011). *African security and the Africa command.* Sterling, VA: Kumarian Press.

Buss, T. F., Redburn, F. S., & Guo, C. (2006). *Modernizing democracy.* Armonk, NY: ME Sharpe.

Butland, B., Jebb, S., Kopelman, P., McPherson, K., Thomas, S., Mardell, J., & Parry, V. (2007). *Tackling obesities – Future choices.* London, UK: Government Office for Science.

C2. (2006). *Borges classification of animals.* Retrieved May 12, 2011, from http://c2.com/cgi/wiki?BorgesClassificationOfAnimals.

C4ISR. (1998). *Levels of information systems interoperability (LISI).* Washington, DC: Department of Defense.

Cable News Network. (2011). *Ronald Reagan's first inaugural address.* Retrieved on March 15, 2011, from http://articles.cnn.com/2011-01-20/politics/reagan.inaugural_1_tax-burden-tax-system-national-history?_s=PM:POLITICS.

Capgemini. (2007). *The user challenge benchmarking: The supply of online public services, 7th measurement.* Retrieved Jan 28, 2011, from http://ec.europa.eu/information_society/eeurope/i2010/docs/benchmarking/egov_benchmark_2007.pdf.

Caro, D. H. J. (2008). Deconstructing symbiotic dyadic e-health networks: Transnational and transgenic perspectives. *International Journal of Information Management, 28,* 94–101. doi:10.1016/j.ijinfomgt.2007.12.002

Carratta, T., Dadayan, L., & Ferro, E. (2006). Electronic government ROI analysis in e-government assessment trials: The case of sistema piemonte. *Lecture Notes in Computer Science, 4084,* 329–340. doi:10.1007/11823100_29

Castanias, R. P., & Helfat, C. E. (2001). The managerial rents model: Theory and empirical analysis. *Journal of Management, 27,* 661–678. doi:10.1177/014920630102700604

Castelnovo, W. (2007). Interorganizational cooperation and cooperability. In *Proceedings of the EGov Interop 2007 Conference.* Retrieved April 12, 2011 from http://80.14.185.155/egovinterop/www.egovinterop.net/Res/10/T10C.pdf.

Castelnovo, W. (2009). Enhancing cooperation among small local government organizations. In A. Kaplan, A. Balci, C. Can Aktan, & O. Dalbay (Eds.), *Advances in eGovernment and eGovernance, Proceedings of ICEGOV 2009.* Ankara, Turkey: ICEGOV.

Castelnovo, W., & Simonetta, M. (2007). The evaluation of e-government projects for small local government organizations. *Electronic Journal of E-Government, 5*(1).

Castelnovo, W. (2011). The governance of partnerships in local government. In Piaggesi, D., Sund, K. J., & Castelnovo, W. (Eds.), *Global Strategy and Practice of E-Governance: Examples from Around the World* (pp. 83–101). Hershey, PA: IGI Global. doi:10.4018/978-1-60960-489-9.ch006

CBS News. (2010). *National debt up $3 trillion on Obama's watch.* Retrieved on April 3, 2011, from http://www.cbsnews.com/8301-503544_162-20019931-503544.html.

CEES. (2009). Citizen-oriented evaluation of e-government services. *EU Marie Curie IAPP Funded Project.* Retrieved from http://www.iapp-cees.eu.

Cegarra-Navarroa, J.-G., & Sánchez-Polo, M. T. (2010). Implementing telemedicine through eListening in hospital-in-the-home units. *International Journal of Information Management, 48*(10), 895–918.

CEMR. (2010). EU subnational government – 2009 key figures. *Council of European Municipalities and Regions.* Retrieved April 12, 2011, from http://www.ccre.org/docs/chiffres_cles_2010_UK_bd.pdf.

Çetin, Y., Medeni, T. D., Özkan, S., Balcı, A., & Dalbay, Ö. (2010). *Improving e-government from citizens' perspectives: An analysis of suggestions for e-government gateway in Turkey.* Paper presented at the ICEGEG 2010 Conference. Antalya, Turkey.

Chae, Y. M., Lee, J. H., Ho, S. H., Kim, H. J., Jun, K. H., & Won, J. U. (2001). Patient satisfaction with telemedicine in home health services for the elderly. *International Journal of Medical Informatics, 61*, 167–173. doi:10.1016/S1386-5056(01)00139-3

Chang, S. (2006). *Are they willing to contribute? Prosumer characteristics among the Australian youth.* Paper presented at the Digital Natives in Australia and Korea, Conference at the University of Melbourne. Melbourne, Australia.

Chang, V., Bacigalupo, D., Wills, G., & De Roure, D. (2010a). *A categorisation of cloud computing business models.* Southampton, UK: University of Southampton.

Chang, V., Wills, G., & De Roure, D. (2010). *A review of cloud business models and sustainability.* Southampton, UK: University of Southampton.

Charette, R. (2004). *IT project failures or blunders?* Retrieved Nov 11, 2004, from http://www.cutter.com/research/2004/edge040427.html.

Chen, D., & Vernadat, F. (2004). *Standards on enterprise integration and engineering – State of the art.* Retrieved from http://www.cimosa.de/Standards/ChVe04.html.

Chief Information Officer. (2008). *Enterprise modernization plan: EA transition strategy, v.3.* Washington, DC: US Department of Housing and Urban Development. Retrieved from www.hud.gov/offices/cio/ea/newea/resources/eatpv2.pdf.

Chief Information Officers Council. (2000). *Architecture alignment and assessment guide.* Washington, DC: CIOC.

Chief Information Officers Council. (2001). *A practical guide to federal enterprise architecture, version 1.0.* Retrieved on January 10, 2011, from http://www.cio.gov/documents/bpeaguide.pdf.

Chief Information Officers Council. (2007). *Architecture principles for the US government.* Washington, DC: CIOC.

Chief Information Officers Council. (2008). *Improving agency performance using information and IT: Enterprise architecture assessment framework, version 3.* Washington, DC: CIOC.

Chong, S. C., & Choi, Y. S. (2005). Critical factors in the successful implementation of knowledge management. Journal of Knowledge Management Practice. Retrieved from http://www.tlainc.com/articl90.htm.

CIO. (2011). *Techstat.* Retrieved from http://www.cio.gov/techstat/.

CIPFA. (2009). New ways of working and innovation in local government. London, UK: CIPFA. Retrieved from http://www.improvementnetwork.gov.uk/imp/aio/1119705.

Cisco, I. B. S. G. (2009). *Realizing the potential of the connected republic: Web 2.0 opportunities in the public sector.* Cisco Systems Incorporated White Paper. Palo Alto, CA: Cisco Systems Incorporated.

CISCO. (2007). *Connected government: Creating a springboard for transformation and innovation.* Retrieved, August 2011 from http://www.cisco.com/web/about/ac79/docs/wp/ctd/Connected_Govt_PoV_1030_finalCB.pdf.

Cisco, I. B. S. G. (2004). *Connected government: Essays from innovators.* London, UK: Premium Publishing.

City of Tacoma. (2006). Deploying SAP® solutions optimizes and consolidates city service processes. Retrieved from http://www.sap.com/portugal/industries/publicsector/pdf/50078756_City_of_Tacoma.pdf.

City of Tacoma. (2009a). City managers evaluation form. Retrieved from http://cms.cityoftacoma.org/CRO/councileval.pdf.

City of Tacoma. (2009b). Green ribbon climate action task force. Retrieved from http://www.cityoftacoma.org/Page.aspx?nid=674.

City of Tacoma. (2011a). *Request for proposal.* Retrieved from http://cms.cityoftacoma.org/Purchasing/FormalBids/HR11-0452F.pdf.

City of Tacoma. (2011b). *Service level agreements.* Retrieved from http://www.cityoftacoma.org/Page.aspx?cid=12951.

City of Tacoma. (2011c). *Waste reduction strategies & residential food waste.* Retrieved from http://cms.cityoftacoma.org/cityclerk/Files/CouncilCommittees/Handouts/2011/EPWHandouts/EPW_20110511handouts.pdf.

Clark, T., & Jones, R. (1999). Organisational interoperability maturity model for C2. In *Proceedings of the Command and Control Research and Technology Symposium*. Retrieved April 12, 2011 from http://www.dodccrp.org/events/1999_CCRTS/pdf_files/track_5/049clark.pdf.

Click! Network. (2007). Welcome to click! network, a division of Tacoma power. Retrieved from http://www.clickcabletv.com/AboutUs.aspx.

CNIPA. (2007). *Monitoraggio dei progetti di e-government - Fase 1: Rapporto finale*. Retrieved April 12, 2011, from http://archivio.cnipa.gov.it/site/_files/EG000_RP05_0007_V1_RapportoSintesiConclusivo.pdf.

Collaboration Project. (2011). *Website.* Retrieved from http://www.collaborationproject.org/display/home/Home.

Committee on Fiscal Futures for the US. (2011). *Choosing the nation's fiscal future*. Washington, DC: National Research Council and National Academy of Public Administration.

Congressional Budget Office. (2011a). *Budget control act of 2011*. Retrieved on August 5, 2011, from http://cbo.gov/ftpdocs/123xx/doc12357/BudgetControlActAug1.pdf.

Congressional Budget Office. (2011b). *The budget and economic outlook: An update*. Retrieved on August 22, 2011, from http://www.cbo.gov/ftpdocs/123xx/doc12316/08-24-BudgetEconUpdate.pdf.

Council of Europe. (2007). *Draft report on inter-municipal cooperation*. Geneva, Switzerland: Council of Europe.

Council, C. I. O. (1999). *Federal enterprise architecture framework*. Retrieved, May 2011 from http://www.cio.gov/Documents/fedarch1.pdf.

Council, C. I. O. (2001). *A practical guide to federal enterprise architecture*. Retrieved, May 2011 from http://www.gao.gov/bestpractices/ bpeaguide.pdf.

Creamer, G., & Freund, Y. (2010). Learning a board balanced scorecard to improve corporate performance. *Decision Support Systems, 49*, 365–385. doi:10.1016/j.dss.2010.04.004

Cresswell, A. M. (2004). *Return on investment in information technology: A guide for managers.* Retrieved from http://www.ctg.albany.edu/publications/reports/advancing_roi.

Cresswell, A. M. (2010). *Public value and government ICT investment*. Paper presented at the Second International Conference on eGovernment and eGovernance. Antalya, Turkey.

Cresswell, A. M., Burke, G. B., & Pardo, T. A. (2006). *Advancing return on investment analysis for government IT - A public value framework*. Retrieved from http://www.ctg.albany.edu/publications/reports/advancing_roi/advancing_roi.pdf.

Cresswell, A. M., Canestraro, D., & Pardo, T. A. (2008). *A multi-dimensional approach to digital government capability assessment*. CTG Working Paper No. 05-2008. Albany, NY: SUNY.

Curtis, G., & Cobham, D. (2002). *Business information systems: Analysis, design and practice* (4th ed.). New York, NY: Prentice Hall.

Dadayan, L. (2006). *Measuring return on government IT investments*. Paper presented at the 13th European Conference on Information Technology Evaluation. Genoa, Italy.

DAMA. (2011). *Website.* Retrieved May 25, 2011, from http://www.dama.org/i4a/pages/index.cfm?pageid=1.

Davenport, T. H., & Harris, J. G. (2007). *Competing on analytics – The new science of winning*. Boston, MA: Harvard Business School Press.

De Toledo, P., Lalinde, W., del Pozo, F., Thurber, D., & Jimenez-Fernandez, S. (2006). Interoperability of a mobile health care solution with electronic healthcare record systems. In *Proceedings of the Engineering in Medicine and Biology Society Conference*. IEEE.

De Vries, J. (2010). Is the new public management really dead? *OECD Journal on Budgeting, 1*, 1–5. doi:10.1787/budget-10-5km8xx3mp60n

Deloitte, & Touché. (2003). *At the dawn of egovernment: The citizen as customer.* Retrieved from http://epractice.eu/files/At%20the%20Dawn%20of%20e-Government%20-%20The%20Citizen%20as%20Customer.pdf.

Demarche Consulting Group. (2006). *Final report to the city of Tacoma public works department: Building and land use division permit process documentation, analysis and resource assessment*. Retrieved from http://www. demarcheconsulting.com.

Demarche Consulting Group. (2009). *Strategic assessment and plan: City of Tacoma permitting*. Retrieved from http://www.demarcheconsulting.com.

Demarche Consulting Group. (2011). *Permitting cost recovery – A comparative investigation of structure and policy*. Retrieved from http://www.demarcheconsulting. com.

Denhardt, J. V., & Denhardt, R. B. (2007). *The new public service: Serving not steering*. Armonk, NY: ME Sharpe.

Department of Defense. (2009). *Department of Defense architecture framework, version 2.0 (Vol. I-III)*. Washington, DC: DOD.

Department of Defense. (2010a). *DOD news briefing with Secretary Gates from the Pentagon*. Retrieved February 7, 2011, from http://www.defense.gov/transcripts/transcript. aspx?transcriptid=4669.

Department of Defense. (2010b). *Defense senior leader development program*. Retrieved on April 25, 2011, from http://www.cpms.osd.mil/ASSETS/2F792DE33C9F4 D1F9E51DE66AAD5F2FB/DSLDP%20Program%20 Brief%20-%20June%202010.pdf.

Department of Defense. (2011). *Meeting our fiscal and national security responsibility*. Retrieved on August 6, 2011, from http://www.defense.gov/home/ features/2011/0711_message1/.

Department of the Navy. (2011a). *Department of the Navy (DON) information technology expenditure approval authorities (ITEAA)*. Retrieved on July 24, 2011, from www.doncio.navy.mil/Download.aspx?AttachID=1756.

Department of the Navy. (2011b). *Department of the Navy (DON) data center consolidation (DCC) policy guidance*. Retrieved on July 24, 2011, from http://www.doncio.navy. mil/Download.aspx?AttachID=1751.

Department of Treasury. (2011). *Frequently asked questions about the public debt*. Retrieved on April 13, 2011, from http://www.treasurydirect.gov/govt/resources/faq/ faq_publicdebt.htm.

DeSanctis, G., & Jackson, B. M. (1994). Coordination of information technology management: Team-based structures and computer-based communication systems. *Journal of Management Information Systems, 10*(4), 85–110.

Dettmer, H. W. (2007). *The logical thinking process: A systems approach to complex problem solving*. New York, NY: ASQ Quality Press.

Dietz, G., Juhrisch, M., & Grossmann, K. (2011). *Inherence of ratios for service identification and evaluation*. Paper presented at the 17th Americas Conference on Information Systems. Detroit, MI.

Digital Sundhed. (2010). *Sammenhængende digital sundhed i Danmark*. Retrieved November 12, 2010, from http://sdsd.dk/.

DigitPA, & PCM. (2010). *Rapporto e-gov Italia 2010, DigitPA and dipartimento per la digitalizzazione della PA e l'Innovazione tecnologica*. Retrieved April 12, 2011 from http://www.innovazionepa.gov.it/media/611301/ rapporto_e-gov_italia_master.pdf.

Dinesen, B., Gustafsson, J., Nøhr, C., Andersen, S. K., Sejersen, H., & Toft, E. (2007). Telehomecare technology across sectors: claims of jurisdiction and emerging controversies. *International Journal of Integrated Care, 7*(21), 1–11.

Dinesen, B., Nøhr, C., Andersen, S. K., Sejersen, H., & Toft, E. (2008). Under surveillance, yet looked after: Telehomecare as viewed by patients and their spouse/ partners. *European Journal of Cardiovascular Nursing, 7*, 239–246. doi:10.1016/j.ejcnurse.2007.11.004

Dodaro, G. L. (2011). *Opportunities to reduce potential duplication in government programs, save tax dollars, and enhance revenue*. Retrieved from http://www.gao.gov.

Doppelt, B. (2010). *Leading change toward sustainability: A change-management guide for business, government and civil society* (2nd ed.). Sheffield, UK: Greenleaf.

Doucet, G., Gøtze, J., Saha, P., & Bernard, S. (2008). *Coherency management: Using enterprise architecture for alignment, agility and assurance*. New York, NY: AuthorHouse.

Doucet, G., Gotze, J., Saha, P., & Bernard, S. A. (2009). *Coherency management: Architecting the enterprise for alignment, agility and assurance*. Bloomington, IN: AuthorHouse.

DPT. (2006). *Bilgi toplumu stratejisi ve eylem plani*. Wincanton, UK: Ariadne Training.

DPT. (2008). *Bilgi toplumu stratejisi ve eylem plan: 1: Değerlendirme raporu*. Wincanton, UK: Ariadne Training.

DPT. (2010). *Bilgi toplumu stratejisi ve eylem plan: 2: Değerlendirme raporu*. Wincanton, UK: Ariadne Training.

Dutta, S., & Mia, I. (2011). *Global information technology report 2010-2011: ICT for sustainability*. Geneva, Switzerland: World Economic Forum.

EARF. (2011). *Website*. Retrieved April 11, 2001, from http://earf.meraka.org.za/earfhome/our-projects-1/completed-projects/.

Ebrahim, Z., & Irani, Z. (2005). E-government adoption: Architecture and barriers. *Business Process Management Journal, 11*(5), 589–611. doi:10.1108/14637150510619902

ECeG Project. (2003). The semantic web techniques for the management of digital identity and the access to norms. *PRIN Project Home Page*. Retrieved January 15, 2008, from http://www.cirsfid.unibo.it/eGov03/.

ECeGov. (2011). *The European commission e-government home page*. Retrieved from http://europa.eu.int/information_society/eeurope/2005/all_about/egovernment/index_en.htm.

Eger, J. M., & Becker, A. M. (2000). *Telecommunications and municipal utilities: Cooperation and competition in the new economy*. Special Report Prepared for the American Public Power Association. Retrieved from http://www.smartcommunities.org/APPA_special_report.pdf.

Eisenberg, D. (2011). Building sustainability into codes: The evolution of building regulation. Paper presented at APEC Green Building Conference. Washington, DC.

Eisenberg, D., Done, R., & Ishida, L. (2002). *Breaking down the barrier: Challenges and solutions to code approval of green buildings*. Tucson, AZ: Development Center for Appropriate Technology.

ePractice.eu. (2011). *eGovernment factsheet – Germany – Strategy*. Retrieved, May 2011 from http://www.epractice.eu/en/document/288242.

Epstein, G., & Mealem, Y. (2009). Group specific public goods, orchestration of interest groups with free riding. *Public Choice, 139*(3/4), 357–369. doi:10.1007/s11127-009-9398-y

Erl, T. (2005). *Service-oriented architecture - Concepts, technology, and design*. Upper Saddle River, NJ: Prentice Hall.

Erl, T. (2009). *SOA design paterns*. Upper Saddle River, NJ: Prentice Hall.

Erradi, A., Anand, S., & Kulkarni, N. (2006). *SOAF: An architectural framework for service definition and realization*. Paper presented at the IEEE International Conference on Services Computing 2006. New York, NY.

Essén, A., & Conrick, M. (2008). New e-service development in the homecare sector: Beyond implementing a radical technology. *International Journal of Medical Informatics, 77*(7), 679–688. doi:10.1016/j.ijmedinf.2008.02.001

EU ICT. (2011). *Policy support programme*. Retrieved from http://ec.europa.eu/information_society/activities/ict_psp/about/index_en.htm.

European Commission. (2010). *A digital agenda for Europe*. Retrieved, January 2011 from http://eur-lex.europa.eu/LexUriServ/LexUriServ.do?uri=COM:2010:0245:FIN:EN:PDF.

European Commission. (2010). *European interoperability framework (EIF) for European public services, version 2.0*. Brussels, Belgium: European Commission. Retrieved from http://ec.europa.eu/isa/strategy/doc/annex_ii_eif_en.pdf.

European Commission. (2010a). *Communication from the commission to the European parliament, the council, the European economic and social committee and the committee of regions 'towards interoperability for european public services': Annex I - European interoperability strategy (EIS) for European public services*. Geneva, Switzerland: European Commission.

European Commission. (2010b). *Communication from the commission to the European parliament, the council, the European economic and social committee and the committee of regions 'towards interoperability for European public services': Annex II - European interoperability framework (EIF) for European public services.* Geneva, Switzerland: European Commission.

European Commission. (2010c). *Communication from the commission to the European parliament, the council, the European economic and social committee and the committee of regions: A digital agenda for Europe.* Geneva, Switzerland: European Commission.

European Parliament. (2006). *Directive 2006/123/EC of the European parliament and of the council of 12 December 2006 on services in the internal market. Official Journal of the European Union.* Geneva, Switzerland: European Union.

European Union. (2006). Consolidated version of the treaty on European Union and of the treaty establishing the European Community. *Official Journal of the European Union.* Geneva, Switzerland: European Union.

Event, I. D. C. (2011). *Webpage.* Retrieved from http://www.idc-cema.com/?showproduct=40681&content_lang=ENG&action=Presentations.

Expect More. (2011). *Website.* Retrieved from http://www.expectmore.gov.

FEA Working Group. (2002). *E-gov enterprise architecture guidance (common reference model).* Retrieved, January 2011 from http://www.feapmo.gov/resources/E-Gov_Guidance_Final_Draft_v2.0.pdf.

FEA Working Group. (2005). *Enabling citizen-centered electronic government: 2005-2006 FEA-PMO action plan.* Retrieved, January 2011 from http://www.whitehouse.gov/omb/egov/documents/2005_FEA_PMO_Action_Plan_FINAL.pdf.

Federal Enterprise Architecture Framework Version 1. (1999). *Website.* Retrieved from http://www.itpolicy.gsa.gov/mke/archplus/fedarch1.pdf.

Federal Enterprise Architecture Program. (2007). *FEA practice guidance.* Retrieved from http://www.whitehouse.gov/sites/default/files/omb/assets/fea_docs/FEA_Practice_Guidance_Nov_2007.pdf.

Federal Republic of Germany. (2008). *Standards and architectures for egovernment applications (SAGA).* Retrieved 18 August, 2011 from http://www.cio.bund.de/saga.

Federal Statistical Office. Germany. (2002). *E-strategy, process analysis and design at the federal statistical office: A practical example.* Retrieved, May 2011 from https://www.bsi.bund.de/SharedDocs/Downloads/EN/BSI/Egovernment/5_StBA_en_pdf.pdf?__blob=publicationFile.

Fereira, N., Kar, J., & Trigeorgis, L. (2009). Option games: The key to competing in capital-intensive industries. *Harvard Business Review.* Retrieved from http://hbr.org/product/option-games-the-key-to-competing-in-capital-inten/an/R0903H-PDF-ENG.

Fichman, R. (2004). Real options and IT platform adoption: Implications for theory and practice. *Information Systems Research, 15*(2), 132–154. doi:10.1287/isre.1040.0021

Figliola, P. M. (2010). *The federal networking and IT research and development program.* Washington, DC: Congressional Research Service.

Finnish Ministry of Finance. (2007). *Overview of enterprise architecture work in 15 countries: Finnish enterprise architecture research project.* Retrieved, May 2011 from http://www.vm.fi/vm/en/04_publications_and_documents/01_publications/04_public_management/20071102Overvi/name.jsp.

Fishenden, J., Johnson, M., Nelson, K., Polin, G., Rijpma, G., & Stolz, P. (2006). *The new world of government work: Transforming the business of government with the power of information technology.* Microsoft Public Services and e-Government Strategy Discussion Paper. Palo Alto, CA: Microsoft.

Fisher, F. M. (1984). The misuse of accounting rates of return. *The American Economic Review, 74*(3), 509–517.

Fisher, F. M., & McGowan, J. J. (1983). On the misuse of accounting rates of return to infer monopoly profits. *The American Economic Review, 73*(1), 82–97.

Fitsilis, P., Anthopoulos, L., & Gerogiannis, V. (2009). An evaluation framework for e-government projects. In *Citizens and E-Government: Evaluating Policy and Management.* Hershey, PA: IGI Global.

Fleisch, E., & Österle, H. (2000). Business networking: A process-oriented framework. In Österle, H., Fleisch, E., & Alt, R. (Eds.), *Business Networking - Shaping Enterprise Relationships on the Internet* (pp. 55–91). Berlin, Germany: Springer.

Flett, P., Curry, A., & Peat, A. (2008). Reengineering systems in general practice—A case study review. *International Journal of Information Management, 28*, 83–93. doi:10.1016/j.ijinfomgt.2007.06.001

Forde, C., Varnus, J., Fehskens, L., Josey, A., Doherty, G., & Fox, C. (2009). *TOGAF version 9: The open group architecture framework (TOGAF)*. Reading, UK: The Open Group.

Franke, U. J. (2002). The competence-based view on the management of virtual web organizations. In Franke, U. J. (Ed.), *Managing Virtual Web Organizations in the 21st Century: Issues and Challenges*. Hershey, PA: IGI Global. doi:10.4018/978-1-930708-24-2.ch001

Frederickson, D. G., & Frederickson, H. G. (2006). *Measuring performance of the hollow state*. Washington, DC: Georgetown University Press.

Frederickson, H. G., Smith, K. B., Larimer, C. W., & Licari, M. (2011). *The PA theory primer*. Boulder, CO: Westwood Press.

Frederiksa, P. J. M., & van der Weideb, T. P. (2006). Information modeling: The process and the required competencies of its participants. *Data & Knowledge Engineering, 58*(1), 4–20. doi:10.1016/j.datak.2005.05.007

French, S. (2003). *Soft modelling and problem formulation*. Retrieved from http://www.sal.hut.fi/TED/slides/Soft_modelling.pdf.

Gall, N., Newman, D., Allega, P., Lapkin, A., & Handler, R. A. (2010). *Introducing hybrid thinking for transformation, innovation and strategy*. Gartner Research ID Number: G00172065. Retrieved from http://www.gartner.com.

Ganesan, E., & Paturi, R. (2008). A unified meta-model for elements can lead to effective business analysis. *Infosys Technologies Limited*. Retrieved, May 2011 from http://www.infosys.com/offerings/IT-services/architecture-services/white-papers/ Documents/enterprise-business-architecture.pdf.

GAO. (2011). *Information technology*. Retrieved from Http://www.gao.gov/highrisk/challenges/information_technology/home_information_technology.php.

Garshnek, V., Logan, J. S., & Hassell, L. H. (1997). The telemedicine frontier: Going the extra mile. *Space Policy, 13*(1), 37–46. doi:10.1016/S0265-9646(96)00036-7

Gartner, Inc. (2010). *Gartner's enterprise architecture hype cycle reveals two generations of enterprise architecture*. Retrieved 08 14, 2011, from http://www.gartner.com/it/page.jsp?id=1417513.

Gattuso, J., & Katz, D. (2011). *Red tape rising*. Washington, DC: Heritage Foundation. Retrieved from http://www.heritage.org/research/reports/2011/07/red-tape-rising-a-2011-mid-year-report.

Gehlert, A., Schermann, M., Pohl, K., & Krcmar, H. (2009). *Towards a research method for theory-driven design research*. Paper presented at the 9th International Conference on Wirtschaftsinformatik. Wien, Austria.

German Federal Government. (2003). *BundOnline 2005: 2003 implementation plan*. Retrieved, May 2011 from http://www.epractice.eu/files/media/media_266.pdf.

Gerson, D. (2006). *Pubic information technology and e-governance: Managing the virtual state*. New York, NY: Jones and Bartlett Learning.

Gil-Garcia, J. R., & Luna-Reyes, L. F. (2003). Towards a definition of electronic government: A comparative review. In Mendez-Vilas, A., Mesa Gonzalez, J. A., Mesa Gonzalez, J., Guerrero Bote, V., & Zapico Alonso, F. (Eds.), *Techno-Legal Aspects of the Information Society and the New Economy: An Overview*. Badajoz, Spain: Formatex.

Ginsberg, W. (2010). *The Obama administration's OGI*. Washington, DC: Congressional Research Service.

Godinez, M., Hechler, E., Koenig, K., & Lockwood, S. (2010). *The art of enterprise information architecture: A systems-based approach for unlocking business insight*. Boston, MA: IBM Press.

Golder, S. A., & Huberman, B. A. (2005). *The structure of collaborative tagging systems*. Retrieved May 17, 2011, from http://arxiv.org/abs/cs.DL/0508082.

Goldsmith, S., & Eggers, W. (2004). *Governing by network: The new shape of the public sector*. Washington, DC: Brookings Institution Press.

Goldstein, H. (2005). Who killed the virtual case file? *IEEE Spectrum Magazine*. Retrieved from http://spectrum.ieee.org/computing/software/who-killed-the-virtual-case-file.

Good, N., Schafer, J. B., Konstan, J. A., Borchers, A., Sarwar, B., Herlocker, J., & Riedl, J. (1999). Combining collaborative filtering with personal agents for better recommendations. In *Proceedings of the 16th National Conference on Artificial Intelligence*, (pp. 439-446). Orlando, FL: ACM.

Government Accountability Office. (1992). *Strategic information planning: Framework for designing and developing system architectures*. Washington, DC: GAO.

Government Accountability Office. (1994). *Executive guide: Improving mission performance through strategic information management and technology*. Washington, DC: GAO.

Government Accountability Office. (2002). *Information technology: Enterprise architecture use across the Federal government can be improved*. Washington, DC: GAO.

Government Accountability Office. (2003). *Information technology: A framework for assessing and improving enterprise architecture management*. Washington, DC: GAO.

Government Accountability Office. (2005). *Managing for results: Enhancing agency use of performance information for management decision making*. Washington, DC: GAO.

Government Accountability Office. (2008). *Military departments need to strengthen management of EA programs*. Washington, DC: GAO.

Government Accountability Office. (2009). *Information technology: Management and oversight of projects totalling billions of dollars need attention*. Washington, DC: GAO.

Government Accountability Office. (2010). *Organizational transformation: A framework for assessing and improving enterprise architecture management (version 2.0)*. Washington, DC: GAO.

Government Accountability Office. (2011a). *High risk list*. Washington, DC: GAO. Retrieved from http://www.gao.gov/highrisk/challenges/information_technology/home_information_technology.php.

Government Accountability Office. (2011b). *Information technology: Investment oversight and management have improved but continued attention is needed*. Washington, DC: GAO.

Government Accountability Office. (2011c). *OMB has made improvements to its dashboard, but further work is needed to ensure data accuracy*. Washington, DC: GAO.

Government Accountability Office. (2011d). *DOD and VA should remove barriers and improve efforts to meet their common system needs*. Washington, DC: GAO.

Government Accountability Office. (2011e). *Better informed decision making needed on Navy's next generation enterprise network acquisition*. Washington, DC: GAO.

Government Accountability Office. (2011f). *Information technology: Continued improvements in investment oversight and management can yield billions in savings*. Washington, DC: GAO.

Government Accountability Office. (2011g). *Information technology: Continued attention needed to accurately report federal spending and improve management*. Washington, DC: GAO.

Government Accountability Office. (2011h). *Opportunities to reduce potential duplication*. Washington, DC: GAO. Retrieved from http://www.gao.gov/ereport/GAO-11-318SP/overview.

Government Accountability Office. (2011i). *Information security: Weaknesses continue amid new federal efforts to implement requirements*. Washington, DC: GAO.

Government Executive Magazine. (2009). Obama team outlines its performance agenda. *GovExec*. Retrieved from http://www.govexec.com/dailyfed/0509/051109e1.htm.

Government Executive. (2011a). *Air Force announces civilian hiring freeze*. Retrieved on August 18, 2011, from http://www.govexec.com/story_page_pf.cfm?articleid=48544&printerfriendlyvers=1.

Government Executive. (2011b). *Gates takes ax to defense programs to end culture of endless money.* Retrieved on March 15, 2011, from http://www.govexec.com/story_page_pf.cfm?articleid=46833&printerfriendlyvers=1.

Government Executive. (2011c). *Plans for closing joint forces command likely ready next month.* Retrieved on March 15, 2011, from http://www.govexec.com/story_page_pf.cfm?articleid=46859&printerfriendlyvers=1.

Government Executive. (2011d). *Army sets stage to slash 8,700 civilian jobs.* Retrieved on August 8, 2011, from http://www.govexec.com/dailyfed/0811/080511cc1.htm.

Graddy, E., & Chen, B. (2006). Influences on the size and scope of networks for social service delivery. *Journal of Public Administration: Research and Theory, 16*(4), 533–552. doi:10.1093/jopart/muj005

Graves, T. (2008). *Adapting the TOGAF ADM for government architectures.* Retrieved from http://www.gtra.org/component/content/article/829?format=pdf.

Graves, T. (2010). *Everyday enterprise architecture.* Colchester, UK: Tetradian Books.

Gruman, G. (2006). *The four stages of enterprise architecture.* Retrieved from http://www.cio.com/article/27079/The_Four_Stages_of_Enterprise_Architecture.

Grundgesetz für die Bundesrepublik Deutschland 65. (1949). *Paper.* Berlin, Germany: Publisher.

Guijarro, L. (2010). Frameworks for fostering cross-agency interoperability in e-government initiatives. *Advances in Management Information Systems, 17*, 280–300.

Guo, X., & Lu, J. (2007). Intelligent e-government services with personalized recommendation techniques. *International Journal of Intelligent Systems, 22*, 401–417. doi:10.1002/int.20206

Halstead, D., Somerville, N., Straker, B., & Ward, C. (2009). *The way to gov 2.0: An enterprise approach to web 2.0 in government.* Microsoft US Public Sector White Paper. Palo Alto, CA: Microsoft.

Hamel, G. (2007). *The future of management.* Boston, MA: Harvard Business School Press.

Handley, J. (2008). *Enterprise architecture best practice handbook: Building, running and managing effective enterprise architecture programs - Ready to use supporting documents bringing enterprise architecture theory into practice.* Brisbane, Australia: Emereo Pty Ltd.

Hashimoto, D., Tanaka, A., & Yokoyama, M. (2007). Case study on RM-ODP and enterprise architecture. In *Proceedings of the Eleventh International IEEE EDOC Conference Workshop,* (pp. 216-223). IEEE Press.

Hatry, H. (2007). *Performance measurement.* Washington, DC: Urban Institute Press.

Health Consumer Powerhouse. (2009). *Euro health consumer index 2009 report.* Danderyd, Sweden: Health Consumer Powerhouse AB.

Heeks, R., & Bailur, S. (2007). Analyzing e-government research: Perspectives, philosophies, theories, methods, and practice. *Government Information Quarterly, 24*, 243–265. doi:10.1016/j.giq.2006.06.005

Hilbel, T., Brown, B. D., de Bie, J., Lux, R. L., & Katus, H. L. (2007). Innovation and advantage of the DICOM ECG standard for viewing, interchange and permanent archiving of the diagnostic electrocardiogram. *Computers in Cardiology, 34*, 633–636.

Hite, R. C. (2003). *Leadership remains key to agencies making progress on enterprise architecture efforts.* Retrieved from http://www.gao.gov/cgi-bin/getrpt?GAO-04-40.

Hite, R. C. (2004). *The federal enterprise architecture and agencies' enterprise architectures are still maturing.* Retrieved from http://www.gao.gov/cgi-bin/getrpt?GAO-04-798T.

Hjort-Madsen, K. (2006). Enterprise architecture implementation and management: A case study on interoperability. In *Proceedings of the 39th Annual Hawaii International Conference on System Sciences (HICSS 39).* Kauai, HI: System Sciences.

Hjort-Madsen, K. (2009). *Architecting government: Understanding enterprise architecture adoption in the public sector.* Doctoral Dissertation. Copenhagen, Denmark: IT University of Copenhagen. Retrieved from http://www.eagov.com/archives/Hjort-MadsenK_March09.pdf.

Hjort-Madsen, K., & Gotze, J. (2004). Enterprise architecture in government – Towards a multi-level framework for managing IT in government. In *Proceedings of European Conference on e-Government*, (pp. 365-374). Dublin, Ireland: ECEG.

Hjort-Madsen, K., & Pries-Heje, J. (2009). *Enterprise architecture in government: Fad or future?* Paper presented at the 42th Hawaii International Conference on System Sciences. Hawaii, HI.

Hjort-Madsen, K. (2007). Institutional patterns of enterprise architecture adoption in government. *Transforming Government: People. Process and Policy*, *1*(4), 333–349.

Hjort-Madsen, K., & Burkard, J. (2006). When enterprise architecture meets government: An institutional case study analysis. *Journal of Enterprise Architecture*, *2*(1), 11–25.

HL7. (2011). *Health level seven international*. Retrieved from http://www.hl7.org/index.cfm.

Ho, A. T. K. (2002). Reinventing local governments and the e-government initiative. *Public Administration Review*, *62*(4), 434–444. doi:10.1111/0033-3352.00197

Hoffmann-Petersen, N., Pedersen, E. B., Bech, J., & Mikkelsen, L. (2009). *Telemedinsk hjemme BT måling: Regionshospitalet holstebro*. Unpublished.

Holt, J., & Perry, S. (2010). *Modelling enterprise architectures*. New York, NY: The Institution of Engineering and Technology.

House of Lords. (1997). *Report on the public service*. London, UK: House of Lords.

Housel, T. J., & Bell, A. H. (2001). *Measuring and managing knowledge*. New York, NY: McGraw-Hill/Irwin. Grenadier, S. (200). Option exercise games: The intersection of real options and game theory. *Journal of Applied Corporate Finance*, *13*(2), 99–107.

Hoverstadt, P. (2008). *The fractal organization: Creating sustainable organizations with the viable system model*. Hoboken, NJ: John Wiley & Sons.

Hrdinová, J., Helbig, N., & Raup-Kounovsky, A. (2009). Enterprise IT governance in state government: State profiles. *Center for Technology in Government*. Retrieved from http://www.ctg.albany.edu.

Huang, H. C. (2009). Designing a knowledge-based system for strategic planning: A balanced scorecard perspective. *Expert Systems with Applications*, *36*, 209–218. doi:10.1016/j.eswa.2007.09.046

Huang, H. K. (2010). Industrial standards (HL7 and DICOM) and integrating the healthcare enterprise (IHE). In *PACS and imaging informatics: Basic principles and applications* (2nd ed.). Hoboken, NJ: John Wiley & Sons, Inc.

HUD. (2011). *Website*. Retrieved from http://www.hud.gov/offices/cio/ea/newea/index.cfm.

Huijboom, N., & Van Den Broek, T. (2011). Open data – An international comparison of strategies. *European Journal of ePractice, 12*, 4 – 16.

Humphrey, W. S. (2002). *Winning with software: An executive strategy*. Pittsburgh, PA: Carnegie Mellon University.

Hwang, J. S. (2005). *e-Government in Korea*. Retrieved, January 2011 from http://www.apiicc.org/apiicc/Lecture/Special/IT_Study_Visit_Program_for_Vietnam/020103.pdf.

IBM. (2006). City of Tacoma: Performance audit services for SAP functionality and departmental operations. Proposal No. IS05-0053F. Retrieved from http://www.ci.tacoma.wa.us/cronews/TacomaSAPAudit.pdf.

ICA. (2006). *Country report - Japan's e-Government*. Retrieved, May 2011 from http://unpan1.un.org/intradoc/groups/public/documents/apcity/unpan027268.pdf.

IDABC. (2004). *European interoperability framework for pan-European egovernment services, version 1.0*. Retrieved from http://ec.europa.eu/idabc/en/document/3473/5585.html#top.

IDABC. (2007). *Preliminary study on mutual recognition of esignatures for egovernment applications*. Brussels, Belgium: IDABC.

InformationWeek Government. (2011). *Army suspends server buys amid cloud plans*. Retrieved on July 18, 2011, from http://www.informationweek.com/news/government/cloud-saas/225300325.

InformationWeek Government. (2011a). *DOD CIO driving enterprise IT structure across military*. Retrieved on August 22, 2011, from http://www.informationweek.com/news/government/policy/231500294.

Institute for Enterprise Architecture Development. (2011). *Website*. Retrieved from http://www.enterprise-architecture.info/.

Institute of Citizen Centred Service. (2011). *Business transformation enablement program (BTEP)*. Retrieved from http://www.iccs-isac.org/en/practice/btep/.

International Code Council. (2010a). 2010 report of the public hearing on public version 1.0 of the international green construction code. Retrieved from http://www.iccsafe.org/cs/IGCC/Documents/PublicComments0810/IGCC2010ROH.pdf.

International Code Council. (2010b). IGCC: A new approach for safe & sustainable construction. Retrieved from http://www.iccsafe.org/cs/IGCC/Documents/Media/IGCC_Flyer.pdf.

International Code Council. (2010c). IGCC public version 2.0 synopsis - International code council. Retrieved from http://www.iccsafe.org/cs/IGCC/Documents/PublicVersion/IGCC_PV2_Synopsis.pdf.

ISO. (1993). *ISO/IEC 2382-1:1993: Information technology – Vocabulary – Part 1: Fundamental terms*. New York, NY: International Organization For Standardization.

ISO/IEC. (2007). *Enterprise integration - Constructs for enterprise modelling. No. ISO/IEC Standard 19440*. Geneva, Switzerland: International Organization for Standardization.

Isomäki, H., & Liimatainen, K. (2008). Challenges of government enterprise architecture work – Stakeholders' views. In M. A. Wimmer, H. J. Scholl, & E. Ferro (Eds.), *International Conference on Electronic Government*, (vol 5184), (pp. 364–374). Berlin, Germany: Springer.

IT Planning Council. (2010). *National e-government strategy*. Washington, DC: IT Planning Council.

ITU. (2006). *Resolution GSC-11/4*. Retrieved from http://www.itu.int/ITU-T/gsc/gsc11/documents/GSC-11_Resolutions_IndexR3.doc.

Jacobson, R. (1987). The validity of ROI as a measure of business performance. *The American Economic Review*, *77*(3), 470–478.

Jahani, B. S., Javadein, & Jafari, H. (2010). Measurement of enterprise architecture readiness within organizations. *Business Strategy Series*, *11*(3), 177–191. doi:10.1108/17515631011043840

Jähn, K., Reiher, T. M., & Stuhl, T. (2005). Telemedical projects in Bavaria—What is the current position and what needs to be done? *International Congress Series*, *1281*, 180–185. doi:10.1016/j.ics.2005.03.296

Jain, H., Chalimeda, N., Ivaturi, N., & Reddy, B. (2001). *Business component identification - A formal approach*. Paper presented at the 5th IEEE International Conference on Enterprise Distributed Object Computing. Seattle, WA.

Janssen, M., & Hjort-Madsen, K. (2007). Analyzing enterprise architecture in national governments: The cases of Denmark and Netherlands. In *Proceedings of the 40th Annual Hawaii International Conference on Systems Sciences (HICSS 2007)*. HICSS.

Janssen, M., & Kuk, G. (2006). *A complex adaptive system perspective of enterprise architecture in electronic government*. Paper presented at the 39th Hawaii International Conference on System Sciences. Hawaii, HI.

Janssen, M. (2011). Sociopolitical aspects of interoperability and enterprise architecture in e-government. *Social Science Computer Review*, *30*, 24–36. doi:10.1177/0894439310392187

Janssen, M., & Creswell, A. M. (2005). An enterprise application integration methodology for e-government. *The Journal of Enterprise Information Management*, *18*(5), 531–547. doi:10.1108/17410390510623990

Japanese Government. (2010). *A new strategy in information and communications technology (IT)*. Retrieved, January 2011 from http://www.kantei.go.jp/foreign/policy/it/100511_full.pdf.

Johns, C. H. W. (1904). *Babylonian and Assyrian Laws, contracts and letters*. New York, NY: Charles Scribner's Sons.

Johnson, N. B. (2011). Citizens less satisfied with government services. *Federal Times*. Retrieved from http://www.federaltimes.com/article/20110125/AGENCY02/101250302/1055/AGENCY.

Johnson, N. B. (2011). Tight budgets prompt IT cutbacks. *Federal Times*. Retrieved from http://www.federaltimes.com/article/20110814/IT03/108140303.

Johnson, S. (2010). Where good ideas come. Paper presented at TED Conference. Long Beach, CA.

Johnson, D., & Turner, C. (2003). *International business: Themes and issues in the modern global economy*. New York, NY: Routledge. doi:10.4324/9780203634141

Johnson, N., & Svara, J. (2011). *Justice for all: Promoting social equity in public administration*. Armonk, NY: ME Sharpe.

Johnston, P. (2006). *21st century networked local government*. White Paper. Retrieved July 20, 2011, from http://www.cisco.com/web/about/ac79/docs/wp/21st_Century_Networked_Local_Government.pdf.

Jordan, A. (2008). The governance of sustainable development: Taking stock and looking forwards. *Environment and Planning. C, Government & Policy*, *26*(1), 17–33. doi:10.1068/cav6

Juhl, A. (2007). *E-health in Denmark*. Conference presentation. New York, NY.

Jun, K.-N., & Weare, C. (2010). Institutional motivations in the adoption of innovations: The case of e-government. *Journal of Public Administration: Research and Theory*, *21*(3), 495–519. doi:10.1093/jopart/muq020

Kaczorowski, W. (Ed.). (2004). *Connected government*. London, UK: Premium Publishing.

Kamarck, E., & Nye, J. S. (2002). *Governance.com: Democracy in the information age*. Washington, DC: Brookings Institute Press.

Kaplan, S. R., & Norton, P. D. (1996). *Translating strategy into action: The balanced scorecard*. Boston, MA: Harvard University Press.

Karokola, G., & Yngstrom, L. (2009). *Discussing e-government maturity models for developing world – Security view*. Paper presented at the 2009 Information Security South Africa (ISSA) Conference. Johannesburg, South Africa.

Kautz, H., Selman, B., & Shah, M. (1997). Referral web: Combining social networks and collaborative filtering. *Communications of the ACM*, *40*, 63–65. doi:10.1145/245108.245123

Kawakami, T. (2005). *Direction of global enterprise architecture*. Retrieved, May 2011 from http://www.n2services.net/Local/Files/4_File_DirectionofGlobalEnterpriseArchitecture_Kawakami.pdf.

KBSt Publication Series. (2003). *SAGA: Standards and architectures for e-government applications, version 2.0*. Retrieved, January 2011 from http://egovstandards.gov.in/egs/eswg5/enterprise-architecture-working-group-folder/standards-and-architectures-v2.pdf/ download.

Keefer, P., & Knack, S. (2007). Boondoggles, rent-seeking, and political checks and balances: Public investment under unaccountable governments. *The Review of Economics and Statistics*, *89*(3), 566–572. doi:10.1162/rest.89.3.566

Kettl, D., & Dilulio, J. J. (1995). *Inside the reinvention machine*. Washington, DC: Brookings Institute Press.

Kettle, D. (2005). *The global public management review*. Washington, DC: Brookings Institute Press.

Kettle, D. (2009). *The next government of the United States*. New York, NY: WW Norton.

Kim, Y. J., Chun, J. U., & Song, J. (2009). Investigating the role of attitude in technology acceptance from an attitude strength perspective. *International Journal of Information Management*, *29*, 67–77. doi:10.1016/j.ijinfomgt.2008.01.011

Klein, H. K., & Myers, M. (1999). A set of principles for conducting and evaluating interpretive field studies in information systems. *Management Information Systems Quarterly*, *23*(1), 67–97. doi:10.2307/249410

Klose, K., Knackstedt, R., & Beverungen, D. (2007). *A stakeholder-based approach to SOA development and its application in the area of production planning*. Paper presented at the European Conference on Information Systems. St. Gallen, Switzerland.

Koch, C., & de Kok, J. (1999). *A human-resource-based theory of the small firm*. EIM Research Report 9906/E. Retrieved from http://www.ondernemerschap.nl/pdf-ez/H199906.pdf.

Kohlborn, T., Korthaus, A., Chan, T., & Rosemann, M. (2009). Identification and analysis of business and software services - A consolidated approach. *IEEE Transactions on Services Computing, 2*(1), 50–64. doi:10.1109/TSC.2009.6

Kotter, J. P. (1995). Leading change: Why transformation efforts fail. *Harvard Business Review, 73*(2), 59–67.

KPMG. (2011). *E-governance: Enabling transparency and efficiency in government.* Retrieved September 4, 2011, from http://www.kpmg.com/IN/en/WhatWeDo/Advisory/Performance-Technology/ITAS/eG_Links/eGovernance.pdf.

Kundra, V. (2010). *25 point implementation plan to reform federal IT management.* Washington, DC: Office of CIO.

Kundra, V. (2010). *State of public sector cloud computing.* Washington, DC: CIO Council.

Kun, L. G. (2001). Telehealth and the global health network in the 21st century: From homecare to public health informatics. *Computer Methods and Programs in Biomedicine, 64,* 155–167. doi:10.1016/S0169-2607(00)00135-8

Kurpjuweit, S., & Winter, R. (2007). *Viewpoint-based meta model engineering.* Paper presented at the 2nd International Workshop on Enterprise Modelling and Information Systems Architectures. St. Goar, Germany.

Kuusik, A., Reilent, E., Loobas, I., & Parve, M. (2011). Software architecture for modern telehealth care systems. *Advances on Information Sciences and Service Sciences, 3*(2).

Lagerström, R., Sommestad, T., Buschle, M., & Ekstedt, M. (2011). Enterprise architecture management's impact on information technology success. In *Proceedings of the 44th Hawaii International Conference on System Sciences.* Hawaii, HI: System Sciences.

Lallana, C. E. (2004). *An overview of ICT policies and e-strategies of select Asian economies.* Retrieved, May 2011 from http://www.apdip.net/publications/ict4d/ict4dlallana.pdf.

Lamore, R., Link, T., & Blackmond, T. (2006). Renewing people and places: Institutional investment policies that enhance social capital and improve the built environment of distressed communities. *Journal of Urban Affairs, 28*(5), 429–442. doi:10.1111/j.1467-9906.2006.00308.x

Land, M., Proper, E., Waage, M., & Cloo, J. (2008). *Enterprise architecture: Creating value by informed governance.* Berlin, Germany: Springer.

Langeni, L. (2010). Ambassador warns SA over media tribunal. *Business Day, 2010/08/19 06:22:27 AM.* Retrieved May 25, 2011, from http://www.businessday.co.za/articles/Content.aspx?id=118388.

Lankhorst, M. (2004). *ArchiMate language primer.* Enschede, The Netherlands: Telematica Instituut.

Lankhorst, M. (Eds.). (2009). *Enterprise architecture at work.* Berlin, Germany: Springer Verlag. doi:10.1007/978-3-642-01310-2

Lee, H., Irani, Z., Osman, I., Balcı, A., Özkan, S., & Medeni, T. (2008). Research note: Toward a reference process model for citizen-oriented evaluation of e-government services. *Transforming Government: People, Process and Policy, 2*(4), 297-310.

Leechul, B. (2010). Building an enterprise architecture for statistics Korea. In *Proceedings of the Management of Statistical Information Systems (MSIS 2010).* Daejeon, Republic of Korea.

Lee, G., & Kwak, Y. H. (2011). *An open government implementation model – Moving to increased public engagement.* Washington, DC: IBM Center for The Business of Government.

Leuf, B. C. (2001). *The wiki way: Quick collaboration on the web.* Reading, MA: Addison-Wesley.

Lewin, K. (1958). Group decision and social change. In Maccoby, E. E., Newcomb, T. N., & Hartley, E. L. (Eds.), *Readings in Social Psychology* (pp. 213–246). New York, NY: Holt, Rinehart, and Winston.

Library of Congress. (2002). *E-government act of 2002: Title II: Federal management and promotion of electronic government services.* Washington, DC: Library of Congress. Retrieved from http://thomas.loc.gov/cgi-bin/bdquery/z?d107:HR02458:@@@L&summ2=m&|TOM:/bss/d107query.html|.

Liegl, P., Mosser, R., Hofreiter, B., Zapletal, M., & Huemer, C. (2007). *Modeling e-government processes with UMM.* Retrieved from http://epress.lib.uts.edu.au/research/handle/10453/5899.

Light, P. C. (1999). *The true size of government.* Washington, DC: Brookings Institution.

Liimataine, K., Hoffman, M., & Jukka, H. (2007). *Overview of enterprise architecture work in 15 countries.* Helsinki, Finland: Finnish Enterprise Architecture Research Project.

Lin, C.-H., Young, S.-T., & Kuo, T.-S. (2007). A remote data access architecture for home-monitoring healthcare applications. *Medical Engineering & Physics, 29,* 199–204. doi:10.1016/j.medengphy.2006.03.002

Linnaean Classification. (2011). *Wikipedia.* Retrieved August 18, 2011, from http://en.wikipedia.org/wiki/Linnaean_taxonomy.

Loebbecke, C. (2009). Furthering distributed participative design - Unlocking the walled gardens. *Scandinavian Journal of Information Systems, 21*(1), 77–106.

Logan, A. G. (2007). Mobile phone-based remote patient monitoring system for management of hypertension in diabetic patients. *American Journal of Hypertension, 20,* 942–948. doi:10.1016/j.amjhyper.2007.03.020

Lukensmeyer, C. J., Goldman, J., & Stern, D. (2011). *Assessing public participation in an open government era: A review of federal agency plans.* Washington, DC: IBM Center for the Business of Government. Retrieved from http://www.federaltimes.com/article/20110814/IT03/108140303.

Lysons, K., & Farrington, B. (2006). *Purchasing and supply chain management.* Upper Saddle River, NJ: Prentice Hall Publishing.

MacFarlane, A., Murphy, A. W., & Clerkin, P. (2006). Telemedicine services in the Republic of Ireland: An evolving policy context. *Health Policy (Amsterdam), 76,* 245–258. doi:10.1016/j.healthpol.2005.06.006

Madhav, R. V., Stefan, R., & Soliman, M. T. (2007). Conservatism, growth, and return on investment. *Review of Accounting Studies, 12,* 325–370. doi:10.1007/s11142-007-9035-2

Madrid, L. (2008). *Measuring the returns from investments on e-government.* Microsoft White Paper. Seattle, WA: Microsoft.

Madsen, L. B., Kirkegaard, P., & Pedersen, E. B. (2008a). Blood pressure control during telemonitoring of home blood pressure: A randomized controlled trial during 6 months. *Blood Pressure, 17,* 78–86. doi:10.1080/08037050801915468

Madsen, L. B., Kirkegaard, P., & Pedersen, E. B. (2008b). Health-related quality of life (SF-36) during telemonitoring of home blood pressure in hypertensive patients: A randomized, controlled study. *Blood Pressure, 17,* 227–232. doi:10.1080/08037050802433701

Mahapatra, R., & Perumal, S. (2007). Enterprise architecture as an enabler for e-governance: An Indian perspective. In Saha, P. (Ed.), *Handbook of Enterprise Systems Architecture in Practice.* Hershey, PA: IGI Global. doi:10.4018/978-1-59904-189-6.ch016

MAMPU. (2003). *Standards, policies and guidelines - Malaysian government interoperability framework (MyGIF) version 1.0.* Kuala Lumpur, Malaysia: MAMPU.

MAMPU. (2008). *Towards one service delivery no wrong door.* Kuala Lumpur, Malaysia: MAMPU.

Markov, R. (2006). *Economical impact of IT investments in the public sector: The case of local electronic government.* Paper presented at the Business Informatics Workshop. Dublin, Ireland.

Marks, J. (2011). *Nearly a quarter of dot-gov domains don't work.* Washington, DC: NextGov. Retrieved from http://www.nextgov.com.

Marks, E., & Lozano, R. (2010). *Executive's guide to cloud computing.* Hoboken, NJ: John Wiley & Sons.

Martin, A., Dimitriev, D., & Akeroyd, J. (2010). A resurgence of interest in information architecture. *International Journal of Information Management, 30,* 6–12. doi:10.1016/j.ijinfomgt.2009.11.008

Mathes, A. (2004). *Folksonomies – Cooperative classification and communication through shared metadata.* Retrieved August 16, 2011, from http://www.adammathes.com/academic/computer-mediated-communication/folksonomies.html.

Mathiassen, L., & Nielsen, P. A. (2008). Engaged scholarship in IS research. *Scandinavian Journal of Information Systems, 20*(2), 3–20.

Matthes, F., Neubert, C., & Steinhoff, A. (2011). *Hybrid wikis: Empowering users to collaboratively structure information.* Paper presented at the 6th International Conference on Software and Data Technologies. Seville, Spain.

May, C., Harrison, R., Finch, T., MacFarlane, A., Mair, F., & Wallace, P. (2003). Understanding the normalization of telemedicine services through qualitative evaluation. *Journal of the American Medical Informatics Association, 10*(6), 596–604. doi:10.1197/jamia.M1145

McAfee, A. P. (2005). Enterprise 2.0: The dawn of emergent collaboration. *MIT Sloan Management Review, 47,* 21–28.

McGovern, J., Ambler, S. W., Stevens, M. E., Linn, J., Sharan, V., & Jo, E. K. (2004). *A practical guide to enterprise architecture.* Upper Saddle River, NJ: Prentice Hall.

McNulty, Y. M., & Tharenou, P. (2005). Expatriate return on investment: A definition and antecedents. *International Studies of Management and Organization, 34*(3), 68–95.

Meadows, D. (1999). *Leverage points: Places to intervene in a system.* Hartland, VT: The Sustainability Institute.

Mecca, T. (2004). Basic concepts for organizational change for administrative leaders. Retrieved from http://www.pcrest.com/PC/FacDev/2010/FI_reading.htm.

Medcom. (2010). *Det danske sundhedsdatanet.* Retrieved April 1, 2011, from http://medcom.dk/wm1.

Medcom. (2011). *Lægesystemer, sende/modtage.* Retrieved April 1, 2011, from http://medcom.dk/wm110032.

Medeni, T., Elwell, M., & Cook, S. (2007). Digitally deaf into games for learning: Towards a theory of reflective and refractive space-time for knowledge management. In *Proceedings of BEYKON 2007.* Turkey: Immersing.

Medeni, T., Erdem, A., Osman, I., Anouze, A., Irani, Z., & Lee, H. … Weerakkody, V. (2011). *Information society strategy & e-government gateway development in Turkey: Moving towards integrated processes and personalized services.* Paper presented in tGov Workshop. West London, UK. Retrieved from http://www.iseing.org/tgovwebsite/tGovWorkshop2011/CRCPDF/tGOV-20/Paper%2020.pdf.

Medeni, T., Iwatsuki, S., & Cook, S. (2008). Reflective ba and refractive ma in cross-cultural learning. In Putnik, G. D., & Cunha, M. M. (Eds.), *Encyclopedia of Networked and Virtual Organizations.* Hershey, PA: IGI Global. doi:10.4018/978-1-59904-885-7.ch178

Medeni, T., Medeni, I. T., Balci, A., & Dalbay, Ö. (2009). *Suggesting a framework for transition towards more interoperable e-government in Turkey: A nautilus model of cross-cultural knowledge creation and organizational learning.* Ankara, Turkey: ICEGOV.

Mickoliet, A., Kounatze, C. R., Serra-Vallejo, C., Vickery, G., & Wunsch-Vincent, S. (2009). *The role of the crisis on ICT and their role in the recovery. Organization for Economic Development and Cooperation (OECD) Report.* Washington, DC: OECD.

Microsoft Corporation. (2007). *Solutions for connected government.* Seattle, WA: Microsoft.

Microsoft Corporation. (2009). *Government service center – A Microsoft vision for high performance citizen service.* Microsoft Corporation White Paper. Palo Alto, CA: Microsoft.

Microsoft Corporation. (2010). *Connected government framework – Strategies to transform government in the 2.0 world.* Microsoft Corporation White Paper. Palo Alto, CA: Microsoft.

Microsoft Open Specifications. (2011). *Microsoft open specification promise (OSP).* Retrieved from http://www.microsoft.com/openspecifications/en/us/programs/osp/default.aspx.

Microsoft. (2011). *Connected government framework: Strategies to transform government in the 2.0 world.* Retrieved, August 2011 from http://www.microsoft.com/download/en/details.aspx?displaylang=en&id=8295.

Microsoft. (2011). *Connected government in a connected world.* White Paper. Retrieved July 20, 2011, from http://www.microsoft.com/download/en/details.aspx?id=8295.

Microsoft. (2011). *Connected health framework architecture and design blueprint, part 1 - 5.* Retrieved July, 15, 2011 from http://www.microsoft.com/health/ww/ict/Pages/Connected-Health-Framework.aspx.

Micrsoft. (2010). *Connected government framework strategies to transform government in the 2.0 world.* Retrieved from http://www.cstransform.com/resources/index.htm.

Ministers of the European Union. (2009). *Ministerial declaration on egovernment.* Geneva, Switzerland: European Union.

Minoli, D. (2008). *Enterprise architecture A to Z: Frameworks, business process modeling, SOA, and infrastructure technology.* Boca Raton, FL: Auerbach Publications. doi:10.1201/9781420013702

Moe, R. (1994). The reinventing government exercise. *Public Administration Review, 54*(2), 111–122. doi:10.2307/976519

Montier, J. (2010). *The little book of behavioral investing.* Hoboken, NJ: John Wiley & Sons.

Moon, J. (2004). *A handbook of reflective and experiential learning: Theory and practice.* London, UK: RoutledgeFalmer.

Moon, M. J. (2002). The evolution of e-government among municipalities: Rhetoric or reality? *Public Administration Review, 62*(4), 424–433. doi:10.1111/0033-3352.00196

Moon, Y. (2010). *Different – Escaping the competitive herd.* New York, NY: Crown Business.

Moorthy, S., & Polley, D. E. (2007). Technological knowledge breadth and depth: Performance impacts. *Journal of Knowledge Management, 14*(3), 359–377. doi:10.1108/13673271011050102

Morganwalp, J., & Andrew, P. (2003). A system of systems focused enterprise architecture framework and an associated architecture development process. In *Information, Knowledge, Systems Management (Vol. 3, pp. 87–105).* Thousand Oaks, CA: Sage.

Muehlfeit, J. (2006). *The connected government framework for local and regional government.* Microsoft Corporation White Paper. Palo Alto, CA: Microsoft.

Muehlfeit, J. (2006). *The connected government framework for local and regional government.* Retrieved from http://download.microsoft.com/download/7/f/0/7f08183b-c84f-491b-9b3f-%20c3d4b0521758/MS_LRG_CGF_Overview_new.pdf.

Mun, J. (2006). *Real options analysis versus traditional DCF valuation in layman's terms.* Retrieved April 09, 2011, from http://www.realoptionsvaluation.com/download.html#CASESTUDIES.

Mun, J., & Housel, T. (2006). *A primer on return on investment and real options for portfolio optimization.* Monterey, CA: Naval Postgraduate School.

Mun, J., & Housel, T. (2010). *A primer on applying Monte Carlo simulation, real options analysis, knowledge value added, forecasting, and portfolio optimization.* Monterey, CA: Naval Postgraduate School.

National Academy of Public Administration. (2003). *Homeland security: Lessons learned from prior government reorganizations.* Washington, DC: NAPA.

National Academy of Public Administration. (2006). *Transforming the FBI.* Washington, DC: NAPA.

National Computerization Agency. (2006). *Government-wide enterprise architecture in Korea.* Retrieved, May 2011 from http://www.opengroup.org/architecture/0310wash/presents/SungBum_Park_GEAF.pdf.

National Institute of Standards and Technology. (1989). *Information management directions: The integration challenge.* Washington, DC: NIST.

National Institute of Standards and Technology. (2010). *Guide for applying the risk management framework to federal information systems.* Washington, DC: NIST.

National Journal. (2011). *Army secretary creates commission to simplify bureaucracy.* Retrieved on August 18, 2011, from http://www.nationaljournal.com/nationalsecurity/mchugh-creates-commission-to-streamline-army-bureaucracy-20110815?mrefid=site_search.

National Research Center. (2011). *BLUS customer satisfaction survey, summary report.* Washington, DC: National Research Center.

Nesterczuk, G. (1996). Reviewing the national performance review. *Regulation, 3,* 31–39.

Net, A. W. C. (2003). Natt Worth & Mr. North: A Tacoma-style ad campaign. 2003 AWC Municipal Achievement Awards. Retrieved from http://www.awcnet.org/Apps/ma/projects/2003tacoma.pdf.

Network Effect. (2011). *Wikipedia.* Retrieved April 9, 2011, from http://en.wikipedia.org/wiki/Network_effect.

Newswire, P. R. (2003). City of Tacoma successfully launches most diverse SAP solution worldwide: Improved customer service, more efficient operation expected. Goliath: Business Knowledge on Demand. Retrieved from http://goliath.ecnext.com/coms2/gi_0199-3324000/ City-of-Tacoma-Successfully-Launches.html.

NextGov. (2011). *Navy CIO envisions defense wide software buys.* Retrieved on August 25, 2011, from http://www.nextgov.com/site_services/print_article. php?StoryID=ng_20110823_4178.

NextGov. (2011). *What transparency means to feds.* Washington, DC: NextGov/Government Business Council. Retrieved from http://www.nextgov.com.

NIA (Ed.). (2010). *Information white paper 2010.* Seoul, South Korea: NIA.

NIA. (2008). *2008 informatization white paper.* Korea: Ministry of Public Administration and Security, Government of Republic of Korea.

NIA. (2009). *2009 yearbook of information society statistics.* Korea: Ministry of Public Administration and Security, Government of Republic of Korea.

Nicolini, D. (2008). The work to make telemedicine work: A social and articulative view. *Social Science & Medicine, 62,* 2754–2767. doi:10.1016/j.socscimed.2005.11.001

NIST. (2011). *National institute of standards and technology.* Retrieved March 25, 2011 from http://www.nist.gov/ itl/csd/cloud-020111.cfm.

Nordfors, L., Ericson, B., Lindell, H., & Lapidus, J. (2009). *eGovernment of tomorrow – Future scenarios for 2020.* Vinnova Report VR 2009:28. Gullers Group. Retrieved from http://www.gullers.se.

Nourizadeh, S., Deroussent, C., Song, Y. Q., & Thomesse, J. P. (2009). Medical and home automation sensor networks for senior citizens telehomecare. In *Proceedings of the First International Workshop on Medical Applications Networking.* IEEE Press.

NUS Institute of Systems Science. (2010). *Enterprise architecture as a platform for connection government.* NUS Government Enterprise Architecture Research Project, Phase 1 Report. Retrieved from http://unpan1.un.org/intra-doc/groups/public/documents/unpan/unpan039390.pdf.

O'Reilly, T., & Battelle, J. (2009). *Web squared: Web 2.0 five years on.* Retrieved from http://assets.en.oreilly. com/1/event/28/web2009_websquared-whitepaper.pdf.

O'Toole, L. J., Jr., Brown, M. M., & Brundey, L. J. (1998). Implementing information technology in government: An empirical assessment of the role of local partnerships. *Journal of Public Administration Research And Theory, 8*(4), 499-525. Retrieved May 1, 2011 from http://www. highbeam.com/doc/1G1-53383712.html.

OASIS eGovernment Member Section. (2010). *Avoiding the pitfalls of egovernment - 10 lessons learnt from egovernment deployments.* Retrieved from http://www. oasis-egov.org/sites/oasis-egov.org/files/eGov_Pitfalls_ Guidance%20Doc_v1.pdf.

OASIS TGF Technical Committee. (2011). *OASIS TGF technical committee, statement of purpose.* Retrieved from https://www.oasis-open.org/committees/tgf/charter.php.

Oasis. (2011). *Oasis transformational government web page.* Retrieved from http://www.oasis-open.org/com-mittees/tgf/charter.php#item-4.

OASIS. (2011). *Transformational government framework (TGF) primer version 1.0.* Committee Note Draft 01 (CND01). Retrieved from http://docs.oasis-open.org/tgf/ TGF-Primer/v1.0/TGF-Primer-v1.0.docx.

Obama, B. (2010). *President's position on modernizing government: Remarks at the forum on modernizing government.* Washington, DC: The White House.

ODPM. (2003). *Rethinking service delivery, volume two - From vision to outline business case.* Office of the Deputy Prime Minister.

OECD. (2007). *E-government as a tool for transformation.* Retrieved April 12, 2011, from http://www.eurim. org.uk/activities/tgdialogues/E-Government_as_a_Tool_ for_Transformation.pdf.

Office of Management and Budget. (1997). *Information technology architectures, memorandum M-97-16.* Washington, DC: OMB.

Office of Management and Budget. (2002a). *The president's management agenda*. Washington, DC: OMB.

Office of Management and Budget. (2002b). *Expanded electronic government in the President's management agenda*. Washington, DC: OMB.

Office of Management and Budget. (2002c). *Rating the performance of federal programs*. Washington, DC: OMB.

Office of Management and Budget. (2005a). *OMB memorandum M-05-23, improving IT project planning and execution*. Washington, DC: OMB.

Office of Management and Budget. (2005b). *OMB memorandum M-06-02, improving public access to and dissemination of government information and using the federal EA data reference model*. Washington, DC: OMB.

Office of Management and Budget. (2007). *FEA practice guidance*. Retrieved on January 13, 2011, from http://www. whitehouse.gov/sites/default/files/omb/assets/fea_docs/FEA_Practice_Guidance_Nov_2007.pdf.

Office of Management and Budget. (2007). *Federal enterprise architecture*. Retrieved March 30, 2011, from http://www.whitehouse.gov/omb/e-gov/fea/.

Office of Management and Budget. (2009a). *A new era of responsibility: Renewing America's promise*. Washington, DC: OMB.

Office of Management and Budget. (2009b). *Improving agency performance using information and information technology, version 3.1*. Washington, DC: OMB.

Office of Management and Budget. (2010). *OMB circular A-11, preparation, execution and submission of the budget*. Washington, DC: OMB.

Office of Management and Budget. (2011a). *Fiscal year 2013 budget guidance*. Retrieved on August 21, 2011, from http://www.whitehouse.gov/sites/default/files/omb/memoranda/2011/m11-30.pdf.

Office of Management and Budget. (2011b). *Delivering an efficient, effective, and accountable government*. Retrieved on August 21, 2011, from http://www.whitehouse.gov/sites/default/files/omb/memoranda/2011/m11-31.pdf.

Office of the Chief Information Officer. (2007). *South Australian government ICT strategy*. Adelaide, Australia: Government of South Australia.

OG. (2009). *The open group cloud cube model: Selecting cloud formations for secure collaboration*. Retrieved April 9, 2011, from http://www.opengroup.org/jericho/publications.htm.

OG. (2010). *The open group building return on investment from cloud computing*. Retrieved April 9, 2011, from http://www.opengroup.org/cloud/whitepapers/ccroi/index.htm.

Ontology. (2011). *Wikipedia*. Retrieved May 1 2011, from http://en.wikipedia.org/wiki/Ontology.

Open Group. (2011). *The open group architecture framework (TOGAF)*. Retrieved May 5, 2011, from http://www.opengroup.org/togaf/.

OPM. (2011). *HCAAF resource center*. Retrieved from http://www.opm.gov/hcaaf_resource_center/.

Oracle. (2011). *Oracle igovernment*. Retrieved from http://www.oracle.com.

Or, C. K. L., & Karsh, B.-T. (2009). A systematic review of patient acceptance of consumer health information technology. *Journal of the American Medical Informatics Association, 16*(4), 550–560. doi:10.1197/jamia.M2888

O'Reilly, T. (2008). *What is web 2.0: Design patterns and business models for the next generation of software*. New York, NY: O'Reilly Media.

Orien, M. A. (2011). Green building: Growing from voluntary to mandatory. Nevada Business Journal Online. Retrieved from http://www.nbj.com/issue/0711/24/2438.

Osborne, D. (1988). *Laboratories of democracy*. Cambridge, MA: Harvard Business School Press.

Osborne, D., & Gaebler, T. (1992). *Reinventing government*. Cambridge, MA: Harvard Business School Press.

Osman, I., Anouze, A., Irani, Z., Lee, H., Balcı, A., Medeni, T., & Weerakkody, V. (2011). *A new cobras framework to evaluate e-government services: A citizen centric perspective*. Paper presented at the Tgovernment workshop. London, UK.

Pallab, S. (2010). *Understanding the impact of enterprise architecture on connected government.* Retrieved April 12, 2011, from http://unpan1.un.org/intradoc/groups/public/documents/unpan/unpan039390.pdf.

Pardo, T. A., & Burke, G. B. (2009). *IT governance capability: Laying the foundation for government interoperability.* Retrieved from http://www.ctg.albany.edu/publications.

Pardo, T. A., & Burke, G. B. (2008). *Improving government interoperability: A capability framework for government managers.* Albany, NY: SUNY Albany.

Parker, S. (Ed.). (2009). More than good ideas: The power of innovation in local government. London, UK: IDeA (Improvement and Development Agency). Retrieved from http://www.idea.gov.uk/idk/aio/9524940.

Parnas, D. L. (1972). On the criteria to be used in decomposing systems into modules. *Communications of the ACM, 15*(12), 1053–1058. doi:10.1145/361598.361623

Patig, S., & Casanova-Brito, V. (2011). *Requirements of process modeling languages – Results from an empirical investigation.* Paper presented at the 10th International Conference on Wirtschaftsinformatik. Zurich, Switzerland.

Pedersen, I. L. (2008). *Hvordan kan sundhedsvæsenets digitalisering styres.* Paper presented at EHR Observers Annual Meeting. Retrieved from http://www.epj-observatoriet.dk/kon-ference2008/sli-des/P2/Pedersen-IvanLund.pdf.

Pedersen, I. L. (2010). *Erfaringer og barrierer ifm: Implementering af tværsektorielle IT-projekter, fx medicin-kortet.* Paper presented at Danish Quality Unit in General Practice. Retrieved from http://www.dak-e.dk/files/157/erfaringer_og_barrierer_ifm_im-plementering_af_tvaer-sektorielle_it-projekter_digital_sundhed.pdf.

Pedersen, M. E. (2010). *The Danish national e-health portal.* Paper presented at Health 2.0 Europe. Retrieved from http://www.slideshare.net/Health2con/health-20-europe-keynote-the-danish-national-ehealth-portal.

Pedersen, K. M., Bech, M., & Vrangbæk, K. (2011). *The Danish health care system: An analysis of strengths, weaknesses, opportunities and threats.* Copenhagen, Denmark: Copenhagen Consensus Center.

Peter, L. J., & Hull, R. (1969). *The Peter principle: Why things always go wrong.* New York, NY: William Morrow and Company, Inc.

Petersen, J. (2011). *ABT koordineringsprojekt - Teknisk delprojekt.* Odense, Denmark: MedCom.

Picard, L., & Buss, T. F. (2009). *A fragile balance: Re-examining the history of foreign aid, security and diplomacy.* Sterling, VA: Kumarian Press.

Potts, C. (2010). *recrEAtion.* Denville, NJ: Technics Publications.

Protti, D., & Johansen, I. (2010). Widespread adoption of information technology in primary care physician offices in Denmark: A case study. *Commonwealth Fund, 1379*(80).

Provan, K. G., & Milward, H. B. (2001). Do networks really work? A framework for evaluating public-sector organizational networks. *Public Administration Review, 61*(4), 414–423. doi:10.1111/0033-3352.00045

Pulkkinen, M. (2006). Systemic management of architectural decisions in enterprise architecture planning: Four dimensions and three abstraction levels. In *Proceedings of the 39th Hawaii International Conference on System Sciences 2006.* Hawaii, HI: System Sciences.

Purser, S. A. (2004). Improving the ROI of the security management process. *Computers & Security, 23,* 542–546. doi:10.1016/j.cose.2004.09.004

Queensland Government. (2010a). *Queensland government business service classification framework definitions.* Retrieved April 28, 2011, from http://www.qgcio.qld.gov.au/SiteCollectionDocuments/Architecture%20and%20Standards/QGEA%202.0/Business%20Services%20Classification%20Framework%20Definitions.pdf.

Queensland Government. (2010b). *Using the business services classification framework.* Retrieved April 28, 2011, from http://www.qgcio.qld.gov.au/SiteCollectionDocuments/Architecture%20and%20Standards/QGEA%202.0/Business%20Services%20Classification%20Framework%20Definitions.pdf.

Queensland Government. (2011). *Queensland government enterprise architecture.* Retrieved March 30, 2011, from http://www.qgcio.qld.gov.au/qgcio/architectureandstandards/qgea2.0/Pages/index.aspx.

Rabaey, M. (2004a). *Decision process of enterprise application integration problems.* Paper presented at Enterprise Application Integration and Software Re-Engineering 2004. Ghent, Belgium.

Rabaey, M. (2011). *Game theoretic real option approach of the procurement of department of defense: Competition or collaboration.* Paper presented at the 8ᵗʰ Annual Acquisition Research Symposium. Monterey, CA.

Rabaey, M., Hoffman, G., & Vandenborre, K. (2004). *Aligning business- and resource-strategy: An interdisciplinary forum.* Paper presented at the 13ᵗʰ International Conference on Management Technology (IAMOT 2004). Washington, DC.

Rabaey, M., Leclercq, J.-M., Vandijck, E., Hoffman, G., & Timmerman, M. (2005a). *Intelligence base: Strategic instrument of an organization.* Paper presented at the Meeting of NATO IST-055 Specialist Meeting. The Hague, The Netherlands.

Rabaey, M., Vandenborre, K., Vandijck, E., Timmerman, M., & Tromp, H. (2007b). Semantic web services and BPEL: Semantic service oriented architecture - Economical and philosophical issues. A. Salam & J. Stevens (Eds.), *Semantic Web Technologies and eBusiness: Toward the Integrated Virtual Organization and Business Process Automation,* (pp. 127-153). Hershey, PA: IGI Global.

Rabaey, M., Vandenborre, K., Vandijck, E., Tromp, H., & Timmerman, M. (2006a). *Business process embedded information systems - For flexibility and adaptability.* Paper presented at 8ᵗʰ International Conference on Enterprise Information Systems: Databases and Information Systems Integration. Paphos, Cyprus.

Rabaey, M., Vandenborre, K., Vandijck, E., Tromp, H., & Timmerman, M. (2006b). *Service oriented investments.* Paper presented at the 17ᵗʰ Information Resource Management Association International Conference. Washington, DC.

Rabaey, M., Vandijck, E., & Hoffman, G. (2005b). *An evaluation framework for enterprise application integration.* Paper presented at the 16ᵗʰ IRMA International Conference. San Diego, CA.

Rabaey, M., Vandijck, E., & Tromp, H. (2003). *Business intelligent agents for enterprise application integration: The link between business process management and web services.* Paper presented at the International Conference Software and Systems Engineering and their Applications 2003. Paris, France.

Rabaey, M., Tromp, H., & Vandenborre, K. (2007a). Holistic approach to align ICT capabilities with business integration. In Cunha, M., Cortes, B., & Putnik, G. (Eds.), *Adaptive Technologies and Business Integration: Social, Managerial, and Organizational Dimensions* (pp. 160–173). Hershey, PA: IGI Global. doi:10.4018/978-1-59904-048-6.ch008

Radin, B. (2006). *Challenging the performance movement.* Washington, DC: Georgetown University Press.

Rahimpoura, M., Lovell, N. H., Celler, B. G., & McCormick, J. (2008). Patients' perceptions of a home telecare system. *International Journal of Medical Informatics, 77*(7), 486–498. doi:10.1016/j.ijmedinf.2007.10.006

Real Options Valuation. (2011). *Wikipedia.* Retrieved March 24, 2011, from http://en.wikipedia.org/wiki/Real_options_valuation.

Reali, R. M. (2011). EA forum - Cape Town. *The Vines Sanlam Head Office, 2011/09/30: 10:00 AM.* Retrieved from http://www.realirm.com.

Rechtin, E., & Maier, M. W. (1997). *The art of systems architecting.* Boca Raton, FL: CRC Press.

Redburn, F. S., Shea, S., & Buss, T. F. (Eds.). (2008). *Performance based management and budgeting.* Armonk, NY: ME Sharpe.

Reddick, C. G. (2011). Citizen interaction and e-government: Evidence for the managerial, consultative, and participatory models. Transforming Government: People. *Process and Policy, 5*(2), 167–184.

Reed, G. E. (2006). Leadership and systems thinking. *Defense AT & L.* Retrieved from http://www.au.af.mil/au/awc/awcgate/dau/ree_mj06.pdf.

Region, H. (2011). *Demonstrationsprojekt til it-understøttelse af forløbsprogrammer.* Copenhagen, Denmark: Region Hovedstaden.

Reid, S. (2002). Tacoma, ho! Billboards in Seattle encourage business to move south. The Stranger. Retrieved from http://www.thestranger.com/seattle/tacoma-ho/Content?oid=12663.

Resnick, P., & Varian, H. R. (1997). Recommender systems. *Communications of the ACM, 40,* 56–58. doi:10.1145/245108.245121

Richard, P. J., Devinney, T. M., Yip, G. S., & Jhonson, G. (2009). Measuring organizational performance: Towards methodological best practice. *Journal of Management, 35*(3), 718–804. doi:10.1177/0149206308330560

Riecken, D. (2000). Personalized views of personalization. *Communications of the ACM, 43,* 26–28. doi:10.1145/345124.345133

Rittel, H., & Webber, M. (1973). Dilemmas in a general theory of planning. *Policy Sciences, 4,* 155–169. doi:10.1007/BF01405730

Ross, J. W. (2003). Creating a strategic IT architecture competency: Learning in stages. *MIS Quarterly Executive, 2*(1), 31–43.

Ross, J. W., Weill, P., & Robertson, D. C. (2006). *Enterprise architecture as strategy: Creating a foundation for business execution.* Boston, MA: Harvard Business School Press.

Ross, J. W., Weill, P., & Robertson, D. C. (2008). *Enterprise architecture as strategy.* Boston, MA: Harvard Business School Press.

Ross, J., Weill, P., & Robertson, D. (2006). *Enterprise architecture as strategy: Creating a foundation for business execution.* Boston, MA: Harvard Business School Press.

Saha, P. (2009). Architecting the connected government: Practices and innovations in Singapore. In *Proceedings of the ICEGOV2009.* ACM Press.

Saha, P. (2010). *Enterprise architecture as platform for connected government: Advancing the whole-of-government enterprise architecture adoption with strategic (systems) thinking.* Retrieved from http://unpan1.un.org.

Saha, P. (2007). *Handbook of enterprise systems architecture in practice.* Hershey, PA: IGI Global. doi:10.4018/978-1-59904-189-6

Saha, P. (2008). *Advances in government enterprise architecture.* Hershey, PA: IGI Global. doi:10.4018/978-1-60566-068-4

Saha, P. (2010a). *Enterprise architecture as platform for connected government: Understanding the impact of enterprise architecture on connected government: A qualitative analysis. Phase 1 Report.* NUS Institute of Systems Science.

Saha, P. (2010b). *Advancing the Whole-of-Government Enterprise Architecture Adoption with Strategic (Systems) Thinking. Phase 2 Report.* Singapore, Singapore: NUS Institute of Systems Science.

Saha, P. (2011). *Architecting for business insight and strategic foresight: A systems approach to management of chronic diseases in Singapore.* Singapore, Singapore: Research Publication of National University of Singapore.

Salamon, G. L. (1985). Accounting rates of return. *The American Economic Review, 75*(3), 495–504.

SAP. (2005). *Enterprise services architecture: Enterprise services design guide.* New York, NY: SAP AG.

Savel, T. (2010). A public health grid (PHGrid): Architecture and value proposition for 21st century public health. *International Journal of Medical Informatics, 79*(7), 523–529. doi:10.1016/j.ijmedinf.2010.04.002

Schachner, L. (1973). Return on investment: Its values, determination and uses. *The CPA Journal, 43*(4), 277–281.

Schein, E. H. (1996). Three cultures of management: The key to organizational learning. *Sloan Management Review, 38*(1), 9–20.

Schekkerman, J. (2005). *Trends in enterprise architecture 2005: How are organizations progressing?* Retrieved, May 2011 from http://www.ea-consulting.com/Reports/Enterprise%20Architecture%20Survey%202005%20IFEAD%20v10.pdf.

Schekkerman, J. (2004). *How to survive in the jungle of enterprise architecture frameworks: Creating or choosing an enterprise architecture framework* (2nd ed.). Victoria, Canada: Trafford Publishing.

Schermann, M., Gehlert, A., Krcmar, H., & Pohl, K. (2009). *Justifying design decisions with theory-based design principles.* Paper presented at the 17th European Conference on Information Systems. Verona, Italy.

Scholl, H. J., & Klischewski, R. (2007). E-government integration and interoperability: Framing the research agenda. *International Journal of Public Administration, 30*(8), 889–920. doi:10.1080/01900690701402668

Schwartz, N. (2011). *Gen. Norton Schwartz.* Retrieved on September 1, 2011, http://www.defensenews.com/story.php?i=7508661&c=FEA&s=INT.

Scott, W. R. (1995). *Institutions and organizations.* Thousand Oaks, CA: Sage.

Scribd. (2011). *GPRA modernization act of 2010.* Retrieved from http://www.scribd.com/doc/47464749/GPRA-Modernization-Act-of-2010-Explained.

Seifert, J. W. (2008). *Federal enterprise architecture and e-government: Issues for information technology management. CRS report for Congress.* Washington, DC: USA Government.

Seifert, J. W. (2008). *Reauthorization of the e-government act.* Washington, DC: Congressional Research Service.

Senge, P. (1990). *The fifth discipline.* New York, NY: Doubleday Currency.

Shapiro, C., & Varian, H. R. (1998). *Information rules: A strategic guide to the network economy.* Watertown, MA: Harvard Business Press Books.

Shillabeer, A., Buss, T. F., & Rousseau, D. (Eds.). (2011). *Evidence based public management.* Armonk, NY: ME Sharpe.

Singapore Government. (2010). *Singapore government enterprise architecture.* Retrieved 2 May, 2011, from http://www.ida.gov.sg/Programmes/20060419144239.aspx?getPagetype=34.

Sistare, H. S., Shiplett, M. H., & Buss, T. (2008). *Innovations in human service management: Getting the public's work done in the 21st century.* Armonk, NY: ME Sharpe.

Sloan Management, M. I. T. (2006). Enterprise architecture: Driving business benefits from IT. Retrieved from http://cisr.mit.edu/blog/documents/2006/04/19/mit_cisrwp359_entarchslctdrsrchbriefs.pdf/.

Smit, H., & Trigeorgis, L. (2009). Valuing infrastructure investment: An option game approach. *California Management Review, 51*(2), 79–100.

Snowden, D. J., & Boone, M. (2007). A leader's framework for decision making. *Harvard Business Review.* Retrieved from http://www.mpiweb.org/CMS/uploadedFiles/Article%20for%20Marketing%20-%20Mary%20Boone.pdf.

Songini, M. L. (2004). $50M SAP rollout runs into trouble in Tacoma. Computerworld. Retrieved from http://www.computerworld.com/s/article/97690/_50M_SAP_Rollout_Runs_Into_Trouble_in_Tacoma.

South African Government Information. (2009). *Key issues.* Retrieved May 25, 2011, from http://www.info.gov.za/issues/index.htm.

Spencer, P. (2007). *Connected government: Creating a springboard for transformation and innovation.* Retrieved from http://www.cisco.com/web/about/ac79/docs/wp/ctd/Connected_Govt_PoV_1030_finalCB.pdf.

Spending, U. S. A. (2011). *Website.* Retrieved from http://it.usaspending.gov/.

Spewak, S. H. (1993). *Enterprise architecture planning: Developing a framework for data, applications, and technology.* New York, NY: Wiley.

Spínola, M. (2009). *An essential guide to possibilities and risks of cloud computing.* Retrieved April 10, 2011, from http://www.mariaspinola.com/cloud-computing/.

State Services Commission. (2006). *Enabling transformation: A strategy for e-government 2006.* Wellington, New Zealand: Ministry of State Services, Government of New Zealand.

Sterman, J. D. (2000). *Business dynamics – Systems thinking and modeling for a complex world.* Boston, MA: Irwin McGraw-Hill.

Stewart, K., Clarke, H., Goillau, P., Verrall, N., & Widdowson, W. (2004). Non-technical interoperability in multinational forces. In *Proceedings of the 9th International Command and Control Research and Technology Symposium*. Copenhagen, Denmark: IEEE.

Stewart, K., Cremin, D., Mills, M., & Phipps, D. (2004). *Non-technical interoperability: The challenge of command leadership in multinational operations.* Paper presented at the 10th International Command and Control Research and Technology Symposium: The Future of C2. Retrieved from http://www.dodccrp.org/events/10th_ICCRTS/CD/papers/298.pdf.

Stich, V., Schmidt, C., Meyer, J. C., & Wienholdt, H. (2009). Viable production system for adaptable and flexible production planning and control processes. Paper presented at the POMS Twentieth Annual Conference. Orlando, FL. Retrieved from http://www.pomsmeetings.org/ConfProceedings/011/FullPapers/011-0269.pdf.

Strandberg-Larsen, M., Schiøtz, M. L., Silver, J. D., Andersen, J. S., Frølich, A., & Krasnik, A. (2010). Is the Kaiser permanente model superior in terms of clinical integration: A comparative study of Kaiser permanente, northern California and the Danish healthcare system. *BMC Health Services Research, 10*(91), 1–13.

Stroh, P. D. (2000). Leveraging change: The power of systems thinking in action. *Reflections: The SoL Journal, 2*(2). doi:10.1162/15241730051092019

Sundhed.dk. (2010a). *Website.* Retrieved from https://www.sundhed.dk/.

Sundhed.dk. (2010b). *Min e-journal.* Retrieved from https://www.sund-hed.dk/profil-.aspx?id=29462.852.

Surowiecki, J. (2004). *The wisdom of crowds.* New York, NY: Random House.

Tacoma Municipal Code. (2011). Title 1: Administration and personnel. Retrieved from http://www.cityoftacoma.org/Page.aspx?hid=1946.

Tamara, R., & Damuth, R. (2009). *Estimating the effects of broadband penetration on GDP and productivity in south east Asia.* Nathan Associates Business Report. Retrieved from http://www.nathaninc.com.

Tambo, T. N., Hoffmann-Petersen, E. B., & Bejder, K. (2010). Coherent national IT infrastructure for telehomecare - A case of hypertension measurement, treatment and monitoring. *World Academy of Science. Engineering and Technology, 6*(71), 757–764.

Tamm, T., Seddon, P. B., Shanks, G., & Reynolds, P. (2011). How does enterprise architecture add value to organisations? *Communications of the Association for Information Systems, 28*(1), 141–168.

The Open Group Architecture Framework. (1999). *Technical reference model, version 5.* Retrieved from http://www.opengroup.org/togaf.

The Open Group. (2009). *TOGAF version 9.* Reading, UK: The Open Group.

Thesauri. (2011). *The free dictionary.* Retrieved May 10, 2011, from http://www.thefreedictionary.com/thesaurus.

Thornett, A. M. (2001). Computer decision support systems in general practice. *International Journal of Information Management, 21*, 39–47. doi:10.1016/S0268-4012(00)00049-9

TOGAF. (2009). *Introduction.* Retrieved May 2011, from http://www.togaf.info/togaf9/chap01.html.

Tolk, A. (2003). Beyond technical interoperability - Introducing a reference model for measures of merit for coalition interoperability. In *Proceedings of the 8th International Command and Control Research and Technology Symposium (ICCRTS)*. Washington, DC: ICCRTS.

Transform, C. S. (2009). *Beyond interoperability – A new policy framework for e-government.* CS Transform White Papers. London, UK: CS Transform Limited. Retrieved on May 4th from http://www.cstransform.com/resources/white_papers/BeyondInteropV1.0.pdf.

Treasury Board of Canada Secretariat. (2004). *Business transformation enablement program (BTEP): GSRM service reference patterns.* Retrieved from http://www.collectionscanada.gc.ca/webarchives/20071125180244/www.tbs-sct.gc.ca/btep-pto/index_e.asp.

Treasury Board of Canada Secretariat. (2007). *Government of Canada service oriented architecture strategy.* Retrieved from http://www.tbs-sct.gc.ca/cio-dpi/webapps/architecture/sd-eo/sd-eotb-eng.asp.

Tsiknakis, M., Katehakis, D. G., & Orphanoudakis, S. C. (2002). An open, component-based information infrastructure for integrated health information networks. *International Journal of Medical Informatics, 68*, 3–26. doi:10.1016/S1386-5056(02)00060-6

Tsilas, N. L. (2007). Enabling open innovation and interoperability: Recommendations for policy makers. In *Proceedings of the 1st International Conference on Theory and Practice of Electronic Governance*. New York, NY: ACM Press.

Tunstall. (2011). *Technical specifications: RTX3371 telehealth monitor, GSM/GPRS*. Retrieved from http://www.tunstall healthcare.com/Spec._RTX 3371_(GSM/GPRS)-2144.aspx.

UK Cabinet Office. (2002). *e-Government interoperability framework (e-GIF), part two: Technical policies and specifications*. Retrieved, January 2011 from http://www.govtalk.gov.uk/documents/e-GIF4Pt2_2002-04-25.pdf.

UK Cabinet Office. (2005). *Transformational government enabled by technology*. Retrieved, September 2010 from http://archive.cabinetoffice.gov.uk/e-government/strategy/.

UK CIO. (2005). *Enterprise architecture for UK government: An overview of the process and deliverables for release 1*. Retrieved, May 2011 from http://tna.europarchive.org/20080727001118/http:/www.cio.gov.uk/documents/cto/pdf/enterprise_architecture_uk.pdf.

UNDESA. (2008). *e-Government survey 2008: From e-government to connected governance*. New York, NY: United Nations.

UNDESA. (2008). *United nations e-government survey 2008: From e-government to connected governance*. New York, NY: United Nations.

UNDESA. (2010). *United nations e-government survey 2010: Leveraging e-government at a time of financial and economic crises*. New York, NY: United Nations.

United Nations Division for Public Economics and Public Administration and the American Society for Public Administration. (2002). *Benchmarking e-government: A global perspective --- Assessing the UN member states*. Retrieved from http://unpan1.un.org/intradoc/groups/public/documents/un/unpan021547.pdf.

United Nations. (2007). *UNDEP e-government interoperability guide: United Nations development programme with the support of IBM, Oracle*. New York, NY: United Nations.

United Nations. (2008). *Connected government survey 2008*. Retrieved, May 2011 from http://unpan1.un.org/intradoc/groups/public/documents/un/unpan028607.pdf.

United Nations. (2008). *E-government survey 2008 - From e-government to connected governance*. New York, NY: United Nations.

United Nations. (2008). UN e-government survey 2008: From e-government to connected governance. New York, NY: UN. Retrieved from http://unpan1.un.org/intradoc/groups/ public/documents/un/unpan028607.pdf.

Uno, Y. (1999). Why the concept of trans-cultural refraction necessary. *Intercultural Communication, 35*.

UNU-IIST-SP. (2008). *15th UNeGov.net school on foundations of electronic governance*. Retrieved April 11, 2011, from http://www.egov.iist.unu.edu/.

US Congress. (1996). *Public law 104-106, 110 Stat. 186*. Washington, DC: US Congress.

US Congress. (2002). *Public law 107-002*. Retrieved on February 8, 2011, from http://www.gpo.gov/fdsys/pkg/BILLS-107hr2458enr/pdf/BILLS-107hr2458enr.pdf.

US Congress. (2011). *Budget control act of 2011*. Retrieved August 11, 2011, from http://www.gpo.gov/fdsys/pkg/BILLS-112s365eah/pdf/BILLS-112s365eah.pdf.

US Government Accountability Office. (2005). *Saving our future requires tough choices today*. Retrieved on March 10, 2011, from http://www.gao.gov/cghome/hrfn20050210/hrfn20050210.pdf.

US Government Accountability Office. (2006). *Enterprise architecture: Leadership remains key to establishing and leveraging architectures for organizational transformation*. Retrieved from http://www.gao.gov/new.items/d06831.pdf.

US Government Accountability Office. (2007). *A call for stewardship: Enhancing the federal government's ability to address key fiscal and other 21st century challenges*. Retrieved on January 6, 2011, from http://www.gao.gov/new.items/d0893sp.pdf.

US Government Accountability Office. (2011a). *Opportunities to reduce potential duplication in government programs, save tax dollars, and enhance revenue.* Retrieved on March 30, 2011, from http://www.gao.gov/new.items/d11318sp.pdf.

US Government Accountability Office. (2011b). *Organizational transformation: Military departments can improve their enterprise architecture programs.* Retrieved on September 24, 2011, from http://www.gao.gov/new.items/d11902.pdf.

US Government Accountability Office. (2011c). *DOD financial management: Improved controls, processes, and systems are needed for accurate and reliable financial information.* Retrieved on September 24, 2011, from http://www.gao.gov/new.items/d11933t.pdf.

US Legal. (2011). *One-subject rule law and legal definition.* Retrieved from http://definitions.uslegal.com/o/one-subject-rule/.

US OMB. (2009). *Open government directive.* Retrieved, December 2010 from http://www.whitehouse.gov/omb/assets/memoranda_2010/m10-06.pdf.

US OMB. (2010). *FY 2009 report to congress on the implementation of the e-government act of 2002.* Retrieved, August 2011 from http://www.whitehouse.gov/sites/default/files/omb/assets/egov_docs/2009_egov_report.pdf.

US Senate. (2011). *Hearing on FY 2012 VA budget request.* Retrieved on April 13, 2011, from http://appropriations.senate.gov/ht-military.cfm?method=hearings.view&id=b8375dc5-1738-4279-bdb9-6670ae3a24d5.

US White House. (2011a). *Presidential memorandum – Disestablishment of the joint forces command.* Retrieved on March 3, 2011, from http://www.whitehouse.gov/the-press-office/2011/01/06/presidential-memorandum-disestablishment-united-states-joint-forces-comm.

US White House. (2011b). *Executive order--Delivering an efficient, effective, and accountable government.* Retrieved on June 18, 2011, from http://www.whitehouse.gov/the-press-office/2011/06/13/executive-order-delivering-efficient-effective-and-accountable-governmen.

USA Department of Defence. (2009). DoD architecture framework, version 2.0: *Vol. 1. Introduction, overview and concepts.* Washington, DC: Department of Defence.

US-CREST. (2000). *Coalition military operations - The way ahead through cooperability.* Retrieved April 12, 2011, from http://www.uscrest.org/CMOfinalReport.pdf.

Van den Berg, M., & Van Steenbergen, M. (2010). *Building an enterprise architecture practice: Tools, tips, best practices, ready-to-use insights.* Berlin, Germany: Springer.

Vander Wal, T. (2007). *Folksonmy coinage and definition.* Retrieved 2 May 2011, from http://www.vanderwal.net/folksonomy.html.

Velitchkov, I. (2011). *All-inclusive enterprise architecture.* Retrieved 08 15, 2011, from http://www.strategicstructures.com/?p=4.

Version, T. O. G. A. F. 9. (2011). *TOGAF 9 online documentation.* Retrieved from http://pubs.opengroup.org/architecture/togaf9-doc/arch/.

Vinnova. (2009). *eGovernment of tomorrow: Future scenarios for 2020.* Retrieved Jan 28, 2011, from http://www.vinnova.se/upload/EPiStorePDF/vr-09-28.pdf.

Wadhwa, V. (2011). The death of open government. *Washington Post.* Retrieved from http://www.transparency-initiative.org/news/kundra-resignation.

Wagter, R., van den Berg, M., Luijpers, J., & van Steenbergen, M. (2005). *Dynamic enterprise architecture: How to make it work.* New York, NY: John Wiley.

Wankel, C., & DeFillippi, R. (2006). *New visions of graduate management education.* New Haven, CT: Information Age Publishing.

Wanscher, C., Pederson, C. D., & Jones, T. (2006). *Medcom, Denmark: Danish health data network.* Bonn, Germany: Empirica.

Washington City Managers Association Awards. (2002). *Website.* Retrieved from http://www.wccma.org/newsletter/0210wcmanews.pdf.

Washington State Constitution. (2011). *Website.* Retrieved from http://www.leg.wa.gov/LAWSANDAGENCYRULES/Pages/constitution.aspx.

Watch, O. M. B. (2010). *Leaders and laggards in agency open government web pages.* Washington, DC: OMB Watch. Retrieved from http://www.ombwatch.org/node/10785.

Waverman, L., Meschi, M., & Fuss, M. (2005). *The impact of telecoms on economic growth in developing countries*. Paper presented at the Telecommunications Policy Research Conference. New York, NY.

Weill, P., & Olson, M. H. (1989). Managing investment in information technology: Mini case examples and implications. *Management Information Systems Quarterly, 13*(1), 3–17. doi:10.2307/248694

Weill, P., & Ross, J. (2004). *IT governance: How top performers manage IT decision rights for superior results*. Boston, MA: Harvard University Press.

Weill, P., & Ross, J. W. (2005). A matrixed approach to designing IT governance. *Sloan Management Review, 46*(2), 26–34.

West, D. M. (2004). E-government and the transformation of service delivery and citizen attitudes. *Public Administration Review, 64*(1), 15–27. doi:10.1111/j.1540-6210.2004.00343.x

White House. (2010). *White house forum on modernizing government overview and next steps*. Retrieved, August 2011 from http://www.whitehouse.gov/sites/default/files/omb/assets/modernizing_government/ModernizingGovernmentOverview.pdf.

White House. (2011). *OMB*. Retrieved from http://www.whitehouse.gov/omb/egov.

Whitehouse. (2011). *Office of e-government & information technology*. Retrieved March 26, 2011, from http://www.whitehouse.gov/omb/e-gov/.

Wiki. (2011). *Wikipedia*. Retrieved 10 May 2011, from http://en.wikipedia.org.

Wilson, E. O. (1998). *Consilience: The unity of knowledge*. New York, NY: Knopf.

Winkler, V. (2007). Identifikation und gestaltung von services - Vorgehen und beispielhafte anwendung im finanzdienstleistungsbereich. *Wirtschaftsinformatik, 49*(4), 257–266. doi:10.1007/s11576-007-0062-1

WITSA. (1999). *Critical information protection (CIP): A framework for government/industry dialogue*. Retrieved from http://www.witsa.org/papers/cip.htm.

World Bank. (2008). *Global economic prospects – Technology diffusion in the developing world*. Washington, DC: The World Bank.

World Bank. (2011). *Website*. Retrieved from http://web.worldbank.org/WBSITE/EXTERNAL/TOPICS/EXTINFORMATIONANDCOMMUNICATIONANDTECHNOLOGIES/EXTEGOVERNMENT/0,contentMDK:20507153~menuPK:702592~pagePK:148956~piPK:216618~theSitePK:702586,00.html.

World Economic Forum. (2009). *ICT for economic growth – A dynamic ecosystem driving the global recovery*. Geneva, Switzerland: World Economic Forum.

World Economic Forum. (2011). *The future of government – Lessons learned from around the world*. Geneva, Switzerland: World Economic Forum.

World Economic Forum. (2011). *The global information technology report 2010/2011 – Transformations 2.0*. Geneva, Switzerland: World Economic Forum.

World, C. I. S. (2002). The "wired city" selects SAP for business systems improvement project. Retrieved from http://www.cisworld.com/news/2002/0916_sap.htm.

WP4. (2005). *D4.2: Set of requirements for interoperability of identity management systems*. Retrieved from http://www.fidis.com.

YCG. (2009). *Enterprise architecture development toolkit*. Riyadh, Saudi Arabia: Yesser Consulting Group.

Yesser. (2005). *The national egovernment strategy and action plan*. Riyadh, Saudi Arabia: Kingdom of Saudi Arabia.

Yesser. (2009a). *Interoperability framework*. Retrieved from http://www.yesser.gov.sa/en/BuildingBlocks/Pages/interoperability_framework.aspx.

Yesser. (2009b). *Government secure network (GSN)*. Retrieved from http://www.yesser.gov.sa/en/BuildingBlocks/Pages/e-Gov._network.aspx.

Yesser. (2009c). *Government service bus (GSB)*. Retrieved from http://www.yesser.gov.sa/en/BuildingBlocks/Pages/government_service_bus.aspx.

Yesser. (2009d). *eGovernment transactions' methodologies & handbooks.* Retrieved from http://www.yesser. gov.sa/en/Methodologies/mechanisms/Pages/e_government_transactions.aspx.

Yesser. (2009e). *Best practices for government agencies' IT managers.* Retrieved from http://www.yesser.gov.sa/en/Methodologies/Pages/best_practices_government.aspx.

Yildirim, G., Medeni, T., Aktaş, M., Kutluoğlu, U., & Kahramaner, Y. (2010). *M-government as an extension of e-government gateway: A case study.* Antalya, Turkey: ICEGEG.

Zachman, J. A. (1987). A framework for information systems architecture. *IBM Systems Journal, 26*(3). Retrieved, January 2011 from http://www.research.ibm.com/journal/sj/263/ibmsj2603E.pdf.

Zachman, J. A. (1996). *The framework for enterprise architecture: Background, description and utility.* Retrieved from http://www.eiminstitute.org/library/eimi-archives/volume-1-issue-4-june-2007-edition/the-framework-for-enterprise-architecture-background-description-and-utility.

Zachman, J. A. (2003). *The Zachman framework: A primer for enterprise engineering and manufacturing.* Retrieved from http://www.zachmaninternational.com.

Zachman, J. (1987). A framework for information systems architecture. *IBM Systems Journal, 26*(3). doi:10.1147/sj.263.0276

Zenghelis, D. (2010). *The economics of network powered growth.* CISCO IBSG White Paper. Palo Alto, CA: CISCO Internet Business Solutions Group (IBSG).

Zokaei, K., Seddon, J., & O'Donovan, B. (2011). *Systems thinking – From heresy to practice.* London, UK: Palgrave Macmillan.

About the Contributors

Pallab Saha is with the National University of Singapore, Institute of Systems Science (NUS-ISS). His current research, consulting, and teaching interests include Enterprise Architecture (EA) and Governance. Dr. Saha has published three books, *Handbook of Enterprise Systems Architecture in Practice, Advances in Government Enterprise Architecture,* and *Coherency Management: Architecting the Enterprise for Alignment, Agility, and Assurance.* His books are widely referred by practitioners and researchers around the world, making it to the Top Seller list in 2008 and 2009. His papers have been translated and published in Korean, Russian, and Polish. Dr. Saha is the primary author of the *Methodology for AGency ENTerprise Architecture (MAGENTA)* and *Government EA Guidebook* for the Government of Singapore, and has led them to international prominence. They are available in IDS Scheer's ARIS Toolset. He is a recipient of the Microsoft research grant in the area of Government EA supported by the UN and the World Bank. He consults extensively and has provided consulting services to the Ministry of Defense, Defense Science and Technology Agency, InfoComm Development Authority of Singapore, Integrated Health Information Systems, IP Office of Singapore, CPF Board, SingHealth, Governments of Oman and Kazakhstan, and Great Eastern Life Assurance, among others. He has been invited as a distinguished speaker to the World Bank, Carnegie Mellon University, UN University, The Open Group, Microsoft, SAP Labs, Denmark IT Society, Korea Institute for IT Architecture, IEEE, SGGovCamp, Nanyang Business School, IIM Bangalore, Governments of South Australia, Jordan, UAE, Macau, Nepal, Korea, Kazakhstan, Colombia, Bangladesh, and several Singapore government agencies. His work has been featured and cited by the UN, WHO, United States DoD, Carlsberg, and The Open Group, and has contributed to the World Bank's EA Guidelines for Vietnam and Bangladesh. Featured as an *Architect in the Spotlight* by the *Journal of EA,* he has been an external examiner for research degrees at the University of New South Wales, a Visiting Researcher to the UN University, an expert reviewer to the ACM Enterprise Architecture Tech Pack, and an invited guest faculty to the Lee Kuan Yew School of Public Policy. Earlier, as Head of Development, he managed Baxter's Offshore Center in Bangalore. He has had engagements in Fortune 100 organizations in various capacities. Dr. Saha holds a Ph.D. in Management (Information Systems) from the Indian Institute of Science, Bangalore, and has received the best research design and best thesis awards. He is an alumnus of the MIT Sloan Executive Program.

* * *

Zakareya Ahmed Al-Khajah is distinguished in combining outstanding academic profile and proven practical background. He obtained B.Sc. and M.Sc. degrees in Computer Science from George Washington University, USA, and PhD in IT Strategic Planning from Brunel University, UK—majoring in eGovernment Strategies. Dr. Al-Khajah has 15 years of exceptional working and professional experience, during which he managed and implemented many specialized strategic projects in different public and private establishments, particularly projects related to developing performance in government sector. Dr. Al-Khajah assumed a number of responsibilities. He was faculty member at the college of Information technology, University of Bahrain. Currently, he is the Director of Policies and Business Processes Re-Engineering Directorate in the eGovernment Authority, Bahrain.

Sukaina Al-Nasrawi is an Associate Social Affairs Officer at the Economic and Social Commission for Western Asia (ESCWA) Centre for Women focusing on women empowerment and Information and Communication Technologies. Ms. Al-Nasrawi joined ESCWA in 2003 as a researcher in the Information and Communication Technology Division (ICTD), during which, she contributed to ESCWA publications, meetings, and regional projects, covering issues related to the Information and Knowledge Societies. In addition, Ms. Al-Nasrawi provides technical training on the ESCWA Statistical Information System to the member countries in the context of ICT capacity building in measuring the Information Society. She is an active member of different technical committees at ESCWA and United Nations secretariat levels. She has also worked as a graduate and research assistant at the American University of Beirut and has written research papers published by renowned societies such as the IEEE Computer Society. Ms. Al-Nasrawi holds a B.S. and M.S. in Computer Science from the American University of Beirut.

Ali Bin Saleh Al-Soma, Advisor to the Minister of Communications and IT, Director General of e-Government Program holds a Master's Degree in Computer Science (networking and distributed processing) from California State University, Long Beach, USA. He has achieved several positions in his career, among which are: Faculty staff member–Institute of Public Administration; Asst. Project Manager for Technical Affairs–The National IT Plan; IT Advisor–The Royal Commission of Jubail and Yanbu; IT Director–The Royal Commission of Jubail and Yanbu; Director of the eServices Planning and Support–The e-Government Program; and currently as the Minister's Advisor for IT and Director General of the e-Government Program–Ministry of Communications and IT. AlSoma has participated in several committees, projects, and consulting studies, which include Member of the e-Government Steering Committee; managing the development of the e-Government National Strategy and Action Plan; Member of the Ministerial Committee Directorate for organizational reform studies taskforce; Member of the National IT Plan project; participation in developing some IT-related regulations through the Expert Bureau Committees; and contributions in several IT and management consultation studies for many governmental and private sector entities.

Ali M. A. Al-Soufi has earned his B.Sc. in Computer Science from University of Bahrain, MSc in Computer Science from Aston University, UK, and Ph.D. in Computer Science from Nottingham University, UK. He worked for 11 years as Lecturer at University of Bahrain, including 4 years as head of Computer Science Department. Ali has 11 years of industrial experience out of which 8 years as a Senior Manager Application Programmes in IS Department at Batelco, where he oversaw a number of teams responsible for developing and supporting the company's critical applications systems such as SAP ERP, Oracle HRMS, NCR Teradata Data Warehouse, various Billing systems, Oracle CRM, various Payment systems and number of web based applications such as Batelco's e-Shop. Between 2007 and 2010, Ali was working as a consultant for Bahrain e-Government Authority (EGA) and Director for Bahrain National Enterprise Architecture Project. He is currently a member of the EGA strategy II development team.

Leonidas G. Anthopoulos is an Assistant Professor at the Project Management Department of the Technological Education Institute (TEI) of Larissa (Greece). At his previous job positions, as an Expert Counselor at the Hellenic Ministry of Foreign Affairs in e-Government and e-Diplomacy areas, as an IT Researcher and Manager at the Research Committee of the Aristotle University of Thessaloniki (Greece), Municipality of Trikala (Greece), Administration of Secondary Education of Trikala (Greece) and Information Society S.A. (Greece), he was responsible for planning and managing the development of multiple IT and e-Government projects for Greek Government and for various Public Organizations. He is the author of several articles published on prestigious scientific journals, books, and international conferences. His research interests concern, among others, e-Government, Enterprise Architecture, and Social Networks.

Don Ashdown was born and raised in Brisbane, Australia. He graduated from the University of Queensland in 1983 with a Bachelor of Science (Computing) and initially worked as a FORTRAN programmer before changing to ICT strategic planning in 1989 and then to enterprise architecture in 1996. He was the sole recipient of the Queensland Government's overseas study award in 1992. He has worked in both the private sector and in government and is currently a senior enterprise architect within the Queensland Government's enterprise architecture unit. His current enterprise architecture focus is on ensuring value is derived from EA activities.

Azlina Azman is presently the Deputy Director of the ICT Policy and Planning Division for the Malaysian Administrative Modernisation and Management Planning Unit (MAMPU), a unit under the Prime Minister Department, which is responsible for 'modernizing' the public sector in the areas of administrative reforms. In this role, she heads the Office of the Government CIO of Malaysia, which is central in formulating policies for the modernization of the Malaysian public sector ICT. An expert in Public Sector ICT Strategic Planning, she has made significant contributions in driving transforming Malaysian government's ICT initiatives. Ms Azlina is also the president of the Malaysian Public Sector ICT Analyst Association (PERJASA).

Karsten Bejder is Ph.D. and Associate Professor at Aarhus University, Institute of Business and Technology. Previous to this, he worked several years in the industry. Karsten received his Ph.D. in Hydraulic and Thermal Analysis of Plate Heat Exchangers from Aalborg University.

Robert Benjamin has spent 23 years in the IT industry, having played a consulting role to a number of private sector enterprises. Besides having actively served in the public sector for a period of eight years in the past, Robert has also, in recent years, been consulting to various Southern African metros. He is a dedicated organizational scientist who invented a nano-engineering methodology. Robert's block-and-arrow models have found use in facilitation sessions, sales proposals, technical solution designs, business processes, and many other artifacts of organizational management. Robert earned a post-graduate Diploma in Business Management at the University of Hull, UK. Prior qualifications included domains of IT, Finance, Education, and Administration. International submissions for Robert included contributions to project management methodology, tacit knowledge engineering as a means of guaranteeing project success, and enabling value-chain management via holistic enterprise-architectural management framework (CAMF).

Dominik Birkmeier is a Ph.D. candidate in the Business Administration and Economics Faculty at the University of Augsburg, Germany. He received his M.Sc. degree in Statistics from the Iowa State University and his Diploma degree in Business Mathematics from the University of Augsburg, in 2008. His research interests include the service-oriented development of information systems (especially the identification and specification of services from business models), the usability of business process modeling notations for business users, as well as methods for the analysis of large data sets. He is a member of the Association for Information Systems and the German Informatics Society.

William S. Boddie is a Professor of Systems Management at the U.S. National Defense University (NDU) iCollege. Dr. Boddie provides graduate-level education in organizational leadership and management, enterprise architecture, and program and project management. Dr. Boddie has over 30 years' experience leading and managing enterprise and information technology environments for public, private, and non-profit-sector organizations. Dr. Boddie supported numerous U.S. Federal Government organizations including the U.S. White House, Treasury Department, Commerce Department, Social Security Administration, and Environmental Protection Agency. Dr. Boddie developed several frameworks and models that enable organizational leaders to improve enterprise performance including the Vision, Integrity, Communication, Inspiration, and Empowerment Transformational Leadership Model and the Transformational Leadership and Enterprise Management Integration Framework. Dr. Boddie published numerous articles and authored book chapters in organizational leadership, enterprise architecture, and program and project management. Dr. Boddie is the NDU iCollege Professor of the Year for 2006 – 2007.

Sabine Buckl is Research Assistant at the Chair for Software Engineering of Business Information Systems at the Technische Universität München, since August, 2006. Her research interests focus on methods, models, and tools for Enterprise Architecture (EA) management. Thereby, she is especially interested in the interaction of organizational aspects and management methods reflecting the socio-technical perspective of EA management. As part of her ongoing research she is further engaged in the development of new research methods that enable collaboration and exchange between academia and practice. Sabine Buckl holds a diploma degree in Informatics (minor: Electrical Engineering) from Technischen Universität München since 2005 and has finished her Ph.D. in May 2011 with her thesis titled "Development of Organization-Specific Enterprise Architecture Management Functions Using a Method Base."

Terry F. Buss, Ph.D., is currently Executive Director and Distinguished Professor of Public Policy at Carnegie Mellon University, in Adelaide, Australia. Buss earned his Doctorate in Political Science and Mathematics at Ohio State University. Over the past 30 years, Buss has built his career in both academe and government. Buss has published 12 books and nearly 350 professional articles on a variety of policy issues. Buss has won numerous awards for research and public service. He was awarded two

Fulbright Scholarships and two fellowships with the Congressional Research Service, where he authored policy studies mandated by Congress. Over the years, Buss has worked overseas on major projects in England, Wales, Italy, Czech Republic, Slovakia, Hungary, Romania, Bulgaria, Albania, Ghana, Haiti, Canada, Colombia, Jamaica, Bahamas, Singapore, Vietnam, and Australia. He also directed projects in Iraq, South Africa, and Botswana from the United States.

Walter Castelnovo is Assistant Professor of Information Systems and Organization at the Department of Theoretical and Applied Sciences of the University of Insubria (Italy). His research interests concern technological and organizational innovation in Public Administration, Interorganizational Information Systems, and Networked Organizational Systems. He is one of the founders of the Research Center for Knowledge and Service Management for Business Applications at the University of Insubria, and he is also a member of the Department of Institutional Reforms, E-Government, Cooperation, and Communitarian Policies of the Association of Municipalities of Lombardia (Italy). He is member of the Program Committee of some international conferences on E-Government and Information Systems and he has been the Conference Chair of the 5th European Conference on Information Management Evaluation hosted by the University of Insubria in 2011.

Sue Coffman leads a dynamic group of engineers, planners, and environmental specialists providing a vital role in ensuring building safety, environmental responsibility and planned land uses within the city of Tacoma. Her experience as an engineer and manager on both the private and government side has helped her lead staff to think outside the box and look for creative solutions to provide more effective and efficient government services. She focuses on administration of an organization guided by a strategic plan and financial management plan. Ms. Coffman has provided a driving force in the integration of Enterprise Architecture into the city of Tacoma's permitting services, enabling the city government to operate more like private organizations. Her passion is in systems thinking and a project based approach to integrate technology solutions into the city's permitting process. Ms. Coffman has a B.S. and M.S. in Civil Engineering from the University of Idaho, and holds an engineering license in the State of Washington.

Anthony M. Cresswell is Deputy Director of the Center for Technology in Government, University at Albany. He works with government, corporate, and university partners to conduct applied research on the policy, management, and technology issues of government IT innovation. His international experience includes information system and policy analysis projects in Africa, Asia, Europe, the Middle East, and Caribbean. Dr. Cresswell joined CTG as a senior research fellow in 1994 and served as interim director in 2008-09. His studies include the public value of investment in government IT, and problems of interorganizational information sharing, organizational capability, and IT impacts on practice. Dr. Cresswell joined the University at Albany in 1979. He holds faculty appointments in Educational Administration and Information Science. He previously served on the faculties of Northwestern University and Carnegie-Mellon University, and as Faculty Advisor in the US Office of Management and Budget. He holds a doctorate from Columbia University.

Awel S. Dico is a Senior Architecture Consultant and Enterprise Architect with experience of over ten years in the creation of the Strategic Enterprise Architecture and technology governance activities for large organization. Dr. Dico is a co-chair of the SOA Working Group at the Open Group. He is a contributor to technical standards related to SOA and led the development of practical guide on using TOGAF to define and govern SOA initiatives. He is also a frequent speaker on enterprise architecture and SOA topics in industry as well as universities. Dr. Dico also serves as a supervisor of Ph.D. candidates in Software engineering at Addis Ababa University.

Vanessa Douglas-Savage is a Senior Enterprise Architect with the Queensland Government with over 10 years' experience in government and academic sectors. She has a particular interest in optimizing the value of organisational information and pragmatically linking enterprise architecture to the business objectives. Vanessa also has a keen interest in investment planning and ICT portfolio management. Vanessa has also worked on contemporary business management issues, such as digital records management and ensuring evidence of business activity is captured for prosperity as organizations increase their reliance on IT systems. Vanessa holds a Ph.D. in Knowledge Management and an undergraduate honors Information Technology degree with majors in IS and Artificial Intelligence.

Alpay Erdem graduated from Computer Engineering department of Bilkent University. He obtained MS. Degree also at Bilkent. He joined and took lectures at Information and Communication Engineering Department at Graduate School of University of Tokyo. He is currently Ph.D. candidate at Informatics Institute of Middle East Technical University. Research topic is Web mining. He has been working in Defense Sector as Senior Software Developer, specialized at command and control systems. Web services and Service Oriented Architecture are among special interest topics. He is also a member of group working on E-Government Services at Turkey.

Andreas Gehlert works as Enterprise Architect for the German Federal Ministry of the Interior. He also serves the European Commission as national expert for the topics enterprise architecture, interoperability, and standards. Andreas Gehlert uses the service concept to establish, maintain, and govern the relationship between business processes and IT systems. He collaborates with researchers to transfer up-to-date theoretical knowledge to the governmental practice. Andreas Gehlert holds a PhD in Information Systems from the Dresden Technical University of Technology (Germany). He has worked in the requirements engineering group of the University Duisburg-Essen (Prof. Pohl, Germany) where he was work package leader in the S-Cube Network of Excellence.

Kirsten Harte is currently employed as a Principal Project Officer within the Queensland Government's enterprise architecture unit. Since commencing with the unit in 2008, Kirsten has contributed to the further development and population of the Queensland Government Enterprise Architecture. This includes developing whole-of-Queensland government information management and information technology policy, frameworks, and guidelines. Prior to this Kirsten worked in information management roles in several Queensland government departments. Kirsten has a Bachelor of Laws and Master of Information Management from the Queensland University of Technology.

Nikolai Hoffmann-Petersen is M.D., is certified as General Practitioner and is assigned as Ph.D. student at Departments of Medical Research and Medicine, Holstebro Hospital and Aarhus University. Nikolai has served as vice-president of the Danish Association of Junior Hospital Doctors.

Hasan Hourani is the Director of Yesser Consulting Group (YCG), a government consulting practice within the e-Government program of the Kingdom of Saudi Arabia. YCG is responsible for providing e-Transformation Consultancy Services for the public sector in Saudi Arabia. Prior to Joining Yesser, Hasan Hourani was the Director of e-government and Adviser to the Minister for ICT-Jordan. He had overall responsibility for the development of Jordan e-Government. Hasan has over 20 years' experience in ICT in both the public and private sectors and has worked for several global organizations in the US, UK, Australia, Europe, and the Middle East. Hasan holds a B.Sc. (Honors) degree in Computing and Informatics from Plymouth University in the UK and a Post Graduate Diploma in Electronic Commerce from Curtin University in Western Australia.

David Johnson brings three decades of technical training and a collaborative leadership style to focus on the integration of Enterprise Architecture (EA) within the permitting division at the City of Tacoma, located in the Pacific Northwest. As structural engineer, project and program manager, owner's representative, and permitting services manager within public and private organizations, his project experience is equivalent to creating a working waterfront community with a population of over 25,000. As a result, David has a depth and breadth of practical knowledge as team member, facilitator, and organizer of talent in creating built environments. While preparing a public enterprise for a half billion dollar building program, he led the development and implementation of a web-based program and project management system. David's familiarity with fostering an organizational culture of trust and the integration of technology into working groups complements the highly motivated and creative cross-functional Building and Land Use Services permitting team.

Young-Joo Lee is a Senior Researcher of the department of IT Infrastructure Service at the National Information Society Agency (NIA), Korea. He received his B.S. in Sociology from Yonsei University and M.S in Management of Information Systems from Korea Advanced Institute of Science and Technology (KAIST), Korea. He has many years of experience in designing and implementing enterprise information system such as ERP, SCM, etc. in manufacturing industry. After joining NIA in 2007, he has been involved in several information system planning and EA programs in the public sector. His research interests include information systems management, Enterprise Architecture, and social issues in information technology.

Ee-Kuan Low has worked across various industries including legal administration, tertiary and professional education and training, local councils, and state government. His career and interests include business and IT strategy, process architecture, investment portfolio management, and software development. His current position as Senior Enterprise Architect within the Queensland Government's enterprise architecture unit is focused on making enterprise architecture accessible and relevant to professionals across diverse business disciplines. His team develops frameworks, policies, tools, and techniques; conducts education and training forums; facilitates workshops; and provides implementation advice and support to agencies across the Queensland Government on the Queensland Government Enterprise Architecture.

Lorenzo Madrid has over 30 years of working experience in the ITC industry, many of them throughout the Latin America region. He joined Microsoft in 2003, was appointed as the Worldwide Director for the Government Interoperability Initiative in 2007, and recently become the Worldwide Director for Technology Office Strategy in Public Sector. Lorenzo has been keynote speaker in several international events, such as COMDEX, The Economist World Forum, the Worldwide Forum in Technology for Tax Systems, the John F. Kennedy School at Harvard, and many others. He has recently been invited to a fellowship at The Center for Technology in Government—University of New York at Albany. Lorenzo Madrid holds a B.Sc. in Engineering from the Polytechnic School – University of São Paulo, where he also had his M.Sc. work in Calculus. He has published four books and several articles about the impact of technology in society.

Dzaharudin Mansor received an Honours Degree in Computer Systems Engineering from Monash University, Australia, and completed his Ph.D. in Computer Science at La Trobe University, Australia. Dzahar has more than 25 years of professional experience in ICT and telecommunications. He also presently holds several associate positions including as a councillor at the Malaysian ICT Industry Association (PIKOM), Adjunct Professor University Tun Hussein Onn Malaysia (UTHM), Senior Management Associate of the Malaysia Industry-Government Group for High Technology (MIGHT) and academic advisor at several public and private universities in Malaysia. In 2010, he was given the honour to lead one of the twelve Economic Transformation Program Labs, a national initiative that was tasked to develop an economic roadmap for Malaysia. His areas of expertise include software engineering, computing architectures, telecommunications, and business systems.

Dato' Mohd Salleh Masduki is Senior Advisor and Head of the Strategy Consulting Practice in the Yesser Consulting Group, Saudi National e-Government Program, Ministry of Communications and Information Technology, Kingdom of Saudi Arabia. He brings with him a wealth of experience in the application of ICT for development. In the 46 years of his career in ICT, he has covered the technological aspects of ICT as a software developer for a major British computer manufacturer, the country head in Malaysia for a major US computer manufacturer, and in the last 20 years working with governments to use ICT for economic, social, and national development.

Florian Matthes holds the chair Software Engineering for Business Information Systems at Technische Universität München. The current focus of his research is on enterprise architecture management, social software engineering, and interactive visualizations of semantic models. As head of the software architecture working group of the Gesellschaft für Informatik, member of the advisory board of the Ernst Denert-Stiftung für Software Engineering and organizer of several workshops and conferences in the area of enterprise architecture he puts special emphasis on the cooperation between practitioners and scientists in informatics and information systems. He is co-founder and chairman of CoreMedia (1996) and infoAsset (1999) with more than 180 employees, co-founder of further small software and service university spin-off, and scientific advisor of UnternehmerTUM, the center of innovation and business creation at TU München.

Ihsan Tolga Medeni works as a specialist in Çankaya University and also as a system analyst in Turksat as a part of his Ph.D. Research. He continues in his Ph.D. in METU Informatics Institute. He received his M.S. in Computer Engineering (2008), B.Sc. in Computer Engineering (2005) and B.Sc. in Business Administration (2004) from Çankaya University. He has numerous academic works in the fields of Knowledge Management, Knowledge Engineering, and e-Government. His works have been funded by Çankaya University and Tubitak, Turkey.

Tunc D. Medeni is a full-time researcher in Turksat and also affiliated to various academic institutions as a part-time staff. He was awarded a Ph.D. degree from the Japan Advanced Institute of Science and Technology (JAIST), Japan; his MS degree from Lancaster University in the UK; and his BS degree from Bilkent University, Turkey. He has contributed to various academic works in his interest areas such as knowledge management and e-government. He has been awarded funding and scholarships from Nakayama Hayao Foundation, JAIST, Japanese State in Japan, Lancaster University in UK, and Turkish State and Bilkent University in Turkey, and European Union for his education and research activities as distinguished individual, group, and institutional works.

Mohamad Rosmadi Mokhtar, Ph.D., obtained his Doctorate in Informatics from The University of Manchester, United Kingdom. He mainly works in the field of information security where he specializes in the area of trust and reputation management. His involvement in this particular work originates from his extensive working experience with one of the consortiums for e-Government service provision for the Malaysian Government. He currently serves as a lecturer at the Faculty of Information Science and Technology, Universiti Kebangsaan Malaysia (UKM).

Christian Neubert studied Computer Science and holds a diploma degree in Informatics from Universität Paderborn since 2006. During his studies, he worked for several companies as an intern and student trainee including SEB AG, Siemens AG, and Wincor Nixdorf AG. From 2006 to 2008, he worked as a software engineer in the area of logistics at Dematic GmbH. Since September 2008, Christian Neubert is Research Assistant at the Chair for Software Engineering of Business Information Systems (SEBIS) at the Technische Universität München. His research interest focuses on Social Software, Enterprise 2.0, Web Technologies, and Software Engineering. From his work at the chair, a new approach to structure information in enterprise wikis emerged, called Hybrid Wikis, which is developed since 2010 and commercialized by the infoAsset AG since 2011.

Sven Overhage currently is an Assistant Professor for Information Systems in the Business Administration and Economics Faculty at the University of Augsburg, Germany. He received the M.S. degree in Information Systems from the Darmstadt University of Technology and the Ph.D. from the University of Augsburg. His research interests are in the areas of systems analysis and design (especially component-based and service-oriented architectures), development methodologies and agile methods, as well as business information systems modeling (especially business process and enterprise modeling). He has had teaching assignments at the Darmstadt University of Technology, the University of Liechtenstein, and the University of Augsburg. He is a member of the Association for Information Systems and the German Informatics Society, where he serves as vice speaker of the special interest group on Software Architecture.

Linda Paralez has spent over 25 years leading highly technical teams in solving complicated engineering and process challenges across a broad spectrum of industries. From civil and geologic engineering to solid rocket booster design, from land use, public housing, and permitting to information technology and workplace culture and diversity awareness, Paralez uses her unique combination of education and experience to save clients time, money, and better use valuable human resources. Known for her compassionate approach to change, Dr. Paralez helps companies succeed by engaging, and enabling their people. She is also the author of numerous books and articles on asset management, benchmarking methodology, strategic planning, entrepreneurship, performance measures, business process management and design, education strategy, and other management strategies.

Marc Rabaey is Senior Officer in the Belgian Ministry of Defense (MOD), where he fulfilled different functions: IT-manager Medical Service, IT-procurement manager Medical Service, CIO of the Assistant Chief of Staff Evaluation, Technical Director Royal Military Academy. He is now System Manager Education of MOD. His main projects were the migration of the applications of the Belgian Medical Service from Mainframe to Client/Server architecture, the implementation of an imaging, workflow, and document management in the Medical Administration and the conceptualization of the information system of Evaluation MOD. His actual project is the implementation of an Education Information System Management in MOD. He holds the degrees of Commercial Engineer (IT) and Master in Social and Military Science. He has a Ph.D. Applied Economics. The main subject is the investment of IT, more specifically in the domain of Cloud Computing for public services. His test case is the move of an application of a federal agency into the Cloud.

Bernard Robertson-Dunn trained as an Electronic and Control Engineer specialising in modelling biological systems. In a career of almost forty years, Bernard has used his modelling skills in a wide variety of areas including information systems development, business process engineering, enterprise architecture, and ICT strategy. Since 1991, Bernard has worked in Canberra, Australia, mainly on Australian Government projects in the areas of Defense, Health, and a range of Whole of Government ICT initiatives. His primary focus has been on problem definition and solution strategies. Bernard spent nearly nine years with IBM in Canberra in their Government Business Unit, where he achieved IT architect certification. At IBM, he undertook a range of roles, including enterprise architect and IT architect on several large Australian Government ICT outsourcing projects. Bernard is currently an independent consultant working for the Australian Government Information Management Office on strategies for the adoption of Cloud Computing.

Sascha Roth is Research Assistant at the chair for Software Engineering of Business Information Systems at the Technische Universität München since February 2010. He holds a Master's degree in Computer Science from Hochschule Darmstadt, University of Applied Sciences since 2009. During his studies, Mr. Roth worked for several global acting enterprises as an intern including SAP AG, Software AG, and Dresdner Bank AG. In his current position as research assistant, he works in the project with the German Federal Government to systematically translate business processes into services. His research centers around enterprise architecture management with a particular focus on decision support and strategically planning of application landscapes by means of dynamically configurable, interactive, and web-based visualizations of system cartography.

Djoko Sigit Sayogo is a Ph.D. candidate in Rockefeller College of Public Administration and Policy, the University at Albany, State University of New York. He is a Fulbright Presidential Scholarship grantee for the period of 2008 to 2011. He is currently working for the Center for Technology in Government in the University at Albany to support research projects on a data interoperability framework to support global food chain governance for sustainable product, in particular fair trade coffee. His international experience includes acting secretary of Indonesian counterpart in international collaboration between: The Netherlands Agency, Indonesian local government, and university, UNESCO-IHE, Afvalzorg of Nauerna and TNO of Utrecht. He has actively participated in key conferences of e-government such as Dg.o, ICEGOV, and e-government track of HICSS, as well as conference in informatics such as SocInfo. His publications involve both empirical and conceptual studies on issues regarding digital government, collaborative networks, and data sharing.

Christian M. Schweda holds a Ph.D. in Computer Science from Technische Universität München, since August 2011. His PhD thesis with the title "Development of Organization-Specific Enterprise Architecture Modeling Languages Using Building Blocks" is the result of his ongoing research in the field of Enterprise Architecture (EA) management with special interests in conceptual modeling of EAs. He seeks to develop architectural models that can serve multiple purposes simultaneously, i.e. support both communication among the architecture stakeholders and computation of architectural properties. As part of his ongoing research, he works on EA analysis models, which can be used to operational-ize, measure, and predict properties of the respective management body. Complementing the theoretic inquiries, Christian M. Schweda is always interested to prove the practical applicability of the findings in a prototypic and experimental tool platform for visualizing EAs.

Anna Shillabeer is currently the Principal of a business consultancy specialising in data management, enterprise architecture, and information security in Adelaide, Australia. She was previously a lecturer in information systems management at Carnegie Mellon University and a fraud and behavioural analyst with the WorkCover Corporation in South Australia. She holds a Ph.D. from Flinders University in Medical Informatics and is currently working on a book focusing on the flow on effects of a cancer diagnosis beyond the immediate patient. She has recently been invited to undertake collaborative research with the Norwegian Centre for Integrated Care and Telemedicine in Tromsø, Norway.

Shinae Shin received the M.S. and Ph.D. degrees in the Department of Computer Science and Engineering from the Korea University, in 1999 and 2009, respectively. In 1993, she joined National Information Society Agency (NIA) in Korea, where she is a director of the department of IT infrastructure service. Also, she is a member of executive committee of KIITA (Korea Institute of Information Technology Architecture), 2008-Present. Since 2003, she has been involved in establishing EA legislation and policies of Korea. Her primary research interests include EA (Enterprise Architecture), IT governance, e-Gov., Metadata, Semantic Web, and Ontology.

Charles Solverson has over 25 years' experience in management and engineering. During his 20-year career with the City of Tacoma, Washington, he has served in a number of management positions, includ-ing special projects and planning. He has extensive experience in strategic initiatives and operational responsibilities grounded in information technology and performance management. Charles currently serves as Planning Manager and City Building Official for the City of Tacoma. He holds a B.S. in Civil Engineering from The University of Illinois. He is a licensed Civil Engineer in the State of Washington.

Torben Tambo is M.Sc., G.D.B.A. and Associate Professor at Aarhus University, Institute of Business and Technology. Previous to this, he served 17 years in IT, management, and consultant roles within manufacturing and trading companies. Research interests include information systems, enterprise architecture, and supply chain management. Torben has previously published with *Journal of Economic Dynamics and Control, Journal of Enterprise Architecture,* and *International Association for Management of Technology.*

Klaus Turowski, born in 1966, received a Diploma degree in Industrial Engineering and Management at the University of Karlsruhe, a Dr. Degree in Business Informatics at the University of Münster, and habilitated in Business Informatics at the Computer Science faculty of the Otto-von-Guericke University Magdeburg. In 2000, he was Visiting Professor at the University of the Federal Armed Forces Munich. From 2001, he held the chair of Business Informatics and Systems Engineering at the University of Augsburg. Since 2011, he is a Professor at the Otto-von-Guericke University Magdeburg. There he holds a chair of Business Informatics (AG WI), heads a research lab for very large business application systems (VLBA Lab), and is the academic director of the world-largest SAP university competence center (SAP UCC Magdeburg). He was Visiting Professor at various universities abroad and had teaching assignments at the Universities of Darmstadt and Konstanz. He (co-)organized a variety of national and international scientific conferences (> 30) and was a member of numerous program committees (> 130) and expert groups. Besides his theoretical background, he has been working in various consulting projects.

Ivo Velitchkov is a consultant and trainer in Enterprise Architecture and Business Process Management. He has Ph.D. in Informatics from Sofia University, Bulgaria. He holds seminars and consults with international companies on BPM, EA, Strategic, and Project Management. He's the author of an IT Strategy Management framework. He co-founded software development and business consulting companies. He managed EA, BPM, and software development projects for Government and private organisations. He's the author of the enterprise architecture and process management blog, strategicstructures.com. He currently works as Senior Architect and BPM Consultant in "e-Commission, Interoperability, Architecture and Methodologies" unit at the European Commission.

Saleem Zoughbi, as a regional adviser for Information and Communication Technology (ICT), provides technical assistance and advisory services to member governments. This includes special technical advice in different applications such as the evaluation of national policies and strategies, evaluation of IT departments within a CIO approach that includes business and process re-engineering, planning, and evaluation in e-government and e-governance, databases, data centres, and others. Dr. Zoughbi worked in several career environments. In academic life, he taught at the Computer Institute of Canada, Concordia University, Montreal, then moved to Jerusalem University and Bethlehem University in the Palestinian Territories. He wrote a couple of books about operating systems and computer organization for academic teaching, in addition to several papers and articles of technical nature. Currently, he focuses on applied research that is of developmental nature.

Index

A

administrative fragmentation 353-355, 361, 372
agile system development 59
Application Development Method (ADM) 58
application domain 154
architecture governance 161
asset portfolio management 94
ASSIMPLER 155
authoring services 268
awareness and feedback services 268

B

Budget Control Act of 2011 496, 511-512
Building and Land Use Services (BLUS) 219, 221
Bureau of Public Debt 495-496
Bush, George W. 412, 416, 420, 496
business domain 154
Business Enterprise Architecture (BEA) 503
Business Information System (BIS) 339
Business Interoperability 378
Business Modularity Architecture 221, 245
business process management 125
Business Process Modeling Notation (BPMN) 264
Business Process Re-Engineering (BPR) 415
Business Reference Model (BRM) 23, 112
business service design 85
business service taxonomies 85
Business Silos Architecture 245
Business Transformation Agency (BTA) 503
Business Transformation Enablement Program
    (BTEP) 179-180, 187, 189, 204

C

change management 125
Chief Financial Officers (CFO) Act 415

Cisco Connected Government Framework 80
citizen centricity 4-5
citizen development 209
Clinton, Bill 412, 415, 496
Cloud Computing 469
Cloud Cube Model (CCM) 485, 487, 492
Cloud Data Center (CDC) 483
collaborative services 5
common infrastructure 5
complex problems 68
Congressional Budget Office (CBO) 496, 511
connected government 4
    evolutionary stages 11
Connected government 4
Connected Government Framework (CGF) 80
Continua Health Alliance 325
cost benchmarks 96
Countries with Volatile Governance (CVG) 208, 211
cross-cultural reflection 394
cross-cultural refraction 394
Cross Enterprise Document Sharing (XDS) 325
cross-Government Enterprise Architecture (xGEA)
    294
Cultural Interoperability 379

D

data architecture 137
Data Reference Model (DRM) 112
Department of Defense (DoD) 49, 106, 172, 181,
    203, 258, 261, 370, 418, 426, 436, 492, 494,
    496-497, 499, 501-503, 506, 509, 511, 514
Department of Homeland Security (DHS) 418
Department of the Navy (DON) 499, 511
designing intervention strategies 39
Digital Agenda 263, 295
dynamic models 65

E

EA Management Maturity Framework (EAMMF) 427
EA taxonomies
    in business management 85
    purpose of 84
    supporting strategic planning 90
e-Government 72, 122
    as a wicked problem 73
    goal 72
    in Saudi Arabia 123
eGovernment Authority (eGA) 152
e-Government Enterprise (eGE) 399
e-Government Gateway (eGG) 389-390
e-Government Interoperability Framework (eGIF) 380
Electronic Content Management (ECM) 231
electronic government (e-Government) 495
Electronic Health Records (EHR) 312, 325
emergent systemic profile 37
Enterprise Architecture Assessment Framework for Connected Government (EAAF-CG) 8
Enterprise Architecture (EA) 2, 46, 58, 78, 105, 121-122, 124, 153-154, 177, 181, 203, 219-220, 246, 248, 264, 288-289, 298, 310, 382, 388, 399, 412, 445, 467-468, 471, 494, 501
    design/evolutionary stages 7
    problem oriented approach 60
    process 58
Enterprise Resource Planning (ERP) 221-222, 240
e-Post Office (e-PO) 297
e-strategies 289
Expeditionary Fighting Vehicle (EFV) 505
extra-governmental 12

F

Federal Bureau of Investigation (FBI) 418
Federal Enterprise Architecture Framework (FEAF) 178-179, 181, 293, 426
folksonomies 79

G

game theory 482
geopolitical changes 209
GovCloud 468, 477, 484
Government 2.0 46-47, 51, 54, 421-423, 432
Government Accountability Office (GAO) 426, 500, 503

governmental reform 209
government EA 15
Government Enterprise Architecture Framework (GEAF) 297
Government of Canada Strategic Reference Model (GSRM) 179
Government Performance and Results Act (GPRA) 415
Government-to-Client (G2C) 476
Government-to-Government (G2G) 476
government transformation 4, 19
Government-wide EA (GEA) 106

H

hard models 65
hierarchies 81
Human Capital Assessment and Accountability Framework (HCAAF) 417

I

I-Choose 442-443, 455-458, 461
ICT governance 125
ICT interoperability 443
ICT investments 91-92, 158, 442-444, 447, 452, 455
identity management 393
Information and Communication Technology (ICT) 4, 19, 205, 375
Information Chaos 390, 408
information domain 154
infrastructure domain 155
Integrated Acquisition Environment (IAE) 290
Integrated System of Local Government (ISLG) 350, 358, 360
inter-governmental 12
Intermunicipal Cooperation 355, 361-363, 370, 373
International Standards Organization (ISO) 376
intra-governmental 11

J

Joint Forces Command (JFCOM) 505

K

keywords 79
Knowledge Value Added (KVA) 481, 490
Kotter's Model 509-510

L

link management services 268

M

Management by Objectives (MBO) 415
Management Information System (MIS) 166, 339
Metcalfe's Law 449
Millenium Bridge 66
Millennium Challenge Corporation (MCC) 418
Ministry of Information and Communications (MIC) 109
modelling 65
    for decision making 71
models 64-65

N

National Data Hub (NDH) 166
national debt 494-496, 510
National Enterprise Architecture Framework (NEAF) 152-153, 171
National Gateway Infrastructure (NGI) 165
National Performance Review (NPR) 415
Net Present Value (NPV) 468, 480
networked organizational model 6
Networks and Information Integration (NII) 505
New Public Management (NPM) 414
nnational deficit 494, 496, 510
Non-Governmental Organizations (NGOs) 417
Non-Technical Interoperability 377

O

Obama, Barack 412, 420, 432-433, 496-497, 505
Object-Oriented Programming (OOP) 474
Office of Management and Budget (OMB) 118, 178, 290, 497, 503
Office of the Director of National Intelligence (ODNI) 418
ontologies 79
open government 6
Open Source Software (OSS) 482
Optimized Core Architecture 220, 233, 246
option games 482
Organizational Interoperability 379

P

Panetta, Leon E 497
Paperwork Reduction Act (PRA) 293
People Interoperability 378

performance management 125
Performance Reference Model (PRM) 112
portfolio balance 94
portfolio management 93, 125, 507
portolio duplication 95
President's Management Agenda (PMA) 416
problem oriented approach
    benefits 61
    business strategy 64
    definition 60
    process 62
problem solving 71
Process Engineer 263, 272-273, 276, 287
Program Assessment Rating Tool (PART) 417
program management 125
prosumer 268
Public Private Partnership (PPP) 330
public sector governance 6
public sector reform 203, 412-415, 420-423, 426, 429-431
public value assessment 452-453, 455-456
public value framework 442-443, 446, 448, 452-455, 460-462, 464, 466

Q

Queensland Government Enterprise Architecture (QGEA) 79
    taxonomies within 82

R

Reagan, Ronald 495, 511
Real Option Valuation (ROV) 468, 480
Recovery Point Objectives (RPO) 485
Recovery Time Objectives (RTO) 485
Regulation Identifier Number (RIN) 293
Return on Investment (ROI) 30, 129, 223, 443, 446, 468

S

Schwartz, Norton 498, 512
search services 268
Semantic Interoperability 379
sense-making tools 79
Service Canada 14
Service Component Reference Model (SRM) 112, 170
Service Delivery Frameworks 385
Service Engineer 272-279, 287
Service Level Agreements (SLA) 468, 478

Service Oriented Architecture (SOA) 122, 137, 146, 166, 177, 180-181, 214, 301, 384-385, 391, 474
Services Directive 249
Single-Subject Rule Making 236-237, 240, 246
social inclusion 6
Social Security Administration (SSA) 398
soft models 65
Soft Systems Methodology (SSM) 66
Solution Owners 273, 275-276, 278-279, 287
Standardized System of Local Government (SSLG) 358
Standard Operational Guidelines (SOG) 340
Standard Operational Procedures (SOP) 340
Standards and Architectures for eGovernment Applications (SAGA) 80, 102
static models 65
Subject Matter Experts (SMEs) 225
System Dynamics (SD) 66
systems thinking 65

T

tagging services 268
tame problems 68
taxonomies 80
    representation 84
Technical Architecture Framework for Information Management (TAFIM) 106, 172
Technical Interoperability 377
Technical Reference Model (TRM) 112, 170
telehealth kit 313
Telehomecare (THC) 313
telemedicine 309

The Open Group Architecture Framework (TOGAF) 58, 79, 102, 121, 153, 156, 172, 177, 181, 204, 382
thesauri 79
Total Quality Management (TQM) 415

U

transparency 6
ubiquitous 12

V

Vendor Neutral Archive (VNA) 325
Veterans Affairs (VA) 506
Viable Systems Model (VSM) 66
vocabularies 79

W

Whole-Of-Government (WOG) 289
wicked problems 68
Worldwide Governance Indicators (WGI) 206

Y

Yesser Enterprise Level Architecture Framework (Y-ELAF) 121, 127-128
    benefits 129
    core components 128

Z

Zachman Framework 80